On Core
Mathematics

Algebra 1

HOUGHTON MIFFLIN HARCOURT

Cover photo: umbrella   Jon Sheer/Flickr/Getty Images

Printed in the U.S.A.

ISBN 978-0-547-61723-7

3 4 5 6 7 8 9 10 1413 20 19 18 17 16 15 14 13 12 11

4500310110   B C D E F G

Contents

▶ Unit 1 Algebraic Modeling and Unit Analysis

▶ Unit 2 Linear Equations and Inequalities

▶ Unit 3 Systems of Equations and Inequalities

Learning the Common Core State Standards

Has your state adopted the Common Core standards? If so, then students will be learning both mathematical content standards and the mathematical practice standards that underlie them. The supplementary material found in *On Core Mathematics Algebra 1* will help students succeed with both.

▶ Here are some of the special features you'll find in *On Core Mathematics Algebra 1*

INTERACTIVE LESSONS

Students actively participate in every aspect of a lesson. They read the mathematical concepts in an Engage, carry out an activity in an Explore, and complete the solution of an Example. This interactivity promotes a deeper understanding of the mathematics.

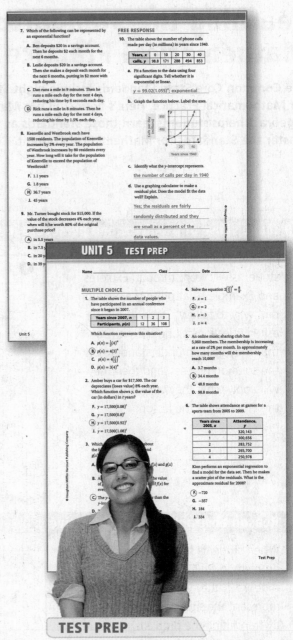

REFLECTIVE LEARNING

Students learn to be reflective thinkers through the follow-up questions after each Engage, Explore, and Example in a lesson. The Reflect questions challenge students to really think about the mathematics they have just encountered and to share their understanding with the class.

TEST PREP

At the end of a unit, students have an opportunity to practice the material in multiple choice and free response formats used on standardized tests.

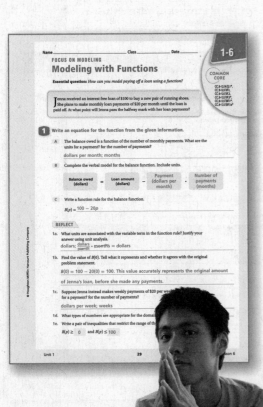

FOCUS ON MODELING

Special lessons that focus on modeling occur near the ends of units. These features help students pull together the mathematical concepts and skills taught in a unit and apply them to real-world situations.

Learning the Standards for Mathematical Practice

The Common Core State Standards include eight Standards for Mathematical Practice. Here's how *On Core Mathematics Algebra 1* helps students learn those standards as they master the Standards for Mathematical Content.

1 Make sense of problems and persevere in solving them.

In *On Core Mathematics Algebra 1*, students will work through Explores and Examples that present a solution pathway to follow. Students will be asked questions along the way so that they gain an understanding of the solution process, and then they will apply what they've learned in the Practice for the lesson.

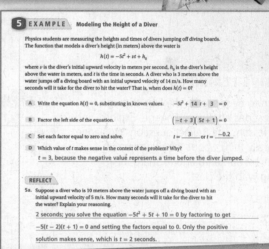

5 EXAMPLE Modeling the Height of a Diver

Physics students are measuring the heights and times of divers jumping off diving boards. The function that models a diver's height (in meters) above the water is

$$h(t) = -5t^2 + vt + h_0$$

where v is the diver's initial upward velocity in meters per second, h_0 is the diver's height above the water in meters, and t is the time in seconds. A diver who is 3 meters above the water jumps off a diving board with an initial upward velocity of 14 m/s. How many seconds will it take for the diver to hit the water? That is, when does $h(t) = 0$?

A Write the equation $h(t) = 0$, substituting in known values. $-5t^2 + 14\ t + 3\ = 0$

B Factor the left side of the equation. $(-t + 3)(5t + 1) = 0$

C Set each factor equal to zero and solve. $t = 3$ or $t = -0.2$

D Which value of t makes sense in the context of the problem? Why?
$t = 3$, because the negative value represents a time before the diver jumped.

REFLECT

5a. Suppose a diver who is 10 meters above the water jumps off a diving board with an initial upward velocity of 5 m/s. How many seconds will it take for the diver to hit the water? Explain your reasoning.

2 seconds; you solve the equation $-5t^2 + 5t + 10 = 0$ by factoring to get

$-5(t - 2)(t + 1) = 0$ and setting the factors equal to 0. Only the positive

solution makes sense, which is $t = 2$ seconds.

2 Reason abstractly and quantitatively.

When students solve a real-world problem in *On Core Mathematics Algebra 1*, they will learn to represent the situation symbolically by translating the problem into a mathematical expression or equation. Students will use these mathematical models to solve the problem and then state the answer in terms of the problem context. Students will reflect on the solution process in order to check their answers for reasonableness and to draw conclusions.

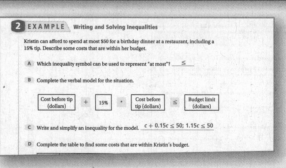

2 EXAMPLE Writing and Solving Inequalities

Kristin can afford to spend at most $50 for a birthday dinner at a restaurant, including a 15% tip. Describe some costs that are within her budget.

A Which inequality symbol can be used to represent "at most"? $\leq$

B Complete the verbal model for the situation.

| Cost before tip (dollars) | + | 15% | · | Cost before tip (dollars) | $\leq$ | Budget limit (dollars) |

C Write and simplify an inequality for the model. $c + 0.15c \leq 50; 1.15c \leq 50$

D Complete the table to find some costs that are within Kristin's budget.

REFLECT

2a. Can Kristin spend $40 on the meal before the tip? Explain.
Yes; substituting 40 into the inequality you get $1.15(40) \leq 50$, or $46 \leq 50$,

which is a true statement. So, Kristin can spend $40 on the meal.

2b. What whole dollar amount is the most Kristin can spend before the tip? Explain.
$43; If Kristin spends $44, the cost with tip will be $1.15(44) = 50.6$, which

is over her budget of $50.

③ Construct viable arguments and critique the reasoning of others.

Throughout *On Core Mathematics Algebra 1*, students will be asked to make conjectures, construct a mathematical arguments, explain their reasoning, and justify their conclusions. Reflect questions offer opportunities for cooperative learning and class discussion. Students will have additional opportunities to critique reasoning in Error Analysis problems.

> **REFLECT**
>
> **1a.** Why should the parts of the domain of a piecewise function $f(x)$ have no common x-values?
>
> You want only one rule to apply to a given x-value so that you get only one
>
> $f(x)$-value, since a function must give a unique output for each input.

> **REFLECT**
>
> **2a.** Describe how the graph of $f(x) = ab^x$ compares with the graph of $f(x) = b^x$ for a given value of b when $a > 1$ and when $0 < a < 1$.
>
> The y-intercept is a rather than 1. When $a > 1$, the graph of $f(x) = ab^x$ is a
>
> vertical stretch of the graph of $f(x) = b^x$. When $0 < a < 1$, the graph of $f(x) = ab^x$
>
> is a vertical shrink of the graph of $f(x) = b^x$.

> **23.** **Error Analysis** A student says that the graph of $g(x) = |x + 3| - 1$ is the graph of the parent function, $f(x) = |x|$, translated 3 units to the right and 1 unit down. Explain what is incorrect about this statement.
>
> When written in the form $g(x) = |x - h| + k$, the function is $g(x) = |x - (-3)| +$
>
> (-1), so the parent graph is translated 3 units to the left and 1 unit down.
>
> **24.** Suppose you translate the graph of $g(x) = |x - 3| + 1$ to the left 4 units and down 1 unit

④ Model with mathematics.

On *Core Mathematics Algebra 1* presents problems in a variety of contexts such as science, business, and everyday life. Students will use mathematical models such as expressions, equations, tables, and graphs to represent the information in the problem and to solve the problem. Then students will interpret their results in context.

> **2 EXAMPLE** Comparing Linear and Exponential Functions
>
> Compare these two salary plans:
> - Job A: $1000 for the first month with a $100 raise every month thereafter
> - Job B: $1000 for the first month with a 1% raise every month thereafter
>
> Will Job B ever have a higher monthly salary than Job A?
>
> **A** Write functions that represent the monthly salaries. Let t represent the number of elapsed months. Then tell whether the function is *linear* or *exponential*.
>
> Job A: $S_A(t) = 1000 + 100\,t$ S_A is a/an ___linear___ function.
>
> Job B: $S_B(t) = 1000 \cdot 1.01^t$ S_B is a/an ___exponential___ function.
>
> **B** Graph the functions on a calculator and sketch them below. Label the functions and include the scale.
>
>
>
> **C** Will Job B ever have a higher monthly salary than Job A? If so, after how many months will this happen? Explain your reasoning.
>
> Yes; 364 months; at that point, the graph of $S_B(t)$ rises above the graph of $S_A(t)$.

> **REFLECT**
>
> **2a.** Revise $S_B(t)$ and use the Table feature on your graphing calculator to find the interval in which the monthly salary for Job B finally exceeds that for Job A if the growth rate is 0.1%. Use intervals of 1,000. Repeat for a growth rate of 0.01%, using intervals of 10,000.
>
> between 6,000 and 7,000 months; between 90,000 and 100,000 months
>
> **2b.** Why does a quantity increasing exponentially eventually exceed a quantity increasing linearly?
>
> The amount of increase is constant in each interval with a linear function, but the
>
> increase per interval grows with an exponential function. Eventually the cumulative
>
> increase with an exponential function exceeds that for a linear function.
>
> **2c.** The table shows values for the monthly salary functions in four-month intervals rather than one-month interval

⑤ Use appropriate tools strategically.

Students will use a variety of tools in *On Core Mathematics Algebra 1*, including manipulatives, paper and pencil, and technology. Students might use manipulatives to develop concepts, paper and pencil to practice skills, and technology (such as graphing calculators, spreadsheets, or geometry software) to investigate more complicated mathematical ideas.

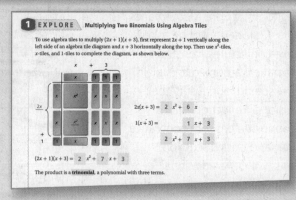

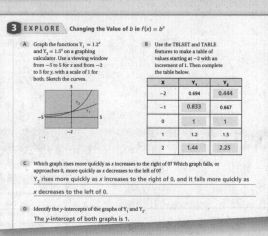

⑥ Attend to precision.

Precision refers not only to the correctness of arithmetic calculations, algebraic manipulations, and geometric reasoning but also to the proper use of mathematical language, symbols, and units to communicate mathematical ideas. Throughout *On Core Mathematics Algebra 1* students will demonstrate their skills in these areas when asked to calculate, describe, show, explain, prove, and predict.

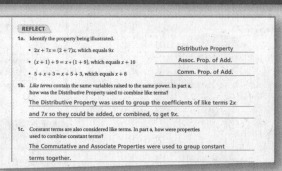

⑦ Look for and make use of structure.

In *On Core Mathematics Algebra 1*, students will look for patterns or regularity in mathematical structures such as expressions, equations, geometric figures, and graphs. Becoming familiar with underlying structures will help students build their understanding of more complicated mathematical ideas.

This method of using the distributive property to multiply two binomials is referred to as the FOIL method. The letters of the word FOIL stand for First, Outer, Inner, and Last and will help you remember how to use the distributive property to multiply binomials.

You apply the FOIL method by multiplying each of the four pairs of terms described below and then simplifying the resulting polynomial.

- **First** refers to the first terms of each binomial.
- **Outer** refers to the two terms on the outside of the expression.
- **Inner** refers to the two terms on the inside of the expression.
- **Last** refers to the last terms of each binomial.

Now multiply $(7x - 1)(3x - 5)$ using FOIL. Again, think of $7x - 1$ as $7x + (-1)$ and $3x - 5$ as $3x + (-5)$. This results in a positive constant term of 5 because $(-1)(-5) = 5$.

$$(7x - 1)(3x - 5) = 21x^2 - 35x - 3x + 5$$

$$(7x - 1)(3x - 5) = 21x^2 - 38x + 5$$

Notice that the trinomials are written with variable terms in descending order of exponents and with the constant term last. This is a standard form for writing polynomials: Starting with the variable term with the greatest exponent, write the other variable terms in descending order of their exponents, and put the constant term last.

⑧ Look for and express regularity in repeated reasoning.

In *On Core Mathematics Algebra 1*, students will have the opportunity to explore and reflect on mathematical processes in order to come up with general methods for performing calculations and solving problems.

Name _____ Class _____ Date _____   **8-6**

Deriving the Quadratic Formula

COMMON CORE

CC-9-12.A.REI.4.A,
CC-9-12.A.REI.4.a,
CC-9-12.A.REI.4.b

Essential question: *What is the quadratic formula and how can you derive it from* $ax^2 + bx + c = 0$*?*

You have learned how to solve quadratic equations by completing the square. In this lesson, you will complete the square on the general form of a quadratic equation to derive a formula that can be used to solve any quadratic equation.

1 EXPLORE Deriving the Quadratic Formula

Solve the general form of the quadratic equation, $ax^2 + bx + c = 0$, by completing the square to find the values of x in terms of a, b, and c.

A Subtract c from both sides of the equation.

$$ax^2 + bx = -c$$

B Multiply both sides of the equation by $4a$ to make the coefficient of x^2 a perfect square.

$$4a^2x^2 + 4ab\,x = -4ac$$

C Add b^2 to both sides of the equation to complete the square. Then write the trinomial as the square of a binomial.

$$4a^2x^2 + 4abx + b^2 = -4ac + b^2$$

$$\left(2ax + b\right)^2 = b^2 - 4ac$$

D Apply the definition of a square root and solve for x.

$$2ax + b = \pm\sqrt{b^2 - 4ac}$$

$$2ax = -b \pm \sqrt{b^2 - 4ac}$$

$$x = \frac{-b \pm \sqrt{b^2 - 4ac}}{2a}$$

The formula $x = \frac{-b \pm \sqrt{b^2 - 4ac}}{2a}$ is called the **quadratic formula**. For any quadratic equation written in standard form, $ax^2 + bx + c = 0$, the quadratic formula gives the solutions of the equation.

UNIT 1

Algebraic Modeling and Unit Analysis

Unit Vocabulary

UNIT 1

Algebraic Modeling and Unit Analysis

Unit Focus

This unit helps you transition from performing operations with numbers to working with variables, expressions, equations, inequalities, and functions, which are the building blocks of algebra. You will apply the order of operations and the distributive property to evaluate and simplify algebraic expressions. You will also apply unit analysis as you learn to write and graph functions to model real-world situations.

Unit at a Glance

COMMON CORE

Lesson		Standards for Mathematical Content
1-1	Evaluating Expressions	CC.9-12.N.Q.1*, CC.9-12.A.SSE.1*, CC.9-12.A.SSE.1a*, CC.9-12.A.SSE.1b*
1-2	Simplifying Expressions	CC.9-12.N.Q.1*, CC.9-12.A.SSE.1*, CC.9-12.A.SSE.1a*, CC.9-12.A.SSE.2
1-3	Writing Expressions	CC.9-12.N.Q.1*, CC.9-12.N.Q.2*, CC.9-12.A.SSE.1*, CC.9-12.A.SSE.1a*, CC.9-12.A.SSE.2
1-4	Writing Equations and Inequalities	CC.9-12.N.Q.2*, CC.9-12.A.CED.1*, CC.9-12.A.CED.3*
1-5	Representing Functions	CC.9-12.N.Q.1*, CC.9-12.F.IF.1, CC.9-12.F.IF.2, CC.9-12.F.IF.5*
1-6	Modeling with Functions	CC.9-12.N.Q.1*, CC.9-12.F.IF.1, CC.9-12.F.IF.2, CC.9-12.F.IF.5*, CC.9-12.F.BF.1*, CC.9-12.F.BF.1a*
	Test Prep	

©Houghton Mifflin Harcourt Publishing Company

Unpacking the Common Core State Standards

Use the table to help you understand the Standards for Mathematical Content that are taught in this unit. Refer to the lessons listed after each standard for exploration and practice.

COMMON CORE Standards for Mathematical Content	What It Means For You
CC.9-12.N.Q.1 Use units as a way to understand problems and to guide the solution of multi-step problems; choose and interpret units consistently in formulas; choose and interpret the scale and the origin in graphs and data displays.* Lessons 1-1, 1-2, 1-3, 1-5, 1-6	You will see how analyzing units can help you better understand the operations involved in algebraic expressions. You will also see that choosing an appropriate scale on a graph will help you better analyze the data.
CC.9-12.N.Q.2 Define appropriate quantities for the purpose of descriptive modeling.* Lessons 1-3, 1-4	You will write expressions, equations, and inequalities to model real-world situations.
CC.9-12.A.SSE.1 Interpret expressions that represent a quantity in terms of its context.* **CC.9-12.A.SSE.1a** Interpret parts of an expression, such as terms, factors, and coefficients.* **CC.9-12.A.SSE.1b** Interpret complicated expressions by viewing one or more of their parts as a single entity.* Lessons 1-1, 1-2, 1-3	In algebra, it is important to interpret and represent parts of an expression, especially when the expression represents a real-world context. This will help you interpret more complex expressions, as well as equations and inequalities.
CC.9-12.A.SSE.2 Use the structure of an expression to identify ways to rewrite it. Lessons 1-2, 1-3	You will use the structure of an expression to help you simplify or regroup terms when you find solutions to problems.
CC.9-12.A.CED.1 Create equations and inequalities in one variable and use them to solve problems.* Lesson 1-4 (Also 1-6)	You will use verbal models to help you write equations and inequalities to represent mathematical relationships.
CC.9-12.A.CED.3 Represent constraints by equations or inequalities, and by systems of equations and/or inequalities, and interpret solutions as viable or nonviable options in a modeling context.* Lesson 1-4	You will see how certain input and output values may or may not result in realistic solutions to problems.
CC.9-12.F.IF.1 Understand that a function from one set (called the domain) to another set (called the range) assigns to each element of the domain exactly one element of the range. If f is a function and x is an element of its domain, then $f(x)$ denotes the output of f corresponding to the input x. The graph of f is the graph of the equation $y = f(x)$. Lessons 1-5, 1-6	You will be introduced to the concept of a function and experience a variety of situations that functions can model. You will apply these concepts throughout algebra and in future math courses.

© Houghton Mifflin Harcourt Publishing Company

Unpacking the Common Core State Standards

This page lists and explains the Standards for Mathematical Content that are addressed in this unit. For information about the Standards for Mathematical Practice, which are integrated throughout the text, see Teacher Edition pages viii–xi.

UNIT 1

UNIT 1

Notes

_____

_____

_____

_____

_____

_____

_____

_____

_____

_____

COMMON CORE Standards for Mathematical Content	What It Means For You
CC.9-12.F.IF.2 Use function notation, evaluate functions for inputs in their domains, and interpret statements that use function notation in terms of a context. Lessons 1-5, 1-6	You will be introduced to function notation and be able to evaluate functions for certain input values. You will also be able to interpret contextual situations by writing equations to represent functions.
CC.9-12.F.IF.5 Relate the domain of a function to its graph and, where applicable, to the quantitative relationship it describes.* Lessons 1-5, 1-6	You will make a table of values, using appropriate input values for the domain, in order to graph functions. You will recognize which input values make sense for a given situation.
CC.9-12.F.BF.1 Write a function that describes a relationship between two quantities.* **CC.9-12.F.BF.1a Determine an explicit expression, a recursive process, or steps for calculation from a context.*** Lesson 1-6	You will write equations to model functions and graph functions on a coordinate grid. You will use functions to model relationships between real-world quantities.

Notes

_____

_____

_____

_____

_____

_____

_____

_____

Notes

_____

_____

_____

_____

_____

_____

_____

_____

_____

_____

_____

_____

_____

_____

_____

_____

_____

_____

_____

_____

_____

_____

_____

_____

_____

Evaluating Expressions

Essential question: *How do you interpret and evaluate algebraic expressions that model real-world situations?*

COMMON CORE Standards for Mathematical Content

CC.9-12.N.Q.1 Use units as a way to understand ... and to guide the solution of multi-step problems ...*

CC.9-12.A.SSE.1 Interpret expressions that represent a quantity in terms of its context.*

CC.9-12.A.SSE.1a Interpret parts of an expression, such as terms, factors, and coefficients.*

CC.9-12.A.SSE.1b Interpret complicated expressions by viewing one or more of their parts as a single entity.*

Vocabulary

expression

numerical expression

algebraic expression

term

coefficient

order of operations

evaluate

Math Background

The transition from arithmetic to algebraic representation and the introduction of variables sometimes causes difficulties for students. Variables, such as t, represent a number, and it is important to recognize that variables are used in a variety of applications. For example, the expression $60t$ represents the distance traveled at a rate of 60 miles per hour. The expression can be evaluated for any value of t (time in hours) greater than or equal to zero. In this lesson, students will learn to use variables in this way.

INTRODUCE

Before introducing variables, review problems such as $3 + \boxed{} = 15$, $3 \cdot \boxed{} = 18$, and $\dfrac{\boxed{}}{2} = 24$. Tell students that in algebra the box replaces a *variable* which represents a number. Then, transition to evaluating simple expressions with variables before evaluating expressions with exponents.

TEACH

1 ENGAGE

Questioning Strategies

- Why is $-16x$ listed as a term rather than $16x$? By definition, a term is added, so the subtraction is rewritten as addition of the inverse; $2x^2 - 16x = 2x^2 + (-16x)$.

- Is it possible to get the correct answer if you simplify an expression in an order different than the order of operations? Give an example. Is it a good idea to do this? Yes; for the given expression, if you square 5 first and then follow the order of operations, the answer is the same. No; you run the risk of getting an incorrect answer.

Teaching Strategy

Ask students to demonstrate their understanding of the words *variable* and *constant* by using them in a real-world context. For example: "The winds were variable, ranging from 5 to 15 mph," or "The water remained a constant 72°F." Ask students to give examples of mathematical variables and constants.

2 EXAMPLE

Questioning Strategies

- In part A, if you subtract 10 from 2 before multiplying by 4 is the answer the same? No; the answer would be −128 instead of −16.

- In part B, why do you simplify powers after multiplying and subtracting within parentheses? Using the order of operations, simplifying inside parentheses for all operations comes before simplifying powers.

EXTRA EXAMPLE

Evaluate the expression $x(-2x + 3)^2$ for $x = 4$. 100

Avoid Common Errors

Remind students that if they do not follow the order of operations, the results of their calculations will vary. For example, if students subtract within parentheses before multiplying within parentheses, the results will differ and be incorrect for the expression $2 \cdot (4 \cdot 2 - 10)^3$.

1-1

Evaluating Expressions

Essential question: *How do you interpret and evaluate algebraic expressions that model real-world situations?*

COMMON
CORE

CC-9-12.N.Q.1*,
CC-9-12.A.SSE.1*,
CC-9-12.A.SSE.1a*,
CC-9-12.A.SSE.1b*

1 ENGAGE   Interpreting Expressions

An **expression** is a mathematical phrase that contains operations, numbers, and/or variables. A **numerical expression** contains only numbers and operations, while an **algebraic expression** contains at least one variable.

A **term** is a part of an expression that is added. The **coefficient** of a term is the numerical factor of the term. A numerical term in an algebraic expression is referred to as a *constant term*.

Algebraic Expression	Terms	Coefficients
$2x^2 - 16x + 32$	$2x^2$, $-16x$, constant term 32	2 is the coefficient of $2x$. −16 is the coefficient of −16x.

Recall that the **order of operations** is a rule for simplifying a numerical expression:

1. **Parentheses** (simplify inside parentheses) $1 - 6 \cdot (7 - 4) + 5^2 = 1 - 6 \cdot 3 + 5^2$

2. **Exponents** (simplify powers) $= 1 - 6 \cdot 3 + 25$

3. **Multiplication and Division** (from left to right) $= 1 - 18 + 25$

4. **Addition and Subtraction** (from left to right) $= 8$

REFLECT

1a. Write the expression $3m - 4n - 8$ as a sum. How does this help you identify the terms of the expression? Identify the terms.

$3m + (-4n) + (-8)$; writing an expression as a sum clarifies the parts

being added and their signs; $3m$, $-4n$, -8

1b. Explain and illustrate the difference between a term and a coefficient.

A term is a part of an expression being added. A coefficient is a numerical factor

of a term. $4x$ is a term of $4x + 1$. Its coefficient is 4.

1c. What is the coefficient of x in the expression $x - 2$? Explain your reasoning.

1; $x = 1 \cdot x$, so the numerical factor of the term is 1.

1d. What is the value of $1 - 18 + 25$ if you subtract then add? If you add then subtract? Why is the order of operations necessary?

8, −42; results will vary if a consistent order isn't followed.

To **evaluate** an algebraic expression, substitute the value(s) of the variable(s) into the expression and simplify using the order of operations.

2 EXAMPLE   Evaluating Algebraic Expressions

Evaluate the algebraic expression $x(4x - 10)^3$ for $x = 2$.

A Substitute 2 for x in the expression. $\boxed{2} \cdot \left(4 \cdot \boxed{2} - 10\right)^3$

B Simplify the expression according to the order of operations.

- Multiply within parentheses. $2 \cdot (8 - 10)^3$

- Subtract within parentheses. $2 \cdot (-2)^3$

- Simplify powers. $2 \cdot (-8)$

- Multiply. -16

REFLECT

2a. Explain why x and $4x - 10$ are factors of the expression $x(4x - 10)^3$ rather than terms of the expression. What are the terms of the factor $4x - 10$?

The expressions x and $4x - 10$ are multiplied, not added, to form $x(4x - 10)^3$,

which makes them factors, not terms; $4x$, -10

2b. Evaluate $5a + 3b$ and $(5 + a)(3 + b)$ for $a = 2$ and $b = 4$. How is the order of the steps different for the two expressions?

22; 49; To evaluate $5a + 3b$, you multiply first, then add. To evaluate

$(5 + a)(3 + b)$, you add first, then multiply.

2c. In what order would you perform the operations to correctly evaluate the expression $2 + (3 - 4) \cdot 9$? What is the result?

Subtract, then multiply, then add; −7

2d. Show how to move the parentheses in the expression $2 + (3 - 4) \cdot 9$ so that the value of the expression is 9.

$(2 + 3 - 4) \cdot 9$

Unit Analysis When evaluating expressions that represent real-world situations, you should pay attention to the units of measurement attached to the parts of the expression. For instance, if p people go to a restaurant and agree to split the $50 cost of the meal equally, then the units in the numerator of the expression $\frac{50}{p}$ are *dollars*, the units in the denominator are *people*, and the units for the value of the expression are *dollars per person*.

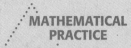

MATHEMATICAL PRACTICE — Highlighting the Standards

Example 2 and its Reflect questions offer an opportunity to address Mathematical Practice Standard 7 (Look for and make use of structure). By analyzing expressions, students learn to differentiate between factors and terms. This provides the structure for writing equations and inequalities. By analyzing the order of steps for the two expressions, students become aware of different usages of the order of operations and why structure is important.

Differentiated Instruction
English language learners may have difficulty with the word "term" because it has so many different meanings. Explain that in mathematics a term is a part of an expression that is added. You may wish to have students highlight the different terms, along with the addition and subtraction signs, in different colors.

 EXAMPLE

Questioning Strategies
- In part B, why does $100 + 12.5t$ represent the total distance? 100 represents the distance on the first day, and 12.5t represents the distance on the second day. Adding the terms together represents the distance traveled on both days.

- In part B, how can you determine if the answer is reasonable? Since the travel time for the second day is about the same as for the first day, the total distance for the two days should be about double the first day, which it is.

EXTRA EXAMPLE
A. On Monday, Carla drives 242 miles in 4 hours. Use the expression $\frac{d}{t}$ where d is the distance traveled and t is the travel time to find her average rate of travel. Include units. 60.5 miles per hour

B. If Carla travels at the same rate on Tuesday, then the expression $242 + 60.5t$ gives the total distance she has traveled after t hours on Tuesday. Evaluate this expression when $t = 9$. Include units. 786.5 miles

Teaching Strategy
Have students create a table of values for the expression $75 + 60t$ showing that as t increases by 1 the value of the expression increases by 60. Viewing a table of values can help students see a pattern.

t	$75 + 60t$
0	$75 + 60 \cdot (0) = 75$
1	$75 + 60 \cdot (1) = 135$
2	$75 + 60 \cdot (2) = 195$
3	$75 + 60 \cdot (3) = 255$

Technology
A graphing calculator or spreadsheet can also be used to quickly evaluate expressions for many values of the variable. Use the table feature of a graphing calculator to evaluate the expression $75 + 60t$ for values of t shown in the table of values above. Again, viewing a table of values can help students see a pattern.

CLOSE

Essential Question
How do you interpret and evaluate algebraic expressions that model real-world situations?
To interpret algebraic expressions, identify each term in the expression and what it represents. Use the order of operations to simplify expressions. To evaluate algebraic expressions, substitute the value of the variable into the expression and solve using the order of operations.

Summarize
Have students create a table listing the vocabulary words. The first column should list the words, the second column should provide the definitions, and the third column should show the examples.

PRACTICE

Where skills are taught	Where skills are practiced
1 ENGAGE	EXS. 1–3
2 EXAMPLE	EXS. 4–12
3 EXAMPLE	EXS. 13–14

3 EXAMPLE Evaluating Real-World Expressions

A   Sheila is participating in a multi-day bike trip. On the first day, she rode 100 miles in 8 hours. Use the expression $\frac{d}{t}$ where d is the distance traveled and t is the travel time to find her average rate of travel. Include units when evaluating the expression.

$$\frac{d}{t} = \frac{100 \text{ miles}}{8 \text{ hours}} = 12.5 \text{ miles per hour}$$

B   If Sheila continues riding at her average rate for the first day, then the expression $100 + 12.5t$ gives the total distance that she has traveled after riding for t hours on the second day. Evaluate this expression when $t = 7$, and include units.

$$100 + 12.5t = 100 \;\text{miles}\; + 12.5 \;\text{miles per hour}\; \cdot 7 \;\text{hours}$$

$$= 187.5 \text{ miles}$$

REFLECT

3a.   What are the terms in the expression $100 + 12.5t$? What does each term represent in the context of Sheila's bike trip?

The term 100 represents the distance (in miles) Sheila traveled on the first day.

The term $12.5t$ represents the distance (in miles) she traveled on the second day.

3b.   What is the coefficient of the term $12.5t$? What does it represent in the context of Sheila's bike trip?

The coefficient 12.5 represents Sheila's average rate of travel in

miles per hour.

3c.   If you write only the units for the expression $100 + 12.5t$, you get $\text{mi} + \frac{\text{mi}}{\text{h}} \cdot \text{h}$ where "mi" is the abbreviation for miles and "h" is the abbreviation for hours. Explain what the following *unit analysis* shows:

$$\text{mi} + \frac{\text{mi}}{\cancel{\text{h}}} \cdot \cancel{\text{h}} = \text{mi} + \text{mi} = \text{mi}$$

When you multiply miles per hour by hours you get miles, and when you add

miles to miles you get miles.

3d.   How can you modify the expression $100 + 12.5t$ so that the units are feet when the expression is evaluated?
Sample answer: $5280(100 + 12.5t)$

© Houghton Mifflin Harcourt Publishing Company

PRACTICE

Identify the terms of each expression and the coefficient of each term.

1. $7x + 8y$
   $7x$ and $8y$; 7 and 8

2. $a - b$
   a and $-b$; 1 and -1

3. $3m^2 - 6n$
   $3m^2$ and $-6n$; 3 and -6

Evaluate each expression for $a = 2$, $b = 3$, and $c = -6$.

4. $7a - 5b + 4$
   3

5. $b^2(c + 4)$
   -18

6. $8 - 2ab$
   -4

7. $a^2 + b^2 - c^2$
   -23

8. $(a - c)(c + 5)$
   -8

9. $12 - 2(a - b)^2$
   10

10. $a + (b - c)^2$
    83

11. $(a + b) - ab$
    -1

12. $5a^2 + bc^2$
    128

13. Henry drives in town at a rate of 25 miles per hour. It takes him 15 minutes to go to the library from his house. The algebraic expression rt represents distance traveled, where r is the average rate (in miles per hour) and t is the travel time (in hours).

   a. Can you multiply 25 and 15 to find the distance Henry traveled to the library? Explain.

   No; The units don't match. You need to convert 15 min to 0.25 h.

   b. Show how to find the distance from Henry's house to the library. Include units in your calculation.
   $25 \frac{\text{miles}}{\cancel{\text{hour}}} \cdot 0.25 \;\cancel{\text{hour}} = 6.25 \text{ miles}$

14. Sarah works 4 hours her first week of a part-time job and earns $60. Her total pay after the second week can be represented by the expression $60 + \frac{p}{t} \cdot s$ where p represents her pay for t hours of work and s represents the hours she works in the second week.

   a. What are the units of the fraction?
   $\frac{\text{dollars}}{\text{hours}} = $ dollars per hour

   b. Rewrite the expression substituting the given values for p and t. What are the units of each term of your new expression? Explain.
   $60 + 15s$; dollars, because $\frac{\text{dollars}}{\cancel{\text{hour}}} \cdot \cancel{\text{hours}} = $ dollars

   c. Evaluate your expression for $s = 5$. Include units.
   60 dollars + 15 dollars per hour $\cdot$ 5 hours = 135 dollars

© Houghton Mifflin Harcourt Publishing Company

1-2 Simplifying Expressions

Essential question: *How can you rewrite algebraic expressions?*

COMMON CORE **Standards for Mathematical Content**

CC.9-12.N.Q.1 Use units as a way to understand ... and to guide the solution of multi-step problems ...*

CC.9-12.A.SSE.1 Interpret expressions that represent a quantity in terms of its context.*

CC.9-12.A.SSE.1a Interpret parts of an expression, such as terms, factors, and coefficients.*

CC.9-12.A.SSE.2 Use the structure of an expression to identify ways to rewrite it.

Vocabulary

Distributive Property

Prerequisites

Evaluating Expressions, Lesson 1-1

Math Background

In algebra, properties of addition and multiplication play a key role in the logical system that makes it possible to simplify expressions. Consider the steps in simplifying the expression $3(x + 5) + x$:

$$3(x + 5) + x = (3x + 15) + x$$
$$= 3x + (15 + x)$$
$$= 3x + (x + 15)$$
$$= (3x + x) + 15$$
$$= 4x + 15$$

Even though many of these steps may be eliminated in a classroom presentation, the steps detail the usage of the Commutative, Associative, and Distributive Properties.

INTRODUCE

Use the Distributive Property to rewrite products using compatible numbers by breaking the greater factor into a sum that contains a multiple of 10. For example:

$$7(104) = 7(100) + 7(4)$$

Tell students that the properties of addition and multiplication allow expressions to be rearranged to make simplifying the expression easier.

TEACH

1 EXPLORE

Questioning Strategies

- Why are the expressions $2l + 2w$ and $2(l + w)$ equivalent? The Distributive Property distributes multiplication over addition and states that $a(b + c) = ab + ac$. Thus, $2(l + w) = 2l + 2w$.

- What is true about the coefficients of two like terms if their sum is 0? The coefficients are additive inverses of each other.

Differentiated Instruction

Tell students that the word "distribute" means to share among many or "to deliver to members of a group." Point out to students how the word's everyday meaning is similar to its mathematical meaning. Also, to help students remember which property is the Commutative Property and which is the Associative Property, have them think of people changing places as they commute back and forth to work. Then have students think of associating with different groups of friends as changing groups.

MATHEMATICAL PRACTICE **Highlighting the Standards**

This Explore and its Reflect questions offer an opportunity to address Mathematical Practice Standard 7 (Look for and make use of structure). By analyzing the properties (Associative, Commutative, and Distributive) used for simplifying expressions, students learn the underlying logical processes that make it possible to simplify and solve expressions and equations. They learn that an operation is associative if it can be grouped in any way without changing the answer. Students also learn that an operation is commutative if the order of the terms can be changed without changing the answer.

Name_____ Class_____ Date_____

1-2

Simplifying Expressions

Essential question: *How can you rewrite algebraic expressions?*

COMMON CORE
CC.9-12.N.Q.1*,
CC.9-12.A.SSE.1*,
CC.9-12.A.SSE.1a*,
CC.9-12.A.SSE.2

1 EXPLORE Comparing Expressions

A soccer field has a length *l* of 105 m and a width *w* of 68 m.

A Use the expression $2l + 2w$ to find the perimeter of the field.

$2l + 2w = 2(105) + 2(68) = 210 + 136 = 346$ m

B Using the expression $2(l + w)$, what is the perimeter of the field?

$2(l + w) = 2(105 + 68) = 2(173) = 346$ m

C What do the results suggest about $2l + 2w$ and $2(l + w)$?

Both expressions give the same perimeter, so they are equivalent.

The Explore above illustrates the **Distributive Property**. The table below summarizes this and other important properties of real numbers.

Property	Addition	Multiplication
Commutative	$a + b = b + a$	$ab = ba$
Associative	$(a + b) + c = a + (b + c)$	$(ab)c = a(bc)$
Distributive	$a(b + c) = ab + ac$ $(b + c)a = ba + ca$	

REFLECT

1a. Identify the property being illustrated.

- $2x + 7x = (2 + 7)x$, which equals $9x$ Distributive Property
- $(x + 1) + 9 = x + (1 + 9)$, which equals $x + 10$ Assoc. Prop. of Add.
- $5 + x + 3 = x + 5 + 3$, which equals $x + 8$ Comm. Prop. of Add.

1b. *Like terms* contain the same variables raised to the same power. In part a, how was the Distributive Property used to combine like terms?

The Distributive Property was used to group the coefficients of like terms $2x$

and $7x$ so they could be added, or combined, to get $9x$.

1c. Constant terms are also considered like terms. In part a, how were properties used to combine constant terms?

The Commutative and Associate Properties were used to group constant

terms together.

1d. You can use the fact that subtracting a number is the same as adding its opposite in order to apply properties of real numbers to subtraction expressions. Identify the property being illustrated.

$2(3x - 4) - 7x = 2(3x + (-4)) + (-7x)$ Add the opposite.

$= 6x + (-8) + (-7x)$ Distributive Property

$= 6x + (-7x) + (-8)$ Comm. Prop. of Add.

$= (6 + (-7))x + (-8)$ Distributive Property

$= -x + (-8)$ Add.

$= -x - 8$ Write without parentheses.

To *simplify* an algebraic expression, you use properties of real numbers to combine like terms and eliminate any grouping symbols.

2 EXAMPLE Using Properties to Simplify Expressions

Simplify each expression.

A For a picnic, you buy p packages of chicken hot dogs at $3.99 per package and p packages of hot dog buns at $2.19 per package. The expression $3.99p + 2.19p$ can be used to represent the total cost.

$3.99p + 2.19p = (3.99 + 2.19) \cdot p$ Distributive Property

$= 6.18p$

B Suppose that you need one more package of hot dogs than buns. Then the expression $3.99(p + 1) + 2.19p$ represents the total cost.

$3.99(p + 1) + 2.19p = 3.99p + 3.99 + 2.19p$ Distributive Property

$= 3.99p + 2.19p + 3.99$ Commutative Property

$= 6.18p + 3.99$ Distributive Property

C Suppose that you need one more package of buns than hotdogs. Then the expression $3.99p + [2.19(p + 1)]$ represents the total cost.

$3.99p + [2.19(p + 1)] = 3.99p + 2.19p + 2.19$ Distributive Property

$= 3.99p + 2.19p + 2.19$ Associative Property

$= 6.18p + 2.19$ Distributive Property

Questioning Strategies

- In part A, what does $6.18p$ represent? What does the coefficient 6.18 represent in the context of the problem? the total cost of p packages of chicken hot dogs and p packages of hot dog buns; $6.18

- In part B, why does p change to $(p + 1)$ only in the first term? The variable p represents the number of packages of both hot dogs and hot dog buns. The expression $(p + 1)$ represents 1 more package of hot dogs than buns. If $(p + 1)$ was used in the second term, there would be an additional one more package of buns.

- In part B, what does $6.18p + 3.99$ represent? the total cost of $p + 1$ packages of chicken hot dogs and p packages of hot dog buns

EXTRA EXAMPLE

A. You buy t new T-shirts for $8.95 each and t pairs of shorts for $13.40 each. The expression $8.95t + 13.40t$ can be used to represent the total cost. Simplify this expression. $22.35t$

B. Suppose you need one more T-shirt than pairs of shorts. The expression $8.95(t + 1) + 13.40t$ represents the total cost. Simplify this expression. $22.35t + 8.95$

Avoid Common Errors

When evaluating an expression such as $7.5(x + 1)$ students sometimes multiply the first term inside a set of parentheses by the outside number 7.5, but forget to distribute that number to the second term. Encourage students to draw arcing arrows from the outside number to each term in the set of parentheses to remind them to complete the distributive process.

CLOSE

Essential Question

How can you rewrite algebraic expressions?
To rewrite algebraic expressions, you simplify the expression using the Associative, Commutative, and Distributive Properties and the order of operations.

Summarize

Have students describe in their journal how the Commutative and Associative Properties are alike and how they differ. Also have students describe how the Distributive Property is useful when simplifying expressions.

PRACTICE

Where skills are taught	Where skills are practiced
1 EXPLORE	EXS. 1–6
2 EXAMPLE	EXS. 7–18

Exercise 19: Students must extend their knowledge from the lesson to identify a mistake in simplifying an expression.

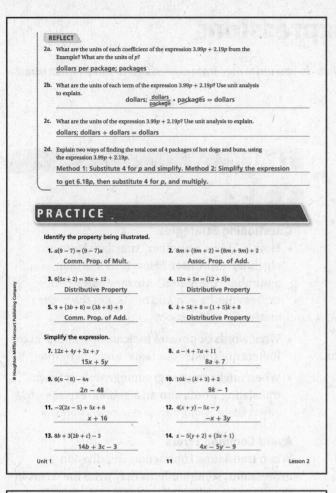

REFLECT

2a. What are the units of each coefficient of the expression $3.99p + 2.19p$ from the Example? What are the units of p?

dollars per package; packages

2b. What are the units of each term of the expression $3.99p + 2.19p$? Use unit analysis to explain.

$$\text{dollars; } \frac{\text{dollars}}{\text{package}} \cdot \text{packages} = \text{dollars}$$

2c. What are the units of the expression $3.99p + 2.19p$? Use unit analysis to explain.

dollars; dollars + dollars = dollars

2d. Explain two ways of finding the total cost of 4 packages of hot dogs and buns, using the expression $3.99p + 2.19p$.

Method 1: Substitute 4 for p and simplify. Method 2: Simplify the expression to get $6.18p$, then substitute 4 for p, and multiply.

PRACTICE

Identify the property being illustrated.

1. $a(9 - 7) = (9 - 7)a$

Comm. Prop. of Mult.

2. $8m + (9m + 2) = (8m + 9m) + 2$

Assoc. Prop. of Add.

3. $6(5x + 2) = 30x + 12$

Distributive Property

4. $12n + 5n = (12 + 5)n$

Distributive Property

5. $9 + (3b + 8) = (3b + 8) + 9$

Comm. Prop. of Add.

6. $k + 5k + 8 = (1 + 5)k + 8$

Distributive Property

Simplify the expression.

7. $12x + 4y + 3x + y$

$15x + 5y$

8. $a - 4 + 7a + 11$

$8a + 7$

9. $6(n - 8) - 4n$

$2n - 48$

10. $10k - (k + 3) + 2$

$9k - 1$

11. $-2(2x - 5) + 5x + 6$

$x + 16$

12. $4(x + y) - 5x - y$

$-x + 3y$

13. $8b + 3(2b + c) - 3$

$14b + 3c - 3$

14. $x - 5(y + 2) + (3x + 1)$

$4x - 5y - 9$

For Exercises 15–17, simplify each expression and identify the units.

15. You purchase n cans of tennis balls at \$4.50 per can from an online retailer. There is a tax of 8% on your order. There are also shipping costs of \$7 per order. The expression $4.5n + 0.08(4.5n) + 7$ can be used to represent the total cost.

$4.86n + 7$; dollars

16. You and two friends all have the same meal for lunch. Each meal costs c dollars plus a tax of 6% of the cost and a tip of 20% of the cost. You use a \$10 gift certificate. You can represent the total cost with the expression $3c + (0.06 + 0.20)(3c) - 10$.

$3.78c - 10$; dollars

17. You are making n loaves of bread for a bake sale and the recipe calls for 3.25 cups of flour per loaf. You are also making $n + 1$ pies for the bake sale, and the pie recipe calls for 2 cups of flour per pie. The expression $3.25n + 2(n + 1)$ can be used to represent the total amount of flour required for the bread and the pies.

$5.25n + 2$; cups

18. You burn calories at a rate of 15 calories per minute when running and 6 calories per minute when walking. Suppose you exercise for 60 minutes by running for r minutes and walking for the remaining time. The expression $15r + 6(60 - r)$ represents the calories burned.

a. What units are associated with r? What units are associated with 15? What does 15r represent? Use unit analysis to explain.

minutes; calories per minute; calories burned running; $\frac{\text{cal}}{\text{min}} \cdot \text{min} = \text{cal}$

b. What does $60 - r$ represent? What units are associated with $6(60 - r)$?

minutes spent walking; calories

c. Simplify $15r + 6(60 - r)$. What units are associated with the expression? Use unit analysis to explain.

$9r + 360$; calories; $\frac{\text{cal}}{\text{min}} \cdot \text{min} + \frac{\text{cal}}{\text{min}} \cdot \text{min} = \text{cal} + \text{cal} = \text{cal}$

19. **Error Analysis** A student says that the perimeter of a rectangle with side lengths $(2x - 1)$ inches and $3x$ inches can be written as $(10x - 1)$ inches, because $2(2x - 1) + 2(3x) = 10x - 1$. Explain why this statement is incorrect.

When you simplify the expression $2(2x - 1) + 2(3x)$, you get $10x - 2$.

The student forgot to distribute the 2 to the -1 inside the parentheses.

Notes

Writing Expressions

Essential question: *How do you write algebraic expressions to model quantities?*

COMMON CORE Standards for Mathematical Content

CC.9-12.N.Q.1 Use units as a way to understand … and to guide the solution of multi-step problems …*

CC.9-12.N.Q.2 Define appropriate quantities for the purpose of descriptive modeling.*

CC.9-12.A.SSE.1 Interpret expressions that represent a quantity in terms of its context.*

CC.9-12.A.SSE.1a Interpret parts of an expression, such as terms, factors, and coefficients.*

CC.9-12.A.SSE.2 Use the structure of an expression to identify ways to rewrite it.

Prerequisites

Simplifying Expressions, Lesson 1-2

Math Background

Students have already evaluated and simplified algebraic expressions. In this lesson, students will write expressions using verbal models and translate the words into algebraic expressions.

Students will learn how algebra can represent words and phrases by using variables, constants, and operation symbols. They will use a consistent, universally understood and accepted system that began with a system developed by the Babylonians.

INTRODUCE

Ask students if they have ever translated a phrase from one language to another. Ask volunteers to translate a simple sentence, such as "My name is Mary," to another language. Remind students that the original sentence and the translation have the same meaning. Tell them that today they will learn how to translate word phrases into algebraic phrases, or expressions, that have the same meaning as the original phrase.

TEACH

1 ENGAGE

Questioning Strategies

- How is "3 less a number" translated into an algebraic expression? How is "3 less than a number" translated? Are they equivalent expressions? 3 — *n* and *n* — 3; no, the order matters in subtraction.

- What words or phrases indicate operations in the Reflect question? "quotient" and "more than"

- When might you use grouping symbols when translating words into an algebraic expression? when there is more than one operation

Avoid Common Errors

When translating subtraction and division expressions, some students may write the terms in the incorrect order. Tell students to double check that the order makes sense within the context of the word phrase when writing a subtraction or division expression.

2 EXAMPLE

Questioning Strategies

- In part A, how do you know to multiply 15% times the price of the meal? A tip is a percentage of the "price of a meal", and "of" signals multiplication.

- In part B, why is it a good idea to choose the letter *p* as the variable? "Price of the meal" starts with a *p* and choosing the same letter that the word or phrase starts with helps you remember what the variable represents.

- In part C, what property is used to factor out the variable *p*? Distributive Property

- What is the total cost if the price of the meal is $12.85? $14.78

continued

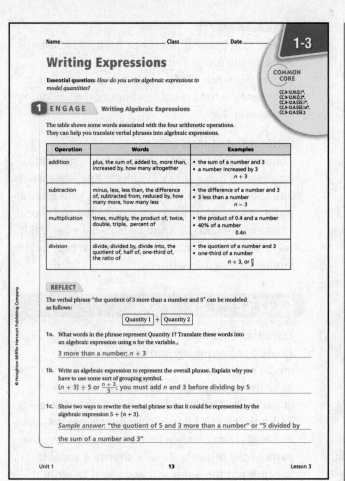

Name _____ **Class** _____ **Date** _____

1-3

Writing Expressions

Essential question: *How do you write algebraic expressions to model quantities?*

COMMON CORE

CC-9-12.N.Q.1*,
CC-9-12.N.Q.2*,
CC-9-12.A.SSE.1*,
CC-9-12.A.SSE.1a*,
CC-9-12.A.SSE.2

1 ENGAGE Writing Algebraic Expressions

The table shows some words associated with the four arithmetic operations. They can help you translate verbal phrases into algebraic expressions.

Operation	Words	Examples
addition	plus, the sum of, added to, more than, increased by, how many altogether	• the sum of a number and 3 • a number increased by 3 $n + 3$
subtraction	minus, less, less than, the difference of, subtracted from, reduced by, how many more, how many less	• the difference of a number and 3 • 3 less than a number $n - 3$
multiplication	times, multiply, the product of, twice, double, triple, percent of	• the product of 0.4 and a number • 40% of a number $0.4n$
division	divide, divided by, divide into, the quotient of, half of, one-third of, the ratio of	• the quotient of a number and 3 • one-third of a number $n \div 3$, or $\frac{n}{3}$

REFLECT

The verbal phrase "the quotient of 3 more than a number and 5" can be modeled as follows:

| Quantity 1 | ÷ | Quantity 2 |

1a. What words in the phrase represent Quantity 1? Translate these words into an algebraic expression using n for the variable.

3 more than a number; $n + 3$

1b. Write an algebraic expression to represent the overall phrase. Explain why you have to use some sort of grouping symbol.

$(n + 3) \div 5$ or $\frac{n + 3}{5}$; you must add n and 3 before dividing by 5

1c. Show two ways to rewrite the verbal phrase so that it could be represented by the algebraic expression $5 \div (n + 3)$.

Sample answer: "the quotient of 5 and 3 more than a number" or "5 divided by the sum of a number and 3"

Unit 1   13   Lesson 3

© Houghton Mifflin Harcourt Publishing Company

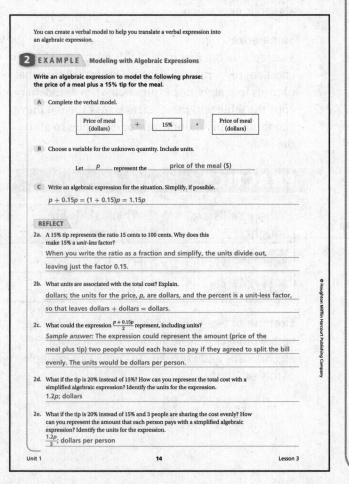

You can create a verbal model to help you translate a verbal expression into an algebraic expression.

2 EXAMPLE Modeling with Algebraic Expressions

Write an algebraic expression to model the following phrase: the price of a meal plus a 15% tip for the meal.

A Complete the verbal model.

| Price of meal (dollars) | + | 15% | • | Price of meal (dollars) |

B Choose a variable for the unknown quantity. Include units.

Let __p__ represent the ___ price of the meal ($) ___

C Write an algebraic expression for the situation. Simplify, if possible.

$p + 0.15p = (1 + 0.15)p = 1.15p$

REFLECT

2a. A 15% tip represents the ratio 15 cents to 100 cents. Why does this make 15% a *unit-less* factor?

When you write the ratio as a fraction and simplify, the units divide out, leaving just the factor 0.15.

2b. What units are associated with the total cost? Explain.

dollars; the units for the price, p, are dollars, and the percent is a unit-less factor, so that leaves dollars + dollars = dollars.

2c. What could the expression $\frac{p + 0.15p}{2}$ represent, including units?

Sample answer: The expression could represent the amount (price of the meal plus tip) two people would each have to pay if they agreed to split the bill evenly. The units would be dollars per person.

2d. What if the tip is 20% instead of 15%? How can you represent the total cost with a simplified algebraic expression? Identify the units for the expression.

1.2p; dollars

2e. What if the tip is 20% instead of 15% and 3 people are sharing the cost evenly? How can you represent the amount that each person pays with a simplified algebraic expression? Identify the units for the expression.

$\frac{1.2p}{3}$; dollars per person

Unit 1   14   Lesson 3

© Houghton Mifflin Harcourt Publishing Company

EXTRA EXAMPLE

Write an algebraic expression to model the following phrase: the price of a video game that is discounted 35%. $p - 0.35p = 0.65p$

Teaching Strategy

Encourage students to highlight all words and phrases that represent operations when translating word phrases to algebraic expressions. This will help students determine the amounts and types of operations to use.

> MATHEMATICAL PRACTICE **Highlighting the Standards**
>
> Example 2, along with its Reflect questions, offers an opportunity to address Mathematical Practice Standard 1 (Make sense of problems and persevere in solving them). By translating verbal phrases into algebraic expressions, students make sense of problems and rewrite them so they can be evaluated mathematically.
>
> Students learn how to explain their reasoning of why they chose certain operations to use in solving problems. When translating a phrase into an algabraic expression, students explore ways for an expression to change when a situation changes.

3 EXAMPLE

Questioning Strategies

- How do you know to use addition? The word "total" represents addition.

- How do you know to use division for the phrase "hours per week"? The word "per" represents division.

- What are the units of the expression you wrote in Reflect Question 3c? Explain. hours; hours $+$ $\frac{hours}{week} \cdot$ weeks $+$ hours $+ \frac{hours}{weeks} \cdot$ weeks $=$ hours $+$ hours $+$ hours $+$ hours $=$ hours

EXTRA EXAMPLE

Arlene did chores at her house for 8 hours last week. In the future she plans to do 2 hours of chores per week. Write an algebraic expression to represent the total number of hours she will do chores. $8 + 2w$

Differentiated Instruction

Translating real-world situations into algebraic expressions may prove difficult for English learners. You may wish to pair English learners with English-proficient students who can explain the real-world situation to them. This can be especially helpful if there are words, such as volunteer, that may not be familiar to English learners.

CLOSE

Essential Question

How do you write algebraic expressions to model quantities?

To write an algebraic expression to model a quantity, first look for key words that indicate which arithmetic operation or operations are involved. Then create a verbal model relating the parts of the quantity. Finally, choose a variable to represent the unknown and use it to write the algebraic expression.

Summarize

The table on the first page of this lesson provides an excellent resource to help students translate verbal phrases into algebraic expressions. Have students copy the table into their journals. Ask them if they can think of any more words or examples to add to the table.

PRACTICE

Where skills are taught	Where skills are practiced
2 EXAMPLE	EXS. 1–3
3 EXAMPLE	EXS. 4–5

Exercise 6: Students are led to realize that some verbal phrases may be ambiguous when written algebraically and are asked to correct an example of this situation.

3 EXAMPLE Using Unit Analysis to Guide Modeling

Lizzie has volunteered 20 hours at her town library. From now on, she plans to volunteer 5 hours per week at the library. Write an algebraic expression to represent the total number of hours she will volunteer.

A Use unit analysis to help you get the correct units for the expression.

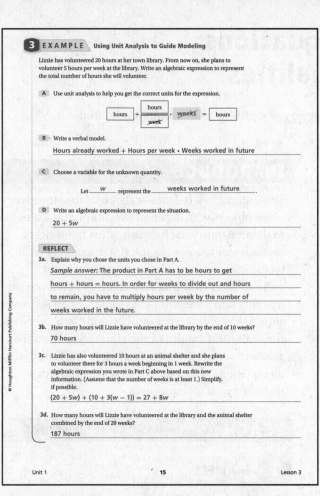

$$\text{hours} + \frac{\text{hours}}{\cancel{\text{week}}} \cdot \cancel{\text{weeks}} = \text{hours}$$

B Write a verbal model.

Hours already worked + Hours per week • Weeks worked in future

C Choose a variable for the unknown quantity.

Let ___w___ represent the ___weeks worked in future___.

D Write an algebraic expression to represent the situation.

20 + 5w

REFLECT

3a. Explain why you chose the units you chose in Part A.

Sample answer: The product in Part A has to be hours to get

hours + hours = hours. In order for weeks to divide out and hours

to remain, you have to multiply hours per week by the number of

weeks worked in the future.

3b. How many hours will Lizzie have volunteered at the library by the end of 10 weeks?

70 hours

3c. Lizzie has also volunteered 10 hours at an animal shelter and she plans to volunteer there for 3 hours a week beginning in 1 week. Rewrite the algebraic expression you wrote in Part C above based on this new information. (Assume that the number of weeks is at least 1.) Simplify, if possible.

$(20 + 5w) + (10 + 3(w - 1)) = 27 + 8w$

3d. How many hours will Lizzie have volunteered at the library and the animal shelter combined by the end of 20 weeks?

187 hours

© Houghton Mifflin Harcourt Publishing Company

PRACTICE

1. Alex purchased a 6-hour calling card. He has used *t* minutes of access time. Write an algebraic expression to represent how many minutes he has remaining and identify the units for the expression.

360 − *t*; minutes

2. It costs $20 per hour to bowl and $3 for shoe rental. Write a verbal model and an algebraic expression to represent the cost for *n* hours and identify the units for the expression.

Cost per hour • Number of hours + Cost of shoes; 20n + 3; dollars

3. Jared earns 0.25 vacation days for every week that he works in a calendar year. He also gets 10 paid company holidays per year. Write a verbal model and an algebraic expression to represent the amount of time he gets off from work in a year after working for w weeks and identify the units for the expression.

Number of holidays + Vacation days earned per week • Number of

weeks; 10 + 0.25w; days

4. To convert dog years to human years, you count 10.5 dog years per human year for the first two human years and then 4 dog years per human year for each human year thereafter.

a. Show how to use unit analysis to get the correct units when you convert dog years to human years.

$$\frac{\text{dog years}}{\text{human years}} \cdot \text{human years} + \frac{\text{dog years}}{\text{human years}} \cdot \text{human years} = \text{dog years}$$

b. Write and simplify an algebraic expression for converting dog years to human years when the number of human years is 2 or more. Define what the variable represents.

$10.5(2) + 4(y - 2) = 13 + 4y$; y = human years

5. Tracie buys tickets to a concert for herself and two friends. There is an 8% tax on the cost of the tickets and an additional $10 booking fee. Write an algebraic expression to represent the cost per person. Simplify the expression, if possible. Define what the variable represents and identify the units for the expression.

$\frac{t + 0.08t + 10}{3} = \frac{(1 + 0.08)t + 10}{3} = \frac{1.08t + 10}{3}$, or $0.36t + 3\frac{1}{3}$;

t = the cost of the tickets; dollars per person

6. Write two different algebraic expressions that could represent the phrase "a number plus 2 times the number." Then rewrite the phrase so that only one of the algebraic expressions could be correct.

n + 2n, or (n + 2)n; *Sample answers:* a number plus twice the number,

or the product of 2 more than a number and the number

© Houghton Mifflin Harcourt Publishing Company

Writing Equations and Inequalities

Essential question: *How do you represent relationships algebraically?*

CC.9-12.N.Q.2 Define appropriate quantities for the purpose of descriptive modeling.*

CC.9-12.A.CED.1 Create equations and inequalities in one variable and use them to solve problems.*

CC.9-12.A.CED.3 Represent constraints by equations or inequalities ... and interpret solutions as viable or nonviable options in a modeling context.*

Vocabulary

equation

solution of an equation

inequality

solution of an inequality

Prerequisites

Writing Expressions, Lesson 1-3

Math Background

Students have previously evaluated, simplified, and written algebraic expressions. In this lesson, students write equations and inequalities. Equations are mathematical sentences that show that two expressions are equivalent, and inequalities compare two expressions that are not strictly equal by using inequality symbols.

One of the basic building blocks of mathematics is the Law of Trichotomy. This axiom states that given any two real numbers, a and b, exactly one of the following is true:

$$a = b, a < b, \text{ or } a > b$$

In the first case, a and b are related by an equation. In the second and third cases, a and b are related by an inequality.

A solution of an inequality is the value or values that make the statement true. Thus, the solution set of $x > 5$ contains every value on a number line to the right of 5 and is an infinite set of numbers.

INTRODUCE

Show students a balance scale. Have the students place objects with different weights on the scales to demonstrate what happens when the weights on each side are not the same. Ask students what would make the scale balance. **equal weight on both sides** Now place 5 weights of equal size on one side and 3 weights of the same size on the other side. Ask students what must be done to balance the scale. **Add 2 more of the equal weights to the side with only 3 weights.** Explain to students that an equation is like a balanced scale: both sides must be equal, or equivalent.

TEACH

1 EXAMPLE

Questioning Strategies

- What words could the equals sign in the verbal model represent? **equals, is, is equal to**

- Six percent is written as 0.06. What percent does 1.06 represent? What does $1.06p$ represent? **106%; 106% of the price of the shirt**

- Why is it more reasonable to begin the guess-and-check strategy with $20 rather than with $30? **The price without tax must be less than $26.50, the price with tax.**

EXTRA EXAMPLE

Arlon paid $24.84 including 8% sales tax for a used video game, but he does not remember the price without tax. Write an equation to represent the situation. $p + 0.08p = 24.84$; $1.08p = 24.84$

Differentiated Instruction

English learners may not have heard the word *equivalent*. Show students the first four letters of the word, *equi*, and ask if they have heard words that sound similar to this or start with this sound. Elicit the word *equal* from them. Explain that if two expressions are equivalent, then their values are equal.

Name_____ Class_____ Date_____

1-4

Writing Equations and Inequalities

Essential question: *How do you represent relationships algebraically?*

COMMON CORE

CC.9-12.N.Q.2*,
CC.9-12.A.CED.1*,
CC.9-12.A.CED.3*

An algebraic expression is a phrase. It represents a value. *Equations* and *inequalities* represent relationships between expressions. An **equation** is a mathematical statement that two expressions are equivalent. The **solution of an equation** is the value or values that make the equation true.

1 EXAMPLE Writing Equations

Leon paid $26.50 for a shirt with a sales tax of 6% included but he doesn't remember the price without tax. Write an equation to represent the situation.

A Complete the verbal model for the situation.

| Price of shirt (dollars) | + | 6% | · | Price of shirt (dollars) | = | Amount paid (dollars) |

B Choose a variable for the unknown quantity. Include units.

Let ___p___ represent the ___price of the shirt ($)___

C Write an equation from the verbal model. Simplify, if possible.

$p + 0.06p = 26.5$; $1.06p = 26.5$

REFLECT

1a. Explain why $20 is not a solution of the equation.

Substituting 20 for p in the equation $1.06p = 26.5$ you get $1.06(20) = 26.5$,

or $21.2 = 26.5$, which is false. So $20 is not a solution.

1b. Explain how to use a guess-and-check strategy to find the solution of the equation. Then find the solution.

Try other possible prices for the shirt, beginning with $21, then $22, etc.,

until you find a price that makes the equation true; $25

1c. What must be true about the units on both sides of an equation?

The units of the expressions on both sides of an equation must be equal.

© Houghton Mifflin Harcourt Publishing Company

An **inequality** is a statement that compares two expressions that are not strictly equal by using one of the following inequality signs.

Symbol	Meaning
<	is less than
≤	is less than or equal to
>	is greater than
≥	is greater than or equal to
≠	is not equal to

A **solution of an inequality** is any value of the variable that makes the inequality true. You can find solutions by making a table.

2 EXAMPLE Writing and Solving Inequalities

Kristin can afford to spend at most $50 for a birthday dinner at a restaurant, including a 15% tip. Describe some costs that are within her budget.

A Which inequality symbol can be used to represent "at most"? ___≤___

B Complete the verbal model for the situation.

| Cost before tip (dollars) | + | 15% | · | Cost before tip (dollars) | ≤ | Budget limit (dollars) |

C Write and simplify an inequality for the model. $c + 0.15c \leq 50$; $1.15c \leq 50$

D Complete the table to find some costs that are within Kristin's budget.

Cost	Substitute	Compare	Solution?
$47	$1.15(47) \leq 50$	$54.05 \leq 50$ ✗	No
$45	$1.15(45) \leq 50$	$51.75 \leq 50$ ✗	No
$43	$1.15(43) \leq 50$	$49.45 \leq 50$ ✓	Yes
$41	$1.15(41) \leq 50$	$47.15 \leq 50$ ✓	Yes

Kristin can spend $43, $41, or any lesser amount and stay within budget.

© Houghton Mifflin Harcourt Publishing Company

Questioning Strategies

- Which inequality symbol can be used to represent "at least"? $\geq$

- Can partial dollar amounts be part of the solution set? Explain. Yes; any amount from $0 to $43 is in the solution set.

- Can any amounts greater than $43 be part of the solution set? Explain. Yes; since $1.15(43) = 49.45$, any amount that has a result from 49.45 to 50 is part of the complete solution set. $43.48 is the greatest amount since $1.15(43.48) = 50.00$.

EXTRA EXAMPLE

Sarah can afford to spend at most $45, including 8% sales tax, on a present for her mother. Write an equation to represent the situation. What is the greatest whole dollar amount that she can spend before the tax is added, and what is the cost including tax? $p + 0.08p \leq 45$; $1.08p \leq 45$; $41; $44.28

Avoid Common Errors

Some students may use the greater than or equal to symbol to represent *at most*, because they see the word "most" and correlate it to "greater than". Help students understand that "at most" means the value given is the greatest the result can be. All other values must be less than the given value. Therefore, *at most* is represented by the less than or equal to symbol, and *at least* is represented by the greater than or equal to symbol.

Technology

Students can use a graphing calculator to create a table to find solutions to an inequality. Enter the expression $x + 0.15x$ into the Y $=$ function of the calculator. Press 2nd then TBLSET and enter 40 after TblStart and 1 after $\triangle$Tbl. Then press 2nd TABLE. The column labeled X will show the cost without the 15% tip, and the column labeled Y_1 will show the cost including the 15% tip. Using a calculator allows students to scroll through a large number of values to find that the inequality in **2** EXAMPLE is true for integer values less than or equal to 43. The $\triangle$Tbl value can be changed to 0.01 to find the maximum value to the nearest cent.

MATHEMATICAL PRACTICE | Highlighting the Standards

2 EXAMPLE , its Reflect questions, and Questioning Strategies offer an opportunity to address Mathematical Practice Standard 2 (Reason abstractly and quantitatively). Students take a situation and represent it symbolically by writing an inequality. Then students analyze the solution set in the parameters of whole dollars. They are then asked if it is possible to expand the solution set to include partial dollar amounts and to explain why this is possible. By analyzing what values are in the solution set if it is restricted to whole dollars, and then expanding the solution set to include partial dollar amounts, students should understand that the solution set changes depending on the units that can be used (dollars or cents).

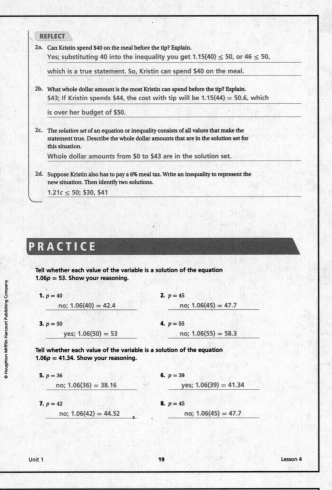

Notes

REFLECT

2a. Can Kristin spend $40 on the meal before the tip? Explain.

Yes; substituting 40 into the inequality you get $1.15(40) \le 50$, or $46 \le 50$,

which is a true statement. So, Kristin can spend $40 on the meal.

2b. What whole dollar amount is the most Kristin can spend before the tip? Explain.

$43; If Kristin spends $44, the cost with tip will be $1.15(44) = 50.6$, which

is over her budget of $50.

2c. The *solution set* of an equation or inequality consists of all values that make the statement true. Describe the whole dollar amounts that are in the solution set for this situation.

Whole dollar amounts from $0 to $43 are in the solution set.

2d. Suppose Kristin also has to pay a 6% meal tax. Write an inequality to represent the new situation. Then identify two solutions.

$1.21c \le 50$; $30, $41

PRACTICE

Tell whether each value of the variable is a solution of the equation $1.06p = 53$. Show your reasoning.

1. $p = 40$

no; $1.06(40) = 42.4$

2. $p = 45$

no; $1.06(45) = 47.7$

3. $p = 50$

yes; $1.06(50) = 53$

4. $p = 55$

no; $1.06(55) = 58.3$

Tell whether each value of the variable is a solution of the equation $1.06p = 41.34$. Show your reasoning.

5. $p = 36$

no; $1.06(36) = 38.16$

6. $p = 39$

yes; $1.06(39) = 41.34$

7. $p = 42$

no; $1.06(42) = 44.52$

8. $p = 45$

no; $1.06(45) = 47.7$

© Houghton Mifflin Harcourt Publishing Company

Essential Question

How do you represent relationships algebraically?
Relationships between expressions that are equal
can be expressed as equations. Relationships
between expressions that involve "at least",
"at most", "less than", or "greater than" can be
expressed as inequalities.

Summarize

Have students describe in their journal the
differences and similarities between expressions,
equations, and inequalities.

PRACTICE

Where skills are taught	Where skills are practiced
1 EXAMPLE	EXS. 1–11
2 EXAMPLE	EXS. 12–16

Tell whether the value is a solution of the inequality. Explain.

12. $x = 36; 3x < 100$
<u>no; 3(36) = 108</u>

13. $m = 12; 5m + 4 > 50$
<u>yes; 5(12) + 4 = 64</u>

14. $b = 5; 60 - 10b \leq 20$
<u>yes; 60 - 10(5) = 10</u>

15. Brent is ordering books for a reading group. Each book costs $11.95. If he orders at least $200 worth of books, he will get free shipping.

   a. Complete the verbal model for the situation.

 ·   ≥

   b. Choose a variable for the unknown quantity. Include units.

   Let <u>b</u> represent the <u>number of books</u>.

   c. Write an inequality from the verbal model.

   <u>$11.95b \geq 200$</u>

   d. Complete the table to find some numbers of books Brent can order and receive free shipping.

Books	Substitute	Compare	Solution?
15	$11.95(15) \geq 200$	$179.25 \geq 200$ ✗	No
16	$11.95(16) \geq 200$	$191.20 \geq 200$ ✗	No
17	$11.95(17) \geq 200$	$203.15 \geq 200$ ✓	Yes
18	$11.95(18) \geq 200$	$215.10 \geq 200$ ✓	Yes

   <u>Brent must order 17 books or more to get free shipping.</u>

16. Farzana has a prepaid cell phone that costs $1 per day plus $.10 per minute she uses. She has a daily budget of $5 for phone costs.

   a. Write an inequality to represent the situation.

   <u>Let m be the daily minutes used; $1 + 0.10m \leq 5$</u>

   b. What is the maximum number of minutes Farzana can use and still stay within her daily budget? Show your reasoning.

   <u>40 min; $1 + 0.10(35) = 4.5$, $1 + 0.10(40) = 5$, $1 + 0.10(45) = 5.5$</u>

   c. Describe the solution set of the inequality.

   <u>Any amount of time between 0 and 40 min is in the solution set.</u>

© Houghton Mifflin Harcourt Publishing Company

Notes

1-5

Representing Functions

Essential question: *How do you represent functions?*

⊙ COMMON **Standards for**
⊙ CORE **Mathematical Content**

CC.9-12.N.Q.1 ...choose and interpret the scale and the origin in graphs and data displays.*

CC.9-12.F.IF.1 Understand that a function from one set (called the domain) to another set (called the range) assigns to each element of the domain exactly one element of the range. If f is a function and x is an element of its domain, then $f(x)$ denotes the output of f corresponding to the input x. The graph of f is the graph of the equation $y = f(x)$.

CC.9-12.F.IF.2 Use function notation, evaluate functions for inputs in their domains, and interpret statements that use function notation in terms of a context.

CC.9-12.F.IF.5 Relate the domain of a function to its graph and, where applicable, to the quantitative relationship it describes.*

Vocabulary

function

domain

range

function notation

independent variable

dependent variable

function rule

Prerequisites

Evaluating Expressions, Lesson 1-1

Math Background

A relation is any set of ordered pairs. A function is a relation in which each domain value pairs with exactly one range value. Thus, every function is a relation, but not every relation is a function. Many students believe incorrectly that functions must be represented by equations. However, a function, by definition, merely pairs each element in its domain with exactly one element in its range. Functions may not be describable by a rule that can be represented as an equation. It is important to stress relations and functions as ordered pairs to help avoid this misconception.

INTRODUCE

Introduce students to functions using concepts and data with which they are familiar, exemplified by the relationship of number of chairs to the number of legs. Have students fill in the following table:

Chairs	1	2	3	4
Legs	4	8	12	16

Ask students to describe the relationship between the number of chairs and the number of legs. **The number of legs is 4 times the number of chairs.**

TEACH

 **1 ENGAGE**

Questioning Strategies

• Would the mapping diagram represent a function if −4 were included in the domain and its arrow pointed to 16 in the range? Explain. **Yes; all elements of the domain would still be paired with only one element in the domain.**

• What would the arrows in the mapping diagram look like if it did not represent a function? **At least one element of the domain would have at least two arrows going from it pointing to at least two different range elements.**

Differentiated Instruction

Some students confuse the domain and the range. Tell students that alphabetically, *domain* comes before *range*, just as *x-values* comes before *y-values* in an ordered pair. This may help students connect the domain to the *x*-values and the range to the *y*-values.

continued

Name_____ Class_____ Date_____

Representing Functions

Essential question: How do you represent functions?

COMMON CORE

CC.9-12.N.Q.1*,
CC.9-12.F.IF.1,
CC.9-12.F.IF.2,
CC.9-12.F.IF.5*

1 ENGAGE Understanding Functions

A *set* is a collection of items called *elements*. A **function** pairs each element in one set, called the **domain**, with exactly one element in a second set, called the **range**. For example, the function below pairs each element in the domain with its square.

Domain   Range

0	→	0
1	→	1
2	→	4
3	→	9
4	→	16

A function can be described using **function notation**. The function f assigns the *output* value $f(x)$ in the range to the corresponding *input* value x from the domain. The notation $f(x)$ is read as "f of x."(It does not indicate the product "f times x.") For the function shown above, $f(3) = 9$.

REFLECT

1a. The domain of the function can be written using *set notation* as {0, 1, 2, 3, 4}. Write the range of the function using set notation.

{0, 1, 4, 9, 16}

1b. Tell how to read the statement $f(4) = 16$. Then interpret what it means in terms of input and output values.

f of 4 is 16; when the input is 4, the output is 16.

1c. Suppose the 3 were paired with the 4 instead of the 9. Would the pairing of the two sets still be a function? Why or why not?

Yes; each input would still be paired with exactly one output.

1d. Suppose the 3 were paired with the 4 and the 9. Would the pairing of the two sets still be a function? Why or why not?

No; each input of a function must have exactly one, not two, outputs.

1e. If you pair each month with all the possible numbers of days in the month, will you get a function? Why or why not?

No; February gets paired with 28 days in most years, but with 29 days

In leap years. Functions must have exactly one output for each input.

© Houghton Mifflin Harcourt Publishing Company

Functions are often used to describe a relationship between two variables. The **independent variable** represents an input value of the function and the **dependent variable** represents an output value.

An algebraic expression that defines a function is a **function rule**. For example, x^2 is the function rule for the squaring function $f(x) = x^2$. If you know a value for the independent variable, you can use a function rule to find the corresponding value for the dependent variable.

2 EXAMPLE Representing Discrete Linear Functions

The cost of sending m text messages at $0.25 per message can be represented by the function $C(m) = 0.25m$.

A Complete the table for the given domain values. Write the results as ordered pairs in the form (independent variable, dependent variable).

Independent variable, m	Dependent variable, $C(m) = 0.25m$	$(m, C(m))$
0	$0.25(0) = 0$	(0, 0)
1	$0.25(1) = 0.25$	(1, 0.25)
2	$0.25(2) = 0.5$	(2, 0.5)
3	$0.25(3) = 0.75$	(3, 0.75)
4	$0.25(4) = 1$	(4, 1)

B Choose a beginning, an end, and a scale for the vertical axis.

Start at 0 and go to at least 1 using a scale of $0.25.

C Graph the function by plotting the ordered pairs. The independent variable goes on the horizontal axis and the dependent variable on the vertical axis. Use scales that will make it easy to read points. Label the graph.

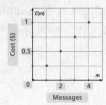

© Houghton Mifflin Harcourt Publishing Company

Teaching Strategy

The characteristic of each element of the domain only being paired with one element of the range is difficult for some students to understand. List elements of a function and a non-function relationship. For example:

A: (9, 2), (10, 5), (12, 2), (13, 7)

B: (3, 2), (5, 5), (7, 6), (7, 3)

Have students diagram the relations as shown in the Engage, drawing arrows from each domain element to its corresponding range element. Help students see that when two arrows point to a range element, the relation is a function. However, if two arrows come from one domain element, the relation is not a function. No domain element can be used twice in this type of diagram or repeated in a list of coordinates.

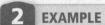

2 EXAMPLE

Questioning Strategies

- Are -2 and 1.5 reasonable values for m? **No; the number of text messages must be a whole number. Anything else is not reasonable.**

- As m increases by 1 what happens to $C(m)$? **As m increases by 1, $C(m)$ increases by 0.25.**

EXTRA EXAMPLE

Derek earns $9.00 per hour at his after-school job. He determined that he is paid $0.15 per minute. His rate of pay per minute can be represented by the function $P(m) = 0.15m$.

A. Complete a table of values using the domain {0, 1, 2, 3, 4, 5}. Write the results as ordered pairs. **(0, 0), (1, 0.15), (2, 0.30), (3, 0.45), (4, 0.60), (5, 0.75)**

B. Choose a beginning, an end, and a scale for the vertical axis. **Start at 0 and go to at least 0.75 using a scale of 0.15**

C. Graph the function by plotting the ordered pairs. Use scales that will make it easy to read the points. Label the graph. **The x-axis should be labeled as "Minutes" and use intervals of 1 starting with 0. The y-axis should be labeled as "Pay" and use intervals of 0.15 starting with 0. The following points should be plotted: (0, 0), (1, 0.15), (2, 0.30), (3, 0.45), (4, 0.60), (5, 0.75).**

Technology

Another way to find the values of the range is to use the table function of a graphing calculator. Input the function into the Y= function of the calculator. Press 2nd then TBLSET and enter 0 after TblStart and 1 after $\triangle$Tbl. Then press 2nd TABLE. The resulting table will display the domain in the column labeled X and the range in the column labeled Y_1.

Students can also graph the function with a graphing calculator. However, if they have used the table function they have to assume the parameters for the graph have been set. Students will need to use the WINDOW function to reset the parameters of the graph to match the situation.

Teaching Strategy

Have students think about the relationship between the input values and the output values before moving on to graphing functions. Have them look for a pattern in the table of values and relate the pattern to the function. Also, have students identify whether the output values are increasing as the input values increase or whether they are decreasing.

MATHEMATICAL PRACTICE Highlighting the Standards

This example and its Reflect questions offer an opportunity to address Mathematical Practice Standard 2 (Reason abstractly and quantitatively). By analyzing the input and output values and their associated units, students can understand that for every text message sent (the input) the output value equals a dollar amount. Students are asked to describe a reasonable domain and range for the function, considering the context of the situation and the units involved. Students are also asked whether it would make sense to connect the points to emphasize that only whole numbers of text messages are reasonable.

Students also relate the function to an input/output diagram, or function machine, representing the symbolic application of a function rule.

REFLECT

2a. Use function notation to represent the cost of sending 15 text messages. Evaluate the function for that value. Include units.

$C(15) = 1.25(15); \$18.75$

2b. Suppose that the domain of the function is not limited as in the Example. Describe a reasonable domain of the function.

It is only possible to send a whole number of text messages, and no limit was given, so the set of whole numbers is a reasonable domain.

2c. Suppose that the domain of the function is not limited as in the Example. Describe a reasonable range of the function.

If the domain is the set of whole numbers, then the range is the set of multiples of 0.25: {0, 0.25, 0.5, 0.75, 1, . . . }

2d. Is the independent variable represented by the *horizontal axis* or the *vertical axis*? Why does this make sense?

horizontal axis; *Sample answer:* You start with a value of the independent variable and find the corresponding value of the dependent variable. Likewise you locate the first coordinate before the second.

2e. Would it make sense to connect the points on the graph with a line? Why or why not?

No; a line would include values of m between whole numbers, but such values are not in the domain of the function.

2f. The figure below shows a representation of the function rule. Explain what is being shown in the context of the situation.

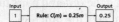

Input
1 → Rule: $C(m) = 0.25m$ → Output 0.25

The input is 1, which represents 1 text message being sent.

The output is 0.25, which means that the cost is $0.25. The rule assigns an output of $0.25 to 1 text message being sent.

2g. Suppose the cost per text message were $0.20 instead of $0.25. Then the cost of sending m text messages could be represented by the function $C(m) = 0.2m$. Describe a reasonable domain and range for this function.

A reasonable domain is the set of whole numbers. A reasonable range is the set of multiples of 0.2: {0, 0.2, 0.4, 0.6, 0.8, ...}.

---

3 EXAMPLE   Representing Discrete Nonlinear Functions

Ben wants to tile part of a floor with 36 square tiles. The tiles come in whole-number side lengths from 2 to 6 inches. If s is the side length of a tile, the area that he can cover is $A(s) = 36s^2$.

A Identify the domain of the function.

{2, 3, 4, 5, 6}

B Make a table of values for this domain. Write the results as ordered pairs in the form (independent variable, dependent variable).

Independent variable, s	Dependent variable, $A(s) = 36s^2$	(s, A(s))
2	$36(2)^2 = 144$	(2, 144)
3	$36(3)^2 = 324$	(3, 324)
4	$36(4)^2 = 576$	(4, 576)
5	$36(5)^2 = 900$	(5, 900)
6	$36(6)^2 = 1296$	(6, 1296)

C Choose a beginning, an end, and a scale for the vertical axis.

Start at 0 and go to at least 1400 using a scale of 200 square inches.

D Graph the function by plotting the ordered pairs.

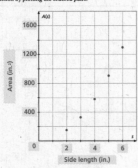

Notes

Questioning Strategies

- Why does the domain start with the value 2 and end with the value 6? **2 is the smallest side length of the squares, and 6 is the longest side length.**

- Why is 0 not part of the domain? **The domain represents side lengths, and a tile cannot have a side length of 0 inches.**

- Would it make sense to connect the points on the graph? Explain. **No, a line would cover values of s that are not whole numbers, and the problem says the tiles come in whole-number side lengths.**

EXTRA EXAMPLE

A pizzeria makes pizzas with radii of 3 to 12 inches. All radii are multiples of 3. If r is the radius of a pizza, the area of each pizza can be approximated with $A(r) = 3.14r^2$.

A. Identify the domain of the function. **{3, 6, 9, 12}**

B. Make a table of values for this domain. Write the results as ordered pairs. **(3, 28.26), (6, 113.04), (9, 254.34), (12, 452.16)**

C. Choose a beginning, an end, and a scale for the vertical axis. **Possible answer: Start at 0 and go to 500 using a scale of 50 square inches.**

D. Graph the function by plotting the ordered pairs. **The x-axis should be labeled as "Radius (in.)" and use intervals of 3 starting with 0 and going to 12. The y-axis should be labeled as "Area (in.²)" and use intervals of 50 starting with 0 and going to 500. The following points should be plotted: (3, 28.26), (6, 113.04), (9, 254.34), (12, 452.16).**

Differentiated Instruction

If students have a difficult time consistently identifying the domain and range of functions, encourage them to use the words "depends on," instead of "is a function of." For example, the function $A(s)$ depends on s. In other words, emphasize that the output value "depends on" the input values just as the area of a room depends on the length of its sides.

Technology

Some students may have difficulty seeing that the points appear to lie along a curve and not a line. Have them graph the function on a graphing calculator using $y = 36x^2$. The calculator will show the entire curve that the points lie along. Be sure to stress that all the points on the curve are not values of the real-world function. The graph just shows the curve containing the ordered pairs that make up the domain and range of the function.

CLOSE

Essential Question

How do you represent functions?
Functions can be represented by ordered pairs, mapping diagrams, function rules, tables, and graphs.

Summarize

Have students explain how to determine if a set of ordered pairs is a function. Then ask them to write a set of ordered pairs that represent a function and graph the function.

PRACTICE

Where skills are taught	Where skills are practiced
1 ENGAGE	EXS. 1–6
2 EXAMPLE	EX. 7
3 EXAMPLE	EX. 8

3a. Identify the range of the function.

{144, 324, 576, 900, 1296}

3b. What does $A(3) = 324$ mean in this context?

$A(3) = 324$ means the area covered by 36 three-inch

square tiles is 324 in.^{2}

3c. Describe another reasonable beginning, end, and scale for the vertical axis.
Include units.

Start at 0 and go to at least 1500 using a scale of 300 square inches.

3d. Do the points appear to lie in a straight line?

No, they appear to lie along a curve.

PRACTICE

Tell whether each pairing of numbers describes a function. If so, identify the domain and the range. If not, explain why not.

1. Each whole number from 0 to 9 is paired with its opposite.

Function; D: {0, 1, 2, 3, 4, 5, 6, 7, 8, 9}, R: {0, −1, −2, −3, −4, −5, −6, −7, −8, −9}

2. Each odd number from 3 to 9 is paired with the next greater whole number.

Function; D: {3, 4, 5, 6, 7, 8, 9}, R: {4, 5, 6, 7, 8, 9, 10}

3. The whole numbers from 10 to 12 are paired with their factors.

Not a function; each of the numbers 10, 11, and 12 has two or more factors, and

functions must have exactly one output for each input.

4. Each even number from 2 to 10 is paired with half the number.

Function; D: {2, 4, 6, 8, 10}, R: {1, 2, 3, 4, 5}

5. {(36, 6), (49, 7), (64, 8), (81, 9), (36, −6), (49, −7), (64, −8), (81, −9)}

Not a function; each input is paired with two outputs, not exactly one output.

6. {(−64, −4), (−27, −3), (−8, −2), (−1, −1), (0, 0), (1, 1), (8, 2), (27, 3), (64, 4)}

Function; D: {−64, −27, −8, −1, 0, 1, 8, 27, 64};

R: {−4, −3, −2, −1, 0, 1, 2, 3, 4}

---

7. Whitley has a $5 gift card for music downloads. Each song costs $1 to download.
The amount of money left on the card can be represented by the function
$M(d) = 5 - d$, where d is the number of songs she has downloaded.

a. Make a table and graph the function.

d	M(d)	(d, M(d))
0	$5 - 0 = 5$	(0, 5)
1	$5 - 1 = 4$	(1, 4)
2	$5 - 2 = 3$	(2, 3)
3	$5 - 3 = 2$	(3, 2)
4	$5 - 4 = 1$	(4, 1)
5	$5 - 5 = 0$	(5, 0)

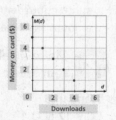

b. Identify the domain and range of the function and the units of the
independent and dependent variables.

D and R: {0, 1, 2, 3, 4, 5}; unit of independent variable:

number of downloads; unit of dependent variable: dollars

8. Ben wants to cover a table that has an area of 864 square inches. The function
$T(s) = \frac{864}{s^2}$ gives the number of tiles he needs with side length s. The tiles come in
side lengths of 1 in., 4 in., 6 in., and 12 in.

a. Make a table and graph the function.

s	T(s)	(s, T(s))
1	$\frac{864}{1^2} = 864$	(1, 864)
4	$\frac{864}{4^2} = 54$	(4, 54)
6	$\frac{864}{6^2} = 24$	(6, 24)
12	$\frac{864}{12^2} = 6$	(12, 6)

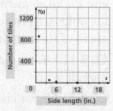

b. Identify the domain and range of the function and the units of the
independent and dependent variables.

D: {1, 4, 6, 12}; R: {864, 54, 24, 6}; unit of independent variable:

side length in inches; unit of dependent variable: tiles

Notes

FOCUS ON MODELING
Modeling with Functions

Essential question: *How can you model paying off a loan using a function?*

COMMON CORE Standards for Mathematical Content

The following standards are addressed in this lesson. (An asterisk indicates that a standard is also a Modeling standard.) For more detailed information, see the correlation for each section of the lesson.

Number and Quantity: CC.9-12.N.Q.1*,

Algebra: CC.9-12.A.CED.1*

Functions: CC.9-12.F.IF.1, CC.9-12.F.IF.2, CC.9-12.F.IF.5*, CC.9-12.F.BF.1*, CC.9-12.F.BF.1.a*

Prerequisites
• Representing Functions, Lesson 1-5

Math Background
In this lesson, students write a function that models paying off a loan. The function is decreasing, meaning its greatest value is the initial value when the independent variable equals zero.

INTRODUCE

Ask students to discuss the implications of paying off a loan on a monthly basis, and how to graph this decreasing function. Explain to students that they will use what they know about functions to model a situation in which a person receives a loan, makes monthly payments, and pays off the loan.

TEACH

1 Write an equation for the function from the given information.

Standards
CC.9-12.N.Q.1 Use units as a way to understand problems and to guide the solution of multi-step problems ...*

CC.9-12.A.CED.1 Create equations ... in one variable and use them to solve problems.*

CC.9-12.F.IF.1 Understand that a function from one set (called the domain) to another set (called the range) assigns to each element of the domain exactly one element of the range. If f is a function and x is an element of its domain, then $f(x)$ denotes the output of f corresponding to the input x. ...

CC.9-12.F.IF.2 Use function notation, evaluate functions for inputs in their domains, and interpret statements that use function notation in terms of a context.

CC.9-12.F.BF.1 Write a function that describes a relationship between two quantities.*

CC.9-12.F.BF.1.a Determine an explicit expression ... from a context.*

Questioning Strategies
• How can you determine how many months it will take to repay the loan? Explain. **Divide the amount of the loan by the payment amount.**

• Why does the balance function involve subtraction? **Jenna is repaying the loan, so the amount she owes each month decreases.**

2 Make a table and a graph to represent the function.

Standards
CC.9-12.N.Q.1 ...choose and interpret the scale and the origin in graphs and data displays.*

CC.9-12.F.IF.1 Understand that a function from one set (called the domain) to another set (called the range) assigns to each element of the domain exactly one element of the range. If f is a function and x is an element of its domain, then $f(x)$ denotes the output of f corresponding to the input x. The graph of f is the graph of the equation $y = f(x)$.

CC.9-12.F.IF.2 ..., evaluate functions for inputs in their domains, ...

CC.9-12.F.IF.5 Relate the domain of a function to its graph ...*

continued

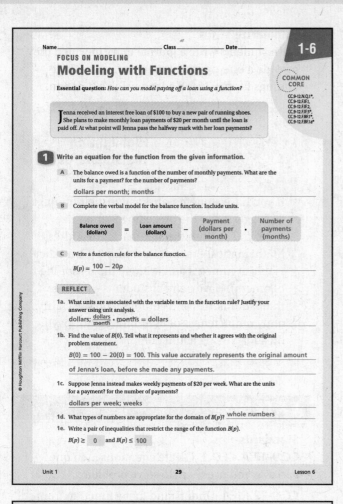

1-6

FOCUS ON MODELING
Modeling with Functions

Essential question: *How can you model paying off a loan using a function?*

COMMON CORE
CC.9-12.N.Q.1*,
CC.9-12.F.IF.1,
CC.9-12.F.IF.2,
CC.9-12.F.IF.5*,
CC.9-12.F.BF.1*,
CC.9-12.F.BF.1a*

> Jenna received an interest free loan of $100 to buy a new pair of running shoes. She plans to make monthly loan payments of $20 per month until the loan is paid off. At what point will Jenna pass the halfway mark with her loan payments?

1 Write an equation for the function from the given information.

A The balance owed is a function of the number of monthly payments. What are the units for a payment? for the number of payments?

dollars per month; months

B Complete the verbal model for the balance function. Include units.

| Balance owed (dollars) | = | Loan amount (dollars) | − | Payment (dollars per month) | · | Number of payments (months) |

C Write a function rule for the balance function.

$B(p) = $ 100 − 20p

REFLECT

1a. What units are associated with the variable term in the function rule? Justify your answer using unit analysis.

dollars; $\frac{dollars}{month}$ · months = dollars

1b. Find the value of $B(0)$. Tell what it represents and whether it agrees with the original problem statement.

$B(0) = 100 − 20(0) = 100$. This value accurately represents the original amount

of Jenna's loan, before she made any payments.

1c. Suppose Jenna instead makes weekly payments of $20 per week. What are the units for a payment? for the number of payments?

dollars per week; weeks

1d. What types of numbers are appropriate for the domain of $B(p)$? whole numbers

1e. Write a pair of inequalities that restrict the range of the function $B(p)$.

$B(p) \geq$ 0 and $B(p) \leq$ 100

© Houghton Mifflin Harcourt Publishing Company

---

2 Make a table and a graph to represent the function.

A Make a table of values for the balance function.

Independent variable, p	Dependent variable, B(p)	(p, B(p))
0	100 − 20(0) = 100	(0, 100)
1	100 − 20(1) = 80	(1, 80)
2	100 − 20(2) = 60	(2, 60)
3	100 − 20(3) = 40	(3, 40)
4	100 − 20(4) = 20	(4, 20)
5	100 − 20(5) = 0	(5, 0)

B Choose a beginning, an end, and a scale for the vertical axis.

Start at 0 and go to at least 100 using a scale of $20.

C Graph the balance function.

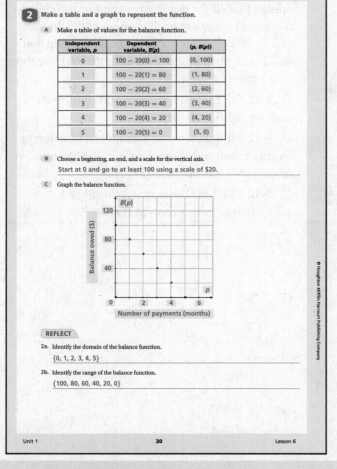

REFLECT

2a. Identify the domain of the balance function.

{0, 1, 2, 3, 4, 5}

2b. Identify the range of the balance function.

{100, 80, 60, 40, 20, 0}

© Houghton Mifflin Harcourt Publishing Company

Notes

2 continued

Questioning Strategies

- Why is 5 the domain's greatest value? At 5 months the balance is $0, so no more payments are made.

- If only five payments are made, why are there six domain values? You include the balance of the loan before any payments are made.

Avoid Common Errors

When students draw the graph of $B(p)$, they may draw a straight line through the points they plotted. Remind them that a reasonable domain of $B(p)$ consists of whole number values of p from 0 to 5, inclusive. Therefore, the graph is actually a set of discrete points rather than a straight line.

 3 Analyze the balance function models.

Standards

CC.9-12.F.IF.5 Relate the domain of a function to its graph and, where applicable, to the quantitative relationship it describes.*

Questioning Strategies

- How do the values of $B(p)$ change as compared to how the values of p change? They consistently decrease as p increases.

- As p increases by 1, by how much does $B(p)$ decrease? $B(p)$ decreases by 20.

CLOSE

Essential Question

How can you model paying off a loan using a function?

Write an expression for the loan amount minus the payment amount times the number of payments made. Use the expression to make a table of values and then graph the function.

Summarize

Have students write a journal entry in which they provide a one-page summary regarding their findings for paying off a loan using a function.

:::: **MATHEMATICAL PRACTICE**   **Highlighting the Standards**

If you have students summarize their findings as suggested in the preceding Summarize note, you can use the summaries to address Mathematical Practice Standard 3 (Construct viable arguments and critique the reasoning of others). Have pairs of students exchange their summaries and comment on the clarity and completeness of their findings for paying off a loan using a function.

EXTEND

Standards

CC.9-12.A.CED.1 Create equations ... in one variable and use them to solve problems.* (Ex. 2)

CC.9-12.F.IF.1 Understand that a function from one set (called the domain) to another set (called the range) assigns to each element of the domain exactly one element of the range. If f is a function and x is an element of its domain, then $f(x)$ denotes the output of f ... (Ex. 1)

CC.9-12.F.IF.2 ... evaluate functions for inputs in their domains... (Ex. 2)

CC.9-12.F.IF.5 Relate the domain of a function to its graph and, where applicable, to the quantitative relationship it describes.* (Ex. 1, 2)

CC.9-12.F.BF.1.a. Determine an explicit expression ... from a context. (Ex. 2)

3 Analyze the balance function models.

A Give the coordinates of the point where the dependent variable is 0. Interpret the meaning of this point in the original situation.

(5, 0); the dependent variable is the balance owed, so this is the point where

the balance is zero. It reaches 0 when the 5th monthly payment is made.

B At what value of p does $B(p)$ have its maximum value? What is the maximum value?

$B(p)$ is at its maximum value when $p = 0$; $B(0) = \$100$ is the maximum.

C At what point will Jenna pass the halfway mark with her loan payments? Explain your reasoning.

Jenna will pass the halfway mark when she makes the 3rd monthly payment.

Sample answer: Half of the original loan amount is $50, but none of the

output values are exactly $50. The first point at which the balance owed is

less than $50 is the point (3, 40).

REFLECT

3a. Will the balance on the loan ever be exactly $70? Why or why not?

The points on the graph represent all the values of the function.

None of the points has a function value of $70.

3b. Is it reasonable to connect the points on the graph with a straight line? Why or why not?

No; *Sample answer*: The number of payments must be a whole number.

3c. Suppose the amount of money borrowed were $120 instead of $100. What would be the domain and the range of the balance function? How long would it take to pay off the loan?

The domain would become {0, 1, 2, 3, 4, 5, 6} and the range would become

{120, 100, 80, 60, 40, 20, 0}; 6 months.

3d. Suppose the monthly loan payments on the $100 loan were $10 per month instead of $20 per month. What would be the domain and the range of the balance function? How long would it take to pay off the loan?

The domain would become {0, 1, 2, 3, 4, 5, 6, 7, 8, 9, 10} and the range would

become {100, 90, 80, 70, 60, 50, 40, 30, 20, 10, 0}; 10 months.

© Houghton Mifflin Harcourt Publishing Company

EXTEND

1. The table shows the balance owed on an interest free loan as a function $B(p)$ of the number of monthly payments p.

a. Identify the domain and the range of the function.

D: {0, 1, 2, 3, 4}, R: {120, 90, 60, 30, 0}

b. What is the initial amount of the loan? What is the monthly payment? Explain.

$120; $30 per month; the output associated

with an input of 0 months is $120; the balance

owed decreases by $30 per month.

p	$(p, B(p))$
0	(0, 120)
1	(1, 90)
2	(2, 60)
3	(3, 30)
4	(4, 0)

c. Compare this function with the function discussed in Steps 1–3?

Sample answer: The initial loan amount for this function is greater, but so is

the payment, so the loan is repaid in 4 months rather than 5.

2. After Jenna pays off her loan, she deposits $20 per month into a savings account with an initial balance of $40.

a. The account balance is a function of the number of deposits. Model this function with an equation, a table, and a graph, using selected domain values and reasonable scales. Include appropriate axis labels.

Equation: $B(d) = 40 + 20d$

d	$B(d)$	$(d, B(d))$
0	40 + 0 = 40	(0, 40)
1	40 + 20 = 60	(1, 60)
2	40 + 40 = 80	(2, 80)
3	40 + 60 = 100	(3, 100)
4	40 + 80 = 120	(4, 120)

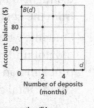

b. Describe the domain and range using set notation. In how many months will Jenna have $120 in the account? Explain.

D: {0, 1, 2, 3, 4, . . .}, R: {40, 60, 80, 100, 120, . . .}; 4 months; the output

is $120 when the input is 4.

© Houghton Mifflin Harcourt Publishing Company

Standard	Items
CC.9-12.N.Q.1*	9, 10
CC.9-12.N.Q.2*	4
CC.9-12.A.SSE.1*	3
CC.9-12.A.SSE.1a*	1
CC.9-12.A.SSE.1b*	9
CC.9-12.A.SSE.2	2
CC.9-12.A.CED.1*	5
CC.9-12.A.CED.3*	6
CC.9-12.F.IF.1	7
CC.9-12.F.IF.2	10
CC.9-12.F.IF.5*	10
CC.9-12.F.BF.1*	8, 10
CC.9-12.F.BF.1a*	8, 10

TEST PREP DOCTOR ✚

Multiple Choice: Item 1
- Students who chose **A** did not square 3 for the first term.
- Students who chose **C** made a sign error.
- Students who chose **D** misunderstood exponents and the order of operations because they multiplied by 2 instead of squaring and they performed the operations from left to right.

Multiple Choice: Item 3
- Students who chose **B** mixed up the values of the hourly rate and the flat service fee.
- Students who chose **C** added the hourly rate and the flat service fee to get the coefficient.
- Students who chose **D** left out the flat service fee.

Multiple Choice: Item 4
- Students who chose **F** may have thought that c represented the tax on both shirts.
- Students who chose **H** calculated the total cost of one shirt including tax.
- Students who chose **J** calculated the total cost of both shirts including tax.

Multiple Choice: Item 6
- Students who chose **F** used the correct inequality except that the less than or equal to symbol should have been used instead of just less than; "at most" means less than or equal to.
- Students who chose **G** misinterpreted the question to be more than instead of less than or equal to, thinking that "at most" means more than.
- Students who chose **H** misinterpreted the question to be more than or equal to instead of less than or equal to, thinking that "at most" means more than or equal to.

Multiple Choice: Item 7
- Students who chose **B**, **C**, or **D** do not understand, or are confused about, the definition of function.

Multiple Choice: Item 8
- Students who chose **F** or **G** only counted the three friends and not themselves, and were looking for an answer that used 3 instead of 4.
- Students who chose **H** chose the wrong operation, multiplication, instead of division.

Free Response: Item 9
- Students may answer item **a** by stating that $10n$ represents the "cost" of the calendars, failing to distinguish the cost to the club, $4 per calendar, from the cost to the customer, $10 per calendar.
- Students who could not answer item **b** correctly did not understand that the 300 calendars in the problem had been multiplied by their cost, $4, to get the total cost of $1200.

Name _____ Class _____ Date _____

MULTIPLE CHOICE

1. Evaluate $x^2 + 3x - 18$ for $x = 3$.

   A. -6

   (B.) 0

   C. 6

   D. 9

2. Simplify $4n + 2(3n - 5) - 8 + n$.

   F. $8n - 13$

   G. $9n - 8$

   H. $10n - 2$

   (J.) $11n - 18$

3. It costs $75 per hour plus a $65 service fee to have a home theater system set up for you. Let t represent the number of hours. Which expression represents the total cost?

   (A.) $75t + 65$

   B. $65t + 75$

   C. $140t$

   D. $75t$

4. Elizabeth and her friend purchase identical team shirts to wear to a football game. There is a 7% sales tax. If c represents the cost of the two shirts without tax, which algebraic expression represents the tax for one shirt?

   F. $\frac{c}{2}$

   (G.) $\frac{0.07c}{2}$

   H. $\frac{1.07c}{2}$

   J. $1.07c$

5. Tia spent $15 on skating. This included a $5 charge for renting skates and a $2.50 per hour fee for skating. How many hours did Tia skate?

   A. 2 hours

   B. 3 hours

   (C.) 4 hours

   D. 5 hours

6. Which inequality represents the situation: "Alex has at most $45 to spend on a basketball, including 8% tax?"

   F. $p + 0.08p < 45$

   G. $p + 0.08p > 45$

   H. $p + 0.08p \geq 45$

   (J.) $p + 0.08p \leq 45$

7. Which set of ordered pairs represents a function?

   (A.) $\{(-1, 1), (0, 0), (1, 1), (2, 2)\}$

   B. $\{(3, -3), (2, -2), (1, -1), (1, 1)\}$

   C. $\{(4, 2), (4, -2), (9, 3), (9, -3)\}$

   D. $\{(-2, -1), (-2, 0), (-2, 1), (-2, 2)\}$

8. You and three friends plan to split the cost b (in dollars) of a large bag of popcorn at a movie. Which function describes the cost for each person as a function of the cost per bag?

   F. $P(b) = 3b$

   G. $P(b) = \frac{3}{b}$

   H. $P(b) = 4b$

   (J.) $P(b) = \frac{b}{4}$

FREE RESPONSE

9. The art club at Lily's school has had 300 calendars printed to sell as a fundraiser. It costs the art club $4 per calendar to have the calendars printed and the club sells them for $10 per calendar. The art club's profit $P(n)$ is given by the following function, where n represents the number of calendars sold.

   $$P(n) = 10n - 1200$$

   a. What does the term "$10n$" represent? What are its units? Explain your reasoning using unit analysis.

   The term $10n$ represents the

   amount the club will collect for

   selling n calendars; dollars;

   $\frac{\text{dollars}}{\text{calendar}} \cdot \text{calendars} = \text{dollars}$

   b. What does the term "1200" represent? Explain your reasoning.

   The term 1200 represents the

   amount the club will pay for

   having the calendars printed;

   $\frac{\$4}{\text{calendar}} \cdot 300 \text{ calendars} = \$1200$

   c. If you were going to graph the function, what scale would you use for the horizontal axis? for the vertical axis?

   Horizontal axis: begin at 0 and

   use intervals of 50 with a max of

   300 calendars; Vertical: begin at

   0 and use intervals of 200 with a

   max of $10(300) - 1200 = \$1800$

10. Henry purchased a roll of 100 stamps. He uses 5 stamps each week.

    a. The number of stamps at the end of each week is a function $S(w)$ of the number of weeks. Write an equation for the function.

    $$S(w) = 100 - 5w$$

    b. What types of numbers are reasonable for the domain and the range?

    Domain: Whole numbers;

    Range: Whole number multiples

    of 5 from 100 down to 0.

    c. Complete the table using selected domain values. Then graph the function.

w	$S(w)$	$(w, S(w))$
0	$100 - 5(0) = 100$	$(0, 100)$
5	$100 - 5(5) = 75$	$(5, 75)$
10	$100 - 5(10) = 50$	$(10, 50)$
15	$100 - 5(15) = 25$	$(15, 25)$
20	$100 - 5(20) = 0$	$(20, 0)$

    d. At the end of how many weeks will Henry have one quarter of the stamps left? Explain your reasoning.

    15 weeks; $\frac{1}{4} \cdot 100 = 25$, and an

    output of 25 has an input of 15.

UNIT 2

Linear Equations and Inequalities

Unit Vocabulary

equivalent
  equations   (2-1)

linear equation
  in two variables   (2-6)

linear inequality
  in two variables   (2-7)

literal equation   (2-4)

solution of an
  equation in
  two variables   (2-6)

solution of an
  inequality in
  two variables   (2-7)

standard form of
  an equation in
  two variables   (2-6)

x-intercept   (2-6)

y-intercept   (2-6)

© Houghton Mifflin Harcourt Publishing Company

UNIT 2

Linear Equations and Inequalities

Unit Focus

In Unit 1 you learned about expressions and how to simplify terms. In this unit you will build on this skill to simplify and solve linear equations and inequalities. You will also work with literal equations and inequalities, which are related to formulas, and practice rewriting formulas so that they focus on a given quantity. Finally, you will write, solve, and graph linear equations and inequalities in two variables.

Unit at a Glance

COMMON CORE

Lesson		Standards for Mathematical Content
2-1	Solving Linear Equations	CC.9-12.A.SSE.2, CC.9-12.A.REI.1, CC.9-12.A.REI.3
2-2	Solving Linear Inequalities	CC.9-12.A.SSE.2, CC.9-12.A.REI.1, CC.9-12.A.REI.3
2-3	Modeling with One-Variable Linear Equations and Inequalities	CC.9-12.N.Q.1*, CC.9-12.N.Q.2*, CC.9-12.A.CED.1*, CC.9-12.A.CED.2*, CC.9-12.A.CED.3*, CC.9-12.F.BF.1*
2-4	Literal Equations and Inequalities	CC.9-12.A.REI.1, CC.9-12.A.REI.3
2-5	Rewriting Formulas	CC.9-12.A.CED.2*, CC.9-12.A.CED.4*
2-6	Linear Equations in Two Variables	CC.9-12.A.REI.10
2-7	Linear Inequalities in Two Variables	CC.9-12.A.REI.12
2-8	Modeling with Two-Variable Linear Equations and Inequalities	CC.9-12.N.Q.1*, CC.9-12.N.Q.2*, CC.9-12.A.CED.2*, CC.9-12.A.CED.3*
	Test Prep	

Unpacking the Common Core State Standards

Use the table to help you understand the Standards for Mathematical Content that are taught in this unit. Refer to the lessons listed after each standard for exploration and practice.

COMMON CORE Standards for Mathematical Content	What It Means For You
CC.9-12.N.Q.1 Use units as a way to understand problems and to guide the solution of multi-step problems; choose and interpret units consistently in formulas; choose and interpret the scale and the origin in graphs and data displays.* Lessons 2-3, 2-8	When you write equations and inequalities for real-world situations, you should consider the units attached to the variables, coefficients, and constants. Keeping units in mind can help you write equations and inequalities correctly.
CC.9-12.N.Q.2 Define appropriate quantities for the purpose of descriptive modeling.* Lessons 2-3, 2-8	When you solve real-world problems, you identify quantities that are unknown or that vary, and you use variables to represent those quantities.
CC.9-12.A.SSE.1 Interpret expressions that represent a quantity in terms of its context.* **CC.9-12.A.SSE.1a** Interpret parts of an expression, such as terms, factors, and coefficients.* Lesson 2-8	When you write expressions to represent real-world quantities, you should be able to recognize the real-world significance of the parts of the expressions.
CC.9-12.A.SSE.2 Use the structure of an expression to identify ways to rewrite it. Lessons 2-1, 2-2	A basic algebraic skill is recognizing how all the parts in an expression work together. Understanding the relationships between these parts will help you simplify or rewrite the expression.
CC.9-12.A.CED.1 Create equations and inequalities in one variable and use them to solve problems.* Lesson 2-3	Equations and inequalities in one variable can be used to solve problems that have an unknown value.
CC.9-12.A.CED.2 Create equations in two or more variables to represent relationships between quantities; graph equations on coordinate axes with labels and scales.* Lessons 2-5, 2-8	An equation in two variables represents the relationship between two quantities. Once you can express this relationship mathematically, you can graph it in a coordinate plane.
CC.9-12.A.CED.3 Represent constraints by equations or inequalities, and by systems of equations and/or inequalities, and interpret solutions as viable or nonviable options in a modeling context.* Lessons 2-3, 2-8	Variable quantities may be able to take on only certain values, and expressing those restrictions, or constraints, algebraically is an important part of modeling with mathematics.

© Houghton Mifflin Harcourt Publishing Company

Unpacking the Common Core State Standards

This page lists and explains the Standards for Mathematical Content that are addressed in this unit. For information about the Standards for Mathematical Practice, which are integrated throughout the text, see Teacher Edition pages viii–xi.

Additional Standards in this Unit

CC.9-12.F.IF.2 Use function notation, evaluate functions for inputs in their domains, and interpret statements that use function notation in terms of a context. Lesson 2-1

CC.9-12.G.MG.1 Use geometric shapes, their measures, and their properties to describe objects (e.g., modeling a tree trunk or a human torso as a cylinder).* Lesson 2-5

Notes

_____

_____

_____

_____

_____

_____

_____

_____

_____

_____

COMMON CORE Standards for Mathematical Content	What It Means For You
CC.9-12.A.CED.4 Rearrange formulas to highlight a quantity of interest, using the same reasoning as in solving equations.* Lesson 2-5	You can apply the same skills you used in solving equations to rearrange a formula. This is good practice for geometry and the sciences, which rely heavily on formulas.
CC.9-12.A.REI.1 Explain each step in solving a simple equation as following from the equality of numbers asserted at the previous step, starting from the assumption that the original equation has a solution. Construct a viable argument to justify a solution method. Lessons 2-1, 2-2, 2-4	Algebraic properties enable you to arrive at a solution of an equation in a logical step-by-step manner. Knowing the properties of equality can not only help you reduce complex equations to simpler ones, but also give you the tools to justify your solution.
CC.9-12.A.REI.3 Solve linear equations and inequalities in one variable, including equations with coefficients represented by letters. Lessons 2-1, 2-2, 2-3, 2-4	Solving linear equations and inequalities in one variable is a basic algebraic skill. Mastering this skill will enable you to solve higher-order equations, such as quadratic equations, later in this course and in more advanced courses in the future.
CC.9-12.A.REI.10 Understand that the graph of an equation in two variables is the set of all its solutions plotted in the coordinate plane, often forming a curve (which could be a line). Lessons 2-6, 2-7	The graph of a linear equation in two variables is a line. Every point on the line is a solution to the equation. Points that are not on the line cannot be solutions to the equation.
CC.9-12.A.REI.12 Graph the solutions to a linear inequality in two variables as a half-plane (excluding the boundary in the case of a strict inequality), and graph the solution set to a system of linear inequalities in two variables as the intersection of the corresponding half-planes. Lessons 2-6, 2-7	The graph of a linear inequality in two variables shows all the possible solutions to the inequality as a shaded region on the coordinate plane. This fact becomes the basis for solving systems of linear inequalities in two variables.
CC.9-12.F.BF.1 Write a function that describes a relationship between two quantities.* **CC.9-12.F.BF.1a** Determine an explicit expression ... from a context.* Lesson 2-8	When an equation in two variables defines one variable in terms of the other, it establishes a functional relationship between the variables. You will write such equations when modeling a fundraiser for a school band.

© Houghton Mifflin Harcourt Publishing Company

Notes

_____

_____

_____

_____

_____

_____

_____

_____

_____

_____

Notes

Solving Linear Equations

Essential question: *How can you use the properties of equality to support your solution to a linear equation?*

COMMON **Standards for**
CORE **Mathematical Content**

CC.9-12.A.SSE.2 Use the structure of an expression to identify ways to rewrite it. . . .

CC.9-12.A.REI.1 Explain each step in solving a simple equation as following from the equality of numbers asserted at the previous step, starting from the assumption that the original equation has a solution. Construct a viable argument to justify a solution method.

CC.9-12.A.REI.3 Solve linear equations . . . in one variable . . .

Also: CC.9-12.F.IF.2

Vocabulary
equivalent equations

Prerequisites
Variables and expressions, Lesson 1-1

Distributive Property, Lesson 1-2

Function notation, Lesson 1-5

Math Background
In Lesson 1-2, students learned how to use the Distributive Property to simplify an expression of the form $a(bx + c)$ to get $abx + ac$. In this lesson, students will use the Distributive Property along with the properties of equality (addition, subtraction, multiplication, and division) to solve equations. Solving equations involves using inverse operations to get the variable alone on one side of the equation and the solution on the other side of the equation. At each step of the solving process, students use properties to derive equivalent equations, or equations with the same solution set. Students will express an equation's solution set using set notation.

INTRODUCE

Emphasize the importance of using steps in order to solve an equation by giving students the following example: Suppose you want to wrap a gift. The steps include cutting a piece of wrapping paper, putting tissue paper into the gift box, adding the gift to the box, putting the paper on the box, and then adding ribbon to the wrapped box. Scramble the steps and have students list the steps in the proper order and justify their steps to a partner.

TEACH

1 ENGAGE

Questioning Strategies
- Why is the Division Property of Equality restricted to real numbers with a nonzero divisor? **Dividing by zero is not defined.**

- How can you tell whether two equations are equivalent? **They have the same solution set.**

2 EXAMPLE

Questioning Strategies
- What property of equality would you use to solve $z - 8 = 20$? Explain. **Addition Property of Equality; 8 is subtracted from the variable, so you would use addition, which is the inverse operation of subtraction.**

- If the Division Property of Equality can be used to solve an equation, what is a *likely* structure for the equation? Explain. **The variable is multiplied by a number and that product is equal to another number. Since you use an inverse operation to solve the equation, and division is the inverse of multiplication, the original equation is a multiplication equation.**

continued

Name_____ Class_____ Date_____

2-1

Solving Linear Equations

Essential question: *How can you use the properties of equality to support your solution to a linear equation?*

COMMON
CORE

CC.9-12.A.SSE.2,
CC.9-12.A.REI.1,
CC.9-12.A.REI.3

1 ENGAGE Equivalent Equations and the Properties of Equality

Two equations are **equivalent equations** if they have the same solution set. The equations below are equivalent because both have the solution $x = 11$.

$$x - 6 = 5 \qquad\qquad x - 11 = 0$$
$$11 - 6 = 5 \qquad\qquad 11 - 11 = 0$$

The solutions of an equation can be given as one or more equations of the form $x = s$ where s is a solution, as in $x = 11$, or listed using set notation, as in $\{11\}$.

To solve an equation, you perform a series of inverse operations to isolate the variable on one side. When these inverse operations are completed, the other side of the equation is the solution. The properties of equality listed below can be used to justify the steps taken in solving an equation.

Addition Property of Equality	If $a = b$, then $a + c = b + c$.
Subtraction Property of Equality	If $a = b$, then $a - c = b - c$.
Multiplication Property of Equality	If $a = b$, then $ac = bc$.
Division Property of Equality	If $a = b$ and $c \neq 0$, then $\frac{a}{c} = \frac{b}{c}$.

Other properties, such as the Distributive Property and the Substitution Property, are also useful when solving equations.

REFLECT

1a. How might you use the Distributive Property to help solve an equation?

If one or both sides of the equation involve an expression with parentheses, you can use the Distributive Property to simplify the expression before starting to isolate the variable. Also, if two terms on one side of the equation are like terms, you can combine them using the Distributive Property.

1b. Are the equations $2x + 14 = 8$ and $x = -3$ equivalent? Explain.

Yes; you know that -3 is the solution of $x = -3$. Substitute -3 for x in $2x + 14 = 8$. Since $2(-3) + 14 = 8$ is a true statement, the equations have the same solution set.

2 EXAMPLE Solving a One-Step Linear Equation

Complete the solution to the linear equation. Justify the solution by using the properties of equality.

A

Equation	Solution step	Reason
$x + 9 = 17$ $\underline{-9 \quad -9}$ $x = \;8$	Subtract 9 from both sides.	Subtraction Property of Equality

The solution set is $\{\,8\,\}$.

B

Equation	Solution step	Reason
$\frac{x}{6} = 12$ $6 \cdot \frac{x}{6} = 6 \cdot 12$ $x = 72$	Multiply both sides by 6.	Multiplication Property of Equality

The solution set is $\{72\}$.

REFLECT

2a. Which property of equality could you use to solve the equation $4x = 68$? Explain.

Division Property of Equality; the variable is multiplied by 4, so you would use division, which is the inverse operation of multiplication.

2b. Give an example of an equation that could be solved using the Addition Property of Equality. Show the steps of the solution.

$x - 4 = 7; \quad x - 4 = 7$
$\underline{\quad\quad x - 4 + 4 = 7 + 4}$
$\quad\quad\quad x = 11$

2c. Solving a linear equation may take more than one step. Show how to solve $2x + 5 = 13$. Justify your steps.

$2x + 5 = 13$	
$2x + 5 - 5 = 13 - 5$	Subtraction Property of Equality
$2x = 8$	Simplify.
$\frac{2x}{2} = \frac{8}{2}$	Division Property of Equality
$x = 4$	Simplify.

Teaching Strategy

Make sure students understand that the goal in solving an equation is to isolate the variable with a coefficient of 1 on one side of the equation.

EXTRA EXAMPLE

Find the solution set for the linear equation. Justify the solution using the properties of equality.

A. $x - 6 = 14$

{20}; Addition Property of Equality

B. $4x = 120$

{30}; Division Property of Equality

3 EXAMPLE

Questioning Strategies

- Why is the Distributive Property used in the first step of the solution? **to eliminate the parentheses on the right side**

- Why are both sides of the equation multiplied by 2 in the second step of the solution? **to eliminate the denominator on the left side**

Differentiated Instruction

Point out that a good pattern to use in solving equations is to clear parentheses by using the Distributive Property, clear fractions by multiplying both sides by the least common denominator, and then finish solving by using the properties of equality.

Avoid Common Errors

Point out that a common error in the second row of the solution is to multiply one side of the equation by 2 but not the other side. Caution students to use the Multiplication Property of Equality correctly.

EXTRA EXAMPLE

Find the solution set for
$\frac{4x}{5} + 6x + 2 = 3(2x + 2)$. Justify the solution by listing each step and the property used.

The solution set is {5}.

Solution step	Property
Distribute the 3 on the right side of the equation.	Distributive Property
Multiply both sides of the equation by 5; then, simplify.	Multiplication Property of Equality; Distributive Property
Combine like terms.	Distributive Property
Subtract 30x from both sides.	Subtraction Property of Equality
Subtract 10 from both sides.	Subtraction Property of Equality
Divide both sides by 4.	Division Property of Equality

4 EXAMPLE

Questioning Strategies

- Why does setting the functions equal to each other help you find the solution? **The solution is the value of x when the functions are equal.**

- How can you check that 2 is the solution? **Find $f(2)$ and $g(2)$ and see whether they are equal.**

- How can the Multiplication Property of Equality be used to replace the last step of the solution? **Multiply each side by $\frac{1}{4}$ rather than divide by 4.**

continued

3 EXAMPLE Solving a Multi-Step Linear Equation

Justify the steps in solving $\frac{3x}{2} + 7x - 7 = 3(2x + 1)$ by using the properties of equality and other properties.

Equation	Solution steps	Reasons
$\frac{3x}{2} + 7x - 7 = 3(2x + 1)$ $\frac{3x}{2} + 7x - 7 = 6x + 3$	Distribute the 3 on the right side of the equation.	Distributive Property
$\frac{3x}{2} + 7x - 7 = 6x + 3$ $2 \cdot \left(\frac{3x}{2} + 7x - 7\right) = 2 \cdot (6x + 3)$ $3x + 14x - 14 = 12x + 6$	Multiply both sides of the equation by 2, then simplify.	Multiplication Property of Equality; Distributive Property
$3x + 14x - 14 = 12x + 6$ $(3 + 14)x - 14 = 12x + 6$ $17x - 14 = 12x + 6$	Combine like terms.	Distributive Property
$17x - 14 = 12x + 6$ $\underline{-12x \qquad -12x}$ $5x - 14 = \qquad 6$	Subtract $12x$ from both sides.	Subtraction Property of Equality
$5x - 14 = \qquad 6$ $\underline{+14 \qquad +14}$ $5x \quad = \quad 20$	Add 14 to both sides.	Addition Property of Equality
$5x = 20$ $\frac{5x}{5} = \frac{20}{5}$ $x = 4$	Divide both sides by 5.	Division Property of Equality

The solution set is $\{\ 4\ \}$.

REFLECT

3a. In the example, could the steps have been performed in a different order? Explain.

Yes; for example, you could multiply both sides by 2 as a first step to
eliminate the fraction and then distribute 6 to simplify the right side
of the equation as the second step.

3b. Would performing the steps in a different order affect the solution to the equation? Why or why not?

No; the solution to the equation is the value that makes it true.

The order of the steps does not change the solution.

---

4 EXAMPLE Determining Equality of Functions

Given the functions $f(x) = 3x + 2$ and $g(x) = -x + 10$, find the set of values of x such that $f(x) = g(x)$. Justify your solution by using the properties of equality.

To find the set of values of x such that $f(x) = g(x)$, set the functions equal to one another to get $3x + 2 = -x + 10$. Now solve this equation.

Equation	Solution step	Reason
$3x + 2 = -x + 10$ $\underline{+x \qquad +x}$ $4x + 2 = 10$	Add x to both sides.	Addition Property of Equality
$4x + 2 = 10$ $\underline{-2 \qquad -2}$ $4x \quad = \quad 8$	Subtract 2 from both sides.	Subtraction Property of Equality
$4x = 8$ $\frac{4x}{4} = \frac{8}{4}$ $x = 2$	Divide both sides by 4.	Division Property of Equality

The solution set is $\{\ 2\ \}$, so $f(x) = g(x)$ when $x = 2$.

REFLECT

4a. In the first step, suppose that you subtracted $3x$ from both sides. How would the rest of the steps change? Would the solution set be different?

The result of subtracting $3x$ from both sides would be $2 = -4x + 10$.

The next step would be to subtract 10 from both sides to get $-8 = -4x$.

The last step would be to divide both sides by -4 to get $2 = x$.

The solution set is the same.

4b. What is the solution set of $x = x$? Why?

It is the set of all real numbers, because x is always equal to itself.

4c. What statement do you get if you try to solve the equation $x + 2 = x$? Is this statement true or false? What does this mean in terms of the solution set?

$2 = 0$; false; the solution set is the empty set, so there are no solutions.

EXTRA EXAMPLE

Given the functions $f(x) = 4x - 2$ and $g(x) = 2x + 4$, find the set of values of x such that $f(x) = g(x)$. Justify your solution by listing each step and the property used.

Solve the equation $4x - 2 = 2x + 4$.
The solution set is {3}.

Solution step	Property
Subtract 2x from both sides.	Subtraction Property of Equality
Add 2 to both sides.	Addition Property of Equality
Divide both sides by 2.	Division Property of Equality

Avoid Common Errors

When students have a variable on both sides of an equation, they often forget to pay attention to the sign of the coefficient of the variable. For the first step in solving $3x + 2 = -x + 10$, students need to add x to both sides because the coefficient of the variable on the right side is -1. Remind students to check their solutions in the original functions to make sure $f(x) = g(x)$ for the value of x they found.

Technology

Encourage students to use technology to check their solution for **4** EXAMPLE. Press **Y=** and enter $f(x)$ as $Y_1 = 3x + 2$ and $g(x)$ as $Y_2 = -x + 10$. Press **GRAPH** and graph both lines, adjusting the window if necessary. Then press **2nd** and **TRACE** (CALC) and select the intersect feature to determine the intersection point of the two lines. Point out that the x-coordinate of the intersection point, which is 2, is the solution.

CLOSE

Essential Question

How can you use the properties of equality to support your solution to a linear equation?

The properties of equality allow you to solve a linear equation by isolating the variable on one side of the equation using inverse operations. You can use these properties to justify the steps in your solution.

Summarize

Have students write a journal entry in which they describe how to find the set of values such that two functions are equal to each other.

If you have students write a journal entry as suggested in the preceding Summarize note, you can use the journal entries to address Mathematical Practice Standard 3 (Construct viable arguments and critique the reasoning of others). Students should recognize that finding the value(s) such that two functions are equal uses the skills of solving an equation. The solution, or argument, is justified using the properties of equality and other properties such as the Distributive Property. Then students need to show that the solution is correct by checking the value(s) in the original functions.

PRACTICE

Where skills are taught	Where skills are practiced
3 EXAMPLE	EXS. 1–4
4 EXAMPLE	EXS. 5, 6

PRACTICE

Find the solution set for the equation. Use the properties of equality and other properties to justify your solution.

1. $2x - 3 = 9 - x$

$2x - 3 + x = 9 - x + x$	Addition property of equality
$3x - 3 = 9$	Simplify.
$3x - 3 + 3 = 9 + 3$	Addition property of equality
$3x = 12$	Simplify.
$\frac{3x}{3} = \frac{12}{3}$	Division property of equality
$x = 4$	Simplify.

The solution set is {4}.

2. $4x - 7 = x + 5$

$4x - 7 - x = x + 5 - x$	Subtraction property of equality
$3x - 7 = 5$	Simplify.
$3x - 7 + 7 = 5 + 7$	Addition property of equality
$3x = 12$	Simplify.
$\frac{3x}{3} = \frac{12}{3}$	Division property of equality
$x = 4$	Simplify.

The solution set is {4}.

3. $25 + 10(12 - x) = 5(2x - 7)$

$25 + 120 - 10x = 10x - 35$	Distributive property
$145 - 10x = 10x - 35$	Simplify.
$145 - 10x - 145 = 10x - 35 - 145$	Subtraction property of equality
$-10x = 10x - 180$	Simplify.
$-10x - 10x = 10x - 180 - 10x$	Subtraction property of equality
$-20x = -180$	Simplify.
$\frac{-20x}{-20} = \frac{-180}{-20}$	Division property of equality
$x = 9$	Simplify.

The solution set is {9}.

© Houghton Mifflin Harcourt Publishing Company

4. $\frac{1}{2}(6x + 4) = x + 2(x + 1)$

$3x + 2 = x + 2x + 2$	Distributive property
$3x + 2 = 3x + 2$	Simplify.
$3x + 2 - 2 = 3x + 2 - 2$	Subtraction property of equality
$3x = 3x$	Simplify.
$\frac{3x}{3} = \frac{3x}{3}$	Division property of equality
$x = x$	Simplify.

The solution set is all real numbers.

5. Given the function $f(x) = 5x - 9$, find the set of values of x such that $f(x) = 6$. Justify your solution by using the properties of equality.

$5x - 9 = 6$	Substitution property of equality
$5x - 9 + 9 = 6 + 9$	Addition property of equality
$5x = 15$	Simplify.
$\frac{5x}{5} = \frac{15}{5}$	Division property of equality
$x = 3$	Simplify.

The solution set is {3}.

6. Given the functions $f(x) = -12x + 7$ and $g(x) = 4x - 9$, find the set of values of x such that $f(x) = g(x)$. Justify your solution by using the properties of equality.

$-12x + 7 = 4x - 9$	Substitution property of equality
$-12x + 7 - 4x = 4x - 9 - 4x$	Subtraction property of equality
$-16x + 7 = -9$	Simplify.
$-16x + 7 - 7 = -9 - 7$	Subtraction property of equality
$-16x = -16$	Simplify.
$\frac{-16x}{-16} = \frac{-16}{-16}$	Division property of equality
$x = 1$	Simplify.

The solution set is {1}.

© Houghton Mifflin Harcourt Publishing Company

Solving Linear Inequalities

Essential question: *How do you justify the solution to a linear inequality?*

⋯ COMMON **Standards for**
⋯ CORE **Mathematical Content**

CC.9-12.A.SSE.2 Use the structure of an expression to identify ways to rewrite it. ...

CC.9-12.A.REI.1 Explain each step in solving a simple equation as following from the equality of numbers asserted at the previous step, starting from the assumption that the original equation has a solution. Construct a viable argument to justify a solution method.

CC.9-12.A.REI.3 Solve linear ... inequalities in one variable ...

Prerequisites

Properties of equality, Lesson 2-1

Solving linear equations, Lesson 2-1

Math Background

In Lesson 2-1, students learned how to solve linear equations using the distributive property and the properties of equality. The properties of inequality almost exactly parallel the properties of equality, with the notable additional stipulation of the Multiplication Property of Inequality and the Division Property of Inequality, which state that the direction of the inequality symbol must reverse if the inequality is multiplied or divided by a negative number. At each step of the solving process, students use properties to derive equivalent inequalities, or inequalities with the same solution set. Students will also graph the solution set on the number line.

INTRODUCE

Use the following game to familiarize students with how to find solutions to inequalities. Have pairs of students express the cost of buying something familiar using "more than" and "less than". Each student gets three tries and then they reverse roles. For example, Student 1 picks a price for an object, and says, "Jeans cost more than $40 and less than $50. Student 2 answers "$45". Student 1 says, "No, they cost more than $41 and less than $44". Student 2 guesses, "$42". Student 1 says, "Correct". Then, the roles reverse.

TEACH

1 EXPLORE

Questioning Strategies

- Why don't you need to reverse the inequality symbol when you add or subtract a negative number? **Adding or subtracting a negative number does not change the order of the numbers.**
- How can you tell whether two inequalities are equivalent? **They have the same solution set.**

Avoid Common Errors

When students solve inequalities, they may want to reverse the inequality symbol whenever there is a division, but never for multiplication. Caution them to pay careful attention to both the operation and the sign of the variable term. Only if the sign is negative will they need to reverse the inequality symbol when multiplying or dividing.

2-2

Solving Linear Inequalities

Essential question: *How do you justify the solution to a linear inequality?*

COMMON
CORE
CC-9-12.A.SSE.2,
CC-9-12.A.REI.1,
CC-9-12.A.REI.3

1 EXPLORE Multiplying or Dividing by a Negative Number

The following two inequalities are true.

$$4 < 5 \qquad\qquad 15 > 12$$

What happens to the inequalities if you multiply both sides of the first inequality by 4 and divide both sides of the second inequality by 3?

$4 < 5$	$15 > 12$
$4(4) < 4(5)$	$15 \div 3 > 12 \div 3$
$16 < 20$	$5 > 4$

Both statements are still true: 16 is less than 20, and 5 is greater than 4.

Now, multiply the first inequality by -4 and divide the second inequality by -3.
Do not change the inequality symbol when you do these multiplications.

$4 < 5$	$15 > 12$
$-4(4) < -4(5)$	$15 \div (-3) > 12 \div (-3)$
$-16 < -20$	$-5 > -4$

Is -16 less than -20? No, -16 is closer to 0 than -20 is, so it is greater than -20.
Is -5 greater than -4? No, -5 is farther from 0 than -4, so it is less than -4.

Repeat the multiplication by -4 and the division by -3, but this time reverse the inequality symbol when you do.

$4 < 5$	$15 > 12$
$-4(4) > -4(5)$	$15 \div (-3) < 12 \div (-3)$
$-16 > -20$	$-5 < -4$

Do you get a true statement in each case? __Yes__

REFLECT

1a. When solving inequalities, if you multiply by a negative number, you

must_____ reverse the inequality symbol _____.

1b. When solving inequalities, if you divide by a negative number,

you must_____ reverse the inequality symbol _____.

© Houghton Mifflin Harcourt Publishing Company

The following properties of inequality are similar to the properties of equality. They can be used to justify the steps in the solution of an inequality. These properties are also true for inequalities involving ≤ and ≥.

Addition Property of Inequality	If $a > b$, then $a + c > b + c$. If $a < b$, then $a + c < b + c$.
Subtraction Property of Inequality	If $a > b$, then $a - c > b - c$. If $a < b$, then $a - c < b - c$.
Multiplication Property of Inequality	If $a > b$ and $c > 0$, then $ac > bc$. If $a < b$ and $c > 0$, then $ac < bc$. If $a > b$ and $c < 0$, then $ac < bc$. If $a < b$ and $c < 0$, then $ac > bc$.
Division Property of Inequality	If $a > b$ and $c > 0$, then $\frac{a}{c} > \frac{b}{c}$. If $a < b$ and $c > 0$, then $\frac{a}{c} < \frac{b}{c}$. If $a > b$ and $c < 0$, then $\frac{a}{c} < \frac{b}{c}$. If $a < b$ and $c < 0$, then $\frac{a}{c} > \frac{b}{c}$.

2 EXAMPLE Justifying the Solution of an Inequality

Justify the solution to the inequality $3x - 5 > 4$ by using the properties of inequality.

Inequality	Solution steps	Reasons
$3x - 5 >\ 4$ $\underline{+5\quad +5}$ $3x\ \ >\ 9$	Add 5 to both sides.	Addition Property of Inequality
$3x > 9$ $\frac{3x}{3} > \frac{9}{3}$ $x > 3$	Divide both sides by 3.	Division Property of Inequality

REFLECT

2a. Suppose the inequality had been $-3x - 5 > 4$. How would the solution have been different?

In the second step of the solution, you would have to divide by -3. This would

require you to reverse the inequality sign. The solution would become $x < -3$.

2b. Give an example of an inequality that could be solved by using the Multiplication Property of Inequality where $c < 0$. Show the steps of the solution.

$$\frac{x}{-5} \geq 7$$
$$-5\left(\frac{x}{-5}\right) \leq -5(7)$$
$$x \leq -35$$

© Houghton Mifflin Harcourt Publishing Company

Notes

Questioning Strategies

- Why didn't you reverse the inequality symbol in any step? **You did not multiply or divide by a negative number.**

- Why isn't the reason for the first step the Subtraction Property of Inequality? **To solve, you use the inverse operation to get an equivalent inequality.**

EXTRA EXAMPLE

Find the solution to the inequality $4x + 2 < 14$ and justify the solution by listing the steps and the property used.

$x > 3$;

Solution step	Property
Subtract 2 from both sides.	Subtraction Property of Inequality
Divide both sides by 4.	Division Property of Inequality

··········
MATHEMATICAL PRACTICE   **Highlighting the Standards**
··········

If you have students compare the properties of equality with the properties of inequalities, you can use their work to address Mathematical Practice Standard 7 (Look for and make use of structure). Students should recognize that the properties of equality and the properties of inequality are structured the same way. If they have difficulty applying the inequality properties to solving inequalities, have them go through how to solve an equation step-by-step; then, change the problem to an inequality so they can make the connection.

Teaching Strategy

Students who have difficulty solving an inequality may benefit from solving the related equation in a column next to the inequality. For this example, create two columns, one with the equation $3x - 5 = 4$, and one with the inequality $3x - 5 > 4$. Show the stepped-out solutions for each problem and make comparisons as you go along. Highlight the similarities and the differences in the two solutions.

Questioning Strategies

- Does using the Addition (Subtraction) Property of Inequality depend on the sign of c? Explain. **No; c can be positive or negative. The inequality is still true if you add (subtract) c to (from) each side of the inequality $a > b$.**

- Why is the endpoint of the graph of the solution set an empty circle? **3 is not a solution.**

Avoid Common Errors

When students graph the solution to an inequality, they will frequently draw the ray in the wrong direction, or incorrectly use a closed or an open circle. Remind students that if the inequality uses < or >, the circle should be open; if the inequality uses ≤ or ≥, the circle should be closed. Students can check if they drew the ray in the correct direction by substituting a value on the ray into the inequality.

Teaching Strategy

Students may be unfamiliar with the use of set-builder notation with inequalities. Point out that the solution set to an equality could be written as $\{x \mid x = 3\}$, but for solution sets with one or a few discrete elements, we write the solution set simply by listing all elements, in this case as $\{3\}$. With inequalities, there is often infinitely many elements in the solution set, so the set is expressed using an inequality, as in $\{x \mid x < 3\}$ or $\{x \mid x \leq 3\}$.

EXTRA EXAMPLE

Complete the solution of $4x + 2 < 14$. Write the solution set using set notation, and graph your solution on a number line.
$\{x \mid x < 3\}$
The graph of the solution is a number line with a left-pointing ray originating from an open circle at 3.

2c. Compare solving a linear inequality to solving a linear equation. How are the processes similar? How are they different?

To solve both equations and inequalities, you use inverse operations to isolate

the variable. When solving inequalities, if you multiply or divide by a negative

number, you must reverse the inequality symbol.

Most linear equations have exactly one solution. Most linear inequalities have infinitely many solutions. When representing the solutions using set notation, it is not possible to list all of the solutions in braces. The solution $x \leq 1$ is written in set notation as $\{x \mid x \leq 1\}$. Read this solution set as "the set of all x such that x is less than or equal to 1."

the set of — all x — such that — x is less than or equal to 1

A graph on a number line can also be used to represent the solution set of a linear inequality.

* To represent < or >, mark the endpoint with an empty circle.

* To represent ≤ or ≥, mark the endpoint with a solid circle.

* Shade the part of the line that contains the solution set.

$x > 1$
$x \geq 1$
$x < 1$
$x \leq 1$

3 EXAMPLE Representing the Solution of a Linear Inequality

Complete the solution of $3x - 5 > 4$. Write the solution set using set notation, and graph your solution on a number line.

$$3x - 5 > 4$$
$$\underline{+5 \qquad +5} \quad \text{Add 5 to both sides.}$$
$$3x > 9$$
$$\frac{3x}{3} > \frac{9}{3} \quad \text{Divide both sides by 3.}$$
$$x > 3$$

Write the solution set using set notation.

$$\{x \mid x > 3\}$$

Graph the solution set on a number line.

$$-4\ -3\ -2\ -1\ \ 0\ \ 1\ \ 2\ \ 3\ \ 4\ \ 5\ \ 6\ \ 7\ \ 8\ \ 9$$

REFLECT

3a. Is 3 in the solution set of the inequality? Why or why not?

No; the inequality symbol is >. The solution set contains only values that are

greater than 3. A number cannot be greater than itself.

© Houghton Mifflin Harcourt Publishing Company

3b. Name three values that are in the solution set.

Answers will vary. Accept any numbers greater than 3.

3c. Suppose the inequality symbol had been ≥. Describe the solution.

The solution would be $x \geq 3$. It would include 3 and the graph would have a solid

circle at 3 with an arrow pointing to the right.

3d. Suppose the inequality symbol had been ≤. Describe the solution.

The solution would be $x \leq 3$. It would include 3 and the graph would have a solid

circle at 3 with an arrow pointing to the left.

PRACTICE

1. Given the function $f(x) = 16 - 9x$, for what values of x is $f(x) \leq 7$? Use the properties of inequality and other properties to justify your solution.

$f(x) \leq 7$	Given
$16 - 9x \leq 7$	Substitution property
$16 - 9x - 16 \leq 7 - 16$	Subtraction property of inequality
$-9x \leq -9$	Simplify.
$\frac{-9x}{-9} \geq \frac{-9}{-9}$	Division property of inequality
$x \geq 1$	Simplify.

Solution set: $\{x \mid x \geq 1\}$

2. Given the functions $f(x) = 3(x - 4)$ and $g(x) = 2(x - 3)$, for what values of x is $f(x) > g(x)$? Use the properties of inequality and other properties to justify your solution.

$f(x) > g(x)$	Given
$3(x - 4) > 2(x - 3)$	Substitution property
$3x - 12 > 2x - 6$	Distributive property
$3x - 12 + 12 > 2x - 6 + 12$	Addition property of inequality
$3x > 2x + 6$	Simplify.
$3x - 2x > 2x + 6 - 2x$	Subtraction property of inequality
$x > 6$	Simplify.

Solution set: $\{x \mid x > 6\}$

© Houghton Mifflin Harcourt Publishing Company

Essential Question

How do you justify the solution to a linear inequality?

The properties of inequality justify the steps required to isolate the variable on one side of the inequality. The properties of inequality almost exactly parallel the properties of equality, with the notable exception of the Multiplication Property of Inequality and the Division Property of Inequality, which state that the direction of the inequality symbol must be reversed if the inequality is multiplied or divided by a negative number.

Summarize

Have students complete the graphic organizer below, comparing the properties of equality and inequality.

Where skills are taught	Where skills are practiced
2 EXAMPLE	EXS. 1–2
3 EXAMPLE	EXS. 3–6

Exercises 1 and 2: Students extend the skills from **2** EXAMPLE to inequalities using function notation.

Properties of Equality	Statement of Properties	Properties of Inequality	Statement of Properties
Addition Property of Equality	If $a = b$, then $a + c = b + c$.	Addition Property of Inequality	If $a > b$, then $a + c > b + c$. If $a < b$, then $a + c < b + c$.
Subtraction Property of Equality	If $a = b$, then $a - c = b - c$.	Subtraction Property of Inequality	If $a > b$, then $a - c > b - c$. If $a < b$, then $a - c < b - c$.
Multiplication Property of Equality	If $a = b$, then $ac = bc$.	Multiplication Property of Inequality	If $a > b$ and $c > 0$, then $ac > bc$. If $a < b$ and $c > 0$, then $ac < bc$. If $a > b$ and $c < 0$, then $ac < bc$. If $a < b$ and $c < 0$, then $ac > bc$.
Division Property of Equality	If $a = b$ and $c \neq 0$, then $\frac{a}{c} = \frac{b}{c}$.	Division Property of Inequality	If $a > b$ and $c > 0$, then $\frac{a}{c} > \frac{b}{c}$. If $a < b$ and $c > 0$, then $\frac{a}{c} < \frac{b}{c}$. If $a > b$ and $c < 0$, then $\frac{a}{c} < \frac{b}{c}$. If $a < b$ and $c < 0$, then $\frac{a}{c} > \frac{b}{c}$.

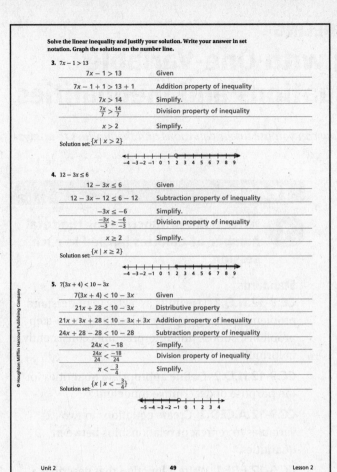

Solve the linear inequality and justify your solution. Write your answer in set notation. Graph the solution on the number line.

3. $7x - 1 > 13$

$7x - 1 > 13$	Given
$7x - 1 + 1 > 13 + 1$	Addition property of inequality
$7x > 14$	Simplify.
$\frac{7x}{7} > \frac{14}{7}$	Division property of inequality
$x > 2$	Simplify.

Solution set: $\{x \mid x > 2\}$

4. $12 - 3x \leq 6$

$12 - 3x \leq 6$	Given
$12 - 3x - 12 \leq 6 - 12$	Subtraction property of inequality
$-3x \leq -6$	Simplify.
$\frac{-3x}{-3} \geq \frac{-6}{-3}$	Division property of inequality
$x \geq 2$	Simplify.

Solution set: $\{x \mid x \geq 2\}$

5. $7(3x + 4) < 10 - 3x$

$7(3x + 4) < 10 - 3x$	Given
$21x + 28 < 10 - 3x$	Distributive property
$21x + 3x + 28 < 10 - 3x + 3x$	Addition property of inequality
$24x + 28 - 28 < 10 - 28$	Subtraction property of inequality
$24x < -18$	Simplify.
$\frac{24x}{24} < \frac{-18}{24}$	Division property of inequality
$x < -\frac{3}{4}$	Simplify.

Solution set: $\{x \mid x < -\frac{3}{4}\}$

6. $-\frac{1}{3}(x + 2) \geq 7x + 3$

$-\frac{1}{3}(x + 2) \geq 7x + 3$	Given
$-\frac{1}{3}x - \frac{2}{3} \geq 7x + 3$	Distributive property
$3\left(-\frac{1}{3}x - \frac{2}{3}\right) \geq 3(7x + 3)$	Multiplication property of inequality
$-x - 2 \geq 21x + 9$	Distributive property
$-x - 2 + 2 \geq 21x + 9 + 2$	Addition property of inequality
$-x - 21x \geq 21x + 11 - 21x$	Subtraction property of inequality
$-22x \geq 11$	Simplify.
$\frac{-22x}{-22} \leq \frac{11}{-22}$	Division property of inequality
$x \leq -\frac{1}{2}$	Simplify.

Solution set: $\{x \mid x \leq -\frac{1}{2}\}$

FOCUS ON MODELING
Modeling with One-Variable Linear Equations and Inequalities

Essential question: *How can you use linear equations and inequalities to analyze a weight-loss plan?*

Standards for Mathematical Content

The following standards are addressed in this lesson. (An asterisk indicates that a standard is also a Modeling standard.) For more detailed information, see the correlation for each section of the lesson.

Number and Quantity: CC.9-12.N.Q.1*, CC.9-12.N.Q.2*

Algebra: CC.9-12.A.CED.1*, CC.9-12.A.CED.2*, CC.9-12.A.CED.3*

Functions: CC.9-12.F.BF.1*

Prerequisites

- Writing and evaluating a function, Lesson 1-5
- Solving a linear equation, Lesson 2-1
- Solving a linear inequality, Lesson 2-2

Math Background

In this lesson, students write linear functions for exercising and dieting. They use the functions to write and solve equations and inequalities to make decisions about a weight-loss program.

INTRODUCE

Ask students to discuss the differences in Calories burned for a given body weight if the time spent walking (or running) is increased or if the intensity (speed) of the exercise increases. Help students understand that the increase in the number of Calories burned is a function of the speed of walking (or running), as well as a function of time.

TEACH

Write a linear function for the total number of Calories burned in each session.

Standards

CC.9-12.N.Q.1 Use units as a way to understand problems and to guide the solution of multi-step problems; choose and interpret units consistently in formulas; …*

CC.9-12.N.Q.2 Define appropriate quantities for the purpose of descriptive modeling.*

CC.9-12.A.CED.2 Create equations in two … variables to represent relationships between quantities.*

CC.9-12.F.BF.1 Write a function that describes a relationship between two quantities.*

Also: CC.9-12.A.SSE.1*, CC.9-12.F.IF.5*

Questioning Strategies

- Why was it convenient to rewrite the table by dividing each value by 60? **Jed wanted an exercise program in terms of minutes, not hours. He started with a table in hours, and dividing by 60 converted it to a table in minutes.**

- How many Calories will Jed burn if he walks 3.0 mph for 45 minutes? How do you know? **230.4 Calories; Jed will burn 5.12 Calories per minute according to the table listing the number of Calories burned per minute for his body weight, 205 pounds. In 45 minutes, he will burn 5.12 × 45 = 230.4 Calories.**

- How can you use $C(t)$ to find the number of Calories that Jed burns when walking 15 minutes and running 15 minutes? **Evaluate $C(t) = 5.12t + 12.42(30 − t)$ for $t = 15$; $C(15) = 5.12(15) + 12.42(30 − 15) = 263.1$ Calories.**

Name _____ Class _____ Date _____

FOCUS ON MODELING

Modeling with One-Variable Linear Equations and Inequalities

2-3

COMMON CORE

CC.9-12.N.Q.1*,
CC.9-12.N.Q.2*,
CC.9-12.A.CED.1*,
CC.9-12.A.CED.2*,
CC.9-12.A.CED.3*,
CC.9-12.F.BF.1*

Essential question: *How can you use linear equations and inequalities to analyze a weight-loss plan?*

Jed is trying to devise a plan to help him lose weight. The weight-loss plan will be supervised by his doctor. His doctor explained to Jed that each pound of body fat is equal to 3500 Calories. So, if Jed eliminates 500 Calories per day through diet and exercise, he will lose one pound per week. The table below shows how many Calories are burned per hour of exercise for people of different weights who are walking or running at various speeds.

Calories Burned per Hour of Exercise by Body Weight				
Exercise (1 hour)	**130 lb**	**155 lb**	**180 lb**	**205 lb**
		Body Weight		
Walking 2.0 mph	148	176	204	233
Walking 3.0 mph	195	232	270	307
Walking 4.0 mph	295	352	409	465
Running, 5.0 mph	472	563	654	745
Running, 6.0 mph	590	704	817	931
Running, 6.7 mph	649	774	899	1024
Running, 7.5 mph	738	880	1022	1163
Running, 8.6 mph	826	985	1144	1303
Running, 10.0 mph	944	1126	1308	1489

Jed currently weighs 205 pounds. Using a pace calculator, he has determined that he walks at a speed of 3 miles per hour and runs at a speed of 5 miles per hour. How can Jed use the table to devise a plan for losing weight? He plans to exercise 30 minutes per day.

© Houghton Mifflin Harcourt Publishing Company

---

1 Write a linear function for the total number of Calories burned in each session.

A Since Jed is exercising 30 minutes per day, divide each value in the table by 60 to determine the number of Calories burned per minute. Round to the nearest hundredth.

Calories Burned per Minute of Exercise by Body Weight				
Exercise (1 min.)	**130 lb**	**155 lb**	**180 lb**	**205 lb**
		Body Weight		
Walking, 2.0 mph	2.47	2.93	3.40	3.88
Walking, 3.0 mph	3.25	3.87	4.50	5.12
Walking, 4.0 mph	4.92	5.87	6.82	7.75
Running, 5 mph	7.87	9.38	10.90	12.42
Running, 6 mph	9.83	11.73	13.62	15.52
Running, 6.7 mph	10.82	12.90	14.98	17.07
Running, 7.5 mph	12.30	14.67	17.03	19.38
Running, 8.6 mph	13.77	16.42	19.07	21.72
Running, 10 mph	15.73	18.77	21.80	24.82

B Let *t* be the number of minutes Jed walks at 3.0 miles per hour. Write an expression for the number of Calories Jed burns while walking.

5.12*t*

C If Jed exercises for 30 minutes, then 30 − *t* is the number of minutes Jed runs at 5.0 miles per hour. Write an expression for the number of Calories Jed burns while running.

12.42(30 − *t*)

D The number of Calories burned while Jed exercises is given below in words. Use this verbal model and your expressions from parts B and C above to write a function *C(t)*, where *C* is the total number of Calories burned.

Total number of Calories burned	=	Calories burned while walking	+	Calories burned while running
C(t)	=	5.12*t*	+	12.42(30 − *t*)

E State the domain of the function.

{*t* | 0 ≤ *t* ≤ 30}

© Houghton Mifflin Harcourt Publishing Company

Differentiated Instruction

Although the stepped-out work in the lesson should be relatively easy for students to complete, some of the Reflect and Extend questions may prove to be challenging. Students may benefit from working in groups to complete them.

Teaching Strategy

If students have difficulty in writing an expression for the number of Calories burned after t minutes, suggest that they make a table showing values of t and the corresponding Calories burned per minute, both for walking and for running. Then, encourage students to look for and describe the linear patterns in the table. A spreadsheet may also be used.

2 Determine whether it is possible for Jed to burn 500 Calories per day.

Standards

CC.9-12.A.CED.1 Create equations ... in one variable and use them to solve problems.*

CC.9-12.A.CED.3 Represent constraints by equations ..., and interpret solutions as viable or nonviable options in a modeling context.*

CC.9-12.A.REI.1 Solve linear equations ... in one variable ...*

Also: CC.9-12.F.IF.2

Questioning Strategies

- What does the equation $C(t) = 500$ represent and why do you solve it for t? **The function $C(t) = 5.12t + 12.42(30 - t)$ represents the total number of Calories Jed can burn in one day. If Jed wants to burn 500 Calories per day, $C(t)$ must equal 500, which results in the equation $C(t) = 500$. You solve $C(t) = 500$ for t to find the number of minutes Jed must spend walking to burn 500 Calories per day.**

- Is it possible to determine if Jed can burn 500 Calories per day without solving the equation in Part A? Explain. **Yes; Jed exercises for 30 minutes per day. Jed burns the most Calories per minute while running, which means the greatest amount of Calories he can burn per day is the product of 12.42 (the number of Calories burned per minute by running) and 30 (the total number of minutes he exercises per day). Because $12.42 \cdot 30 = 372.6$, Jed can only burn at most 372.6 Calories per day.**

Differentiated Instruction

Visual learners can benefit from graphing the function $C(t) = 5.12t + 12.42(30 - t)$ on a graphing calculator. Students should graph the function without regard to its real world domain of $\{t | 0 \leq t \leq 30\}$ and select a viewing window so that the y-value of 500 is visible on the graph. By using the TRACE function, students can find the point on the graph that has a y-value of 500. They will see that the x-value for that point is about -17.5. Lead students to understand that -17.5 represents the number of walking minutes necessary to burn 500 Calories per day. Students should realize that because time cannot be negative, Jed cannot burn 500 Calories per day.

3 Revise Jed's exercise plan so that he burns 500 Calories per day.

Standards

CC.9-12.A.CED.1 Create equations ... in one variable and use them to solve problems.*

CC.9-12.A.CED.3 Represent constraints by equations ..., and interpret solutions as viable or nonviable options in a modeling context.*

CC.9-12.A.REI.1 Solve linear equations ... in one variable ...*

Also: CC.9-12.F.IF.2

Questioning Strategies

- Rewrite both original function $C(t)$ and new function $C(t)$ in slope intercept form. Compare the functions. How are they the same; how are they different? **Original function: $C(t) = -7.3t + 372.6$; new function: $C(t) = -7.3t + 558.9$; Both functions have slope -7.3. The y-intercept of the original function is 372.6. The y-intercept of the new function is 558.9.**

- How is the graph of the new function related to the graph of the original function? **The graph of the new function is a vertical translation of the graph of the old function up 186.3 units. The graphs are parallel lines.**

- What do the y-intercepts of the two graphs represent? How is this useful in determining if Jed's exercise plan will allow him to burn 500 Calories per day? **The y-intercept of each graph represents the maximum number of Calories Jed can burn under each exercise plan if he runs for the entire time. Under the original plan, Jed could burn a maximum of 372.6 Calories, so he could not burn 500 Calories per day. Under the new plan, he could burn a maximum of 558.9 Calories, so he could burn 500 Calories per day.**

REFLECT

1a. Why did you divide the rates in the original table by 60 to determine the rates in the second table?

To convert the values in the original table from Calories per hour to

Calories per minute, multiply by the conversion factor $\frac{1 \text{ hour}}{60 \text{ minutes}}$:

$$x \frac{\text{Calories}}{\text{hour}} \cdot \frac{1 \text{ hour}}{60 \text{ minutes}} = \frac{x}{60} \frac{\text{Calories}}{\text{minute}}$$

1b. What unit of measurement does each term of $C(t)$, $5.12t$ and $12.42(30 - t)$, have? How do you know?

Calories; the coefficients 5.12 and 12.42 are measured in Calories per minute,

while the variables t and $30 - t$ are measured in minutes, so the products $5.12t$

and $12.42(30 - t)$ are measured in $\frac{\text{Calories}}{\text{minutes}} \cdot \text{minutes} = \text{Calories}$.

1c. What unit of measurement do the values of $C(t)$ have? How do you know?

Calories; $C(t)$ is the sum of two terms measured in Calories, and

Calories + Calories = Calories.

2 Determine whether it is possible for Jed to burn 500 Calories per day from exercise alone.

A Solve the equation $C(t) = 500$ for t. Justify the steps.

$5.12t + 12.42(30 - t) = 500$	Given equation
$5.12t + 372.6 - 12.42t = 500$	Distributive Property
$-7.3t + 372.6 = 500$	Distributive Property (combining like terms)
$-7.3t = 127.4$	Subtraction Property of Equality
$t \approx -17.5$	Division Property of Equality

B Interpret the solution. Is it possible for Jed to burn 500 Calories per day by exercising for 30 minutes? Explain.

Since t represents time spent walking, t must be nonnegative; the value of t in

part A is negative, so it is not possible to burn 500 Calories in 30 minutes.

REFLECT

2a. The possible values of t range from 0 to 30. For what value of t does Jed burn the fewest number of Calories? For what value of t does Jed burn the greatest number of Calories? Explain your reasoning.

$t = 30$ results in the fewest number of Calories burned because Jed spends all

of his exercise time walking, which burns fewer Calories than running does;

$t = 0$ results in the greatest number of Calories burned because Jed spends all

of his exercise time running.

2b. Find the value of $C(0)$. How is this number relevant to the question of whether Jed can burn 500 Calories per day by exercising for 30 minutes?

$C(0) = 372.6$; this represents the greatest number of Calories that Jed can

burn, and it is less than his goal of 500 Calories.

3 Revise Jed's exercise plan so that he burns 500 Calories per day.

A If he wants to burn 500 Calories per day, one option that Jed has is to exercise for more than 30 minutes. Suppose he decides to exercise for 45 minutes. Give the new rule for $C(t)$.

$C(t) = 5.12t + 12.42(45 - t)$

B Solve the equation $C(t) = 500$ for t. Show and justify the steps that you take.

$5.12t + 12.42(45 - t) = 500$	Substitute the rule for $C(t)$.
$5.12t + 558.9 - 12.42t = 500$	Distributive Property
$-7.3t + 558.9 = 500$	Distributive Property (combining like terms)
$-7.3t = -58.9$	Subtraction Property of Equality
$t \approx 8$	Division Property of Equality

C Interpret the solution. Is it possible for Jed to burn 500 Calories per day by exercising for 45 minutes? If so, how?

Yes; Jed should spend about 8 minutes walking and about 37 minutes running.

Notes

4 If Jed chooses not to exercise every day, design a diet and exercise plan that will result in a weight loss of 1 pound per week.

Standards

CC.9-12.A.CED.1 Create ... inequalities in one variable and use them to solve problems.*

CC.9-12.A.CED.2 Create equations in two ... variables to represent relationships between quantities ...*

CC.9-12.A.CED.3 Represent constraints by ... inequalities ... and interpret solutions as viable or nonviable options in a modeling context.*

CC.9-12.A.REI.3 Solve linear ... inequalities in one variable ...*

CC.9-12.F.BF.1 Write a function that describes a relationship between two quantities.*

Also: CC.9-12.F.IF.2

Questioning Strategies

- What is the range of the function $C(d)$? Is the function discrete or continuous? Explain. **The range is {0, 500, 1000, 1500, 2000, 2500, 3000, 3500}. Discrete; the function consists of the ordered pairs (0, 3500), (1, 3000), (2, 2500), (3, 2000), (4, 1500), (5, 1000), (6, 500) and (7, 0).**

- Why must Jed exercise at least 5 days? **The solution to $C(d) \leq 1400$ is $d \geq 4.2$. Thus, Jed must exercise more than 4.2 days. Since d is the number of days of exercise during a week, d must be a whole number between 0 and 7. Therefore, Jed can exercise 5, 6, or 7 days a week.**

CLOSE

Essential Question

How can you use linear equations and inequalities to analyze a weight-loss program?
By writing functions that model Calories burned from exercising and Calories eliminated through dieting, you can impose constraints on the functions, which lead to equations and inequalities whose solutions help you make decisions about the weight-loss program.

Summarize

Have students write a journal entry in which they provide a one-page summary of examples of diet and exercise plans Jed could follow. Ask them to include a plan for losing 1 pound per week.

MATHEMATICAL PRACTICE	Highlighting the Standards

If you have students summarize their findings as suggested in the preceding Summarize note, you can use the summaries to address Mathematical Practice Standard 3 (Construct viable arguments and critique the reasoning of others). Have pairs of students exchange their summaries and comment on the clarity and completeness of the argument made by their partners to design a diet and exercise plan for Jed. Ask students to describe and justify to their partners their choices for a combination of walking and running and how that affects the number of Calories that need to be eliminated through dieting in order to lose 1 pound per week.

EXTEND

Standards
CC.9-12.A.CED.1 Create equations and inequalities in one variable and use them to solve problems.* (Exs. 1, 2)

CC.9-12.A.CED.3 Represent constraints by equations and inequalities, ... and interpret solutions as viable or nonviable options in a modeling context.* (Exs. 1, 2)

CC.9-12.A.REI.3 Solve linear equations and inequalities in one variable ...* (Exs. 1, 2)

REFLECT

3a. What is the minimum amount of time that Jed must exercise to burn 500 Calories per day? Explain.

About 40.3 minutes; dividing 500 Calories by 12.42 Calories per minute (the rate of burn while running) gives about 40.3 minutes.

3b. What is the maximum amount of time that Jed must exercise to burn 500 Calories per day? Explain.

About 97.7 minutes; dividing 500 Calories by 5.12 Calories per minute (the rate of burn while walking) gives about 97.7 minutes.

3c. If the total number of Calories burned is held constant at 500, what happens to the amounts of time spent walking and running as exercise time increases from the minimum to the maximum?

The amount of time spent walking increases while the amount of time spent running decreases.

4 **If Jed chooses not to exercise every day, design a diet and exercise plan that will result in a weight loss of 1 pound per week.**

A Suppose Jed decides to exercise d days per week. On days that he exercises, he will burn 500 Calories. But if he doesn't exercise *every* day, he must diet to make up for any shortfall in his goal of eliminating 3500 Calories per week. Use the verbal model below to write a function $C(d)$, where C is the number of Calories that Jed must make up through dieting.

Number of Calories eliminated through dieting	=	Weekly number of Calories to be eliminated	−	Number of Calories eliminated through exercise
$C(d)$	=	3500	−	$500d$

B What is the domain of the function? Explain.

Since d is the number of days of exercise during a week, the domain is {0, 1, 2, 3, 4, 5, 6, 7}.

C Suppose Jed decides that he will eliminate at most 200 Calories per day through dieting. This means that he will eliminate at most how many Calories per week through dieting? Explain.

1400 Calories, because 7 days • 200 Calories per day = 1400 Calories

D Based on the supposition in part C, use the function $C(d)$ to write and solve an inequality to find the number of days during a week that Jed must exercise. Show and justify the steps that you take.

$C(d) \leq 1400$	Calories from dieting must be at most 1400.
$3500 - 500d \leq 1400$	Substitute the rule for $C(d)$.
$-500d \leq -2100$	Subtraction Property of Inequality
$d \geq 4.2$	Division Property of Inequality

REFLECT

4a. Interpret the solution in part D in terms of Jed's diet and exercise plan. Take into consideration what the possible values of d are.

Jed must exercise at least 5 days during a week if he plans to eliminate at most 200 Calories per day through dieting.

EXTEND

1. Suppose Jed decides to run twice the number of minutes that he walks. How many Calories will he burn during 45 minutes of exercise? Show your work.

Let t equal the number of minutes spent walking. Then $2t$ is the number of minutes spent running. If Jed exercises for 45 minutes, then $t + 2t = 45$, so $t = 15$. $C(15) = 5.12(15) + 12.42(30) = 449.4$ Calories.

2. Suppose Jed decides to eliminate at least 150 Calories per day through dieting. How many days during a week must he exercise? Show your work.

The inequality that models the situation is $C(d) \geq 7(150)$. Solving $3500 - 500d \geq 1050$ gives $d \leq 4.9$, so Jed must exercise at most 4 days during a week.

Literal Equations and Inequalities

Essential question: *How do you solve literal equations and inequalities?*

COMMON **Standards for**
CORE **Mathematical Content**

CC.9-12.A.REI.1 Explain each step in solving a simple equation as following from the equality of numbers asserted at the previous step, starting from the assumption that the original equation has a solution. Construct a viable argument to justify a solution method.

CC.9-12.A.REI.3 Solve linear equations and inequalities in one variable, including equations with coefficients represented by letters.

Vocabulary

literal equation

literal inequalilty

Prerequisites

Solving linear equations, Lesson 2-1

Solving linear inequalities, Lesson 2-2

Math Background

In this lesson students will extend their skill at solving specific linear equations and inequalities to solving entire classes of linear equations and inequalities by replacing the numbers in an equation or inequality with letters. For instance, the equation $3x = 12$ has the general form $ax = b$, which also represents other equations like $2x = -4$ and $-5x = 17$. The general forms of equations and inequalities are called *literal* equations and inequalities. (The word *literal* refers to *letter*.) Restrictions must be placed on the letters used for the coefficients of a variable in a literal equation or inequality. One common restriction is that the coefficient of a variable cannot be 0; otherwise, the variable term drops out of the equation or inequality. Further restrictions are needed for the coefficient of a variable in an inequality in order to know what to do with the inequality sign when dividing both sides by the coefficient (or multiplying both sides by its reciprocal).

When solving literal equations and inequalities, students will follow the same steps as when solving specific equations and inequalities. Once they have solved a literal equation or inequality, they should recognize that it represents the solutions of all members of that class of equations or inequalities. For instance, $x = \frac{b}{a}$ gives the solution of all equations of the form $ax = b$. Students just need to substitute the values of a and b into $x = \frac{b}{a}$ and simplify to obtain the solution of a specific equation like $3x = 12$. This is the idea behind the quadratic formula, which gives the solution of the literal equation $ax^2 + bx + c = 0$. It is also the idea behind calculator or computer programs that allow you to enter an equation or inequality having a particular form and obtain the solution automatically.

INTRODUCE

Show the following graphic organizer to help students see that solving literal equations uses the same steps as solving non-literal linear equations. Leave the steps on the right side blank until the appropriate part of the lesson.

$4x + 3 = 15$		$ax + b = c$	
-3	-3	$-b$	$-b$
$4x$	$= 12$	ax	$= c - b$
$\dfrac{4x}{4}$	$= \dfrac{12}{4}$	$\dfrac{ax}{a}$	$= \dfrac{c - b}{a}$
x	$= 3$	x	$= \dfrac{c - b}{a}$

Name_____ Class_____ Date_____

Literal Equations and Inequalities

COMMON CORE

CC.9-12.A.REI.1
CC.9-12.A.REI.3

Essential question: *How do you solve literal equations and inequalities?*

A **literal equation** is an equation in which the coefficients and constants have been replaced by letters. In the following Explore, you will see how a literal equation can be used to represent specific equations having the same form.

1 EXPLORE   Understanding Literal Equations

A For each equation given below, solve the equation by writing two equivalent equations: one where the x-term is isolated and then one where x is isolated.

$3x + 1 = 7$	$-2x + 5 = 11$	$4x + 3 = -1$
$3x = 6$	$-2x = 6$	$4x = -4$
$x = 2$	$x = -3$	$x = -1$

B Identify the two properties of equality that you used in part A. List them in the order that you used them.

Subtraction Property of Equality; Division Property of Equality

C Each equation in part A has the general form $ax + b = c$ where $a \neq 0$. Solve this literal equation for x using the properties of equality that you identified in part B.

$ax + b = c$ Write the literal equation.

$ax = c - b$ Subtract b from both sides.

$x = \dfrac{c - b}{a}$ Divide both sides by a.

D Show that the solution of the literal equation gives the same solution of $3x + 1 = 7$ as you found in part A. Recognize that when $a = 3$, $b = 1$, and $c = 7$, the literal equation $ax + b = c$ gives the specific equation $3x + 1 = 7$.

$x = \dfrac{c - b}{a}$ Write the literal equation's solution.

$x = \dfrac{7 - 1}{3}$ Substitute 3 for a, 1 for b, and 7 for c.

$x = 2$ Simplify.

REFLECT

1a. Why must the restriction $a \neq 0$ be placed on the literal equation $ax + b = c$?

The equation would have no variable term if $a = 0$.

© Houghton Mifflin Harcourt Publishing Company

1b. Choose one of the other specific equations from part A. Show that the solution of the literal equation gives the solution of the specific equation.

For $-2x + 5 = 11$, $x = \dfrac{c - b}{a} = \dfrac{11 - 5}{-2} = -3$.

For $4x + 3 = -1$, $x = \dfrac{c - b}{a} = \dfrac{-1 - 3}{4} = -1$.

When you solve a literal equation, you use properties of equality and other properties to isolate the variable. The result is not a number, but rather an expression involving the letters that represent the coefficients and constants.

2 EXAMPLE   Solving a Literal Equation and Evaluating Its Solution

Solve the literal equation $a(x + b) = c$ where $a \neq 0$. Then use the literal equation's solution to obtain the solution of the specific equation $2(x + 7) = -6$.

A Solve $a(x + b) = c$ for x. Use the properties of equality to justify your solution steps.

Equation	Solution step	Reason
$a(x + b) = c$		
$x + b = \dfrac{c}{a}$	Divide both sides by a.	**Division** Property of Equality
$x = \dfrac{c}{a} - b$	Subtract b from both sides.	**Subtraction** Property of Equality

B Obtain the solution of $2(x + 7) = -6$ from the literal equation's solution by letting $a = 2$, $b = 7$, and $c = -6$.

$x = \dfrac{c}{a} - b$ Write the literal equation's solution.

$x = \dfrac{-6}{2} - 7$ Substitute 2 for a, 7 for b, and -6 for c.

$x = -10$ Simplify.

REFLECT

2a. When solving $a(x + b) = c$, why do you divide by a before you subtract b?

The order of operations for $a(x + b)$ tells you that b is added to x before the sum is multiplied by a. When undoing these operations, you perform the inverse operations in reverse order: dividing by a before subtracting b.

© Houghton Mifflin Harcourt Publishing Company

Questioning Strategies

- Could you use other letters besides *a, b,* and *c* to write the literal equation? If so, give an example. **Yes; you could write the literal equation as $mx + n = p$, for instance.**

- How does the solution of the literal equation differ from the solution of a specific equation of that form? **Unlike a specific equation, the literal equation's solution is not a number; it is an expression that involves the letters representing the coefficients and constants in the literal equation.**

- How is the solution of a literal equation useful? **It provides a rule for calculating the solution of any specific equation having the form of the literal equation; there is no need to go through the steps of solving the specific equation.**

Teaching Strategy

After completing the Explore, have students work in pairs. One student should write an equation of the form $ax + b = c$, share it with his or her partner, and then solve it on his or her own. The partner should determine the solution of the equation from the general solution $x = \frac{c - b}{a}$. The partners should then compare their two solutions to make sure they are the same. (If not, they should check each other's work to see where a mistake was made.) The partners can then switch roles and repeat the process.

Questioning Strategies

- In part A, is it possible to use the Multiplication Property of Equality rather than the Subtraction Property of Equality as the first step of solving $a(x + b) = c$? If so, how? **Yes; you could multiply both sides by the reciprocal of *a*.**

- In part A, is it possible to use the Addition Property of Equality rather than the Division Property of Equality as the second step of solving $a(x + b) = c$? If so, how? **Yes; you could add the opposite of *b* to both sides.**

- In part B, what mental calculations do you perform in going from $x = \frac{-6}{2} - 7$ to $x = -10$? **Divide −6 by 2 to get −3, then subtract 7 from −3 to get −10.**

Avoid Common Errors

Because the letters in the solution of a literal equation appear in a different order than they do in the equation, students may substitute the wrong values for the letters. To slow down the process of substituting values for so many letters, have them work with one letter at a time, as shown below when using $x = \frac{c}{a} - b$ to solve $2(x + 7) = -6$.

Step	Result
Identify the value of *a*.	2
Substitute the value of *a*.	$x = \frac{c}{2} - b$
Identify the value of *b*.	7
Substitute the value of *b*.	$x = \frac{c}{2} - 7$
Identify the value of *c*.	−6
Substitute the value of *c*.	$x = \frac{-6}{2} - 7$

EXTRA EXAMPLE

Solve the literal equation $\frac{x - a}{b} = c$ where $b \neq 0$. Then use the literal equation's solution to obtain the solution of $\frac{x - 3}{2} = -4$. $x = bc + a$; $x = 2(-4) + 3 = -5$

2b. Write an equation that has the form $a(x + b) = c$. Find the solution of your equation using the literal equation's solution.

Answers will vary. Sample answer: $-3(x + 4) = 6$; $x = \frac{6}{-3} - 4 = -6$

2c. Another way to solve $a(x + b) = c$ is to start by using the Distributive Property. Show and justify the solution steps using this method.

$a(x + b) = c$	Write the literal equation.
$ax + ab = c$	Distributive Property
$ax = c - ab$	Subtraction Property of Equality
$x = \frac{c - ab}{a}$	Division Property of Equality

2d. When you start solving $a(x + b) = c$ by dividing by a, you get $x = \frac{c}{a} - b$. When you start solving $a(x + b) = c$ by distributing a, you get $x = \frac{c - ab}{a}$. Use the fact that you can rewrite $\frac{c - ab}{a}$ as the difference of two fractions to show that the two solutions are equivalent.

$$\frac{c - ab}{a} = \frac{c}{a} - \frac{ab}{a} = \frac{c}{a} - b$$

A **literal inequality** is an inequality in which the coefficients and constants have been replaced by letters. When solving a linear inequality, you need to pay attention to the restriction placed on the coefficient of the variable because it will affect the direction of the inequality symbol when you divide by that coefficient.

3 EXAMPLE Solving a Literal Inequality and Evaluating Its Solution

Solve the literal inequality $ax + b > c$ where $a > 0$. Then use the literal inequality's solution to obtain the solution of the specific inequality $3x + 1 > -2$.

A Solve $ax + b > c$ for x. Use the properties of inequality to justify your solution steps.

Equation	Solution step	Reason
$ax + b > c$		
$x + b > \boxed{c - b}$	Subtract b from both sides.	Subtraction Property of Inequality
$x > \dfrac{\boxed{c - b}}{a}$	Divide both sides by a.	Division Property of Inequality

B Obtain the solution of $3x + 1 > -2$ from the literal inequality's solution by letting $a = 3$, $b = 1$, and $c = -2$.

$x > \dfrac{c - b}{a}$	Write the literal inequality's solution.
$x > \dfrac{\boxed{-2} - \boxed{1}}{3}$	Substitute 3 for a, 1 for b, and -2 for c.
$x > \boxed{-1}$	Simplify.

REFLECT

3a. Show and justify the steps for solving $ax + b > c$ where $a < 0$.

$ax + b > c$	Write the literal inequality.
$ax > c - b$	Subtraction Property of Inequality
$x < \frac{c - b}{a}$	Division Property of Inequality

3b. How is the solution of $ax + b > c$ where $a > 0$ different from the solution of $ax + b > c$ where $a < 0$? Why?

The directions of the inequality symbols in the two solutions are different. In the case where $a < 0$, dividing by a requires reversing the direction of the inequality.

When the variable appears more than once in a literal inequality, you must consider the restriction on all the coefficients of the variable.

4 EXAMPLE Solving a Literal Inequality and Evaluating Its Solution

Solve the literal inequality $ax \le bx + c$ where $a > b$. Then use the literal inequality's solution to obtain the solution of the specific inequality $x \le -3x + 8$.

A Solve $ax \le bx + c$ for x. Use the properties of inequality to justify your solution steps.

Equation	Solution step	Reason
$ax \le bx + c$		
$ax - \boxed{bx} \le c$	Subtract bx from both sides.	Subtraction Property of Inequality
$(\boxed{a} - b)x \le c$	Combine like terms.	Distributive Property
$x \le \dfrac{c}{\boxed{a - b}}$	Divide both sides by $a - b$.	Division Property of Inequality

Questioning Strategies

- In part A, when you divide both sides by a, why does the direction of the inequality symbol *not* change? **You know that $a > 0$.**

- In part B, what mental calculations do you perform in going from $x > \frac{-2-1}{3}$ to $x > -1$? **Subtract 1 from −2 to get −3, then divide −3 by 3 to get −1.**

EXTRA EXAMPLE

Solve the literal inequality $\frac{x}{a} - b > c$ where $a < 0$. Then use the literal inequality's solution to obtain the solution of $\frac{x}{-3} - 1 > 2$. $x < a(c + b)$; $x < -3(2 + 1)$, or $x < -9$

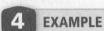

Questioning Strategies

- In part A, why do you begin by subtracting bx from both sides? **You subtract bx from both sides to get the variable terms on one side of the inequality.**

- In part B, what mental calculations do you perform in going from $x \le \frac{8}{1 - (-3)}$ to $x \le 2$? **Subtract −3 from 1 to get 4, then divide 8 by 4 to get 2.**

EXTRA EXAMPLE

Solve the literal inequality $ax + b \le cx$ where $a < c$. Then use the literal inequality's solution to obtain the solution of $-2x + 5 \le 3x$. $x \ge \frac{b}{c - a}$; $x \ge \frac{5}{3 - (-2)}$, or $x \ge 1$

Essential Question

How do you solve literal equations and inequalities? To solve literal equations and inequalities, you must isolate the variable on one side of the equation, using the same steps and properties as when solving specific equations and inequalities. You must also pay attention to any restrictions on the coefficient(s) of the variables.

Summarize

Have students write a journal entry in which they summarize the steps for solving a literal equation or inequality and then use the literal solution to obtain the solution of a specific equation or inequality. Have students give their own examples and challenge them to determine appropriate restriction on the coefficient(s) of the variable in the equation or inequality.

⋮ **MATHEMATICAL PRACTICE**   **Highlighting the Standards**

The journal entry provides a connection to Mathematical Practice Standard 6 (Attend to precision). Placing a restriction on the coefficient(s) of the variable in a literal equation or inequality is an essential part of generalizing a class of equations or inequalities because it guarantees that the literal equation or inequality will have a variable term and determines what happens to the inequality sign when solving a literal inequality.

PRACTICE

Where skills are taught	Where skills are practiced
2 EXAMPLE	EXS. 1–3
3 EXAMPLE	EX. 4
4 EXAMPLE	EX. 5

B Obtain the solution of $x \leq -3x + 8$ from the literal inequality's solution by letting $a = 1$, $b = -3$, and $c = 8$.

$x \leq \dfrac{c}{a-b}$ Write the literal inequality's solution.

$x \leq \dfrac{8}{1 - -3}$ Substitute 1 for a, -3 for b and 8 for c.

$x \leq 2$ Simplify.

REFLECT

4a. In solving $ax \leq bx + c$ where $a > b$, why do you *not* need to reverse the direction of the inequality symbol?

The restriction $a > b$ tells you that $a - b > 0$, so when you divide both sides of $(a - b)x < c$ by $a - b$, you do not need to reverse the direction of the inequality.

4b. Show and justify the steps for solving $ax \leq bx + c$ where $a < b$.

$ax \leq bx + c$	Write the literal inequality.
$ax - bx \leq c$	Subtraction Property of Inequality
$(a - b)x \leq c$	Distributive Property
$x \geq \dfrac{c}{a - b}$	Division Property of Inequality

PRACTICE

1. Show and justify the steps for solving $x + a = b$. Then use the literal equation's solution to obtain the solution of $x + 2 = -4$.

$x + a = b$	Write the literal equation.
$x = b - a$	Subtraction Property of Equality

Substitute 2 for a and -4 for b to get the solution of $x + a = b$: $x = 4 - (-2) = 6$.

2. Show and justify the steps for solving $ax = b$ where $a \neq 0$. Then use the literal equation's solution to obtain the solution of $3x = -15$.

$ax = b$	Write the literal equation.
$x = \dfrac{b}{a}$	Division Property of Equality

Substitute 3 for a and -15 for b to get the solution of $3x = -15$: $x = \dfrac{-15}{3} = -5$.

3. Show and justify the steps for solving $ax = bx + c$ where $a \neq b$. Then use the literal equation's solution to obtain the solution of $2x = x + 7$.

$ax = bx + c$	Write the literal equation.
$ax - bx = c$	Subtraction Property of Equality
$(a - b)x = c$	Distributive Property
$x = \dfrac{c}{a - b}$	Division Property of Equality

Substitute 2 for a, 1 for b, and 7 for c to get the solution of $2x = x + 7$: $x = \dfrac{7}{2 - 1} = 7$.

4. Show and justify the steps for solving $a(x + b) \geq c$ where $a > 0$. Then use the literal inequality's solution to obtain the solution of $5(x + 3) \geq -10$.

$a(x + b) \geq c$	Write the literal inequality.
$x + b \geq \dfrac{c}{a}$	Division Property of Inequality
$x \geq \dfrac{c}{a} - b$	Subtraction Property of Inequality

Substitute 5 for a, 3 for b, and -10 for c to get the solution of $5(x + 3) \geq -10$: $x \geq \dfrac{-10}{5} - 3$, or $x \geq -5$.

5. Show and justify the steps for solving $ax + b < cx + d$ where $a < c$. Then use the literal inequality's solution to obtain the solution of $-x + 4 < 2x + 13$.

$ax + b < cx + d$	Write the literal inequality.
$ax - cx + b < d$	Subtraction Property of Inequality
$(a - c)x + b < d$	Distributive Property
$(a - c)x < d - b$	Subtraction Property of Inequality
$x > \dfrac{d - b}{a - c}$	Division Property of Inequality

Substitute -1 for a, 4 for b, 2 for c, and 13 for d to get the solution of $-x + 4 < 2x + 13$: $x > \dfrac{13 - 4}{-1 - 2}$, or $x > -3$.

Notes

Rewriting Formulas

Essential question: *How do you rewrite formulas?*

CC.9-12.A.CED.2 Create equations in two or more variables to represent relationships between quantities; ... *

CC.9-12.A.CED.4 Rearrange formulas to highlight a quantity of interest, using the same reasoning as in solving equations. ... *

Also: CC.9-12.G.MG.1*

Prerequisites

Solving literal equations, Lesson 2-4

Math Background

Formulas are literal equations that relate two or more variables. If you solve a formula for an unknown quantity in terms of the other (known) quantities, you can substitute the known quantities to find the unknown quantity. You may also get another formula in its own right. For example, the chemistry formula relating the pressure, P, and volume, V, of an ideal gas is $PV = nRT$, where n is the number of moles of gas (a constant), R is a constant for the ideal gas, and T is the temperature held constant. This literal equation can be rearranged in several ways, as needed, to give different formulas.

If the volume is known, solving for P gives $P = \frac{nRT}{V}$. If the pressure is known, solving for V gives $V = \frac{nRT}{P}$. If you want to find the constant for the ideal gas under known pressure, volume, and temperature conditions, the formula is $R = \frac{VP}{nT}$. Each of these forms of the ideal gas law is also a formula.

INTRODUCE

Have students state formulas that they are familiar with. Point out that while these formulas are usually solved for one of the variables, they could be solved for any of the other variables by treating the formulas as literal equations.

TEACH

1 EXAMPLE

Questioning Strategies

- In part A, what would you get if you solve for w instead of h? $w = \frac{A}{lh}$

- How can you tell whether a rewritten formula is correct? Choose values for the variables that make the original formula a true statement. Then substitute those values in the rewritten formula to see if it is a true statement.

Name_____ Class_____ Date_____

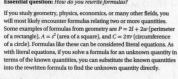

Rewriting Formulas

2-5

COMMON CORE

CC.9-12.A.CED.2*,
CC.9-12.A.CED.4*

Essential question: *How do you rewrite formulas?*

If you study geometry, physics, economics, or many other fields, you will most likely encounter formulas relating two or more quantities. Some examples of formulas from geometry are $P = 2l + 2w$ (perimeter of a rectangle), $A = s^2$ (area of a square), and $C = 2\pi r$ (circumference of a circle). Formulas like these can be considered literal equations. As with literal equations, if you solve a formula for an unknown quantity in terms of the known quantities, you can substitute the known quantities into the rewritten formula to find the unknown quantity directly.

1 EXAMPLE Solving a Formula for a Variable

Solve the formula for the given variable. Justify each step in your solution.

A The formula $V = lwh$ gives the volume of a rectangular prism with length l, width w, and height h. Solve the formula for h to find the height of a rectangular prism with a given volume, length, and width.

Equation	Property
$V = lwh$ $\dfrac{V}{lw} = \dfrac{lwh}{lw}$	Division Property of Equality

$$h = \frac{V}{lw}$$

B The formula $E = \frac{1}{2}kx^2$ gives the potential energy E of a spring with spring constant k that has been stretched by length x. Solve the formula for k to find the constant of a spring with a given potential energy and stretch.

Equation	Property
$E = \frac{1}{2}kx^2$ $2 \cdot E = 2 \cdot \frac{1}{2}kx^2$	Multiplication Property of Equality
$2E = kx^2$ $\dfrac{2E}{x^2} = \dfrac{kx^2}{x^2}$	Division Property of Equality

$$k = \frac{2E}{x^2}$$

© Houghton Mifflin Harcourt Publishing Company

REFLECT

1a. The formula $T = p + sp$ gives the total cost of an item with price p and sales tax s, expressed as a decimal. Describe a situation in which you would want to solve the formula for s.

You know the total cost and the item price, and want to find the sales tax rate.

1b. What is true about the restrictions on the value of a variable in a formula that might not be true of other literal equations?

If the variable represents a measurable quantity such as length or volume, then

the value cannot be negative or 0.

2 EXAMPLE Writing and Rearranging a Formula

The flower garden at the right is made up of a square and an isosceles triangle. Write a formula for the perimeter P in terms of x, and then solve for x to find a formula for the side length of the square in terms of P.

A Write a formula for the perimeter of each shape. Use only the sides of the square and the triangle that form the outer edges of the figure.

Perimeter of square = ____$3x$____

Perimeter of triangle = ____$\frac{7}{4}x$____

B Combine the formulas. $P = $ $3x + \frac{7}{4}x$

C Solve the formula for x.

$P = $ $3x + \frac{7}{4}x$ Write the combined formula.

$P = x\left(3 + \frac{7}{4} \right)$ Distributive Property

$P = x\left(\dfrac{19}{4} \right)$ Find the sum. Write the result as an improper fraction.

$P\left(\dfrac{4}{19} \right) = x\left(\dfrac{19}{4} \right)\left(\dfrac{4}{19} \right)$ Multiplication Property of Equality

$\dfrac{4P}{19} = x$ Simplify.

© Houghton Mifflin Harcourt Publishing Company

EXTRA EXAMPLE

Solve the formula for the given variable.

A. The formula $I = prt$ gives the simple interest on a savings account with principal p at a decimal rate r for t years. Solve for r to find the rate of a savings account with a given interest, principal, and time.

$$r = \frac{I}{pt}$$

B. The formula $A = \frac{1}{2}d_1 d_2$ gives the area of a rhombus with diagonal lengths d_1 and d_2. Solve for d_1 to find the length of one diagonal with a given area and known length of the other diagonal.

$$d_1 = \frac{2A}{d_2}$$

Teaching Strategies

Students may become confused when working with formulas with three or more variables. You may wish to begin with pairs of formulas with only two variables, such as formulas for converting units of measurement.

Converting feet and inches: $i = 12f; f = \frac{1}{12}i$

Converting Fahrenheit and Celsius temperatures: $F = \frac{9}{5}C - 32; C = \frac{5}{9}(F + 32)$

2 EXAMPLE

Questioning Strategies

• In part A, why does the formula have the term $3x$ instead of $4x$? The perimeter of the figure only includes the outside lengths. The fourth side of the square, represented by the dashed line, is not part of the perimeter of the figure.

> **MATHEMATICAL PRACTICE** **Highlighting the Standards**
>
> Reflect Question 2b, rewriting a formula for the area of a square in terms of its perimeter, provides a connection to Mathematical Practice Standard 4 (Model with mathematics). If the figure shown in **2 EXAMPLE** models a piece of land and the perimeter is the length of a fence enclosing the land, then the area of the square piece can be found in terms of the perimeter of the entire piece of land.

EXTRA EXAMPLE

The figure shown below is made up of a square and a rectangle. Write a formula for the perimeter P in terms of x, and then solve for x to find a formula for the side length of the square in terms of P.

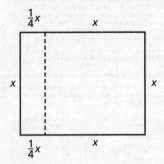

$$P = 4x + \tfrac{1}{2}x; \; \frac{2P}{9} = x$$

CLOSE

Essential Question

How do you rewrite formulas?
Because formulas are essentially literal equations with specific meaning, you rewrite a formula in exactly the same way that you would solve a literal equation for a given variable, by isolating the desired variable on one side of the equation.

Summarize

Have students write a journal entry in which they summarize the steps for rewriting a formula as in **1 EXAMPLE**.

PRACTICE

Where skills are taught	Where skills are practiced
1 EXAMPLE	EXS. 1–6
2 EXAMPLE	EXS. 7–9

REFLECT

2a. What are the restrictions on the values of P and x? Explain.

$P > 0$, $x > 0$; the variables represent lengths, which cannot be negative or 0.

2b. How could you write a formula for the area of the square in terms of P?

The area is $A = x^2$. Substitute $\frac{4P}{19}$ for x to get $\left(\frac{4P}{19}\right)^2 = \frac{16P^2}{361}$. The formula is $A = \frac{16P^2}{361}$.

PRACTICE

Solve the formula for the given variable.

1. Formula for distance traveled:
$d = rt$, for t

$t = \frac{d}{r}$

2. Formula for the flow of a current in an electric circuit: $V = IR$, for I

$I = \frac{V}{R}$

3. Formula for density:
$D = \frac{m}{V}$, for V

$DV = m$

$V = \frac{m}{D}$

4. Formula for the lateral surface area of a cylinder: $SA = 2\pi rh$, for r

$SA = 2\pi rh$

$\frac{SA}{2\pi h} = \frac{2\pi rh}{2\pi h}$

$\frac{SA}{2\pi h} = r$

5. Formula for the surface area of rectangular prism: $SA = 2(lw + hw + hl)$, for w

$SA = 2(lw + hw + hl)$

$SA - 2hl = 2lw + 2hw + 2hl - 2hl$

$SA - 2hl = 2lw + 2hw$

$SA - 2hl = w(2l + 2h)$

$\frac{SA - 2hl}{2l + 2h} = \frac{w(2l + 2h)}{2l + 2h}$

$\frac{SA - 2hl}{2l + 2h} = w$

6. Formula for the area of a trapezoid:
$A = \frac{1}{2}(a + b)h$, for b

$A = \frac{1}{2}(a + b)h$

$\frac{A}{h} = \frac{\frac{1}{2}(a + b)h}{h}$

$\frac{A}{h} = \frac{1}{2}(a + b)$

$2 \cdot \frac{A}{h} = 2 \cdot \frac{1}{2}(a + b)$

$\frac{2A}{h} = a + b$

$\frac{2A}{h} - a = a + b - a$

$\frac{2A}{h} - a = b$

7. An electrician sent Bonnie an invoice in the amount of a dollars for 6 hours of work that was done on Saturday. The electrician charges a weekend fee f in addition to an hourly rate r. Bonnie knows what the weekend fee is. Write a formula Bonnie can use to find r, the rate the electrician charges per hour.

$a = f + 6r$

$a - f = 6r$

$\frac{a - f}{6} = \frac{6r}{6}$

$\frac{a - f}{6} = r$

8. The swimming pool below is made up of a square and two semicircles. Write a formula for the perimeter P in terms of x, and then solve for x to find a formula for the side length of the square in terms of P.

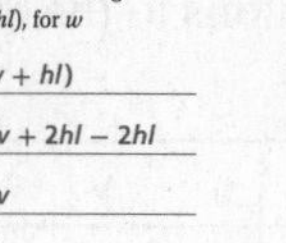

$P = 2x + 2\pi\left(\frac{1}{2}x\right)$

$P = 2x + \pi x$

$P = x(2 + \pi)$

$\frac{P}{2 + \pi} = \frac{x(2 + \pi)}{2 + \pi}$

$\frac{P}{2 + \pi} = x$

9. Kai purchased a plot of land shaped like the figure below. How can he find the length of the side labeled x if he knows the area A of his lot?

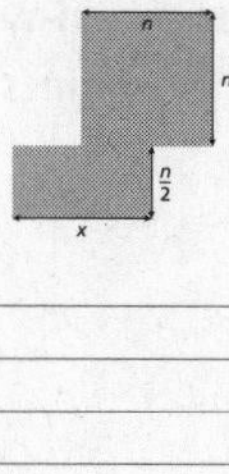

$A = n^2 + \frac{n}{2}x$

$A - n^2 = n^2 + \frac{n}{2}x - n^2$

$A - n^2 = \frac{n}{2}x$

$\frac{2}{n}(A - n^2) = \frac{2}{n}\left(\frac{n}{2}x\right)$

$\frac{2}{n}(A - n^2) = x$ or

$\frac{2A}{n} - 2n = x$

Linear Equations in Two Variables

Essential question: *How do you graph the solutions to a linear equation in two variables?*

COMMON **Standards for**
CORE **Mathematical Content**

CC.9-12.A.REI.10 Understand that the graph of an equation in two variables is the set of all its solutions plotted in the coordinate plane, often forming a curve (which could be a line).

Vocabulary

linear equation in two variables

standard form of a linear equation

solution of an equation in two variables

x-intercept

y-intercept

Prerequisites

Evaluating expressions, Lesson 1-1

Math Background

To determine when an ordered pair (x, y) is a solution of a linear equation in two variables, substitute the values of x and y into the linear equation. For example, $(4, 1)$ is a solution of $2x + 4y = 12$ because $2(4) + 4(1) = 12$, while $(-2, 3)$ is not a solution because $2(-2) + 4(3) \neq 12$. If all solutions are graphed in the coordinate plane, the solutions form a line. If the line is vertical, then the coordinates of the solutions are of the form (c, y), where c is a constant. If the line is horizontal, then the coordinates of the solutions are of the form (x, c), where c is a constant.

INTRODUCE

Review plotting ordered pairs on a coordinate grid with students. Plot the points $(0, 2)$ and $(2, 0)$ and draw a line through them. Ask students to make a table listing in columns the x- and y-coordinates of four other points on the line. Next, have them add the x- and y-coordinates and write the sum in a third column. In each case, the third column will contain the number 2. Tell students that the line represents all solutions to the equation $x + y = 2$. For example:

x	y	$x + y$
-1	3	2
1	1	2
3	-1	2
4	-2	2

TEACH

 **EXPLORE**

Questioning Strategies

- In the standard form for a linear equation in two variables, $Ax + By = C$, what are the restrictions on the values of A, B, and C? **A, B, and C represent real numbers where A and B are not both zero.**

- What is the relationship between an ordered pair that is a solution to a linear equation and the graph of the linear equation? **The ordered pair represents a point on the graph.**

- Do the solutions to a linear equation have to be connected in a straight line? **Yes, unless the linear equation represents a real-world application where connecting the points is not appropriate.**

Name_____ Class_____ Date_____

2-6

COMMON CORE

CC.9-12.A.REI.10

Linear Equations in Two Variables

Essential question: *How do you graph the solutions to a linear equation in two variables?*

An equation in two variables x and y that can be written in the form $Ax + By = C$ for real numbers A, B, and C is a **linear equation in two variables**.

The form $Ax + By = C$ where A and B are not both 0 is called the **standard form of a linear equation**.

A **solution of an equation in two variables** x and y is any ordered pair (x, y) that makes the equation true.

1 EXPLORE Definition of a Linear Equation in Two Variables

A Complete the table of values to find solutions of the linear equation $x + y = 5$.

B Plot the ordered pairs on a coordinate grid.

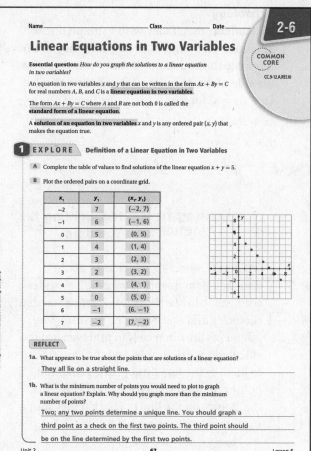

x_1	y_1	(x_1, y_1)
−2	7	(−2, 7)
−1	6	(−1, 6)
0	5	(0, 5)
1	4	(1, 4)
2	3	(2, 3)
3	2	(3, 2)
4	1	(4, 1)
5	0	(5, 0)
6	−1	(6, −1)
7	−2	(7, −2)

REFLECT

1a. What appears to be true about the points that are solutions of a linear equation?

They all lie on a straight line.

1b. What is the minimum number of points you would need to plot to graph a linear equation? Explain. Why should you graph more than the minimum number of points?

Two; any two points determine a unique line. You should graph a

third point as a check on the first two points. The third point should

be on the line determined by the first two points.

Unit 2   67   Lesson 6

To determine whether an ordered pair (x_1, y_1) is a solution of a linear equation, substitute the values of x_1 and y_1 into the linear equation. If the two sides of the equation are equal, then the ordered pair is a solution.

2 EXAMPLE Determining Whether an Ordered Pair is a Solution

Which ordered pair is a solution to $3x + 5y = 15$?

A (0, 3)

$3(0) + 5(3) = 15$

$0 + 15 = 15$

(0, 3) ___is___ a solution to $3x + 5y = 15$.

B (8, 1)

$3(8) + 5(1) = 15$

$24 + 6 = 15; 30 \neq 15$

(8, 1) ___is not___ a solution to $3x + 5y = 15$.

REFLECT

2a. What do you know about the point (0, 3) and its relationship to the graph of $3x + 5y = 15$?

The point (0, 3) is on the graph of the line $3x + 5y = 15$.

2b. Explain how you know that $3x + 5y = 15$ is a linear equation.

It is written in the form $Ax + By = C$, where A, B, and C are real numbers.

The graph of a linear equation is a line. To graph a line, it is necessary to plot only two points. However, it is a good idea to plot a third point as a check. For linear equations written in standard form, two good points to plot are where the line crosses each axis. The x-coordinate of the point where the line crosses the x-axis is called the **x-intercept** and is found by substituting 0 for y in the equation of the line. The y-coordinate of the point where the line crosses the y-axis is called the **y-intercept** and is found by substituting 0 for x in the equation of the line.

3 EXAMPLE Graphing a Linear Equation in Standard Form

Graph $2x + y = 4$.

A Make a table of values. Each row in the table of values makes an ordered pair (x, y).

B Substitute 0 for x in the equation and solve for y.

$2(0) + y = 4$

$y = $ __4__

Write the value for y next to the 0 in the first row of the table.

x	y
0	4
2	0
1	2

Unit 2   68   Lesson 6

EXAMPLE

Questioning Strategies

- How can you tell whether an ordered pair is a solution to a linear equation? Substitute the x- and y-values from the ordered pair into the linear equation, and if the result is a true statement, then the ordered pair is a solution.

- Can an ordered pair of irrational numbers be a solution? Yes; x and y can be any real numbers, unless the equation represents a real-world application with constraints on the values of x and y.

EXTRA EXAMPLE
Which ordered pair is a solution to $2x - 3y = 6$?

A $(0, -2)$ yes   **B** $(4, 1)$ no

Teaching Strategy
Point out that if an ordered pair is a solution to a linear equation, then the point it represents will be on the graph of the linear equation. An ordered pair that is not a solution will not lie on the same line as the points that are solutions.

3 **EXAMPLE**

Questioning Strategies

- How is making a table of values helpful in finding the solutions to a linear equation? Each row in the table represents an ordered pair that is a solution to the linear equation.

- Why should you make a table with at least three rows? The third point acts as a check on the other two points. The three points should lie in a straight line.

EXTRA EXAMPLE
Graph $3x - y = 3$.

The graph is a line that passes through the points $(0, -3)$ and $(1, 0)$.

Technology
Tell students that if they wish to graph linear equations on a graphing calculator, they will have to rewrite the equations so that y is isolated on one side of the equation. Ask students to solve $Ax + By = C$ for y.

$$Ax + By = C$$

$$By = C - Ax$$

$$y = \frac{C - Ax}{B} \text{ or } y = -\frac{A}{B}x + \frac{C}{B}$$

4 **EXAMPLE**

Questioning Strategies

- What is true about all points on the graph of $x = 3$? What is true about all points on the graph of $y = -4$? All points have an x-coordinate of 3; all points have a y-coordinate of -4.

- What is an equation of the horizontal line through $(4, 2)$? a vertical line through $(-1, 3)$? $y = 2$; $x = -1$

EXTRA EXAMPLE
Graph $x = -2$ and $y = 3$.

The graph of $x = -2$ is a vertical line that passes through $(-2, 0)$; the graph of $y = 3$ is a horizontal line that passes through $(0, 3)$.

C Next substitute 0 for y in the equation and solve for x.

$$2x + (0) = 4$$
$$2x = 4$$
$$x = \boxed{2}$$

Write the value for x before the 0 in the second row of the table.

D Choose another value for x and solve for y. It is usually easiest to choose a simple value such as 1.

$$2(1) + y = 4$$
$$\boxed{2} + y = 4$$
$$y = \boxed{2}$$

Write the value for y after the 1 in the third row of the table.

E Plot the first two points on the coordinate grid. Then plot the third point. If you have done your calculations correctly, all three points should lie on a straight line. Draw a line through the points.

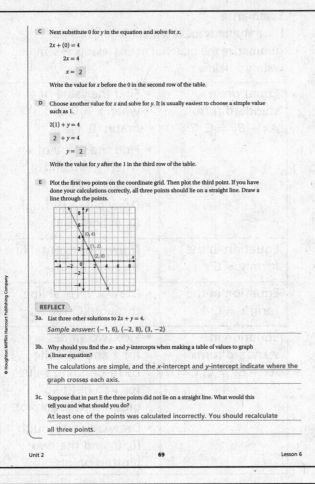

REFLECT

3a. List three other solutions to $2x + y = 4$.

Sample answer: $(-1, 6), (-2, 8), (3, -2)$

3b. Why should you find the x- and y-intercepts when making a table of values to graph a linear equation?

The calculations are simple, and the x-intercept and y-intercept indicate where the graph crosses each axis.

3c. Suppose that in part E the three points did not lie on a straight line. What would this tell you and what should you do?

At least one of the points was calculated incorrectly. You should recalculate all three points.

© Houghton Mifflin Harcourt Publishing Company

---

4 EXAMPLE Vertical and Horizontal Lines

Graph $x = 3$ and $y = -4$.

Note that the equation $x = 3$ can be written as $1x + 0y = 3$. All points with an x-value of 3 are solutions to the equation. These points lie on a vertical line that passes through $(3, 0)$.

Note that the equation $y = -4$ can be written as $0x + 1y = -4$. All points with a y-value of -4 are solutions to the equation. These points lie on a horizontal line that passes through $(0, -4)$.

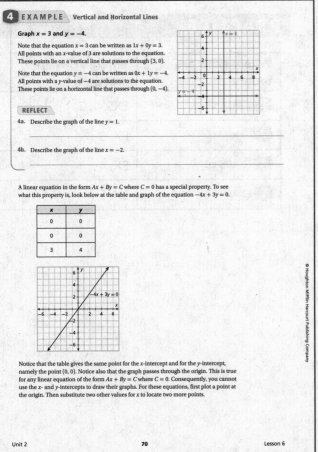

REFLECT

4a. Describe the graph of the line $y = 1$.

4b. Describe the graph of the line $x = -2$.

A linear equation in the form $Ax + By = C$ where $C = 0$ has a special property. To see what this property is, look below at the table and graph of the equation $-4x + 3y = 0$.

x	y
0	0
0	0
3	4

Notice that the table gives the same point for the x-intercept and for the y-intercept, namely the point $(0, 0)$. Notice also that the graph passes through the origin. This is true for any linear equation of the form $Ax + By = C$ where $C = 0$. Consequently, you cannot use the x- and y-intercepts to draw their graphs. For these equations, first plot a point at the origin. Then substitute two other values for x to locate two more points.

© Houghton Mifflin Harcourt Publishing Company

Questioning Strategies

- Is it sufficient to find the intercepts when you want to graph lines through the origin? Explain. No; both the *x*- and *y*-intercepts are 0, so they give you the same point, (0, 0), and one point is not enough to graph a line.

Teaching Strategy

Before students graph lines that pass through the origin, suggest that they use integer multiples of the coefficient of the *y*-coordinate as the values for the *x*-coordinates in a table of values. If they do, the *y*-coordinates will also all be integers and the resulting points will be easier to graph.

EXTRA EXAMPLE

Graph $4x - 2y = 0$.

The graph is a line that passes through the points (0, 0), (2, 4), and (4, 8).

CLOSE

Essential Question

How do you graph the solutions to a linear equation in two variables?

Use a table of values to find three ordered pairs that are solutions to the linear equation. Then, plot these three points on a coordinate plane. Draw a line through the points. The line is the graph of the solutions to the linear equation.

Summarize

Have students make a graphic organizer to summarize the material in this lesson. A sample is shown below.

Equation in standard form $Ax + By = C$, $C \neq 0$	• Find the value of *y* when $x = 0$ and graph (0, *y*). • Find the value of *x* when $y = 0$ and graph (*x*, 0). • Draw a line through (0, *y*) and (*x*, 0).
Equation in the form $y = C$	• Draw a horizontal line through (0, *C*).
Equation in the form $x = C$	• Draw a vertical line through (*C*, 0).
Equation in standard form $Ax + By = C$, $C = 0$	• Pick two values for *x* and find the corresponding values for *y* to get two ordered pairs to plot. • Draw a line through (0, 0) and the two plotted points.

PRACTICE

Where skills are taught	Where skills are practiced
2 EXAMPLE	EXS. 1, 2
3 EXAMPLE	EX. 3
4 EXAMPLE	EX. 4
5 EXAMPLE	EX. 5

5 EXAMPLE Lines Through the Origin

Graph $2x - 3y = 0$.

A   Complete the table of values.

B   Plot the points on the coordinate grid.

C   Check that all three points are collinear.

D   Draw a line through the points.

x	y
0	0
1	$\frac{2}{3}$
2	$\frac{4}{3}$

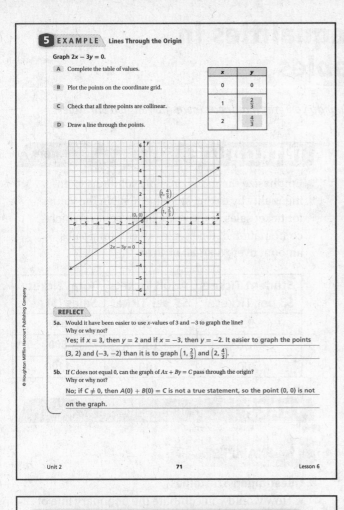

REFLECT

5a. Would it have been easier to use x-values of 3 and -3 to graph the line? Why or why not?

Yes; if $x = 3$, then $y = 2$ and if $x = -3$, then $y = -2$. It easier to graph the points

$(3, 2)$ and $(-3, -2)$ than it is to graph $\left(1, \frac{2}{3}\right)$ and $\left(2, \frac{4}{3}\right)$.

5b. If C does not equal 0, can the graph of $Ax + By = C$ pass through the origin? Why or why not?

No; if $C \neq 0$, then $A(0) + B(0) = C$ is not a true statement, so the point $(0, 0)$ is not

on the graph.

PRACTICE

Tell whether the ordered pair is a solution to the equation.

1. $-5x + 2y = 4$; $(4, 8)$

     no

2. $2x - 7y = 1$; $(11, 3)$

     yes

Complete the table and graph the equation.

3. $-2x + y = 3$

x	y
0	3
$\frac{3}{2}$	0
1	5

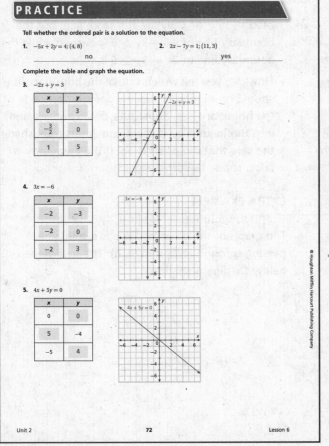

4. $3x = -6$

x	y
-2	-3
-2	0
-2	3

5. $4x + 5y = 0$

x	y
0	0
5	-4
-5	4

Linear Inequalities in Two Variables

Essential question: *How do you graph a linear inequality in two variables?*

COMMON CORE **Standards for Mathematical Content**

CC.9-12.A.REI.12 Graph the solutions to a linear inequality in two variables as a half-plane (excluding the boundary in the case of a strict inequality) …

Vocabulary

linear inequality in two variables

solution of an inequality in two variables

Prerequisites

Graphing linear equations in two variables, Lesson 2-6

Math Background

There are infinitely many solutions to linear inequalities in two variables, and they are represented by a shaded half-plane. First, graph the boundary line of the solution set by graphing the associated linear equation. If the inequality is > or <, the boundary line consists of points that are not solutions and should be dashed. If the inequality is ≥ or ≤, the boundary line consists of points that are solutions, and should be a solid line. Since there are only two half-planes on either side of the boundary line, choose a point on either side of the boundary line to check in the original inequality. If the point is a solution, shade that side of the boundary line. If the point is not a solution, shade the other side of the boundary line, the side not containing that point.

INTRODUCE

Emphasize the many possible solutions to an inequality by asking students to fill in the values for ticket sales to the school play below. Which combination of ticket sales gives a total sales amount over $500? all of them

Student Tickets $3 per Ticket	Adult Tickets $5 per Ticket	Total Ticket Sales ($)
50	100	650
100	100	800
200	100	1100

TEACH

1 EXAMPLE

Questioning Strategies

- How would you compare the boundary line of the inequality $2x - 3y > 6$ to the boundary line of $2x - 3y \geq 6$? They are the same line, but the boundary line of $2x - 3y > 6$ is dashed while the boundary line of $2x - 3y \geq 6$ is solid.

- How can you tell which side of the boundary line should be shaded? Choose a point on one side of the boundary line. Substitute the x- and y-values into the inequality. If the inequality is true, shade the side that the point is on. If the inequality is false, shade the other side.

EXTRA EXAMPLE

Graph the solution set for $3x + 4y \leq 12$. The graph of the boundary line is a solid line passing through (0, 3) and (4, 0). The half-plane below the line is shaded.

2-7

Linear Inequalities in Two Variables

COMMON CORE
CC.9-12.A.REI.12

Essential question: How do you graph a linear inequality in two variables?

A **linear inequality in two variables**, such as $2x - 3y \geq 6$, results when you replace the = sign in an equation by $<$, $>$, $\leq$, or $\geq$. A **solution of an inequality in two variables** x and y is any ordered pair (x, y) that makes the inequality true.

1 EXAMPLE   Graphing a Linear Inequality

Graph the solution set for $2x - 3y \geq 6$.

A Start by graphing $2x - 3y = 6$. The inequality is true for every point on this line because the inequality symbol is less than or equal to. The line is called the *boundary line* of the solution set.

x	y
0	−2
3	0
−3	−4

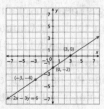

B Test several other points in the plane that are not on the boundary line to determine whether the inequality is true.

Point	Above or Below the Line?	Inequality	True or False?
(0, 0)	Above	$2(0) - 3(0) \geq 6$	False
(5, 0)	Below	$2(5) - 3(0) \geq 6$	True
(0, 3)	Above	$2(0) - 3(3) \geq 6$	False
(4, 2)	Above	$2(4) - 3(2) \geq 6$	False
(6, 1)	Below	$2(6) - 3(1) \geq 6$	True

The solutions of $2x - 3y \geq 6$ lie on or ___below___ $2x - 3y = 6$.

© Houghton Mifflin Harcourt Publishing Company

C Shade the set of solutions to the inequality $2x - 3y \geq 6$. The shaded region and the boundary line make up the graph of $2x - 3y \geq 6$. This area is referred to as a *half-plane*.

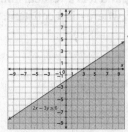

REFLECT

1a. How would the graph of $2x - 3y \leq 6$ be like the graph of $2x - 3y \geq 6$? How would it be different?

The graph of $2x - 3y \leq 6$ would have the same boundary line as the graph

of $2x - 3y \geq 6$, but the opposite side of the line would be shaded.

1b. Would the points on the boundary line $2x - 3y = 6$ be included in the graph of the inequality $2x - 3y > 6$? Why or why not?

No; for every point on the line, the left side of the inequality is equal to 6.

Because $6 \not> 6$, the inequality is false for the points on the line.

1c. Error Analysis A student says that you shade above the boundary line when the inequality is $>$ or $\geq$ and you shade below it when the inequality is $<$ or $\leq$. Use the example to explain why this is not always true.

The inequality symbol in $2x - 3y \geq 6$ is $\geq$, but you shade below the line, not above

it, because the solution does not include (0, 0)

To graph a linear inequality in the coordinate plane:

1. Graph the boundary line. If the symbol is $\leq$ or $\geq$, draw a solid line. If the symbol is $<$ or $>$, draw a dashed line.

2. Choose a test point (x, y) that is not on the line. Substitute the values of x and y into the inequality and determine whether it is true or false.

3. If the inequality is true for the test point, shade the half-plane on the side of the boundary line that contains the test point. If not, shade the half-plane on the opposite side of the line.

© Houghton Mifflin Harcourt Publishing Company

Notes

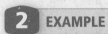

2 EXAMPLE

Questioning Strategies

- How is graphing a linear inequality similar to graphing a linear equation? In both cases, you graph a linear equation. For a linear inequality, you start by graphing the associated linear equation. You then go further, however, and shade a half-plane.

- When is the boundary line dashed? When is it solid? when the inequality symbol is $>$ or $<$; when the inequality symbol is $\geq$ or $\leq$

- When does the boundary line contain the point $(0, 0)$? when the equation of the boundary line is of the form $Ax + By = 0$

Teaching Strategy

Summarize the graphs of linear inequalities by using the table below.

$Ax + By \leq C$, $Ax + By \geq C$ Vertical boundary line: $Ax \leq C$ or $Ax \geq C$ Horizontal boundary line: $By \leq C$ or $By \geq C$	Solid boundary line with half-plane shaded
$Ax + By < C$, $Ax + By > C$ Vertical boundary line: $Ax < C$ or $Ax > C$ Horizontal boundary line: $By < C$ or $By > C$	Dashed boundary line with half-plane shaded

Avoid Common Errors

Students who have trouble remembering whether to use a solid or open circle when graphing an inequality on a number line probably will have trouble remember whether to use a solid or dashed line when graphing an inequality on the coordinate plane. Make sure to point out to students that the *solid* circle and the *solid* line are used with $\leq$ and $\leq$, and the open circle and dashed line are used with $<$ and $>$.

Teaching Strategy

Make sure to point out that if a point is a solution to a linear inequality, that point will either be on the boundary line of the linear inequality, if the line is solid, or in the shaded half-plane. Any point that is not a solution will be either on the side of the boundary line that is not shaded or on the boundary line itself if the boundary line is dashed.

Avoid Common Errors

The most common error students make when graphing a linear inequality is choosing the wrong half-plane to shade. Caution them to choose only $(0, 0)$ as a test point if $(0, 0)$ is not on the boundary line. For other test points, tell them to make sure they shade the half-plane opposite the test point if the test point is not a solution.

not a solution → shade the other side

solution → shade the same side

EXTRA EXAMPLE

Graph the inequality $4x - 2y > 8$.
The graph of the boundary line is a dashed line passing through $(0, -4)$ and $(2, 0)$. The half-plane below the line is shaded.

Teaching Strategy

Before assigning the Practice, review that the graph of a linear equation is a horizontal line when it is of the form $y = c$, and it is a vertical line when it is of the form $x = c$, where c is a constant.

2 EXAMPLE Graphing a Linear Inequality in Two Variables

Graph the inequality $7x - y < 13$.

A Write the equation of the boundary line. ___$7x - y = 13$___

B Graph the boundary line. The inequality symbol is >, so the line will be dashed.

C Test a point that is not on the line, such as (0, 0).

$7\left(\,0\,\right) - \,0\, < 13$ True or false? ___true___

Shade the part of the plane on the correct side of the line.

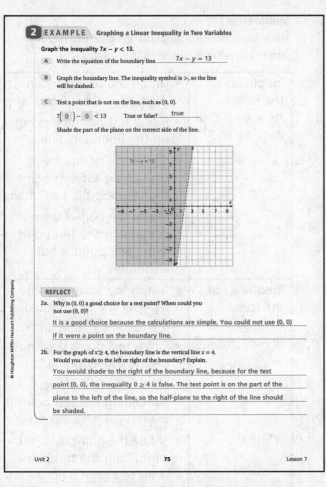

REFLECT

2a. Why is (0, 0) a good choice for a test point? When could you not use (0, 0)?

It is a good choice because the calculations are simple. You could not use (0, 0)

if it were a point on the boundary line.

2b. For the graph of $x \geq 4$, the boundary line is the vertical line $x = 4$. Would you shade to the left or right of the boundary? Explain.

You would shade to the right of the boundary line, because for the test

point (0, 0), the inequality $0 \geq 4$ is false. The test point is on the part of the

plane to the left of the line, so the half-plane to the right of the line should

be shaded.

PRACTICE

Graph the inequality.

1. $y \geq 2$

2. $x < -3$

MATHEMATICAL PRACTICE · Highlighting the Standards

Reflect Question 2b on graphing a boundary line that is a vertical line provides a connection to Mathematical Practice Standard 7 (Look for and make use of structure). Students should recall from Lesson 2-6 that a vertical line has a certain structure. It is of the form $x = c$, where c is a constant. Likewise, the graph of a horizontal line is of the form $y = c$, where c is a constant. Students can then extend what they know about the graphs of vertical or horizontal lines to include how to graph a linear inequality that has a vertical or horizontal boundary line. The half-plane that is the solution set is found in the same way (by using a test point) as it is for linear inequalities that do not have a vertical or horizontal boundary line.

CLOSE

Essential Question

How do you graph a linear inequality in two variables?

Graph the linear inequality as if it were a linear equation. This is the boundary line. If the inequality symbol used is $<$ or $>$, the boundary line is dashed. If it is $\leq$ or $\geq$, the boundary line is solid. To determine which side of the boundary line to shade, choose at least one test point and check whether it is a solution to the inequality. If it is, shade the side of the boundary line on which the test point lies. If it is not, shade the other side.

Summarize

Have students complete the graphic organizer to summarize the material in this lesson.

Inequality of the form $Ax + By \geq C$ or $Ax + By \leq C$	• Graph the boundary line $Ax + By = C$ as a solid line. • Pick a test point (x, y) not on the boundary line. • Shade the half-plane containing the test point if the test point is a solution. • Shade the half-plane not containing the test point if the test point is not a solution.
Inequality of the form $Ax + By > C$ or $Ax + By < C$	• Graph the boundary line $Ax + By = C$ as a dashed line. • Pick a test point (x, y) not on the boundary line. • Shade the half-plane containing the test point if the test point is a solution. • Shade the half-plane not containing the test point if the test point is not a solution.

PRACTICE

Where skills are taught	Where skills are practiced
1 EXAMPLE	EXS. 1–6
2 EXAMPLE	EXS. 1–6

3. $x + 4y < 9$

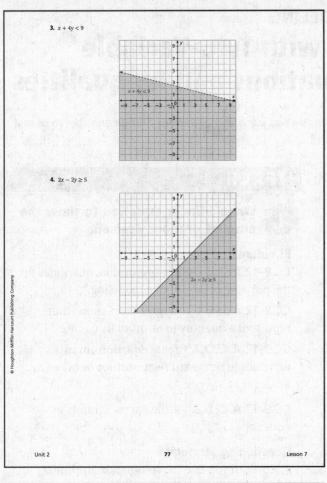

4. $2x - 2y \geq 5$

5. $-3x + 6y \geq 2$

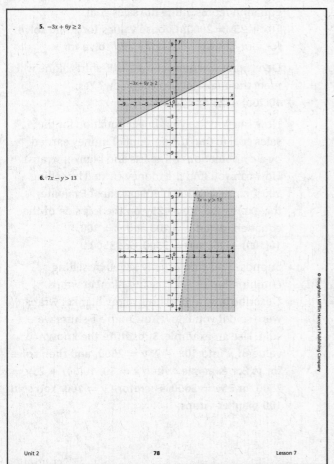

6. $7x - y > 13$

Notes

FOCUS ON MODELING
Modeling with Two-Variable Linear Equations and Inequalities

Essential question: *How can you use linear equations and inequalities to model the results of a fundraiser?*

Standards for Mathematical Content

The following standards are addressed in this lesson. (An asterisk indicates that a standard is also a Modeling standard.) For more detailed information, see the correlation for each section of the lesson.

Number and Quantity: CC.9-12.N.Q.1*, CC.9-12.N.Q.2*

Algebra: CC.9-12.A.SSE.1*, CC.9-12.A.CED.2*, CC.9-12.A.CED.3*

Prerequisites
- Graphing a linear equation, Lesson 2-6
- Graphing a linear inequality, Lesson 2-7

Math Background
In this lesson, students write a linear equation to show the total amount of money that can be raised by selling T-shirts for $10 each and blanket wraps for $25 each. Students also use the graph of a linear inequality to show the sales required to raise a minimum of $1000. In both cases, the variables are constrained to positive x- and y-values. Standard CC.9-12.A.CED.3 uses the term *constraint* in a mathematical way, that students may not be familiar with. Constraints are used in college- and graduate-level mathematics, as well as in more advanced high school mathematics courses. This lesson is the first step in learning to work with constraints.

INTRODUCE

Ask students how they can calculate the amount of money they can raise if they sell one item for a certain price and another item for another price. Ask students to discuss how they would find out how many of each item to sell to break even and then go on to meet a sales goal. Tell students that these questions can be answered by finding the solutions to linear equations and inequalities.

TEACH

1 **Write a linear equation to show the amount of money raised.**

Standards
CC.9-12.N.Q.2 Define appropriate quantities for the purpose of descriptive modeling.*

CC.9-12.A.SSE.1 Interpret expressions that represent a quantity in terms of its context.*

CC.9-12.A.CED.2 Create equations in two … variables to represent relationships between quantities …*

CC.9-12.A.CED.3 Represent constraints by equations …*

Questioning Strategies
- How can you find the solutions to the linear equation representing the sales goal, $10x + 25y = 2000$? **Choose values for x and solve for y or choose values of y and solve for x.**

- Determine whether selling 200 T-shirts alone will meet the goal. How do you know? **Yes; $10(200) + 25(0) = 2000$**

- How can you use your linear equation for the sales goal to find the amount of money earned by a combination of T-shirts and blanket wraps? How can you find the money earned by selling 100 T-shirts and 100 blanket wraps? **Evaluate the expression $10x + 25y$ on the left side of the equation; when $x = 100$ and $y = 100$, $10(100) + 25(100) = 3500$, or $3500.**

- Suppose you earn *exactly* $2500 by selling a combination of T-shirts and blanket wraps. Describe how to find how many blanket wraps were sold if you know how many T-shirts were sold. Use an example. **Substitute the known value of x into $10x + 25y = 2500$, and then solve for y. For example, when $x = 50$, $10(50) + 25y = 2500$, or $25y = 2000$. Therefore $y = 100$. You sold 100 blanket wraps.**

continued

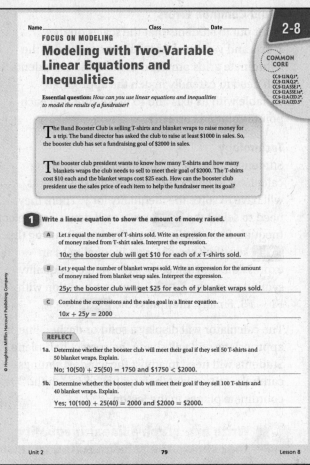

Name _____ Class _____ Date _____

2-8

FOCUS ON MODELING

Modeling with Two-Variable Linear Equations and Inequalities

COMMON CORE

CC.9-12.N.Q.1*
CC.9-12.N.Q.2*
CC.9-12.A.SSE.1*
CC.9-12.A.SSE.1a*
CC.9-12.A.CED.2*
CC.9-12.A.CED.3*

Essential question: *How can you use linear equations and inequalities to model the results of a fundraiser?*

The Band Booster Club is selling T-shirts and blanket wraps to raise money for a trip. The band director has asked the club to raise at least $1000 in sales. So, the booster club has set a fundraising goal of $2000 in sales.

The booster club president wants to know how many T-shirts and how many blankets wraps the club needs to sell to meet their goal of $2000. The T-shirts cost $10 each and the blanket wraps cost $25 each. How can the booster club president use the sales price of each item to help the fundraiser meet its goal?

1 Write a linear equation to show the amount of money raised.

A Let x equal the number of T-shirts sold. Write an expression for the amount of money raised from T-shirt sales. Interpret the expression.

$10x$; the booster club will get $10 for each of x T-shirts sold.

B Let y equal the number of blanket wraps sold. Write an expression for the amount of money raised from blanket wrap sales. Interpret the expression.

$25y$; the booster club will get $25 for each of y blanket wraps sold.

C Combine the expressions and the sales goal in a linear equation.

$10x + 25y = 2000$

REFLECT

1a. Determine whether the booster club will meet their goal if they sell 50 T-shirts and 50 blanket wraps. Explain.

No; $10(50) + 25(50) = 1750$ and $\$1750 < \$2000$.

1b. Determine whether the booster club will meet their goal if they sell 100 T-shirts and 40 blanket wraps. Explain.

Yes; $10(100) + 25(40) = 2000$ and $\$2000 = \$2000$.

Unit 2   79   Lesson 8

---

2 Graph the linear equation.

A Calculate three pairs of values for x and y. Enter your results in the table.

x	y
0	80
200	0
50	60

B Plot the ordered pairs on the coordinate grid. Connect the points to graph the equation.

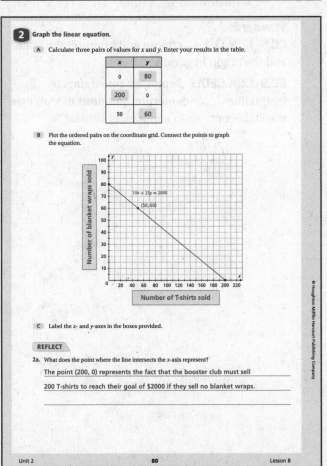

$10x + 25y = 2000$

(50, 60)

Number of blanket wraps sold

Number of T-shirts sold

C Label the x- and y-axes in the boxes provided.

REFLECT

2a. What does the point where the line intersects the x-axis represent?

The point (200, 0) represents the fact that the booster club must sell

200 T-shirts to reach their goal of $2000 if they sell no blanket wraps.

Unit 2   80   Lesson 8

Teaching Strategy

If students have difficulty answering Reflect Questions 1a and 1b, suggest that they make a table with three columns: x, y, and $10x + 25y$. Test various values of x and y by using multiples of 10. Those rows that have $10x + 25y = 2000$ are solutions of the linear equation. Have students adjust their values for x and y to try to achieve a value of 2000 in the third column.

2 **Graph the linear equation.**

Standards

CC.9-12.N.Q.1 ... choose and interpret the scale and the origin in graphs ...*

CC.9-12.A.CED.2 ... graph equations on coordinate axes with labels and scales.*

CC.9-12.A.CED.3 ... interpret solutions as viable or nonviable options in a modeling context.*

Questioning Strategies

• What do points on the graph of $10x + 25y = 2000$ represent? the combination of T-shirts for $10 and blanket wraps for $25 that must be sold to raise $2000

• Do all the points on the line represent solutions in the context of the problem? Why or why not? No; you cannot sell fractional parts of T-shirts or blanket wraps. While all points on the line are solutions of $10x + 25y = 2000$ in a mathematical sense, only the points that have integer values for both x and y are solutions of the problem in a real-world sense.

Avoid Common Errors

Point out to students that the scales on the x-axis and y-axis are not the same for any of the coordinate grids provided in this lesson. Students will need to carefully match the appropriate variable with its axis and to make sure that each point is plotted correctly.

Technology

Students can graph inequalities on a graphing calculator to check their graphs. First, students will have to solve the inequality for y. Then, they need to select the APPS key, scroll down, and select Inequalz from the list of applications. By using the Y= key, they can enter an inequality as an expression, and select the approprate inequality symbol using the ALPHA key in combination with F1 — F5. Finally, they press the GRAPH key.

The calculator will display a solid or dashed line, as appropriate, and will shade the correct half-plane. Students will need to adjust the window settings carefully if they want their graphs to match the coordinate planes in the lesson.

3 **Write and graph a linear inequality that shows the sales required to raise a minimum of $1000.**

Standards

CC.9-12.N.Q.1 ... choose and interpret the scale and the origin in graphs ...*

CC.9-12.A.CED.3 Represent constraints by ... inequalities, ... and interpret solutions as viable or nonviable options in a modeling context.*

continued

2b. Explain what the point (100, 40) represents on this graph.

The point (100, 40) represents the fact that if the booster club sells 100

T-shirts, they must sell 40 blanket wraps to meet their goal of $2000.

2c. Suppose the Band Booster Club sells 25 blanket wraps during a chilly football game. Use the graph to determine about how many T-shirts they need to sell.

about 140 T-shirts

3 Write and graph a linear inequality that shows the sales required to raise a minimum of $1000.

A Use the expressions for the amount of money raised from T-shirts and blanket wraps and the minimum goal of $1000 to write a linear inequality.

$$10x + 25y \geq 1000$$

B Calculate three pairs of values for x and y. Enter your results in the table. Then, graph the boundary line of the linear inequality.

x	y
0	40
100	0
50	20

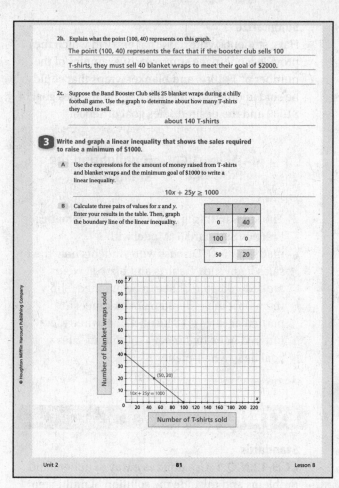

Number of blanket wraps sold / Number of T-shirts sold

(50, 20)

$10x + 25y = 1000$

C Use the test point (0, 0) to determine which side of the boundary line to shade.

$10x$	$+ \ 25y$	$\geq$	1000	Write the inequality.
$10(0)$	$+ \ 25(0)$	$\geq$	1000	Substitute 0 for x and 0 for y.
0	$+ \ 0$	$\geq$	1000	Simplify each product.
	0	$\ngeq$	1000	Simplify the sum and check the inequality.

D Shade the correct part of the plane. Label the x- and y-axes in the boxes provided.

Number of blanket wraps sold / Number of T-shirts sold

(50, 20)

$10x + 25y = 1000$

REFLECT

3a. Suppose the manufacturer made an error and none of the blanket wraps were sellable. At least how many T-shirts would the Band Booster Club need to sell to raise $1000?

At least 100 T-shirts

3b. If the booster club sells 18 blanket wraps, what is the minimum number of T-shirts they need to sell to make $1000?

The inequality would be $10x + 25(18) \geq 1000$, or $10x \geq 550$. Dividing both

sides by 10 gives $x \geq 55$. They would need to sell at least 55 T-shirts.

Questioning Strategies

- Why does the sales goal involve a linear inequality? **Sales can exceed the goal of $1000.**

- Why are the intercepts of the boundary line important to find? **They are endpoints of the boundary line since the variables must be nonnegative.**

- How will the progressive sales of T-shirts affect the number of blanket wraps that need to be sold, or vice versa? **The more you sell of one item, the less you need to sell of the other item.**

- Which values of x and y will result in a need to do another fundraiser to make the minimum goal of $1000? How do you know? **Any solutions of the inequality $10x + 25y < 1000$ would necessitate another fundraiser because they would represent not making a total of $1000. These are the points in the first quadrant below the boundary line $10x + 25y = 1000$.**

CLOSE

Essential Question

How can you use linear equations and inequalities to model the results of a fundraiser?

Linear equations can be used to model the total amount raised from selling two different items. Whether or not the total amount raised meets a minimum fundraising goal can be expressed as an inequality, where the amount raised must be greater than or equal to the goal. Sale amounts that meet or exceed the goal are solutions of the inequality.

Summarize

Have students write a journal entry in which they provide a one-page summary of examples of the number of T-shirts and blanket wraps that could be sold in order to meet the minimum sales goal of $1000 and the desired sales goal of $2000.

> ## MATHEMATICAL PRACTICE Highlighting the Standards
>
> The steps in this lesson address Mathematical Practice Standard 5 (Model with mathematics). Discuss with students how the sales figures for T-shirts and blanket wraps are ordered pairs that can be graphed. Show them how the ordered pairs that meet a particular sales goal lie on a line, while the ordered pairs that meet a minimum sales goal lie in a half-plane.

EXTEND

Standards

CC.9-12.N.Q.1 Use units as a way to understand problems and to guide the solution of multi-step problems ...* (Ex. 1)

CC.9-12.N.Q.2 Define appropriate quantities for the purpose of descriptive modeling.* (Exs. 3, 5)

CC.9-12.A.CED.2 ...graph equations on coordinate axes with labels and scales.* (Ex. 2)

CC.9-12.A.CED.3 Represent constraints by equations or inequalities, ... and interpret solutions as viable or nonviable options in a modeling context.* (Exs. 3, 4, 5, 6)

EXTEND

1. Use unit analysis to determine the unit of measurement for the expression $10x + 25y$.

$\frac{\text{dollars}}{\text{T-shirt}} \cdot \text{T-shirts} + \frac{\text{dollars}}{\text{wrap}} \cdot \text{wraps} = \text{dollars} + \text{dollars} = \text{dollars}$

_____

2. Describe where the lines would be in relation to each other if you graphed the linear equation and the linear inequality on the same coordinate grid.

The line for the linear equation would be above the boundary line for

the linear inequality.

_____

3. The booster club sold 30 more T-shirts than blanket wraps at a fundraising event and made exactly $1000. How many of each did they sell?

Let b equal the number of blanket wraps sold. So, the money raised by the

blanket wraps is $25b$ and the money raised by T-shirts is $10(b + 30)$.

$$10(b + 30) + 25b = 1000$$
$$\begin{array}{r} 10b + 300 + 25b = 1000 \\ -300 \qquad\qquad -300 \end{array}$$
$$10b \quad + 25b = \ 700$$
$$35b = 700$$
$$\frac{35b}{35} = \frac{700}{35}$$
$$b = 20$$

The booster club sold 20 blanket wraps and $20 + 30 = 50$ T-shirts.

_____

4. If the booster club orders at least 100 blanket wraps, they get a reduced price on them. Does it make sense for the booster club to order at least 100 blanket wraps if the goal is to raise a minimum of $1000? Explain your answer.

Sample answer: No. Even if the club sold no T-shirts at all, the maximum

number of blanket wraps they need to sell to make their goal is 80.

Unless the savings is significant, the booster club does not need to order at

least 100 blanket wraps.

---

5. The booster club will earn $5 profit for every T-shirt sold and $10 profit for every blanket wrap sold. Write an inequality to show how many T-shirts and blanket wraps the club would need to sell to make a profit of at least $1000.

Let x equal the number of T-shirts sold and y equal the number of blanket

wraps sold.

$5x + 10y \geq 1000$

6. Find a solution to the linear inequality you wrote in Problem 5. How much money would the booster club raise in *sales* if they sold that many T-shirts and blanket wraps? *Sample answer*: Let $x = 40$.

$$5(40) + 10y \geq 1000$$
$$\begin{array}{r} 200 + 10y \geq 1000 \\ -200 \qquad\quad -200 \end{array}$$
$$10y \geq 800$$
$$y \geq 80$$

So, if the booster club sells 40 T-shirts and 80 blanket wraps, the club will

earn a $1000 profit.

$$10(40) + 25(80) = \text{sales}$$
$$400 + 2000 = 2400$$

The booster club would raise $2400 in sales to earn a $1000 profit.

_____

CORRELATION

Standard	Items
CC.9-12.A.CED.1*	6
CC.9-12.A.CED.2*	5, 16
CC.9-12.A.CED.4*	9
CC.9-12.A.REI.1	1, 4
CC.9-12.A.REI.3	2, 3, 7, 8
CC.9-12.A.REI.10	10, 11, 12
CC.9-12.A.REI.12	13, 14 ,15

TEST PREP DOCTOR ✛

Multiple Choice: Item 1
- Students who chose **A** may not understand what substitution is. There is no substitution in this solution, so choice **A** could be eliminated immediately.
- Students who chose **B** may have confused summation with addition. There is no Summation Property of Equality.
- Students who chose **D** may have been thinking of subtraction because $10x$ is being subtracted in the equation.

Multiple Choice: Item 3
- Students who chose **B** or **D** did not divide by the coefficient of x. They should have divided by -4.
- Students who chose **C** forget to reverse the inequality when dividing by a negative number.

Multiple Choice: Item 5
- Students who chose **B** or **D** did not calculate the time left from 45 minutes after running for t minutes. Also, students who chose **D** used the wrong units in creating the equation. A rate of 3.25 Calories per minute corresponds to the walking time, not to the running time.
- Students who chose **C** used an equal time for running and walking and did not include the condition that the total time must be 45 minutes.

Multiple Choice: Item 10
- Students who chose **F**, **G**, or **J** gave ordered pairs that are solutions, not ordered pairs that are not solutions.

Free Response: Item 15
- Students who graphed the wrong half-plane may have substituted the test point incorrectly into the inequality.
- Students who graphed the boundary line in the second and fourth quadrants did not find points of the line correctly when they were constructing their tables. Suggest that they use the intercepts to help them graph the boundary line.

Free Response: Item 16
- Students who answered $20x + 12y = 600$, with x being the cost of a box of stationery and y being the cost of a pen, confused the units for each item sold. Suggest that they use a test point after writing the linear equation to check their equation. Is the sum $600 with the point they chose?
- Students whose graph included an x-intercept of 30 for the number of boxes of stationery and a y-intercept of 50 for the number of pens sold confused the units for each item sold. Suggest that they use a test point on the line to check their equation.

Name _____ Class _____ Date _____

MULTIPLE CHOICE

1. Which property of equality can be used to justify this step?

$$15 - 10x = 6x$$
$$\underline{+ 10x + 10x}$$
$$15 = 16x$$

- **A.** Substitution Property of Equality
- **B.** Summation Property of Equality
- **(C.)** Addition Property of Equality
- **D.** Subtraction Property of Equality

2. Find the solution set for $8x - 3 = 2(x - \frac{1}{2})$.

- **F.** $\{-\frac{1}{3}\}$
- **(H.)** $\{\frac{1}{3}\}$
- **G.** $\{\frac{1}{5}\}$
- **J.** $\{\frac{2}{5}\}$

3. What is the next and most efficient step in solving the inequality for x?

$$-4x > 12$$

- **(A.)** $\frac{-4x}{-4} < \frac{12}{-4}$
- **C.** $\frac{-4x}{-4} > \frac{12}{-4}$
- **B.** $\frac{-4x}{4} > \frac{12}{4}$
- **D.** $\frac{-4x}{4} < \frac{12}{4}$

4. Given $-\frac{1}{3}x - \frac{2}{3} \geq 7x + 3$, which property is used below?

$$3\left(-\frac{1}{3}x - \frac{2}{3}\right) \geq 3(7x + 3)$$

- **F.** Distributive Property
- **(G.)** Multiplication Property of Inequality
- **H.** Subtraction Property of Inequality
- **J.** Associative Property of Multiplication

5. A 130-pound woman burns 9.83 Calories per minute while running. She burns 3.25 Calories per minute while walking during her cool-down. She runs for t minutes and exercises for a total of 45 minutes. Write an equation to find how many total Calories, C, she burns.

- **(A.)** $C = 9.83t + 3.25(45 - t)$
- **B.** $C = 9.83t + 3.25(t - 45)$
- **C.** $C = 9.83t + 3.25t$
- **D.** $C = 9.83(t - 45) + 3.25t$

6. It costs \$5 to have a tote bag monogrammed with up to 12 letters and \$.50 for each additional letter. A club has a budget of \$8 maximum per tote bag. Write an inequality for the amount the club can spend on monogramming a tote bag.

- **F.** $5 + 0.5x > 8$
- **H.** $5 + 0.5x < 8$
- **G.** $5 + 0.5x \geq 8$
- **(J.)** $5 + 0.5x \leq 8$

7. Solve the inequality for x, given $b < c$.

$$a + bx > cx - d$$

- **A.** $x < \frac{a+d}{b-c}$
- **(B.)** $x < \frac{a+d}{c-b}$
- **C.** $x > \frac{a+d}{c-b}$
- **D.** $x > \frac{-d-a}{b-c}$

8. Solve $q = \frac{r}{2}(s + t)$ for t.

- **F.** $t = \frac{qr}{2} - s$
- **(H.)** $t = \frac{2q}{r} - s$
- **G.** $t = \frac{2q - s}{r}$
- **J.** $t = \frac{q}{2r} - s$

© Houghton Mifflin Harcourt Publishing Company

---

9. Solve $V = \frac{1}{3}\pi r^2 h$ for h.

- **(A.)** $h = \frac{3V}{\pi r^2}$
- **C.** $h = \frac{\pi V}{3r^2}$
- **B.** $h = \frac{3\pi V}{r^2}$
- **D.** $h = r\sqrt{\frac{3V}{\pi}}$

10. Which ordered pair is *not* a solution to $2x + 3y = 12$?

- **F.** $(0, 4)$
- **(H.)** $(2, 3)$
- **G.** $(3, 2)$
- **J.** $(6, 0)$

11. Which statement about the graphs of $x = 2$ and $y = 4$ is true?

- **(A.)** The two lines intersect at $(2, 4)$.
- **B.** The two lines intersect at $(4, 2)$.
- **C.** The graph of $x = 2$ is horizontal and the graph of $y = 4$ is vertical.
- **D.** Both lines pass through the origin $(0, 0)$.

12. Which ordered pair is a solution to $mx + ny = 0$?

- **F.** (m, n)
- **H.** $(0, n)$
- **(G.)** $(0, 0)$
- **J.** (n, m)

13. Which description fits the graph of $x > 4$?

- **A.** A vertical solid line, shaded to the right of the line
- **B.** A horizontal dashed line, shaded above the line
- **C.** A horizontal solid line, shaded above the line
- **(D.)** A vertical dashed line, shaded to the right of the line

14. Which ordered pair is a solution to $-5x + 3y > 12$?

- **F.** $(3, 9)$
- **H.** $(3, -6)$
- **G.** $(-2, -5)$
- **(J.)** $(2, 8)$

FREE RESPONSE

15. Graph the solution to $3x - 4y \leq 1$.

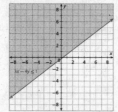

16. A charity raised \$600 at a holiday bazaar selling stationery and fountain pens. A box of stationery sold for \$12 and a pen sold for \$20. Let x represent how many boxes of stationery were sold. Let y represent how many pens were sold.

a. Write a linear equation you can use to represent all possible numbers of boxes of stationery and pens that were sold. Identify a possible solution.

$$12x + 20y = 600; \ (25, 15)$$

b. Graph the equation on the coordinate grid. Be sure to label the graph.

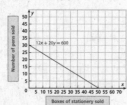

© Houghton Mifflin Harcourt Publishing Company

Systems of Equations and Inequalities

Unit Vocabulary

Systems of Equations and Inequalities

Unit Focus

In this unit, you will learn how to write and solve systems of linear equations and inequalities. You will begin by graphing two equations of a linear system and seeing how the solution to the system can be determined by looking at the graph. Then, you will explore different ways to solve linear systems algebraically. You will extend those skills to learn how to graph systems of linear inequalities and interpret the solutions. Finally, you will apply your knowledge to a real-world situation in which you will write and solve systems of equations and inequalities to model a shopping trip.

Unit at a Glance

COMMON CORE

Lesson		Standards for Mathematical Content
3-1	Solving Linear Systems by Graphing	CC.9-12.A.REI.6
3-2	Solving Linear Systems by Substitution	CC.9-12.A.REI.6
3-3	Solving Linear Systems by Adding or Subtracting	CC.9-12.A.REI.6
3-4	Solving Linear Systems by Multiplying	CC.9-12.A.REI.5, CC.9-12.A.REI.6
3-5	Solving Systems of Linear Inequalities	CC.9-12.A.REI.12
3-6	Modeling with Linear Systems	CC.9-12.N.Q.1*, CC.9-12.N.Q.2*, CC.9-12.A.CED.2*, CC.9-12.A.CED.3*, CC.9-12.A.REI.6, CC.9-12.A.REI.12
	Test Prep	

Unpacking the Common Core State Standards

Use the table to help you understand the Standards for Mathematical Content that are taught in this unit. Refer to the lessons listed after each standard for exploration and practice.

COMMON CORE Standards for Mathematical Content	What It Means For You
CC.9-12.N.Q.1 Use units as a way to understand problems and to guide the solution of multi-step problems; choose and interpret units consistently in formulas; choose and interpret the scale and the origin in graphs and data displays.* Lesson 3-6	When you model real-world situations with systems of linear equations and inequalities, it is important to check that the units of the equations and inequalities make sense. When you solve systems of linear equations and inequalities by graphing, you will need to choose appropriate units and scales for the axes in order to read your solutions from the graphs.
CC.9-12.N.Q.2 Define appropriate quantities for the purpose of descriptive modeling.* Lesson 3-6	You will write systems of linear equations and inequalities to model the relationships between quantities in real-world situations.
CC.9-12.A.CED.2 Create equations in two or more variables to represent relationships between quantities; graph equations on coordinate axes with labels and scales.* Lesson 3-6	You will create and graph linear systems of equations in two variables to model relationships between quantities in real-world situations.
CC.9-12.A.CED.3 Represent constraints by equations or inequalities, and by systems of equations and/or inequalities, and interpret solutions as viable or nonviable options in a modeling context.* Lesson 3-6	You will learn to create systems of linear equations and inequalities to model situations that include restrictions on the values of the variables. You will incorporate those restrictions into your model by writing equations or inequalities. In addition, you will analyze solutions to determine when they are possible in the context of a situation.
CC.9-12.A.REI.5 Prove that, given a system of two equations in two variables, replacing one equation by the sum of that equation and a multiple of the other produces a system with the same solutions. Lesson 3-4	An important strategy for solving systems of equations is to eliminate variables. You will prove that an equation in a system can be replaced with a constant multiple of itself, or the sum of itself and another equation in the system, and use this fact to eliminate variables.
CC.9-12.A.REI.6 Solve systems of linear equations exactly and approximately (e.g., with graphs), focusing on pairs of linear equations in two variables. Lessons 3-1, 3-2, 3-3, 3-4, 3-6	You will learn a variety of ways to solve systems of linear equations in two variables, including graphing, substitution, and elimination. You will learn which methods give exact solutions and which give approximate solutions.
CC.9-12.A.REI.12 Graph the solutions to a linear inequality in two variables as a half-plane (excluding the boundary in the case of a strict inequality), and graph the solution set to a system of linear inequalities in two variables as the intersection of the corresponding half-planes. Lessons 3-5, 3-6	You will solve systems of linear inequalities by representing the solution of each inequality as a shaded region of a graph. The solution of the system will be the area where the shaded regions overlap.

Unit 3   88   Systems of Equations and Inequalities

Unpacking the Common Core State Standards

This page lists and explains the Standards for Mathematical Content that are addressed in this unit. For information about the Standards for Mathematical Practice, which are integrated throughout the text, see Teacher Edition pages viii–xi.

Notes

Solving Linear Systems by Graphing

Essential question: How do you approximate the solution of a system of linear equations by graphing?

COMMON
CORE

Standards for Mathematical Content

CC.9-12.A.REI.6 Solve systems of linear equations ... approximately (e.g., with graphs), focusing on pairs of linear equations in two variables.

Vocabulary

system of linear equations

solution of a system of linear equations

Prerequisites

Graphing linear equations, Lesson 2-6

Math Background

In Unit 2, students learned to graph linear equations of the form $Ax + By = C$ by finding the x- and y-intercepts and connecting those points with a line. They also learned that a third point can be graphed as a check that the intercepts are valid. Students also learned to graph equations such as $y = 4$ and $x = -1$.

The solution of a system of linear equations can be found by graphing each line, approximating the point of intersection, and then checking the solution algebraically. When the intersection point has integer coordinates, the solution can be found exactly from the graph and will check exactly when the values of x and y are substituted back into each equation.

When the point of intersection does not have integer coordinates, the coordinates must be approximated from the graph, and the values of x and y may not satisfy either equation exactly when an algebraic check is performed. In this case, $Ax + By$ should be approximately equal to C for each equation in the system of equations.

INTRODUCE

Review the process for graphing equations of the form $Ax + By = C$. Have students graph the equation $3x + 2y = 6$ by finding the x-intercept $(2, 0)$, the y-intercept $(0, 3)$, and connecting those points with a line. Emphasize the concept that each point on the line is a solution of the equation by asking students to substitute values of x and y for various points on the line to check that they satisfy the equation.

TEACH

Questioning Strategies

- Look at the graphs of the two equations. Does the linear system have exactly one solution? How do you know? **The system has exactly one solution because the two lines intersect at exactly one point.**

- Is $(1, 4)$ also a solution of the system $-x + y = 3$ and $y = 4$? Explain your reasoning. **Yes, when each equation is graphed, the lines intersect at $(1, 4)$.**

Teaching Strategies

After students have identified and checked $(1, 4)$ as the solution of the system, have them also check several points that are either on one line only or on neither line to verify that these ordered pairs are *not* solutions of the system.

EXTRA EXAMPLE

Solve the system of equations below by graphing.

$$\begin{cases} 2x - y = 2 \\ x + 2y = 6 \end{cases}$$

The graph of $2x - y = 2$ has an x-intercept of 1 and a y-intercept of -2, the graph of $x + 2y = 6$ has an x-intercept of 6 and a y-intercept of 3, and the lines intersect at $(2, 2)$.

3-1

Solving Linear Systems by Graphing

COMMON CORE
CC.9-12.A.REI.6

Essential question: *How do you approximate the solution of a system of linear equations by graphing?*

A **system of linear equations** consists of two or more linear equations that have the same variables. A **solution of a system of linear equations** with two variables is an ordered pair that satisfies both equations in the system. The values of the variables in the ordered pair make each equation in the system true.

Systems of linear equations can be solved by graphing and by using algebra. In this lesson you will learn to solve linear systems by graphing the equations of the system and analyzing how those graphs are related.

1 EXAMPLE Solving a Linear System by Graphing

Solve the system of equations below by graphing. Check your answer.

$$\begin{cases} -x + y = 3 \\ 2x + y = 6 \end{cases}$$

A Graph each equation.

Step 1: Find the intercepts for $-x + y = 3$, plus a third point for a check. Graph the line.

x-intercept: ___−3___   *y*-intercept: ___3___

Check: The *y*-value for $x = 2$ is $y =$ ___5___,

Is that point (x, y) on the line? ___yes___

Step 2: Find the intercepts for $2x + y = 6$ and graph the line.

x-intercept: ___3___   *y*-intercept: ___6___

Check: The *y*-value for $x = 2$ is $y =$ ___2___,

Is that point (x, y) on the line? ___yes___

B Find the point of intersection.

The two lines appear to intersect at ___(1, 4)___

How is the point of intersection related to the solution of the linear system?

The point of intersection is the ordered pair that satisfies both equations in the

system. It is the solution of the system.

C Check if the ordered pair is a solution.

The solution of the system appears to be ___(1, 4)___.

To check, substitute the ordered pair (x, y) into each equation.

$-x + y = 3$	
− 1 + 4	3
3	3 ✓

$2x + y = 6$	
2(1) + 4	6
2 + 4	6
6	6 ✓

The ordered pair ___(1, 4)___ makes both equations ___true___.

So, ___(1, 4)___ is a solution of the system.

REFLECT

1a. How is the graph of each equation related to the solutions of the equation?

All solutions of a linear equation are represented by points on its graph; each

point corresponds to an ordered pair that makes the equation true.

1b. Explain why the solution of a linear system with two equations is represented by the point where the graphs of the two equations intersect.

Since all solutions for each equation are on its graph, a point that is on both

graphs represents a solution for both equations.

1c. Describe the graphs of $x = 4$ and $y = 2$. Explain how to solve the linear system by graphing.

$$\begin{cases} x = 4 \\ y = 2 \end{cases}$$

What would the graph look like? What is the solution of the linear system? Can systems of this type be solved by examining the equations without graphing them?

The graph of $x = 4$ is a vertical line 4 units right of the *y*-axis and the graph of

$y = 2$ is a horizontal line 2 units above the *x*-axis; Graph the two equations

and find the point of intersection; the graph shows two perpendicular lines

intersecting at (4, 2); the solution is (4, 2); Yes, for systems of this type $x = a$ gives

the *x*-value and $y = b$ gives the *y*-value, so the solution is (a, b).

2 EXAMPLE

Questioning Strategies

- In part A, is it *always* true that if a system of linear equations consists of two equations whose graphs are parallel lines, then the system has no solution? Yes; for any linear system composed of two equations, if the graphs of the equations are parallel lines, then there is no point of intersection and there is no solution.

- In part B, is it *always* true that if a system of linear equations consists of two equations whose graphs are the same line, then the system has infinitely many solutions? Yes; for any linear system composed of two equations, if the graphs of the equations are the same line, then every point on that line is a solution and there are infinitely many points on that line.

EXTRA EXAMPLE

Solve each system of equations below by graphing.

a. $\begin{cases} 4x + 2y = 8 \\ 2x + y = -4 \end{cases}$

No solution; the graphs of the two equations are parallel lines.

b. $\begin{cases} x + 3y = 3 \\ 2x + 6y = 6 \end{cases}$

Infinitely many solutions; the graphs of the two equations are the same line.

Differentiated Instruction

When looking at the linear system in part A, analytic thinkers might recognize that the second equation can be rewritten as $x + y = 3$, and therefore the system has no solution, because there is no ordered pair (x, y) for which the sum $x + y$ is both 3 and 7. In part B, analytic thinkers will recognize that since the first equation can be rewritten as $x + y = 3$, the graphs of the equations are the same line and the system has infinitely many solutions. Visual learners, on the other hand, will benefit by looking at the graphs for both systems first, and then relating the visual and algebraic representations.

3 EXAMPLE

Questioning Strategies

- Which solution is a more accurate estimate: $\left(4\frac{1}{4}, -1\frac{1}{8}\right)$ or $(4, -1)$? How would you decide? The first ordered pair; both ordered pairs are solutions of $x + 2y = 2$, but $\left(4\frac{1}{4}, -1\frac{1}{8}\right)$ is closer to the point where the lines intersect than $(4, 1)$ is.

- Which scale would help you make a more accurate estimate: each grid square represents two units or half a unit? Half a unit; if fractional units are used, the point of intersection can be identified with greater precision.

EXTRA EXAMPLE

Estimate the solution for the linear system below by graphing.

$$\begin{cases} x - 2y = -4 \\ 3x + y = 6 \end{cases}$$

The graph of $x - 2y = -4$ has an x-intercept of -4 and a y-intercept of 2, and the graph of $3x + y = 6$ has an x-intercept of 2 and a y-intercept of 6. The lines appear to intersect at $\left(1\frac{1}{4}, 2\frac{1}{2}\right)$, which is an approximate solution.

> **MATHEMATICAL PRACTICE** **Highlighting the Standards**
>
> Example 3 and its Reflect questions offer an opportunity to address Mathematical Practice Standard 5 (Use appropriate tools strategically). By graphing each equation in a linear system and looking at the intersection of the lines to approximate the solution of the system, students use a visual tool to solve an algebraic problem. Students should recognize that they can adjust the scale of a graph, setting each grid square to represent a smaller unit, in order to estimate a more accurate solution. They should also recognize when the intersection of graphed lines represents an exact rather than an approximate solution.

2 EXAMPLE   Solving Special Systems by Graphing

Use the graph to solve each system of linear equations.

A $\begin{cases} x + y = 7 \\ 2x + 2y = 6 \end{cases}$

Is there a point of intersection? Explain.

No, the lines appear to be parallel; they have

no points in common.

Does this linear system have a solution? Use the graph to explain.

This system has no solution; the lines have no points in common, which means

there is no ordered pair that will make both equations true.

B $\begin{cases} 2x + 2y = 6 \\ x + y = 3 \end{cases}$

Is there a point of intersection? Explain.

Yes, the graphs are the same line; all points are points of intersection.

Does this linear system have a solution? Use the graph to explain.

This system has infinitely many solutions; all ordered pairs on the line will make

both equations true.

REFLECT

2a. Use the graph to identify two lines that represent a linear system with exactly one
solution. What are the equations of the lines? Explain your reasoning.

Sample answer: $x + y = 7$ and $3x - y = 1$; the lines intersect at one point.

2b. If each equation in a system of two linear equations is represented by a different line
when graphed, what is the greatest number of solutions the system can have? Explain
your reasoning.

One; because the two lines are different, they are either parallel and there is no

solution, or they intersect at only one point.

2c. Identify the three possible numbers of solutions for a system of linear equations.
Explain when each type of solution occurs.

One solution when the lines intersect at a single point, no solution when the lines

are parallel, infinitely many solutions when the lines are the same line.

---

3 EXAMPLE   Estimating a Solution by Graphing

Estimate the solution for the linear system by graphing.

$$\begin{cases} x + 2y = 2 \\ 2x - 3y = 12 \end{cases}$$

A Graph each equation by finding intercepts.

$x + 2y = 2$ $2x - 3y = 12$

x-intercept: 2   x-intercept: 6

y-intercept: 1   y-intercept: −4

B Find the point of intersection.

The two lines appear to intersect at $\left(4\frac{1}{4}, -1\frac{1}{8}\right)$

C Check if the ordered pair is an approximate solution.

$x + 2y$	$= 2$
$4\frac{1}{4} + 2\left(-1\frac{1}{8}\right)$	2
$4\frac{1}{4} + \left(-2\frac{1}{4}\right)$	2
2	2 ✓

$2x - 3y$	$= 12$
$2\left(4\frac{1}{4}\right) - 3\left(-1\frac{1}{8}\right)$	12
$8\frac{1}{2} - \left(-3\frac{3}{8}\right)$	12
$11\frac{7}{8}$	12 ✓

Does the approximate solution make both equations true? If not, explain why not and
whether the approximate solution is acceptable.

No; the sides of the equation are not exactly equal in the second equation

because the solution is approximate. The approximate solution is acceptable

because it makes the left side of the equation very close to the right side, 12.

REFLECT

3a. How could you adjust the graph to make your estimate more accurate?

Sample answer: Change the scale on the graph so that each grid square

represents half a unit.

3b. Can an approximate solution make both equations true? Explain.

Yes; the estimate of the solution could turn out to be the exact solution.

Notes

Essential Question

How do you approximate the solution of a system of linear equations by graphing?
Graph each equation by finding the *x*- and *y*-intercepts and drawing a line through the points. Find the point of intersection and estimate its *x*- and *y*-coordinates. Substitute the *x*- and *y*-values into both equations to check if the ordered pair is an approximate solution.

Summarize

Have students make a graphic organizer to show how they can determine whether a system of two linear equations has no solution, exactly one solution, or infinitely many solutions. One possibility is shown below.

Where skills are taught	Where skills are practiced
1 EXAMPLE	Exs. 1, 2, 4, and 5
2 EXAMPLE	Exs. 3 and 6
3 EXAMPLE	Exs. 7–10

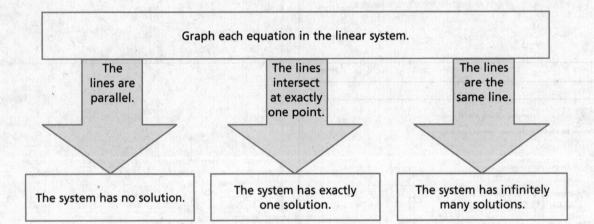

Graph each equation in the linear system.

The lines are parallel.	The lines intersect at exactly one point.	The lines are the same line.
The system has no solution.	The system has exactly one solution.	The system has infinitely many solutions.

PRACTICE

Solve each system by graphing. Check your answer.

1. $\begin{cases} x - y = -2 \\ 2x + y = 8 \end{cases}$

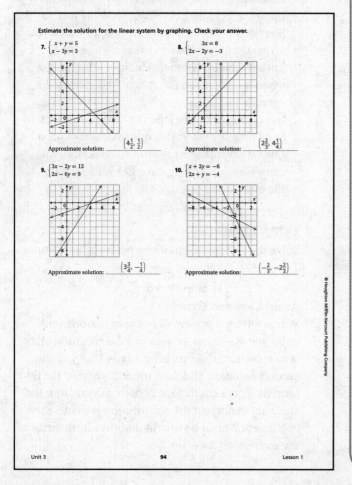

Solution: _____(2, 4)_____

2. $\begin{cases} x - y = -5 \\ 2x + 4y = -4 \end{cases}$

Solution: _____(−4, 1)_____

3. $\begin{cases} x + 2y = -8 \\ -2x - 4y = 4 \end{cases}$

Solution: _____no solution_____

4. $\begin{cases} 2x + y = 1 \\ y = -3 \end{cases}$

Solution: _____(2, −3)_____

5. $\begin{cases} x + 2y = 6 \\ x = 2 \end{cases}$

Solution: _____(2, 2)_____

6. $\begin{cases} 2x - y = -6 \\ 4x - 2y = -12 \end{cases}$

Solution: _____infinitely many solutions_____

Estimate the solution for the linear system by graphing. Check your answer.

7. $\begin{cases} x + y = 5 \\ x - 3y = 3 \end{cases}$

Approximate solution: _____$\left(4\frac{1}{2}, \frac{1}{2}\right)$_____

8. $\begin{cases} 3x = 8 \\ 2x - 2y = -3 \end{cases}$

Approximate solution: _____$\left(2\frac{2}{3}, 4\frac{1}{4}\right)$_____

9. $\begin{cases} 3x - 2y = 12 \\ 2x - 6y = 9 \end{cases}$

Approximate solution: _____$\left(3\frac{3}{4}, -\frac{1}{4}\right)$_____

10. $\begin{cases} x + 2y = -6 \\ 2x + y = -4 \end{cases}$

Approximate solution: _____$\left(-\frac{2}{3}, -2\frac{2}{3}\right)$_____

3-2

Solving Linear Systems by Substitution

Essential question: *How do you use substitution to solve a system of linear equations?*

COMMON CORE Standards for Mathematical Content

CC.9-12.A.REI.6 Solve systems of linear equations exactly ... , focusing on pairs of linear equations in two variables.

Vocabulary

substitution method

Prerequisites

Solve an equation for a given variable, Lesson 2-4

Math Background

In Unit 2, students learned to solve an equation for a given variable. In a system of two linear equations with two variables, x and y, students can solve for y in one equation, and then substitute the resulting expression for y in the other equation and solve for x. Or, they can solve for x in one equation, and then substitute the resulting expression for x in the other equation and solve for y. An important skill students will learn in this lesson is how to decide which approach is more efficient for a given system of linear equations.

Students will also revisit the concept of linear systems that have either no solution or infinitely many solutions. In the previous lesson, they visualized such linear systems by graphing. In this lesson, they will relate these graphic representations to corresponding algebraic representations.

INTRODUCE

Review the process for rewriting equations of the form $Ax + By = C$ so that one variable is isolated on one side of the equation and an equivalent expression containing the other variable is on the other side. Emphasize that it is easier to do this when at least one variable in an equation has a coefficient of 1.

TEACH

1 EXAMPLE

Questioning Strategies

- After you found the value of x, could you have found the value of y by substituting $x = 1$ in $4x + y = 8$ instead of in $-3x + y = 1$? **Yes, in both cases the solution is $y = 4$.**

- Can any system of two linear equations in two variables be solved by substitution? **Yes, although substitution is easiest if at least one variable in one of the equations has a coefficient of 1.**

 MATHEMATICAL PRACTICE **Highlighting the Standards**

Example 1 and its Reflect questions offer an opportunity to address Mathematical Practice Standard 7 (Look for and make use of structure). When using substitution to solve a system of linear equations, students look for structure when they examine the system and identify the variable that is easier to isolate. Students make use of structure when they rewrite one equation in a linear system so that one variable is isolated on one side of the equation and an equivalent expression containing the other variable is on the other side.

EXTRA EXAMPLE

Solve the system of equations below by substitution.

$$\begin{cases} 3x + y = 7 \\ 2x + 4y = 8 \end{cases} \quad \textbf{(2, 1)}$$

Avoid Common Errors

When solving a system of linear equations such as $3x - y = -1$ and $4x + 2y = 12$, a common error is to substitute the expression $3x + 1$ for y in the second equation and then to multiply only the first term $3x$ by the coefficient 2 when solving. Remind students that when the substitution is made, the coefficient 2 must be distributed over both terms of the expression $3x + 1$.

Solving Linear Systems by Substitution

COMMON CORE
CC.9-12.A.REI.6

Essential question: *How do you use substitution to solve a system of linear equations?*

The **substitution method** is used to solve systems of linear equations by solving an equation for one variable and then substituting the resulting expression for that variable into the other equation. The steps for this method are as follows:

1. Solve one of the equations for one of its variables.

2. Substitute the expression from step 1 into the other equation and solve for the other variable.

3. Substitute the value from step 2 into either original equation and solve to find the value of the variable in step 1.

1 EXAMPLE   Solving a Linear System by Substitution

Solve the system of linear equations by substitution. Check your answer.

$$\begin{cases} -3x + y = 1 \\ 4x + y = 8 \end{cases}$$

A   Solve an equation for one variable.

$-3x + y = 1$ Select one of the equations.

$y = \underline{3x + 1}$ Solve for the variable *y*. Isolate *y* on one side.

B   Substitute the expression for *y* in the other equation and solve.

$4x + (\,\underline{3x + 1}\,) = 8$ Substitute the expression for the variable *y*.

$\underline{7x} + 1 = 8$ Combine like terms.

$\underline{7x} = 7$ Subtract __1__ from each side.

$x = \underline{1}$ Divide each side by __7__.

C   Substitute the value of *x* you found into one of the equations and solve for the other variable, *y*.

$-3(\,\underline{1}\,) + y = 1$ Substitute the value of *x* into the first equation.

$\underline{-3} + y = 1$ Simplify.

$y = \underline{4}$ Add __3__ to each side.

So, __(1, 4)__ is the solution of the system.

D   Check the solution by graphing.

$-3x + y = 1$	$4x + y = 8$
x-intercept: $-\dfrac{1}{3}$	*x*-intercept: __2__
y-intercept: __1__	*y*-intercept: __8__

The point of intersection is __(1, 4)__.

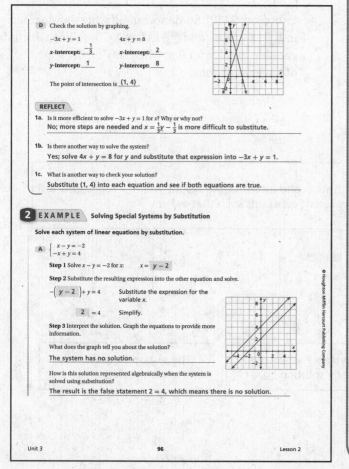

REFLECT

1a. Is it more efficient to solve $-3x + y = 1$ for *x*? Why or why not?

No; more steps are needed and $x = \frac{1}{3}y - \frac{1}{3}$ is more difficult to substitute.

1b. Is there another way to solve the system?

Yes; solve $4x + y = 8$ for *y* and substitute that expression into $-3x + y = 1$.

1c. What is another way to check your solution?

Substitute (1, 4) into each equation and see if both equations are true.

2 EXAMPLE   Solving Special Systems by Substitution

Solve each system of linear equations by substitution.

A $\begin{cases} x - y = -2 \\ -x + y = 4 \end{cases}$

Step 1 Solve $x - y = -2$ for *x*: $x = \underline{y - 2}$

Step 2 Substitute the resulting expression into the other equation and solve.

$-(\,\underline{y - 2}\,) + y = 4$ Substitute the expression for the variable *x*.

$\underline{2} = 4$ Simplify.

Step 3 Interpret the solution. Graph the equations to provide more information.

What does the graph tell you about the solution?

The system has no solution.

How is this solution represented algebraically when the system is solved using substitution?

The result is the false statement 2 = 4, which means there is no solution.

Questioning Strategies

- After solving one equation for one variable and substituting the resulting expression in the other equation, the variable is eliminated when you try to solve the other equation. What does this tell you about the solution of the system of linear equations? **The system has either no solution or infinitely many solutions.**

- In part A, if you solve $-x + y = 4$ for y and substitute the resulting expression for y in $x - y = -2$, will you still arrive at the result $2 = 4$? **Yes, you will arrive first at the statement $-4 = -2$, which can be rewritten as $2 = 4$.**

Teaching Strategies

Relate the algebraic solutions to the corresponding graphs. The resulting statement in part A is false, and the graphs of the equations have no point of intersection. In part B, the statement is always true, and the graphs have infinitely many points of intersection because they are the same line.

EXTRA EXAMPLE

Solve each system of equations below by substitution.

a. $\begin{cases} -2x + 2y = -4 \\ x - 2y = 6 \end{cases}$

no solution

b. $\begin{cases} 3x + y = 5 \\ 6x + 2y = 10 \end{cases}$

infinitely many solutions

CLOSE

Essential Question

How do you use substitution to solve a system of linear equations?

Solve one equation for one variable and substitute the resulting expression into the other equation. Solve for the value of the other variable, then substitute that value into either equation and solve for the value of the first variable. Graph the equations or substitute the x- and y-values into both equations to check the solution.

Summarize

Have students make a graphic organizer to show how they can determine whether a system of two linear equations has no solution, exactly one solution, or infinitely many solutions when solving by substitution. One possibility is shown below.

PRACTICE

Where skills are taught	Where skills are practiced
1 EXAMPLE	Exs. 1–4, 6, 7, 9
2 EXAMPLE	Exs. 5, 8, 10

Exercises 9–10: Students extend what they learned in **1** EXAMPLE and **2** EXAMPLE by telling which variable to solve for first when solving the system of linear equations.

Solve a system of linear equations by substitution and interpret the results where x represents a variable and a and b represent constants such that $a \neq b$.

$a = b$	$x = a$	$a = a$
The system has no solution.	The system has exactly one solution.	The system has infinitely many solutions.

B $\begin{cases} 2x + y = -2 \\ 4x + 2y = -4 \end{cases}$

Step 1 Solve $2x + y = -2$ for y: $y = \underline{-2x - 2}$

Step 2 Substitute the resulting expression into the other equation and solve.

$4x + 2\left(\boxed{-2x - 2}\right) = -4$ Substitute the expression for the variable y.

$\boxed{-4} = -4$ Simplify.

Step 3 Interpret the solution. Graph the equations to provide more information.

What does the graph tell you about the solution?
The graphs are the same line, so the

system has infinitely many solutions.

How is this solution represented algebraically when the linear system is solved using substitution?
The result is the statement $-4 = -4$, which is

always true. This means that the system has

infinitely many solutions.

REFLECT

2a. If x represents a variable and a and b represent constants such that $a \neq b$, interpret what each result means when solving a system of linear equations by substitution.

$x = a$ The system has one solution.

$a = b$ The system has no solution.

$a = a$ The system has infinitely many solutions.

2b. In part B of Example 2, why is it more efficient to solve and substitute for y than to solve and substitute for x?
Solving for x first would require more steps; after isolating the x-term, each side

would have to be divided by a constant.

2c. Give two possible solutions of the system in part B of Example 2. How are all the solutions of this system related to one another?
$(0, -2)$ and $(-1, 0)$; all the solutions of this system are on the graph of the line.

© Houghton Mifflin Harcourt Publishing Company

PRACTICE

Solve each system by substitution. Check your answer.

1. $\begin{cases} x + y = 3 \\ 2x + 4y = 8 \end{cases}$
Solution: __(2, 1)__

2. $\begin{cases} x + 2y = 7 \\ 4x + 3y = 3 \end{cases}$
Solution: __(-3, 5)__

3. $\begin{cases} -4x + y = 3 \\ 5x - 2y = -9 \end{cases}$
Solution: __(1, 7)__

4. $\begin{cases} 8x - 7y = -2 \\ -2x - 3y = 10 \end{cases}$
Solution: __(-2, -2)__

5. $\begin{cases} 2x - 2y = 5 \\ 4x - 4y = 9 \end{cases}$
Solution: __no solution__

6. $\begin{cases} 2x + 7y = 2 \\ 4x + 2y = -2 \end{cases}$
Solution: __$\left(-\frac{3}{4}, \frac{1}{2}\right)$__

7. $\begin{cases} 2x - y = 7 \\ 2x + 7y = 31 \end{cases}$
Solution: __(5, 3)__

8. $\begin{cases} x - 2y = -4 \\ 4y = 2x + 8 \end{cases}$
Solution: __infinitely many solutions__

For each linear system, tell whether it is more efficient to solve for x and then substitute for x or to solve for y and then substitute for y. Explain your reasoning. Then solve the system.

9. $\begin{cases} 6x - 3y = 15 \\ x + 3y = -8 \end{cases}$

Solve for x first; if solving for y first, each side would have to be divided by a

constant after isolating the y-term.

Solution: __(1, -3)__

10. $\begin{cases} \frac{x}{2} + y = 6 \\ \frac{x}{4} + \frac{y}{2} = 3 \end{cases}$

Solve for y first; if solving for x first, each side would have to be multiplied by a

constant after isolating the x-term.

Solution: __infinitely many solutions__

Notes

Solving Linear Systems by Adding or Subtracting

Essential question: How do you solve a system of linear equations by adding or subtracting?

COMMON CORE Standards for Mathematical Content

CC.9-12.A.REI.6 Solve systems of linear equations exactly ..., focusing on pairs of linear equations in two variables.

Vocabulary

elimination method

Prerequisites

Add and subtract expressions, Lesson 1-2

Math Background

Students have learned to add and subtract expressions by identifying and combining like terms. In this lesson, students identify systems of linear equations that contain like terms with coefficients that are opposites or the same and then combine those like terms to eliminate one or both variables. When like terms are opposites, one or both variables can be eliminated by adding the equations. When like terms are the same, one or both variables can be eliminated by subtracting the equations.

INTRODUCE

After reviewing the process for adding and subtracting expressions, show how these skills can be extended to adding and subtracting equations. Point out that in a system of linear equations, the *x*-terms are like terms, the *y*-terms are like terms, and the constants are like terms.

TEACH

1 EXAMPLE

Questioning Strategies

• Is it possible to eliminate the variable *x* by adding the two equations? **No, 4*x* plus *x* equals 5*x*. So, the variable *x* is not eliminated by adding.**

• How do you know by looking if a linear system has a variable that can be eliminated by adding? **The equations have two like terms that are opposites.**

EXTRA EXAMPLE

Solve the system of equations below by addition.

$$\begin{cases} 5x - 3y = 1 \\ x + 3y = 11 \end{cases} \quad (2, 3)$$

2 EXAMPLE

Questioning Strategies

• When eliminating the variable *x* by subtracting, does it matter which equation is subtracted from the other equation? **No. Since the *x*-terms are the same in both equations, the variable *x* will be eliminated whether the second equation is subtracted from the first or the first equation is subtracted from the second.**

• Is it possible to eliminate the variable *y* by subtracting one equation from the other? **No, 6*y* minus −*y* equals 7*y*, and −*y* minus 6*y* equals −7*y*. So, the variable *y* is not eliminated by subtracting.**

Teaching Strategies

Explain that subtracting an equation is the same as adding the opposite of each of its terms. Emphasize the importance of aligning like terms when equations are being added or subtracted vertically.

Avoid Common Errors

When subtracting a term with a negative coefficient, such as $3y - (-2y)$, students may subtract $2y$ instead of adding $2y$. Emphasize that subtracting a term with a negative coefficient is the same as adding the opposite of that term.

EXTRA EXAMPLE

Solve the system of equations below by subtraction.

$$\begin{cases} 4x + 2y = 2 \\ 4x - y = -7 \end{cases} \quad (-1, 3)$$

continued

Name _____ Class _____ Date _____

Solving Linear Systems by Adding or Subtracting

COMMON CORE

CC.9-12.A.REI.6

Essential question: *How do you solve a system of linear equations by adding or subtracting?*

The **elimination method** is another method used to solve a system of linear equations. In this method, one variable is *eliminated* by adding or subtracting the two equations of the system to obtain a single equation in one variable. The steps for this method are as follows:

1. Add or subtract the equations to eliminate one variable.

2. Solve the resulting equation for the other variable.

3. Substitute the value into either original equation to find the value of the eliminated variable.

1 EXAMPLE Solving a Linear System by Adding

Solve the system of equations by adding. Check your answer.

$$\begin{cases} 4x - 2y = 12 \\ x + 2y = 8 \end{cases}$$

A Add the equations.

$4x - 2y = 12$ Write the equations so that like terms are aligned.

$+\ x + 2y = 8$ Notice that the terms $\underline{-2y}$ and $\underline{2y}$ are opposites.

$5x + 0 = 20$ Add to eliminate the variable $\underline{y}$.

$5x = 20$ Simplify and solve for x.

$\dfrac{5x}{5} = \dfrac{20}{5}$ Divide both sides by 5.

$x = \underline{4}$ Simplify.

B Substitute the solution into one of the equations and solve for y.

$x + 2y = 8$ Use the second equation.

$(\ \underline{4}\ ) + 2y = 8$ Substitute $\underline{4}$ for the variable $\underline{x}$.

$2y = \underline{4}$ Subtract $\underline{4}$ from each side.

$y = \underline{2}$ Divide each side by $\underline{2}$.

C Write the solution as an ordered pair: $\underline{(4,\ 2)}$

D Check the solution by graphing.

$4x - 2y = 12$ $x + 2y = 8$

x-intercept: $\underline{3}$ x-intercept: $\underline{8}$

y-intercept: $\underline{-6}$ y-intercept: $\underline{4}$

The point of intersection is $\underline{(4,\ 2)}$.

REFLECT

1a. Can this linear system be solved by subtracting one of the original equations from the other? Why or why not?

No; if either of the original equations in the system is subtracted from the other, neither variable will be eliminated.

1b. What is another way to check your solution?

Substitute (4, 2) into each equation and see if both equations are true.

2 EXAMPLE Solving a Linear System by Subtracting

Solve the system of equations by subtracting. Check your answer.

$$\begin{cases} 2x + 6y = 6 \\ 2x - y = -8 \end{cases}$$

A Subtract the equations.

$2x + 6y = 6$ Write the equations so that like terms are aligned.

$-(2x - y = -8)$ Notice that both equations contain the term $\underline{2x}$.

$0 + 7y = 14$ Subtract to eliminate the variable $\underline{x}$.

$7y = 14$ Simplify and solve for y.

$\dfrac{7y}{7} = \dfrac{14}{7}$ Divide both sides by 7.

$y = \underline{2}$ Simplify.

B Substitute the solution into one of the equations and solve for x.

$2x - y = -8$ Use the second equation.

$2x - (\ \underline{2}\ ) = -8$ Substitute $\underline{2}$ for the variable $\underline{y}$.

$2x = -6$ Add $\underline{2}$ to each side.

$x = -3$ Divide each side by $\underline{2}$.

C Write the solution as an ordered pair: $\underline{(-3,\ 2)}$

MATHEMATICAL PRACTICE

Highlighting the Standards

Example 2 and its Reflect questions offer an opportunity to address Mathematical Practice Standard 8 (Look for and express regularity in repeated reasoning). When solving a system of linear equations by adding or subtracting, students repeatedly notice that linear systems with equations that have like terms with coefficients that are opposites can be solved by adding and that linear systems with equations that have two identical terms can be solved by subtracting. As they use this strategy over and over again, they look for and express regularity by recognizing adding and subtracting as a general method for solving systems of linear equations and by being able to identify the linear systems for which that method can be used.

CLOSE

Essential Question

How do you solve a system of linear equations by adding or subtracting?

If the equations have like terms with coefficients that are opposites, add the equations to eliminate one variable; if two terms are identical, subtract the equations to eliminate one variable. Solve for the value of the remaining variable, then substitute that value into either equation and solve for the value of the first variable. Graph the equations or substitute the *x*- and *y*-values into both equations to check the solution.

Summarize

Have students make a graphic organizer to show how they can determine if a system of two linear equations can be solved by adding or subtracting and, if so, which variable can be eliminated and whether addition or subtraction should be used. One possibility is shown below.

PRACTICE

Where skills are taught	Where skills are practiced
1 EXAMPLE	Exs. 1, 4–6
2 EXAMPLE	Exs. 2, 3

Exercises 7–8: Students generalize that a system of linear equations has no solution if a false statement results after adding or subtracting the equations, and infinitely many solutions if a true statement results after adding or subtracting the equations.

Exercise 9: Students extend what they learned in **1** EXAMPLE and **2** EXAMPLE by identifying correct and incorrect solutions for a system of linear equations solved by subtracting, and describing the error made when finding the incorrect solution.

Exercise 10: Students compare using substitution and elimination to solve the system from **1** EXAMPLE to determine which method is more efficient.

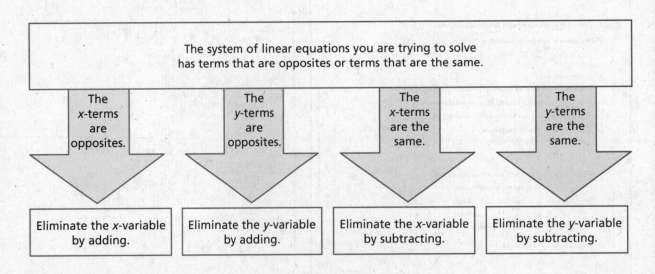

The system of linear equations you are trying to solve has terms that are opposites or terms that are the same.

The *x*-terms are opposites.	The *y*-terms are opposites.	The *x*-terms are the same.	The *y*-terms are the same.
Eliminate the *x*-variable by adding.	Eliminate the *y*-variable by adding.	Eliminate the *x*-variable by subtracting.	Eliminate the *y*-variable by subtracting.

D Check the solution by graphing.

$2x + 6y = 6$ $2x - y = -8$

x-intercept: __3__   x-intercept: __−4__

y-intercept: __1__   y-intercept: __8__

The point of intersection is __(−3, 2)__.

REFLECT

2a. What would happen if you added the original equations instead of subtracting?

You would get $4x + 5y = -2$, which would not help to solve the system because

neither variable would be eliminated.

2b. Instead of subtracting $2x - y = -8$ from $2x + 6y = 6$, what equation can you add to get the same result? Explain.

$-2x + y = 8$; subtracting an equation is the same as adding the opposite of

each of its terms.

2c. How can you decide whether to add or subtract to eliminate a variable in a linear system? Explain your reasoning.

If the equations have two terms that are opposites, then you can add to eliminate

a variable; if the equations have two terms that are the same, then you can

subtract to eliminate a variable.

PRACTICE

Solve each system by adding or subtracting. Check your answer.

1. $\begin{cases} -5x + y = -3 \\ 5x - 3y = -1 \end{cases}$

Solution: __(1, 2)__

2. $\begin{cases} 2x + y = -6 \\ -5x + y = 8 \end{cases}$

Solution: __(−2, −2)__

3. $\begin{cases} 2x - 3y = -2 \\ 2x + y = 14 \end{cases}$

Solution: __(5, 4)__

4. $\begin{cases} 6x - 3y = 15 \\ 4x + 3y = -5 \end{cases}$

Solution: __(1, −3)__

5. $\begin{cases} -4x + y = -3 \\ 4x - y = -2 \end{cases}$

Solution: __no solution__

6. $\begin{cases} x - 6y = 7 \\ -x + 6y = -7 \end{cases}$

Solution: __infinitely many solutions__

---

7. If a linear system has no solution, what happens when you try to solve the system by adding or subtracting?

When the equations are added or subtracted, the result is a false statement,

such as $0 = 5$; this means there is no solution.

8. If a linear system has infinitely many solutions, what happens when you try to solve the system by adding or subtracting?

When the equations are added or subtracted, the result is a true statement,

$0 = 0$, which means there are infinitely many solutions.

9. Error Analysis Which solution is incorrect? Explain the error.

A

$\begin{cases} x + y = -4 \\ 2x + y = -3 \end{cases}$ $\begin{array}{r} x + y = -4 \\ -(2x + y = -3) \\ \hline -x = -7 \\ x = 7 \end{array}$

$7 + y = -4$

$y = -11$

Solution is $(7, -11)$.

B

$\begin{cases} x + y = -4 \\ 2x + y = -3 \end{cases}$ $\begin{array}{r} x + y = -4 \\ -(2x + y = -3) \\ \hline -x = -1 \\ x = 1 \end{array}$

$1 + y = -4$

$y = -5$

Solution is $(1, -5)$.

Solution A is incorrect; the x and y terms were subtracted, but the constants

−4 and −3 were added.

10. Is it possible to solve the system in the first Example by using substitution? If so, explain how. Which method is easier to use? Why?

Yes; Solve the second equation for x to get $x = -2y + 8$. Substitute $-2y + 8$

for x in the first equation to get $4(-2y + 8) - 2y = 12$. Solve this equation for y

to get $y = 2$. Then substitute 2 for y in either original equation to get $x = 4$. The

elimination method is easier because there are fewer calculations involved and

they are simpler to do.

Solving Linear Systems by Multiplying

Essential question: *How do you solve a system of linear equations by multiplying?*

COMMON CORE **Standards for Mathematical Content**

CC.9-12.A.REI.5 Prove that, given a system of two equations in two variables, replacing one equation by the sum of that equation and a multiple of the other produces a system with the same solutions.

CC.9-12.A.REI.6 Solve systems of linear equations exactly and approximately (e.g., with graphs), focusing on pairs of linear equations in two variables.

Prerequisites

Multiplying polynomials by a constant, Lesson 1-2

Solving linear systems by adding and subtracting, Lesson 3-3

Math Background

In Lesson 3-3, students learned to solve systems of linear equations by adding or subtracting. In this lesson, students solve linear systems by first multiplying one or both equations by a constant, and then applying the skills they learned in Lesson 3-3.

Students begin the lesson by exploring graphs of equations in linear systems when one equation is multiplied by a constant and added to the other equation. This exploration leads them to prove algebraically that a system of linear equations that is solved by multiplying one or both equations by a constant has the same solution as the original system.

INTRODUCE

Review the process for solving a system of linear equations by adding or subtracting, emphasizing that the technique can only be used when the system has like terms whose coefficients are opposites or the same. Point out that the use of the technique can be extended to systems of linear equations that do not meet these requirements by multiplying one or both equations in the system by a constant so that the result is a "new" system of linear equations that does have terms whose coefficients are opposites or the same.

TEACH

1 EXPLORE

Questioning Strategies

- How is the graph of a linear equation that has been multiplied by a constant related to the graph of the original equation? **The graph is the same line.**

- Is the solution of a linear equation in two variables that has been multiplied by a constant the same as the solution of the original equation? **Yes; multiplying by a constant does not change the solution.**

Differentiated Instruction

Encourage students to reinforce their understanding of the proof they completed in the Reflect section by relating the abstract algebraic representation of the process of solving a system of linear equations to more concrete representations. Visual learners may benefit from relating the algebraic proof to the graphs of the equations for the linear system given in parts A, B, and C of **1 EXPLORE**. Kinesthetic learners may benefit from writing both the algebraic proof and the solution for the linear system in **1 EXPLORE** on the board, and mapping abstract representations of coefficients and constants to their corresponding concrete representations.

MATHEMATICAL PRACTICE — Highlighting the Standards

This Explore and its Reflect questions offer an opportunity to address Mathematical Practice Standard 3 (Construct viable arguments and critique the reasoning of others). Graphs are used to show that given a system of two equations in two variables, replacing one equation by the sum of that equation and a multiple of the other produces a system with the same solutions. Students move from this concrete representation of an argument to the more abstract algebraic proof of that argument completed in Reflect question 1b.

Name _____ Class _____ Date _____

3-4

COMMON CORE

CC.9-12.A.REI.5,
CC.9-12.A.REI.6

Solving Linear Systems by Multiplying

Essential question: *How do you solve a system of linear equations by multiplying?*

In some linear systems, neither variable can be eliminated by adding or subtracting the equations directly. In systems like these, you need to multiply one or both of the equations by a constant so that adding or subtracting the equations will eliminate one variable. The steps for this method are as follows:

1. Decide which variable to eliminate.

2. Multiply one or both equations by a constant so that adding or subtracting will eliminate that variable.

3. Solve the system using the elimination method.

1 EXPLORE Understanding Linear Systems and Multiplication

A Use the equations in the linear system below to write a third equation.

$$\begin{cases} 2x - y = 1 \\ x + y = 2 \end{cases}$$

$x + y = 2$	Write the second equation in the system.
$2(x + y = 2)$	Multiply each term in the equation by 2.
$2x + 2y = 4$	Simplify.
$+\ \ 2x - y = 1$	Write the first equation in the system.
$4\ x +\ 1\ y =\ 5$	Add the equations to write a third equation.

B Graph and label each equation in the original linear system.

The solution of the system is __(1, 1)__ .

C Graph and label the third equation.

How is the graph of the third equation related to the graphs of the two equations in the original system?

It passes through the intersection point of the two

original lines.

Is the solution of the original system also a solution of the system formed by the equation $2x - y = 1$ and the third equation? Explain.

Yes; (1, 1) is a point of intersection for $2x - y = 1$ and $4x + y = 5$.

© Houghton Mifflin Harcourt Publishing Company

REFLECT

1a. Examine your results from the Explore. Does it appear that a new linear system composed of one of the equations from the original system and a new equation created by adding a multiple of one original equation to the other equation will have the same solution as the original system? Explain.

Yes; if a multiple of one original equation is added to the other original equation

to create a third equation, the graph of that new equation will pass through the

point of intersection of the two original equations.

1b. If the two equations in the original system are represented by $Ax + By = C$ and $Dx + Ey = F$, where $A, B, C, D, E,$ and F are constants, then the third equation you wrote can be represented by doing the following:

Multiply the second equation by a nonzero constant k to get $kDx + kEy = kF$.

Then add this equation to the first equation to get the third equation.

$$\begin{array}{r} Ax +\ \ \ \ \ \ By = C \\ +\ \ kDx +\ \ \ \ kEy =\ \ \ kF \\ \hline (A + kD)x + (B + kE)y = C + kF \end{array}$$

Complete the proof below to show that if (x_1, y_1) is a solution of the original system, then it is also a solution of the new system below.

$$\begin{cases} Ax + By = C \\ (A + kD)x + (B + kE)y = C + kF \end{cases}$$

$Ax_1 + By_1 = C$	(x_1, y_1) is a solution of $Ax + By = C$.
$Dx_1 + Ey_1 = F$	(x_1, y_1) is a solution of $Dx + Ey = F$.
$k\ (Dx_1 + Ey_1) = kF$	Multiplication Property of __Equality__
$kDx_1 + kEy_1 = kF$	__Distributive__ Property
$C + kDx_1 + kEy_1 =\ \ C\ + kF$	__Addition__ Property of Equality
$Ax_1 +\ By_1\ + kDx_1 + kEy_1 = C + kF$	Substitute $Ax_1 + By_1$ for C on the left side.
$Ax_1 + kDx_1 +\ By_1\ + kEy_1 = C + kF$	__Commutative__ Property of Addition
$(Ax_1 + kDx_1) + (By_1 + kEy_1) = C + kF$	Associative Property of Addition
$(A + kD)x_1 + (\ B\ + kE)y_1 = C + kF$	Distributive Property

Since $(A + kD)x_1 + (B + kE)y_1 = C + kF$, (x_1, y_1) is a solution of the new system.

© Houghton Mifflin Harcourt Publishing Company

2 EXAMPLE

Questioning Strategies

- In part B, how is the graph of the equation created by adding the multiple of $2x - 2y = -10$ to $3x + 8y = 7$ related to the graphs of the original two equations in the system? **All graphs pass through the point (−3, 2).**

- How can you check that the solution is correct? **Graph the equations or substitute the x- and y-values into both equations to check the solution.**

Teaching Strategies

Help students identify systems of linear equations that can be solved by multiplying only one equation by a constant. Start by having them look at the coefficients for the x-terms and ask, "Can either coefficient be multiplied by a constant so that the resulting coefficient is the opposite of, or the same as, the other coefficient?" Repeat the process for the coefficients of the y-term.

Students will recognize that the coefficient of $-2y$ can be multiplied by 4 to get $-8y$, which is the opposite of the other y-term $8y$. Guide them to discover that 8 is a multiple of -2, and lead them to the generalization that when a variable in a linear system has one coefficient that is a multiple of the other, the system can be solved by multiplying only one equation by a constant.

Avoid Common Errors

When multiplying an equation of the form $Ax + By = C$ by a constant k in order to solve a system of linear equations, students sometimes multiply the coefficients A and B but forget to multiply the constant C. Remind students that the form of the resulting equation is $kAx + kBy = kC$.

EXTRA EXAMPLE

Solve the system of equations below by multiplying.

$$\begin{cases} 2x + 9y = 1 \\ 3x - 3y = -15 \end{cases} \quad (-4, 1)$$

3 EXAMPLE

Questioning Strategies

- Is it possible to solve this system of linear equations by adding or subtracting after multiplying only one of the equations by an integer? **No; neither the x-term nor the y-term can be eliminated by multiplying only one equation.**

- How can you use the substitution method to solve this system of linear equations by an integer? **Solve the first equation for x to get x = 3y + 1. Then, substitute the expression 3y + 1 for x in the second equation and solve for y. Finally, substitute the value of y into either equation and solve for x.**

Teaching Strategies

Remind students that when they solve systems of linear equations by multiplying, some systems will have no solution and some systems will have infinitely many solutions. Ask students to recall the results when they solved systems with no solution and infinitely many solutions by adding and subtracting. Guide them to discover that the results will be the same if one or both equations in a linear system are multiplied by a constant before adding or subtracting: a false statement means that the system has no solution and a true statement means that the system has infinitely many solutions.

Avoid Common Errors

When each equation in a linear system is multiplied by a different constant in order to eliminate a variable, one equation is often multiplied by a positive constant while the other equation is multiplied by a negative constant in order to make the coefficients of the variable opposites. Remind students to pay close attention to signs as they multiply, and then add or subtract the equations.

EXTRA EXAMPLE

Solve the system of equations below by multiplying.

$$\begin{cases} -5x + 4y = -2 \\ 2x - 7y = 17 \end{cases} \quad (-2, -3)$$

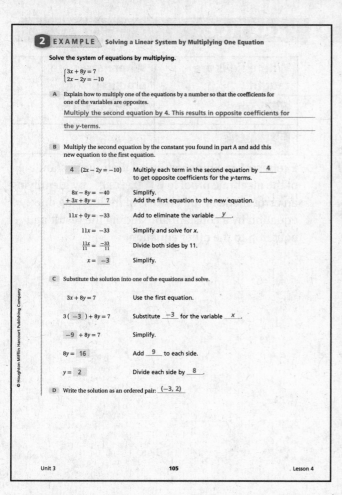

2 EXAMPLE Solving a Linear System by Multiplying One Equation

Solve the system of equations by multiplying.

$$\begin{cases} 3x + 8y = 7 \\ 2x - 2y = -10 \end{cases}$$

A Explain how to multiply one of the equations by a number so that the coefficients for one of the variables are opposites.

Multiply the second equation by 4. This results in opposite coefficients for the y-terms.

B Multiply the second equation by the constant you found in part A and add this new equation to the first equation.

| 4 $(2x - 2y = -10)$ | Multiply each term in the second equation by __4__ to get opposite coefficients for the y-terms. |

$8x - 8y = -40$	Simplify.
$+ \ 3x + 8y = \ \ \ 7$	Add the first equation to the new equation.
$11x + 0y = -33$	Add to eliminate the variable __y__.
$11x = -33$	Simplify and solve for x.
$\frac{11x}{11} = \frac{-33}{11}$	Divide both sides by 11.
$x = -3$	Simplify.

C Substitute the solution into one of the equations and solve.

$3x + 8y = 7$	Use the first equation.
$3(\ -3 \ ) + 8y = 7$	Substitute __-3__ for the variable __x__.
$-9 + 8y = 7$	Simplify.
$8y = 16$	Add __9__ to each side.
$y = 2$	Divide each side by __8__.

D Write the solution as an ordered pair: __$(-3, 2)$__

© Houghton Mifflin Harcourt Publishing Company

REFLECT

2a. How can you solve this linear system by subtracting? Which is more efficient, adding or subtracting? Explain your reasoning.

Multiply the second equation by -4 and then subtract. Adding is more efficient because the y-terms already have opposite signs.

2b. Can this linear system be solved by adding or subtracting without multiplying? Why or why not?

No; without multiplying, neither variable will be eliminated.

2c. What would you need to multiply the second equation by to eliminate x by adding? Why might you choose to eliminate y instead of x?

You would need to multiply the second equation by $-\frac{3}{2}$ or -1.5; it is simpler to multiply by the whole number 4.

3 EXAMPLE Solving a Linear System by Multiplying Both Equations

Solve the system of equations by multiplying.

$$\begin{cases} -3x + 9y = -3 \\ 4x - 13y = 5 \end{cases}$$

A Explain how to multiply both of the equations by different integers so that the coefficients for one of the variables are opposites.

Multiply the first equation by 4 and the second equation by 3 to get opposite x-coefficients.

B Multiply both of the equations and add.

4 $(-3x + 9y = -3)$	Multiply the first equation by __4__.
3 $(4x - 13y = 5)$	Multiply the second equation by __3__.
$-12x + 36y = -12$	Simplify the multiple of the first equation.
$+ \ 12x - 39y = \ \ 15$	Simplify the multiple of the second equation.
$-3y = 3$	Add to eliminate the variable __x__.
$\frac{-3y}{-3} = \frac{3}{-3}$	Divide both sides by -3.
$y = -1$	Simplify.

© Houghton Mifflin Harcourt Publishing Company

Notes

Essential Question

How do you solve a system of linear equations by multiplying?

First, check if a coefficient for either variable is a multiple of the other coefficient for that variable. If so, multiply one equation so that the coefficients for one variable are opposites or the same, and then solve the system by adding or subtracting. If neither variable has coefficients that are multiples, multiply each equation so that the coefficients for one variable are opposites or the same, and then solve the system by adding or subtracting. Graph the equations or substitute the *x*- and *y*-values into both equations to check the solution.

Summarize

Have students make a graphic organizer to show how they can determine whether only one or both equations in a linear system must be multiplied by a constant before the system can be solved by adding or subtracting. One possibility is shown below.

Where skills are taught	Where skills are practiced
2 EXAMPLE	Exs. 1–3, 7, 10
3 EXAMPLE	Exs. 4–6, 8, 9

Exercise 11: Students extend their understanding of the algebraic proof in 1 EXPLORE by identifying an error made in the process of multiplying one equation by a constant and adding the resulting equation to the other equation.

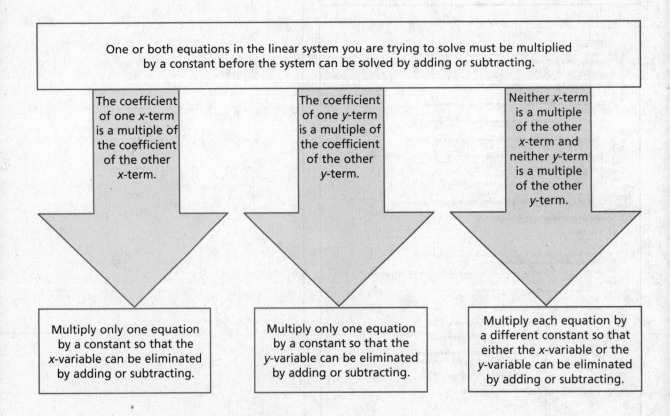

One or both equations in the linear system you are trying to solve must be multiplied by a constant before the system can be solved by adding or subtracting.

The coefficient of one *x*-term is a multiple of the coefficient of the other *x*-term.

The coefficient of one *y*-term is a multiple of the coefficient of the other *y*-term.

Neither *x*-term is a multiple of the other *x*-term and neither *y*-term is a multiple of the other *y*-term.

Multiply only one equation by a constant so that the *x*-variable can be eliminated by adding or subtracting.

Multiply only one equation by a constant so that the *y*-variable can be eliminated by adding or subtracting.

Multiply each equation by a different constant so that either the *x*-variable or the *y*-variable can be eliminated by adding or subtracting.

C Substitute the solution into one of the equations and solve.

$4x - 13y = 5$ Use the second equation.

$4x - 13(\,-1\,) = 5$ Substitute __−1__ for the variable __y__.

$4x - (\,-13\,) = 5$ Simplify.

$4x = \,-8$ Add __−13__ to each side.

$\frac{4x}{4} = \frac{-8}{4}$ Divide each side by __4__.

$x = \,-2$ Simplify.

D Write the solution as an ordered pair: $(-2, -1)$

REFLECT

3a. What numbers would you need to multiply both equations by to eliminate y? Why might you choose to eliminate x instead?

You would multiply the first equation by 13 and the second by 9; the numbers used to eliminate x are smaller and easier to work with.

3b. Describe how to find the numbers by which you would multiply both equations to eliminate a variable.

Find the least common multiple of the coefficients for one variable. Then multiply the equations so that the coefficients for that variable both equal the LCM or one coefficient equals the LCM and the other equals the opposite of the LCM.

3c. If both equations must be multiplied in order to eliminate a variable, how can you decide which variable will be easier to eliminate?

The variable whose coefficients have the lower LCM may be easier to eliminate.

3d. Explain what would happen if you multiplied both equations in the system $-3x + 9y = -3$ and $4x - 12y = 5$ in order to eliminate a variable.

If you multiply the first equation by 4 and the second equation by 3, when you add them you get $0 = 3$, which is false. The system has no solution.

3e. Explain what would happen if you multiplied both equations in the system $9x - 15y = 24$ and $6x - 10y = 16$ and subtracted them to eliminate a variable.

If you multiply the first equation by 2 and the second by 3, when you subtract you get $0 = 0$, which is always true. The system has infinitely many solutions.

PRACTICE

Solve each system by multiplying. Check your answer.

1. $\begin{cases} -2x + 2y = 2 \\ 5x - 6y = -9 \end{cases}$

Solution: _____ $(3, 4)$ _____

2. $\begin{cases} 3x + 3y = 12 \\ -6x - 11y = -14 \end{cases}$

Solution: _____ $(6, -2)$ _____

3. $\begin{cases} 4x + 3y = 11 \\ 2x - 2y = -12 \end{cases}$

Solution: _____ $(-1, 5)$ _____

4. $\begin{cases} 6x + 3y = -24 \\ 7x - 5y = 6 \end{cases}$

Solution: _____ $(-2, -4)$ _____

5. $\begin{cases} 3x + 8y = 17 \\ -2x + 9y = 3 \end{cases}$

Solution: _____ $(3, 1)$ _____

6. $\begin{cases} 11x + 6y = -20 \\ 15x + 9y = -33 \end{cases}$

Solution: _____ $(2, -7)$ _____

7. $\begin{cases} 2x + 3y = -6 \\ 10x + 15y = -30 \end{cases}$

Solution: _____ infinitely many solutions

8. $\begin{cases} 12x - 6y = 12 \\ 8x - 16y = -16 \end{cases}$

Solution: _____ $(2, 2)$ _____

9. $\begin{cases} 5x + 9y = -3 \\ -4x - 7y = 3 \end{cases}$

Solution: _____ $(-6, 3)$ _____

10. $\begin{cases} 3x - 4y = -1 \\ -6x + 8y = 3 \end{cases}$

Solution: _____ no solution

11. **Error Analysis** A linear system has two equations, $Ax + By = C$ and $Dx + Ey = F$. A student multiplies the x- and y-coefficients in the second equation by a constant k to get $kDx + kEy = F$. The student then adds the result to $Ax + By = C$ to write a new equation.

a. What is the new equation that the student wrote?

$(A + kD)x + (B + kE)y = C + F$

b. If the ordered pair (x_1, y_1) is a solution of the original system, will it also be a solution of $Ax + By = C$ and the new equation? Why or why not?

No; the student did not multiply F in the second equation by the constant k before adding it to the first equation. The systems are not equivalent.

Solving Systems of Linear Inequalities

Essential question: How do you solve a system of linear inequalities?

COMMON
CORE

Standards for Mathematical Content

CC.9-12.A-REI.12 Graph the solutions to a linear inequality in two variables as a half-plane (excluding the boundary in the case of a strict inequality), and graph the solution set to a system of linear inequalities in two variables as the intersection of the corresponding half-planes.

Vocabulary

system of linear inequalities

solutions of a system of linear inequalities

Prerequisites

Graphing a single inequality in two variables, Lesson 2-7

Math Background

Students have learned to graph a single linear inequality in two variables in the coordinate plane by graphing its boundary line and then shading the half-plane above or below the line, depending on the inequality symbol. In this lesson, students extend those skills by graphing systems of inequalities containing two or more linear inequalities and identifying the solution set as the region where the shaded half-planes overlap.

INTRODUCE

After reviewing the process for graphing a single linear inequality in two variables, explain that the process can also be used to solve a system of linear inequalities containing two or more inequalities.

Point out that, unlike a system of linear equations in two variables which usually has a single ordered pair as a solution, a system of linear inequalities has a solution set that consists of all ordered pairs that satisfy all inequalities in that system. Explain that, for this reason, graphs are useful for representing the solutions of systems of linear inequalities.

TEACH

1 EXAMPLE

Questioning Strategies

- Why is (0, 0) a good point to use for checking the answer to this system of linear inequalities? The point (0, 0) does not lie on a boundary line, and it is easy to evaluate each inequality in the system for $x = 0$ and $y = 0$.

- Is $(-1, 3)$ a solution of this system of inequalities? Yes; it lies on a solid boundary line for the inequality $-x + y \leq 4$ and is within the shaded region for the inequality $x + 2y > 2$.

Teaching Strategies

After students have graphed $x + 2y > 2$, ask if various points on the boundary line are solutions of the inequality. Remind students that points on the boundary line are excluded from the solution when the inequality symbol is $<$ or $>$. Explain that the solutions of the system of linear inequalities will only include ordered pairs that are solutions of $x + 2y > 2$, not $x + 2y = 2$.

Avoid Common Errors

Emphasize that an ordered pair must satisfy *both* inequalities in order to be a solution of a system of two linear inequalities. The point of intersection of two boundary lines is *not* a solution if only one of those boundary lines is solid.

EXTRA EXAMPLE

Solve the system of inequalities below by graphing.

$$\begin{cases} x + y < -1 \\ -2x + y \geq 2 \end{cases}$$

The graph of $x + y < -1$ is a dashed line passing through $(-1, 0)$ and $(0, -1)$ with shading below. The graph of $-2x + y \geq 2$ is a solid line passing through $(-1, 0)$ and $(0, 2)$ with shading above. The solutions are represented by the overlapping shaded regions.

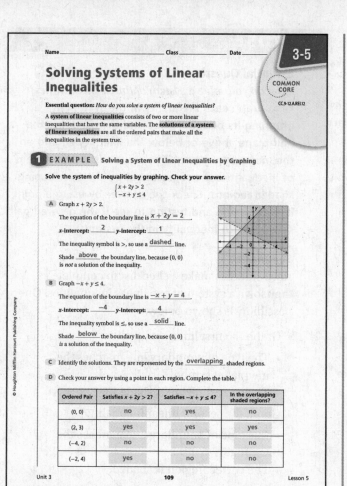

Name_____ Class_____ Date_____

3-5

Solving Systems of Linear Inequalities

COMMON CORE

CC.9-12.A.REI.12

Essential question: *How do you solve a system of linear inequalities?*

A **system of linear inequalities** consists of two or more linear inequalities that have the same variables. The **solutions of a system of linear inequalities** are all the ordered pairs that make all the inequalities in the system true.

1 **EXAMPLE** Solving a System of Linear Inequalities by Graphing

Solve the system of inequalities by graphing. Check your answer.

$$\begin{cases} x + 2y > 2 \\ -x + y \le 4 \end{cases}$$

A Graph $x + 2y > 2$.

The equation of the boundary line is $\underline{x + 2y = 2}$.

x-intercept: __2__ y-intercept: __1__

The inequality symbol is >, so use a __dashed__ line.

Shade __above__ the boundary line, because (0, 0) is *not* a solution of the inequality.

B Graph $-x + y \le 4$.

The equation of the boundary line is $\underline{-x + y = 4}$.

x-intercept: __−4__ y-intercept: __4__

The inequality symbol is ≤, so use a __solid__ line.

Shade __below__ the boundary line, because (0, 0) *is* a solution of the inequality.

C Identify the solutions. They are represented by the __overlapping__ shaded regions.

D Check your answer by using a point in each region. Complete the table.

Ordered Pair	Satisfies $x + 2y > 2$?	Satisfies $-x + y \le 4$?	In the overlapping shaded regions?
(0, 0)	no	yes	no
(2, 3)	yes	yes	yes
(−4, 2)	no	no	no
(−2, 4)	yes	no	no

© Houghton Mifflin Harcourt Publishing Company

REFLECT

1a. How does testing specific ordered pairs tell you that the solution you graphed is correct?

Only ordered pairs that satisfy both inequalities should be in the overlapping shaded region.

1b. Is (−2, 2) a solution of the system of inequalities? Why or why not?

No, a solution must satisfy both inequalities; although (−2, 2) is a solution of $-x + y \le 4$, it is on the dashed boundary line of $x + 2y > 2$ and, thus, is not a solution of $x + 2y > 2$.

The graphs of linear inequalities in a system can have parallel boundary lines. Unlike systems of linear equations, this does not always mean the system has no solution.

2 **EXAMPLE** Graphing Systems with Parallel Boundary Lines

Graph each system of linear inequalities.

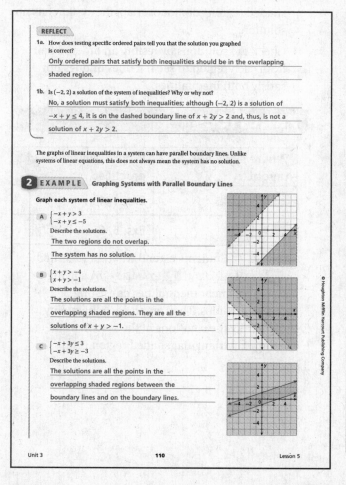

A $\begin{cases} -x + y > 3 \\ -x + y \le -5 \end{cases}$

Describe the solutions.

The two regions do not overlap.

The system has no solution.

B $\begin{cases} x + y > -4 \\ x + y > -1 \end{cases}$

Describe the solutions.

The solutions are all the points in the overlapping shaded regions. They are all the solutions of $x + y > -1$.

C $\begin{cases} -x + 3y \le 3 \\ -x + 3y \ge -3 \end{cases}$

Describe the solutions.

The solutions are all the points in the overlapping shaded regions between the boundary lines and on the boundary lines.

© Houghton Mifflin Harcourt Publishing Company

Questioning Strategies

- Look at the graph in part A. What would the graph look like if the system of linear inequalities were $-x + y < 3$ and $-x + y \geq -5$? The boundary lines would be the same, but the area between the two parallel lines would be an overlapping shaded region.

EXTRA EXAMPLE

Graph the system of inequalities below and describe the solutions.

$$\begin{cases} x + y \geq 2 \\ x + y < -4 \end{cases}$$

The graph of $x + y \geq 2$ is a solid line passing through (2, 0) and (0, 2) with shading above. The graph of $x + y < -4$ is a dashed line passing through (−4, 0) and (0, −4) with shading below. The shaded regions do not overlap, so the system of linear inequalities has no solution.

MATHEMATICAL PRACTICE **Highlighting the Standards**

Example 2 and its Reflect questions offer an opportunity to address Mathematical Practice Standard 7 (Look for and make use of structure). When solving a system of linear inequalities in two variables, students build upon strategies they have used before. For example, when solving compound inequalities in one variable, students graphed each inequality on a number line and identified the solution as the intersection of the graphs. When graphing a single linear inequality in two variables, students graphed the boundary line and then decided where to shade by testing points on either side of the boundary line to see whether or not the ordered pair satisfied the inequality.

CLOSE

Essential Question

How do you solve a system of linear inequalities?
First, graph each inequality in the system by graphing its boundary line and then shading the half-plane above or below the line, depending on the inequality symbol. The solutions of the system of inequalities are represented by the overlapping shaded regions. Check the answer by using a point in each region and testing to see if the ordered pair satisfies each inequality in the system.

Summarize

Have students make a checklist to complete as they solve a system of two linear inequalities. One possibility is shown below.

- Graph the first linear inequality.
  - The type of boundary line matches the inequality symbol.
  - The correct region is shaded.
- Graph the second linear inequality.
  - The type of boundary line matches the inequality symbol.
  - The correct region is shaded.
- Identify the overlapping shaded regions. If the shaded regions do not overlap, the system has no solution.
- Check the solutions by testing an ordered pair from each region to see if it does or does not satisfy both inequalities.

PRACTICE

Where skills are taught	Where skills are practiced
1 EXAMPLE	Exs. 1–4
2 EXAMPLE	Exs. 5, 6

Exercise 7: Students extend what they learned in **1** EXAMPLE and **2** EXAMPLE by solving a system of linear inequalities consisting of three inequalities. They graph each inequality and identify the solutions of the system as the overlapping triangular shaded region.

REFLECT

2a. Is $(1, -2)$ a solution of the system $x + y > -4$ and $x + y > -1$? Explain.

No; although $(1, -2)$ is a solution of $x + y > -4$, it is on the boundary line

of $x + y > -1$ and, thus, is not a solution of $x + y > -1$.

2b. Is $(3, 2)$ a solution of the system $-x + 3y \leq 3$ and $-x + 3y \geq -3$? Explain.

Yes; $(3, 2)$ is on the boundary line $-x + 3y = 3$. The inequality symbol is

$\leq$, so points on the boundary line are included in the solution.

2c. Can the solution of a system of inequalities be a line? If so, give an example.

Yes; the system $-x + 3y \leq 3$ and $-x + 3y \geq 3$ has only the boundary

line $-x + 3y = 3$ as its solution.

2d. Does the system $3x - 2y < 4$ and $3x - 2y > 4$ have a solution? Explain.

No; the graphs have only the boundary line $3x - 2y = 4$ in common, but the

boundary line is not part of either graph.

2e. Is it possible for a system of two linear inequalities to have every point in the plane as solutions? Why or why not?

No; each boundary line divides the plane into two half-planes, one of each being

the solution to each inequality. It is not possible for the two solution half-planes

to overlap and completely cover the plane.

PRACTICE

Solve each system of linear inequalities by graphing. Check your answers.

1. $\begin{cases} x + y \leq -2 \\ -x + y > 1 \end{cases}$

2. $\begin{cases} x + 2y \geq 8 \\ x - 2y < -4 \end{cases}$

3. $\begin{cases} y \geq -2 \\ 4x + y \geq 2 \end{cases}$

4. $\begin{cases} x < 1 \\ 2x + y > 1 \end{cases}$

5. $\begin{cases} x - y \leq -3 \\ x - y > 3 \end{cases}$

6. $\begin{cases} 4x + y \geq 4 \\ 4x + y \geq -4 \end{cases}$

7. Graph the system of linear inequalities.

$\begin{cases} x + 4y > -4 \\ x + y \leq 2 \\ x - y \geq 2 \end{cases}$

a. Describe the solutions of the system.

The solutions are all the points in the

overlapping triangular region, including points

on all but the bottom edge of the triangle.

b. Is $(2, 0)$ a solution of the system? Explain your reasoning.

Yes; $(2, 0)$ is a solution because it is at the intersection

of two boundary lines that are both included in the solution.

c. Is $(4, -2)$ a solution of the system? Explain your reasoning.

No; even though $(4, -2)$ is at the intersection of two boundary lines, only one

of those lines is included in the solution.

3-6

FOCUS ON MODELING
Modeling with Linear Systems

Essential question: *How can you use systems of linear equations or inequalities to model and solve contextual problems?*

The following standards are addressed in this lesson. (An asterisk indicates that a standard is also a Modeling standard.) For more detailed information, see the correlation for each section of the lesson.

Number and Quantity: CC.9-12.N.Q.1*, CC.9-12.N.Q.2*

Algebra: CC.9-12.A.CED.2*, CC.9-12.A.CED.3*, CC.9-12.A.REI.6, CC.9-12.A.REI.12

Prerequisites
- Solving Linear Systems by Substitution, Lesson 3-2
- Solving Systems of Linear Inequalities, Lesson 3-5

Math Background
In this lesson, students write and solve a system of linear equations that models purchasing jeans and T-shirts. Students explore ways to represent relationships between quantities of items purchased and purchase costs by writing a system of equations in two variables and graphing those equations. Students reflect upon units associated with the number of items purchased and the cost, and understand which solutions are viable given the context of the situation. Students extend the model for this real-world situation by writing and solving a system of linear inequalities that represents constraints on the number of items purchased and the total amount spent.

INTRODUCE

Ask students to discuss how they would plan a shopping trip when they know how much money they have to spend, the cost for two different items, and the combined number of those two items they want to buy. Explain to students that they will use what they know about systems of linear equations to model a situation in which they have a given amount of money to buy jeans and T-shirts, with the requirement that they purchase a total of 5 items.

TEACH

1 **Write a system of linear equations to model the situation.**

Standards
CC.9-12.N.Q.1 Use units as a way to understand problems and to guide the solution of multi-step problems; choose and interpret units consistently ...*

CC.9-12.N.Q.2 Define appropriate quantities for the purpose of descriptive modeling.*

CC.9-12.A.CED.2 Create equations in two or more variables to represent relationships between quantities ...*

Questioning Strategies
- How would the system of equations be changed if the total amount you plan on spending is increased to $200? **The first equation would be changed to $35x + 15y = 200$.**
- How would the system of equations be changed if the total number of items you plan to purchase is increased to 8? **The second equation would be changed to $x + y = 8$.**

Teaching Strategies
If students have difficulty writing the system of equations to model the situation, have them first use numbers instead of variables to represent the quantities in the problem. Ask questions such as, "What is the total amount spent if you purchase 1 pair of jeans and 4 T-shirts?" and "What is the total number of items if you purchase 1 pair of jeans and 4 T-shirts?"

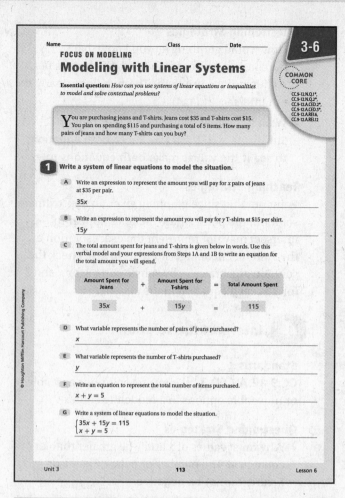

FOCUS ON MODELING

Modeling with Linear Systems

3-6

COMMON CORE

CC-9-12.N.Q.1*,
CC-9-12.N.Q.2*,
CC-9-12.A.CED.2*,
CC-9-12.A.CED.3*,
CC-9-12.A.REI.6,
CC-9-12.A.REI.12

Essential question: *How can you use systems of linear equations or inequalities to model and solve contextual problems?*

You are purchasing jeans and T-shirts. Jeans cost $35 and T-shirts cost $15. You plan on spending $115 and purchasing a total of 5 items. How many pairs of jeans and how many T-shirts can you buy?

1 **Write a system of linear equations to model the situation.**

A Write an expression to represent the amount you will pay for *x* pairs of jeans at $35 per pair.

35x

B Write an expression to represent the amount you will pay for *y* T-shirts at $15 per shirt.

15y

C The total amount spent for jeans and T-shirts is given below in words. Use this verbal model and your expressions from Steps 1A and 1B to write an equation for the total amount you will spend.

Amount Spent for Jeans	+	Amount Spent for T-shirts	=	Total Amount Spent
35x	+	15y	=	115

D What variable represents the number of pairs of jeans purchased?

x

E What variable represents the number of T-shirts purchased?

y

F Write an equation to represent the total number of items purchased.

$x + y = 5$

G Write a system of linear equations to model the situation.

$$\begin{cases} 35x + 15y = 115 \\ x + y = 5 \end{cases}$$

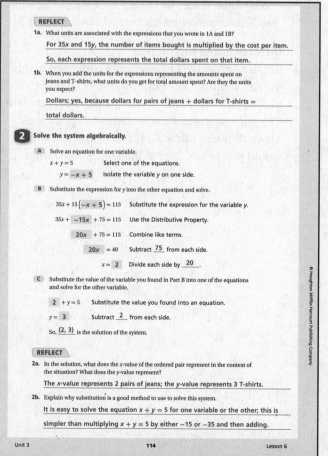

REFLECT

1a. What units are associated with the expressions that you wrote in 1A and 1B?

For 35x and 15y, the number of items bought is multiplied by the cost per item.

So, each expression represents the total dollars spent on that item.

1b. When you add the units for the expressions representing the amounts spent on jeans and T-shirts, what units do you get for total amount spent? Are they the units you expect?

Dollars; yes, because dollars for pairs of jeans + dollars for T-shirts =

total dollars.

2 **Solve the system algebraically.**

A Solve an equation for one variable.

$x + y = 5$ Select one of the equations.

$y = -x + 5$ Isolate the variable *y* on one side.

B Substitute the expression for *y* into the other equation and solve.

$35x + 15(-x + 5) = 115$ Substitute the expression for the variable *y*.

$35x + -15x + 75 = 115$ Use the Distributive Property.

$20x + 75 = 115$ Combine like terms.

$20x = 40$ Subtract 75 from each side.

$x = 2$ Divide each side by 20 .

C Substitute the value of the variable you found in Part B into one of the equations and solve for the other variable.

$2 + y = 5$ Substitute the value you found into an equation.

$y = 3$ Subtract 2 from each side.

So, (2, 3) is the solution of the system.

REFLECT

2a. In the solution, what does the *x*-value of the ordered pair represent in the context of the situation? What does the *y*-value represent?

The *x*-value represents 2 pairs of jeans; the *y*-value represents 3 T-shirts.

2b. Explain why substitution is a good method to use to solve this system.

It is easy to solve the equation $x + y = 5$ for one variable or the other; this is

simpler than multiplying $x + y = 5$ by either -15 or -35 and then adding.

2 Solve the system algebraically.

Standards
CC.9-12.N.Q.2 Define appropriate quantities for the purpose of descriptive modeling.*

CC.9-12.A.REI.6 Solve systems of linear equations exactly ..., focusing on pairs of linear equations in two variables.

Questioning Strategies
- Is it easier to solve the system of equations if you solve for x first instead of y? **No; if you solve for x first, the next step is to substitute $-y + 5$ for x and multiply the expression by 35; it is easier to multiply $-x + 5$ by 15.**

- Why would you solve this system algebraically instead of by graphing? **Graphing may result in an approximation instead of an exact solution because the x- and y-intercepts of $35x + 15y = 115$ are not whole numbers.**

Avoid Common Errors
When substituting an expression containing two terms for a variable that has a coefficient, students often multiply only the first term of the expression by the coefficient, forgetting to multiply the second term as well. Remind students that after substituting $-x + 5$ for y in the equation $35x + 15y = 115$, *both* terms in the expression must be multiplied by 15 when solving the resulting equation for x.

3 Check the solution by graphing.

Standards
CC.9-12.N.Q.1 ... choose and interpret the scale and the origin in graphs and data displays.*

CC.9-12.A.CED.2 ... graph equations on coordinate axes with labels and scales.*

CC.9-12.A.REI.6 Solve systems of linear equations ... approximately (e.g., with graphs), focusing on pairs of linear equations in two variables.

Questioning Strategies
- How would graphing let you know that purchasing 1 pair of jeans and 4 T-shirts is *not* a solution of the problem? **The two lines clearly do not intersect at (1, 4).**

- What is another way to check the solution? **Substitute $x = 2$ and $y = 3$ into both equations to see if the values make both equations true.**

Teaching Strategies
Point out that since graphing gives an approximate solution, the point where the lines appear to intersect may not represent the exact solution of the system. Encourage students to also check the solution algebraically by substituting 2 for x and 3 for y in each equation in the system.

4 Interpret the solution.

Standards
CC.9-12.A.CED.3 ... interpret solutions as viable or nonviable options in a modeling context.*

Questioning Strategies
- Why must values of x and y be greater than or equal to 0? **The number of pairs of jeans or T-shirts cannot be negative.**

- Why must values of x and y be less than or equal to 5? **The combined number of both items is 5.**

Differentiated Instruction
English Language Learners may benefit by acting out the solution. For example, they can draw pictures on the board showing 2 pairs of jeans with $35 price tags and 3 T-shirts with $15 price tags. Then, they can calculate the total amount they would pay to a cashier at the checkout counter.

3 Check the solution by graphing.

A Graph each equation.

Step 1: Find the intercepts for $35x + 15y = 115$ and graph the line.

x-intercept: $3\frac{2}{7}$ y-intercept: $7\frac{2}{3}$

Step 2: Find the intercepts for $x + y = 5$ and graph the line.

x-intercept: 5 y-intercept: 5

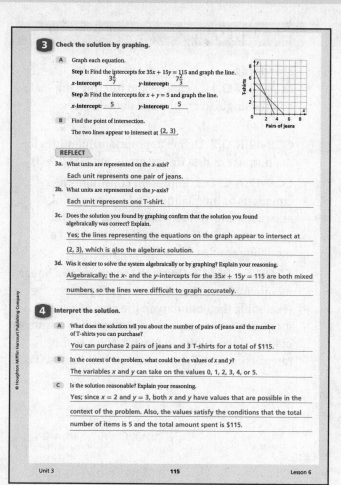

B Find the point of intersection.

The two lines appear to intersect at $(2, 3)$.

REFLECT

3a. What units are represented on the x-axis?

Each unit represents one pair of jeans.

3b. What units are represented on the y-axis?

Each unit represents one T-shirt.

3c. Does the solution you found by graphing confirm that the solution you found algebraically was correct? Explain.

Yes; the lines representing the equations on the graph appear to intersect at

(2, 3), which is also the algebraic solution.

3d. Was it easier to solve the system algebraically or by graphing? Explain your reasoning.

Algebraically; the x- and the y-intercepts for the $35x + 15y = 115$ are both mixed

numbers, so the lines were difficult to graph accurately.

4 Interpret the solution.

A What does the solution tell you about the number of pairs of jeans and the number of T-shirts you can purchase?

You can purchase 2 pairs of jeans and 3 T-shirts for a total of $115.

B In the context of the problem, what could be the values of x and y?

The variables x and y can take on the values 0, 1, 2, 3, 4, or 5.

C Is the solution reasonable? Explain your reasoning.

Yes; since x = 2 and y = 3, both x and y have values that are possible in the

context of the problem. Also, the values satisfy the conditions that the total

number of items is 5 and the total amount spent is $115.

REFLECT

4a. Is the solution you found the only solution for this linear system? Explain how you know.

Yes, (2, 3) is the only solution for the system $35x + 15y = 115$ and $x + y = 5$;

the lines representing each equation intersect at exactly one point.

EXTEND

1. Suppose you want to buy at least 5 items and spend no more than $115. How can you modify the system of linear equations you wrote to model this new situation?

The system of linear equations can be rewritten as a system of linear

inequalities.

2. Write an inequality to represent buying at least 5 items.

$x + y \geq 5$

3. Write an inequality to represent spending no more than $115.

$35x + 15y \leq 115$

4. Are there any other conditions on the system, based on the context of the problem? If so, what are they?

Yes; $x \geq 0$ and $y \geq 0$ because the number of items purchased cannot be

less than 0.

5. Write a system of linear inequalities to model the situation. Include any new conditions from Question 4.

$\begin{cases} x + y \geq 5 \\ 35x + 15y \leq 115 \\ x \geq 0 \\ y \geq 0 \end{cases}$

6. What constraints do the additional conditions based on the context of the problem place on where in the plane the solution region will be located?

The solution region must be located in the first quadrant.

Essential Question

How can you use systems of linear equations or inequalities to model and solve contextual problems? Write expressions to represent the quantities in the problem. Next, write a system of linear equations or inequalities to represent the relationships between those quantities. Then, solve the system and check the solution. Finally, interpret the solution in the context of the real-world situation, making sure that the solution is viable.

Summarize

Have students write a journal entry in which they provide a one-page summary of their findings for modeling the purchase of jeans and T-shirts by writing and solving a system of linear equations.

MATHEMATICAL PRACTICE **Highlighting the Standards**

Students learn to construct algebraic and graphical models of a real-world situation, addressing Mathematical Practice standard 4 (Model with Mathematics). Make sure students understand how an ordered pair in this model represents a number of pairs of jeans and a number of T-shirts. Students can demonstrate their understanding of the model by completing the Extend exercises and showing how the new conditions affect the graphical model. Stress the importance of checking the model with different values, including values on the boundary lines.

Standards

CC.9-12.N.Q.1 ... choose and interpret the scale and the origin in graphs and data displays.* (Exs. 7, 12)

CC.9-12.N.Q.2 Define appropriate quantities for the purpose of descriptive modeling.* (Exs. 1–3)

CC.9-12.A.CED.3 Represent constraints by equations or inequalities, and by systems of equations and/or inequalities, and interpret solutions as viable or nonviable options in a modeling context.* (Exs. 1–6, 8–12)

CC.9-12.A.REI.12 Graph the solutions to a linear inequality in two variables as a half-plane (excluding the boundary in the case of a strict inequality), and graph the solution set to a system of linear inequalities in two variables as the intersection of the corresponding half-planes. (Ex. 7)

7. Graph the system of inequalities.

Step 1 Graph $x + y \geq 5$.

The equation of the boundary line is $\underline{x + y = 5}$.

x-intercept: $\underline{5}$ y-intercept: $\underline{5}$

The inequality symbol is ≥, use a $\underline{\text{solid}}$ line.

Shade $\underline{\text{above}}$ the boundary line, because $(0, 0)$ is *not* a solution of the inequality.

Step 2 Graph $35x + 15y \leq 115$.

The equation of the boundary line is $\underline{35x + 15y = 115}$.

x-intercept: $\underline{3\frac{2}{7}}$ y-intercept: $\underline{7\frac{2}{3}}$

The inequality symbol is ≤, use a $\underline{\text{solid}}$ line.

Shade $\underline{\text{below}}$ the boundary line line, because $(0, 0)$ is a solution of the inequality.

Step 3 Identify the solutions.

The solutions of the system are represented by the $\underline{\text{overlapping}}$ shaded regions that form a $\underline{\text{triangle}}$ to the $\underline{\text{right}}$ of the y-axis.

8. In the context of the situation, are all points in the overlapping shaded region possible solutions? Why or why not? Explain.

No, since jeans and T-shirts cannot be purchased in fractional parts, only ordered pairs of whole numbers are viable solutions.

9. Is the ordered pair that was the solution of the system of linear equations for this situation a solution of this system of inequalities?

Yes, since both boundary lines that intersect at (2, 3) are solid lines, (2, 3) is included in the solutions of the system of inequalities.

10. If you buy at least 5 items and spend no more than $115, what is the greatest number of jeans you can buy? Explain your reasoning.

2; if 3 pairs of jeans are purchased, there will not be enough money left to buy any more items; so, it will not be possible to purchase at least 5 items.

11. If you buy at least 5 items and spend no more than $115, what is the greatest number of T-shirts you can buy? Explain your reasoning.

If you don't buy any jeans, you can buy 7 T-shirts for a total of $105.

Buying 8 T-shirts will cost $120, which is too much.

---

12. Use the graph to make a list of all the possible solutions for the number of pairs of jeans and number of T-shirts you can purchase if you buy at least 5 items and spend no more than $115.

Pairs of Jeans	T-Shirts	Total Items	Total Cost
0	5	5	$75
0	6	6	$90
0	7	7	$105
1	4	5	$95
1	5	6	$110
2	3	5	$115

Standard	Items
CC.9-12.N.Q.1*	10
CC.9-12.A.CED.2*	6
CC.9-12.A.CED.3*	11, 12
CC.9-12.A.REI.5	9
CC.9-12. A.REI.6	1, 2, 3, 4, 7, 8
CC.9-12. A.REI.12	5

TEST PREP DOCTOR ⊕

Multiple Choice: Item 1

- Students who answered **A** or **D** did not correctly evaluate that the ordered pair (1, 3), which is the point of intersection, does not satisfy the second equation of the given system.

- Students who answered **C** did not correctly evaluate that the ordered pair (1, 3) does not satisfy the first equation of the given system.

Multiple Choice: Item 2

- Students who answered **F** or **G** made an error when solving the first equation for x.

- Students who answered **J** used the wrong signs when solving the first equation for y.

Multiple Choice: Item 4

- Students who answered **F** or **G** identified the wrong equation to multiply before adding or subtracting in order to eliminate a variable.

- Students who answered **J** identified the correct equation to be multiplied, but the incorrect constant to multiply by. If the equation is multiplied by -3, y will be eliminated by subtracting, instead of by adding.

Multiple Choice: Item 5

- Students who answered **A** or **B** identified points that are in the overlapping shaded region and are therefore solutions of the system of inequalities.

- Students who answered **D** identified a point that is in the shaded region for one inequality and on a solid boundary of the other inequality, which means it is a solution of the system. Students who made this choice may have been thinking about the situation where a point is at the intersection of a solid boundary line and a dashed one, and is therefore not a solution of the system of inequalities.

Free Response: Item 9

- Students who said that the two systems do not have the same solution either did not understand the proof that, given a system of two equations in two variables, replacing one equation by the sum of that equation and a multiple of the other produces a system with the same solutions, or they did not recognize these two systems as an example of that proof.

Free Response: Item 11

- Students who did not correctly describe the constraint $x + y = 10$ did not understand $x + y$ represents the total number of items purchased.

- Students who did not correctly describe the constraint $\frac{1}{2}x + \frac{1}{4}y = 4$ did not understand how to express the cost of pens and pencils in dollars.

Free Response: Item 12

- Students who did not correctly identify the additional constraints $x \geq 0$ and $y \geq 0$ either did not understand that the number of pens and pencils cannot be negative or they did not remember that this constraint must be included to make sure the solution is viable.

UNIT 3 TEST PREP

Name _____ Class _____ Date _____

MULTIPLE CHOICE

1. Which system of linear equations is represented by the graph shown below?

A. $\begin{cases} x + y = 4 \\ 2x + y = 1 \end{cases}$ C. $\begin{cases} x - y = 4 \\ 2x - y = -1 \end{cases}$

B. $\begin{cases} x + y = 4 \\ 2x - y = -1 \end{cases}$ D. $\begin{cases} x + y = 4 \\ x - 2y = 1 \end{cases}$

2. Katy is solving the linear system below by substitution.

$$\begin{cases} 2x + y = 7 \\ 3x - 2y = -7 \end{cases}$$

Which of the following would be a step in solving the system?

F. Substitute $y + 7$ for x in $3x - 2y = -7$.

G. Substitute $-y + 7$ for x in $3x - 2y = -7$.

H. Substitute $-2x + 7$ for y in $3x - 2y = -7$.

J. Substitute $2x - 7$ for y in $3x - 2y = -7$.

3. Which step can be taken to eliminate a variable from the linear system below?

$$\begin{cases} -4x + 2y = -2 \\ 4x - 3y = -1 \end{cases}$$

A. Add to eliminate the variable x.

B. Subtract to eliminate the variable x.

C. Add to eliminate the variable y.

D. Subtract to eliminate the variable y.

4. Frank wants to eliminate the variable y from the system below by adding.

$$\begin{cases} 7x - 6y = 8 \\ 2x + 2y = 6 \end{cases}$$

First, he will have to multiply one of the equations by a number. Which step will enable him to eliminate y by adding?

F. Multiply each term in $7x - 6y = 8$ by 3.

G. Multiply each term in $7x - 6y = 8$ by −3.

H. Multiply each term in $2x + 2y = 6$ by 3.

J. Multiply each term in $2x + 2y = 6$ by −3.

5. Which ordered pair is *not* a solution of the system of linear inequalities graphed below?

A. $(1, 7)$ C. $(3, 2)$

B. $(2, 5)$ D. $(4, 3)$

6. You are purchasing paint and paintbrushes for an art project. Tubes of paint cost $6 each and paintbrushes cost $8 each. You plan on spending $60 and purchasing a total of 9 items. Which linear system best represents the situation?

F. $\begin{cases} 6x + 8y = 9 \\ x + y = 60 \end{cases}$ H. $\begin{cases} 9x + 9y = 60 \\ 6x + 8y = 60 \end{cases}$

G. $\begin{cases} 6x + 9y = 60 \\ 9x + 8y = 60 \end{cases}$ J. $\begin{cases} x + y = 9 \\ 6x + 8y = 60 \end{cases}$

FREE RESPONSE

7. A system of two linear equations has no solution. Describe the graph of the system.

The lines representing the equations are parallel; there are no points of intersection.

8. Solve the linear system below. Describe the steps you used to solve it.

$$\begin{cases} 2x + 3y = 13 \\ x - 2y = 3 \end{cases}$$

(5, 1); rewrite $x - 2y = 3$ as $x = 2y + 3$, substitute $2y + 3$ for x in the other equation and solve for y, substitute the value you found for y into one of the equations and solve for x.

9. Pilar says that the two linear systems below have the same solution.

$\begin{cases} 3x + 2y = 2 \\ 5x + 4y = 6 \end{cases}$ $\begin{cases} 3x + 2y = 2 \\ 11x + 8y = 10 \end{cases}$

Is she correct? Explain.

Yes, given a system of two equations in two variables, replacing one equation by the sum of that equation and a multiple of the other produces a system with the same solutions; $3x + 2y = 2$ is multiplied by 2 and added to $5x + 4y = 6$ to get $11x + 8y = 10$.

Use the information below to complete Items 10–12.

Terrance purchased a total of 10 pens and pencils for $4. Pens cost 50 cents and pencils cost 25 cents. Terrance wrote the system of equations below to represent the situation.

$$\begin{cases} x + y = 10 \\ \frac{1}{2}x + \frac{1}{4}y = 4 \end{cases}$$

10. What units are associated with the expressions in the second equation?

The number of items is multiplied by the cost in dollars per item; each expression represents the total dollars spent on the item.

11. Describe the constraint that each equation places on the system.

$x + y = 10$ limits the total number of items to 10; $\frac{1}{2}x + \frac{1}{4}y = 4$ limits the total cost of the items to $4.

12. Are there any other constraints on the system? If so, what are they?

Yes; $x \geq 0$ and $y \geq 0$ because the number of pens and pencils purchased cannot be less than 0.

Linear Functions

Unit Vocabulary

constant function	(4-3)
correlation	(4-8)
correlation coefficient	(4-8)
extrapolation	(4-9)
interpolation	(4-9)
inverse of a function	(4-7)
linear function	(4-1)
linear regression	(4-10)
rate of change	(4-3)
residual	(4-9)
residual plot	(4-9)
rise	(4-3)
run	(4-3)
slope	(4-3)

UNIT 4

Linear Functions

Unit Focus

In this unit you will examine the characteristics of linear functions and their graphs. You will learn to write linear functions, perform operations with them, and find their inverses. You will also learn to model paired data using linear functions.

Unit at a Glance

COMMON CORE

Lesson		Standards for Mathematical Content
4-1	Discrete Linear Functions	CC.9-12.F.IF.2, CC.9-12.F.IF.3, CC.9-12.F.IF.5*, CC.9-12.F.IF.7*, CC.9-12.F.IF.7a*, CC.9-12.F.BF.2*
4-2	Continuous Linear Functions	CC.9-12.N.Q.1*, CC.9-12.F.IF.1, CC.9-12.F.IF.2, CC.9-12.F.IF.5*, CC.9-12.F.IF.9
4-3	Using Slope	CC.9-12.N.Q.1*, CC.9-12.A.CED.2*, CC.9-12.F.IF.4*, CC.9-12.F.IF.6*, CC.9-12.F.IF.7*, CC.9-12.F.IF.7a*
4-4	Changing the Values of m and b in $f(x) = mx + b$	CC.9-12.F.IF.4*, CC.9-12.F.BF.3, CC.9-12.F.LE.5*
4-5	Writing Linear Functions	CC.9-12.A.CED.2*, CC.9-12.A.REI.11*, CC.9-12.F.IF.4*, CC.9-12.F.IF.6*, CC.9-12.F.BF.1*, CC.9-12.F.LE.2*
4-6	Operations with Linear Functions	CC.9-12.A.APR.1, CC.9-12.A.CED.2*, CC.9-12.F.BF.1*, CC.9-12.F.BF.1b*, CC.9-12.F.LE.2*, CC.9-12.F.LE.5*
4-7	Linear Functions and Their Inverses	CC.9-12.F.IF.1, CC.9-12.F.IF.2, CC.9-12.F.BF.4, CC.9-12.F.BF.4a
4-8	Correlation	CC.9-12.S.ID.8*, CC.9-12.S.ID.9*, CC.9-12.S.IC.6*
4-9	Fitting Lines to Data	CC.9-12.F.LE.5*, CC.9-12.S.ID.6*, CC.9-12.S.ID.6a*, CC.9-12.S.ID.6b*, CC.9-12.S.ID.6c*, CC.9-12.S.ID.7*
4-10	Linear Regression	CC.9-12.F.LE.5*, CC.9-12.S.ID.6a*, CC.9-12.S.ID.6b*, CC.9-12.S.ID.6c*, CC.9-12.S.ID.7*, CC.9-12.S.ID.8*
	Test Prep	

Unpacking the Common Core State Standards

Use the table to help you understand the Standards for Mathematical Content that are taught in this unit. Refer to the lessons listed after each standard for exploration and practice.

COMMON CORE Standards for Mathematical Content	What It Means For You
CC.9-12.N.Q.1 Use units as a way to understand problems and to guide the solution of multi-step problems; choose and interpret units consistently in formulas; choose and interpret the scale and the origin in graphs and data displays.* Lessons 4-2, 4-3 (Also 4-5, 4-6)	Because linear functions that model real-world situations involve rates of change, it's important that you check the units involved to make sure they are compatible and give the desired units for the models.
CC.9-12.A.APR.1 Understand that polynomials form a system analogous to the integers, namely, they are closed under the operations of addition, subtraction, and multiplication; add, subtract, and multiply polynomials. Lesson 4-6	As you will learn later in the course, the rules for linear functions are polynomials having degree 1. You will learn to combine linear functions by adding and subtracting their rules as well as multiplying their rules by constants.
CC.9-12.A.CED.2 Create equations in two or more variables to represent relationships between quantities; graph equations on coordinate axes with labels and scales.* Lessons 4-2, 4-3, 4-5, 4-6 (Also 4-7)	You will use linear functions to model real-world situations and real-world data, and you will graph the linear models in the coordinate plane.
CC.9-12.A.REI.11 Explain why the x-coordinates of the points where the graphs of the equations $y = f(x)$ and $y = g(x)$ intersect are the solutions of the equation $f(x) = g(x)$; find the solutions approximately, e.g., using technology to graph the functions, make tables of values, or find successive approximations. Include cases where $f(x)$ and/or $g(x)$ are linear, polynomial, rational, absolute value, exponential, and logarithmic functions.* Lesson 4-5	You will solve real-world problems by writing two linear models and determining where their graphs intersect.
CC.9-12.F.IF.1 Understand that a function from one set (called the domain) to another set (called the range) assigns to each element of the domain exactly one element of the range. If f is a function and x is an element of its domain, then $f(x)$ denotes the output of f corresponding to the input x. The graph of f is the graph of the equation $y = f(x)$. Lessons 4-2, 4-7 (Also 4-1)	You will learn how to recognize restrictions on the domains and ranges of linear functions that model real-world situations.

Unpacking the Common Core State Standards

This page lists and explains the Standards for Mathematical Content that are addressed in this unit. For information about the Standards for Mathematical Practice, which are integrated throughout the text, see Teacher Edition pages viii–xi.

Additional Standards in This Unit

CC.9-12.N.Q.2 Define appropriate quantities for the purpose of descriptive modeling.* Lesson 4-5

Notes

_____

_____

_____

_____

_____

_____

_____

_____

_____

_____

COMMON CORE Standards for Mathematical Content	What It Means For You
CC.9-12.F.IF.2 Use function notation, evaluate functions for inputs in their domains, and interpret statements that use function notation in terms of a context. Lessons 4-1, 4-2, 4-7 (Also 4-6)	You will learn to move flexibly between writing an equation in x and y and writing the equation using $f(x)$ in place of y when y is a function of x.
CC.9-12.F.IF.3 Recognize that sequences are functions, sometimes defined recursively, whose domain is a subset of the integers. Lesson 4-1	You will learn that the outputs of a discrete linear function are a sequence of numbers known as an arithmetic sequence for certain domains from the set of integers.
CC.9-12.F.IF.4 For a function that models a relationship between two quantities, interpret key features of graphs and tables in terms of the quantities, and sketch graphs showing key features given a verbal description of the relationship. Key features include: intercepts; intervals where the function is increasing, decreasing, positive, or negative; relative maximums and minimums; symmetries; end behavior; and periodicity.* Lessons 4-3, 4-4, 4-5	You will learn to graph a linear function by recognizing its slope and y-intercept from the function's rule. You will also see that a positive slope means that the function is an increasing function while a negative slope means that the function is a decreasing function.
CC.9-12.F.IF.5 Relate the domain of a function to its graph and, where applicable, to the quantitative relationship it describes.* Lessons 4-1, 4-2 (Also 4-4)	You will learn to distinguish between situations where the graph of a linear function is a set of distinct points that lie on a line and situations where the graph is an unbroken line or part of a line.
CC.9-12.F.IF.6 Calculate and interpret the average rate of change of a function (presented symbolically or as a table) over a specified interval. Estimate the rate of change from a graph.* Lessons 4-3, 4-5	You will learn that the rate of change of a linear function is constant and that it tells you the slope of the function's graph. Being able to calculate or estimate the rate of change is particularly useful when modeling real-world situations or real-world data.
CC.9-12.F.IF.7 Graph functions expressed symbolically and show key features of the graph, by hand in simple cases and using technology for more complicated cases.* **CC.9-12.F.IF.7a** Graph linear and quadratic functions and show intercepts, maxima, and minima.* Lessons 4-1, 4-2, 4-3, 4-5 (Also 4-7, 4-10)	You will learn to graph linear functions using slopes and y-intercepts.
CC.9-12.F.IF.9 Compare properties of two functions each represented in a different way (algebraically, graphically, numerically in tables, or by verbal descriptions). Lesson 4-2	Functions can be represented in several ways, including input-output tables, graphs, algebraic rules, and verbal descriptions. In order to compare two functions represented in different ways, you need to be able to convert them to a common representation.

© Houghton Mifflin Harcourt Publishing Company

UNIT 4

Notes

UNIT 4

COMMON CORE Standards for Mathematical Content	What It Means For You
CC.9-12.F.BF.1 Write a function that describes a relationship between two quantities.* **CC.9-12.F.BF.1a Determine an explicit expression, a recursive process, or steps for calculation from a context.*** **CC.9-12.F.BF.1b Combine standard function types using arithmetic operations.*** Lessons 4-5, 4-6, 4-9 (Also 4-7)	Given a graph of a linear function, a table of function values, or a verbal description of a linear relationship, you will learn to write a function rule. You will also be able to combine function rules to create new linear functions.
CC.9-12.F.BF.2 Write arithmetic and geometric sequences both recursively and with an explicit formula, use them to model situations, and translate between the two forms.* Lesson 4-1	You will analyze discrete linear functions, also known as arithmetic sequences, that model real-world situations.
CC.9-12.F.BF.3 Identify the effect on the graph of replacing $f(x)$ by $f(x) + k$, $k\,f(x)$, $f(kx)$, and $f(x + k)$ for specific values of k (both positive and negative); find the value of k given the graphs. Experiment with cases and illustrate an explanation of the effects on the graphs using technology. Lesson 4-4	You will investigate what happens to the graph of a linear function in the form $f(x) = mx + b$ when you change the values of m and b.
CC.9-12.F.BF.4 Find inverse functions. **CC.9-12.F.BF.4a Solve an equation of the form $f(x) = c$ for a simple function f that has an inverse and write an expression for the inverse.** Lesson 4-7	You will learn to find the inverse of a linear function, and you will see that the inverse undoes, in the reverse order, the operations that the function performs on inputs to obtain outputs.
CC.9-12.F.LE.2 Construct linear and exponential functions, including arithmetic and geometric sequences, given a graph, a description of a relationship, or two input-output pairs (include reading these from a table).* Lessons 4-5, 4-6	You will write the rule for a linear function when given a graph, table, or verbal description. This is particularly useful when you fit a line to data and want to know the equation of the line.
CC.9-12.F.LE.5 Interpret the parameters in a linear or exponential function in terms of a context.* Lessons 4-4, 4-5, 4-6, 4-9, 4-10	A linear function has the form $f(x) = mx + b$ where the parameter m is the slope of the function's graph and the parameter b is the y-intercept of the graph. You will learn to recognize the real-world meaning of these parameters when working with linear models.

Notes

_____

_____

_____

_____

_____

_____

_____

_____

_____

_____

COMMON CORE Standards for Mathematical Content	What It Means For You
CC.9-12.S.ID.6 **Represent data on two quantitative variables on a scatter plot, and describe how the variables are related.** CC.9-12.S.ID.6a **Fit a function to the data; use functions fitted to data to solve problems in the context of the data.*** CC.9-12.S.ID.6b **Informally assess the fit of a function by plotting and analyzing residuals.*** CC.9-12.S.ID.6c **Fit a linear function for a scatter plot that suggests a linear association.*** Lessons 4-9, 4-10	You will learn to model real-world data using linear functions. The models will allow you to make predictions, and the goodness of fit will, to some degree, determine the accuracy of your predictions.
CC.9-12.S.ID.7 **Interpret the slope (rate of change) and the intercept (constant term) of a linear model in the context of the data.*** Lessons 4-9, 4-10	Once you have a linear model for a set of data, you should be able to recognize what the model is telling you about the data.
CC.9-12.S.ID.8 **Compute (using technology) and interpret the correlation coefficient of a linear fit.*** Lessons 4-8, 4-10	The correlation coefficient is a measure of the strength of a linear relationship between two variables. It helps you decide whether it makes sense to model data using a linear function.
CC.9-12.S.ID.9 **Distinguish between correlation and causation.*** Lesson 4-8	Just because two real-world variables have a strong correlation does not mean that a change in one variable causes a change in the other variable. You must be cautious when moving from correlation to causation.
CC.9-12.S.IC.6 **Evaluate reports based on data.*** Lesson 4-8	You will decide whether two sets of data show correlation, causation, or neither.

Notes

_____

_____

_____

_____

_____

_____

_____

_____

_____

Notes

_____

_____

_____

_____

_____

_____

_____

_____

_____

_____

_____

_____

_____

_____

_____

_____

_____

_____

_____

_____

_____

_____

_____

_____

Discrete Linear Functions

Essential question: *What are the characteristics of a discrete linear function?*

COMMON CORE Standards for Mathematical Content

CC.9-12.F.IF.2 Use function notation, evaluate functions for inputs in their domains, and interpret statements that use function notation in terms of a context.

CC.9-12.F.IF.3 Recognize that sequences are functions, sometimes defined recursively, whose domain is a subset of the integers.

CC.9-12.F.IF.5 Relate the domain of a function to its graph and, where applicable, to the quantitative relationship it describes.*

CC.9-12.F.IF.7 Graph functions expressed symbolically and show key features of the graph, by hand in simple cases and using technology for more complicated cases.*

CC.9-12.F.IF.7a Graph linear ... functions and show intercepts ...*

CC.9-12.F.BF.2 Write arithmetic ... sequences with an explicit formula, use them to model situations, ...*

Also: CC.9-12.F.IF.1

Vocabulary
linear function

Prerequisites
Functions, Lesson 1-5

Math Background
In this lesson, students will examine linear functions for which the domain is a subset of the set of integers. Their graphs consist of isolated points that lie along a line. Such functions are called *discrete*, and their output values form *arithmetic sequences*. (Students will learn much more about arithmetic sequences in Algebra 2.)

INTRODUCE

Ask students to suppose they are buying music CDs for $10 each. Ask them to calculate and describe the pattern in the costs for 1, 2, 3, 4, 5, and 6 CDs.

TEACH

1 EXPLORE

Questioning Strategies
- What would be the function relating the cost of operating the printer if each cartridge cost $20? $f(x) = 20n + 80$, where n is the number of cartridges

2 ENGAGE

Questioning Strategies
- What is another name for the value of b in the graph of a linear function? the y-intercept

CLOSE

Essential Question
What are the characteristics of a discrete linear function?
A discrete linear function is of the form $f(x) = mx + b$, and its graph consists of isolated points.

Summarize
Have students summarize how to analyze a discrete real-world function in terms of its domain, range, and graph.

PRACTICE

Where skills are taught	Where skills are practiced
1 EXPLORE	EXS. 1a–d
2 ENGAGE	EX. 1e

Name_____ Class_____ Date_____

4-1

Discrete Linear Functions

Essential question: *What are the characteristics of a discrete linear function?*

COMMON
CORE

CC-9-12.F.IF.2,
CC-9-12.F.IF.3,
CC-9-12.F.IF.5*,
CC-9-12.F.IF.7*,
CC-9-12.F.IF.7a*,
CC-9-12.F.BF.2*

1 EXPLORE Analyzing a Discrete Real-World Function

You buy a printer for $80 and then pay $15 for each ink cartridge that you use. A function relating the cost, C (in dollars), of operating the printer to the number of cartridges used, n, is $C(n) = 15n + 80$.

A Complete the table to represent the total cost for 0 to 4 cartridges.

Number of cartridges, n	Cost, C (dollars)
0	80
1	95
2	110
3	125
4	140

B Graph the function from Part A. Specify the scale you use.

C What is the initial value of the cost function? What does it represent? What number of cartridges corresponds to the initial cost?

$80; the cost of the printer by itself; 0 cartridges

D Compare the differences in cost with each unit increase in the number of cartridges purchased.

The differences in cost are always $15 per unit increase in the number of cartridges purchased, or the cost per cartridge.

REFLECT

1a. Identify the domain and range for the function $C(n)$ using set notation.

Domain: {0, 1, 2, 3, 4, ...}   Range: {80, 95, 110, 125, 140, ...}

1b. Describe the pattern formed by the points in the graph.

The points lie along a straight line that slants up from left to right.

1c. How do your answers change if the price of the printer is $90?

The initial value becomes $90. The difference per unit increase remains $15. The domain stays the same. The range becomes {90, 105, 120, 135, 150,...}. The points still lie along a line slanting up from left to right.

Unit 4   127   Lesson 1

---

2 ENGAGE Recognizing Linear Functions

A function whose output values have a *common difference* for each unit increase in the input values is a *linear function*. A **linear function** can be represented by the equation $f(x) = mx + b$, where m and b are constants. The graph of a linear function forms a straight line.

When a linear function is *discrete*, its graph consists of isolated points along a straight line. If a discrete linear function has inputs that are a set of equally spaced integers, then its outputs are a sequence of numbers called an *arithmetic sequence*.

REFLECT

2a. Give three reasons why the cost function in the Explore is linear.

There is a common difference of $15 per unit increase in the input. The function has the form $f(x) = mx + b$. The graph is a series of points that lie along a line.

2b. What are m and b and what do they represent for the cost function?

$m = $15 per cartridge; $b = $80, or the initial cost of the printer when $n = 0$

PRACTICE

1. Andrea receives a $40 gift card to use a town pool. It costs her $8 per visit to swim. A function relating the value of the gift card, v, to the number of visits, n, is $v(n) = 40 - 8n$.

a. Graph the function. Label axes and scales.

b. What is the initial value?

$40

c. What is the difference between a given card value and the previous card value?

−8 dollars per visit

d. Identify the domain and the range of the function using set notation.

Domain: {0, 1, 2, 3, 4, 5}; Range: {0, 8, 16, 24, 32, 40}

e. Is the function a discrete linear function? Are its outputs an arithmetic sequence? Why or why not?

Yes, because it can be written in the form of a linear function [$v(n) = -8n + 40$] and the graph consists of individual points that lie along a line; Yes, because the function is discrete and linear and the outputs correspond to evenly spaced input values from the set of integers.

Unit 4   128   Lesson 1

Continuous Linear Functions

Essential question: *How are discrete and continuous linear functions alike, and how are they different?*

COMMON **Standards for**
CORE **Mathematical Content**

CC.9-12.N.Q.1 Use units as a way to understand problems and to guide the solution of multi-step problems; ... choose and interpret the scale and the origin in graphs and data displays.*

CC.9-12.F.IF.1 Understand that a function from one set (called the domain) to another set (called the range) assigns to each element of the domain exactly one element of the range. If f is a function and x is an element of its domain, then $f(x)$ denotes the output of f corresponding to the input x. The graph of f is the graph of the equation $y = f(x)$.

CC.9-12.F.IF.2 Use function notation, evaluate functions for inputs in their domains, and interpret statements that use function notation in terms of a context.

CC.9-12.F.IF.5 Relate the domain of a function to its graph and, where applicable, to the quantitative relationship it describes.*

CC.9-12.F.IF.9 Compare properties of two functions each represented in a different way (algebraically, graphically, numerically in tables, or by verbal descriptions).

Prerequisites

Writing functions, Lesson 1-5

Discrete linear functions, Lesson 4-1

Math Background

If $f(x)$ is a discrete linear function and $g(x)$ is a continuous linear function, then you can compare them to see how they are alike and how they are different. The domain of the discrete linear function is a subset of the set of integers, while the domain of the continuous linear function is the set of real numbers or an interval of real numbers. The graph of the discrete linear function consists of isolated points, while the graph of the continuous linear function is an unbroken line or a part of a line.

INTRODUCE

Ask students to identify the domain and range of {(11, 5), (−4, 2), (1, 3)}. **domain: {−4, 1, 11}; range: {2, 3, 5}** Then have them graph the points. Do the points lie in a line? **yes** Ask them if they should connect the points with a line. **no**

TEACH

1 EXPLORE

Questioning Strategies

• What does the term "a reasonable domain" mean? **the set of numbers that make sense for a given situation**

• Why is the graph of $C(g)$ continuous? **You can buy any fraction of a pound of green beans, so the domain of $C(g)$ is the set of all real numbers greater than or equal to 0. Since every nonnegative number is in the domain, the points of the graph are connected.**

Differentiated Instruction

Some students may confuse the meaning of "discrete" with the meaning of "discreet." Point out that "discreet" means careful, while "discrete" means "separate."

Name_____ Class_____ Date_____

4-2

COMMON CORE
CC-9-12.N.Q.1*,
CC-9-12.F.IF.1,
CC-9-12.F.IF.2,
CC-9-12.F.IF.5*,
CC-9-12.F.IF.9

Continuous Linear Functions

Essential question: *How are discrete and continuous linear functions alike, and how are they different?*

1 EXPLORE   Comparing Linear Functions

A   Avocados cost $1.50 each. Green beans cost $1.50 per pound. The total cost of *a* avocados is $C(a) = 1.5a$ and the total cost of *g* pounds of green beans is $C(g) = 1.5g$. Complete the tables to find a few values.

Cost of Avocados		
a	C(a) = 1.5a	(a, C(a))
0	0	(0, 0)
1	1.50	(1, 1.5)
2	3.00	(2, 3)
3	4.50	(3, 4.5)

Cost of Green Beans		
g	C(g) = 1.5g	(g, C(g))
0	0	(0, 0)
1	1.50	(1, 1.5)
2	3.00	(2, 3)
3	4.50	(3, 4.5)

B   What is a reasonable domain for $C(a)$? for $C(g)$? Explain.

$C(a)$ domain: the set of whole numbers. You can't buy part of an avocado;

$C(g)$ domain: the set of real numbers $g \geq 0$. You can buy any fraction of a pound of green beans.

C   Graph the two cost functions for all appropriate domain values from the given scales below.

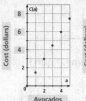
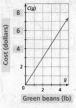

D   Compare the graphs. How are they alike? How are they different?

Sample answer: Both vertical axes represent cost in dollars, but the horizontal axis

for C(a) represents numbers of avocados and for C(g) represents weights of green

beans. The graph of C(a) is a set of isolated points, whereas the points are

connected on the graph of C(g).

REFLECT

1a.   Describe the range for $C(a)$ and for $C(g)$.

The range for C(a) is the set {0, 1.5, 3, 4.5, ...} The range for C(g) is all real numbers

greater than or equal to 0.

1b.   How do the units of *a* and *g* imply that their graphs will be different?

The units for *a*, number of avocados, imply that the domain is whole numbers

so fractional inputs do not make sense. The units for *g*, pounds, imply that the

domain is nonnegative real numbers so there are no gaps between input values.

1c.   A function whose graph is unbroken is a *continuous* function. Tell which cost function is *continuous* and which is *discrete*.

C(a) is a discrete function. C(g) is a continuous function.

2 EXAMPLE   Comparing Functions Given a Table and a Rule

The functions $f(x)$ and $g(x)$ below are linear. Find the initial value and the range of each function. Then compare the functions.

- The table gives the values of the function $f(x)$. The domain of $f(x)$ is {4, 5, 6, 7}.
- Let the domain of the function $g(x) = 2x + 3$ be all real numbers such that $4 \leq x \leq 7$.

x	f(x)
4	8
5	10
6	12
7	14

A   The initial value is the output that is paired with the least input.

The initial value of $f(x)$ is $f(\underline{4}) = \underline{8}$.

The initial value of $g(x)$ is $g(\underline{4}) = \underline{11}$.

B   The range of $f(x)$ is $\underline{\{8, 10, 12, 14\}}$.

Because $g(x)$ is a continuous linear function the range is

$g(4) \leq g(x) \leq g(7)$, or $\{g(x) \mid \underline{11} \leq g(x) \leq \underline{17}\}$.

C   How are the functions alike? How are they different? Consider their domains, initial values, and ranges.

Sample answer: Both functions are defined over a domain from 4 to 7, but the

domain of f(x) consists of whole numbers while the domain of g(x) consists of

real numbers. The initial value occurs at the same input, 4, for both functions, but

the initial value for g(x), 11, is greater than the initial value for f(x), 8. The range

of f(x) is even whole numbers from 8 to 14, whereas the range of g(x) is real

numbers from 11 to 17.

Questioning Strategies
- How do the domain and range of each function help you determine whether the function is discrete or continuous? **The domain and range of $f(x)$ contain only four values, so it is discrete. The domain and range of $g(x)$ contains an infinite number of values, so it is continuous.**

EXTRA EXAMPLE
The functions below are linear. Find the initial value and the range of each function. Then compare the functions.

x	$f(x)$
3	6
4	9
5	12
6	15

$g(x) = 3x - 1$
for $3 \leq x \leq 6$

Initial value: for $f(x) = 6$; for $g(x) = 8$
Range: for $f(x)$ is {6, 9, 12, 15}; for $g(x)$ is $8 \leq g(x) \leq 17$

Possible answer: Both functions are defined over a domain from 3 to 6, but the domain of $f(x)$ consists of whole numbers, while the domain of $g(x)$ consists of all real numbers. The initial value for $g(x)$ is greater than the initial value for $f(x)$. The range of $f(x)$ is four whole numbers: the range of $g(x)$, real numbers from 8 to 17.

3 **EXAMPLE**

Questioning Strategies
- Why is the graph of the violent storm a segment and not a line or a ray? **The storm has a beginning point ($t = 0$) and an ending point ($t = 2$), so its graph must be a segment to reflect this situation.**

⟂ **MATHEMATICAL PRACTICE** **Highlighting the Standards**

3 EXAMPLE addresses Mathematical Practice Standard 2 (Reason abstractly and quantitatively) because the description of the heavy storm is not accompanied by a graph. Comparing the heavy storm to the graph of the violent storm will help students visualize how to represent the heavy storm graphically.

EXTRA EXAMPLE
Compare the following functions.
- Hannah walked 3.5 hours at an average rate of 3 miles per hour. The function $d_h(t)$ represents the distance Hannah walked in t hours.
- The graph below shows the distance Penelope walked, $d_p(t)$ (in miles), as a function of time t (in hours).

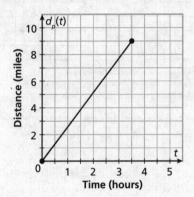

Hannah walked 10.5 miles in 3.5 hours, while Penelope walked 9 miles in 3.5 hours. Hannah walked at a faster speed, and she walked 1.5 miles farther than Penelope.

CLOSE

Essential Question
How are discrete and continuous linear functions alike, and how are they different?
They are alike because the points on their graphs lie on a line. They differ because the graph of a discrete function consists of isolated points, while the graph of a continuous function is an unbroken line or part of a line.

Summarize
Have students write a journal entry about the similarities and differences between discrete and continuous functions.

PRACTICE

Where skills are taught	Where skills are practiced
1 EXPLORE	EX. 1
2 EXAMPLE	EX. 1
3 EXAMPLE	EX. 2

REFLECT

2a. Find and compare the common differences per unit increase in the input values for the functions $f(x)$ and $g(x)$ in the Example.

The common difference for $f(x)$ is $10 - 8 = 2$. The common difference for $g(x)$ is

$g(5) - g(4) = 13 - 11 = 2$. Both functions have a common difference of 2.

2b. How can you tell that $f(x)$ and $g(x)$ in the Example are linear?

$f(x)$: the output values have a common difference per unit increase in the input

values: $10 - 8 = 12 - 10 = 14 - 12 = 2$. $g(x)$: its form is $g(x) = mx + b$, where
$m = 2$ and $b = 3$.

3 EXAMPLE   Comparing Descriptions and Graphs of Functions

Compare the following functions.

- A heavy rainstorm lasted for 2.5 hours during which time it rained at a steady rate of 0.5 inches per hour. The function $A_h(t)$ represents the amount of rain that fell in t hours.
- The graph at the right shows the amount of rain that fell during a violent rainstorm $A_v(t)$ (in inches) as a function of time t (in hours).

A How long did each storm last? Explain your reasoning.

The heavy storm lasted 2.5 hours, as stated. The

violent storm lasted 2 hours, as shown on the graph.

B Calculate the amount of rainfall during the heavy storm. Then compare the amounts of rainfall for the two storms.

Heavy rainfall: (__0.5__ inches per hour) · (__2.5__ hours) = __1.25__ inches of rain

The graph shows that the violent storm produced 5 inches of rain, which was

more than the 1.25 inches of rain from the heavy storm.

C Calculate how many inches of rain fell per hour during the violent rainstorm. Then compare the rainfall rates for the two storms.

Violent rainfall rate: (__5__ inches) ÷ (__2__ hours) = __2.5__ inches per hour

$2.5 - 0.5 = 2$, so 2 more inches of rain fell per hour during the violent rain storm.

REFLECT

3a. How would the graphs of $A_h(t)$ and $A_v(t)$ compare with one another?

The graph of $A_h(t)$ would be a segment from (0, 0) to (2.5, 1.25) rather than

from (0, 0) to (2, 5).

PRACTICE

1. The functions $f(x)$ and $g(x)$ are defined by the table and graph below.

x	f(x)
0	−2
1	1
2	4
3	7
4	10
5	13

a. Compare the domains, initial values, and ranges of the functions.

The domain of $f(x)$ is the set of whole numbers from 0 to 5. The domain of $g(x)$

is the set of real numbers from 0 to 5. The initial values are both −2. The range

of $f(x)$ is $\{-2, 1, 4, 7, 10, 13\}$. The range of $g(x)$ is $\{g(x) \mid -2 \le g(x) \le 18\}$.

b. Explain why the functions are linear. Tell whether each function is *discrete* or *continuous*

Sample answer: $f(x)$ is linear because there is a common difference of 3 per unit

increase in x. $g(x)$ is linear because its graph is a line. $f(x)$ is discrete because its

graph would consist of isolated points. $g(x)$ is continuous because its graph is

unbroken over its domain.

2. Grace works between 10 and 20 hours per week while attending college. She earns $9.00 per hour. Her hours are rounded to the nearest quarter hour. Her roommate Frances also has a job. Her pay for t hours is given by the function $f(t) = 10t$, where $5 \le t \le 15$. Her hours are not rounded.

a. Find the domain and range of each function.

Domain for Grace: $\{10, 10.25, 10.5, 10.75, 11, \ldots, 20\}$; Range for Grace:

$\{90, 92.25, 94.50, 96.75, 99, \ldots, 180\}$; Domain for Frances: $\{t \mid 5 \le t \le 15\}$;

Range for Frances: $\{f(t) \mid 50 \le f(t) \le 150\}$.

b. Compare their hourly wages and the amount they each earn per week.

Grace earns $9 per hour and from $90 to $180 per week. Frances earns $10 per

hour and from $50 to $150 per week.

Using Slope

Essential question: *What is the slope of a linear function and how can you use it to graph the function?*

Standards for Mathematical Content

CC.9-12.N.Q.1 Use units as a way to understand problems; ... choose and interpret the scale and the origin in graphs and data displays.*

CC.9-12.A.CED.2 Create equations in two ... variables to represent relationships between quantities; graph equations on coordinate axes with labels and scales.*

CC.9-12.F.IF.4 For a function that models a relationship between two quantities, interpret key features of graphs and tables in terms of the quantities, and sketch graphs showing key features given a verbal description of the relationship.*

CC.9-12.F.IF.6 Calculate and interpret the average rate of change of a function (presented symbolically or as a table) over a specified interval. Estimate the rate of change from a graph.*

CC.9-12.F.IF.7 Graph functions expressed symbolically and show key features of the graph ...*

CC.9-12.F.IF.7a Graph linear ... functions and show intercepts ...*

Vocabulary

rate of change

rise

run

slope

constant function

Prerequisites

Continuous linear functions, Lesson 4-2

Math Background

Given a linear function $f(x) = mx + b$, the graph of $f(x)$ is a line, the slope of $f(x)$ is the value of m, and the y-intercept of the graph of $f(x)$ is the value of b. If two points of a line have coordinates $(x_1, f(x_1))$ and $(x_2, f(x_2))$, then the slope of the line is equal to the ratio of the change in the function values, $f(x_2) - f(x_1)$, to the change in the x-values, $x_2 - x_1$. The slope may be expressed as

$$m = \frac{\text{rise}}{\text{run}} = \frac{f(x_2) - f(x_1)}{x_2 - x_1} = \frac{\text{change in } f(x)}{\text{change in } x}.$$

The value of m can be positive, negative, or 0. If $m = 0$, then $f(x)$ is a constant function. If the slope of a line is undefined, then the graph is not the graph of a function, but rather a vertical line. You can graph $f(x) = mx + b$ using only the slope m and the y-intercept b. First, locate the point $(0, b)$ on the y-axis. Next, use the rise and run of the slope to locate another point on the line. Draw the line through the two points.

INTRODUCE

Remind students that they graphed continuous linear functions in Lesson 4-2. In that lesson, students restricted the domain to one that was appropriate for the situation, and the range consisted of the output values for the given domain. Students also found the initial value of the linear function, or the range value that was paired with the least input value.

TEACH

Questioning Strategies

- What is true about the ratio of the change in $f(x)$ and the change in x over the three intervals listed in the table? The ratio is the same for each interval.

continued

Name_____ Class_____ Date_____

Using Slope

**COMMON
CORE**

CC-9-12.N.Q.1*,
CC-9-12.A.CED.2*,
CC-9-12.F.IF.4*,
CC-9-12.F.IF.6*,
CC-9-12.F.IF.7*,
CC-9-12.F.IF.7a*

Essential question: *What is the slope of a linear function and how can you use it to graph the function?*

If $f(x)$ is a linear function, then its graph is a line. The ordered pairs $(x_1, f(x_1))$ and $(x_2, f(x_2))$ can be used to name two points on the line. The change in the independent variables between these points is $x_2 - x_1$. The change in the dependent variables is $f(x_2) - f(x_1)$.

1 EXPLORE   Changes in Independent and Dependent Variables

A Use the function $f(x) = 2x + 1$ to complete the table for each interval.

Interval	From $x = 1$ to $x = 2$	From $x = 1$ to $x = 3$	From $x = 1$ to $x = 4$
Change in x, the independent variable	$2 - 1 = 1$	$3 - 1 = 2$	$4 - 1 = 3$
Change in $f(x)$, the dependent variable	$f(2) - f(1) = 5 - 3 = 2$	$f(3) - f(1) = 7 - 3 = 4$	$f(4) - f(1) = 9 - 3 = 6$
$\dfrac{\text{Change in } f(x)}{\text{Change in } x}$	$\dfrac{2}{1} = 2$	$\dfrac{4}{2} = 2$	$\dfrac{6}{3} = 2$

B The ratio $\dfrac{f(x_2) - f(x_1)}{x_2 - x_1}$ over each interval simplifies to ___2___.

REFLECT

1a. What is the relationship between the ratio of $f(x_2) - f(x_1)$ to $x_2 - x_1$ and the function rule?

The ratio of $f(x_2) - f(x_1)$ to $x_2 - x_1$ is the coefficient of x in the function rule.

1b. Is the ratio of $f(x_2) - f(x_1)$ to $x_2 - x_1$ the same over the interval from $x = 2$ to $x = 4$? Explain.

Yes; $\dfrac{f(4) - f(2)}{4 - 2} = \dfrac{9 - 5}{2} = \dfrac{4}{2} = 2$

1c. Suppose the function rule was $f(x) = 2x + 5$ instead of $f(x) = 2x + 1$. Would the ratio of $f(x_2) - f(x_1)$ to $x_2 - x_1$ remain the same? Explain.

Yes; $x_2 - x_1$ would be the same for each ratio. $f(x_2)$ and $f(x_1)$ would each increase by 4, but their difference $f(x_2) - f(x_1)$ would remain the same because the 4's would subtract out. Therefore, the ratio of $f(x_2) - f(x_1)$ to $x_2 - x_1$ would still be 2.

© Houghton Mifflin Harcourt Publishing Company

2 ENGAGE   Understanding Slope of a Linear Function

The ratio of $f(x_2) - f(x_1)$ to $x_2 - x_1$ for a linear function $f(x)$ is the **rate of change** of $f(x)$ with respect to x. The rate of change is the same for any two points on the graph of a given linear function.

You can interpret the rate of change of a linear function $f(x)$ geometrically as the *slope* of its graph. The diagram at the right shows the graph of $f(x)$, where the vertical axis represents the function values. The **rise** is the change in function values, $f(x_2) - f(x_1)$, and the **run** is the change in x-values, $x_2 - x_1$. The **slope** of the line is the ratio of the rise to the run.

Several ways of expressing the slope of a line are given below.

$$\text{slope} = \frac{\text{rise}}{\text{run}} = \frac{f(x_2) - f(x_1)}{x_2 - x_1} = \frac{\text{change in } f(x)}{\text{change in } x}$$

REFLECT

2a. Complete the following to show that the y-intercept of the graph of a linear function $f(x)$ is the value of b in the equation $f(x) = mx + b$.

The y-intercept of the graph of an equation occurs where $x = 0$.

So, the y-intercept of the graph of $f(x) = mx + b$ is as follows.

$$f(0) = m \cdot \boxed{0} + b$$

$$f(0) = \boxed{0} + b$$

$$f(0) = b$$

2b. Complete the following to show that the slope of the graph of a linear function $f(x)$ is the value of m in the equation $f(x) = mx + b$.

To find the slope of the graph of $f(x) = mx + b$, choose any two points on the line. Two convenient points are $(x_1, f(x_1)) = (0, b)$ and $(x_2, f(x_2)) = (1, m + b)$.

$$\frac{f(x_2) - f(x_1)}{x_2 - x_1} = \frac{\boxed{m + b} - \boxed{b}}{\boxed{1} - \boxed{0}} = \frac{\boxed{m}}{\boxed{1}} = m$$

2c. Show that the y-intercept of the graph of the function $f(x) = 4x + 1$ is 1 and that the rate of change of $f(x)$ with respect to x is 4.

Sample answer: $f(0) = 4(0) + 1 = 0 + 1 = 1$; two points on the graph are (0, 1) and (2, 9). The rate of change is $\dfrac{\text{change in } f(x)}{\text{change in } x} = \dfrac{9 - 1}{2 - 0} = \dfrac{8}{2} = 4$

© Houghton Mifflin Harcourt Publishing Company

Questioning Strategies

- Suppose the function rule was $f(x) = 3x + 1$ instead of $f(x) = 2x + 1$. Would the ratio of $f(x_2) - f(x_1)$ to $x_2 - x_1$ still be 2? Explain. No; the ratio of $f(x_2) - f(x_1)$ to $x_2 - x_1$ represents the coefficient of x, so the new ratio would be 3.

Differentiated Instruction

Visual learners may benefit from expanding the middle row of the table in part A to include the intermediate steps needed to find the change in the dependent variable. For example, use $f(2) - f(1) = (2(2) + 1) - (2(1) + 1) = 5 - 3 = 2$ for the interval from $x = 1$ to $x = 2$, $f(3) - f(1) = (2(3) + 1) - (2(1) + 1) = 7 - 3 = 4$ for the interval from $x = 1$ to $x = 3$, and $f(4) - f(1) = (2(4) + 1) - (2(1) + 1) = 9 - 3 = 6$ for the interval from $x = 1$ to $x = 4$.

2 ENGAGE

Questioning Strategies

- For Reflect Question 2b, why is $f(x_2) = m + b$? If $x_2 = 1$, $f(x_2) = f(1) = m(1) + b = m + b$.

- What would be the rate of change for the linear function $f(x) = 5x - 4$? 5

- Would the rate of change be different if the function in Reflect Question 2c were $f(x) = 4x - 2$? No; it would still be 4.

Teaching Strategy

Help students read the rise and the run of the diagram for **2** ENGAGE correctly. Use the analogy of running up the stairs. The rise is analogous to the stair going or rising up and matches the up arrow. The run is analogous to the part of the stair you would step on if you were running up the stairs and matches the right arrow.

---

2 ENGAGE addresses Mathematical Practice Standard 2 (Reason abstractly and quantitatively). Draw students' attention to the use of function notation to represent the change in the output values. Specifically, ask students why the change in input values is called the "run", and why the change in the output values is called the "rise".

3 ENGAGE

Questioning Strategies

- For a nonvertical line, what is true about the run as you move from left to right? The run is always positive.

- Would the graph of the linear function $f(x) = 3x - 2$ rise or fall as the run moves from left to right? rise

- What is an equation of the graph with an undefined slope? $x = a$

Avoid Common Errors

If students have difficulty remembering which kind of line has undefined slope, tell them that U and V "go together", both in the order of the alphabet and in relating the Undefined slope to a Vertical line: Undefined ⟺ Vertical.

4 EXAMPLE

Questioning Strategies

- Does the line in the graph for part A have positive or negative slope? negative

- Does the line in the graph for part A rise or fall as the run moves from left to right? fall

- Why does the graph in part B have a y-intercept of 1? The pitcher starts out containing 1 cup of juice.

continued

3 ENGAGE   Classifying Slopes of Lines

The slope of a line, can be positive, negative, 0, or undefined. If the slope is undefined, the line is not the graph of a function.

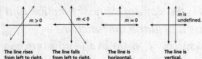

$m > 0$	$m < 0$	$m = 0$	m is undefined.
The line rises from left to right.	The line falls from left to right.	The line is horizontal.	The line is vertical.

REFLECT

3a. When you move from left to right between two points on a line with a positive slope, is the rise *positive*, *negative*, or 0? Is the run *positive*, *negative*, or 0? Use your answers to explain why the slope of a line that rises from left to right is positive.

The rise is positive and the run is positive, so $\frac{\text{rise}}{\text{run}} =$ _____

positive number ÷ positive number = positive number.

3b. When you move from left to right between two points on a line with a negative slope, is the rise *positive*, *negative*, or 0? Is the run *positive*, *negative*, or 0? Use your answers to explain why the slope of a line that falls from left to right is negative.

The rise is negative and the run is positive, so $\frac{\text{rise}}{\text{run}} =$ _____

negative number ÷ positive number = negative number.

3c. When you move from left to right between two points on a horizontal line, is the rise *positive*, *negative*, or 0? Is the run *positive*, *negative*, or 0? Use your answers to explain why the slope of a horizontal line is 0.

The rise is 0 and the run is positive, so $\frac{\text{rise}}{\text{run}} = 0 \div$ positive number = 0.

3d. When you move up from one point to another on a vertical line, is the rise *positive*, *negative*, or 0? Is the run *positive*, *negative*, or 0? Use your answers to explain why the slope of a vertical line is undefined.

The rise is positive and the run is 0, so $\frac{\text{rise}}{\text{run}} =$ positive number ÷ 0, which

is undefined.

3e. A **constant function** is a function that has a rate of change of 0. Describe the graph of a constant function and the form of its equation.

The graph of a constant function is a horizontal line. Its equation has the

form $f(x) = b$ where b is the y-intercept of the function's graph.

Graphing Lines You can graph the linear function $f(x) = mx + b$ using only the slope m and the y-intercept b. First, locate the point $(0, b)$ on the y-axis. Next, use the rise and run of the slope to locate another point on the line. Draw the line through the two points.

When using m to locate a second point, bear in mind that m is a ratio, so many values of rise and run are possible. For instance, if $m = \frac{1}{2}$, then you could use a rise of $\frac{1}{2}$ and a run of 1, a rise of 1 and run of 2, a rise of -2 and a run of -4, and so on. Your choice of rise and run often depends on the scales used on the coordinate plane's axes.

4 EXAMPLE   Graphing a Line Using the Slope and y-Intercept

Graph each function.

A $f(x) = -\frac{2}{3}x + 4$

• The y-intercept is ___4___. Plot the point that corresponds to the y-intercept.

• The slope is ___$\frac{2}{3}$___. If you use -2 as the rise, then the run is ___3___.

• Use the slope to move from the first point to a second point. Begin by moving down ___2___ units, because the rise is negative. Then move right ___3___ units, because the run is positive. Plot a second point.

• Draw the line through the two points.

• The domain is the set of ___real___ numbers.

The range is the set of ___real___ numbers.

B   A pitcher with a maximum capacity of 4 cups contains 1 cup of apple juice concentrate. A faucet is turned on filling the pitcher at a rate of 0.25 cup per second. The amount of liquid in the pitcher (in cups) is a function $A(t)$ of the time t (in seconds) that the water is running.

• The y-intercept is the initial amount in the pitcher at time 0, or ___1___ cup. Plot the point that corresponds to the y-intercept.

• The slope is the rate of change: ___0.25___ cup per second, or 1 cup in ___4___ seconds. So, the rise is ___1___ and the run is ___4___.

• Use the rise and run to move from the first point to a second point on the line by moving up ___1___ unit and right ___4___ units. Plot a second point.

• Connect the points and extend the line to the maximum value of the function, where $A(t) = $ ___4___ cups.

• The domain is the set of numbers ___0___ $\leq t \leq$ ___12___.

The range is the set of numbers ___1___ $\leq A(t) \leq$ ___4___.

Questioning Strategies

- Why is the graph in part B a segment, not a line? The pitcher starts with 1 cup in it at $t = 0$ and reaches full capacity at $t = 12$. The graph is limited by the 4-cup capacity of the pitcher.

Technology

Students may benefit from using a graphing calculator to see the graph in part A. Ask them to graph $Y_1 = -\left(\frac{2}{3}\right)X + 4$ and then verify that the graph matches the one in the example. Also ask them to verify that $(0, 4)$ and $(3, 2)$ are points of the graph either by using the Trace feature or by looking at points in the Table function.

Avoid Common Errors

Students may have difficulty graphing a function that has a fractional rate of change as shown in this Example. Remind them that the fraction can be looked at as rise over run, so the rise and run can be used to move from one point to a second point. That is, if the rate of change is expressed as a fraction, use the numerator to move the appropriate number of units up or down (the rise) and use the denominator to move the appropriate number of units right (the run) to plot a second point given the first point.

EXTRA EXAMPLE

Graph each function.

A. $f(x) = -\frac{1}{2}x - 3$ The graph is a line with y-intercept -3 and slope $-\frac{1}{2}$. The domain is all real numbers.

B. An oil storage tank with a volume of 6000 gallons starts off full and empties at a rate of 60 gallons per minute. The graph is a line with y-intercept 6000 and slope -60. The maximum value is 6000, and the minimum value is 0. The domain is $0 \leq x \leq 100$.

CLOSE

Essential Question

What is the slope of a linear function and how can you use it to graph the function?

The slope is the ratio of the difference in two function values to the difference in the corresponding x-values. To graph the function, plot the y-intercept and then use the slope to locate a second point on the graph. Draw a line through these points.

Summarize

Have students fill in the blanks in the graphic organizer below.

The line ...	The slope is ...
rises from left to right.	positive.
falls from left to right.	negative.
is horizontal.	zero.
is vertical.	undefined.

Teaching Strategy

Before assigning Practice Exercise 3, remind students that the graph of a discrete function has isolated points, but that the slope can still be found for the line connecting those points.

PRACTICE

Where skills are taught	Where skills are practiced
1 EXPLORE	EX. 1
2 ENGAGE	EXS. 2, 3
4 EXAMPLE	EXS. 4–9

Exercises 10–11: Students use the skills taught in the lesson to graph a function and extend these skills to make a prediction about the function.

REFLECT

4a. How could you use the slope and y-intercept to graph the function $f(x) = 3$?

Write the rule as $f(x) = 0x + 3$. Start at the point (0, 3). The slope $m = 0$, so the rise is 0 when the run is 1. Plot (1, 3) and draw a horizontal line through (0, 3) and (1, 3).

4b. What are the units of the rise in Part B? What are the units of the run?

The units of the rise are cups. The units of the run are seconds.

4c. How long does it take to fill the pitcher? Explain.

12 seconds; the input associated with a maximum output of 4 cups is 12 seconds.

4d. Why is the function rule $A(t) = \frac{1}{4}t + 1$? Use units to justify your answer.

Sample answer: If the function rule is written as $f(x) = mx + b$, then m is the rate of change and b is the y-intercept, or the initial value where $x = 0$. Since the pitcher starts with 1 cup of water at time 0, $b = 1$ cup. The rate of change is 0.25 cup per second $= \frac{1}{4}$ cup per second, and $\frac{cups}{second} \cdot$ seconds $+$ cups $=$ cups.

PRACTICE

1. Calculate the rate of change of the function in the table. **$.75 per ticket**

Tickets for rides	10	12	14	16
Total cost of carnival ($)	12.50	14.00	15.50	17.00

Estimate the change in the dependent variable over the given interval from the domain of the independent variable. Estimate the rate of change.

2.

Given interval: $20 \le t \le 40$

Change in $D(t)$: about -1.3 miles

Rate of change: about -0.065 mi/min

3.

Given interval: $3 \le s \le 5$

Change in $f(s)$: about 5 yards

Rate of change: about 2.5 yards/shirt

Graph each linear function.

4. $f(x) = 3x - 4$

5. $f(x) = \frac{1}{2}x + 2$

6. $f(x) = -1$

7. $f(x) = \frac{4}{3}x$

8. $f(x) = \frac{1}{4}x - 3$

9. $f(x) = -5x + 1$

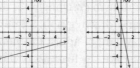

Graph each linear function and answer the question. Explain your answer.

10. A plumber charges $50 for a service call plus $75 per hour. The total of these costs (in dollars) is a function $C(t)$ of the time t (in hours) on the job. For how many hours will the cost be $200? $300?

2 hours; the input value associated with an output of $200 is 2 hours; about 3.3 hours; the input associated with an output of $300 is about 3.3 hours.

11. A bamboo plant is 10 centimeters tall at noon and grows at a rate of 5 centimeters every 2 hours. The height (in centimeters) is a function $h(t)$ of the time t it grows. When will the plant be 20 centimeters tall?

about 4:00 P.M.; the input value associated with an output of 20 cm is about 4 hours, and 4 hours after noon is 4:00 P.M.

© Houghton Mifflin Harcourt Publishing Company

Changing the Values of *m* and *b* in $f(x) = mx + b$

Essential question: How do the values of m and b affect the graph of the function $f(x) = mx + b$?

COMMON CORE **Standards for Mathematical Content**

CC.9-12.F.IF.4 For a function that models a relationship between two quantities, interpret key features of graphs and tables in terms of the quantities, and sketch graphs showing key features given a verbal description of the relationship.*

CC.9-12.F.BF.3 Identify the effect on the graph of replacing $f(x)$ by $f(x) + k$, ... $f(kx)$, ... for specific values of k (both positive and negative); find the value of k given the graphs. Experiment with cases and illustrate an explanation of the effects on the graphs using technology.

CC.9-12.F.LE.5 Interpret the parameters in a linear ... function in terms of a context.*

Also: CC.9-12.F.IF.5*

Prerequisites

Continuous linear functions, Lesson 4-2

Using slope, Lesson 4-3

Math Background

As students learned in the previous lesson, since $f(x) = mx + b$ is a linear function, the graph of $f(x)$ is a line, the slope of the graph of $f(x)$ is the value of m, and the y-intercept of the graph of $f(x)$ is the value of b. The graph of the parent function $f(x) = x$ has a slope of 1 and a y-intercept of 0. The graph of the function $g(x) = x + b$ can be described as a vertical translation of the graph of $f(x) = x$ so that the slope is still 1 and the y-intercept is b. In other words, the graph of $g(x)$ is a vertical translation of the graph of $f(x) = x$ by b units.

The graph of a function of the form $g(x) = mx$ where $m > 0$ is a graph that is steeper or less steep than the graph of the function $f(x) = x$ by a factor of m. If $m < 0$, then the graph of $g(x)$ is also a reflection of the graph of $f(x)$ in the x-axis. If $m > 0$, then $g(x)$ is an increasing function; if $m < 0$, then $g(x)$ is a decreasing function; and if $m = 0$, then $g(x)$ is the constant function $g(x) = 0$.

INTRODUCE

Ask students to graph the line $y = 2x$ on grid paper. Have them draw a rectangle (mimicking a calculator screen) around their graph. Then, ask them to describe the domain and range for the view of the graph in the rectangle.

TEACH

1 EXPLORE

Questioning Strategies

- What types of lines are represented by the functions graphed in part C? **parallel lines**

- What can be said about parallel graphs of linear functions? **They all have the same slope but different y-intercepts.**

- Compare the graphs of $f(x) = x + 4$ and $f(x) = x - 3$. How many units apart are the graphs? **The graphs have the same slope but different y-intercepts (4 and −3) and are parallel; the graphs are 7 units apart vertically.**

Technology

Be certain that students make the connection between adjusting the size of the viewing window and drawing rectangles of different sizes around a hand-drawn graph. Students can use ZOOM ZStandard or adjust the viewing window manually to see the key features of the graph. Emphasize that the graphs will not be shown at a 45° angle with the x-axis unless ZOOM ZSquare is used to adjust the aspect ratio of the screen to 3:2.

Teaching Strategy

For part C, suggest to students that they do not erase graphs in the Y= screens before entering another graph with a different b-value. This should help them understand why each graph is a vertical translation of the graph of $f(x) = x$.

continued

Name_____ Class_____ Date_____

COMMON CORE
CC.9-12.F.IF.4*,
CC.9-12.F.BF.3,
CC.9-12.F.LE.5*

4-4

Changing the Values of *m* and *b* in $f(x) = mx + b$

Essential question: *How do the values of m and b affect the graph of the function* $f(x) = mx + b$?

1 EXPLORE Changing the Value of *b* in $f(x) = x + b$

Investigate what happens to the graph of $f(x) = x + b$ when you change the value of *b*.

A Use a graphing calculator. Start with the standard viewing window, which you can obtain by pressing **ZOOM** and selecting ZStandard. Because the distances between consecutive tick marks on the *x*-axis and on the *y*-axis are not equal, you can make them equal by pressing **ZOOM** again and selecting ZSquare.

What interval on each axis does the viewing window now show? (Press **WINDOW** to find out.)

Approximately $-15.16 \leq x \leq 15.16$; $-10 \leq y \leq 10$

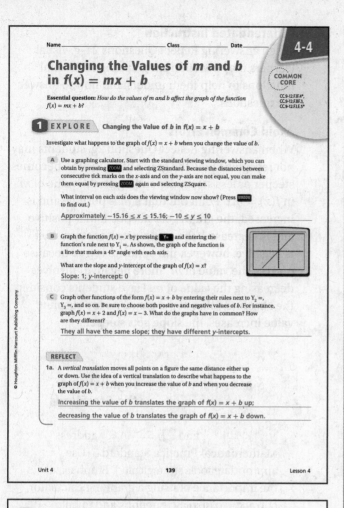

B Graph the function $f(x) = x$ by pressing **Y=** and entering the function's rule next to $Y_1 =$. As shown, the graph of the function is a line that makes a 45° angle with each axis.

What are the slope and *y*-intercept of the graph of $f(x) = x$?

Slope: 1; *y*-intercept: 0

C Graph other functions of the form $f(x) = x + b$ by entering their rules next to $Y_2 =$, $Y_3 =$, and so on. Be sure to choose both positive and negative values of *b*. For instance, graph $f(x) = x + 2$ and $f(x) = x - 3$. What do the graphs have in common? How are they different?

They all have the same slope; they have different *y*-intercepts.

REFLECT

1a. A *vertical translation* moves all points on a figure the same distance either up or down. Use the idea of a vertical translation to describe what happens to the graph of $f(x) = x + b$ when you increase the value of *b* and when you decrease the value of *b*.

Increasing the value of *b* translates the graph of $f(x) = x + b$ up;

decreasing the value of *b* translates the graph of $f(x) = x + b$ down.

2 EXPLORE Changing the Value of *m* in $f(x) = mx$

Investigate what happens to the graph of $f(x) = mx$ when you change the value of *m*.

A Use a graphing calculator. Press **Y=** and clear out all but the function $f(x) = x$ from the previous Explore. Then graph other functions of the form $f(x) = mx$ by entering their rules next to $Y_2 =$, $Y_3 =$, and so on. Use only values of *m* that are greater than 1. For instance, graph $f(x) = 2x$ and $f(x) = 6x$.

What do the graphs have in common? How are they different?

They all have the same *y*-intercept; they have different slopes.

As the value of *m* increases from 1, does the graph become more vertical or more horizontal?

More vertical

B Again press **Y=** and clear out all but the function $f(x) = x$. Then graph other functions of the form $f(x) = mx$ by entering their rules next to $Y_2 =$, $Y_3 =$, and so on. This time use only values of *m* that are less than 1 but greater than 0. For instance, graph $f(x) = 0.5x$ and $f(x) = 0.2x$.

As the value of *m* decreases from 1 toward 0, does the graph become more vertical or more horizontal?

More horizontal

C Again press **Y=** and clear out all but the function $f(x) = x$. Then graph the function $f(x) = -x$ by entering its rule next to $Y_2 =$.

What are the slope and *y*-intercept of the graph of $f(x) = -x$?

Slope: −1; *y*-intercept: 0

How are the graphs of $f(x) = x$ and $f(x) = -x$ geometrically related?

They are reflections across the *x*-axis.

D Again press **Y=** and clear out all the functions. Graph $f(x) = -x$ by entering its rule next to $Y_1 =$. Then graph other functions of the form $f(x) = mx$ where $m < 0$ by entering their rules next to $Y_2 =$, $Y_3 =$, and so on. Be sure to choose values of *m* less than −1 as well as values of *m* between −1 and 0.

Describe what happens to the graph of $f(x) = mx$ as the value of *m* decreases from −1 and as it increases from −1 to 0.

The graph becomes more vertical; the graph becomes more horizontal.

Questioning Strategies

- For part A, what is the ratio of the function values for the graphs of $f(x) = 2x$ and $f(x) = 6x$? The values for $f(x) = 6x$ are three times as great as the values for $f(x) = 2x$.

- Suppose you did parts A and B by changing the value of m for the function $f(x) = mx + 4$. Would your results be the same? Explain. Yes; all the functions would have the same y-intercept (4) but different slopes.

- Why are the functions $f(x) = x$ and $f(x) = -x$ reflections across the x-axis? The y-values are opposites, so the points of the graphs have opposite y-coordinates.

- How can you tell whether a linear function is increasing or decreasing without graphing it? If the slope is negative, then the function will be decreasing. If the slope is positive, then the function will be increasing.

- What does it mean for the graph of one linear function to be "more vertical" than the graph of another linear function? The absolute value of the slope of the graph that is more vertical is greater than the absolute value of the other slope.

- In terms of steepness, what does it mean for the graph of one linear function to be more horizontal than the graph of another linear function? The absolute value of the slope of the function that is more horizontal is less than the absolute value of the slope of the other function.

Teaching Strategy

You may want groups of students to compare their answers for both the Explore questions and the Reflect questions. Emphasize that the actual values they use are not important as long as the sign is the same. What is important is how an increase or a decrease in the value can be used to determine whether the graph is more vertical or more horizontal.

Differentiated Instruction

When answering Reflect Questions 2a–g, visual learners may benefit from graphing additional functions to help them understand how to answer the questions.

Avoid Common Errors

When answering Reflect Question 2g, students may not recognize how the graph of a function becomes steeper or less steep, depending on the value of m in $f(x) = mx$. Point out that if m is positive and is increased, the graph gets steeper. If m is positive and is decreased, the graph gets less steep. If m is negative, however, the opposite is true because making the value of m "more negative" involves decreasing the value of m. Have students consider the absolute value of the slope. As the absolute value increases, the slope gets steeper.

MATHEMATICAL PRACTICE — **Highlighting the Standards**

1 EXPLORE and **2 EXPLORE** address Mathematical Practice Standard 5 (Use appropriate tools strategically). Emphasize the importance of using a graphing calculator correctly to display functions and to help make conclusions about how different graphs are related geometrically. Specifically, ask students why the viewing window is important. Then have them detail how to use a graphing calculator correctly to graph a pair of linear functions that have different y-intercepts and a pair of linear functions that have different slopes.

REFLECT

2a. A function $f(x)$ is called an *increasing function* when the value of $f(x)$ always increases as the value of x increases. For what values of m is the function $f(x) = mx$ an increasing function? How can you tell from the graph of a linear function that it is an increasing function?

$m > 0$; the graph rises from left to right.

2b. A function $f(x)$ is called a *decreasing function* when the value of $f(x)$ decreases as the value of x increases. For what values of m is the function $f(x) = mx$ a decreasing function? How can you tell from the graph of a linear function that is a decreasing function?

$m < 0$; the graph falls from left to right.

2c. When $m > 0$, increasing the value of m results in an increasing linear function that increases *faster*. What effect does increasing m have on the graph of the function?

It makes the graph more vertical.

2d. When $m > 0$, decreasing the value of m toward 0 results in an increasing linear function that increases *slower*. What effect does decreasing m have on the graph of the function?

It makes the graph more horizontal.

2e. When $m < 0$, decreasing the value of m results in a decreasing linear function that decreases *faster*. What effect does decreasing m have on the graph of the function?

It makes the graph more vertical.

2f. When $m < 0$, increasing the value of m toward 0 results in a decreasing linear function that decreases *slower*. What effect does increasing m have on the graph of the function?

It makes the graph more horizontal.

2g. The *steepness* of a line refers to the absolute value of its slope. A steeper line is more vertical; a less steep line is more horizontal. Complete the table to summarize, in terms of steepness, the effect of changing the value of m on the graph of $f(x) = mx$.

How the Value of m Changes	Effect on the Graph of $f(x) = mx$
Increase m when $m > 0$.	Graph becomes steeper.
Decrease m toward 0 when $m > 0$.	Graph becomes less steep.
Decrease m when $m < 0$.	Graph becomes steeper.
Increase m toward 0 when $m < 0$.	Graph becomes less steep.

---

3 EXAMPLE Modeling with Changes in m and b

A gym charges a one-time joining fee of $50 and then a monthly membership fee of $25. The total cost C of being a member of the gym is given by the function $C(t) = 25t + 50$ where t is the time (in months) since joining the gym. For each situation described below, *sketch* a graph using the given graph of $C(t) = 25t + 50$ as a reference.

A The gym decreases its one-time joining fee. (Remember: You are not graphing a specific function for this situation. Rather, you are sketching a representative graph of a function related to $C(t) = 25t + 50$, whose graph is shown.)

What change did you make to the graph of $C(t) = 25t + 50$ to obtain the graph that you drew?

lowered the vertical intercept but

left the slope the same

B The gym increases its monthly membership fee.

What change did you make to the graph of $C(t) = 25t + 50$ to obtain the graph that you drew?

increased the slope but left the vertical

intercept the same

REFLECT

3a. Suppose the gym increases its one-time joining fee *and* decreases its monthly membership fee. Describe how you would alter the graph of $C(t) = 25t + 50$ to illustrate the new cost function.

Translate the graph up to show the increase in the one-time joining

fee, and make the graph less steep to show the decrease in the monthly

membership fee.

3b. Suppose the gym increases its one-time joining fee *and* decreases its monthly membership fee, as in Question 3a. Does this have any impact on the domain of the function? Does this have any impact on the range of the function? Explain your reasoning.

No; the domain is still any number of months. Yes; the range has a new minimum

value equal to the new joining fee.

Questioning Strategies

- Why are the graphs in part A parallel? **The slopes are the same but the *y*-intercepts are different. One graph is a vertical translation of the other.**

- Why do the graphs in part B intersect at the same point on the *y*-axis? **They both have the same *y*-intercept, the initial value of 50.**

- Why are the graphs in parts A and B first quadrant graphs only? **Only nonnegative domain and range values make sense in these situations.**

Teaching Strategy

Emphasize the following statements: If the slope stays the same but the *y*-intercept changes, the graphs are parallel, and they are vertical translations of each other. If the *y*-intercept stays the same and the slope changes, one graph is steeper than the other.

Extra Example

A satellite dish company charges a one-time installation fee of $75 and then a monthly usage charge of $40. The total cost C of using that satellite service is given by the function $C(t) = 40t + 75$, where t is the time (in months) since starting the service. For each situation given below, sketch a graph using the graph of $C(t) = 40t + 75$ as a reference.

A. The satellite dish company reduces its one-time installation fee to $60. What change did you make to the graph of $C(t) = 40t + 75$ to obtain the new graph? **Change the vertical intercept to 60, but leave the slope the same.**

B. The satellite dish company decreases its monthly fee to $30. What change did you make to the graph of $C(t) = 40t + 75$ to obtain the new graph? **Change the slope from 40 to 30, but leave the vertical intercept the same.**

CLOSE

Essential Question

How do the values of m and b affect the graph of the function $f(x) = mx + b$?
The value of *m* affects the steepness of the graph of $f(x) = mx + b$, while the value of *b* affects the *y*-intercept.

Summarize

Have students fill out the graphic organizer below.

PRACTICE

Where skills are taught	Where skills are practiced
3 EXAMPLE	EXS. 1–3

Exercises 4–5: These exercises extend the lesson concepts by interpreting operations performed either on the output or on the input of a function as transformations of the function's graph.

How the Value of *m* Changes	Effect on the Graph of $f(x) = mx$	How the Value of *b* Changes	Effect on the Graph of $f(x) = x + b$
Increase *m* when $m > 0$.	becomes steeper	Increase *b*.	translate up
Decrease *m* when $m > 0$.	becomes less steep	Decrease *b*.	translate down
Decrease *m* when $m < 0$.	becomes steeper		
Increase *m* when $m < 0$.	becomes less steep		

PRACTICE

1. A salesperson earns a base monthly salary of $2000 plus a 10% commission on sales. The salesperson's monthly income I (in dollars) is given by the function $I(s) = 0.1s + 2000$ where s is the sales (in dollars) that the salesperson makes. Sketch a graph to illustrate each situation using the graph of $I(s) = 0.1s + 2000$ as a reference.

a. The salesperson's base salary is increased.

b. The salesperson's commission rate is decreased.

2. Mr. Resnick is driving at a speed of 40 miles per hour to visit relatives who live 100 miles away from his home. His distance d (in miles) from his destination is given by the function $d(t) = 100 - 40t$ where t is the time (in hours) since his trip began. Sketch a graph to illustrate each situation.

a. He increases his speed to get to his destination sooner.

b. He encounters a detour that increases the driving distance.

3. Use the graph of $d(t) = 100 - 40t$ in Exercise 2 to identify the domain and range of the function. Then tell whether the domain, the range, neither, or both are affected by the changes described in each part.

$D = \{t \mid 0 \le t \le 2.5\}$; $R = \{d(t) \mid 0 \le d(t) \le 100\}$; part (a): domain changes;

part (b): both change

Transformations In Exercises 4 and 5, use the following information.

Given a linear function $f(x) = mx + b$, you can create new linear functions by using a constant k in combination with the rule for $f(x)$. For instance, you can create the functions $g(x) = f(x) + k$ and $h(x) = f(kx)$. The graph of each of these new functions is geometrically related to the graph of f through transformations.

Consider the function $f(x) = x + 1$ as well as the related functions $g(x) = f(x) + 2$ and $h(x) = f\left(\frac{x}{2}\right)$. In the case of g, adding 2 is performed on the *output* of f. In the case of h, dividing by 2 is performed on the *input* of f. Each of these cases is illustrated below using -2, 0, and 2 as a few sample inputs of f.

4. The graphs of f and g are shown along with arrows to indicate what happened to the points on the graph of f with x-coordinates -2, 0, and 2. The graph of g is a *vertical translation* of the graph of f. Is the slope or the y-intercept of f affected by the vertical translation? Show that this is true by writing the rule for $g(x) = f(x) + 2$.

y-intercept changes; $g(x) = (x + 1) + 2 = x + 3$

5. The graphs of f and h are shown along with arrows to indicate what happened to the points on the graph of f with x-coordinates -2, 0, and 2. The graph of h is a *horizontal stretch* of the graph of f by a factor of 2. Is the slope or the y-intercept of f affected by the horizontal stretch? Show that this is true by writing the rule for $h(x) = f\left(\frac{x}{2}\right)$.

slope changes; $h(x) = \frac{x}{2} + 1 = \frac{1}{2}x + 1$

Writing Linear Functions

Essential question: *How can you represent a function symbolically from a graph, a verbal description, or a table of values?*

COMMON CORE Standards for Mathematical Content

CC.9-12.A.CED.2 Create equations in two ... variables to represent relationships between quantities; graph equations on coordinate axes with labels and scales.*

CC.9-12.A.REI.11 Explain why the *x*-coordinates of the points where the graphs of the equations $y = f(x)$ and $y = g(x)$ intersect are the solutions of the equation $f(x) = g(x)$; ... Include cases where $f(x)$ and/or $g(x)$ are linear ... functions.*

CC.9-12.F.IF.4 For a function that models a relationship between two quantities, interpret key features of graphs and tables in terms of the quantities, and sketch graphs showing key features given a verbal description of the relationship.*

CC.9-12.F.IF.6 Calculate and interpret the average rate of change of a function (presented symbolically or as a table) over a specified interval. Estimate the rate of change from a graph.*

CC.9-12.F.BF.1 Write a function that describes a relationship between two quantities.*

CC.9-12.F.LE.2 Construct linear ... functions, ... given a graph, a description of a relationship, or two input-output pairs (include reading these from a table).*

Also: CC.9-12.N.Q.1*, CC.9-12.N.Q.2*

Prerequisites

Using slope, Lesson 4-3

The values of m and b in $f(x) = mx + b$, Lesson 4-4

Math Background

A linear function of the form $f(x) = mx + b$ can be written if the slope and the *y*-intercept are known. The slope can be determined as long as the coordinates of two points are known or can be obtained from a graph. Calculate the slope from the coordinates of two points as follows:

$$m = \frac{\text{rise}}{\text{run}} = \frac{f(x_2) - f(x_1)}{x_2 - x_1}.$$

You can then find the value of b using m and one of the known points. If the known point is $(x_1, f(x_1))$, then $b = f(x_1) - mx_1$, or

$$b = f(x_1) - \frac{f(x_2) - f(x_1)}{x_2 - x_1}(x_1).$$ The function $f(x) = mx + b$ can then be rewritten as $f(x) =$

$$mx + b = \frac{f(x_2) - f(x_1)}{x_2 - x_1}(x) + f(x_1) - \frac{f(x_2) - f(x_1)}{x_2 - x_1}(x_1).$$

INTRODUCE

Ask students to graph the function $f(x) = 3x + 4$ on graph paper and identify the slope and the *y*-intercept. Have them identify several points of the graph and verify that each pair of points has the same slope.

TEACH

1 EXAMPLE

Questioning Strategies

- For part B, do you get the same slope no matter which two ordered pairs you choose? **yes**

- For part B, what would be the linear function if you used known points $(-1, 5)$ and $(7, -11)$? $f(x) = -2x + 3$

continued

Name_____ Class_____ Date_____

4-5

Writing Linear Functions

COMMON CORE

Essential question: How can you represent a function symbolically from a graph, a verbal description, or a table of values?

CC.9-12.A.CED.2*,
CC.9-12.A.REL.11*,
CC.9-12.F.IF.4*,
CC.9-12.F.IF.6*,
CC.9-12.F.BF.1*,
CC.9-12.F.LE.2*

1 EXAMPLE Writing a Linear Function

Write the linear function f using the given information.

A The graph of the function has a slope of 3 and a y-intercept of -1.

A linear function has the form $f(x) = mx + b$ where m is the slope and b is the y-intercept. Substitute ___3___ for m and ___-1___ for b.

So, the function is $f(x) = $ ___$3x - 1$___.

B A different function has the values shown in the table.

First calculate the slope using any two ordered pairs from the table. For instance, let $(x_1, f(x_1)) = (-1, 5)$ and $(x_2, f(x_2)) = (3, -3)$.

x	f(x)
-1	5
3	-3
7	-11

$m = \dfrac{f(x_2) - f(x_1)}{x_2 - x_1}$　　Write the slope formula.

$= \dfrac{-3 - 5}{3 - (-1)}$　　Substitute values.

$= \dfrac{-8}{4}$　　Simplify numerator and denominator.

$= -2$　　Simplify fraction.

Then find the value of b using the fact that $m = $ ___-2___ and $f(-1) = 5$.

$f(x) = $ ___-2___ $x + b$　　Write the function with the known value of m.

$5 = $ ___-2___ $\left(-1 \right) + b$　　Substitute -1 for x and 5 for $f(x)$.

$5 = $ ___2___ $+ b$　　Simplify the right side of the equation.

___3___ $= b$　　Solve for b.

So, the function is $f(x) = $ ___$-2x + 3$___.

REFLECT

1a. In Part B, use the ordered pair $(7, -11)$ to check your answer.

$f(7) = -2(7) + 3 = -14 + 3 = -11$

© Houghton Mifflin Harcourt Publishing Company

Unit 4　　　145　　　Lesson 5

---

2 EXAMPLE Writing a Linear Function from a Graph

The graph shows the increase in pressure (measured in pounds per square inch) as a scuba diver descends from a depth of 10 feet to a depth of 30 feet.

Pressure is the result of the weight of the column of water above the diver as well as the weight of the column of Earth's atmosphere above the water. Pressure is a linear function of depth.

What is the pressure on the diver at the water's surface?

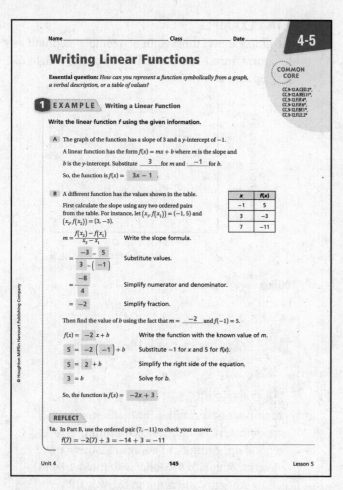

Scuba Diving

(graph with $P(d)$ on vertical axis, Pressure (lb/in.²) and Depth (feet) on horizontal axis; points $(10, 19.1)$ and $(30, 28.0)$ shown)

A Interpret the question.

Let d represent depth and P represent pressure. At the water's surface, $d = $ ___0___. For this value of d, what meaning does $P(d)$ have in terms of the line that contains the line segment shown on the graph?

It is the line's P-intercept.

B Find the value of m in $P(d) = md + b$. Use the fact that $P(10) = 19.1$ and $P(30) = 28.0$.

$m = \dfrac{P(d_2) - P(d_1)}{d_2 - d_1}$　　Write the slope formula.

$= \dfrac{28.0 - 19.1}{30 - 10}$　　Substitute values.

$= \dfrac{8.9}{20}$　　Simplify numerator and denominator.

$= $ ___0.445___　　Write in decimal form.

C Find the value of b in $P(d) = md + b$. Use the value of m from Part B as well as the fact that $P(10) = 19.1$.

$P(d) = $ ___0.445___ $d + b$　　Write the function with the known value of m.

$19.1 = $ ___0.445___ $\left(10 \right) + b$　　Substitute 10 for d and 19.1 for $P(d)$.

$19.1 = $ ___4.45___ $+ b$　　Simplify the right side of the equation.

___14.7___ $\approx b$　　Solve for b. Round to the nearest tenth.

So, the pressure at the water's surface is $P(0) = b \approx$ ___14.7___ lb/in.²

© Houghton Mifflin Harcourt Publishing Company

Unit 4　　　146　　　Lesson 5

Avoid Common Errors

When calculating the slope using ordered pairs with negative coordinates, students will sometimes forget the negative sign when subtracting values. For example, for $(-1, 5)$ and $(3, -3)$, $x_2 - x_1$ should be $3 - (-1)$, not $3 - 1$. Remind students that they must retain any negative signs in an ordered pair when using the slope formula.

Teaching Strategy

Encourage students to use the third point in the table to check that they have the correct function.

EXTRA EXAMPLE

Write the linear function f using the given information.

A. The graph of the function has a slope of -5 and a y-intercept of 1. $f(x) = -5x + 1$

B. The function has values shown in the table.

x	$f(x)$
-1	-2
1	6
3	14

$f(x) = 4x + 2$

2 EXAMPLE

Questioning Strategies

• Why can you extend the graph so that it intersects the y-axis? The depths of the diver from 0 to 10 feet are reasonable to include in the domain of the function.

• What would be the pressure at a depth of 40 feet? Explain how you found your answer. 32.5 lb/in.²; $P(40) = 0.445(40) + 14.7 = 32.5$

• Why is the graph a first-quadrant graph only? Only nonnegative domain and range values make sense in this situation.

Technology

Have students substitute the function in Reflect Question 2b into a graphing calculator and then use the Table feature to find additional points on the graph.

EXTRA EXAMPLE

The graph shows the weight of a female elephant as she grows from 1 to 3 years. What was the weight of the elephant at birth?

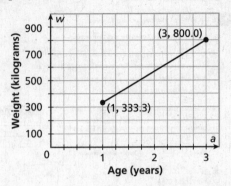

100 kg

```
⋰ MATHEMATICAL   Highlighting
⋱ PRACTICE        the Standards
```

2 EXAMPLE is a real-world problem that includes opportunities for mathematical modeling, reasoning, and computation. It is a good opportunity to address Mathematical Practice Standard 4 (Model with mathematics). Draw students' attention to the way they interpret the values of m and b. The value of m gives the rate of change in pressure with respect to depth: The pressure on the diver increases 0.445 lb/in.² for every additional foot of depth. The value of b gives the pressure on the diver at the water's surface, which is just the pressure due to the weight of the column of Earth's atmosphere above the water: The pressure at the water's surface is 14.7 lb/in.²

REFLECT

2a. Interpret the value of m in the context of the problem.

m is the rate of change in pressure with respect to depth.

2b. Write the function $P(d) = md + b$ using the calculated values of m and b. Use the function to find the pressure on the diver at a depth of 20 feet.

$P(d) = 0.445d + 14.7;\ P(20) = 23.6\ \text{lb/in.}^2$

3 EXAMPLE Writing and Solving a System of Equations

Mr. Jackson takes a commuter bus from his suburban home to his job in the city. He normally gets on the bus in the town where he lives, but today he is running a little late. He gets to the bus stop 2 minutes after the bus has left. He wants to catch up with the bus by the time it gets to the next stop in a neighboring town 5 miles away.

The speed limit on the road connecting the two stops is 40 miles per hour, but Mr. Jackson knows that the bus travels the road at 30 miles per hour. He decides to drive at 40 miles per hour to the next stop. Does he successfully catch the bus there?

A Identify the independent and dependent variables, how they are measured, and how you will represent them.

The independent variable is ___time___, measured in minutes. Let t represent the time since Mr. Jackson began driving to the next bus stop.

The dependent variable is ___distance___, measured in miles. Let d represent the distance traveled. Since you need to track the distances traveled by both Mr. Jackson and the bus, use subscripts: d_J will represent the distance traveled by Mr. Jackson, and d_B will represent the distance traveled by the bus.

B Write a distance-traveled function for Mr. Jackson and for the bus.

Each function has the form $d(t) = rt + d_0$ where r is the rate of travel and d_0 is any initial distance. Although you know the rates of travel, they are given in miles per hour, which is incompatible with the unit of time (minutes). So, you need to convert miles per hour to miles per minute. In the conversions below, express the miles as simplified fractions.

Mr. Jackson: $\dfrac{40\ \text{miles}}{\text{hour}} \cdot \dfrac{1\ \text{hour}}{60\ \text{minutes}} = \boxed{\dfrac{2}{3}}$ mile per minute

Bus: $\dfrac{30\ \text{miles}}{\text{hour}} \cdot \dfrac{1\ \text{hour}}{60\ \text{minutes}} = \boxed{\dfrac{1}{2}}$ mile per minute

Continued on next page

At the moment Mr. Jackson begins driving to the next bus stop, the bus has traveled for 2 minutes. If you use Mr. Jackson's position as the starting point, then the initial distance for Mr. Jackson is 0 miles, and the initial distance for the bus is $\dfrac{1}{2} \cdot 2 = \boxed{1\ \text{mile}}$.

So, the distance-traveled functions are:

Mr. Jackson: $d_J(t) = \boxed{\dfrac{2}{3}}\,t + \boxed{0}$ Bus: $d_B(t) = \boxed{\dfrac{1}{2}}\,t + \boxed{1}$

C Determine the value of t for which $d_J(t) = d_B(t)$. You can do this by graphing the two functions and seeing where the graphs intersect. Carefully draw the graphs on the coordinate plane below, and label the intersection point.

The t-coordinate of the point of intersection is ___6___, so

Mr. Jackson catches up with the bus in ___6 minutes___.

D Check the result against the conditions of the problem, and then answer the problem's question.

The problem states that the next bus stop is ___5___ miles away, and the

graph shows that Mr. Jackson catches up with the bus in ___4___ miles.

So, does Mr. Jackson successfully catch the bus? ___Yes___

REFLECT

3a. Explain how you can use algebra rather than a graph to find the time when Mr. Jackson catches up with the bus. Then show that you get the same result.

Solve the equation: $\dfrac{1}{2}t + 1 = \dfrac{2}{3}t$: $1 = \dfrac{1}{6}t$, so $t = 6$.

3b. In terms of the context of the problem, explain why the t-coordinate of the intersection point (and not some other point) determines how long it takes Mr. Jackson to catch up with the bus.

The two graphs are distance-traveled graphs, and their intersection point is the

only point on the two graphs where the distances are equal. The t-coordinate of

this point gives the time at which this occurs.

Questioning Strategies

- What do the coordinates of the intersection point represent in the context of this situation? The distance at which Mr. Jackson catches up with the bus (4 miles) and the time it took Mr. Jackson to reach that distance (6 minutes).

- Why are conversions necessary in part B? The speeds given are in miles per hour, but the elapsed time is in minutes. Both measures need to use the same unit of time to solve and graph the functions.

- Why is each graph only in the first quadrant? Only nonnegative domain and range values make sense in this situation.

EXTRA EXAMPLE

You are participating in a 2-mile run for charity. You are at the back of the group of runners and leave the starting line 0.5 minute after the first runners have left. You would like to catch up to the first runners by the time you reach the halfway point of the race at 1 mile. The first runners run at a rate of 7.2 miles per hour, and you run at a rate of 7.5 miles per hour. Do you successfully catch up to the lead runners by the time you reach the halfway point of the event? No; you catch up 12 minutes after the race starts, when both you and the lead runners have run 1.5 miles.

Essential Question

How can you represent a function symbolically from a graph, a verbal description, or a table of values? From a graph, find the y-intercept b and use two points on the graph to find the value of m; then substitute those values into $f(x) = mx + b$. From a verbal description, identify the independent and dependent variables, determine the coordinates of points that fit the situation, and write the function $f(x) = mx + b$. From a table of values, use two ordered pairs to find the value of m and then use m and an ordered pair to find b; then substitute those values into $f(x) = mx + b$.

Summarize

Have students complete a graphic organizer showing the steps for writing a linear function from two given points. A sample is shown below.

Where skills are taught	Where skills are practiced
1 EXAMPLE	EXS. 1–8
2 EXAMPLE	EXS. 9–11
3 EXAMPLE	EX. 12

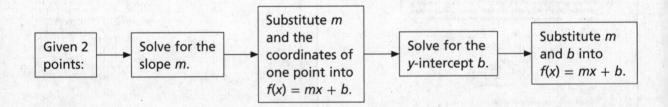

Given 2 points: → Solve for the slope m. → Substitute m and the coordinates of one point into $f(x) = mx + b$. → Solve for the y-intercept b. → Substitute m and b into $f(x) = mx + b$.

PRACTICE

Write the linear function *f* using the given information.

1. The graph of the function has a slope of 4 and a *y*-intercept of 1.

$f(x) = 4x + 1$

2. The graph of the function has a slope of 0 and a *y*-intercept of 6.

$f(x) = 6$

3. The graph of the function has a slope of $-\frac{2}{3}$ and a *y*-intercept of 5.

$f(x) = -\frac{2}{3}x + 5$

4. The graph of the function has a slope of $\frac{7}{4}$ and a *y*-intercept of 0.

$f(x) = \frac{7}{4}x$

5.

x	f(x)
–3	8
0	5
3	2

$f(x) = -x + 5$

6.

x	f(x)
0	–3
2	0
4	3

$f(x) = \frac{3}{2}x - 3$

7.

x	f(x)
1	–1
2	5
3	11

$f(x) = 6x - 7$

8.

x	f(x)
5	–2
10	–6
15	–10

$f(x) = -\frac{4}{5}x + 2$

9.

$f(x) = 2x - 1$

10.

$f(x) = -\frac{1}{2}x + 3$

11. The graph shows the amount of gas remaining in the gas tank of Mrs. Liu's car as she drives at a steady speed for 2 hours. How long can she drive before her car runs out of gas?

Fuel Consumption

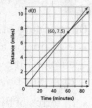

a. Interpret the question by describing what aspect of the graph would answer the question.

Want to know the *t*-intercept if the graph were extended to the *t*-axis.

b. Write a linear function whose graph includes the segment shown.

$g(t) = -2t + 10$

c. Describe how to use the function to answer the question, and then answer the question.

Set $g(t)$ equal to 0 and solve for *t*; she can drive for 5 hours.

12. Jamal and Nathan exercise by running one circuit of a basically circular route that is 5 miles long and takes them past each other's home. The two boys run in the same direction, and Jamal passes Nathan's home 12 minutes into his run. Jamal runs at a rate of 7.5 miles per hour while Nathan runs at a rate of 6 miles per hour. If the two boys start running at the same time, when, if ever, will Jamal catch up with Nathan before completing his run?

a. Identify the independent and dependent variables, how they are measured, and how you will represent them.

Independent variable is time *t* measured in minutes; dependent variable is distance *d* measured in miles.

b. Write distance-run functions for Jamal and Nathan.

$d_J(t) = \frac{1}{8}t$; $d_N(t) = \frac{1}{10}t + 1.5$

c. Graph the functions, find the intersection point, and check the point against the conditions of the problem to answer the question.

Jamal does not catch up with Nathan.

Operations with Linear Functions

Essential question: *How can you use operations to combine functions that model real-world situations?*

COMMON **Standards for**
CORE **Mathematical Content**

CC.9-12.A.APR.1 … add, subtract, and multiply polynomials.

CC.9-12.A.CED.2 Create equations in two … variables to represent relationships between quantities …*

CC.9-12.F.BF.1 Write a function that describes a relationship between two quantities.*

CC.9-12.F.BF.1a Determine an explicit expression … from a context.*

CC.9-12.F.BF.1b Combine standard function types using arithmetic operations.*

CC.9-12.F.LE.2 Construct linear … functions … given a graph, a description of a relationship, or two input-output pairs (include reading these from a table).*

CC.9-12.F.LE.5 Interpret the parameters in a linear … function in terms of a context.*

Also: CC.9-12.N.Q.1*, CC.9-12.F.IF.2

Prerequisites

Ways of representing functions, Lesson 1-5

Modeling with functions, Lesson 1-6

Math Background

If $f(x)$ and $g(x)$ are linear functions, you can perform addition and subtraction on the functions. For example, let $f(x) = 2x + 3$ and $g(x) = 4 - x$. Then $f(x) + g(x)$ is defined over the set of real numbers and is equal $x + 7$. Similarly, $f(x) - g(x)$ is defined over the set of real numbers and is equal to $3x - 1$. Finally, let $h(x)$ be the constant function $h(x) = 7$. You can find the product $h(x) \cdot f(x)$ by multiplying $h(x)$ and $f(x)$. The product $h(x) \cdot f(x)$ is defined over the set of real numbers and is equal to $14x + 21$. Note that in Lesson 8-1, students will learn to find the product $f(x) \cdot g(x)$ where $f(x)$ and $g(x)$ are both non-constant linear functions by using FOIL.

INTRODUCE

In Lessons 4-1 through 4-5, students studied various aspects of linear functions, including using linear functions as models for real-world situations. Ask students how they would determine the total enrollment function for a school if they had an enrollment function for males and an enrollment function for females.

TEACH

1 EXAMPLE

Questioning Strategies

- Why can you represent the sum, difference, or product of linear functions $f(x)$ and $g(x)$ as a function $h(x)$? **Performing an operation on two linear functions produces a new function, so you can represent the sum, difference, or product as a function.**

- What does the middle column of the table in Reflect Question 1a represent? **the sum of the output values for $f(x)$ and $g(x)$**

EXTRA EXAMPLE

A. Given $f(x) = 2x + 4$ and $g(x) = -4x - 3$, find $h(x) = f(x) + g(x)$. $h(x) = -2x + 1$

B. Given $f(x) = 3x - 5$ and $g(x) = 5x - 1$, find $h(x) = f(x) - g(x)$. $h(x) = -2x - 4$

C. Given $f(x) = 5$ and $g(x) = -\frac{1}{5}x - 2$, find $h(x) = f(x) \cdot g(x)$. $h(x) = -x - 10$

2 EXAMPLE

Questioning Strategies

- Why do you add $g(t)$ and $b(t)$ to find $T(t)$? **total enrollment over time = girls enrollment over time plus boys enrollment over time**

- In terms of the situation, explain why $m = 13$ and $b = 100$ in $T(t)$. **There is an increase of 13 campers each year and the initial number of campers was 100.**

continued

4-6

Operations with Linear Functions

Essential question: *How can you use operations to combine functions that model real-world situations?*

COMMON
CORE

CC.9-12.A.APR.1.
CC.9-12.A.CED.2*.
CC.9-12.F.BF.1*.
CC.9-12.F.BF.1b*.
CC.9-12.F.LE.2*.
CC.9-12.F.LE.5*

Just as you can perform operations with numbers, you can perform operations with functions. In this lesson you will add and subtract linear functions as well as multiply a linear function by a nonzero constant function. Performing an operation on two functions $f(x)$ and $g(x)$ produces a new function $h(x)$.

1 EXAMPLE Performing Operations with Functions

A Given $f(x) = 3x - 1$ and $g(x) = -2x + 2$, find $h(x) = f(x) + g(x)$.

$h(x) = f(x) + g(x)$ Write the general form of $h(x)$.

$= (3x - 1) + \left(\boxed{-2x + 2} \right)$ Substitute the rules for $f(x)$ and $g(x)$.

$= \left(3x + \boxed{-2x} \right) + \left(-1 + \boxed{2} \right)$ Collect like terms for adding.

$= \boxed{x} + \boxed{1}$ Simplify.

B Given $f(x) = x + 5$ and $g(x) = 4x - 2$, find $h(x) = f(x) - g(x)$.

$h(x) = f(x) - g(x)$ Write the general form of $h(x)$.

$= (x + 5) - \left(\boxed{4x - 2} \right)$ Substitute the rules for $f(x)$ and $g(x)$.

$= \left(x - \boxed{4x} \right) + \left(5 - \boxed{-2} \right)$ Collect like terms for subtracting.

$= \boxed{-3x} + \boxed{7}$ Simplify.

C Given $f(x) = 3$ and $g(x) = \frac{1}{3}x - 2$, find $h(x) = f(x) \cdot g(x)$.

$h(x) = f(x) \cdot g(x)$ Write the general form of $h(x)$.

$= \boxed{3} \left(\frac{1}{3}x - 2 \right)$ Substitute the rules for $f(x)$ and $g(x)$.

$= \boxed{x} - \boxed{6}$ Multiply using the distributive property.

REFLECT

1a. The table shows the values of the sum $f(x) + g(x)$ for several values of x using the functions $f(x)$ and $g(x)$ from part A. Use the rule that you found for $h(x)$ in part A to complete the third column of the table. What do you notice?

For any x, values of $f(x) + g(x)$ and $h(x)$ are equal.

x	$f(x) + g(x)$	$h(x)$
−2	−7 + 6 = −1	−1
−1	−4 + 4 = 0	0
0	−1 + 2 = 1	1
1	2 + 0 = 2	2
2	5 + (−2) = 3	3

1b. Error Analysis A student wrote the rule for $h(x)$ in part A as $5x + 1$. After letting $x = 0$ and observing that $f(0) + g(0) = -1 + 2 = 1$ and $h(0) = 1$, the student concluded that the rule must be correct. Describe what is incorrect about the student's reasoning, and describe what the student should have done to check the rule for $h(x)$.

The values of $f(x) + g(x)$ and $h(x)$ should be equal for all values of x,

not just one value of x. The student should have checked more than

one value of x.

2 EXAMPLE Adding Linear Models

For the initial year of a soccer camp, 44 girls and 56 boys enrolled. Each year thereafter, 5 more girls and 8 more boys enrolled in the camp. Let t be the time (in years) since the camp opened. Write a rule for each of the following functions:

- $g(t)$, the number of girls enrolled as a function of time t
- $b(t)$, the number of boys enrolled as a function of time t
- $T(t)$, the total enrollment as a function of time t

A For the function $g(t)$, the initial value is $\underline{44}$ and the rate of

change is $\underline{5}$. So, $g(t) = \underline{5t + 44}$

B For the function $b(t)$, the initial value is $\underline{56}$ and the rate of

change is $\underline{8}$. So, $b(t) = \underline{8t + 56}$

C The total enrollment is the sum of the functions $g(t)$ and $b(t)$.

$T(t) = g(t) + b(t)$ Write the general form of $T(t)$.

$= \boxed{5t + 44} + \boxed{8t + 56}$ Substitute the rules for $g(t)$ and $b(t)$.

$= \boxed{13t + 100}$ Simplify.

REFLECT

2a. Use unit analysis to show that the rule for $g(t)$ makes sense.

In the rule $5t + 44$, the unit associated with 5 is girls per year, the unit associated

with t is years, and the unit associated with 44 is girls; $\frac{girls}{year} \cdot$ years + girls =

girls + girls = girls, so the rule makes sense.

EXTRA EXAMPLE

For the initial month of a computer/printer package purchase, you pay $200 for the computer and $50 for the printer. Each month thereafter, you make payments of $45 for the computer and $12 for the printer. Let t be the time (in months) since you bought the computer and printer. Write a rule for each of the following functions:

- $c(t)$, the amount paid for the computer as a function of time t: $c(t) = 45t + 200$

- $p(t)$, the amount paid for the printer as a function of time t: $p(t) = 12t + 50$

- $T(t)$, the total amount paid as a function of time t: $T(t) = 57t + 250$

3 EXAMPLE

Questioning Strategies

- Sue multiplied $C(t)$ and $T(t)$ and got $R(t) = 2,600t + 100$. Explain what Sue did wrong and how to fix it. She did not distribute the 200; she should multiply 200 and 100 to get 20,000 as the constant term.

- If you found the revenue function for girls and the revenue function for boys, could you add them to get $R(t)$? Yes; the revenue function for girls is $1,000t + 8,800$; the revenue function for boys is $1,600t + 11,200$. Adding them together gives $R(t)$.

EXTRA EXAMPLE

The computer store in the previous example sold 100 computer/printer packages during the first month and then stopped the sale. Let t be the time in months since the package was first offered for sale. Write a rule for each of the following functions:

- $S(t)$, the number of packages sold as a function of the time t: $S(t) = 100$

- $R(t)$, the revenue generated for the computer store as a function of time t: $R(t) = S(t) \cdot T(t) = 5,700t + 25,000$

Avoid Common Errors

Students may not understand why $C(t)$ does not contain the variable t. Explain that C is a constant function and does not depend on t.

> **MATHEMATICAL PRACTICE** | **Highlighting the Standards**
>
> **2 EXAMPLE** and **3 EXAMPLE** address Mathematical Practice Standard 4 (Model with mathematics). Students create linear functions to model enrollment and revenue for a soccer camp. Draw students' attention to how the total enrollment, total revenue, and profit functions are generated. Have them explain why the profit function is the difference of the revenue function and the expense function.

CLOSE

Essential Question

How can you use operations to combine functions that model real-world situations?

You can add, subtract, or multiply the rules for functions that model the real-world situations provided the operations have meaning in the real world.

Summarize

Have students write a journal entry describing how to add and subtract linear functions and how to multiply a linear function by a constant function.

PRACTICE

Where skills are taught	Where skills are practiced
1 EXAMPLE	EXS. 1–3
2 EXAMPLE	EXS. 5, 6
3 EXAMPLE	EXS. 5, 6

Exercise 4: This exercise extends students' skills by having them perform an addition followed by a multiplication to find a new function.

3 EXAMPLE Multiplying Linear Models

For the soccer camp in the previous example, the cost per child each year was $200. Let t be the time (in years) since the camp opened. Write a rule for each of the following functions:

- $C(t)$, the cost per child of the camp as a function of time t
- $R(t)$, the revenue generated by the total enrollment as a function of time t

A For the function $C(t)$, the initial value is ___200___ and the rate of change is ___0___. So, $C(t) = $ ___200___

B The revenue generated by the total enrollment is the product of the cost function $C(t)$ and the total enrollment function $T(t)$, which was found in the previous example.

$R(t) = C(t) \cdot T(t)$ Write the general form of $R(t)$.

$\quad = \boxed{200} \cdot \left(\boxed{13t + 100} \right)$ Substitute the rules for $C(t)$ and $T(t)$.

$\quad = \boxed{2{,}600t + 20{,}000}$ Multiply using the distributive property.

REFLECT

3a. Explain why $C(t)$ is a constant function.

There is no change in the cost of the camp from year to year.

3b. Use unit analysis to explain why you multiply the cost function $C(t)$ and the enrollment function $T(t)$ to get the revenue function $R(t)$.

The unit associated with $C(t)$ is dollars per child, and the unit associated with $T(t)$ is children; $\frac{\text{dollars}}{\text{child}} \cdot$ children = dollars, which is the unit you want for the revenue function.

3c. What was the initial revenue for the camp? What was the annual rate of change in the revenue?

$20,000; $2,600 per year

3d. The camp's organizer had initial expenses of $18,000, which increased each year by $2,500. Write a rule for the expenses function $E(t)$. Then write a rule for the profit function $P(t)$ based on the fact that profit is the difference between revenue and expenses.

$E(t) = 2{,}500t + 18{,}000; \ P(t) = R(t) - E(t) = 100t + 2{,}000$

PRACTICE

1. Given $f(x) = -2x$ and $g(x) = 4x - 8$, find $h(x) = f(x) + g(x)$.

$h(x) = 2x - 8$

2. Given $f(x) = 3x - 5$ and $g(x) = -2x + 1$, find $h(x) = f(x) - g(x)$.

$h(x) = 5x - 6$

3. Given $f(x) = -2$ and $g(x) = 5x - 6$, find $h(x) = f(x) \cdot g(x)$.

$h(x) = -10x + 12$

4. Given $f(x) = 4$, $g(x) = x + 1$, and $h(x) = x$, find $j(x) = f(x) \cdot [g(x) + h(x)]$.

$j(x) = 8x + 4$

5. To raise funds, a club is publishing and selling a calendar. The club has sold $500 in advertising and will sell copies of the calendar for $20 each. The cost of printing each calendar is $6. Let c be the number of calendars to be printed and sold.

a. Write a rule for the function $R(c)$, which gives the revenue generated by the sale of the calendars.

$R(c) = 20c + 500$

b. Write a rule for the function $E(c)$, which gives the expense of printing the calendars.

$E(c) = 6c$

c. Describe how the function $P(c)$, which gives the club's profit from the sale of the calendars, is related to $R(c)$ and $E(c)$. Then write a rule for $P(c)$.

$P(c) = R(c) - E(c) = 14c + 500$

6. The five winners of a radio station contest will spend a day at an amusement park with all expenses paid. The per-person admission cost is $10, and each person can spend $20 on food. The radio station will pay for all rides, which cost $2 each. Assume that each person takes the same number r of rides.

a. Write a rule for the function $C(r)$, which gives the cost per person.

$C(r) = 2r + 30$

b. Write a rule for the function $P(r)$, which gives the number of people.

$P(r) = 5$

c. Describe how the function $T(r)$, which gives the radio station's total cost, is related to $C(r)$ and $P(r)$. Then write a rule for $T(r)$.

$T(r) = P(r) \cdot C(r) = 10r + 150$

Linear Functions and Their Inverses

Essential question: *What is the inverse of a function, and how can you find the inverse of a linear function?*

Standards for Mathematical Content

CC.9-12.F.IF.1 Understand that a function from one set (called the domain) to another set (called the range) assigns to each element of the domain exactly one element of the range. If f is a function and x is an element of its domain, then $f(x)$ denotes the output of f corresponding to the input x. The graph of f is the graph of the equation $y = f(x)$.

CC.9-12.F.IF.2 Use function notation, evaluate functions for inputs in their domains, and interpret statements that use function notation in terms of a context.

CC.9-12.F.BF.4 Find inverse functions.

CC.9-12.F.BF.4a Solve an equation of the form $f(x) = c$ for a simple function f that has an inverse and write an expression for the inverse.

Also: CC.9-12.A.CED.2, CC.9-12.F.IF.7*, CC.9-12.F.IF.7a*, CC.9-12.F.BF.1*, CC.9-12.F.BF.1a*

Vocabulary
inverse of a function

Prerequisites
Solving literal equations, Lesson 2-4

Continuous linear functions, Lesson 4-2

Math Background
In the simple case, the inverse of a function with input-output pairs $\{(0, 1), (3, 5), (-2, 7)\}$ is a relation with the inputs and outputs switched, or $\{(1, 0), (5, 3), (7, -2)\}$. In the broader sense, however, the inverse of a linear function $f(x)$ is another linear function $g(x)$ such that $f(g(x)) = x$. Graphically, the functions are reflections of each other across the line $y = x$. To find the rule for the inverse of a linear function, f, let $y = f(x)$ and solve for x in terms of y. You now have a function g, where $x = g(y)$. Now switch x and y to obtain $y = g(x)$.

INTRODUCE

Suppose you plan to vacation in Japan and you exchanged dollars for Japanese yen to spend on the trip. Ask students how they would determine how many yen could be exchanged for $100. Then ask students to consider how they would change the yen back to dollars at the end of the trip.

TEACH

1 EXPLORE

Questioning Strategies

- Are the functions $f(x)$ and $g(x)$ in the tables for Reflect Question 1a inverses of each other? Explain. **Yes; the outputs of f are the inputs of g, and the inputs of f are the outputs of g.**

- What operations would you use to find the inverse $g(x)$ for $f(x) = 3x + 4$? **Subtract 4 and then divide by 3 to get $g(x) = \dfrac{x - 4}{3}$.**

Teaching Strategy

Some students may have difficulty following the steps used to find the inverse of a function. You may want to describe an inverse function as one that "undoes" a function. That is, to undo adding a number, you subtract the number. To undo multiplying by a number, you divide by the number, and so on. Show students that you can find the inverse of a function by undoing the operations that have been done to x, but in the reverse order of the order of operations. For example, point out that in **1 EXPLORE**, subtracting 1 undoes adding 1, and dividing by 2 undoes multiplying by 2. Since the order of operations is to multiply by 2 first, you undo that operation last.

Linear Functions and Their Inverses

Essential question: *What is the inverse of a function, and how can you find the inverse of a linear function?*

Recall that inverse operations are operations that undo each other. Similarly, the **inverse of a function** is another function that undoes everything that the original function does.

1 EXPLORE   Using Inverse Operations to Find Inverse Functions

Find the inverse of $f(x) = 2x + 1$ using inverse operations.

A List the operations that the function performs on an input value x in the order that the function performs them. Illustrate these steps using $x = 3$.

$x \longrightarrow$ Multiply by 2. $\longrightarrow$ **Add 1.**

$3 \longrightarrow 2 \cdot 3 = 6 \longrightarrow$ $6 + 1 = 7$

B List the *inverse operations* in the *reverse order*. Illustrate these steps using $x = 7$.

$x \longrightarrow$ Subtract 1. $\longrightarrow$ **Divide by 2.**

$7 \longrightarrow 7 - 1 = 6 \longrightarrow$ $\dfrac{6}{2} = 3$

C Write a rule for the function $g(x)$ that performs the inverse operations in the reverse order. Check your rule by finding $g(7)$.

$g(x) = \dfrac{x - 1}{2}$, so $g(7) = \dfrac{7 - 1}{2} = $ **3**

REFLECT

1a. The first table at the right shows some input-output pairs for the function f. The outputs of f are then listed as inputs for the function g in the second table. Complete the second table.

x	f(x)
−2	−3
0	1
2	5

x	g(x)
−3	−2
1	0
5	2

1b. The function g is the inverse of the function f. If $f(a) = b$, then what is $g(b)$?

$g(b) = a$

1c. Is it reasonable to describe f as the inverse of g? Explain.

Yes; f undoes what g does just as g undoes what f does.

To find the rule for the inverse of a linear function f, let $y = f(x)$ and solve for x in terms of y. Whatever sequence of operations f performs on x to obtain y, the process of solving for x will introduce the inverse operations in the reverse order. You now have a function g where $g(y) = x$. Since x is commonly used as a function's input variable and y as its output variable, as a final step switch x and y to obtain $g(x) = y$.

2 EXAMPLE   Finding the Inverse by Solving $y = f(x)$ for x

Find the inverse of $f(x) = \frac{1}{2}x - 1$.

A Let $y = f(x)$. Solve for x in terms of y.

$y = \frac{1}{2}x - 1$ Write $y = f(x)$.

$y + 1 = \frac{1}{2}x$ Add 1 to both sides.

$2\left(y + 1\right) = x$ Multiply both sides by 2.

$2y + 2 = x$ Distribute.

B Switch x and y and then write the rule for the inverse function g.

$2x + 2 = y$ Switch x and y.

The inverse of $f(x) = \frac{1}{2}x - 1$ is $g(x) = $ $2x + 2$

REFLECT

2a. Find $f(4)$. Then use this value as the input x for $g(x)$. What output value do you get? Why is this expected?

$f(4) = 1$; $g(1) = 4$; g is the inverse of f, so g produces f's

input when given f's output.

2b. When solving $y = f(x)$ for x, you multiplied both sides by 2 instead of dividing both sides by $\frac{1}{2}$. In other words, instead of using an *inverse operation*, you used a *multiplicative inverse*. Why is this acceptable?

Multiplying by 2, the multiplicative inverse of $\frac{1}{2}$, is equivalent to dividing by $\frac{1}{2}$.

In general, $a \div b = a \cdot \frac{1}{b}$ provided $b \neq 0$.

2c. When you switch x and y to find the inverse function, are you solving the function for y? Why or why not?

No; you are just switching the positions of x and y. If you solved the function for

y, you would get the original function back.

Notes

Questioning Strategies

- For part A, if $f(6) = 2$, what would be the value of $g(2)$? How do you know? **6; since g is the inverse of f, g produces the same output value as the input value of f.**

- How does switching x and y in part B help you write the rule for the inverse? **Switching x and y allows you to write the inverse as a function of x.**

- If $(8, 3)$ is a point on the graph of $f(x)$, what is a corresponding point on the graph of $g(x)$? **(3, 8)**

Teaching Strategy

Ask students to graph $f(x)$, $y = x$, and $g(x)$ on the same coordinate plane to help visual learners understand inverse functions. Then ask them to reflect points on the graph of $f(x)$ across the line $y = x$. Point out that the reflected points are points on the graph of $g(x)$.

EXTRA EXAMPLE

Find the inverse of $f(x) = \frac{2}{3}x - 6$. $g(x) = \frac{3}{2}x + 9$

3 EXAMPLE

Questioning Strategies

- What information does the inverse function give you in this situation? **the number of rides you can go on if you have a fixed amount of money to spend at the amusement park**

- If you have $50 to spend at the amusement park, how much can you spend on rides? How do you know? **$10; substituting 50 for A in $r(A)$ gives the output value 10.**

EXTRA EXAMPLE

The function $E(c) = 0.75c + 200$ gives the total expenses for producing c greeting cards if there are $200 in fixed expenses and the materials cost $0.75 per card. Find the inverse function. $c(E) = \frac{E - 200}{0.75}$

Essential Question

What is the inverse of a function, and how can you find the inverse of a linear function?

The inverse of a function interchanges the input and output values of the function. To find the inverse of a linear function, write the original function in terms of x and y, solve for x in terms of y, and then switch x and y. For functions that model real-world situations, the final step of switching the variables is not done because the variables carry real-world meaning.

Summarize

Have students explain how to find the inverse of a linear function by using a graphic organizer. An example is shown below for the function $f(x) = 2x - 4$.

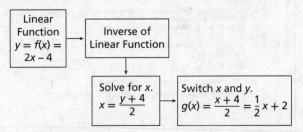

MATHEMATICAL PRACTICE   Highlighting the Standards

Practice Exercises 7 and 8 provide opportunities to address Mathematical Practice Standard 4 (Model with mathematics). Draw students' attention to the formula for converting Fahrenheit to Celsius in Exercise 7. Point out that the inverse of this formula is also a formula; that is, it is the formula for converting Celsius to Fahrenheit.

PRACTICE

Where skills are taught	Where skills are practiced
2 EXAMPLE	EXS. 1–6
3 EXAMPLE	EXS. 7–8

Exercise 9: This exercise extends what students learned in **2** EXAMPLE to the general linear function.

Exercise 10: Students extend their knowledge about inverse functions to determine whether a constant function has an inverse.

2d. The graph of $f(x) = \frac{1}{2}x - 1$ is shown. Graph the inverse function g. Also graph $y = x$ as a dashed line. How are the graphs of f and g related to the line $y = x$?

The graphs of f and g are reflections in
the line $y = x$.

2e. The point $(4, 1)$ is on the graph of f. What is the corresponding point on the graph of g? In general, if (a, b) is a point on the graph of f, what is the corresponding point on the graph of g?

$(1, 4); (b, a)$

---

3 EXAMPLE Finding Inverses of Real-World Functions

The function $A(r) = 2r + 30$ gives the total amount A that you will spend at an amusement park if you spend \$30 on admission and food and you go on r rides that cost \$2 each. Find the inverse function.

$A = 2r + 30$ Write the function using A for $A(r)$.

$A - 30 = 2r$ Subtract 30 from both sides.

$\dfrac{A - 30}{2} = r$ Divide both sides by 2.

REFLECT

3a. Write the inverse function using function notation.

$r(A) = \dfrac{A - 30}{2}$

3b. Explain how the inverse function would be useful if you have a fixed amount of money that you can spend at the amusement park.

If you plan to spend a fixed amount A, then you can input that value into the

inverse function and find the number r of rides that you will be able to go on

(after rounding down to the nearest whole number).

3c. When finding the inverse of a real-world function, why shouldn't you switch the variables as the final step?

The variables have specific real-world meanings that cannot be interchanged.

PRACTICE

Find the inverse $g(x)$ of each function.

1. $f(x) = x - 1$

$g(x) = x + 1$

2. $f(x) = -x + 4$

$g(x) = -x + 4$

3. $f(x) = 2x - 3$

$g(x) = \frac{1}{2}x + \frac{3}{2}$

4. $f(x) = \frac{2}{3}x + 6$

$g(x) = \frac{3}{2}x - 9$

5. $f(x) = 3x - \frac{3}{4}$

$g(x) = \frac{1}{3}x + \frac{1}{4}$

6. $f(x) = -\frac{5}{2}x - \frac{15}{2}$

$g(x) = -\frac{2}{5}x - 3$

7. The formula to convert a temperature F measured in degrees Fahrenheit to a temperature C measured in degrees Celsius is $C = \frac{9}{5}(F - 32)$. You can think of this formula as function $C(F)$. Find the inverse function $F(C)$ and describe what it does.

$F(C) = \frac{5}{9}C + 32$; the function converts degrees Celsius to degrees Fahrenheit.

8. A cylindrical candle 10 inches tall burns at rate of 0.5 inch per hour.

a. Write a rule for the function $h(t)$, the height (in inches) of the candle at time t (in hours since the candle was lit). State the domain and range of the function.

$h(t) = -0.5t + 10; D = \{t \mid 0 \le t \le 20\}; R = \{h \mid 0 \le h \le 10\}$

b. Find the inverse function $t(h)$. State the domain and range of the function.

$t(h) = -2h + 20; D = \{h \mid 0 \le h \le 10\}; R = \{t \mid 0 \le t \le 20\}$

c. Explain how the inverse function is useful.

If you input the height of the candle, the inverse function tells you how

long the candle has burned.

9. Prove that the inverse of a non-constant linear function is another non-constant linear function by starting with the general linear function $f(x) = mx + b$ where $m \ne 0$ and showing that the inverse function $g(x)$ is also linear. Identify the slope and y-intercept of the graph of $g(x)$.

$g(x) = \frac{x - b}{m} = \frac{1}{m}x - \frac{b}{m}$; the slope is $\frac{1}{m}$, and the y-intercept is $-\frac{b}{m}$.

10. Can a constant function have an inverse function? Why or why not?

No; a constant function is a many-to-one pairing, so the inverse would have to be

a one-to-many pairing, but a function must pair each input with a single output.

Correlation

Essential question: *How can you decide whether a correlation exists between paired numerical data?*

```
....................
: COMMON :  Standards for
:  CORE  :  Mathematical Content
....................
```

CC.9-12.S.ID.8 Compute ... and interpret the correlation coefficient of a linear fit.*

CC.9-12.S.ID.9 Distinguish between correlation and causation.*

CC.9-12.S.IC.6 Evaluate reports based on data.*

Vocabulary

correlation

correlation coefficient

Prerequisites

Slope, Lesson 4-3

Math Background

A scatter plot is a graph of numerical data (x, y) that are paired, such as height and weight. If the y-values tend to increase as the x-values increase, then the data have a positive correlation. If the y-values tend to decrease as the x-values increase, then the data have a negative correlation. The strength of the correlation depends on how tightly the points lie about a line. The correlation coefficient of the data, r, is a number between -1 and 1 ($|r| \leq 1$) that measures how well a line fits the data points. If $r = 1$, then the points are all on a non-horizontal line and the slope is positive; if $r = -1$, then the points are all on a non-horizontal line and the slope is negative. A value of r close to 1 indicates a strong positive correlation, while a value of r close to -1 indicates a strong negative correlation. If $|r|$ is about 0.5, then the correlation is considered to be weak. If r is very close to 0, there is no correlation.

INTRODUCE

Point out that up until this lesson, students have worked with data that are perfectly linear and can be modeled by linear functions. In this lesson and those that follow, students will work with data that are not perfectly linear, and they will fit lines to data only in cases where the data have a strong positive or negative correlation.

TEACH

1 ENGAGE

Questioning Strategies

- How does y change in relation to x for each graph shown? *y increases as x increases; y decreases as x increases; y increases as x increases; y decreases as x increases*

- Is the slope of a line equal to the correlation coefficient? Explain. *No; slope is the ratio of the change in y-values over the change in the corresponding x-values and can be any real number. The correlation coefficient is a measure of how closely the points of a scatter plot fit a line and is always a number between -1 and 1.*

Differentiated Instruction

Visual learners may have difficulty in relating the value of r to the scatter plot. You may want them to look at r as a value on a continuum as shown below.

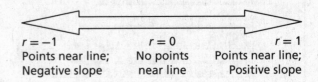

$r = -1$	$r = 0$	$r = 1$
Points near line; Negative slope	No points near line	Points near line; Positive slope

Name_____ Class_____ Date_____

Correlation

Essential question: *How can you decide whether a correlation exists between paired numerical data?*

1 ENGAGE   Understanding Correlation

When two real-world variables (such as height and weight or latitude and average temperature) are measured from the same things (the same people, places, etc.), you obtain a set of paired numerical data that you can plot as points in the coordinate plane to create a data display called a *scatter plot*. Sometimes the scatter plot will show a linear pattern. When it does, the linear pattern may be tight (that is, the points lie very close to a line), or it may be loose (that is, the points are more dispersed about a line). The degree to which a scatter plot shows a linear pattern is an indicator of the strength of a **correlation** between the two variables.

Mathematicians have defined a measure of the direction and magnitude of a correlation. This measure is called the **correlation coefficient** and is denoted by *r*. When the points in a scatter plot all lie on a line that is not horizontal, *r* has a value of 1 if the line has a positive slope and a value of −1 if the line has a negative slope. The correlation coefficient takes on values between −1 and 1 in cases where the points are not perfectly linear.

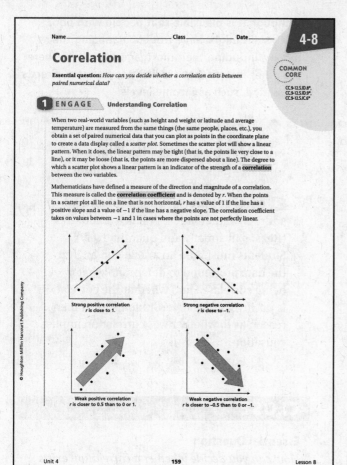

Strong positive correlation
r is close to 1.

Strong negative correlation
r is close to −1.

Weak positive correlation
r is closer to 0.5 than to 0 or 1.

Weak negative correlation
r is closer to −0.5 than to 0 or −1.

REFLECT

1a. What conclusion would you draw about the value of *r* for the scatter plot shown at the right? Why?

The value of *r* is close to 0 because the points do not show any linear pattern.

1b. If the variables *x* and *y* have a strong positive correlation, what generally happens to *y* as *x* increases? What if *x* and *y* have a strong negative correlation?

y increases as *x* increases; *y* decreases as *x* increases.

2 EXAMPLE   Estimating Correlation Coefficients

The table lists the latitude and average annual temperature for various cities in the Northern Hemisphere. Describe the correlation and estimate the correlation coefficient.

City	Latitude	Avg. Annual Temperature
Bangkok, Thailand	13.7°N	82.6°F
Cairo, Egypt	30.1°N	71.4°F
London, England	51.5°N	51.8°F
Moscow, Russia	55.8°N	39.4°F
New Delhi, India	28.6°N	77.0°F
Tokyo, Japan	35.7°N	58.1°F
Vancouver, Canada	49.2°N	49.6°F

A Make a scatter plot. The data pair for Bangkok has been plotted.

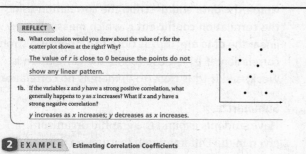

B Describe the correlation, and estimate the correlation coefficient.

Because the plotted points appear to lie very close to a line with a __negative__ slope, the scatter plot shows a __strong negative__ correlation. So, the correlation coefficient is close to __−1__.

Questioning Strategies

• Phoenix, Arizona, is at latitude 33.45°N and has an average annual temperature of 72.6°F. If you include this data pair in the data set, how would it affect the correlation? Why? **It would not affect the correlation because it is a point very close to the others.**

EXTRA EXAMPLE

The graph shows the latitude and average rainfall for the same cities used in **2 EXAMPLE**. Describe the correlation, and estimate the correlation coefficient.

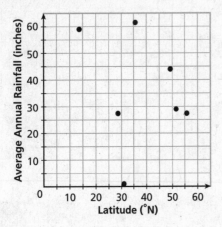

no correlation; correlation coefficient close to 0

3 EXAMPLE

Questioning Strategies

• If amygdala size was found to also correlate with age, how should the scientists change their study of social network size? **Compare groups of people of similar ages.**

EXTRA EXAMPLE

Read the article, and decide whether correlation implies causation in this case.

Math and Mortgages

Researchers at the Federal Reserve Bank and Columbia University have found a correlation between math skills ("financial literacy") and how well people keep up with their home mortgage payments. The researchers tested subjects with a few simple math questions and found that people with poor math skills are likelier to fall behind on their mortgage payments.

Although it is plausible that people with poor math skills might have trouble managing their money, including their mortgage payments, there are other factors that are likely to be more directly correlated, such as income levels.

```
MATHEMATICAL   Highlighting
PRACTICE       the Standards
```

3 EXAMPLE provides opportunities to address Mathematical Practice Standard 2 (Reason abstractly and quantitatively). Students must read an article and analyze the data presented to determine what is being correlated and whether the correlation is positive or negative. Students must then reason as to whether this correlation implies causation.

CLOSE

Essential Question

How can you decide whether a correlation exists between paired numerical data?

Graph the data and describe the correlation using the correlation coefficient r, which measures how linear the data are. If $|r|$ is close to 1, there is a strong correlation; if $|r|$ is close to 0.5, the correlation is weak; and if $|r|$ is close to 0, there is no correlation.

Summarize

Have students expand the graphic organizer given in the Differentiated Instruction note on the previous page. Students should include entries for 0.5 and −0.5 and indicate the type of correlation for each entry.

PRACTICE

Where skills are taught	Where skills are practiced
2 EXAMPLE	EX. 1
3 EXAMPLE	EX. 2

REFLECT

2a. Mexico City, Mexico, is at latitude 19.4°N and has an average annual temperature of 60.8°F. If you include this data pair in the data set, how would it affect the correlation? Why?

It would weaken the correlation because the data point is not close to the line

that the other data points are near.

Correlation and Causation In the preceding example, you would expect that a city's latitude has an effect on the city's average annual temperature. While it does, there are other factors that contribute to a city's weather, such as whether a city is located on a coast or inland.

A common error when interpreting paired data is confusing correlation and causation. If a correlation exists between two variables, this does not necessarily mean that one variable causes the other. When one variable increases, the other variable may increase (or decrease) as a result of other variables not being considered. Such variables are sometimes called *lurking variables*.

3 EXAMPLE Distinguishing Causation from Correlation

Read the article. Decide whether correlation implies causation in this case.

A Identify the two variables that the scientists correlated. Was the correlation positive or negative?

size of amygdala, size of social

network; positive

B Decide whether correlation implies causation in this case. Explain your reasoning.

Causation is possible, but which variable

controls the other is not known. It's

possible that having a larger amygdala

might cause a person to have a larger social

network, and it's possible that increasing

the size of the network may cause the

amygdala to grow in response. However,

neither variable may be in control because

a lurking variable may be causing both the

social network and the amygdala to grow.

BRAIN'S AMYGDALA CONNECTED TO SOCIAL BEHAVIOR

An almond-shaped part of the brain called the amygdala has long been known to play a role in people's emotional states. Now scientists studying the amygdala have discovered a connection between its size and the size of a person's social network. The scientists used a brain scanner to determine the size of the amygdala in the brains of 58 adults. They also gave each person a survey that measured the size of the person's social network. Their analysis of the data found that there is a correlation between the two: People with larger amygdalas tend to have larger social networks.

Unit 4   161   Lesson 8

REFLECT

3a. Suppose scientists study a group of people over time and find that those who increased the size of their social networks also had an increase in the size of their amygdalas. Does this result establish a cause-and-effect relationship? Explain.

No; it is still not possible to determine which variable controls the other or to

rule out the possibility of a lurking variable.

PRACTICE

1. The table lists the heights and weights of the six wide receivers who played for the New Orleans Saints during the 2010 football season.

a. Make a scatter plot.

Wide Receiver	Height (inches)	Weight (pounds)
Arrington	75	192
Colston	76	225
Henderson	71	200
Meachem	74	210
Moore	69	190
Roby	72	189

b. Describe the correlation, and estimate the correlation coefficient using one of these values: −1, −0.5, 0, 0.5, 1.

Weak positive correlation; 0.5

2. Read the article shown at the right. Describe the correlation and decide whether correlation implies causation in this case. Explain your reasoning.

Walking speed is positively correlated to

life span; causation is not likely; there is

probably a lurking variable such as general

health that causes people to walk faster and

live longer.

WALKING SPEED MAY PREDICT LIFE SPAN

Researchers who looked at data from nearly 35,000 senior citizens discovered that an elderly person's walking speed is correlated to that person's chance of living 10 more years. For instance, the researchers found that only 19 percent of the slowest-walking 75-year-old men lived for 10 more years compared with 87 percent of the fastest-walking 75-year-old men. Similar results were found for elderly women.

Unit 4   162   Lesson 8

Fitting Lines to Data

Essential question: *How do you find a linear model for a set of paired numerical data, and how do you evaluate the goodness of fit?*

Standards for Mathematical Content

CC.9-12.F.BF.1 Write a function that describes a relationship between two quantities.*

CC.9-12.F.BF.1a Determine an explicit expression ... from a context.*

CC.9-12.F.LE.5 Interpret the parameters in a linear ... function in terms of a context.*

CC.9-12.S.ID.6 Represent data on two quantitative variables on a scatter plot, and describe how the variables are related.*

CC.9-12.S.ID.6a Fit a function to the data; use functions fitted to data to solve problems in the context of the data.*

CC.9-12.S.ID.6b Informally assess the fit of a function by plotting and analyzing residuals.*

CC.9-12.S.ID.6c Fit a linear function for a scatter plot that suggests a linear association.*

CC.9-12.S.ID.7 Interpret the slope (rate of change) and the intercept (constant term) of a linear model in the context of the data.*

Vocabulary

residual

residual plot

interpolation

extrapolation

Prerequisites

Graphing linear functions, Lesson 4-3

Writing linear functions, Lesson 4-5

Math Background

In this lesson, students will make a scatter plot for a set of paired numerical data, draw a line of fit on the scatter plot, and then find the equation of the line of fit. To find a line of fit in the form $y = mx + b$, use two given data points close to the line and then find the line's slope, $m = \dfrac{y_2 - y_1}{y_2 - x_1}$. Then use m and one of the points to find the y-intercept, b, where

$$b = y_1 - \dfrac{y_2 - y_1}{y_2 - x_1}(x_1).$$

Residuals can be used to assess how well a model fits a data set. Residuals that are small and random indicate a good fit. If there are many large residuals or if there is a pattern to the residuals, then a new model may be needed. For a data point (x, y_d) and the corresponding point (x, y_m) on the model, the residual is $y_d - y_m$.

INTRODUCE

Remind students that in a linear relationship, as the input values increase by one unit, the differences in the consecutive output values are constant, as shown in the table below.

College Tuition	
Year	Amount ($)
0	10,000
1	11,000
2	12,000
3	13,000

Remind students how to find the slope of a line containing the points $(-4, 1)$ and $(3, 6)$. $\dfrac{5}{7}$

continued

Name_____ Class_____ Date_____

4-9

Fitting Lines to Data

COMMON CORE

CC.9-12.F.LE.5*,
CC.9-12.S.ID.6*,
CC.9-12.S.ID.6a*,
CC.9-12.S.ID.6b*,
CC.9-12.S.ID.6c*,
CC.9-12.S.ID.7*

Essential question: *How do you find a linear model for a set of paired numerical data, and how do you evaluate the goodness of fit?*

When paired numerical data have a strong positive or negative correlation, you can find a linear model for the data. The process is called *fitting a line to the data* or *finding a line of fit for the data.*

1 EXAMPLE Finding a Line of Fit for Data

The table lists the median age of females living in the United States based on the results of the U.S. Census over the past few decades. Determine whether a linear model is reasonable for the data. If so, find a linear model for the data.

Year	Median Age of Females
1970	29.2
1980	31.3
1990	34.0
2000	36.5
2010	38.2

A Identify the independent and dependent variables, and specify how you will represent them.

The independent variable is time, so use the variable t. Rather than let t take on the values 1970, 1980, and so on, define t as the number of years since 1970.

The dependent variable is the median age of females. Although you could simply use the variable a, you can use F as a subscript to remind yourself that only median *female* ages are being considered. So, the dependent variable is a_F.

B Make a table of paired values of t and a_F. Then draw a scatter plot.

t	a_F
0	29.2
10	31.3
20	34.0
30	36.5
40	38.2

Time (years since 1970)

C Draw a line of fit on the scatter plot.

Using a ruler, draw a line that passes as close as possible to the plotted points. Your line does not necessarily have to pass through any of the points, but you should try to balance points above and below the line.

D Find the equation of the line of fit.

Suppose that a student drew a line of fit that happens to pass through the data points (20, 34.0) and (30, 36.5). Complete the steps below to find the equation of the student's line. (Note that x and y are used as the independent and dependent variables for the purposes of finding the line's slope and y-intercept.)

1. Find the slope.

$m = \dfrac{y_2 - y_1}{x_2 - x_1}$

$m = \dfrac{36.5 - 34.0}{30 - 20}$

$m = 0.25$

2. Find the y-intercept using (20, 34.0).

$y = mx + b$

$34.0 = 0.25 (20) + b$

$34.0 = 5 + b$

$29.0 = b$

So, in terms of the variables t and a_F, the equation of the line of fit is

$a_F = 0.25t + 29$

Perform similar calculations to find the equation of your line of fit.

Equation of your line of fit: Answers will vary.

REFLECT

1a. What type of correlation does the scatter plot show?

A strong positive correlation

1b. Before you placed a ruler on the scatter plot to draw a line of fit, you may have thought that the plotted points were perfectly linear. How does the table tell you that they are not?

If the points were perfectly linear, the difference in consecutive values of the

dependent variable would be constant because the values of the independent

variable are equally spaced. But the median age increased by 2.1 from 1970 to

1980 and by 2.7 from 1980 to 1990.

1c. For your line of fit, interpret the slope and a_F-intercept in the context of the data.

The slope is the rate of change in median female age per year; the a_F-intercept

is the median female age in the initial year (1970).

EXAMPLE

Questioning Strategies

- Why is a linear model reasonable for the data?
  The points of the scatter plot roughly follow
  a line.

- When can there be more than one reasonable
  equation of the line of fit for a data set? **when the**
  data points are not perfectly linear

- Why does the scatter plot show points with a
  strong positive correlation? **The correlation is**
  strong because the points are very tight along
  the line of fit; the correlation is positive because
  the dependent values are increasing as the
  independent values are increasing.

Avoid Common Errors

Students may have difficulty drawing a line of fit on
a scatter plot if they are trying to include actual data
points on the line. While it is desirable to include
points on the line, they should try to balance the
number of points above the line with the number
of points below the line. Tell students it is more
important to locate the line so that the points are
evenly distributed above and below the line.

EXTRA EXAMPLE

The table lists the estimated number of wireless
industry (primarily cellular telephone) subscribers
in the United States over a five-year period,
measured in June of each year. Determine whether
a linear model is reasonable for the data. If so, find
a linear model for the data.

Year (as of June)	Number of Subscribers (millions)
2005	194.5
2006	219.7
2007	243.4
2008	262.7
2009	276.6

A scatter plot shows that a linear model is
reasonable for the data. Sample answer for line
of fit: $s = 20.7t + 197.9$ where t is the number of
years since 2005 (answers will vary but the value
of the coefficients should be similar to this answer).

2 EXAMPLE

Questioning Strategies

- Why do two points in part A have residuals of 0?
  They are data points used to find the model.

- How would you describe the suitability of the
  model if a pattern in the residuals showed
  that they are decreasing as the values of x are
  increasing? **The model may not be suitable.**

Differentiated Instruction

Help visual learners understand how to interpret
the scatter plot of the residuals for the model and
how their scatter plot compares with a scatter plot
of residuals that shows a random tight distribution
of points about the x-axis.

EXTRA EXAMPLE

A student fit the line $s = 19.3t + 204.8$ to the data
in the previous example. Make a residual plot and
evaluate the goodness of fit.
Residuals are −10.3, −4.4, 0, 0, and −5.4. There
are two residuals with a value of zero, but there
are no positive residuals, so there is not a balance
between the positive and negative residuals. So,
the distribution is not random. The absolute values
of the residuals are small compared with the
values, and the only pattern is the lack of positive
residuals. The line fits the data somewhat but is
a relatively poor model. A model with a mix of
positive and negative residuals would be better.

Residuals You can evaluate a linear model's goodness of fit using *residuals*. A **residual** is the difference between an actual value of the dependent variable and the value predicted by the linear model. After calculating residuals, you can draw a **residual plot**, which is a scatter plot of points whose *x*-coordinates are the values of the independent variable and whose *y*-coordinates are the corresponding residuals.

Whether the fit of a line to data is suitable and good depends on the distribution of the residuals, as illustrated below.

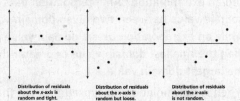

Distribution of residuals about the *x*-axis is random and tight. A linear fit to the data is suitable and strong.

Distribution of residuals about the *x*-axis is random but loose. A linear fit to the data is suitable but weak.

Distribution of residuals about the *x*-axis is not random. A linear fit to the data may not be suitable.

2 EXAMPLE Creating a Residual Plot and Evaluating Fit

A student fit the line $a_F = 0.25t + 29$ to the data in the previous example. Make a residual plot and evaluate the goodness of fit.

A Calculate the residuals. Substitute each value of *t* into the equation to find the value predicted for a_F by the linear model. Then subtract predicted from actual to find the residual.

t	a_F actual	a_F predicted	Residual
0	29.2	29.0	0.2
10	31.3	31.5	−0.2
20	34.0	34.0	0
30	36.5	36.5	0
40	38.2	39.0	−0.8

B Plot the residuals.

C Evaluate the suitability of a linear fit and the goodness of the fit.

- Is there a balance between positive and negative residuals?
  There is one positive and two negatives, but the negatives have a greater
  absolute value than the positive if you add them.

- Is there a pattern to the residuals? If so, describe it.
  The residuals have no apparent pattern.

- Is the absolute value of each residual small relative to a_F (actual)? For instance, when $t = 0$, the residual is 0.2 and the value of a_F is 29.2, so the relative size of the residual is $\frac{0.2}{29.2} \approx 0.7\%$, which is quite small.
  The absolute values of the residuals are all small.

- What is your overall evaluation of the suitability and goodness of the linear fit?
  The line is an appropriate model for the data and fits the data fairly well.

REFLECT

2a. Use the table and graph below to find the residuals for your line of fit from the first Example and then make a residual plot. Answers will vary.

t	a_F actual	a_F predicted	Residual
0	29.2		
10	31.3		
20	34.0		
30	36.5		
40	38.2		

2b. Evaluate the suitability and goodness of the fit for your line of fit.
Answers will vary.

2c. Suppose the line of fit with equation $a_F = 0.25t + 29$ is changed to $a_F = 0.25t + 28.8$. What effect does this change have on the residuals? On the residual plot? Is the new line a better fit to the data? Explain.
Residuals increase by 0.2; points in plot are translated 0.2 unit up; now there are
3 positive residuals and 1 negative one, but the sum of the residuals is now closer
to 0, so the fit may be slightly better.

Avoid Common Errors

Some students may expect that since the lesson is about linear models, a graph of the residuals should form a straight line. Make sure students understand that the residuals indicate a good fit only if they cluster randomly around the *x*-axis, preferably with a tight distribution that resembles a horizontal line. However, if the residuals have a tight linear distribution that veers away from the *x*-axis, this indicates a poor fit.

Differentiated Instruction

Advanced students may be interested in knowing that they can find more than one equation of the line of fit, and that they can compare their models with other students to determine which one may be the best fitting model.

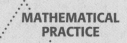

MATHEMATICAL PRACTICE   **Highlighting the Standards**

2 EXAMPLE addresses Standard 2 (Reason abstractly and quantitatively). Draw students' attention to the use of multiple representations for the residuals, both as a table and as a scatter plot. Specifically, ask students why a scatter plot of residuals is helpful in determining whether a model for data is suitable and good.

3 EXAMPLE

Questioning Strategies

- What is the difference between an interpolation and an extrapolation? An interpolation uses a domain value between two given domain values, while an extrapolation uses a domain value less than the smallest domain value or greater than the largest domain value.

- When is extrapolation most useful? when the domain value of the extrapolation is close to the given domain values

- If the independent variable is time, is a prediction about a future value interpolation or extrapolation? extrapolation

- If the independent variable is time, is a prediction about a past value interpolation or extrapolation? It could be either, depending on whether the date in question is before or after the earliest date in the given data set.

Technology

Students may benefit from using a spreadsheet to find the interpolated values of the model for the years 1970 to 2010. Ask them to enter 1970 as year 0 in cell A1; then, have students enter $\boxed{=A1 + 1}$ in cell A2 and the model for 1970 as $\boxed{0.25*A1 + 29}$ in cell B1. Then, they should use the FILL DOWN feature of the spreadsheet to find the values for all years between 1970 and 2010.

EXTRA EXAMPLE

Using the model $s = 20.7t + 197.9$, predict the total number of wireless subscribers in December 2006 (midway between the 2006 and 2007 data in Extra Example 1) and in June 2015. Identify each prediction as an interpolation or an extrapolation. Dec. 2006: 229 million, interpolation; June 2015: 405 million, extrapolation

Making Predictions A linear model establishes the dependent variable as a linear function of the independent variable, and you can use the function to make predictions. The accuracy of a prediction depends not only on the model's goodness of fit but also on the value of the independent variable for which you're making the prediction.

A model's domain is determined by the least and greatest values of the independent variable found in the data set. For instance, the least and greatest t-values for the median age data are 0 (for 1970) and 40 (for 2010), so the domain of any model for the data is $\{t \mid 0 \le t \le 40\}$. Making a prediction using a value of the independent variable from *within* the model's domain is called **interpolation**. Making a prediction using a value from *outside* the domain is called **extrapolation**. As you might expect, you can have greater confidence in an interpolation than in an extrapolation.

3 EXAMPLE   Making Predictions Using a Linear Model

Using the model $a_F = 0.25t + 29$, predict the median age of females in 1995 and in 2015. Identify each prediction as an interpolation or as an extrapolation.

A   To make a prediction about 1995, let $t = $ __25__ . Then to the nearest

   tenth, the predicted value of a_F is $a_F = 0.25 \left(\boxed{25} \right) + 29 \approx $ __35.3__ .

   Because the t-value falls __within__ the model's domain,

   the prediction is an __interpolation__.

B   To make a prediction about 2015, let $t = $ __45__ . Then to the nearest

   tenth, the predicted value of a_F is $a_F = 0.25 \left(\boxed{45} \right) + 29 \approx $ __40.3__ .

   Because the t-value falls __outside__ the model's domain, the

   prediction is an __extrapolation__.

REFLECT

3a. Use your linear model to predict the median age of females in 1995 and 2015.

   Answers will vary.

3b. The Census Bureau gives 35.5 as the median age of females for 1995 and an estimate of 38.4 for 2015. Which of your predictions using your linear model was more accurate? Explain.

   Answers will vary but should be based on comparing differences between

   actual and predicted values.

PRACTICE

Answers to parts c–e are based on the sample answer in part b.
1. The table lists the median age of males living in the United States based on the results of the U.S. Census over the past few decades.

Year	1970	1980	1990	2000	2010
Median Age of Males	26.8	28.8	31.6	34.0	35.5

a. Let t represent time (in years since 1970), and let a_M represent the median age of males. Make a table of paired values of t and a_M. Then draw a scatter plot.

t	a_M
0	26.8
10	28.8
20	31.6
30	34.0
40	35.5

b. Draw a line of fit on the scatter plot and find an equation of the line.

   Sample answer: $a_M = 0.24t + 26.6$

c. Calculate the residuals, and make a residual plot.

t	a_M actual	a_M predicted	Residual
0	26.8	26.6	0.02
10	28.8	29.0	−0.02
20	31.6	31.4	0.02
30	34.0	33.8	0.02
40	35.5	36.2	−0.07

d. Evaluate the suitability of a linear fit and the goodness of the fit.

   The line is an appropriate model for the data and fits the data fairly well.

© Houghton Mifflin Harcourt Publishing Company

Essential Question

How do you find a linear model for a set of paired numerical data, and how do you evaluate the goodness of fit?

Identify the independent and dependent variables, make a scatter plot of the data, draw a line of fit on the scatter plot, and find the equation of the line of fit. To determine the goodness of fit, find the residuals and see whether the distribution of residuals about the x-axis is random and tight.

Summarize

Have students complete the graphic organizer below.

Distribution of residuals about the x-axis is...	Goodness of fit is ...
random and tight.	suitable and strong.
random and loose.	suitable and weak.
not random.	not suitable.

PRACTICE

Where skills are taught	Where skills are practiced
1 EXAMPLE	EXS. 1a, 1b, 4a, 4b, 4c
2 EXAMPLE	EXS. 1c, 1d, 4d, 4e
3 EXAMPLE	EX. 1e

Exercise 2: Students compare data from two different models. Students should focus on the characteristics of the models, in particular slope and intercepts.

Exercise 3: Students will have to consider reasons why a model that works over a known data range may not hold up in the future. This should help reinforce the statement in the lesson that extrapolations tend to be less reliable than interpolations.

e. Predict the median age of males in 1995 and 2015. Identify each prediction as an interpolation or an extrapolation, and then compare the predictions with these median ages of males from the Census Bureau: 33.2 in 1995 and an estimated 35.9 in 2015.

1995 age is 32.6 and is an interpolation; 2015 age is 37.4 and is an extrapolation.

The 1995 interpolation is a better approximation to the Census Bureau data

than the 2015 extrapolation.

2. Compare the equations of your lines of fit for the median age of females and the median age of males. When referring to any constants in those equations, be sure to interpret them in the context of the data.

Answers will vary, but students should find that the slopes (rates of change in

median age) are roughly equal while the a-intercepts (median ages in 1970)

differ by about 2.

3. Explain why it isn't reasonable to use linear models to predict the median age of females or males far into the future.

The predictions made from a linear model will grow at a constant rate from year

to year but median ages will not. The growth in median ages is likely to slow

down and might even reverse (start decreasing).

4. The table lists, for various lengths (in centimeters), the median weight (in kilograms) of male infants and female infants (ages 0−36 months) in the United States.

Length (cm)	50	60	70	80	90	100
Median Weight (kg) of Male Infants	3.4	5.9	8.4	10.8	13.0	15.5
Median Weight (kg) of Female Infants	3.4	5.8	8.3	10.6	12.8	15.2

a. Let l represent an infant's length in excess of 50 centimeters. (For instance, for an infant whose length is 60 cm, $l = 10$.) Let w_M represent the median weight of male infants, and let w_F represent the median weight of female infants. Make a table of paired values of l and either w_M or w_F (whichever you prefer).

l	0	10	20	30	40	50
w						

Answers will vary.

---

b. Draw a scatter plot of the paired data. Answers will vary.

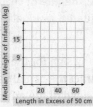

Median Weight of Infants (kg)

Length in Excess of 50 cm

c. Draw a line of fit on the scatter plot and find the equation of the line. According to your model, at what rate does weight change with respect to length?

Answers will vary. Sample answers: $w_M = 0.244l + 3.4$; $w_F = 0.238l + 3.4$.

Weight increases 0.244 kg (boys) or 0.238 kg (girls) per 1 cm increase in length.

d. Calculate the residuals, and make a residual plot. Answers will vary.

l	w actual	w predicted	Residual
0			
10			
20			
30			
40			
50			

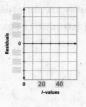

Residuals

l-values

e. Evaluate the suitability of a linear fit and the goodness of the fit.

Answers will vary.

4-10

Linear Regression

Essential question: *How do you use a graphing calculator to perform linear regression on a set of paired numerical data?*

CC.9-12.F.LE.5 Interpret the parameters in a linear ... function in terms of a context.*

CC.9-12.S.ID.6 Represent data on two quantitative variables on a scatter plot, and describe how the variables are related.*

CC.9-12.S.ID.6a Fit a function to the data; use functions fitted to data to solve problems in the context of the data.*

CC.9-12.S.ID.6b Informally assess the fit of a function by ... analyzing residuals.*

CC.9-12.S.ID.6c Fit a linear function for a scatter plot that suggests a linear association.*

CC.9-12.S.ID.7 Interpret the slope (rate of change) and the intercept (constant term) of a linear model in the context of the data.*

CC.9-12.S.ID.8 Compute (using technology) and interpret the correlation coefficient of a linear fit.*

Also: CC.9-12.F.IF.7*, CC.9-12.F.IF.7a*

Vocabulary

linear regression

Prerequisites

Correlation, Lesson 4-8

Fitting lines to data, Lesson 4-9

Math Background

In the previous lesson, students fit a line to data "by eye" and then calculated the residuals. If the line of fit was drawn such that as many points fell above the line as below, then the number of residuals with positive values should equal the number of residuals with negative values.

In this lesson, students first learn to compare different hand-drawn lines of fit by comparing the sum of the squares of the residuals. The students learn that minimizing the sum of the squares of the residuals improves the fit of the model. Finally, students learn how use their calculators to generate a line of best fit that minimizes the sum of the squares of the residuals.

INTRODUCE

Remind students about how to graph a function with a graphing calculator by asking them to graph $y = 50x + 100$ in the first quadrant. Tell them to adjust their viewing window so that only the first quadrant is showing, but also so that they can see the y-intercept.

TEACH

 EXPLORE

Questioning Strategies

• Why are the squares of the residuals used to perform a linear regression? Using the squares guarantees that the values will be nonnegative and their sum will not be 0 unless the points are perfectly linear.

• Why are two lines of fit analyzed by finding the squares of the residuals? Which line of fit should be chosen? to determine which line of fit was a better model for the data; the line of fit that has the smaller sum of the squared residuals

Avoid Common Errors

Students often have the wrong sign for their residuals because they subtract the actual value from the predicted value instead of the other way around. Point out that finding the squares of the residuals will mask this error, since the square of a real number is always nonnegative, but that they should be careful to calculate the residuals correctly if they want to know whether the model's predicted value is an underestimate (positive residual) or an overestimate (negative residual) of the actual value.

Name_____ Class_____ Date_____

4-10

COMMON CORE

CC-9-12.F.LE.5*,
CC-9-12.S.ID.6a*,
CC-9-12.S.ID.6b*,
CC-9-12.S.ID.6c*,
CC-9-12.S.ID.7*,
CC-9-12.S.ID.8*

Linear Regression

Essential question: *How can you use a graphing calculator to perform linear regression on a set of paired numerical data?*

You can use a graphing calculator to fit a line to a set of paired numerical data that have a strong positive or negative correlation. The calculator uses a method called **linear regression**, which involves minimizing the sum of the squares of the residuals.

1 EXPLORE   Comparing Sums of Squared Residuals

In Lesson 4-9 you fit a line to the data in the table at the right. Because each person in your class fit a line by eye, any two people are likely to have gotten slightly different lines of fit. Suppose one person came up with the equation $a_F = 0.25t + 29.0$ while another came up with $a_F = 0.25t + 28.8$ where, in each case, t is the time in years since 1970 and a_F is the median age of females.

Time	Median Age of Females
1970	29.2
1980	31.3
1990	34.0
2000	36.5
2010	38.2

A Complete each table below in order to calculate the squares of the residuals for each line of fit.

		$a_F = 0.25t + 29.0$		
t	a_F (actual)	a_F (predicted)	Residuals	Square of Residuals
0	29.2	29.0	0.2	0.04
10	31.3	31.5	−0.2	0.04
20	34.0	34.0	0	0
30	36.5	36.5	0	0
40	38.2	39.0	−0.8	0.64

		$a_F = 0.25t + 28.8$		
t	a_F (actual)	a_F (predicted)	Residuals	Square of Residuals
0	29.2	28.8	0.4	0.16
10	31.3	31.3	0	0
20	34.0	33.8	0.2	0.04
30	36.5	36.3	0.2	0.04
40	38.2	38.8	−0.6	0.36

© Houghton Mifflin Harcourt Publishing Company

B Find the sum of the squared residuals for each line of fit.

Sum of squared residuals for $a_F = 0.25t + 29.0$: __2(0.04) + 0.64 = 0.72__

Sum of squared residuals for $a_F = 0.25t + 28.8$: __0.16 + 2(0.04) + 0.36 = 0.6__

C Identify the line that has the smaller sum of the squared residuals.

__$a_F = 0.25t + 28.8$__

REFLECT

1a. Complete the table to calculate the squares of the residuals and then the sum of the squares for your line of fit from Lesson 4-9. Answers will vary.

t	a_F (actual)	a_F (predicted)	Residuals	Square of Residuals
0	29.2			
10	31.3			
20	34.0			
30	36.5			
40	38.2			

Sum of squared residuals: _____

1b. If you use a graphing calculator to perform linear regression on the data, you obtain the equation $a_F = 0.232t + 29.2$. Complete the table to calculate the squares of the residuals and then the sum of the squares for this line of fit.

		$a_F = 0.232t + 29.2$		
t	a_F (actual)	a_F (predicted)	Residuals	Square of Residuals
0	29.2	29.2	0	0
10	31.3	31.52	−0.22	0.0484
20	34.0	33.84	0.16	0.0256
30	36.5	36.16	0.34	0.1156
40	38.2	38.48	−0.28	0.0784

Sum of squared residuals: _0.268_

1c. Explain why the model $a_F = 0.232t + 29.2$ is a better fit to the data than $a_F = 0.25t + 29.0$, $a_F = 0.25t + 28.8$, and even your own model.

The sum of the squared residuals is less than the sum for any other model.

© Houghton Mifflin Harcourt Publishing Company

2 EXAMPLE

Questioning Strategies

- Why is the value of r^2 less than the value of r in part D? Since r^2 is the square of r, and since $0 < r < 1, r^2 < r$.

- How does the residual plot in part F relate to the graph of the equation of the line of best fit in part E? The residuals that are below the x-axis represent data points that are below the line of fit, and the residuals that are above the x-axis represent data points that are above the line of fit.

Differentiated Instruction

Students may need practice with each of the steps in graphing the line of best fit before doing **2 EXAMPLE**. Have them practice the steps for graphing the line of best fit using the data in the table below. Tell them to use the data to find an equation of the line of best fit and the value of the correlation coefficient.

x	y
0	10
4	15
8	21
12	27
16	32

$y = 1.4x + 9.8; r = 0.9994$

Help visual learners understand how to interpret the scatter plot of the residuals. Point out that a scatter plot of residuals should show a random distribution of points about the x-axis.

Teaching Strategy

Before doing Reflect Question 2b, remind students about the meaning of interpolation and extrapolation from Lesson 4-8.

EXTRA EXAMPLE

The table lists the number of different events in the Olympic Winter Games from 1972 to 2010. Use a graphing calculator to find the line of best fit, to find the correlation coefficient, and to evaluate the goodness of fit.

Year of Olympic Winter Games	Number of Events
1972	35
1976	37
1980	38
1984	39
1988	46
1992	57
1994	61
1998	68
2002	78
2006	84
2010	86

$y = 1.5428x + 27.73; r = 0.97$; the fit is good because r is very close to 1 and the plotted residuals have a random, tight distribution about the x-axis.

MATHEMATICAL PRACTICE — Highlighting the Standards

You can address Mathematical Practice Standard 5 (Use appropriate tools strategically) in a class discussion about **2 EXAMPLE**. Ask students to describe the advantages of using a graphing calculator to find the line of best fit and to do a residuals plot from the data. Students should understand that it may be cumbersome to find a line of fit by hand as in Lesson 4-9, and that saving time by using a graphing calculator gives them more time to analyze their graphs and results.

Because linear regression produces an equation for which the sum of the squared residuals is as small as possible, the line obtained from linear regression is sometimes called the *least-squares regression line*. It is also called the *line of best fit*. Not only will a graphing calculator automatically find the equation of the line of best fit, but it will also give you the correlation coefficient and display the residual plot.

2 EXAMPLE Performing Linear Regression on a Graphing Calculator

The table gives the distances (in meters) that a discus was thrown by men to win the gold medal at the Olympic Games from 1920 to 1964. (No Olympic Games were held during World War II.) Use a graphing calculator to find the line of best fit, to find the correlation coefficient, and to evaluate the goodness of fit.

A Identify the independent and dependent variables, and specify how you will represent them.

The independent variable is time. Since the graphing calculator uses the variables x and y, let x represent time. To simplify the values of x, define x as years since 1920 so that, for instance, $x = 0$ represents 1920 and $x = 44$ represents 1964. Then $x = \underline{\quad 4 \quad}$ represents 1924, $x = \underline{\quad 8 \quad}$ represents 1928, $x = \underline{\quad 12 \quad}$ represents 1932, and so on.

The dependent variable is the distance that won the gold medal for the men's discus throw. Let y represent that distance.

Year of Olympic Games	Men's Gold Medal Discus Throw (meters)
1920	44.685
1924	46.155
1928	47.32
1932	49.49
1936	50.48
1940	No Olympics
1944	No Olympics
1948	52.78
1952	55.03
1956	56.36
1960	59.18
1964	61.00

B Enter the paired data into two lists, L_1 and L_2, on your graphing calculator after pressing `STAT`.

Do the distances increase or decrease over time? What does this mean for the correlation?

The distances increase, so the correlation will

be positive.

C Create a scatter plot of the paired data using STAT PLOT. The calculator will choose a good viewing window and plot the points automatically if you press `ZOOM` and select ZoomStat.

Describe the correlation.

There is a strong positive correlation because the

data points are quite linear and they increase

from left to right.

D Perform linear regression by pressing `STAT` and selecting LinReg ($ax + b$) from the CALC menu. The calculator reports the slope a and y-intercept b of the line of best fit. It also reports the correlation coefficient r.

Does the correlation coefficient agree with your description of the correlation in Part C? Explain.

Yes; the value of r is very close to 1, which

supports the assertion that the correlation is

strong and positive.

E Graph the line of best fit by pressing `Y=`, entering the equation of the line of best fit, and then pressing `GRAPH`. You should round the values of a and b when entering them so that each has at most 4 significant digits.

What is the equation of the line of best fit?

$y = 0.3461x + 44.63$

F Create a residual plot by replacing L_2 with RESID in STAT PLOT as the choice for Ylist. (You can select RESID from the NAMES menu after pressing `2nd` `STAT`.)

Evaluate the suitability and goodness of the fit.

The points are randomly distributed about the

x-axis, so a linear fit is suitable. The points are

close to the x-axis, so the fit is good.

Notes

Essential Question

How do you use a graphing calculator to perform linear regression on a set of paired numerical data?
Identify the independent and dependent variables, enter the data into a graphing calculator, do a scatter plot of the data, find the line of best fit, use the calculator to draw the line of best fit on the scatter plot, and make a plot of the residuals. To determine the goodness of fit, analyze the residual plot and see whether the distribution of residuals about the x-axis is random and tight. Use the correlation coefficient as well to tell whether the correlation is weak or strong.

Summarize

Have students explain how to perform linear regression with a graphing calculator in a graphic organizer. An example is shown below.

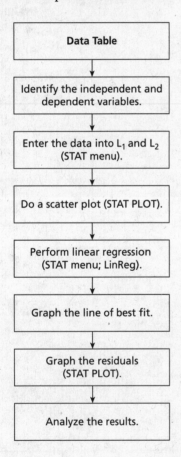

Teaching Strategy

For Practice Exercise 3, you may want to discuss that linear models are not the only models that may fit a set of data. Emphasize the need for the data points to cluster closely to the line of fit and for the correlation coefficient to indicate a strong correlation before a linear model is used. More advanced students may be interested to know that there exist quadratic, cubic, and power regressions that are used to find curves of best fit.

Where skills are taught	Where skills are practiced
2 EXAMPLE	EXS. 1, 2, 4

Exercise 3: Students research data values that do not fit a linear model. This will help students understand that not all data sets are linear, even when they are similar in nature to data for which a linear model is reasonable.

REFLECT

2a. Interpret the slope and *y*-intercept of the line of best fit in the context of the data.

The distances increased about 0.35 meter per year (1.38 meters every 4 years);

the initial distance (in 1920) was about 44.63 meters.

2b. Use the line of best fit to make predictions about the distances that would have won gold medals if the Olympic Games had been held in 1940 and 1944. Are the predictions interpolations or extrapolations?

1940: 51.55 meters; 1944: 52.94 meters; interpolations

2c. Several Olympic Games were held prior to 1920. Use the line of best fit to make a prediction about the distance that would have won a gold medal in the 1908 Olympics. What value of *x* must you use? Is the prediction an interpolation or an extrapolation? How does the prediction compare with the actual value of 40.89 meters?

Use $x = -12$; prediction: 40.48 meters; extrapolation; prediction is

remarkably accurate.

PRACTICE

Throughout these exercises, use a graphing calculator.

1. The table gives the distances (in meters) that a discus was thrown by men to win the gold medal at the Olympic Games from 1968 to 2008.

a. Find the equation of the line of best fit.

$y = 0.1173x + 65.04$ where x = years since 1968

b. Find the correlation coefficient.

$r \approx 0.78$

c. Evaluate the suitability and goodness of the fit.

Residual plot is random, so a linear fit is suitable,

but the correlation is weak, so the fit is poor.

d. Does the slope of the line of best fit for the 1968–2008 data equal the slope of the line of best fit for the 1920–1964 data? If not, speculate about why this is so.

No, the slope for 1968–2008 is much less; perhaps

distances are approaching an upper limit.

Year of Olympic Games	Men's Gold Medal Discus Throw (meters)
1968	64.78
1972	64.40
1976	67.50
1980	66.64
1984	66.60
1988	68.82
1992	65.12
1996	69.40
2000	69.30
2004	69.89
2008	68.82

2. Women began competing in the discus throw in the 1928 Olympic Games. The table gives the distances (in meters) that a discus was thrown by women to win the gold medal at the Olympic Games from 1928 to 1964.

a. Find the equation of the line of best fit.

$y = 0.46125x + 39.64$ where x = years since 1928

b. Find the correlation coefficient.

$r \approx 0.89$

c. Evaluate the suitability and goodness of the fit.

Residual plot is random, so a linear fit is suitable,

but the correlation isn't particularly strong, so the

fit is acceptable but not great.

Year of Olympic Games	Women's Gold Medal Discus Throw (meters)
1928	39.62
1932	40.58
1936	47.63
1940	No Olympics
1944	No Olympics
1948	41.92
1952	51.42
1956	53.69
1962	55.10
1964	57.27

3. Research the distances that a discus was thrown by women to win the gold medal at the Olympic Games from 1968 to 2008. Explain why a linear model is not appropriate for the data.

The data appear to follow an inverted U-shaped curve.

4. The table lists the median heights (in centimeters) of girls and boys from age 2 to age 10. Choose either the data for girls or the data for boys.

a. Identify the real-world variables that x and y will represent.

x = age; y = median height

b. Find the equation of the line of best fit.

Girls: $y = 6.61x + 73.9$;

boys: $y = 6.51x + 75.5$

c. Find the correlation coefficient.

Girls: $r \approx 0.9975$; boys: $r \approx 0.9975$

d. Evaluate the suitability and goodness of the fit.

Residual plot shows a pattern, which suggests that some non-linear model is

more appropriate; linear fit is still good, however.

Age (years)	Median Height (cm) of Girls	Median Height (cm) of Boys
2	84.98	86.45
3	93.92	94.96
4	100.75	102.22
5	107.66	108.90
6	114.71	115.39
7	121.49	121.77
8	127.59	128.88
9	132.92	133.51
10	137.99	138.62

COMMON CORE CORRELATION

Standard	Items
CC.9-12.F.IF.1	8
CC.9-12.F.IF.4	5, 6, 7
CC.9-12.F.IF.5	8
CC.9-12.F.IF.6	3, 4
CC.9-12.F.IF.7	1
CC.9-12.F.IF.7a	1
CC.9-12.F.IF.9	3
CC.9-12.F.BF.3	7
CC.9-12.F.BF.1b	9
CC.9-12.F.BF.4a	10
CC.9-12.F.LE.2	2, 3
CC.9-12.F.LE.5	12
CC.9-12.S.ID.6a	12
CC.9-12.S.ID.6b	12
CC.9-12.S.ID.6c	12
CC.9-12.S.ID.7	12
CC.9-12.S.ID.8	11, 12

TEST PREP DOCTOR ✛

Multiple Choice: Item 1

- Students who chose **A** did not recognize that the slope should be positive.

- Students who chose **B** or **C** confused the x- and y-intercepts or thought that the value of the x-intercept, -1, appears in the function.

Multiple Choice: Item 2

- The cost of the mechanical pencil is the initial cost, or y-intercept of the function's graph. The cost of each refill pack is the slope of the function's graph. Students who chose **F** or **J** confused the slope with the y-intercept.

- Students who chose **H** did not include the initial cost of the pencil, $8, as the y-intercept.

Multiple Choice: Item 3

- The monthly increase in the cost of Plan B is $50. This is the slope of the graph of the function $B(t)$. Students who chose **A** or **C** confused slope with y-intercept.

- Students who chose **B** chose the plan for which the cost is less for 6 months rather than more.

Multiple Choice: Item 5

- Students who chose **C** or **D** confused slope with y-intercept for a linear function of the form $f(x) = mx + b$.

- Students who chose **B** confused the charateristics of increasing and decreasing functions. If the slope is negative, then the function is decreasing as you move from left to right along the horizontal axis.

Multiple Choice: Item 10

- Students who chose **G** added 7 to each side rather than subtracted 7 from each side.

- Students who chose **H** switched the variables C and w but did not solve for w.

- Students who chose **J** switched the variables C and w and then took the opposites of the terms rather than solving for w.

Free Response: Item 12

- For Item **12a**, remind students to draw a line that will result in about the same number of points being above the line as below the line.

- For Item **12b**, remind student to calculate the slope using two points that fall closest to the line they drew in Item **12a**. The equation in Item **12c** was derived using the points $(158, 250)$ and $(428, 400)$. Other pairs of points may be equally valid but give slightly different results.

- The model appears to be such a good fit that students may think it is a good predictor of the initial value without really considering whether an initial value of over 150° is reasonable. Remind students that the initial value is an extrapolation of this data set, and will be less reliable than an interpolation would be.

Name _____ Class _____ Date _____

MULTIPLE CHOICE

1. Which function is represented by the graph?

A. $f(x) = -x + 2$ C. $f(x) = 2x - 1$

B. $f(x) = x - 1$ (D.) $f(x) = 2x + 2$

2. Jorge bought a mechanical pencil for $8. A lead and eraser refill pack costs $2. Write a linear function to describe the cost of using the pencil as a function of the number of refill packs.

F. $C(r) = 8r - 2$ H. $C(r) = 2r$

(G.) $C(r) = 2r + 8$ J. $C(r) = 8r + 2$

3. The function $A(t) = 99t$ describes the cost of Cell Phone Plan A (in dollars) for t months. The table shows the cost of Cell Phone Plan B for t months. Which plan will cost more for 6 months, and which function describes the cost of Plan B?

t	1	2	3
$B(t)$	$150	$200	$250

A. Plan B; $B(t) = 100t + 50$

B. Plan B; $B(t) = 50t + 100$

C. Plan A; $B(t) = 100t + 50$

(D.) Plan A; $B(t) = 50t + 100$

4. Pat pays $250 to be a gym member for 2 months and $550 to be a member for 6 months. What is the monthly cost of a gym membership?

F. $50   H. $150

(G.) $75   J. $300

5. For $f(x) = -\frac{2}{5}x + 3$, find the slope and y-intercept, and determine whether the graph is increasing or decreasing.

(A.) $m = -\frac{2}{5}, b = 3$, decreasing

B. $m = -\frac{2}{5}, b = 3$, increasing

C. $m = 3, b = -\frac{2}{5}$, decreasing

D. $m = 3, b = -\frac{2}{5}$, increasing

6. The graph shows the distance Tiana walks as a function of time. How would the graph change if she walked 1 mi/h faster?

F. The line in the graph would not change.

G. The line would be less steep.

(H.) The line would be steeper.

J. The line would shift up on the y-axis.

7. How would the graphs of $f(x) = 2x + 6$ and $g(x) = 2x + 3$ compare if graphed on the same coordinate plane?

A. The graphs would intersect at $(0, 2)$.

B. The graph of $f(x)$ would be twice as steep as the graph of $g(x)$.

(C.) The graph of $f(x)$ would be 3 units above the graph of $g(x)$.

D. The graph of $f(x)$ would be 6 units above the graph of $g(x)$.

8. Gary works no more than 9 hours on weekends and gets paid $10 per hour. He works whole-hour shifts. His pay P is a function of the number of hours he works n. What is the range of this function?

F. $0 \le n \le 9$

G. $0 \le P \le 90$

H. {0, 1, 2, 3, 4, 5, 6, 7, 8, 9}

(J.) {0, 10, 20, 30, 40, 50, 60, 70, 80, 90}

9. Given $f(x) = 3x + 2$ and $g(x) = -2x - 4$, find $h(x) = f(x) - g(x)$.

A. $h(x) = x - 2$

B. $h(x) = x + 6$

(C.) $h(x) = 5x + 6$

D. $h(x) = 5x - 2$

10. The cost to ship a package is $C(w) = 0.23w + 7$ where w is the weight in pounds. Write the inverse function to find the weight of a package as a function $w(C)$ of the cost.

(F.) $w(C) = \frac{C - 7}{0.23}$

G. $w(C) = \frac{C + 7}{0.23}$

H. $w(C) = 0.23C + 7$

J. $w(C) = -0.23C - 7$

11. Which number best approximates the correlation coefficient for the data below?

(A.) −0.8   C. 0.2

B. −0.2   D. 0.8

FREE RESPONSE

12. The table shows the temperature T displayed on an oven while it was heating as a function of the amount of time a since it was turned on.

a (sec)	T (°F)	a (sec)	T (°F)
31	175	250	300
61	200	285	325
104	225	327	350
158	250	380	375
202	275	428	400

a. Draw a line of fit on the scatter plot.

b. Find an equation of your line of fit.

Answer will vary.

c. Perform linear regression to find the equation of the line of best fit and the correlation coefficient.

$T = 0.5602a + 162.8; 0.9991$

d. Create a residual plot on a graphing calculator. Evaluate the suitability and goodness of fit of the regression equation.

The points are randomly distributed about the x-axis, so a linear fit is suitable. The correlation is strong and the points are close to the x-axis, so the fit is good.

e. Is the model a good predictor of the initial value? Why or why not?
Sample answer: The temperature at time 0 should be room temperature, but for the model, T is about 162°F when $a = 0$. The relationship may not be linear initially, or the oven display may not show temperatures below 162°F to 175°F.

Exponential Functions

Unit Vocabulary

exponential
decay model (5-3)

exponential
function (5-1)

exponential
growth model (5-2)

Exponential Functions

Unit Focus

In this unit you will learn what exponential functions are and use them for modeling and solving problems that involve increasing or decreasing quantities. You will learn how the graph of an exponential function changes when the function rule changes in certain ways. You will learn how to solve exponential equations. You will learn how to use a graphing calculator to write an exponential function model for data that are approximately exponential. You will learn how an exponential function compares with a linear function.

Unit at a Glance

COMMON CORE

Lesson		Standards for Mathematical Content
5-1	Discrete Exponential Functions	CC.9-12.A.CED.2*, CC.9-12.F.IF.2, CC.9-12.F.IF.3, CC.9-12.F.IF.5*, CC.9-12.F.IF.7e*, CC.9-12.F.LE.2*
5-2	Exponential Growth Functions	CC.9-12.F.IF.1, CC.9-12.F.IF.5*, CC.9-12.F.IF.7e*, CC.9-12.F.LE.1c*, CC.9-12.F.LE.2*, CC.9-12.F.LE.5*
5-3	Exponential Decay Functions	CC.9-12.F.IF.4*, CC.9-12.F.IF.7*, CC.9-12.F.IF.7e*, CC.9-12.F.LE.1c*, CC.9-12.F.LE.2*, CC.9-12.F.LE.5*
5-4	Changing the Values of a and b in $f(x) = ab^x$	CC.9-12.F.IF.4*, CC.9-12.F.BF.3
5-5	Solving Equations Involving Exponents	CC.9-12.A.CED.1*, CC.9-12.A.CED.2*, CC.9-12.A.REI.11*, CC.9-12.F.BF.1*, CC.9-12.F.BF.1a*, CC.9-12.F.LE.2*
5-6	Performing Exponential Regression	CC.9-12.A.CED.2*, CC.9-12.F.BF.1a*, CC.9-12.F.LE.1c*, CC.9-12.F.LE.5*, CC.9-12.S.ID.6a*, CC.9-12.S.ID.6b*
5-7	Comparing Linear and Exponential Functions	CC.9-12.F.LE.1*, CC.9-12.F.LE.1a*, CC.9-12.F.LE.1b*, CC.9-12.F.LE.1c*, CC.9-12.F.LE.3*
5-8	Modeling with Exponential Functions	CC.9-12.A.REI.11*, CC.9-12.F.BF.1a*, CC.9-12.F.LE.1c*, CC.9-12.F.LE.2*, CC.9-12.F.LE.5*, CC.9-12.S.ID.6a*
	Test Prep	

© Houghton Mifflin Harcourt Publishing Company

Unpacking the Common Core State Standards

Use the table to help you understand the Standards for Mathematical Content that are taught in this unit. Refer to the lessons listed after each standard for exploration and practice.

COMMON CORE Standards for Mathematical Content	What It Means For You
CC.9-12.A.CED.1 Create equations and inequalities in one variable and use them to solve problems.* Lesson 5-5	You will write and solve exponential equations to solve problems such as when a sales goal will be achieved or when a changing population will reach a certain number.
CC.9-12.A.CED.2 Create equations in two or more variables to represent relationships between quantities; graph equations on coordinate axes with labels and scales.* Lessons 5-1, 5-5, 5-6, 5-8 (Also 5-2, 5-3, 5-4)	A function is often in the form of an equation in two variables, such as $y = 3x$, or the alternate form $f(x) = 3x$. You will write and graph functions and use those skills to solve problems throughout this unit.
CC.9-12.A.REI.11 Explain why the x-coordinates of the points where the graphs of the equations $y = f(x)$ and $y = g(x)$ intersect are the solutions of the equation $f(x) = g(x)$; find the solutions approximately, e.g., using technology to graph the functions, make tables of values, or find successive approximations. Include cases where $f(x)$ and/or $g(x)$ are linear, polynomial, rational, absolute value, exponential and logarithmic functions.* Lessons 5-5, 5-8	One way to solve an equation is to graph two functions and find where the graphs intersect. For example, you could solve the equation $2x = x + 4$ by graphing the functions $f(x) = 2x$ and $g(x) = x + 4$ and then finding where the graphs intersect. You will apply this idea to solving exponential equations with a graphing calculator. You will also solve exponential equations using paper-and-pencil techniques.
CC.9-12.F.IF.1 Understand that a function from one set (called the domain) to another set (called the range) assigns to each element of the domain exactly one element of the range. If f is a function and x is an element of its domain, then $f(x)$ denotes the output of f corresponding to the input x. The graph of f is the graph of the equation $y = f(x)$. Lesson 5-2 (Also 5-1)	A function is a set of ordered pairs, usually denoted (x, y) or $(x, f(x))$. The domain is the set of all x-values. The range is the set of all y-values (or $f(x)$-values). You will represent exponential functions in several different ways: by a list of the ordered pairs, by an equation that tells the function rule, and by a graph.
CC.9-12.F.IF.2 Use function notation, evaluate functions for inputs in their domains, and interpret statements that use function notation in terms of a context. Lesson 5-1	You will use function notation as you model situations with exponential functions. You will revisit the fact that $f(x)$ means the value of the function for the given value of x.
CC.9-12.F.IF.3 Recognize that sequences are functions, sometimes defined recursively, whose domain is a subset of the integers. Lesson 5-1	You will be introduced to discrete exponential functions, which are one type of sequence where the ratio between consecutive values is constant.

Unpacking the Common Core State Standards

This page lists and explains the Standards for Mathematical Content that are addressed in this unit. For information about the Standards for Mathematical Practice, which are integrated throughout the text, see Teacher Edition pages viii–xi.

Notes

_____

_____

_____

_____

_____

_____

_____

_____

_____

_____

_____

COMMON CORE Standards for Mathematical Content	What It Means For You
CC.9-12.F.IF.4 For a function that models a relationship between two quantities, interpret key features of graphs and tables in terms of the quantities, and sketch graphs showing key features given a verbal description of the relationship.* Lessons 5-3, 5-4 (Also 5-2)	You will use graphs and tables as models to help solve problems. You will learn to interpret key features of exponential graphs. One key feature is end behavior, which concerns the shape of the graph as you move infinitely far left or right.
CC.9-12.F.IF.5 Relate the domain of a function to its graph and, where applicable, to the quantitative relationship it describes.* Lessons 5-1, 5-2, 5-8 (Also 5-3)	For a function denoted by $f(x)$, the domain is a set of x-values. You will learn that in many cases, there are x-values in a domain that do not make sense for the problem you are working on. In those cases, you need to choose an appropriate domain by deciding what x-values make sense in context.
CC.9-12.F.IF.7 Graph functions expressed symbolically and show key features of the graph, by hand in simple cases and using technology for more complicated cases.* **CC.9-12.F.IF.7e** Graph exponential and logarithmic functions, showing intercepts and end behavior, and trigonometric functions, showing period, midline, and amplitude.* Lessons 5-1, 5-2, 5-3, 5-8	You will graph exponential functions and then compare the graphs with each other. You will learn how a graph changes when the function rule changes in certain ways, and you will describe those changes by discussing intercepts and end behavior.
CC.9-12.F.BF.1 Write a function that describes a relationship between two quantities.* **CC.9-12.F.BF.1a** Determine an explicit expression, a recursive process, or steps for calculation from a context.* Lessons 5-5, 5-6, 5-8 (Also 5-2, 5-3)	When you write a function rule, you are determining an explicit expression. You will use the recursive nature of exponential growth to write expressions for real-world situations.
CC.9-12.F.BF.3 Identify the effect on the graph of replacing $f(x)$ by $f(x) + k$, $kf(x)$, $f(kx)$, and $f(x + k)$ for specific values of k (both positive and negative); find the value of k given the graphs. Experiment with cases and illustrate an explanation of the effects on the graphs using technology. Lesson 5-4	You will explore the effects of changing key parameters of an exponential function to see how they affect the behavior of the graph.

Notes

_____

_____

_____

_____

_____

_____

_____

_____

_____

_____

COMMON CORE Standards for Mathematical Content	What It Means For You
CC.9-12.F.LE.1 Distinguish between situations that can be modeled with linear functions and with exponential functions.* **CC.9-12.F.LE.1a Prove that linear functions grow by equal differences over equal intervals, and that exponential functions grow by equal factors over equal intervals.*** **CC.9-12.F.LE.1b Recognize situations in which one quantity changes at a constant rate per unit interval relative to another.*** **CC.9-12.F.LE.1c Recognize situations in which a quantity grows or decays by a constant percent rate per unit interval relative to another.*** Lessons 5-2, 5-3, 5-6, 5-7, 5-8	You will use properties of equations and properties of exponents to prove key facts about the behavior of linear and exponential functions over intervals of the same size. You will learn to distinguish linear growth from exponential growth. You will learn to recognize exponential growth by comparing consecutive function values and looking for a constant ratio.
CC.9-12.F.LE.2 Construct linear and exponential functions, including arithmetic and geometric sequences, given a graph, a description of a relationship, or two input-output pairs (include reading these from a table).* Lessons 5-1, 5-2, 5-3, 5-5, 5-8	You will write function rules for discrete and continuous exponential functions based on a verbal description of the relationship or given values from which you can calculate the key parameters and write the function.
CC.9-12.F.LE.3 Observe using graphs and tables that a quantity increasing exponentially eventually exceeds a quantity increasing linearly, quadratically, or (more generally) as a polynomial function.* Lesson 5-7	You will graph an increasing linear function and an exponential growth function on the same viewing window of a graphing calculator. Then you will experiment with different window sizes to see that the exponential function always rises above the linear function.
CC.9-12.F.LE.5 Interpret the parameters in a linear or exponential function in terms of a context.* Lessons 5-2, 5-3, 5-6, 5-8	In the function $y = mx + b$, the slope, m, and the y-intercept, b, are called *parameters*. Exponential functions also have parameters. You will identify those parameters and describe what they represent in different situations.
CC.9-12.S.ID.6 Represent data on two quantitative variables on a scatter plot, and describe how the variables are related.* **CC.9-12.S.ID.6a Fit a function to the data; use functions fitted to data to solve problems in the context of the data.*** **CC.9-12.S.ID.6b Informally assess the fit of a function by plotting and analyzing residuals.*** Lessons 5-6, 5-8	You will use a graphing calculator to find best-fit exponential functions for data sets and then use those functions to solve problems. You will use residuals to assess (judge) fit. A residual is the difference between an actual data value and a corresponding model function value. You will learn to make a scatter plot to show all the residuals for a data set and its model. Then, by looking at the scatter plot, you can assess how well the model fits the data.

UNIT 5

© Houghton Mifflin Harcourt Publishing Company

Notes

_____

_____

_____

_____

_____

_____

_____

_____

_____

Discrete Exponential Functions

Essential question: *What are discrete exponential functions and how can you represent them?*

......COMMON **Standards for**
: CORE : **Mathematical Content**
......

CC.9-12.A.CED.2 Create equations in two ... variables to represent relationships between quantities; graph equations on coordinate axes with labels and scales.*

CC.9-12.F.IF.2 Use function notation, evaluate functions for inputs in their domains, and interpret statements that use function notation in terms of a context.

CC.9-12.F.IF.3 Recognize that sequences are functions ... whose domain is a subset of the integers. ...

CC.9-12.F.IF.5 Relate the domain of a function to its graph and, where applicable, to the quantitative relationship it describes. ...*

CC.9-12.F.IF.7e Graph exponential ... functions, showing intercepts and end behavior, ...*

CC.9-12.CC.9-F.LE.2 Construct ... exponential functions, including ... geometric sequences, given a graph, a description of a relationship, or two input-output pairs (include reading these from a table).*

Also: CC.9-12.F.IF.1

Vocabulary
exponential function

Prerequisites
Functions, Lesson 1-5

Math Background
In this lesson, students will learn that if the ratios of successive output values of the function $f(x)$ are equal for each unit increase in the input value, then the function is an exponential function of the form $f(x) = ab^x$, where x is a real number, b is the ratio of output values, and $b > 0$ and $b \neq 1$. The value of a is found by determining $f(x)$ for $x = 0$. The value of b helps determine the behavior of the exponential function, as shown in the following table.

Values of b	$f(x)$ behavior	Graph behavior
$0 < b < 1$, $a > 0$	decreases as x increases	falls from left to right
$b > 1$, $a > 0$	increases as x increases	rises from left to right

INTRODUCE

The table shows the tuition at two colleges for four consecutive years. Ask students to explain the pattern of the tuition increases for both colleges. If students cannot find the pattern for College B, have them divide each tuition figure by the preceding year's tuition.

College Tuition

Year	College A ($)	College B ($)
0	10,000	10,000
1	11,000	11,000
2	12,000	12,100
3	13,000	13,310

TEACH

 ENGAGE

Questioning Strategies
- How are the tables for the functions alike? How are they different? They are alike because they have the same domain. They are different because successive output values of the linear function have a common difference, while successive output values of the exponential function have a common ratio.

- What is the difference between a discrete function and a continuous function? The graph of a discrete function is made up of isolated points. In a continuous function, the points representing the ordered pairs are connected by an unbroken line or curve.

- Suppose you know that successive values of a discrete function are consecutive multiples of 2. How would you determine whether the function is exponential? Find the ratio of consecutive output values. It is always 2, so the function is exponential with a constant ratio of 2.

Name_____ Class_____ Date_____

5-1

COMMON CORE

Discrete Exponential Functions

Essential question: *What are discrete exponential functions and how can you represent them?*

CC.9-12.A.CED.2*,
CC.9-12.F.IF.2,
CC.9-12.F.IF.3,
CC.9-12.F.IF.5*,
CC.9-12.F.IF.7e*,
CC.9-12.F.LE.2*

1 ENGAGE Understanding Discrete Exponential Functions

Recall that a discrete function has a graph that consists of isolated points. The function shown is a discrete *linear* function, because the isolated points lie along a line. Note that the *differences* of successive output values are all equal.

Tickets	Dollars
0	0
1	10
2	20
3	30
4	40
5	50

The function shown here is a discrete *exponential* function relating attendance at an annual event to the number of years since the initial event. Note that the *ratios* of successive output values are equal.

Events	Attendance
0	3
1	6
2	12
3	24
4	48
5	96

REFLECT

1a. Describe the limitations on the domains of these discrete functions.

Numbers of tickets and numbers of events must be whole numbers.

1b. How are the graphs alike? How are they different?

Sample answer: Both represent discrete and increasing functions. The points on the linear function lie along a line. The points on the exponential function lie along a curve.

1c. What was the attendance at the initial seminar? What is the ratio of successive output values? How has attendance grown over time?

3 people; 2 : 1; attendance has doubled each year.

Unit 5   183   Lesson 1

A function whose successive output values have a *constant ratio* for each unit increase in the input values is an *exponential function*. An **exponential function** can be represented by the equation, $f(x) = ab^x$, where x is a real number, $a \neq 0$, $b > 0$, and $b \neq 1$. The constant ratio is the base b.

If a discrete exponential function has inputs that are a set of equally spaced integers, then its outputs are a sequence of numbers called a *geometric sequence*.

When evaluating exponential functions, you will need to remember these properties of exponents.

Zero and Negative Exponents		
Words	**Algebra**	**Example**
Any nonzero number raised to the zero power is 1.	$c^0 = 1$, $c \neq 0$	$12^0 = 1$
Any nonzero number raised to a negative power is equal to 1 divided by the number raised to the opposite power.	$c^{-n} = \frac{1}{c^n}$, $c \neq 0$	$2^{-3} = \frac{1}{2^3} = \frac{1}{8}$

2 EXAMPLE Representing an Exponential Function

Make a table for the function $f(x) = 2\left(\frac{2}{3}\right)^x$ for the domain $\{-2, -1, 0, 1, 2, 3\}$. Then graph the function for this domain.

A Complete the following to calculate $f(-2)$.

$2\left(\frac{2}{3}\right)^{-2} = 2\left(\frac{1}{\left(\frac{2}{3}\right)^2}\right) = 2\left(\frac{1}{\frac{4}{9}}\right) = 2\left(\frac{9}{4}\right) = \frac{9}{2}$

B Complete the table of values.

x	f(x)	(x, f(x))
−2	$\frac{9}{2}$	$\left(-2, \frac{9}{2}\right)$
−1	3	$(-1, 3)$
0	2	$(0, 2)$
1	$\frac{4}{3}$	$\left(1, \frac{4}{3}\right)$
2	$\frac{8}{9}$	$\left(2, \frac{8}{9}\right)$
3	$\frac{16}{27}$	$\left(3, \frac{16}{27}\right)$

C Graph the function.

Unit 5   184   Lesson 1

Questioning Strategies

- Why is $f(x)$ a discrete exponential function?
  The domain is a subset of the integers and the
  graph is made up of isolated points, so the
  function is discrete. The function is of the form
  $f(x) = ab^x$, with $a \neq 0$, $b > 0$, $b \neq 1$, and x a real
  number, so the function is exponential.

- What is the ratio of successive output values for
  the table? $\frac{2}{3}$

Avoid Common Errors

Students may have difficulty completing the table
of values for $f(x)$ because they have to divide by
a fraction. Remind them that a nonzero number
raised to a negative power is equal to the reciprocal
of the number raised to the opposite power. So,
$2\left(\frac{2}{3}\right)^{-2} = 2\left(\frac{3}{2}\right)^2 = 2\left(\frac{3}{2}\right)\left(\frac{3}{2}\right) = \frac{9}{2}$, which is the same as
the value students found in Part A.

EXTRA EXAMPLE

Make a table for and graph the function
$f(x) = 3\left(\frac{3}{4}\right)^x$ for the domain $\{-3, -1, 0, 1, \text{ and } 3\}$.

The graph is a discrete graph, decreasing as x
increases, and it contains the points: $\left(-3, \frac{64}{9}\right)$,
$(-1, 4)$, $(0, 3)$, $\left(1, \frac{9}{4}\right)$, $\left(3, \frac{81}{64}\right)$

Questioning Strategies

- Is the function decreasing or increasing? Explain.
  increasing; $b = 2$, so each successive value is two
  times the value that precedes it.

EXTRA EXAMPLE

The number of a certain bacteria doubles in a lab
culture every day. Suppose there are 100 bacteria
to start an experiment. Write an equation for the
number of bacteria, n, as a function of the number
of days, d. $n(d) = 100(2)^d$

Questioning Strategies

- Is the function decreasing or increasing? Explain.
  decreasing; $b = 0.5$, so each successive value is
  one-half the value that precedes it.

Avoid Common Errors

Students may make an error when calculating the
value of b. They should choose two outputs whose
inputs differ by one unit. Also, remind them that
they should always divide an output value by the
preceding output value. For example, if they are
using the first two output values, the second output
value would be the numerator and the first output
value would be the denominator. The first output
value will never be the numerator for calculating
the ratio.

EXTRA EXAMPLE

The value of a car, v, is an exponential function of
the number of years, n, since it was purchased. A
car cost \$30,000 when it was new. After 1 year, it
was worth \$27,000. Write an equation for the value
of the car as a function of the number of years.
$v(n) = 30,000(0.9)^n$

MATHEMATICAL PRACTICE   **Highlighting the Standards**

Examples 3 and 4 address Mathematical
Practice Standard 4 (Model with
mathematics). Be sure students understand
how to identify the value of a, which is the
initial value when $x = 0$, and how to identify
the value of b, which is the ratio of successive
output values for each unit increase in the
input values. They may be given the value of b
directly, as in Example 3, or they may have to
calculate b as in Example 4.

REFLECT

2a. Identify the values of a and b for the function $f(x) = 2\left(\frac{2}{3}\right)^x$.

$a = 2,\ b = \frac{2}{3}$

2b. Describe how the value of the function changes as x increases.

The function decreases as x increases.

2c. Explain why each of the following statements is true.

- For $0 < b < 1$ and $a > 0$, the function $f(x) = ab^x$ *decreases* as x increases.

When you multiply a number a by a fraction b between 0 and 1, the product is

less than the original number a. When you multiply by this fraction b repeatedly,

the results decrease further.

- For $b > 1$ and $a > 0$, the function $f(x) = ab^x$ *increases* as x increases.

When you multiply a number a by a number b greater than 1, the product

is greater than the original number a. When you multiply by this number b

repeatedly, the results increase further.

Writing Equations You can write an equation for an exponential function as long as you can identify or calculate the values of a and b. The value of a is the value of the function where x is 0, because $f(0) = ab^0 = a \cdot 1 = a$. The value of b is the factor that is the ratio of successive function values.

3 EXAMPLE   Writing an Equation from a Verbal Description

When a piece of paper is folded in half, the total thickness doubles. Suppose an unfolded piece of paper is 0.1 millimeter thick. Write an equation for the total thickness, t, as a function of the number of folds, n.

A   The value of a is the thickness before any folds are made, or   0.1 millimeter

B   Because the thickness doubles with each fold, the value of b is   2 .

C   An equation for the function is $t(n) = $ $0.1(2)^n$

REFLECT

3a. Why is the exponential function in Part A of the Example discrete?

The paper can only be folded a whole number of times.

3b. If the paper were twice as thick to begin with, what would be an equation for the function?

$t(n) = 0.2(2)^n$

4 EXAMPLE   Writing an Equation from Input-Output Pairs

The height, h, of a dropped ball is an exponential function of the number of bounces, n. On its first bounce, a certain ball reached a height of 15 inches. On its second bounce, the ball reached a height of 7.5 inches. Write an equation for the height of the ball as a function of the number of bounces.

A   Divide successive function values, or heights, to find the value of b.

$b = 7.5 \div 15 = 0.5$

B   Use your value for b and a known ordered pair to find the value of a.

$h(n) = ab^n$	Write the general form.
$h(n) = a\left(0.5\right)^n$	Substitute the value for b.
$15 = a\left(0.5\right)^1$	Substitute the input and output values for the first bounce.
$15 = 0.5a$	Simplify.
$30 = a$	Solve for a.

C   An equation for the function is $h(n) = 30(0.5)^n$

REFLECT

4a. Use unit analysis to explain why b is a unit-less factor in Part B above.

When you divide two heights to find b, the units "inches" divide out, leaving just

the factor 0.5.

4b. Show that using the values for the second bounce will give the same result for a.

Using (2, 7.5), you get $7.5 = a(0.5)^2$, $7.5 = 0.25a$, $30 = a$.

4c. What was the initial height? What was the height for the fifth bounce? Explain.

30 inches, because the value of a is 30; about 1 inch, because the value of the

function where n is 5 is 0.9375 inch

4d. What is the ratio of the height on the fifth bounce to the initial height? How is this ratio related to the constant ratio for this exponential function? Explain.

0.03125; the ratio is equal to the fifth power of the constant ratio, or

0.5^5; the ratio of the height on the fifth bounce to the initial height is

$\frac{30(0.5)^5}{30(0.5)^0} = (0.5)^5$.

Essential Question

What are discrete exponential functions and how can you represent them?

A discrete exponential function is a function of the form $f(x) = ab^x$, with $a \neq 0$, $b > 0$, and $b \neq 1$ in which only distinct values make sense in the domain. Such a function can be represented by a set of input and output values in a table or by a graph of ordered pairs.

Summarize

Have students make a graphic organizer to distinguish between linear and exponential functions. One possibility is shown below.

Where skills are taught	Where skills are practiced
2 EXAMPLE	EXS. 1–3
3 EXAMPLE	EXS. 8, 9
4 EXAMPLE	EXS. 4–7

	Linear	**Exponential**
Equation	$f(x) = mx + b$	$f(x) = ab^x$, $a \neq 0$, $b > 0$, $b \neq 1$
Change in output values per unit increase in input values	Output values increase or decrease by a constant amount.	The ratio of successive output values remains constant.

PRACTICE

Make a table of values and a graph for each function.

1. $f(x) = 2^x$

x	f(x)
−3	1/8
−2	1/4
−1	1/2
0	1
1	2
2	4
3	8

2. $f(x) = 2\left(\frac{3}{4}\right)^x$

x	f(x)
−3	128/27
−2	32/9
−1	8/3
0	2
1	3/2
2	9/8
3	27/32

3. $f(x) = 0.9(0.6)^x$

x	f(x)
−3	4.17
−2	2.5
−1	1.5
0	0.9
1	0.54
2	0.324
3	0.1944

Use two points to write an equation for each function shown.

4.

x	−3	−2	−1	0
f(x)	8	4	2	1

$$f(x) = \left(\frac{1}{2}\right)^x$$

5.

x	1	2	3	4
f(x)	8	6.4	5.12	4.096

$$f(x) = 10(0.8)^x$$

6.

$$f(x) = 3\left(\frac{2}{3}\right)^x$$

7.

$$f(x) = \frac{1}{4}(2)^x$$

---

8. The area of the top surface of an 8.5 inch by 11 inch piece of paper is a function of the number of times it is folded in half.

  a. Write an equation for the function that models this situation. Explain why this is an exponential function.

    $A(n) = 93.5(0.5)^n$; the area decreases by a constant factor with each fold.

  b. Identify the value of *a*. What does it represent in this situation?

    $a = 93.5$ square inches; *a* is the area of the original piece of paper.

  c. What is the area of the top surface after 4 folds? Round to the nearest tenth of a square inch.

    5.8 square inches

  d. What would the equation be if the original piece of paper had dimensions 11 inches by 17 inches? Compare this equation with the equation in Part (a).

    $A(n) = 187(0.5)^n$; *a* is doubled but *b* stays the same.

9. Suppose you do a favor for 3 people. Then you ask each of them to do a favor for 3 more people, passing along the request that each person who receives a favor does a favor for 3 more people. Suppose you do your 3 favors on Day 1, each recipient does 3 favors on Day 2, and so on.

Day n	Favors f(n)
1	3
2	9
3	27
4	81
5	243

  a. Complete the table for the first five days.

  b. Write an equation for the exponential function that models this situation.

    $f(n) = 3^n$

  c. Describe the domain and range of this function.

    The domain is the set of positive integers: {1, 2, 3, 4, ...}. The range is the set of positive integral powers of three: {3, 9, 27, ...}.

  d. According to the model, how many favors will be done on Day 10?   59,049

  e. How is the number of favors done on Day 10 related to the number done on Day 5? Explain your reasoning.

    Sample answer: The number of favors done on Day 10 is 243 times, or 3^5 times, the number done on Day 5.

  f. What would the equation be if everyone did a favor for 4 people rather than 3 people?

    $f(n) = 4^n$

Exponential Growth Functions

Essential question: *How do you write, graph, and interpret an exponential growth function?*

COMMON **Standards for**
CORE **Mathematical Content**

CC.9-12.F.IF.1 Understand that a function from one set (called the domain) to another set (called the range) assigns to each element of the domain exactly one element of the range. If f is a function and x is an element of its domain, then $f(x)$ denotes the output of f corresponding to the input x. The graph of f is the graph of the equation $y = f(x)$.

CC.9-12.F.IF.5 Relate the domain of a function to its graph and, where applicable, to the quantitative relationship it describes. ...*

CC.9-12.F.IF.7e Graph exponential ... functions, showing intercepts and end behavior, ...*

CC.9-12.F.LE.1c Recognize situations in which a quantity grows or decays by a constant percent rate per unit interval relative to another.*

CC.9-12.F.LE.2 Construct ... exponential functions ... given ... a description of a relationship...*

CC.9-12.F.LE.5 Interpret the parameters in a ... exponential function in terms of a context.*

Also: CC.9-12.A.CED.2*, CC.9-12.F.IF.4*, CC.9-12.F.BF.1a*

Vocabulary
exponential growth model

Prerequisites
Exponential functions, Lesson 5-1

Math Background
The end behavior of a function $f(x)$ is a description of what happens to a function $f(x)$ as x increases or decreases without bound. The value of an exponential growth function $f(x) = ab^x$, where $b > 1$ and $a > 0$, increases without bound as x increases without bound, and approaches 0 as x decreases without bound.

The symbol ∞ represents infinity. In future math courses, such end behavior will use the notation $f(x) \to \infty$ as $x \to \infty$ and $f(x) \to 0$ as $x \to -\infty$.

If b is replaced by $1 + r$ and x is replaced by t, the exponential growth function becomes an exponential growth model $y = a(1 + r)^t$, where a is the *initial amount*, $(1 + r)$ is the *growth factor*, r is the *growth rate*, and t is the *time interval*.

Example: Suppose you buy a new home for $300,000. If it appreciates (gains value) by 5% per year, an exponential growth model for the situation is $y = 300,000(1 + 0.05)^t$, where t is the number of years.

INTRODUCE

Remind students that an exponential function has the form $f(x) = ab^x$, where $a \neq 0$, $b > 0$ and $b \neq 1$, and b is the constant ratio. Ask them to use domain values $\{-2, -1, 0, 1, 2\}$ to graph $f(x) = 1.1^x$ and describe what they see: discrete points along a curve that rises as x increases. Ask students to recall how they represented exponential functions in different forms in Lesson 5-1.

TEACH

1 EXPLORE

Questioning Strategies
- For what values of x is $f(x) = 200(1.10)^x$ less than 200? when x is less than 0.

- Describe the x-intercepts of the function. There are no x-intercepts for this function because there are no values of x for which $f(x) = 0$.

- Are there any asymptotes for this function other than $y = 0$? Explain. No; the graph gets closer and closer to 0 as x decreases without bound, and it is ever-increasing as x increases without bound.

Name_____ Class_____ Date_____

5-2

Exponential Growth Functions

COMMON CORE

CC.9-12.F.IF.1,
CC.9-12.F.IF.5*,
CC.9-12.F.IF.7e*,
CC.9-12.F.LE.1c*,
CC.9-12.F.LE.2*,
CC.9-12.F.LE.5*

Essential question: *How do you write, graph, and interpret an exponential growth function?*

When you graph a function $f(x)$ in a coordinate plane, the x-axis represents the independent variable and the y-axis represents the dependent variable. Therefore, the graph of $f(x)$ is the same as the graph of the equation $y = f(x)$. You will use this form when you use a calculator to graph functions.

1 EXPLORE **Describing End Behavior of a Function**

A Use a graphing calculator to graph the exponential function $f(x) = 200(1.10)^x$ using Y_1 for $f(x)$. Use a viewing window from -20 to 20 for x, with a scale of 2, and from -100 to 1000 for y, with a scale of 50. Make a copy of the curve below.

B To describe the *end behavior* of a function, you describe the function values as x increases or decreases without bound. Using the TRACE feature, move the cursor to the right along the curve. Describe the end behavior as x increases without bound.

The value of the function increases without bound.

C Using the TRACE feature, move the cursor to the left along the curve. Describe the end behavior as x decreases without bound.

The value of the function approaches, but never reaches, 0.

REFLECT

1a. Describe the domain and the range of the function.

Domain: all real numbers; Range: all real numbers greater than 0

1b. Identify the y-intercept of the graph of the function. _____ 200 _____

1c. An *asymptote* of a graph is a line the graph approaches more and more closely. Identify an asymptote of this graph _____ $y = 0$ _____

1d. Why is the value of the function always greater than 0?

All powers of 1.10 are positive and 200 times a positive number is positive.

Unit 5   189   Lesson 2

A function of the form $y = ab^x$ represents exponential growth when $a > 0$ and $b > 1$. If b is replaced by $1 + r$ and x is replaced by t, then the function is the **exponential growth model** $y = a(1 + r)^t$, where a is the *initial amount*, the base $(1 + r)$ is the *growth factor*, r is the *growth rate*, and t is the *time interval*. The value of the model increases with time.

2 EXAMPLE **Modeling Exponential Growth**

Alex buys a rare trading card for $4. The value of the card increases 40% per year for four years.

A Identify the initial amount and the growth rate.

$a =$ _____ $4 _____

$r =$ _____ 40% _____

B Write an exponential growth equation for this situation:

$y = $ 4 $\left(1 + \right.$ 0.4 $\left.\right)^t$

C Copy and complete the table. Round to the nearest cent.

Time (years) t	Value ($) y
0	4.00
1	5.60
2	7.84
3	10.98
4	15.37

D Graph the points from the table using appropriate scales. Draw a smooth curve connecting the points. Label the axes.

Unit 5   190   Lesson 2

Questioning Strategies

- In the exponential growth equation, why is 40% written as 0.4? **The growth rate is written as a decimal and 40% = 0.4.**

- Is 5 part of the domain of the function? Why or why not? **No; the function is defined for a period of 4 years, so 5 is outside the domain.**

- Describe the end behavior of the graph. **The lowest point on the graph is (0, 4) and the highest point on the graph is (4, 15.37).**

Technology

Tell students that they can enter $Y_1 = 4(1 + 0.40)^{\wedge}X$ into a graphing calculator for Part C and then use the Table or Trace feature of the calculator to find the y-values when x is not a whole number as in Question 2c.

Teaching Strategies

Ask students to predict the value of the trading card after 2.5 years and explain how they can use the graph to verify their prediction.

EXTRA EXAMPLE

Hannah buys a new comic book for $5. The value of the comic book increases 15% each year for 4 years.

A Identify the initial amount and the growth rate. **$5; 15%**

B Write an exponential growth equation for this situation. $y = 5(1 + 0.15)^t$

C Find y for $t = \{0, 1, 2, 3, 4\}$. **(0, 5), (1, 5.75), (2, 6.61), (3, 7.60), (4, 8.75).**

D Graph the points from part C and draw a smooth curve connecting them. **The left-most point is the y-intercept, (0, 5). The graph passes through the points in part C and is continuous and increasing over the domain $0 \le x \le 4$.**

CLOSE

Essential Question

How do you write, graph, and interpret an exponential growth function?

If r is the known growth rate, a is the initial amount, and t is the time interval, substitute r and a into the equation $y = a(1 + r)^t$. To graph the function, determine the appropriate domain, complete a table of values and graph the points in the table. To interpret the function, connect the points with a smooth curve, and look at the end behavior of the function.

Summarize

Have students create a graphic organizer to define the role of each variable in the exponential growth model and show any constraints.

Variable	Role	Constraint
a	initial amount	$a > 0$
r	growth rate	$r > 0$
t	time interval	$t \ge 0$
y	amount over time	$y > 0$

⋰ MATHEMATICAL PRACTICE   **Highlighting the Standards**

Exercise 8 addresses Mathematical Practices Standard 2 (Reason abstractly and quantitatively). Students are asked to make predictions about the future value of an investment. This requires them to take a problem situation and represent it symbolically, then understand the meaning of the representation and use it to predict a result.

PRACTICE

Where skills are taught	Where skills are practiced
2 EXAMPLE	EXS. 1–7

Exercise 8: Students extend what they learned in **2** EXAMPLE to making predictions about the value of an investment in the future.

REFLECT

2a. Identify the *y*-intercept of the graph. What does it represent?

$4; the value of the card when Alex bought it ✓

2b. What is the growth factor $(1 + r)$ written as a percent? _____140%_____

2c. Use the graph to estimate the value of the card in 3.5 years. Then explain why it makes sense to connect the points from the table with a smooth curve when graphing this function.

about $13; it makes sense to talk about the value of the card at any

point in the year, and the value doesn't have to be a whole number.

2d. Describe the domain and range of the function $y = 4(1.4)^t$ outside of the context of this problem. Do all of these values make sense in the context of this situation? Why or why not?

Domain: all real numbers; Range: all real numbers greater than 0; no;

the domain is limited to values from 0 to 4 years, so the range is

limited to values from $4 to $15.37.

PRACTICE

Complete the table for each function.

	Function	Initial Amount	Growth Rate	Growth Factor
1.	$y = 1250(1 + 0.02)^t$	1250	0.02	1.02
2.	$y = 40(1 + 0.5)^t$	40	0.50	1.50
3.	$y = 50(1.06)^t$	50	0.06	1.06

Write an equation for each exponential growth function.

4. Eva deposits $1500 in an account that earns 4% interest each year.

$y = 1500(1.04)^t$

5. Lamont buys a house for $255,000. The value of the house increases 6% each year.

$y = 255,000(1.06)^t$

6. Brian invests $2000. His investment grows at a rate of 16% per year.

$y = 2000(1.16)^t$

---

7. Sue is a coin collector. At the end of 2005 she bought a coin for $2.50 whose value had been growing 20% per year for 3 years. The value continued to grow at this rate until she sold the coin 4 years later.

a. Write an exponential growth equation for this situation, using the amount Sue paid as the value at time 0.

$y = 2.50(1 + 0.20)^t$

b. Complete the table.

Time (years) *t*	Value ($) *y*
−3	1.45
−2	1.74
−1	2.08
0	2.50
1	3.00
2	3.60
3	4.32
4	5.18

c. Graph and connect the points.

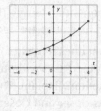

d. Describe the domain and range for this situation.

Domain: all real numbers from −3 to 4; Range: all real numbers from

about $1.45 to about $5.18

e. Identify the *y*-intercept. What does it represent?

$2.50; it represents the amount Sue paid for the coin.

f. What was the value of the coin at the end of 2003? at the time Sue sold the coin? Explain your reasoning.

$1.74; $5.18; $1.74 is the value of the function at $t = -2$, which

corresponds to the end of 2003; $5.18 is the value of the function

at $t = 4$, which corresponds to the end of 2009 when Sue sold the coin.

8. Suppose you invest $1600 on your 16th birthday and your investment earns 8% interest each year. What will be the value of the investment on your 30th birthday? Explain your reasoning.

$4699.51; On your 30th birthday, $t = 14$, so $y = 1600(1.08)^{14} = 4699.51.

Exponential Decay Functions

Essential question: *How do you write, graph, and interpret an exponential decay function?*

COMMON **Standards for**
CORE **Mathematical Content**

CC.9-12.F.IF.4 For a function that models a relationship between two quantities, interpret key features of graphs and tables in terms of the quantities, and sketch graphs showing key features given a verbal description of the relationship.*

CC.9-12.F.IF.7 Graph functions expressed symbolically and show key features of the graph, by hand in simple cases and using technology for more complicated cases.*

CC.9-12.F.IF.7e Graph exponential ... functions, showing intercepts and end behavior ...*

CC.9-12.F.LE.1c Recognize situations in which a quantity grows or decays by a constant percent rate per unit interval relative to another.*

CC.9-12.F.LE.2 Construct ... exponential functions ... given a graph, a description of a relationship, or two input-output pairs ...*

CC.9-12.F.LE.5 Interpret the parameters in a ... exponential function in terms of a context.*

Also: CC.9-12.A.CED.2*, CC.9-12.F.IF.5*, CC.9-12.F.BF.1a*

Vocabulary
exponential decay model

Prerequisites
Exponential growth functions, Lesson 5-2

Math Background
If $a > 0$ and $0 < b < 1$, then a function of the form $f(x) = ab^x$ is an exponential decay function. The value of an exponential decay function approaches 0 as x increases without bound, and increases without bound as x decreases without bound.

The symbol ∞ represents infinity. In future math courses, such end behavior will use the notation $f(x) \to 0$ as $x \to \infty$ and $f(x) \to \infty$ as $x \to -\infty$.

If b is replaced by $1 - r$ and x is replaced by t, then the function becomes an exponential decay model $y = a(1 - r)^t$, where a is the initial amount, the base $(1 - r)$ is the decay factor, r is the decay rate, and t is the time interval.

Example: Suppose you buy a new boat for $30,000. If it depreciates (loses value) by 10% per year, an exponential decay model for the situation is $y = 30,000(1 - 0.10)^t$, where t is the number of years.

INTRODUCE

Ask students to use a calculator to explore the end behavior of the exponential function $f(x) = 0.8^x$ as x increases without bound. Ask them to identify the y-intercept of the function (1) and identify an asymptote for the graph ($y = 0$).

TEACH

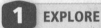 **EXPLORE**

Questioning Strategies
- Why does the function $f(x) = 500(0.8)^x$ represent exponential decay? **The function is exponential and its values are decreasing as x is increasing.**

- What does it mean for a function to approach 0 as x increases without bound? Is 0 a value of the function? Explain. **The value of the function gets closer and closer to 0 over time but never reaches 0.**

- Why is a window setting of $-500 < y < 5000$ used for the graph of $f(x) = 500(0.8)^x$? **The values are sufficient to show the end behavior of the function.**

Name _____ **Class** _____ **Date** _____

Exponential Decay Functions

Essential question: *How do you write, graph, and interpret an exponential decay function?*

COMMON
CORE

CC.9-12.F.IF.4*,
CC.9-12.F.IF.7*,
CC.9-12.F.IF.7e*,
CC.9-12.F.LE.1c*,
CC.9-12.F.LE.2*,
CC.9-12.F.LE.5*

1 EXPLORE Describing End Behavior of a Decay Function

A Use a graphing calculator to graph the exponential function $f(x) = 500(0.8)^x$ using Y_1 for $f(x)$. Use a viewing window from -10 to 10 for x, with a scale of 1, and from -500 to $5,000$ for y, with a scale of 500. Make a copy of the curve below.

5,000

-10   10

-500

B Using the TRACE feature, move the cursor to the right along the curve. Describe the end behavior as x increases without bound.

The value of the function approaches 0.

C Using the TRACE feature, move the cursor to the left along the curve. Describe the end behavior as x decreases without bound.

The value of the function increases without bound.

REFLECT

1a. Describe the domain and the range of the function.

Domain: all real numbers; Range: all real numbers greater than 0

1b. Identify the y-intercept of the graph of the function. _____ 500 _____

1c. Identify an asymptote of this graph. Why is this line an asymptote?

$y = 0$; As x increases, $500(0.8)^x$ approaches, but never reaches, 0.

A function of the form $f(x) = ab^x$ represents exponential decay when $a > 0$ and $0 < b < 1$. If b is replaced by $1 - r$ and x is replaced by t, then the function is the **exponential decay model** $y = a(1 - r)^t$, where a is the *initial amount*, the base $(1 - r)$ is the *decay factor*, r is the *decay rate*, and t is the *time interval*.

© Houghton Mifflin Harcourt Publishing Company

Unit 5   193   Lesson 3

---

2 EXAMPLE Modeling Exponential Decay

You pay \$12,000 for a car. The value then depreciates at a rate of 15% per year. That is, the car loses 15% of its value each year.

A Write an exponential decay equation for this situation.

$$y = 12,000\left(1 - 0.15\right)^t$$

B Complete the table. Round to the nearest dollar.

Time (years) t	Value (\$) y
0	12,000
1	10,200
2	8,670
3	7,370
4	6,264
5	5,324
6	4,526

C Graph the points and connect them with a smooth curve. Label the axes.

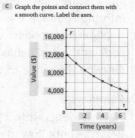

REFLECT

2a. Identify the y-intercept of the graph. What does it represent?

\$12,000; the value of the car when it was purchased

2b. What is the decay factor $(1 - r)$ written as a percent?

85%

2c. What values make sense for the domain and range of this function?

Domain: nonnegative real numbers

Range: real numbers greater than 0 and less than or equal to 12,000

2d. Predict the value of the car after 10 years.

\$2362

2e. In how many years was the value of the car \$8000?

about 2.5 years

2f. Explain why exponential functions of this type are referred to as exponential *decay* functions.

Sample answer: The initial value decreases, or decays, with the passage of time.

© Houghton Mifflin Harcourt Publishing Company

Unit 5   194   Lesson 3

Questioning Strategies

- Why can you connect the points of the graph with a smooth curve? **The domain of the function is nonnegative real numbers.**

- What is the decay factor written as a decimal? **0.85**

EXTRA EXAMPLE

You pay $495 for a new tablet computer. The value then depreciates by 10% per year. That is, the computer loses 10% of its value each year.

A Write an exponential decay equation for this situation. $y = 495(1 - 0.10)^t$

B Find y for $t = \{0, 1, 2, 3, 4, 5, 6\}$. Round to the nearest dollar. (0, 495), (1, 446), (2, 401), (3, 361) (4, 325), (5, 292), (6, 263)

C Graph the points from part B and draw a smooth curve connecting them. **The left-most point is the y-intercept, (0, 495). The graph passes through the points in part B and is continuous and decreasing over the domain $x \geq 0$.**

:::: MATHEMATICAL PRACTICE | **Highlighting the Standards**

Example 2 provides an opportunity to address Mathematical Practices Standard 4 (Model with mathematics). Ask students what they know about the price of a new car compared with the price of a used car. As they work through the Example, they can relate what they know about real-world prices to the changes over time shown in the table and the graph.

---

3 EXAMPLE

Questioning Strategies

- What does the intersection point of the graphs represent? **The time in years and the amount in dollars when the stocks have equal value.**

EXTRA EXAMPLE

The graph shows the value of two different shares of technology stocks over the period of 5 years since they were purchased. The values have been changing exponentially. Describe and compare the behaviors of the two stocks.

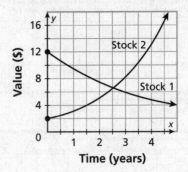

The value of Stock 1 decreases over time by a factor of about 0.8. The value of Stock 2 increases over time by a factor of about 1.6. The initial value of Stock 1, $12, is greater than the initial value of Stock 2, $2. After less than 3 years, the value of Stock 1 is less than that of Stock 2.

CLOSE

Essential Question

How do you write, graph, and interpret an exponential decay function?

If r is the known decay rate, a is the initial amount, and t is the time interval, then substitute r and a into the equation $y = a(1 - r)^t$. Plot points for the function and connect them with a smooth curve. Look at the end behavior of the function and describe the range of the function.

Summarize

Have students write a journal entry in which they describe both how to represent an exponential decay function as a table or a graph and how to find the equation for the situation.

PRACTICE

Where skills are taught	Where skills are practiced
2 EXAMPLE	EXS. 1–3
3 EXAMPLE	EX. 4

3 EXAMPLE Comparing Exponential Growth and Exponential Decay

The graph shows the value of two different shares of stock over the period of four years since they were purchased. The values have been changing exponentially. Describe and compare the behaviors of the two stocks.

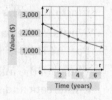

A The model for the graph representing Stock A is an exponential ___decay___ model. The initial value is ___$16.00___ and the decay factor is $12 \div 16 = 0.75$.

B The model for the graph representing Stock B is an exponential ___growth___ model. The initial value is ___$5.00___ and the growth factor is $6 \div 5 = 1.2$.

C The value of Stock A is going ___down___ over time. The value of Stock B is going ___up___ over time. The initial value of Stock A is ___greater___ than the initial value of Stock B. However, after about ___2.5___ years, the value of Stock A becomes less than the value of Stock B.

REFLECT

3a. What is the growth rate for the increasing function above? Explain your reasoning.

20%; the growth factor is 1.2, so $1 + r = 1.2$, and growth rate $r = 0.2$.

3b. What is the decay rate for the decreasing function above? Explain your reasoning.

25%; the decay factor is 0.75, so $1 - r = 0.75$, and decay rate $r = 0.25$.

3c. How did the values of the stocks compare initially? after four years?

Initially, Stock A was worth $11 more per share than Stock B. After four years, Stock B was worth just over $5 more per share than Stock A.

3d. In how many years was the value of Stock A about equal to the value of Stock B? Explain your reasoning.

about 2.5 years; in 2.5 years, the value of both stocks was about $8 per share

3e. In how many years was the value of Stock A about twice the value of Stock B? Explain your reasoning.

about 1 year; in 1 year, the value of Stock B was about $6 and the value of Stock A was about $12, which was twice the value of Stock B.

PRACTICE

1. Identify the initial amount, the decay factor, and the decay rate for the function $y = 2.50(0.4)^t$. Explain how you found the decay rate.

2.50, 0.4, 0.6; $1 - r = 0.4$, so $r = 0.6$

2. Mr. Nevin buys a car for $18,500. The value depreciates 9% per year. Write an equation for this function

$y = 18,500(0.91)^t$

3. You are given a gift of $2,500 in stock on your 16th birthday. The value of the stock declines 10% per year.

a. Write an exponential decay equation for this situation.

$y = 2,500(0.9)^t$

b. Complete the table.

Time (years), t	Value ($), y
0	2,500
1	2,250
2	2,025
3	1,823
4	1,640
5	1,476

c. Graph and connect the points. Label the axes.

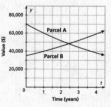

d. Predict the value of the stock on your 22nd birthday. $1329

4. The value of two parcels of land has been changing exponentially in the years since they were purchased, as shown in the graph. Describe and compare the values of the two parcels of land.

Parcel A's value is decreasing exponentially by a decay rate of about 14%. Parcel B's value is increasing exponentially at a growth rate of about 14%. Parcel A is worth more than Parcel B initially ($70,000 vs. $35,000), but after about 2.5 years, Parcel B is worth more than Parcel A.

Notes

Changing the Values of *a* and *b* in $f(x) = ab^x$

Essential question: *How does the graph of $f(x) = ab^x$ change when a and b are changed?*

Standards for Mathematical Content

CC.9-12.F.IF.4 For a function that models a relationship between two quantities, interpret key features of graphs and tables in terms of the quantities, and sketch graphs showing key features ...*

CC.9-12.F.BF.3 Identify the effect on the graph of replacing $f(x)$ by ... $k f(x)$ ... for specific values of k .... Experiment with cases and illustrate an explanation of the effects on the graphs using technology....*

Also: CC.9-12.A.CED.2*

Prerequisites

Exponential functions, Lessons 5-2 and 5-3

Math Background

A calculator is a good tool with which to study the effect of changing the value of a or b in the exponential function $f(x) = ab^x$ with $a \neq 0$ and $b > 0$. If $a > 0$ and $b > 1$ for a given exponential function, then increasing b will make the graph rise more quickly as x increases. If $a > 0$ and $0 < b < 1$ for a given exponential function, increasing b will make the graph fall less quickly as x increases. In either case, increasing the value of a will stretch the graph of the given function vertically and decreasing the value of a will shrink the graph vertically. This lesson focuses on exponential functions where $a > 0$.

INTRODUCE

Show students graphs of the linear functions $f(x) = x$, $f(x) = \frac{1}{3}x$, and $f(x) = 3x$. Ask students to compare the values of the three functions when $x = 1$ and then again when $x = 3$.

TEACH

1 ENGAGE

Questioning Strategies

- Suppose you dilated a figure in the plane with the origin as the center of dilation and with scale factor 2. How would you complete the ordered pair $(x, y) \rightarrow \left(\boxed{}, \boxed{} \right)$ to show the dilation? $(x, y) \rightarrow (2x, 2y)$

- Suppose each point in the plane is dilated with the origin as the center of dilation and with a scale factor of $\frac{1}{2}$. What will be the coordinates of $(12, 5)$? **(6, 2.5)**

- One point of $f(x)$ is $(4, 7)$. If $f(x)$ is stretched horizontally by a factor of 2, what will be the new coordinates? **(8, 7)**

- One point of $f(x)$ is $(5, 3)$. If $f(x)$ is stretched vertically by a factor of 2, what will be the new coordinates? **(5, 6)**

2 EXPLORE

Questioning Strategies

- How does using the table feature of a graphing calculator help you compare functions? For two functions, you can see the values of each function for the same value of *x*.

- Why is Y_1 the parent of each of the functions in Part A? They all have the same base value, 1.5.

- Which of the following functions has the greatest x-intercept and which has the least x-intercept: $Y_1 = (2.5)^x$, $Y_2 = \frac{1}{2}(2.5)^x$, $Y_3 = 2(2.5)^x$, or $Y_4 = 4(2.5)^x$? Explain. Y_4; Y_2; $(2.5)^0 = 1$, and $\frac{1}{2} \cdot 1 < 1 \cdot 1 < 2 \cdot 1 < 4 \cdot 1$

Name_____ Class_____ Date_____

Changing the Values of *a* and *b* in $f(x) = ab^x$

COMMON
CORE

CC.9-12.F.IF.4*,
CC.9-12.F.BF.3,

Essential question: *How does the graph of $f(x) = ab^x$ change when a and b are changed?*

1 ENGAGE   Stretching Figures

Recall that when you *dilate* a figure on a coordinate plane, its coordinates are all multiplied by the same scale factor. In other words, the figure is stretched horizontally and vertically by the same scale factor so that the new figure is similar to the original. If you stretch a figure in only one direction, vertically or horizontally, you do not produce a dilation.

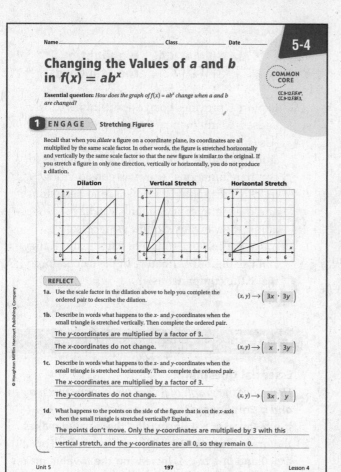

Dilation   Vertical Stretch   Horizontal Stretch

REFLECT

1a. Use the scale factor in the dilation above to help you complete the ordered pair to describe the dilation.

$(x, y) \rightarrow \left(3x \ , \ 3y \right)$

1b. Describe in words what happens to the *x*- and *y*-coordinates when the small triangle is stretched vertically. Then complete the ordered pair.

The *y*-coordinates are multiplied by a factor of 3.

The *x*-coordinates do not change.

$(x, y) \rightarrow \left(x \ , \ 3y \right)$

1c. Describe in words what happens to the *x*- and *y*-coordinates when the small triangle is stretched horizontally. Then complete the ordered pair.

The *x*-coordinates are multiplied by a factor of 3.

The *y*-coordinates do not change.

$(x, y) \rightarrow \left(3x \ , \ y \right)$

1d. What happens to the points on the side of the figure that is on the *x*-axis when the small triangle is stretched vertically? Explain.

The points don't move. Only the *y*-coordinates are multiplied by 3 with this

vertical stretch, and the *y*-coordinates are all 0, so they remain 0.

A *family* of functions is a group of functions that all have something in common. For exponential functions, every different base determines a different *parent function* for its own family of functions. You can explore the behavior of an exponential function by examining *parameters a* and *b*.

2 EXPLORE   Transforming a Parent Function

A Graph parent function $Y_1 = (1.5)^x$ and functions $Y_2 = 2(1.5)^x$ and $Y_3 = 3(1.5)^x$ on a graphing calculator. Use a viewing window from -5 to 5 for *x* and from -1 to 6 for *y*, using a scale of 1. Sketch the curves.

B Use the CALC feature while viewing the graphs to calculate the value of Y_1 when $x = -2$. Then use the up and down arrow keys to jump to the other curves and calculate their values when $x = -2$. Round to the nearest thousandth if necessary. Repeat this process until you have completed the table at the right.

X	Y₁	Y₂	Y₃
−2	0.444	0.889	1.333
−1	0.667	1.333	2
0	1	2	3
1	1.5	3	4.5
2	2.25	4.5	6.75

C What is the value of *a* for the parent function Y_1? for Y_2? for Y_3? How do the values in the table for Y_2 and Y_3 compare with the values for Y_1 for a given value of *x*? Describe a stretch of the graph of Y_1 that will produce the graph of Y_2 and another that will produce the graph of Y_3.

1, 2, 3; The values for Y_2 are twice those for Y_1. The values for Y_3 are three times

those for Y_1. Y_2's graph is a vertical stretch of Y_1's graph by a factor of 2. Y_3's

graph is a vertical stretch of Y_1's graph by a factor of three.

D Graph the function $Y_4 = 0.5(1.5)^x$. Explain why it is considered a vertical *shrink* of the parent function $Y_1 = (1.5)^x$.

All points on the curve Y_4 are half as high as on the curve Y_1 for a

given *x*-value.

REFLECT

2a. Describe how the graph of $f(x) = ab^x$ compares with the graph of $f(x) = b^x$ for a given value of *b* when $a > 1$ and when $0 < a < 1$.

The *y*-intercept is *a* rather than 1. When $a > 1$, the graph of $f(x) = ab^x$ is a

vertical stretch of the graph of $f(x) = b^x$. When $0 < a < 1$, the graph of $f(x) = ab^x$

is a vertical shrink of the graph of $f(x) = b^x$.

Questioning Strategies

- How do the following graphs compare: $Y_1 = 2(2.5)^x$ and $Y_2 = 2(2.8)^x$? Discuss end behavior and the y-intercept. **The graph of Y_2 rises more quickly as x increases to the right of 0 and it falls more quickly as x decreases to the left of 0 compared with the graph of Y_1, but both graphs have the same y-intercept of 2.**

- Which of the following functions has the graph that rises more quickly as x increases to the right of 0: $Y_1 = 600(1.04)^x$ or $Y_2 = 600(1.06)^x$? **Y_2**

- If $0 < b < 1$ and a is a positive constant, how can you alter b to make the graph of $f(x) = ab^x$ fall more gradually? **increase the value of b**

- Which graph rises more quickly as x decreases to the left of 0: $Y_1 = (0.5)^x$ or $Y_2 = (0.7)^x$? **Y_1**

- How does the y-intercept change as b increases for $f(x) = 2b^x$, where $b > 0$? **The y-intercept is always equal to 2.**

> **MATHEMATICAL PRACTICE**   **Highlighting the Standards**
>
> Explore 3 provides good opportunities to address Mathematical Practices Standard 5 (Use appropriate tools strategically) because students will be using graphing calculators to compare functions. They will consider how quickly the graph rises or falls, end behavior, and the y-intercept. Students will have to adjust the viewing window as necessary to make the comparisons. For Parts B and F, they can use the TABLE feature of the calculator to make the comparisons.

CLOSE

Essential Question

How does the graph of $f(x) = ab^x$ change when a and b are changed?

If $a > 0$ and $b > 1$, increasing the b-value makes the graph rise more quickly as x increases. For $a > 0$ and $0 < b < 1$, increasing the b-value makes the graph fall more gradually as x increases.

Summarize

Have students make a graphic organizer like the one below to describe how changing the values of a and b in $f(x) = ab^x$ for $b > 1$ and $0 < b < 1$ affects the graph of $f(x)$ when $a > 0$.

Function	Increase *b*	Decrease *b*	Increase *a*	Decrease *a*
$f(x) = ab^x$; $b > 1$; $a > 0$	Graph rises more quickly as x increases.	Graph rises less quickly as x increases.	Graph stretches vertically.	Graph shrinks vertically.
$f(x) = ab^x$; $0 < b < 1$; $a > 0$	Graph falls less quickly as x increases.	Graph falls more quickly as x increases.	Graph stretches vertically.	Graph shrinks vertically.

3 **EXPLORE** Changing the Value of b in $f(x) = b^x$

A Graph the functions $Y_1 = 1.2^x$ and $Y_2 = 1.5^x$ on a graphing calculator. Use a viewing window from -5 to 5 for x and from -2 to 5 for y, with a scale of 1 for both. Sketch the curves.

B Use the TBLSET and TABLE features to make a table of values starting at -2 with an increment of 1. Then complete the table below.

X	Y_1	Y_2
−2	0.694	0.444
−1	0.833	0.667
0	1	1
1	1.2	1.5
2	1.44	2.25

C Which graph rises more quickly as x increases to the right of 0? Which graph falls, or approaches 0, more quickly as x decreases to the left of 0?

Y_2 rises more quickly as x increases to the right of 0, and it falls more quickly as

x decreases to the left of 0.

D Identify the y-intercepts of the graphs of Y_1 and Y_2.

The y-intercept of both graphs is 1.

E Using the same window as above, graph the functions $Y_3 = 0.6^x$ and $Y_4 = 0.9^x$. Sketch the curves.

F Make a table of values starting at -2 with an increment of 1. Then complete the table.

X	Y_3	Y_4
−2	2.778	1.235
−1	1.667	1.111
0	1	1
1	0.6	0.9
2	0.36	0.81

G Which graph rises more quickly as x decreases to the left of 0? Which graph falls more quickly as x increases to the right of 0?

Y_3 rises more quickly as x decreases to the left of 0, and it falls more quickly as

x increases to the right of 0.

H Identify the y-intercepts of the graphs of Y_3 and Y_4.

The y-intercept of both graphs is 1.

© Houghton Mifflin Harcourt Publishing Company

REFLECT

3a. Consider the function $Y_5 = 1.3^x$. How will its graph compare with the graphs of Y_1 and Y_2? Discuss end behavior and the y-intercept.

All three graphs have the same y-intercept, 1. The graph of Y_5 falls between the

other two. It rises more quickly than the graph of Y_1, but less quickly than the

graph of Y_2 as x increases to the right of 0. It falls more quickly than the graph

of Y_1 but less quickly than the graph of Y_2 as x decreases to the left of 0.

3b. Consider the function $Y_6 = 0.7^x$. How will its graph compare with the graphs of Y_3 and Y_4? Discuss end behavior and the y-intercept.

All three graphs have the same y-intercept, 1. The graph of Y_6 falls between the

other two. It rises more quickly than the graph of Y_4 but less quickly than the

graph of Y_3 as x decreases to the left of 0. It falls more quickly than the graph of

Y_4 but less quickly than the graph of Y_3 as x increases to the right of 0.

3c. Describe how the graph of $f(x) = ab^x$ changes for a given positive value of a as you increase the value of b when $b > 1$. Discuss end behavior and the y-intercept.

The y-intercept equals a for all values of $b > 1$, because $ab^0 = a$. As the value of

b increases, the graph rises more quickly as x increases to the right of 0, and it

falls more quickly as x decreases to the left of 0.

3d. Describe how the graph of $f(x) = ab^x$ changes for a given positive value of a as you decrease the value of b when $0 < b < 1$. Discuss end behavior and the y-intercept.

The y-intercept equals a for all values of b between 0 and 1. As the value of b

decreases, the graph rises more quickly as x decreases to the left of 0, and the

graph falls more quickly as x increases to the right of 0.

3e. Consider the functions $Y_1 = (1.02)^x$ and $Y_2 = (1.03)^x$. Which function increases more quickly as x increases to the right of 0? How do the growth factors support your answer?

Y_2; Y_2 has the greater growth rate (3% rather than 2%) so you would

expect Y_2 to increase more quickly as x increases to the right of 0.

3f. Consider the functions $Y_1 = (0.94)^x$ and $Y_2 = (0.98)^x$. Which function decreases more quickly as x increases to the right of 0? How do the decay factors support your answer?

Y_1; Y_1 has the greater decay rate (6% rather than 2%) so you would

expect Y_1 to decrease more quickly as x increases to the right of 0.

© Houghton Mifflin Harcourt Publishing Company

Solving Equations Involving Exponents

Essential question: *How can you solve problems modeled by equations involving variable exponents?*

COMMON **Standards for**
CORE **Mathematical Content**

CC.9-12.A.CED.1 Create equations … in one variable and use them to solve problems.*

CC.9-12.A.CED.2 Create equations in two or more variables to represent relationships between quantities; graph equations on coordinate axes with labels and scales.*

CC.9-12.A.REI.11 Explain why the x-coordinates of the points where the graphs of the equations $y = f(x)$ and $y = g(x)$ intersect are the solutions of the equation $f(x) = g(x)$; find the solutions approximately, e.g., using technology to graph the functions … or find successive approximations. Include cases where $f(x)$ and/or $g(x)$ are…, exponential …functions.*

CC.9-12.F.BF.1 Write a function that describes a relationship between two quantities.*

CC.9-12.F.BF.1a Determine an explicit expression, a recursive process, or steps for calculation from a context.*

CC.9-12.F.LE.2 Construct … exponential functions, … given … a description of a relationship …*

Prerequisites

Solving equations, Lesson 1-4

Writing an exponential function, Lessons 5-1, 5-2, 5-3

Math Background

An equation of the form $b^x = c$ can be solved using mental math if c can be expressed as a whole number power of b. If $b > 0$ and $b \neq 1$, then $b^x = b^y$ if and only if $x = y$. For example, $2^x = 64$ can be solved using the fact that 64 can be expressed as 2^6. Rewrite the equation as $2^x = 2^6$ and solve: $x = 6$. If c is not a power of base b, each side of the equation can be graphed with a graphing calculator so that the INTERSECT feature can be used to find the x-coordinate of the intersection point of the graphs, which is the solution of the original equation.

INTRODUCE

Remind students how to solve an equation using a graphing calculator by asking them to graph each side of the linear equation $3x + 5 = 4x$. They should enter $Y_1 = 3X + 5$ and $Y_2 = 4X$. Then they should press **2nd CALC** and then **5:INTERSECT** and move the cursor near the point of intersection. Next they should press **ENTER** when prompted by **First curve?**, **Second curve?**, and **Guess?**. The x-value at the bottom of the screen, in this case 5, is the solution.

TEACH

1 EXAMPLE

Questioning Strategies

- In Part A, why is 32 written as a power of 2?
  If you write 32 as a power of 2, you can use the property that if $b^x = b^y$, then $x = y$.

- In Part B, each side of the equation is multiplied by $\frac{1}{4}$ to isolate the power $\left(\frac{5}{3}\right)^x$. How does this compare to isolating a variable on one side of a linear equation? It is done for the same reason. By isolating the power, you have isolated the variable as well and then you can compare the exponents in the final equivalent expression.

EXTRA EXAMPLE

Solve each equation.

A $36(2)^x = 576$ 4

B $8\left(\frac{3}{2}\right)^x = \frac{243}{4}$ 5

continued

Name_____ Class_____ Date_____

5-5

Solving Equations Involving Exponents

COMMON CORE

CC.9-12.A.CED.1*,
CC.9-12.A.CED.2*,
CC.9-12.A.REI.11*,
CC.9-12.F.BF.1*,
CC.9-12.F.BF.1a*,
CC.9-12.F.LE.2*

Essential question: *How can you solve problems modeled by equations involving variable exponents?*

You can apply the properties of equations you already know to solve equations involving exponents. You will also need the following property.

	Equating Exponents when Solving Equations	
Words	**Algebra**	**Example**
Two powers with the same positive base other than 1 are equal if and only if the exponents are equal.	If $b > 0$ and $b \neq 1$, then $b^x = b^y$ if and only if $x = y$.	If $2^x = 2^9$, then $x = 9$. If $x = 9$, then $2^x = 2^9$.

1 EXAMPLE Solving Equations by Equating Exponents

Solve each equation.

A $\frac{5}{2}(2)^x = 80$

$\frac{2}{5} \cdot \frac{5}{2}(2)^x = \frac{2}{5} \cdot 80$ Multiply to isolate the power $(2)^x$.

$(2)^x = 32$ Simplify.

$(2)^x = 2^5$ Write 32 as a power of 2.

$x = 5$ $b^x = b^y$ if and only if $x = y$.

B $4\left(\frac{5}{3}\right)^x = \frac{500}{27}$

$\frac{1}{4} \cdot 4\left(\frac{5}{3}\right)^x = \frac{1}{4} \cdot \frac{500}{27}$ Multiply to isolate the power.

$\left(\frac{5}{3}\right)^x = \frac{125}{27}$ Simplify.

$\left(\frac{5}{3}\right)^x = \left(\frac{5}{3}\right)^3$ Write the fraction as a power of $\frac{5}{3}$.

$x = 3$ $b^x = b^y$ if and only if $x = y$.

© Houghton Mifflin Harcourt Publishing Company

Unit 5   201   Lesson 5

REFLECT

1a. How can you check a solution?

Substitute it into the original equation and check that it makes the equation true.

1b. How can you work backward to write $\frac{125}{27}$ as a power of $\frac{5}{3}$?

Sample answer: Divide 125 by 5 repeatedly and divide 27 by 3 repeatedly.

1c. Is it possible to solve the equation $2^x = 96$ using the method in the Example? Why or why not?

No, because 96 is not a whole power of 2. It has 3 as another factor.

Some equations can't be solved using the method in the Example because it isn't possible to write both sides of the equation as a whole number power of the same base. Instead, you can consider the expressions on either side of the equation as the rules for two different functions. You can then solve the original equation in one variable by graphing the two functions. The solution is the input value for the point where the two graphs intersect.

2 EXAMPLE Writing an Equation and Solving by Graphing

A town has 78,918 residents. The population is increasing at a rate of 6% per year. The town council is offering a prize for the best prediction of how long it will take for the population to reach 100,000. Make a prediction.

A Write an exponential model to represent the situation. Let y represent the population and x represent time (in years).

$y = 78{,}918\left(1 + \boxed{0.06}\right)^x$

B Write an equation in one variable to represent the time, x, when the population reaches 100,000.

$\boxed{100{,}000} = 78{,}918\left(1 + \boxed{0.06}\right)^x$

C Write functions for the expressions on either side of the equation.

$f(x) = \boxed{100{,}000}$

$g(x) = 78{,}918\left(1 + \boxed{0.06}\right)^x$

D What type of function is $f(x)$? What type of function is $g(x)$?

$f(x)$ is a constant function; $g(x)$ is an exponential growth function

© Houghton Mifflin Harcourt Publishing Company

Unit 5   202   Lesson 5

An animal reserve has 20,000 elk. The population is increasing at a rate of 8% per year. There is concern that food will be scarce when the population doubles. How long will it take for the population to reach 40,000? Make a prediction.

The equation $y = 20{,}000(1 + 0.08)^x$ solved using the intersect feature of a graphing calculator has the solution 9.0064683, or just over 9 years.

MATHEMATICAL PRACTICE — Highlighting the Standards

Example 1 provides opportunities to address Mathematical Practices Standard 7 (Look for and make use of structure). When solving an equation involving a variable exponent, students should try to structure the solution so that they are solving an equation of the form $b^x = c^y$. Then if $c = b$, $x = y$; if $c \neq b$, then they should solve by graphing.

CLOSE

Essential Question

How can you solve problems modeled by equations involving variable exponents?

If an equation of the form $b^x = c$ can be used to model a problem, and c can be expressed as a whole number power y of the same base b, then the equation can be solved by setting x equal to y and solving. If c is not a whole number power of base b, each side of the equation can be graphed as a separate function with a graphing calculator and solved by finding the x-coordinate of the point of intersection of the graphs.

Summarize

Have students create a graphic organizer like the one below that shows whether to solve an equation involving a variable exponent algebraically or graphically.

2 EXAMPLE

Questioning Strategies

- In Part D, why is $g(x)$ described as an exponential growth function? **The value of the base is greater than 1.**

- In part G, why is it appropriate to round the prediction to the nearest year? **Since a prediction is usually just an estimate, it is appropriate to round the value you found in part F.**

Teaching Strategies

Students may need to review how to find an appropriate viewing window for the graph of a function. Point out that since the value of a in $g(x) = 78{,}918(1 + 0.06)^x$ is so large and since the constant function equals 100,000, they can start with a window of $Y_{max} = 110{,}000$.

Avoid Common Errors

Students may think that the y-coordinate of the intersection point in part F is the solution to the equation. Point out that the x-coordinate is used because that is the input value that produces the same output value for each function.

PRACTICE

Where skills are taught	Where skills are practiced
1 EXAMPLE	EXS. 1–6, 10
2 EXAMPLE	EXS. 7–9, 11–12

Equation; $b, c > 0, b, c \neq 1$	Relationship Between Bases	Solution Method
$b^x = c^d$	$c = b$	algebraic: $x = d$
$b^x = c^d$	$c \neq b$	graph: intersection of $f(x) = b^x$ and $g(d) = c^d$

E   Graph the functions on a graphing calculator. Let $Y_1 = f(x)$ and $Y_2 = g(x)$. Sketch the graph of Y_2 below. (Y_1 is already graphed for you.) Include the missing window values.

F   Use the intersect feature on the CALC menu to find the input value where the graphs intersect. (Do not round.)

   4.063245

G   Make a prediction as to the number of years until the population reaches 100,000.

   The population will reach 100,000 in just over 4 years.

REFLECT

2a. Suppose the contest is announced on January 1, and the town has 78,918 residents on that date. Explain how to predict *the date* on which the population will be 100,000.

   The number of years, 4.063245, represents 4 years plus 0.063245 of a year. There are 365 days in a year. Convert 0.063245 of a year to days: $0.063245 \times 365 \approx$ 23.084425. The predicted date is January 24, 4 years later.

2b. Explain why the *x*-coordinate of the point where the graphs of $Y_1 = f(x)$ and $Y_2 = g(x)$ intersect is the solution of the equation in Part B.

   Sample answer: The solution of the equation $100{,}000 = 78{,}918(1.06)^x$ is the value of *x* where the expression on the left equals the expression on the right. That is the input value that produces the same output value for both functions $f(x) = 100{,}000$ and $g(x) = 78{,}918(1.06)^x$. The input value where this occurs is the *x*-coordinate of the point where the graphs of the functions intersect.

PRACTICE

Solve each equation without graphing.

1. $5(3)^x = 405$

$x = \underline{\quad 4 \quad}$

2. $\frac{1}{5}(5)^x = 5$

$x = \underline{\quad 2 \quad}$

3. $10(4)^x = 640$

$x = \underline{\quad 3 \quad}$

4. $7\left(\frac{1}{2}\right)^x = \frac{7}{8}$

$x = \underline{\quad 3 \quad}$

5. $\frac{3}{4}\left(\frac{2}{3}\right)^x = \frac{4}{27}$

$x = \underline{\quad 4 \quad}$

6. $3\left(\frac{3}{10}\right)^x = \frac{27}{100}$

$x = \underline{\quad 2 \quad}$

Solve each equation by graphing. Round to the nearest hundredth.

7. $6^x = 150$

$x \approx \underline{\quad 2.80 \quad}$

8. $5^x = 20$

$x \approx \underline{\quad 1.86 \quad}$

9. $(2.5)^x = 40$

$x \approx \underline{\quad 4.03 \quad}$

10. Last year a debate club sold 972 fundraiser tickets on their most successful day. This year the 4 club officers plan to match that number on a single day as follows:

To start off, on Day 0, each of the 4 officers of the club will sell 3 tickets and ask each buyer to sell 3 more tickets the next day. Every time a ticket is sold, the buyer of the ticket will be asked to sell 3 more tickets the next day.

If the plan works, on what day will the number of tickets sold be 972?

a. Write an equation in one variable to model the situation. $\underline{972 = 12(3)^x}$

b. If the plan works, on what day will the number sold be 972? $\underline{\text{Day 4}}$

11. There are 175 deer in a state park. The population is increasing at the rate of 12% per year. At this rate, when will the population reach 300?

a. Write an equation in one variable to model the situation. $\underline{300 = 175(1.12)^x}$

b. How long will it take for the population to reach 300?

   4.7560465 years or about 4.76 years

c. Suppose there are 200 deer in another state park and that the deer population is increasing at a rate of 10% per year. Which park's deer population will reach 300 sooner? Explain.

   This park's population will reach 300 sooner; Solve $300 = 200(1.1)^x$. This park's population reaches 300 in about 4.25 years as opposed to 4.76 years.

12. A city has 642,000 residents on July 1, 2011. The population is decreasing at the rate of 2% per year. At that rate, in what month and year will the population reach 500,000? Explain how you found your answer.

   November, 2023; Solve $642{,}000(0.98)^x = 500{,}00$ to find $x \approx 12.373599$ years;

   0.373599×12 months ≈ 4.48 months. Add 12 years 4.48 months to July 1, 2011.

Performing Exponential Regression

Essential question: *How can you use exponential regression to model data?*

COMMON CORE Standards for Mathematical Content

CC.9-12.A.CED.2 Create equations in two or more variables to represent relationships between quantities; graph equations on coordinate axes with labels and scales.*

CC.9-12.F.BF.1a Determine an explicit expression, a recursive process, or steps for calculation from a context.*

CC.9-12.F.LE.1c Recognize situations in which a quantity grows or decays by a constant percent rate per unit interval relative to another.*

CC.9-12.F.LE.5 Interpret the parameters in a … exponential function in terms of a context.*

CC.9-12.S.ID.6a Fit a function to the data; use functions fitted to data to solve problems in the context of the data.*

CC.9-12.S.ID.6b Informally assess the fit of a function by plotting and analyzing residuals.*

Prerequisites

Linear regression, Lesson 4-10

Discrete exponential functions, Lesson 5-1

Math Background

Regression can be used to create exponential models for data. Residuals can be used to assess how well a model fits a data set. For data point (x, y_d), the residual is the difference in the y-value y_d of the data point and the y-value on the model itself. If the point on the model is (x, y_m), then the residual is $y_d - y_m$. Residuals that are small in absolute value relative to the data and randomly distributed between positive and negative values indicate a good data fit. If there are many large residuals or if there is a pattern to the residuals as the x-values vary, a different model may be needed.

INTRODUCE

Review linear regression with the students, reminding them that residuals are used to assess how well a model fits the data. Tell students that regression can also be used to produce an equation for a curve that fits exponential data. As with linear regression, residuals are used to assess goodness of fit. An exponential model that is a good fit for the data will have a correlation coefficient close to 1.

TEACH

1 EXAMPLE

Questioning Strategies

- Does the model show growth or decay in the number of Internet hosts? Explain. **Growth;** $b > 1$

- How can the model be used to predict the number of internet hosts in 2015? **Substitute 14 for x in the model; then simplify.**

EXTRA EXAMPLE

The table shows the number of cell phone subscribers in the United States from 2000 to 2007. Use a graphing calculator to find the exponential regression model and correlation coefficient. Record the results rounded to three significant digits.

Years Since 2000	0	1	2	3	4	5	6	7
Number (millions)	109	128	141	159	182	208	233	255

function: $y = 111(1.13)^x$

correlation coefficient: $r = 0.999$

Technology

The Exponential Regression program is found by pressing the **STAT** key on the graphing calculator, selecting **CALC**, and then scrolling down to **0:EXPREG**.

Performing Exponential Regression

Essential question: *How can you use exponential regression to model data?*

COMMON CORE
CC.9-12.A.CED.2*,
CC.9-12.F.BF.1a*,
CC.9-12.F.LE.1c*,
CC.9-12.F.LE.5*,
CC.9-12.S.ID.6a*,
CC.9-12.S.ID.6b*

1 EXAMPLE Fitting a Function to Data

The table shows the number of internet hosts from 2001 to 2007.

Number of Internet Hosts							
Years since 2001	0	1	2	3	4	5	6
Number (millions)	110	147	172	233	318	395	490

A Enter the data from the table on a graphing calculator, with years since 2001 in List 1 and number of internet hosts in List 2. Then set up a scatter plot of the data, as shown, and graph it. Copy the points below.

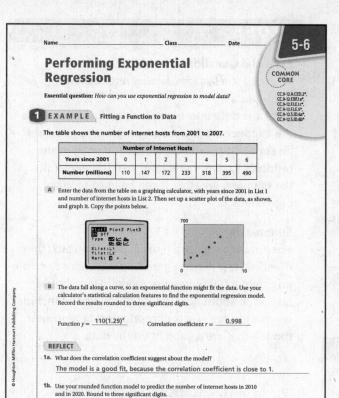

B The data fall along a curve, so an exponential function might fit the data. Use your calculator's statistical calculation features to find the exponential regression model. Record the results rounded to three significant digits.

Function $y = $ __110(1.29)^x__   Correlation coefficient $r = $ __0.998__

REFLECT

1a. What does the correlation coefficient suggest about the model?

The model is a good fit, because the correlation coefficient is close to 1.

1b. Use your rounded function model to predict the number of internet hosts in 2010 and in 2020. Round to three significant digits.

2010: __1,090,000,000 hosts__   2020: __13,900,000,000 hosts__

1c. Are these predictions likely to be accurate? Explain.

Sample answer: The trend may or may not continue over time, but 2010 is closer

to the actual data, so that prediction may be more accurate.

Residuals You have used residuals to assess how well a linear model fits a data set. You can also use residuals for exponential and other models. Remember that if (x, y_d) is a data point and the corresponding point on the model is (x, y_m), then the corresponding *residual* is the difference $y_d - y_m$.

Recall that a model is a good fit for the data when the following are true:

- The numbers of positive and negative residuals are roughly equal.
- The residuals are randomly distributed about the *x*-axis, with no pattern.
- The absolute values of the residuals are small relative to the data.

2 EXAMPLE Plotting and Analyzing Residuals

Continue working with the data from the first Example to plot and analyze the residuals.

A Enter the regression equation from your calculator as the rule for equation Y_1. (It can be found with the statistical variables on the variables menu.) Then view the table to find the function values y_m for the model. Record the results in the table at the right. Round to three significant digits.

B Use the results of Part A to complete the residuals column of the table.

Number of Internet Hosts (millions)		
x	y_d	y_m	Residual $y_d - y_m$
0	110	110	0
1	147	142	5
2	172	183	−11
3	233	235	−2
4	318	303	15
5	395	390	5
6	490	502	−12

C Set up a residual scatter plot of the data, as shown, and graph it. Adjust the viewing window as needed. Copy the points below.

D At first glance, does the model fit the data well? Explain.

Yes. The number of residuals is the same above and below the *x*-axis and they

appear to be fairly randomly distributed.

Questioning Strategies

- Why is it useful to store the exponential function model as Y_1? You can use the TABLE feature to find model values without calculating them.

- Look at the table of residuals and at the graph of the residuals. Is there a pattern in the residuals for y_m? no

EXTRA EXAMPLE

Continue working with the data from the first Extra Example to plot and analyze the residuals.

A Enter the regression equation from your calculator as the rule for equation Y_1. Then, view the table to find the function values, y_m, for the model. Record the results in the table below.

Number of Cell Phone Subscribers (millions)			
x	y_d	y_m	Residual $y_d - y_m$
0	109	111	−2
1	128	125	3
2	141	142	−1
3	159	160	−1
4	182	181	1
5	208	204	4
6	233	231	2
7	255	261	−6

B Set up a residual scatter plot of the data and graph it. At first glance, does the model fit the data well? Explain. Yes; the numbers of positive and negative residuals are roughly equal; the residuals are randomly distributed about the x-axis, with no pattern; and the absolute values of the residuals are small relative to the data.

CLOSE

Essential Question

How can you use exponential regression to model data?

Enter the data into a graphing calculator and use the exponential regression program to generate an equation for the data. Plot and analyze the residuals to determine how well the model fits the data and whether it can be used to make predictions.

Summarize

Have students write a journal entry in which they describe how to use a graphing calculator to create an exponential regression model. They should also write about how to find residuals and include sample graphs of sets of residuals that represent models that are a good fit for the data.

MATHEMATICAL PRACTICE	Highlighting the Standards

Exercises 1-6 provide opportunities to address Mathematical Practices Standard 4 (Model with mathematics). Draw students' attention to the residual plot in Exercise 6 that shows a random distribution in the points with the residuals tightly and evenly distributed about the x-axis. Analyzing residuals helps students evaluate how well a model fits the data.

PRACTICE

Where skills are taught	Where skills are practiced
1 EXAMPLE	EXS. 1–2
2 EXAMPLE	EXS. 3–6

REFLECT

2a. Use the model $y = 110(1.29)^x$ from Part B of the first Example to find the function value for $x = 4$. Round to three significant digits. Compare the result with the value in the table above and with the actual value.

Model value: 305,000,000 hosts; Table value: 303,000,000 hosts. Both values are

reasonably close to the actual value of 318,000,000 hosts.

2b. Are the residuals in the calculator plotted on the residual plot exactly the same as the residuals in the table? Why or why not?

No. The residuals in the residual plot were based on the calculator model with all

its digits. The residuals in the table are based on rounded values.

2c. One reason the model is a good fit for the data is that the absolute values of the residuals are small relative to the data. What does this claim mean? Give examples from the table to support this claim.

The absolute values of the residuals are small as a percent of the actual data

values. These percents range from about 0% to about 6%.

2d. Another reason the model fits the data well is that the residuals are randomly distributed about the x-axis with no pattern. Use a graphing calculator to find a *linear* regression model for these data. Describe the residual plot. What does it tell you about the model?

$y = 63.6x + 75.5$; the number of positive and negative residuals is about the same,

but the residuals aren't randomly distributed. They form a U-shaped pattern. This

indicates that a linear model does not fit the data well.

2e. Describe what the parameters a and b in the model represent. Is the number of internet hosts growing or decaying? Explain your reasoning. What is the growth or decay rate?

In the model $y = 110(1.29)^x$, 110 represents the number, in millions, of internet

hosts in the year 2001, and 1.29 represents the growth factor; the number of

internet hosts is growing at a growth rate of about 29%.

PRACTICE

The first two columns of the table show the population of Arizona (in thousands) in census years from 1900 to 2000.

1. Find an exponential function model for the data. Round to four significant digits.

$y = 135.9(1.037)^x$

2. Identify the parameters in the model, including the growth or decay rate, and explain what they represent.

$a = 135.9$ is the population in 1900;

$b = 1.037$ is the growth factor;

the yearly growth rate is about 3.7%.

3. Use the more precise model stored on your calculator to complete the third column of the table with population values based on the model. Round to three significant digits.

4. Use the results of Exercise 3 to complete the residuals column of the table.

5. Use your model from Exercise 1 to predict the population of Arizona in 1975 and in 2030, to the nearest thousand. Discuss the accuracy of the results. Which result is likely to be more accurate? Why?

1975: about 2,073 thousand; 2030: about 15,292 thousand; the prediction for 1975;

it falls within the given time period, not 30 years later, when the pattern might

have changed.

Arizona Population y (in thousands) in Years x Since 1900			
x	y_d	y_m	$y_d - y_m$
0	123	136	−13
10	204	196	8
20	334	283	51
30	436	407	29
40	499	587	−88
50	750	847	−97
60	1,302	1,220	82
70	1,771	1,760	11
80	2,718	2,540	178
90	3,665	3,660	5
100	5,131	5,280	−149

6. Make a residual plot. Does the model fit the data well? Explain.

Yes; the points look randomly distributed. About

half are positive and about half are negative.

A few residuals are between 10% and 20% of

the data values, but the rest are 10% of the data

values or less.

Comparing Linear and Exponential Functions

Essential question: *How can you recognize, describe, and compare linear and exponential functions?*

COMMON CORE **Standards for Mathematical Content**

CC.9-12.F.LE.1 Distinguish between situations that can be modeled with linear functions and with exponential functions.*

CC.9-12.F.LE.1a Prove that linear functions grow by equal differences over equal intervals, and that exponential functions grow by equal factors over equal intervals.*

CC.9-12.F.LE.1b Recognize situations in which one quantity changes at a constant rate per unit interval relative to another.*

CC.9-12.F.LE.1c Recognize situations in which a quantity grows or decays by a constant percent rate per unit interval relative to another.*

CC.9-12.F.LE.3 Observe using graphs and tables that a quantity increasing exponentially eventually exceeds a quantity increasing linearly, ….*

Prerequisites

Writing linear functions, Lesson 4-5

Exponential functions, Lessons 5-2 and 5-3

Math Background

If a function increases at a constant rate, then the function is linear. A constant percent change can be modeled by an exponential function. An exponential growth function may "lag behind" a linear function for values of x close to zero, but as x increases without bound, the exponential function will overtake and then rapidly exceed the linear function.

INTRODUCE

Ask students to recall how to find the rate of change in a linear function, $y = mx + b$. The rate of change is the value of m, or the slope. Example: You initially have $100 in a noninterest savings account and put $20 per month into the account. The linear function for this situation is $y = 20x + 100$, where x is the number of months and y is the amount of money in the account after x months. The rate of change is $20 per month and the y-intercept is $100.

TEACH

1 ENGAGE

Questioning Strategies

- What kind of function fits a rate of change of $100 per month? Explain. **Linear; if x = the number of months, then $100x$ = the change in x months**

- How do your calculations differ as you make the entries in the $100 column and in the 10% column? **Sample answer: You add $100 each time for the $100 column; you multiply by 1.10 each time for the 10% column.**

- How do you find the change per unit interval for the $100 column versus the 10% column? **$100 column: Find two inputs that are one unit apart. Subtract the output for the lesser input from the output for the greater input; 10% column: Find two inputs that are one unit apart. Divide the output for the greater input by the outcome for the lesser input.**

- What accounts for the difference in the amounts for Month 2 of the $100 column versus Month 2 of the 10% column? **The extra $10 in the 10% column is explained by receiving 10% of the $1100 in Month 1 as a raise, or $110 versus $100 in the $100 column.**

Name _____ Class _____ Date _____

5-7

Comparing Linear and Exponential Functions

COMMON CORE
CC.9-12.F.LE.1*,
CC.9-12.F.LE.1a*,
CC.9-12.F.LE.1b*,
CC.9-12.F.LE.1c*,
CC.9-12.F.LE.3*

Essential question: *How can you recognize, describe, and compare linear and exponential functions?*

1 ENGAGE · Comparing Constant Change and Constant Percent Change

Suppose you are offered a job that pays $1000 the first month with a raise every month after that. You can choose a $100 raise or a 10% raise. Which option would you choose? What if the raise were 8%, 6%, or 4%?

A Work in groups and use multiple calculators to find the monthly salaries by following the steps described below. For the first three months, record the results in the table below, rounded to the nearest dollar.

- For the $100 raise, enter 1000, press [ENTER], enter +100, press [ENTER], and then press [ENTER] repeatedly.
- For the 10% raise, enter 1000, press [ENTER], enter ×1.10, press [ENTER], and then press [ENTER] repeatedly.
- For the other raises, replace 1.10 with these factors: 1.08, 1.06, and 1.04.

Month	\$100	10%	8%	6%	4%
			Monthly Salary After Indicated Monthly Raise		
0	\$1000	\$1000	\$1000	\$1000	\$1000
1	\$1100	\$1100	\$1080	\$1060	\$1040
2	\$1200	\$1210	\$1166	\$1124	\$1082
3	\$1300	\$1331	\$1260	\$1191	\$1125

B Continue until you find the number of months it takes for each salary with a percent raise to exceed that month's salary with the $100 raise. Record the number of months in the table below.

\$100	10%	8%	6%	4%
		Number of Months Until Salary with Percent Raise Exceeds Salary with \$100 Raise		
─────	2	7	18	43

REFLECT

1a. What is the change per unit interval in monthly salary for each option? Which of these is a constant rate of change in dollars per month? Explain your reasoning.

$100 per month; 10% per month; 8% per month; 6% per month; 4% per month;

$100 per month; with % change, the raise increases each month.

1b. Why are the differences from row to row in each percent column not constant? What *is* constant about the changes from row to row?

Sample answer: Each raise is a constant multiple (percent) of the previous

salary, but because the salaries are increasing, this product gets bigger with

each raise. What is constant is the percent of change.

2 EXAMPLE · Comparing Linear and Exponential Functions

Compare these two salary plans:

- Job A: $1000 for the first month with a $100 raise every month thereafter
- Job B: $1000 for the first month with a 1% raise every month thereafter

Will Job B ever have a higher monthly salary than Job A?

A Write functions that represent the monthly salaries. Let t represent the number of elapsed months. Then tell whether the function is *linear* or *exponential*.

Job A: $S_A(t) = 1000 + 100\,t$ S_A is a/an __linear__ function.

Job B: $S_B(t) = 1000 \cdot 1.01^t$ S_B is a/an __exponential__ function.

B Graph the functions on a calculator and sketch them below. Label the functions and include the scale.

C Will Job B ever have a higher monthly salary than Job A? If so, after how many months will this happen? Explain your reasoning.

Yes; 364 months; at that point, the graph of $S_B(t)$ rises above the graph of $S_A(t)$.

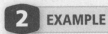

2 EXAMPLE

Questioning Strategies

- How can you recognize whether the function is linear or exponential by looking at the parameters in Job A and Job B? **The salary for Job A changes by a constant rate per month, so that function is linear. The salary for Job B changes by a constant percent per month, so that function is exponential.**

- What does the intersection point of the graphs of the linear and exponential functions tell you? **The intersection point tells how many months it will take for each of the salary plans to pay the same amount.**

Differentiated Instruction

It will be helpful for visual learners to study the graph in part B. They can see that the exponential graph starts off below the linear graph; thus, the salary represented by that graph is less. They can also see that at some point the exponential graph crosses the linear graph and goes above it, thus indicating that the salary represented by the exponential graph eventually will exceed the salary represented by the linear graph.

Technology

Remind students how to find an appropriate viewing window for the functions in part A. Suggest that they start with the **0:ZOOMFIT** feature of the calculator. They should then keep adjusting the window until they can see the intersection point of both graphs.

Avoid Common Errors

Students may not express the exponential function (Job B) correctly in part A. Remind them that the raise (expressed as a decimal) is added to 1 to find the value of the growth factor, or 1.01.

EXTRA EXAMPLE

Compare these two salary plans:

Plan 1: $100 for the first week with a $25 raise every week thereafter.

Plan 2: $100 for the first week with a 10% raise every week thereafter.

Will Plan 2 ever have a higher weekly salary than Plan 1?

Yes; by week 18, the graph of Plan 2 rises above the graph of Plan 1.

CLOSE

Essential Question

How can you recognize, describe, and compare linear and exponential functions?

Linear functions are of the form $y = mx + b$, while exponential functions are of the form $y = ab^x$, where $a \neq 0$, $b > 0$, and $b \neq 1$. Both types of functions can be described by rules, tables, or graphs, and they can be compared by using tables or graphs.

REFLECT

2a. Revise $S_B(t)$ and use the Table feature on your graphing calculator to find the interval in which the monthly salary for Job B finally exceeds that for Job A if the growth rate is 0.1%. Use intervals of 1,000. Repeat for a growth rate of 0.01%, using intervals of 10,000.

between 6,000 and 7,000 months; between 90,000 and 100,000 months

2b. Why does a quantity increasing exponentially eventually exceed a quantity increasing linearly?

The amount of increase is constant in each interval with a linear function, but the

increase per interval grows with an exponential function. Eventually the cumulative

increase with an exponential function exceeds that for a linear function.

2c. The table shows values for the monthly salary functions in four-month intervals rather than one-month intervals.

t	$S_A(t)$	$S_B(t)$
0	1000	1000.00
4	1400	1040.60
8	1800	1082.86
12	2200	1126.83
16	2600	1172.58
20	3000	1220.19

• Does $S_A(t)$ grow by equal differences over each four-month interval? Explain your reasoning.

Yes. The difference is 400 over each four-month interval.

• Does $S_A(t)$ grow by the same difference over the first eight-month interval as it does over the first four-month interval? Explain your reasoning.

No. The difference is 800, not 400, over the first eight-month interval.

• Does $S_B(t)$ grow by equal factors over each four-month interval? Explain your reasoning.

Yes. The growth factor is just over 1.04 for each four-month interval.

• Does $S_B(t)$ grow by the same factor over the first eight-month interval as it does over the first four-month interval? Explain your reasoning.

No. The growth factor is about 1.083, not 1.04, for the first eight-month interval.

Later you will prove that linear functions grow by the same difference over equal intervals and that exponential functions grow by equal factors over equal intervals.

PRACTICE

Tell whether each quantity is changing at a *constant rate* per unit of time, at a *constant percent rate* per unit of time, or *neither*.

1. Amy's salary is $40,000 in her first year on a job with a $2,000 raise every year thereafter.

constant rate

2. Carla's salary is $50,000 in her first year on a job plus a 1% commission on all sales.

neither

3. Enrollment at a school is 976 students initially and then it declines 2.5% each year thereafter.

constant percent rate

4. Companies X and Y each have 50 employees. If Company X increases its workforce by 2 employees per month, and Company Y increases its workforce by 2% per month, will Company Y ever have more employees than Company X? If so, when?

Yes; in 65 months

5. Centerville and Easton each have 2500 residents. Centerville's population decreases by 80 people per year, and Easton's population decreases by 3% per year. Will Centerville ever have a greater population than Easton? If so, when? Explain your reasoning.

No; Centerville's population decreases by 80 each year, while Easton's

population decreases by 75 the first year and by smaller amounts each year

thereafter. So Easton will always have the greater population.

Complete each statement with the correct function from the table at the right.

x	f(x)	g(x)
0	50	100
1	54	104
2	58	108
3	63	112
4	68	116
5	73	120

6. $g(x)$ grows at a constant rate per unit interval.

7. $f(x)$ grows at a constant percent rate per unit interval.

8. An equation for the linear function is as follows:

$g(x) = 100 + 4x$

9. An equation for the exponential function is as follows:

$f(x) = 50(1.08)^x$

Summarize

Have students explain in their journals how to verify that the linear function $f(x) = 100 + 25x$ grows at a constant rate per unit interval (**25**) and that the exponential function $g(x) = 100(1.10)^x$ grows by a constant factor (percent rate) per unit interval (**1.10**).

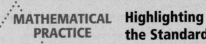

MATHEMATICAL PRACTICE   **Highlighting the Standards**

Exercises 10 and 11 give students the opportunity to demonstrate Mathematical Practice Standard 6 (Attend to precision). When writing algebraic proofs, students have to present the steps in a logical order. They also have to use mathematical notation clearly and accurately to communicate their reasoning effectively.

Where skills are taught	Where skills are practiced
1 ENGAGE	EXS. 1–7
2 EXAMPLE	EXS. 8–9

Exercises 10–11: Students extend what they learned in **2** EXAMPLE by completing a proof that linear functions grow by a constant rate per unit interval and a proof that exponential functions grow by a constant percent per unit interval.

10. Complete the proof that linear functions grow by equal differences over equal intervals.

Given: $x_2 - x_1 = x_4 - x_3$,
            f is a linear function of the form $f(x) = mx + b$.

Prove: $f(x_2) - f(x_1) = f(x_4) - f(x_3)$

Proof:

$x_2 - x_1 = x_4 - x_3$	Given
$m(x_2 - x_1) = m\ (x_4 - x_3)$	Mult. Prop. of Equality
$mx_2 - mx_1 = mx_4 - mx_3$	Distributive Property
$mx_2 + b - mx_1 - b = mx_4 + b - mx_3 - b$	Add. and Subt. Prop. of Equality
$(mx_2 + b) - (mx_1 + b) = (mx_4 + b) - (mx_3 + b)$	Distributive Property
$f(x_2) - f(x_1) = f(x_4) - f(x_3)$	Definition of $f(x)$

11. Complete the proof that exponential functions grow by equal factors over equal intervals.

Given: $x_2 - x_1 = x_4 - x_3$
            g is an exponential function of the form $g(x) = ab^x$.

Prove: $\dfrac{f(x_2)}{f(x_1)} = \dfrac{f(x_4)}{f(x_3)}$

Proof:

$x_2 - x_1 = x_4 - x_3$	Given
$b^{x_2 - x_1} = b^{x_4 - x_3}$	If $x = y$, then $b^x = b^y$.
$\dfrac{b^{x_2}}{b^{x_1}} = \dfrac{b^{x_4}}{b^{x_3}}$	Quotient of Powers Prop.
$\dfrac{ab^{x_2}}{ab^{x_1}} = \dfrac{ab^{x_4}}{ab^{x_3}}$	Mult. Prop. of Equality
$\dfrac{f(x_2)}{f(x_1)} = \dfrac{f(x_4)}{f(x_3)}$	Definition of $f(x)$

FOCUS ON MODELING
Modeling with Exponential Functions

Essential question: *How can you model changes in population using an exponential function?*

Standards for Mathematical Content

The following standards are addressed in this lesson. (An asterisk indicates that a standard is also a Modeling standard.) For more detailed information, see each section of the lesson.

Algebra: CC.9-12.A.CED.2*, CC.9-12.A.REI.11*

Functions: CC.9-12.F.IF.5*, CC.9-12.F.IF.7*, CC.9-12.F.IF.7e*, CC.9-12.F.BF.1*, CC.9-12.F.BF.1a*, CC.9-12.F.LE.1*, CC.9-12.F.LE.1c*, CC.9-12.F.LE.2*, CC.9-12.F.LE.5*

Statistics and Probability: CC.9-12.S.ID.6*, CC.9-12.S.ID.6a*, CC.9-12.S.ID.6b*

Prerequisites

- Graphing a discrete exponential function, Lesson 5-1

- Writing an exponential function, Lesson 5-2

- Performing exponential regression, Lesson 5-6

- Comparing linear and exponential functions, Lesson 5-7

Math Background

In this lesson, students analyze population data and decide between a linear and an exponential model to fit the data. Students find an exponential model, sketch a graph of the model, and draw a smooth curve through the points. They decide on certain aspects of the graph, including whether the curve is a discrete or continuous graph, and they use the regression model to help them decide about building a new high school for Middleton.

INTRODUCE

The United States conducts a population census every 10 years, as was done in 2010. Show students the population figures from the 1950 census to the 2010 census. Ask students to predict whether the data show a linear or an exponential pattern. Then, ask them to validate their predictions.

TEACH

1 Choose and write a model for the function.

Standards

CC.9-12.F.BF.1 Write a function that describes a relationship between two quantities.*

CC.9-12.F.BF.1a Determine an explicit expression, a recursive process, or steps for calculation from a context.*

CC.9-12.F.LE.1 Distinguish between situations that can be modeled with linear functions and with exponential functions.*

CC.9-12.F.LE.1c Recognize situations in which a quantity grows or decays by a constant percent rate per unit interval relative to another.*

CC.9-12.F.LE.2 Construct ... exponential functions, ... given ... two input-output pairs (include reading these from a table).*

CC.9-12.F.LE.5 Interpret the parameters in a linear or exponential function in terms of a context.*

Questioning Strategies

- Why is it important to list more than one ratio between consecutive *y*-values in Part B? **You need to check more than one ratio to see whether there is a pattern in the ratios. Using only one data pair would not distinguish the data between linear and exponential.**

- What ratio would you expect between the data pairs for year 7 and year 8? How do you know? **approximately 1.2; 1.2 represents the mean of the known ratios, so you would expect it to accurately predict the ratio for data close to the data used to calculate the actual ratio.**

continued

FOCUS ON MODELING

Modeling with Exponential Functions

5-8

COMMON CORE
CC.9-12.A.REL11*,
CC.9-12.F.BF.1a*,
CC.9-12.F.LE.1c*,
CC.9-12.F.LE.2*,
CC.9-12.F.LE.5*,
CC.9-12.S.ID.6a*

Essential question: *How can you model changes in population using an exponential function?*

The table shows the population *y* of Middleton, where *x* is the number of years since the end of 2000.

The director of Middleton's planning committee needs a model for the data to make predictions. What model should the director use? How can the director justify that the model is a good one?

Years since 2000, x	Population, y
0	5,005
1	6,010
2	7,203
3	8,700
4	10,521
5	12,420
6	14,982
7	18,010

1 Choose and write a model for the function.

A What are the differences between consecutive *y*-values?

1005, 1193, 1497, 1821, 1899, 2562, 3028

B What are the approximate ratios between consecutive *y*-values?

1.201, 1.199, 1.208, 1.209, 1.180, 1.206, 1.202

C What type of model makes sense for these data? Explain your reasoning.

Exponential; consecutive function values appear to be changing by a constant factor, not by a constant difference.

D Describe in words how the population has been changing during this time period.

Sample answer: the population for a given year is about 1.2 times the population of the previous year.

E Write an equation that models this function.

$y = 5005(1.2)^x$

REFLECT

1a. Identify the parameters of the function and explain what they represent in this situation.

a = 5005, which represents the population of Middleton in 2000;

b = 1.2, which represents the approximate growth factor.

1b. Did the population grow at a constant rate per year or at a constant percent rate per year? Identify the growth rate.

The population grew at a constant percent rate; 20%.

1c. If you assume that the function you wrote in Step 1 applies only to the time period in the table, what are the domain and range of the function?

Domain: All real numbers from 0 to 7 years;

Range: Whole numbers of people from 5005 to *f*(7) = 17,933

1d. If you assume that the function you wrote in Step 1 applies beyond the time period in the table, what are the domain and range of the function?

Domain: All real numbers greater than or equal to 0;

Range: Whole numbers of people greater than or equal to 5005

1e. The population of Brookville was 3500 in the year 2000. Brookville had the same growth rate as Middleton from 2000 to 2007. Assume that both populations continue to grow at that rate indefinitely.

• Write an equation to model the growth of Brookville's population.

$y = 3500(1.2)^x$

• How does the population graph of Brookville compare with that of Middleton over time? Discuss the *y*-intercepts and end behavior.

Sample answer: The *y*-intercept of the graph for Middleton is the initial

population, or 5005 people. The *y*-intercept of the graph for Brookville

is 3500 people. As time passes, both graphs increase without bound.

However, the graph for Middleton is always higher than the graph for

Brookville, because $y = 5005(1.2)^x$ is a greater vertical stretch of the graph

of $y = 1.2^x$ than is $y = 3500(1.2)^x$.

Differentiated Instruction

Make sure students understand the information in the table and can read it correctly. Although students may not have difficulty with the stepped-out work in the lesson, some of the Reflect and Extend questions are challenging. Students may benefit from working in groups to complete them. You may also provide a visual connection by displaying the data table on an overhead projector and drawing arrows from one *y*-value to another. Then, show the differences or ratios under the arrows.

Avoid Common Errors

Students often confuse the parameters in an exponential function. Make sure they think of *a* as the *first* letter of the alphabet ↔ *first* *y*-value, and *b* as the *base* ↔ *base* for the exponent.

2 **Use a calculator to fit a function to the data.**

Standards

CC.9-12.A.CED.2 Create equations in two or more variables to represent relationships between quantities; graph equations on coordinate axes with labels and scales.*

CC.9-12.F.IF.7 Graph functions expressed symbolically ... using technology for more complicated cases.*

CC.9-12.F.IF.7e Graph exponential ... functions, showing intercepts ...*

CC.9-12.F.LE.2 Construct ... exponential functions, ... given a graph, a description of a relationship, or two input-output pairs (include reading these from a table).*

CC.9-12.F.LE.5 Interpret the parameters in a linear or exponential function in terms of a context.*

CC.9-12.S.ID.6 Represent data on two quantitative variables on a scatter plot, and describe how the variables are related.*

CC.9-12.S.ID.6a Fit a function to the data; use functions fitted to data to solve problems in the context of the data.*

Questioning Strategies

- How does the exponential regression model differ from the model you found for part 1E? **$a = 5011$ instead of 5005; *b*, the regression growth factor, is more accurate (1.201 instead of 1.2).**

- How closely does the regression model fit the data? How do you know? **Very closely; the correlation coefficient, *r*, is almost 1 (0.9999).**

- Use the stored regression model to predict the population by the end of 2010. Then use the model in part 1E to predict the population. **stored model: 31,286; part 1E: 30,990**

Differentiated Instruction

Students may have difficulty performing an exponential regression. Encourage them to practice the steps by first solving a simpler problem. For example, have them find an exponential regression for the table points below.

x	0	1	2	3
y	10	20	40	80

$y = 10(2)^x$

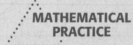

MATHEMATICAL PRACTICE **Highlighting the Standards**

Performing an exponential regression addresses Mathematical Practice Standard 4 (Model with mathematics). Draw students' attention to the way in which they interpret the population model to predict the population in Questions 2a and 2b. Stress the importance of checking the model with actual values and not assuming that the model is a good fit for the data. Explain that the model may be more accurate for years closer in to the given data than for years farther out.

2 Use a calculator to fit a function to the data.

A Use a graphing calculator to make a scatter plot of the data in Step 1. Copy the points below. Label the axes with their minimum and maximum values.

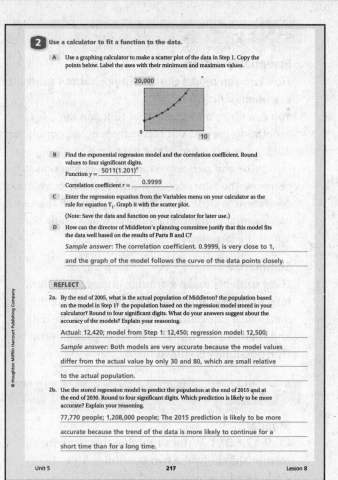

B Find the exponential regression model and the correlation coefficient. Round values to four significant digits.

Function $y = $ _5011(1.201)^x_

Correlation coefficient $r = $ _0.9999_

C Enter the regression equation from the Variables menu on your calculator as the rule for equation Y_1. Graph it with the scatter plot.

(Note: Save the data and function on your calculator for later use.)

D How can the director of Middleton's planning committee justify that this model fits the data well based on the results of Parts B and C?

Sample answer: The correlation coefficient, 0.9999, is very close to 1,

and the graph of the model follows the curve of the data points closely.

REFLECT

2a. By the end of 2005, what is the actual population of Middleton? the population based on the model in Step 1? the population based on the regression model stored in your calculator? Round to four significant digits. What do your answers suggest about the accuracy of the models? Explain your reasoning.

Actual: 12,420; model from Step 1: 12,450; regression model: 12,500;

Sample answer: Both models are very accurate because the model values

differ from the actual value by only 30 and 80, which are small relative

to the actual population.

2b. Use the stored regression model to predict the population at the end of 2015 and at the end of 2030. Round to four significant digits. Which prediction is likely to be more accurate? Explain your reasoning.

77,770 people; 1,208,000 people; The 2015 prediction is likely to be more

accurate because the trend of the data is more likely to continue for a

short time than for a long time.

3 Solve an equation using a graph to make a decision.

Suppose Middleton's town council decides to build a new high school when its population exceeds 25,000. When will the population likely exceed 25,000?

A Write an equation in one variable to represent the time x when the population will reach 25,000.

$25{,}000 = 5011(1.201)^x$

B Enter the function $y = 25{,}000$ as Y_2 on your graphing calculator. Graph Y_1 and Y_2 together. Sketch the graphs below. Label the axes with their minimum and maximum values.

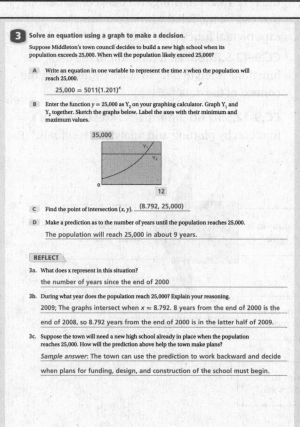

C Find the point of intersection (x, y). _(8.792, 25,000)_

D Make a prediction as to the number of years until the population reaches 25,000.

The population will reach 25,000 in about 9 years.

REFLECT

3a. What does x represent in this situation?

the number of years since the end of 2000

3b. During what year does the population reach 25,000? Explain your reasoning.

2009; The graphs intersect when $x \approx 8.792$. 8 years from the end of 2000 is the

end of 2008, so 8.792 years from the end of 2000 is in the latter half of 2009.

3c. Suppose the town will need a new high school already in place when the population reaches 25,000. How will the prediction above help the town make plans?

Sample answer: The town can use the prediction to work backward and decide

when plans for funding, design, and construction of the school must begin.

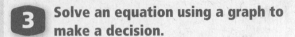

3 Solve an equation using a graph to make a decision.

Standards

CC.9-12.A.REI.11 Explain why the x-coordinates of the points where the graphs of the equations $y = f(x)$ and $y = g(x)$ intersect are the solutions of the equation $f(x) = g(x)$; find the solutions approximately, e.g., using technology to graph the functions, ... Include cases where $f(x)$ and/or $g(x)$ are ..., exponential ... functions.*

CC.9-12.F.IF.7e Graph exponential ... functions ...*

CC.9-12.S.ID.6a ... use functions fitted to data to solve problems in the context of the data.*

Questioning Strategies

- Why is it useful to connect the plotted points with a smooth curve? so you can use the curve to estimate values between points and beyond the given points

- Why is the viewing window $0 < Y < 35,000$? Does this window show the end behavior of the regression model? The viewing window needs to show the equation $Y_2 = 25,000$. It does not show the end behavior of the model because the values of x end at 12.

- How would you use the graph to predict when the population of Middleton will be double its 2007 population? Change the viewing window to $0 < Y < 40,000$. Graph Y_1 as in the lesson along with $Y_3 = 2(18,010)$. Then find the point of intersection ($X \approx 10.8$).

Essential Question

How can you model changes in population using an exponential function?

You can write an exponential function by estimating the growth factor from given population data, or you can graph the data on a graphing calculator and perform exponential regression to generate the function, checking that the correlation coefficient is close to 1. Then, you can use the exponential regression model to make predictions about the population.

Summarize

Have students make a graphic organizer to show how to choose and write a model for population data, use a calculator to fit a function to the data, and then use the function to make predictions. One possibility is shown below.

Standards

CC.9-12.F.BF.1 Write a function that describes a relationship between two quantities.* (Ex. 1)

CC.9-12.F.LE.1 Distinguish between situations that can be modeled with linear functions and with exponential functions.* (Exs. 2, 3, 4)

CC.9-12.S.ID.6a Fit a function to the data; use functions fitted to data to solve problems in the context of the data.* (Ex. 1)

CC.9-12.S.ID.6b Informally assess the fit of a function by plotting and analyzing residuals.* (Ex. 4)

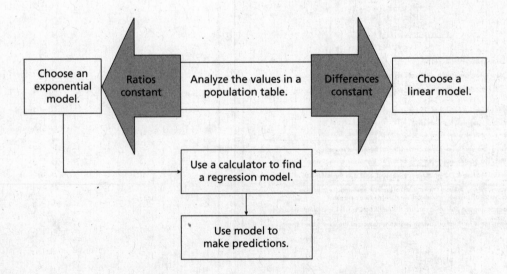

EXTEND

Step 1 shows that an exponential model is better than a linear model for the data given at the beginning of the lesson, based on comparing differences between consecutive y-values and comparing factors between consecutive y-values. Below are some other ways to evaluate the fit of a model.

1. Perform a linear regression on the given data. Round a, b, and r to four significant digits.

Function y = ___1826x + 3966___   Correlation coefficient r = ___0.9844___

2. Based on the correlation coefficients, which model is a better fit? Explain your reasoning.

The r-value for the exponential model, 0.9999, is closer to 1 than that for the

linear model, 0.9844. This indicates that the exponential model is a better fit.

3. Use the exponential and linear regression models with rounded parameters. Predict the population for 2005 to four significant digits. Based on the results, which model is a better fit? Explain your reasoning.

Population from exponential model: 12,520; population from linear model: 13,100;

The exponential model is a better fit. It's value for 2005 is closer to the actual

population of 12,420.

4. Complete the residual plots below. Label the axes with their minimum and maximum values. Use them to decide which model is a better fit. Explain your reasoning. (Note: The residuals list on a graphing calculator stores the residuals for the most recent regression model calculated.)

Residuals for linear model

Residuals for exponential model

The exponential model is a better fit. *Sample answer*: The residuals for the

linear model aren't randomly distributed, because they form a U-shaped pattern.

The residuals for the exponential model do look randomly distributed, about half

are positive and about half are negative, and they are all 0% or 1% of the actual

values in absolute value.

Notes

COMMON CORE CORRELATION

Standard	Items
CC.9-12.A.CED.1*	4, 9
CC.9-12.A.CED.2*	1, 2
CC.9-12.A.REI.11*	5
CC.9-12.F.IF.4*	3
CC.9-12.F.IF.7e*	10
CC.9-12.F.BF.3	3
CC.9-12.F.LE.1b*	8
CC.9-12.F.LE.1c*	7, 10
CC.9-12.F.LE.2*	1, 2, 10
CC.9-12.F.LE.3*	8
CC.9-12.F.LE.5*	10
CC.9-12.S.ID.6a*	6, 10
CC.9-12.S.ID.6b*	6, 10

TEST PREP DOCTOR ⊕

Multiple Choice: Item 1
- Students who chose **A**, **C**, or **D** did not correctly find the ratio between successive $p(n)$ values, or did not know where to place this ratio in the function.

Multiple Choice: Item 2
- If a car loses 8% of its value per year, then each year the car is worth 92% of what it was worth the previous year. Students who chose **F** or **G** did not subtract the depreciation rate from 1. For **G**, they also made a decimal error.
- Students who chose **J** added 0.08 to 1 and used an exponential growth equation instead of an exponential decay equation.

Multiple Choice: Item 3
- Students who chose **A**, **B**, or **D** may not have read the exercise correctly and thus chose a true statement.

Multiple Choice: Item 5
- Students who chose **A** used 1.2, not 1.02, as the growth rate.
- Students who chose **C** calculated $\frac{10,000 - 5060}{0.02 \times 5060}$.
- Students who chose **D** calculated $(10,000 - 5060) \cdot 0.02$.

Multiple Choice: Item 6
- Students who chose **G** gave the residual for 2006.
- Students who chose **H** gave the residual for 2005.
- Students who chose **J** gave the residual for 2009.

Multiple Choice: Item 8
- Students who chose **F** used $y = 1500x^{1.03}$.
- Students who chose **G** used $y = 1580$ instead of $y = 1500 + 80x$.
- Students who chose **J** simply calculated 3% of 1500.

Free Response: Item 10
- Students who answered $y = 18.3x + 14.68$ for Part (a) gave a linear model instead of an exponential model.
- Students who answered $y = 1.055(0.9902)^t$ for Part (a) confused the y-intercept with the ratio value.
- Students who answered $y = 99.02(1.55)^t$ for Part (a) gave a growth factor of 55% instead of 5.5%.

UNIT 5   TEST PREP

Name _____ Class _____ Date _____

MULTIPLE CHOICE

1. The table shows the number of people who have participated in an annual conference since it began in 2007.

Years since 2007, n	1	2	3
Participants, $p(n)$	12	36	108

Which function represents this situation?

A. $p(n) = \frac{1}{3}(4)^n$

B. $p(n) = 4(3)^n$ ✓

C. $p(n) = 4\left(\frac{1}{3}\right)^n$

D. $p(n) = 3(4)^n$

2. Amber buys a car for $17,500. The car depreciates (loses value) 8% each year. Which function shows y, the value of the car (in dollars) in t years?

F. $y = 17,500(0.08)^t$

G. $y = 17,500(0.8)^t$

H. $y = 17,500(0.92)^t$ ✓

J. $y = 17,500(1.08)^t$

3. Which statement is **NOT** true about the functions $f(x) = 1.2(1.05)^x$ and $g(x) = 1.2(1.07)^x$?

A. As x increases without bound, $f(x)$ and $g(x)$ both increase without bound.

B. As x increases to the right of 0, the value of $g(x)$ is greater than the value of $f(x)$ for every value of x.

C. The y-intercept of $g(x)$ is greater than the y-intercept of $f(x)$. ✓

D. The y-intercept of $g(x)$ is equal to the y-intercept of $f(x)$.

4. Solve the equation $2\left(\frac{2}{3}\right)^x = \frac{8}{9}$.

F. $x = 1$

G. $x = 2$ ✓

H. $x = 3$

J. $x = 4$

5. An online music sharing club has 5,060 members. The membership is increasing at a rate of 2% per month. In approximately how many months will the membership reach 10,000?

A. 3.7 months

B. 34.4 months ✓

C. 48.8 months

D. 98.8 months

6. The table shows attendance at games for a sports team from 2005 to 2009.

Years since 2005, x	Attendance, y
0	320,143
1	300,656
2	283,752
3	265,700
4	250,978

Kion performs an exponential regression to find a model for the data set. Then he makes a scatter plot of the residuals. What is the approximate residual for 2008?

F. −720 ✓

G. −357

H. 184

J. 334

7. Which of the following can be represented by an exponential function?

A. Ben deposits $20 in a savings account. Then he deposits $2 each month for the next 6 months.

B. Leslie deposits $20 in a savings account. Then she makes a deposit each month for the next 6 months, putting in $2 more with each deposit.

C. Dan runs a mile in 9 minutes. Then he runs a mile each day for the next 4 days, reducing his time by 6 seconds each day.

D. Rick runs a mile in 8 minutes. Then he runs a mile each day for the next 4 days, reducing his time by 1.5% each day. ✓

8. Keenville and Westbrook each have 1500 residents. The population of Keenville increases by 3% every year. The population of Westbrook increases by 80 residents every year. How long will it take for the population of Keenville to exceed the population of Westbrook?

F. 1.1 years

G. 1.8 years

H. 36.7 years ✓

J. 45 years

9. Mr. Turner bought stock for $15,000. If the value of the stock decreases 4% each year, when will it be worth 80% of the original purchase price?

A. in 5.5 years ✓

B. in 7.5 years

C. in 20 years

D. in 39 years

FREE RESPONSE

10. The table shows the number of phone calls made per day (in millions) in years since 1940.

Years, x	0	10	20	30	40
calls, y	98.8	171	288	494	853

a. Fit a function to the data using four significant digits. Tell whether it is exponential or linear.

$y = 99.02(1.055)^x$; exponential

b. Graph the function below. Label the axes.

c. Identify what the y-intercept represents.

the number of calls per day in 1940

d. Use a graphing calculator to make a residual plot. Does the model fit the data well? Explain.

Yes; the residuals are fairly randomly distributed and they are small as a percent of the data values.

e. Predict the calls per day in 1975 and in 1995. Which is more likely to be accurate? Explain.

645,000,000; 1,882,000,000; the prediction for 1975 is more likely to be accurate because it falls within the range of data values.

Piecewise and Absolute Value Functions

Unit Vocabulary

absolute value
  function   (6-2)

greatest integer
  function   (6-1)

piecewise
  function   (6-1)

step function   (6-1)

UNIT 6

Piecewise and Absolute Value Functions

Unit Focus

In this unit you will learn that a piecewise function has two or more parts in its rule, creating two or more pieces in its graph. Two special cases of piecewise functions are step functions, whose graphs look like steps, and absolute value functions, whose graphs are V-shaped. You will learn about transforming the graphs of absolute value functions, solving absolute value equations, and modeling with absolute value functions.

Unit at a Glance

COMMON CORE

Lesson	Standards for Mathematical Content
6-1 Piecewise Functions	CC.9-12.A.CED.2*, CC.9-12.F.IF.2, CC.9-12.F.IF.4*, CC.9-12.F.IF.5*, CC.9-12.F.IF.7b*, CC.9-12.F.BF.1*
6-2 Translating the Graph of $f(x) = |x|$	CC.9-12.A.CED.2*, CC.9-12.F.IF.2, CC.9-12.F.IF.7*, CC.9-12.F.IF.7b*, CC.9-12.F.BF.1*, CC.9-12.F.BF.3
6-3 Stretching, Shrinking, and Reflecting the Graph of $f(x) = |x|$	CC.9-12.A.CED.2*, CC.9-12.F.IF.2, CC.9-12.F.IF.7*, CC.9-12.F.IF.7b*, CC.9-12.F.BF.1*, CC.9-12.F.BF.3
6-4 Combining Transformations of the Graph of $f(x) = |x|$	CC.9-12.A.CED.2*, CC.9-12.F.IF.2, CC.9-12.F.IF.7*, CC.9-12.F.IF.7b*, CC.9-12.F.BF.1*, CC.9-12.F.BF.3
6-5 Solving Absolute Value Equations	CC.9-12.A.CED.1*, CC.9-12.A.CED.2*, CC.9-12.A.REI.11*
6-6 Modeling with Absolute Value Functions	CC.9-12.A.CED.2*, CC.9-12.F.IF.2, CC.9-12.F.IF.4*, CC.9-12.F.IF.5*, CC.9-12.F.IF.7b*, CC.9-12.F.BF.1*
Test Prep	

Unit 6   223   Piecewise and Absolute Value Functions

© Houghton Mifflin Harcourt Publishing Company

UNIT 6

UNIT 6

Unpacking the Common Core State Standards

Use the table to help you understand the Standards for Mathematical Content that are taught in this unit. Refer to the lessons listed after each standard for exploration and practice.

COMMON CORE Standards for Mathematical Content	What It Means For You
CC.9-12.A.CED.1 Create equations and inequalities in one variable and use them to **solve problems.*** Lesson 6-5	You will use absolute value functions to write absolute value equations in one variable, and you will solve the equations by graphing or by using algebra.
CC.9-12.A.CED.2 Create equations in two or more **variables to represent relationships between quantities; graph equations on coordinate axes with labels and scales.*** Lessons 6-1, 6-2, 6-3, 6-4, 6-5, 6-6	You will graph piecewise and absolute value functions from their equations, and you will write equations for them when given their graphs.
CC.9-12.A.REI.11 Explain why the *x*-coordinates of the points where the graphs of the equations $y = f(x)$ and $y = g(x)$ intersect are the solutions of the equation $f(x) = g(x)$; find the solutions approximately, e.g., using technology to graph the functions, make tables of values, or find successive approximations. **Include cases where** $f(x)$ **and/or** $g(x)$ **are linear, polynomial, rational, absolute value, exponential and logarithmic functions.*** Lessons 6-5	One way to solve an equation in one variable is to treat each side of the equation as a function, graph the functions, and find where the graphs intersect. You will use this method to solve absolute value equations.
CC.9-12.F.IF.2 Use function notation, evaluate functions for inputs in their domains, and interpret statements that use function notation in terms of a **context.** Lessons 6-1, 6-2, 6-3, 6-4, 6-6 (Also 6-5)	You will write piecewise and absolute value functions using function notation, and you will interpret the notation when using those functions to solve real-world problems.
CC.9-12.F.IF.4 For a function that models a relationship between two quantities, interpret key features of graphs and tables in terms of the quantities, and sketch graphs showing key features given a verbal description of the relationship.* Lessons 6-1, 6-6 (Also 6-2, 6-3, 6-4, 6-5)	You will learn that the graph of an absolute value function has the shape of a V or an inverted V. The symmetry of the graph is particularly useful as a model for the path of a rolling ball that strikes a flat surface and bounces off.

Unpacking the Common Core State Standards

This page lists and explains the Standards for Mathematical Content that are addressed in this unit. For information about the Standards for Mathematical Practice, which are integrated throughout the text, see Teacher Edition pages viii–xi.

Notes

_____

_____

_____

_____

_____

_____

_____

_____

_____

_____

Additional Standards in This Unit

CC.9-12.N.Q.1 Use units as a way to understand problems and to guide the solution of multi-step problems; ... choose and interpret the scale and the origin in graphs ...* Lessons 6-1, 6-5, 6-6

CC.9-12.N.Q.2 Define appropriate quantities for the purpose of descriptive modeling.* Lessons 6-5, 6-6

CC.9-12.A.CED.1 Create equations ... in one variable and use them to solve problems.* Lesson 6-6

CC.9-12.A.REI.3 Solve linear equations ... in one variable ... Lesson 6-6

COMMON CORE Standards for Mathematical Content	What It Means For You
CC.9-12.F.IF.5 Relate the domain of a function to its graph and, where applicable, to the quantitative relationship it describes.* Lessons 6-1, 6-6 (Also 6-2, 6-3, 6-4)	When writing equations for piecewise functions whose graphs are given, you must pay close attention to the domain for each piece of the graph because the domain becomes part of the function's rule. Also, although absolute value functions are defined for all real numbers, the domain may be restricted when using the functions to model real-world situations.
CC.9-12.F.IF.7 Graph functions expressed symbolically and show key features of the graph, by hand in simple cases and using technology for more complicated cases.* **CC.9-12.F.IF.7b Graph square root, cube root, and piecewise-defined functions, including step functions and absolute value functions.*** Lessons 6-1, 6-2, 6-3, 6-4, 6-6 (Also 6-5)	You will graph piecewise functions, including two important special cases: step functions and absolute value functions. For absolute value functions, you will learn to identify the vertex, a key feature of their graphs.
CC.9-12.F.BF.1 Write a function that describes a relationship between two quantities.* **CC.9-12.F.BF.1a Determine an explicit expression, a recursive process, or steps for calculation from a context.*** Lessons 6-1, 6-2, 6-3, 6-4, 6-6	When you write a rule for an absolute value function in this unit, you will be finding an expression of the form $a|x - h| + k$ where a, h, and k are constants.
CC.9-12.F.BF.3 Identify the effect on the graph of replacing $f(x)$ by $f(x) + k$, $kf(x)$, $f(kx)$, and $f(x + k)$ for specific values of k (both positive and negative); find the value of k given the graphs. Experiment with cases and illustrate an explanation of the effects on the graphs using technology. Lessons 6-2, 6-3, 6-4	By comparing equations and graphs of absolute value functions, you will learn how changes in an equation cause a graph to be translated, vertically stretched or shrunk, reflected in the x-axis, or some combination of these transformations. Learning these concepts will enable you to graph an absolute value function without the need to create a table of values. In particular, you will be able to immediately identify the vertex and tell whether the graph's shape is a V or an inverted V.

© Houghton Mifflin Harcourt Publishing Company

Notes

_____

_____

_____

_____

_____

_____

_____

_____

_____

Notes

_____

_____

_____

_____

_____

_____

_____

_____

_____

_____

_____

_____

_____

_____

_____

_____

_____

_____

_____

_____

_____

_____

Piecewise Functions

Essential question: *How are piecewise functions and step functions different from other functions?*

○ **COMMON** **Standards for**
○ **CORE** **Mathematical Content**

CC.9-12.A.CED.2 Create equations in two ... variables to represent relationships between quantities; graph equations on coordinate axes with labels and scales.*

CC.9-12.F.IF.2 Use function notation, evaluate functions for inputs in their domains, and interpret statements that use function notation in terms of a context.

CC.9-12.F.IF.4 For a function that models a relationship between two quantities, interpret key features of graphs and tables in terms of the quantities, and sketch graphs showing key features given a verbal description of the relationship.*

CC.9-12.F.IF.5 Relate the domain of a function to its graph and, where applicable, to the quantitative relationship it describes.*

CC.9-12.F.IF.7 Graph functions expressed symbolically and show key features of the graph ...*

CC.9-12.F.IF.7b Graph ... piecewise-defined functions, including step functions ...*

CC.9-12.F.BF.1 Write a function that describes a relationship between two quantities.*

CC.9-12.F.BF.1a Determine an explicit expression ... from a context.*

Also: CC.9-12.N.Q.1*

Vocabulary

greatest integer function

piecewise function

step function

Prerequisites

Functions, Lesson 1-5

Linear functions, Lesson 4-2

Math Background

A piecewise function is defined by at least two different rules that apply to different parts of the domain. To evaluate a piecewise function, substitute the value of x into the rule for the part of the domain that includes that value of x. If the graph of a piecewise function resembles a set of stairs, the function is defined by a constant value over each part of its domain. This type of piecewise function is referred to as a "step" function. An example of this is the greatest integer function, $f(x) = [\![x]\!]$. The greatest integer function can also be written as shown below.

$$f(x) = \begin{cases} \vdots & \\ -2 & \text{if } -2 \le x < -1 \\ -1 & \text{if } -1 \le x < 0 \\ 0 & \text{if } 0 \le x < 1 \\ 1 & \text{if } 1 \le x < 2 \\ 2 & \text{if } 2 \le x < 3 \\ \vdots & \end{cases}$$

INTRODUCE

The table below shows U.S. postal rates in 2011 for first class letters. Ask students the following questions: What is the cost of mailing a letter that weighs 0.8 ounce? 1.5 ounces? 2 ounces? 2.9 ounces? $0.44; $0.61; $0.61; $0.78

Weight Not Over	Postage
1 oz	$0.44
2 oz	$0.61
3 oz	$0.78

© Houghton Mifflin Harcourt Publishing Company

Piecewise Functions

Essential question: *How are piecewise functions and step functions different from other functions?*

A **piecewise function** has different rules for different parts of its domain. The **greatest integer function** is a piecewise function whose rule is denoted by [x], which represents the greatest integer less than or equal to x. To evaluate a piecewise function for a given value of x, substitute the value of x into the rule for the part of the domain that includes x.

1 EXAMPLE Evaluating Piecewise Functions

A Find $f(-3), f(-0.2), f(0),$ and $f(2)$ for $f(x) = \begin{cases} -x & \text{if } x < 0 \\ x+1 & \text{if } x \geq 0 \end{cases}$

$-3 < 0$, so use the rule $f(x) = -x$: $f(-3) = -(-3) = \underline{3}$

$-0.2 < 0$, so use the rule $\underline{f(x) = -x}$: $f(-0.2) = -(-0.2) = \underline{0.2}$

$0 \geq 0$, so use the rule $f(x) = x + 1$: $f(0) = 0 + 1 = \underline{1}$

$2 \geq 0$, so use the rule $\underline{f(x) = x + 1}$ $f(2) = \underline{2} + 1 = \underline{3}$

B Find $f(-3), f(-2.9), f(0.7),$ and $f(1.06)$ for $f(x) = [x]$.

The greatest integer function $f(x) = [x]$ can also be written as shown below. Complete the rules for the function before evaluating it.

$f(x) = \begin{cases} \vdots \\ -3 & \text{if } -3 \leq x < -2 \\ -2 & \text{if } -2 \leq x < -1 \\ -1 & \text{if } -1 \leq x < 0 \\ 0 & \text{if } 0 \leq x < 1 \\ 1 & \text{if } 1 \leq x < 2 \\ 2 & \text{if } 2 \leq x < 3 \\ \vdots \end{cases}$ ← For any number x that is less than −2 and greater than or equal to −3, the greatest of the integers less than or equal to x is −3.

-3 is in the interval $-3 \leq x < -2$, so $f(-3) = -3$.

-2.9 is in the interval $-3 \leq x < -2$, so $f(-2.9) = \underline{-3}$

0.7 is in the interval $\underline{0 \leq x < 1}$, so $f(0.7) = \underline{0}$

1.06 is in the interval $\underline{1 \leq x < 2}$, so $f(1.06) = \underline{1}$

REFLECT

1a. Why should the parts of the domain of a piecewise function $f(x)$ have no common x-values?

You want only one rule to apply to a given x-value so that you get only one f(x)-value, since a function must give a unique output for each input.

1b. For positive numbers, how is applying the greatest integer function different from the method of rounding to the nearest whole number?

When you round a positive number to the nearest whole number, you round down if the tenths digit is 4 or less and you round up if the tenths digit is 5 or greater. For the greatest integer function, you always round down.

2 EXAMPLE Graphing Piecewise Functions

Graph each function.

A $f(x) = \begin{cases} -x & \text{if } x < 0 \\ x+1 & \text{if } x \geq 0 \end{cases}$

Complete the table. Use the values to help you complete the graph. Extend the pattern to cover the entire domain on the grid.

x	−3	−2	−1	−0.9	−0.1
f(x)	3	2	1	0.9	0.1

x	0	0.1	0.9	1	2
f(x)	1	1.1	1.9	2	3

The transition from one rule, −x, to the other, x + 1, occurs at x = 0. Show an open dot at (0, 0) because the point is not part of the graph. Show a closed dot at (0, 1) because the point is part of the graph.

B $f(x) = [x]$

Complete the table. Use the values to help you complete the graph. Extend the pattern to cover the entire domain on the grid.

x	−4	−3.9	−3.1	−3	−2.9
f(x)	−4	−4	−4	−3	−3

x	−2.1	−2	−1.5	−1	0
f(x)	−3	−2	−2	−1	0

x	1	1.5	2	3	4
f(x)	1	1	2	3	4

1 EXAMPLE

Questioning Strategies

- What are the domain and range of the function in part A? domain: all real numbers; range: all real numbers

- What are the domain and range of the function in part B? domain: all real numbers; range: all integers

Teaching Strategy

Help students remember that you always round down for the greatest integer function by telling them that the function is sometimes called the "floor" function.

EXTRA EXAMPLE

A. Find $f(-3), f(-0.1), f(0),$ and $f(1)$
   for the following: $f(x) = \begin{cases} x & \text{if } x < 0 \\ -x - 1 & \text{if } x \geq 0 \end{cases}$.

   $-3, -0.1, -1, -2$

B. Find $f(-2), f(-1.3), f(0.9),$ and $f(2.12)$
   for $f(x) = [\![x]\!]$. $-2, -2, 0, 2$

2 EXAMPLE

Questioning Strategies

- How is the graph of $g(x) = -x$ with domain negative real numbers related to the graph of $f(x)$ in part A? The graph of $g(x)$ is the left side of the graph of $f(x)$.

- Why are the "steps" in the graph of $f(x)$ in part B closed on the left and open on the right? $f(x) = x$ when x is an integer.

Avoid Common Errors

Students make errors when they use the normal rules of rounding to find values for $f(x) = [\![x]\!]$. Caution them to always round down.

EXTRA EXAMPLE

Graph each function.

A. $f(x) = \begin{cases} x & \text{if } x < 0 \\ -x - 1 & \text{if } x \geq 0 \end{cases}$

The graph consists of two rays; one ray has an open circle at (0, 0) continuing downward and left, passing through the points (−1, −1) and (−3, −3); the other ray has a closed circle at (0, −1) and continues downward and right, passing through (1, −2), and (3, −4).

B. $f(x) = [\![x]\!] - 1$

The graph has solid circles at ..., (−2, −3), (−1, −2), (0, −1), (1, 0), (2, 1), ... each of which is connected by a solid line to an open circle one unit to the right.

3 EXAMPLE

Questioning Strategies

- Why is the graph in part C continuous? A gap in either time or distance traveled would not make sense in the context of the problem.

- Why does the graph in part C include a section that is horizontal? The student stopped traveling for one minute, so the distance traveled during that time period did not change.

> **MATHEMATICAL PRACTICE** — **Highlighting the Standards**
>
> Example 3 addresses Mathematical Practice Standard 4 (Model with mathematics). Draw students' attention to the use of multiple representations for the piecewise function. Specifically, ask students why using a table or graph may be helpful in visualizing the different rules for a specific piecewise function representing a real-world situation.

Teaching Strategy

In the table for part B, stress the importance of recognizing the t-values that correspond to the endpoints of each part of the domain.

continued

REFLECT

2a. Why does the first graph use rays and not lines?

Each rule has a separate domain. If the graph contained lines, the domains would

overlap. Since each rule is an inequality with one endpoint, the graph contains rays.

2b. The greatest integer function is an example of a **step function**, a piecewise function that is constant for each rule. Use the graph of the greatest integer function to explain why such a function is called a step function.

The sections of the graph are horizontal segments and look like a set of stairs.

2c. Does the greatest integer function have a maximum or minimum value? Explain.

No; there is no point on the graph that is higher or lower than all other points.

---

3 EXAMPLE Writing and Graphing a Piecewise Function

On his way to class from his dorm room, a college student walks at a speed of 0.05 mile per minute for 3 minutes, stops to talk to a friend for 1 minute, and then to avoid being late for class, runs at a speed of 0.10 mile per minute for 2 minutes. Write a piecewise function for the student's distance from his dorm room during this time. Then graph the function.

A Express the student's distance traveled d (in miles) as a function of time t (in minutes). Write an equation for the function $d(t)$.

$$d(t) = \begin{cases} 0.05\ t & \text{if } 0 \le t \le 3 \quad \leftarrow \text{He travels at 0.05 mile per minute for 3 minutes.} \\ 0.15 & \text{if } 3 < t \le 4 \quad \leftarrow \text{Distance traveled is constant for 1 minute.} \\ 0.15 + 0.10\,(t-4) & \text{if } 4 < t \le 6 \quad \leftarrow \text{Add the distance traveled at 0.10 mile per minute to the distance already traveled.} \end{cases}$$

B Complete the table.

t	0	1	2	3
$d(t)$	0	0.50	0.10	0.15

t	4	5	6
$d(t)$	0.15	0.25	0.35

C Complete the graph.

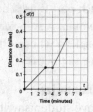

REFLECT

3a. Why is the second rule for the function $d(t) = 0.15$ instead of $d(t) = 0$?

$d(t)$ represents distance traveled, and the student has traveled 0.15 mile when $t = 3$.

3b. Why is the third rule for the function $d(t) = 0.15 + 0.10(t-4)$?

The distance already traveled during the first 4 minutes is 0.15 mile. During the next

2 minutes, he is traveling at 0.10 mile per minute for only the time beyond 4 minutes.

---

4 EXAMPLE Writing a Function When Given a Graph

Write the equation for each function whose graph is shown.

A

B

Find the equation for each ray:

• Find the slope m of the line that contains the ray on the left. Use $(-4, -2)$ and $(-1, 1)$.

$$m = \frac{1 - \left(-2 \right)}{-1 - \left(-4 \right)} = \frac{3}{3} = 1$$

Substitute this value of m along with the coordinates of $(-1, 1)$ into $y = mx + b$ and solve for b.

$$y = mx + b$$
$$1 = 1\left(-1 \right) + b$$
$$2 = b$$

So, $y = 1x + 2$.

• The equation of the line that contains the horizontal ray is $y = 3$.

The equation for the function is:

$$f(x) = \begin{cases} x + 2 & \text{if } x \le -1 \\ 3 & \text{if } x > -1 \end{cases}$$

Write a rule for each horizontal line segment.

$$f(x) = \begin{cases} -4 & \text{if } -2 \le x < -1 \\ -2 & \text{if } -1 \le x < 0 \\ 0 & \text{if } 0 \le x < 1 \\ 2 & \text{if } 1 \le x < 2 \\ 4 & \text{if } 2 \le x < 3 \end{cases}$$

Although the graph shows the function's domain to be $-2 \le x < 3$, assume that the domain consists of all real numbers and that the graph continues its stair-step pattern for $x < -2$ and $x \ge 3$.

Notice that each function value is __2__ times the corresponding value of the greatest integer function.

The equation for the function is:

$$f(x) = 2\ [x]$$

EXTRA EXAMPLE

A parent drives from home to the grocery store at 0.9 mile per minute for 4 minutes, stops to buy snacks for the team for 2 minutes, and then drives to the soccer field at a speed of 0.7 mile per minute for 3 minutes. Write a piecewise function for the parent's distance from home to the soccer field during this time. Then graph the function.

$$d(t) = \begin{cases} 0.9t & \text{if } 0 \le t \le 4 \\ 3.6 & \text{if } 4 < t \le 6 \\ 3.6 + 0.7(t-6) & \text{if } 6 < t \le 9 \end{cases}$$

The graph is a line segment from (0, 0) to (4, 3.6), a line segment from (4, 3.6) to (6, 3.6) and a line segment from (6, 3.6) to (9, 5.7).

4 **EXAMPLE**

Questioning Strategies

• How is the graph in part A related to the graph of $g(x) = 3$? The graph of $g(x) = 3$ restricted to the domain values $x > -1$ is the upper part of the graph of $f(x)$.

• In part B, how are $f(x)$ and the greatest integer function related? The range values of $f(x)$ are twice those of the corresponding range values of the greatest integer function.

EXTRA EXAMPLE

Write the equation for each function whose graph is shown.

A.

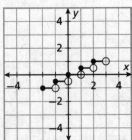

$f(x) = \frac{1}{2} [\![x]\!]$ for $-2 \le x < 3$

B.

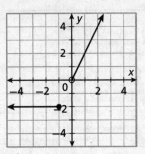

$$f(x) = \begin{cases} -2 & \text{if } x \le -1 \\ 2x & \text{if } x > 0 \end{cases}$$

CLOSE

Essential Question

How are piecewise functions and step functions different from other functions?
A piecewise function's rule has two or more parts; each part is applied to a different subset of the domain. A step function is a special piecewise function whose graph consists of horizontal line segments.

Summarize

Have students write a journal entry in which they describe how to graph a step function and explain why the function is called a step function.

PRACTICE

Where skills are taught	Where skills are practiced
2 EXAMPLE	EXS. 1–3
3 EXAMPLE	EXS. 7–8
4 EXAMPLE	EXS. 4–6

4a. When writing a piecewise function from a graph, how do you determine the domain of each rule?

For each piece of the function, determine the interval on the x-axis that corresponds to that piece. An open circle on the graph indicates the x-value is not in the domain for that piece.

4b. How can you use y-intercepts to check that your answer in part A is reasonable?

Extend the first ray to see that it passes through (0, 2), which agrees with the equation $y = x + 2$. The second ray passes through (0, 3), which agrees with the equation $y = 0x + 3$.

PRACTICE

Graph each function.

1. $f(x) = \begin{cases} -x + 1 & \text{if } x < 0 \\ x & \text{if } x \geq 0 \end{cases}$

2. $f(x) = \begin{cases} -1 & \text{if } x < 1 \\ 2x - 2 & \text{if } x \geq 1 \end{cases}$

3. $f(x) = [\![x]\!] + 1$

Write the equation for each function whose graph is shown.

4.

5.

6.

$f(x) = \begin{cases} x + 1 & \text{if } x < 0 \\ 2 & \text{if } x \geq 0 \end{cases}$

$f(x) = \begin{cases} -x - 1 & \text{if } x < 0 \\ 1 & \text{if } 0 \leq x < 2 \\ \frac{1}{2}x + 1 & \text{if } x \geq 2 \end{cases}$

$f(x) = [\![x]\!] - 2$

7. A garage charges the following rates for parking (with an 8 hour limit):

    $4 per hour for the first 2 hours
    $2 per hour for the next 4 hours
    No additional charge for the next 2 hours

a. Write a piecewise function that gives the parking cost C (in dollars) in terms of the time t (in hours) that a car is parked in the garage.

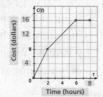

$C(t) = \begin{cases} 4t & \text{if } 0 \leq t \leq 2 \\ 8 + 2(t - 2) & \text{if } 2 < t \leq 6 \\ 16 & \text{if } 6 < t \leq 8 \end{cases}$

b. Graph the function. Include labels to show what the axes represent and to show the scales on the axes.

8. The cost to send a package between two cities is $8.00 for any weight less than 1 pound. The cost increases by $4.00 when the weight reaches 1 pound and again each time the weight reaches a whole number of pounds after that.

a. For a package having weight w (in pounds), write a function in terms of $[\![w]\!]$ to represent the shipping cost C (in dollars).

$C(w) = 8 + 4 [\![w]\!]$

b. Complete the table.

Weight (pounds) w	Cost (dollars) C(w)
0.5	8
1	12
1.5	12
2	16
2.5	16

c. Graph the function. Show the costs for all weights less than 5 pounds.

Translating the Graph of $f(x) = |x|$

Essential question: *What are the effects of the constants h and k on the graph of $y = |x - h| + k$?*

COMMON **Standards for**
CORE **Mathematical Content**

CC.9-12.A.CED.2 Create equations in two ... variables to represent relationships between quantities; graph equations on coordinate axes with labels and scales.*

CC.9-12.F.IF.2 Use function notation, evaluate functions for inputs in their domains ...

CC.9-12.F.IF.7 Graph functions expressed symbolically and show key features of the graph ...*

CC.9-12.F.IF.7b Graph ... piecewise-defined functions, including ... absolute value functions.*

CC.9-12.F.BF.1 Write a function that describes a relationship between two quantities.*

CC.9-12.F.BF.3 Identify the effect on the graph of replacing $f(x)$ by $f(x) + k$ ... and $f(x + k)$ for specific values of k (both positive and negative); find the value of k given the graphs. ...

Vocabulary
absolute value function

Prerequisites
Piecewise functions, Lesson 6-1

Translations, Grade 8

Math Background
In Grade 8, students learned to translate figures in the coordinate plane. (Standard 8.G.3: Describe the effect of dilations, translations, rotations, and reflections on two-dimensional figures using coordinates.) In this lesson, students will apply translations to the graph of the parent absolute value function $y = |x|$. You can derive the equation of the translated graph as follows:

The notation $(x, y) \rightarrow (x + h, y + k)$ defines a translation of h units horizontally and k units vertically of any point (x, y). To distinguish between the pre-image and image coordinates, denote the image coordinates as (x', y') so that $x' = x + h$ and $y' = y + k$. Solving for x and y gives $x = x' - h$ and $y = y' - k$, and substituting into $y = |x|$ gives $y' - k = |x' - h|$. So, the equation of the translated graph is $y - k = |x - h|$, or $y = |x - h| + k$.

INTRODUCE

Remind students that a translation, or slide, moves all points in a coordinate plane the same distance in the same direction. For instance, the translation that moves points 4 units left and 6 units up will move the point $(3, 2)$ to the point $(3 - 4, 2 + 6)$, or $(-1, 8)$. Ask students: If a translation moves points 4 units to the right and 6 units down, the point $(3, 2)$ has what coordinates when translated? **(7, −4)**

TEACH

1 **ENGAGE**

Questioning Strategies
• Look at the piecewise rule for the function. Is the function defined for all x-values or just certain x-values? What is the function's domain? **Defined for all x-values; {real numbers}**

• Look at the graph of the function. Does the function take on all y-values or just certain y-values? What is the function's range? **Takes on only nonnegative y-values; {y | y ≥ 0}**

2 **EXAMPLE**

Questioning Strategies
• In part A, what is the vertex of the translated graph? Since the vertex of the parent graph is $(0, 0)$, what translation has moved $(0, 0)$ to the vertex of the translated graph? **(0, 2); translate 2 units up**

• In part B, note that the least value that the function takes on is 0 because the value of $|x - 4|$ is never negative. So what x-value makes $x - 4$ equal to 0? How does this help you choose x-values for the table? **4; choose x-values on each side of 4**

continued

Translating the Graph of
$f(x) = |x|$

COMMON
CORE

Essential question: *What are the effects of the constants h and k on the graph of* $y = |x - h| + k$?

CC 9-12.A.CED.2*,
CC 9-12.F.IF.2,
CC 9-12.F.IF.7*,
CC 9-12.F.IF.7b*,
CC 9-12.F.BF.1*,
CC 9-12.F.BF.3

1 ENGAGE Understanding the Parent Absolute Value Function

The most basic **absolute value function** is a piecewise function given by the following rule.

$$f(x) = |x| = \begin{cases} x & \text{if } x \geq 0 \\ -x & \text{if } x < 0 \end{cases}$$

This function is sometimes called the *parent* absolute value function.

To graph the function, you can make a table of values like the one shown below, plot the ordered pairs, and draw the graph.

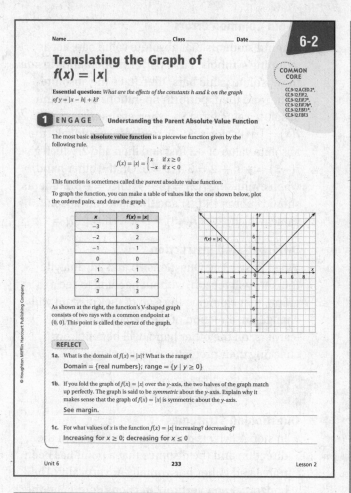

x	f(x) = |x|
−3	3
−2	2
−1	1
0	0
1	1
2	2
3	3

As shown at the right, the function's V-shaped graph consists of two rays with a common endpoint at (0, 0). This point is called the *vertex* of the graph.

REFLECT

1a. What is the domain of $f(x) = |x|$? What is the range?

Domain = {real numbers}; range = {y | y ≥ 0}

1b. If you fold the graph of $f(x) = |x|$ over the y-axis, the two halves of the graph match up perfectly. The graph is said to be *symmetric* about the y-axis. Explain why it makes sense that the graph of $f(x) = |x|$ is symmetric about the y-axis.

See margin.

1c. For what values of x is the function $f(x) = |x|$ increasing? decreasing?

Increasing for $x \geq 0$; decreasing for $x \leq 0$

© Houghton Mifflin Harcourt Publishing Company

2 EXAMPLE Graphing Functions of the Form $g(x) = |x - h| + k$

Graph each absolute value function. (The graph of the parent function $f(x) = |x|$ is shown in gray.)

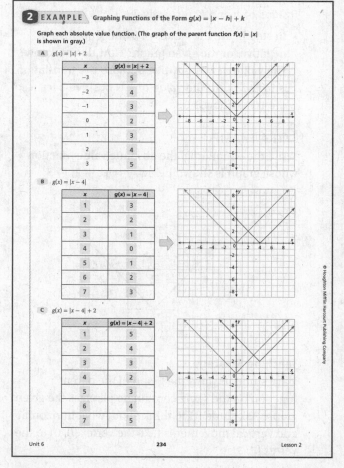

A $g(x) = |x| + 2$

x	g(x) = |x| + 2
−3	5
−2	4
−1	3
0	2
1	3
2	4
3	5

B $g(x) = |x - 4|$

x	g(x) = |x − 4|
1	3
2	2
3	1
4	0
5	1
6	2
7	3

C $g(x) = |x - 4| + 2$

x	g(x) = |x − 4| + 2
1	5
2	4
3	3
4	2
5	3
6	4
7	5

© Houghton Mifflin Harcourt Publishing Company

1b. The graph consists of the mirror-image points (a, a) and $(-a, a)$ for any $a > 0$.

Notes

EXTRA EXAMPLE

Graph each absolute value function.

A. $y = |x| - 3$ The graph of $y = |x| - 3$ is the graph of $y = |x|$ translated 3 units down.

B. $y = |x + 1|$ The graph of $y = |x + 1|$ is the graph of $y = |x|$ translated 1 unit left.

C. $y = |x + 1| - 3$ The graph of $y = |x + 1| - 3$ is the graph of $y = |x|$ translated 1 unit left and 3 units down.

△ **MATHEMATICAL PRACTICE** **Highlighting the Standards**

This example and its Reflect questions offer an opportunity to address Mathematical Practice Standard 7 (Look for and make use of structure). By analyzing graphs and making predictions, students look for a pattern when constants are added or subtracted inside or outside the parent function $y = |x|$. Students should predict that a constant added or subtracted inside the parent function results in a horizontal translation of the graph, while a constant added or subtracted outside the parent function results in a vertical translation of the graph. Students should also predict that when constants are added or subtracted both inside and outside the parent function, the result is both a horizontal and vertical translation of the graph.

Students who recognize that the graph of $y = |x - h| + k$ involves a translation of the graph of the parent function h units horizontally and k units vertically may very well wonder why h is subtracted while k is added. They are looking for a symmetry in the structure of the function's rule that is not evident unless they rewrite the equation as $y - k = |x - h|$. In this form, both h (which produces a horizontal translation and is therefore associated with x) and k (which produces a vertical translation and is therefore associated with y) are subtracted from their associated variables. While the equation $y - k = |x - h|$ is not in "function form" (expressing y as a function of x), students may prefer it because it helps them identify the directions of translations before graphing.

Avoid Common Errors

Remind students that absolute value bars act as grouping symbols: First, perform operations inside the absolute value bars; then, take the absolute value; and then, perform operations outside the absolute value bars. So, when evaluating $f(x) = |x| + 2$ for $x = -3$, students should take the absolute value of -3 first and then add 2, which gives $f(-3) = -3| + 2 = 3 + 2 = 5$. On the other hand, when evaluating $f(x) = |x - 4|$ for $x = -3$, students should subtract 4 first and then take the absolute value, which gives $f(-3) = |-3 - 4| = |-7| = 7$.

Differentiated Instruction

When answering Questions 2b and 2d, analytic thinkers will reason, without needing to see a graph, that changing the sign of the constant will change the direction of the translation. Visual learners, on the other hand, will benefit from checking their predictions by graphing.

3 EXAMPLE

Questioning Strategies

• In step A, why is it important to note both the direction and the distance that a point has been translated either horizontally or vertically? **The horizontal and vertical directions determine the signs of h and k, respectively.**

• In step B, are the values of h and k positive or negative for the given graph? How do you know? **The value of h is positive because the translation is to the right; the value of k is positive because the translation is up.**

EXTRA EXAMPLE

Write the equation of the absolute value function whose graph is shown below. $y = |x + 2| - 3$

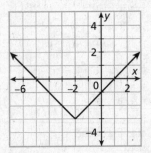

Teaching Strategy

Have students draw the graph of the parent function on the same coordinate plane as the given graph. Ask students to think about what horizontal and vertical movements take the vertex $(0, 0)$ to the vertex $(2, 3)$.

REFLECT

2a. How is the graph of $g(x) = |x| + 2$ related to the graph of the parent function $f(x) = |x|$?

Vertical translation of 2 units up

2b. How do you think the graph of $g(x) = |x| - 2$ would be related to the graph of the parent function $f(x) = |x|$?

Vertical translation of 2 units down

2c. How is the graph of $g(x) = |x - 4|$ related to the graph of the parent function $f(x) = |x|$?

Horizontal translation of 4 units to the right

2d. How do you think the graph of $g(x) = |x + 4|$ would be related to the graph of the parent function $f(x) = |x|$?

Horizontal translation of 4 units to the left

2e. How is the graph of $g(x) = |x - 4| + 2$ related to the graph of the parent function $f(x) = |x|$?

Horizontal translation of 4 units to the right and vertical translation

of 2 units up

2f. Predict how the graph of $g(x) = |x + 3| - 5$ is related to the graph of the parent function $f(x) = |x|$. Then check your prediction by making a table of values and graphing the function. (The graph of $f(x) = |x|$ is shown in gray.)

Horizontal translation of 3 units to the left and vertical

translation of 5 units down

x	$g(x) = |x + 3| - 5$
−6	−2
−5	−3
−4	−4
−3	−5
−2	−4
−1	−3
0	−2

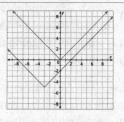

2g. In general, how is the graph of $g(x) = |x - h| + k$ related to the graph of $f(x) = |x|$?

Translation of h units horizontally (to the right if $h > 0$, to the left if $h < 0$)

and k units vertically (up if $k > 0$, down if $k < 0$)

---

3 **EXAMPLE**   Writing Equations for Absolute Value Functions

Write the equation for the absolute value function whose graph is shown.

A Compare the given graph to the graph of the parent function $f(x) = |x|$.

Complete the table to describe how the parent function must be translated to get the graph shown here.

Type of Translation	Number of Units	Direction
Horizontal Translation	2	To the right
Vertical Translation	3	Up

B Determine the values of h and k for the function $g(x) = |x - h| + k$.

* h is the number of units that the parent function is translated horizontally. For a translation to the right, h is positive; for a translation to the left, h is negative.

* k is the number of units that the parent function is translated vertically. For a translation up, k is positive; for a translation down, k is negative.

So, $h = $ ___2___ and $k = $ ___3___. The function is $g(x) = |x - 2| + 3$

REFLECT

3a. What can you do to check that your equation is correct?

Graph the equation to see if the graph is identical to the

given one.

3b. If the graph of an absolute value function is a translation of the graph of the parent function, explain how you can use the vertex of the translated graph to help you determine the equation for the function.

If the vertex has coordinates (h, k), then the function has

equation $g(x) = |x - h| + k$.

3c. Suppose the graph in the Example is shifted left one unit so that the vertex is at $(1, 3)$. What will be the equation of that absolute value function?

$g(x) = |x - 1| + 3$

Essential Question

What are the effects of the constants h and k on the graph of $y = |x - h| + k$?

The constant h produces a horizontal translation of the graph of the parent function $y = |x|$ where the movement is to the right if $h > 0$ and to the left if $h < 0$. The constant k produces a vertical translation of the graph of the parent function $y = |x|$ where the movement is up if $k > 0$ or down if $k < 0$.

Summarize

Have students make a graphic organizer to show how horizontal and vertical translations of the graph of $y = |x|$ are related to the equation of the translated graph. One possibility is shown below.

Where skills are taught	Where skills are practiced
2 EXAMPLE	EXS. 1–12
3 EXAMPLE	EXS. 13–16

Exercises 17–22: Students extend what they learned in **3** EXAMPLE . In these exercises, students should see that the domain of the function $y = |x - h| + k$ consists of all real numbers (just like the parent function $y = |x|$), and that the range consists of real numbers greater than or equal to k.

Exercise 23: Students must pay attention to the form of the general function $y = |x - h| + k$. While h is subtracted inside the absolute value, k is added outside.

Exercise 24: Students should see that a translated graph can itself be translated by simply increasing or decreasing the given values of h and k.

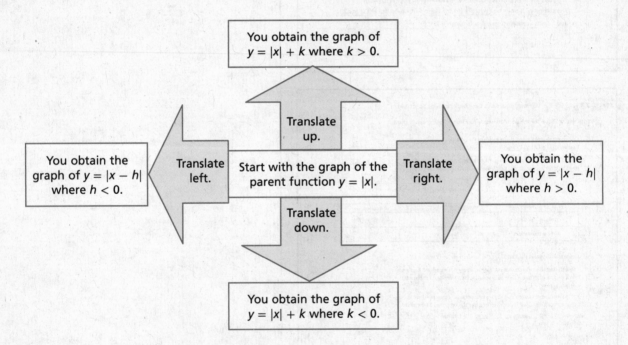

You obtain the graph of $y = |x| + k$ where $k > 0$.

Translate up.

You obtain the graph of $y = |x - h|$ where $h < 0$.

Translate left.

Start with the graph of the parent function $y = |x|$.

Translate right.

You obtain the graph of $y = |x - h|$ where $h > 0$.

Translate down.

You obtain the graph of $y = |x| + k$ where $k < 0$.

PRACTICE

Graph each absolute value function.

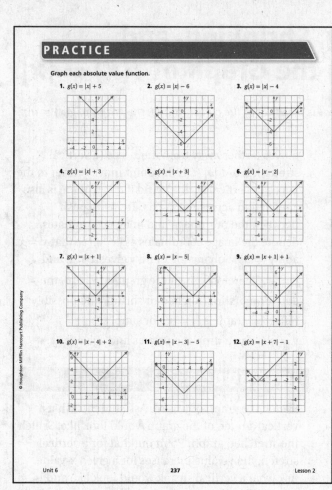

1. $g(x) = |x| + 5$

2. $g(x) = |x| - 6$

3. $g(x) = |x| - 4$

4. $g(x) = |x| + 3$

5. $g(x) = |x + 3|$

6. $g(x) = |x - 2|$

7. $g(x) = |x + 1|$

8. $g(x) = |x - 5|$

9. $g(x) = |x + 1| + 1$

10. $g(x) = |x - 4| + 2$

11. $g(x) = |x - 3| - 5$

12. $g(x) = |x + 7| - 1$

© Houghton Mifflin Harcourt Publishing Company

Write the equation of each absolute value function whose graph is shown.

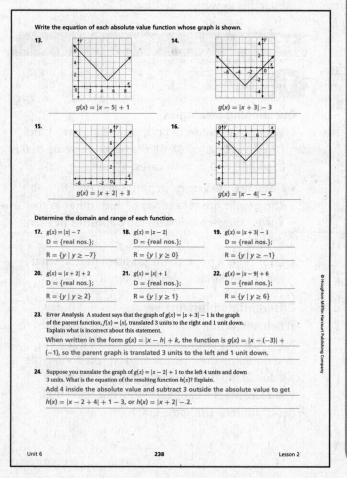

13.

$g(x) = |x - 5| + 1$

14.

$g(x) = |x + 3| - 3$

15.

$g(x) = |x + 2| + 3$

16.

$g(x) = |x - 4| - 5$

Determine the domain and range of each function.

17. $g(x) = |x| - 7$
D = {real nos.};
R = {$y \mid y \geq -7$}

18. $g(x) = |x - 2|$
D = {real nos.};
R = {$y \mid y \geq 0$}

19. $g(x) = |x + 3| - 1$
D = {real nos.};
R = {$y \mid y \geq -1$}

20. $g(x) = |x + 2| + 2$
D = {real nos.};
R = {$y \mid y \geq 2$}

21. $g(x) = |x| + 1$
D = {real nos.};
R = {$y \mid y \geq 1$}

22. $g(x) = |x - 9| + 6$
D = {real nos.};
R = {$y \mid y \geq 6$}

23. **Error Analysis** A student says that the graph of $g(x) = |x + 3| - 1$ is the graph of the parent function, $f(x) = |x|$, translated 3 units to the right and 1 unit down. Explain what is incorrect about this statement.

When written in the form $g(x) = |x - h| + k$, the function is $g(x) = |x - (-3)| +$

(-1), so the parent graph is translated 3 units to the left and 1 unit down.

24. Suppose you translate the graph of $g(x) = |x - 2| + 1$ to the left 4 units and down 3 units. What is the equation of the resulting function $h(x)$? Explain.

Add 4 inside the absolute value and subtract 3 outside the absolute value to get

$h(x) = |x - 2 + 4| + 1 - 3$, or $h(x) = |x + 2| - 2$.

© Houghton Mifflin Harcourt Publishing Company

Stretching, Shrinking, and Reflecting the Graph of $f(x) = |x|$

Essential question: What is the effect of the constant a on the graph of $g(x) = a|x|$?

COMMON **Standards for**
CORE **Mathematical Content**

CC.9-12.A.CED.2 Create equations in two ... variables to represent relationships between quantities; graph equations on coordinate axes with labels and scales.*

CC.9-12.F.IF.2 Use function notation, evaluate functions for inputs in their domains, and interpret statements that use function notation in terms of a context.

CC.9-12.F.IF.7 Graph functions expressed symbolically and show key features of the graph ...*

CC.9-12.F.IF.7b Graph ... absolute value functions.*

CC.9-12.F.BF.1 Write a function that describes a relationship between two quantities.*

CC.9-12.F.BF.1a Determine an explicit expression ... from a context.*

CC.9-12.F.BF.3 Identify the effect on the graph of replacing $f(x)$ by ... $kf(x)$, $f(kx)$, ... for specific values of k (both positive and negative); find the value of k given the graphs. ...

Also: CC.9-12.F.IF.4*, CC.9-12.F.IF.5*

Prerequisites
Piecewise functions, Lesson 6-1
Absolute value functions, Lesson 6-2

Math Background
The absolute value function $f(x) = |x|$ is a piecewise function because $f(x) = -x$ if $x < 0$, and $f(x) = x$ if $x \geq 0$. It is the parent function of functions of the form $g(x) = a|x|$. If $a > 1$, the graph is stretched vertically. If $0 < a < 1$, the graph is shrunk vertically. Both graphs are symmetric in the y-axis and have vertices at $(0, 0)$. If the value of a is negative, the graph is reflected in the x-axis and opens downward.

When the graph of $y = |x|$ has been vertically stretched, shrunk, or reflected, you can derive the equation for the transformed graph using the notation $(x, y) \rightarrow (x, ay)$, which defines a transformation that changes a point's distance from the x-axis by a factor of $|a|$ but leaves the point's horizontal position unchanged. If $|a| > 1$, the point

moves farther away from the x-axis (a vertical stretch). If $0 < |a| < 1$, the point moves closer to the x-axis (a vertical shrink). And if $a < 0$, there is also a reflection across the x-axis. To distinguish between the pre-image and image coordinates, denote the image coordinates as (x', y') so that $x' = x$ and $y' = ay$. Solving for x and y gives $x = x'$ and $y = \frac{y'}{a}$. Therefore, given the graph of $y = |x|$, the equation of the stretched or shrunk and possibly reflected graph is $\frac{y'}{a} = |x'|$, or simply $y = a|x|$ if you drop the primes and solve for y.

INTRODUCE

Sketch the graph of $y = |x|$. Ask students what a vertical stretch of the graph would look like. Sketch the stretched graph. Point out that for a vertical stretch, the y-value increases for a given x-value. Ask what a vertical shrink would look like and sketch this as well.

TEACH

1 EXAMPLE

Questioning Strategies

- What is the vertex of both graphs in parts A and B? Why is this so? **(0, 0); the absolute value of 0 is 0, so $g(0) = 0$ in both cases.**

- Compare the graphs in part A and part B. **The graphs are reflections of each other in the x-axis. The y-coordinates are opposites of each other.**

- If (5, 10) is a point of the graph in part A, what is the corresponding point in part B? **(5, −10)**

Differentiated Instruction
When answering Reflect Question 1b, analytic thinkers will reason, without needing a graph, that doubling the coefficient of $|x|$ will double the y-value of the function and therefore stretch it. Visual learners will benefit from checking their description by using the graph.

continued

6-3

COMMON
CORE

Stretching, Shrinking, and Reflecting the Graph of $f(x) = |x|$

CC.9-12.A.CED.2*,
CC.9-12.F.IF.2,
CC.9-12.F.IF.7*,
CC.9-12.F.IF.7b*,
CC.9-12.F.BF.1*,
CC.9-12.F.BF.3

Essential question: *What is the effect of the constant a on the graph of $g(x) = a|x|$?*

To understand the effect of the constant a on the graph of $g(x) = a|x|$, you will graph the function using various values of a.

1 EXAMPLE Graphing $g(x) = a|x|$ when $|a| > 1$

Graph each absolute value function using the same coordinate plane. (The graph of the parent function $f(x) = |x|$ is shown in gray.)

A $g(x) = 2|x|$

x	−3	−2	−1	0	1	2	3
$g(x) = 2\|x\|$	6	4	2	0	2	4	6

B $g(x) = -2|x|$

x	−3	−2	−1	0	1	2	3
$g(x) = -2\|x\|$	−6	−4	−2	0	−2	−4	−6

REFLECT

1a. The graph of the parent function $f(x) = |x|$ includes the point $(-1, 1)$ because $f(-1) = |-1| = 1$. The corresponding point on the graph of $g(x) = 2|x|$ is $(-1, 2)$ because $g(-1) = 2|-1| = 2$. In general, how does the y-coordinate of a point on the graph of $g(x) = 2|x|$ compare with the y-coordinate of a point on the graph of $f(x) = |x|$ when the points have the same x-coordinate?

The y-coordinate of a point on the graph of $g(x)$ is 2 times the y-coordinate of a point on the graph of $f(x)$.

1b. Describe how the graph of $g(x) = 2|x|$ compares with the graph of $f(x) = |x|$. Use either the word *stretch* or *shrink*, and include the direction of the movement.

The graph of $g(x)$ is a vertical stretch of the graph of $f(x)$.

1c. What other transformation occurs when the value of a in $g(x) = a|x|$ is negative?

Reflection across the x-axis

---

2 EXAMPLE Graphing $g(x) = a|x|$ when $|a| < 1$

Graph each absolute value function using the same coordinate plane. (The graph of the parent function $f(x) = |x|$ is shown in gray.)

A $g(x) = \frac{1}{4}|x|$

x	−8	−4	0	4	8
$g(x) = \frac{1}{4}\|x\|$	2	1	0	1	2

B $g(x) = -\frac{1}{4}|x|$

x	−8	−4	0	4	8
$g(x) = -\frac{1}{4}\|x\|$	−2	−1	0	−1	−2

REFLECT

2a. How does the y-coordinate of a point on the graph of $g(x) = \frac{1}{4}|x|$ compare with the y-coordinate of a point on the graph of $f(x) = |x|$ when the points have the same x-coordinate?

The y-coordinate of a point on the graph of $g(x)$ is $\frac{1}{4}$ times the y-coordinate of a point on the graph of $f(x)$.

2b. Describe how the graph of $g(x) = \frac{1}{4}|x|$ compares with the graph of $f(x) = |x|$. Use either the word *stretch* or *shrink*, and include the direction of the movement.

The graph of $f(x) = \frac{1}{4}|x|$ is a vertical shrink of the graph of $f(x) = |x|$.

2c. What other transformation occurs when the value of a in $g(x) = a|x|$ is negative?

Reflection across the x-axis

2d. Compare the domain and range of $g(x) = a|x|$ when $a > 0$ and when $a < 0$.

When $a > 0$: domain of $g = \{$real numbers$\}$, and range of $g = \{$nonnegative real numbers$\}$; when $a < 0$: domain of $g = \{$real numbers$\}$, and range of $g = \{$nonpositive real numbers$\}$.

Notes

EXTRA EXAMPLE
Graph each absolute value function using the same coordinate plane. (The graph of the parent function $f(x) = |x|$ is shown in gray.)

A. $g(x) = 4|x|$ **B.** $g(x) = -4|x|$

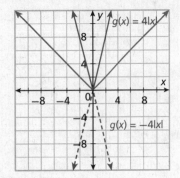

2 EXAMPLE

Questioning Strategies

• What is the vertex of both graphs in part A and part B? Why is this so? **(0, 0); the absolute value of 0 is 0, so $g(0) = 0$ in both cases.**

• Compare the graphs in part A and part B. **The graphs are reflections of each other in the x-axis. The y-coordinates are opposites of each other.**

• If $(12, 3)$ is a point of the graph in part A, what is the corresponding point in part B? **(12, −3)**

Differentiated Instruction

When answering Reflect Question 2d, analytic thinkers will reason, without needing a graph, that if a is positive, the range of the function in part A will be all nonnegative real numbers, and that if a is negative, the range in part B will be all nonpositive real numbers. Visual learners, on the other hand, will benefit from checking the range by using the graphs in parts A and B.

EXTRA EXAMPLE
Graph each absolute value function using the same coordinate plane. (The graph of the parent function $f(x) = |x|$ is shown in gray.)

A. $g(x) = \frac{1}{3}|x|$ **B.** $g(x) = -\frac{1}{3}|x|$

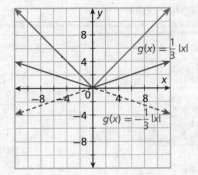

3 EXAMPLE

Questioning Strategies

• If the given point is $(4, -3)$, will the equation for the function be the same? How do you know? **Yes; after substituting into $g(x) = a|x|$, you get the same equation you do when you use the point $(-4, -3)$.**

• How does knowing a point on the graph other than the vertex help you find the value of a? **If you have a point other than $(0, 0)$, you can substitute the coordinates into $g(x) = a|x|$ and solve for a.**

EXTRA EXAMPLE
Write the equation for the absolute value function whose graph is shown.

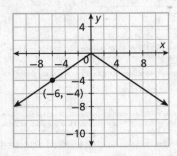

$$g(x) = -\frac{2}{3}|x|$$

2e. Summarize your observations about the graph of $g(x) = a|x|$.

Value of *a*	Vertical stretch or shrink?	Reflection across *x*-axis?
$a > 1$	Vertical stretch	No
$0 < a < 1$	Vertical shrink	No
$-1 < a < 0$	Vertical shrink	Yes
$a < -1$	Vertical stretch	Yes

An absolute value function whose graph's vertex is at $(0, 0)$ has the form $g(x) = a|x|$. To write the equation for the function, you can use the coordinates of a point (x_1, y_1) on the graph to write $g(x_1) = a|x_1| = y_1$, and then solve for *a*.

3 EXAMPLE Writing the Equation for an Absolute Value Function

Write the equation for the absolute value function whose graph is shown.

Use the point $(-4, -3)$ to find *a*.

$g(x) = a|x|$ Function form

$g(-4) = a|-4| = -3$ Substitute.

$a(\boxed{4}) = -3$ Simplify.

$a = \dfrac{-3}{4}$ Solve for a.

The equation for the function is $g(x) = -\dfrac{3}{4}|x|$

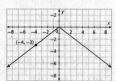

REFLECT

3a. The fact that the given graph lies on or below the *x*-axis tells you what about the value of *a*? Does this agree with the value of *a* that you found? Explain.

    $a < 0$; yes, because $-\dfrac{3}{4} < 0$

3b. The angle between the two rays that make up the graph of the parent function $f(x) = |x|$ is a right angle. What happens to this angle when the graph is vertically stretched? When the graph is vertically shrunk?

    The angle becomes acute; the angle becomes obtuse.

3c. Based on your answer to Question 3b, does the given graph represent a vertical stretch or a vertical shrink of the graph of the parent function? Does this fact agree with the value of *a* that you found? Explain.

    Vertical shrink; yes, because $0 < \left|-\dfrac{3}{4}\right| < 1$

Modeling with Absolute Value Functions When a rolling ball, such as a billiard ball, strikes a flat surface, such as an edge of the billiard table, the ball bounces off the surface at the same angle at which the ball hit the surface. (The angles are measured off a line perpendicular to the surface, as shown in the diagram.) A ray of light striking a mirror behaves in the same way.

The symmetry of the graph of an absolute value function makes the graph a perfect model for the path of a rolling ball or a ray of light.

Angle that ball strikes surface   Angle that ball rebounds

4 EXAMPLE Modeling a Real-World Situation

Inez is playing miniature golf. Her ball is at point $A(-4, 6)$. She wants to put the ball into the hole at $C(2, 3)$ with a bank shot, as shown. If the ball hits the edge at $B(0, 0)$, find the equation for the absolute value function whose graph models the path of the ball. How does the equation tell you whether the ball will go into the hole (if the ball is hit with sufficient force)?

A Use the point $A(-4, 6)$ to write the equation for a function of the form $g(x) = a|x|$.

$g(x) = a|x|$ Function form

$g(-4) = a\,\boxed{-4} = \boxed{6}$ Substitute.

$a\left(\boxed{4}\right) = \boxed{6}$ Simplify.

$a = \boxed{\dfrac{3}{2}}$ Solve for a.

So, the equation for the function is $g(x) = \dfrac{3}{2}|x|$

B Check to see whether the point $C(2, 3)$ lies on the path of the ball.

$g(2) = \dfrac{3}{2}|2| = \boxed{3}$, so the ball   __will__   go into the hole.

REFLECT

4a. If you reflect point *C* in the *x*-axis, what do you notice about points *A*, *B*, and the reflection of *C*? Explain why this is so.

    The points all lie on the same line; the equation for the line passing through *B*

    and *C* is $y = \dfrac{3}{2}x$, and reflecting in the *x*-axis puts the reflection of *B* (which is

    the same point as *B*) and the reflection of *C* on the line $y = -\dfrac{3}{2}x$, which is the line

    containing *B* and *A*.

1 EXAMPLE , **2** EXAMPLE , and **3** EXAMPLE
provide opportunities to address Mathematical
Practice Standard 7 (Look for and make use
of structure). Draw students attention to how
graphs of $g(x) = a|x|$ have the same structure
as the graph of $f(x) = |x|$ but are stretched
or shrunk vertically and possibly reflected
over the x-axis. Point out that relating
transformations to a parent graph is also done
with other types of functions.

CLOSE

Essential Question
What is the effect of the constant a on the graph of
$g(x) = a|x|$?
The constant a results in a vertical stretch or shrink
of the graph of the parent absolute value function.
If the constant is negative, the absolute value
graph is also reflected in the x-axis. The constant
does not change the parent graph's vertex at the
origin.

Summarize
Have students copy the graphic organizer from
Reflect Question 2e that summarizes the effect of a
on $f(x) = a|x|$ into their journals as a reference.

4 EXAMPLE

Questioning Strategies

- If the hole is located at point $C(2, 3)$, what is
  another point on the path of the ball? **(−2, 3)**

- How does having a point of the path of the ball
  other than the vertex help you find the value of a?
  **If you have a point other than (0, 0), you can
  substitute the coordinates into $g(x) = a|x|$ and
  solve for a.**

- Could you use the point $C(2, 3)$ to find the
  equation of the absolute value function? If so,
  how would this change what you need to check?
  **Yes; using $C(2, 3)$ gives the same equation as that
  in the Example. However, you would need to
  check that the initial point of the ball, $A(−4, 6)$, is
  on the graph.**

EXTRA EXAMPLE

Elle is playing pool. A ball is at point $A(−1, 2)$. Elle
wants to hit the ball into the center pocket at $C(2, 4)$
with a bank shot. If the ball hits the edge at $B(0, 0)$,
find the equation for the absolute value function
that models the path of the ball. Write an equation
for this situation. How does the equation tell you
whether the ball will go into the pocket (if the ball is
hit with sufficient force)?

$g(x) = 2|x|$; $g(2) = 4$; since $C(2, 4)$ lies on the path of
the ball, the ball will go into the pocket.

PRACTICE

Where skills are taught	Where skills are practiced
1 EXAMPLE	EXS. 1–2
2 EXAMPLE	EXS. 3–5
3 EXAMPLE	EXS. 6–9
4 EXAMPLE	EX. 10

PRACTICE

Graph each absolute value function.

1. $g(x) = 3|x|$

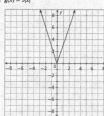

2. $g(x) = -2.5|x|$

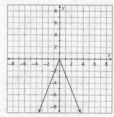

3. $g(x) = \frac{1}{2}|x|$

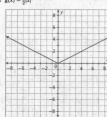

4. $g(x) = -\frac{2}{3}|x|$

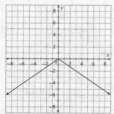

5. a. Complete the table and graph all the functions on the same coordinate plane.

x	−6	−3	0	3	6
$g(x) = \frac{1}{3}|x|$	2	1	0	1	2
$g(x) = |\frac{1}{3}x|$	2	1	0	1	2
$g(x) = -\frac{1}{3}|x|$	−2	−1	0	−1	−2
$g(x) = |-\frac{1}{3}x|$	2	1	0	1	2

b. How do the graphs of $f(x) = a|x|$ and $g(x) = |ax|$ compare?

For $a > 0$, they are the same; for $a < 0$, they are reflections across the x-axis.

Write the equation of each absolute value function whose graph is shown.

6.

$f(x) = 4|x|$

7.

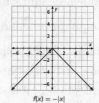

$f(x) = -|x|$

8.

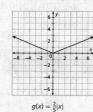

$g(x) = \frac{2}{5}|x|$

9.

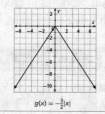

$g(x) = -\frac{3}{2}|x|$

10. From his driveway at point P, Mr. Carey's direct view of the traffic signal at point Q is blocked. In order to see the traffic signal, he places a mirror at point R and aligns it with the x-axis as shown.

a. Use point Q to write an equation for a function of the form $g(x) = a|x|$ whose graph models the path that light from the traffic signal takes when it strikes the mirror at R.

$g(x) = \frac{7}{4}|x|$

b. Explain why the mirror is positioned correctly.

$g(-8) = \frac{7}{4}|-8| = 14$, so P is on the

path that the light takes.

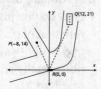

Combining Transformations of the Graph of $f(x) = |x|$

Essential question: *What are the effects of the constants a, h, and k on the graph of* $g(x) = a|x - h| + k$?

COMMON **Standards for**
CORE **Mathematical Content**

CC.9-12.A.CED.2 Create equations in two ... variables to represent relationships between quantities; graph equations on coordinate axes with labels and scales.*

CC.9-12.F.IF.2 Use function notation, evaluate functions for inputs in their domains, and interpret statements that use function notation in terms of a context.

CC.9-12.F.IF.7 Graph functions expressed symbolically and show key features of the graph, by hand in simple cases ...*

CC.9-12.F.IF.7b Graph ... absolute value functions.*

CC.9-12.F.BF.1 Write a function that describes a relationship between two quantities.*

CC.9-12.F.BF.1a Determine an explicit expression ... from a context.*

CC.9-12.F.BF.3 Identify the effect on the graph of replacing $f(x)$ by $f(x) + k$, $kf(x)$, $f(kx)$, and $f(x + k)$ for specific values of k (both positive and negative); find the value of k given the graphs. ...

Also: CC.9-12.F.IF.4*, CC.9-12.F.IF.5*

Prerequisites

Absolute value functions, Lessons 6-2 and 6-3

Math Background

In this lesson, students will see that the graph of $g(x) = a|x - h| + k$ is a combination of the transformations of the graph of $f(x) = |x|$ discussed in Lessons 6-2 and 6-3: a translation of h units horizontally and k units vertically as well as a vertical stretch or shrink by a factor of $|a|$ and possibly (if $a < 0$) a reflection across the x-axis. Although students will graph functions of the form $g(x) = a|x - h| + k$ by plotting points, you may want to have students obtain the graphs through a sequence of transformations of the graph of the parent function $f(x) = |x|$ instead. If so, students should follow the order of operations in the function's rule, drawing a sequence of intermediate graphs to obtain the final graph.

1. Perform a horizontal translation of h units.

2. Perform a vertical stretch or shrink by a factor of $|a|$, coupled with a reflection across the x-axis if $a < 0$.

3. Perform a vertical translation of k units.

Note that it is important *not* to perform the vertical translation before the vertical stretch or shrink (and possible reflection across the x-axis). The reason for this prohibition is that the stretching/shrinking and reflecting transformation is performed in relation to the x-axis. Points on the x-axis are not affected by this transformation. If the graph's vertex has been prematurely moved off the x-axis by the vertical translation, then it will be affected by the transformation, resulting in an incorrect graph.

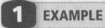

INTRODUCE

Review with students the forms of the absolute value functions studied in the preceding lessons.

Graph the function $f(x) = |x|$. Ask students what the graphs of $g(x) = 2|x|$ and $g(x) = \frac{1}{2}|x|$ look like. How do the graphs change if 2 is replaced by -2 and $\frac{1}{2}$ by $-\frac{1}{2}$? Ask students to think about how the function might change to show a translation of the graph 2 units right, or 2 units down.

TEACH

1 EXAMPLE

Questioning Strategies

- How do you justify that $f(x) = |x|$ is the parent function of $g(x) = a|x - h| + k$? **The graph of $g(x) = a|x - h| + k$ is translated h units horizontally and k units vertically from the graph of $h(x) = a|x|$. The graph of $h(x) = a|x|$ is the graph of $f(x) = |x|$ stretched or shrunk by a factor of a. Hence, $f(x)$ is the parent function.**

- How would you know whether the graph of $g(x) = a|x - h| + k$ were reflected in the x-axis without graphing? **a is negative.**

continued

Name_____ Class_____ Date_____

6-4

COMMON
CORE

Combining Transformations
of the Graph of $f(x) = |x|$

CC.9-12.A.CED.2*,
CC.9-12.F.IF.2,
CC.9-12.F.IF.7*,
CC.9-12.F.IF.7b*,
CC.9-12.F.BF.1*,
CC.9-12.F.BF.3

Essential question: *What are the effects of the constants a, h, and k on the graph of $g(x) = a|x - h| + k$?*

1 EXAMPLE Graphing $g(x) = a|x - h|$ and $g(x) = a|x| + k$

Graph each absolute value function. (The graph of the parent function $f(x) = |x|$ is shown in gray.)

A $g(x) = \frac{1}{2}|x - 3|$

x	−3	−1	1	3	5	7	9
y	3	2	1	0	1	2	3

B $g(x) = 3|x| - 7$

x	−3	−2	−1	0	1	2	3
y	2	−1	−4	−7	−4	−1	2

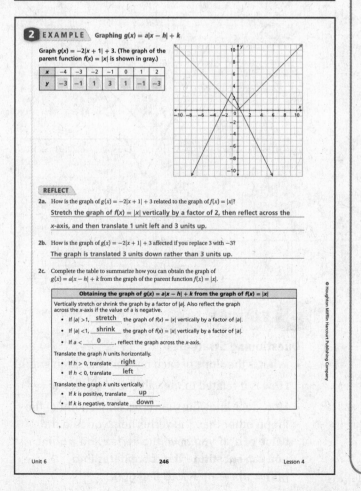

REFLECT

1a. How is the graph of $g(x) = \frac{1}{2}|x - 3|$ related to the graph of $f(x) = |x|$?

Shrink the graph of $f(x) = |x|$ vertically by a factor of $\frac{1}{2}$ and then

translate 3 units right.

1b. How is the graph of $g(x) = 3|x| - 7$ related to the graph of $f(x) = |x|$?

Stretch the graph of $f(x) = |x|$ vertically by a factor of 3 and then translate
7 units down.

1c. How is the graph of $g(x) = \frac{1}{2}|x - 3|$ affected if you replace $\frac{1}{2}$ with $-\frac{1}{2}$ and 3 with −3?

The graph is reflected in the x-axis, and it is translated 3 units left rather

than 3 units right.

Unit 6   245   Lesson 4

---

2 EXAMPLE Graphing $g(x) = a|x - h| + k$

Graph $g(x) = -2|x + 1| + 3$. (The graph of the parent function $f(x) = |x|$ is shown in gray.)

x	−4	−3	−2	−1	0	1	2
y	−3	−1	1	3	1	−1	−3

REFLECT

2a. How is the graph of $g(x) = -2|x + 1| + 3$ related to the graph of $f(x) = |x|$?

Stretch the graph of $f(x) = |x|$ vertically by a factor of 2, then reflect across the

x-axis, and then translate 1 unit left and 3 units up.

2b. How is the graph of $g(x) = -2|x + 1| + 3$ affected if you replace 3 with −3?

The graph is translated 3 units down rather than 3 units up.

2c. Complete the table to summarize how you can obtain the graph of
$g(x) = a|x - h| + k$ from the graph of the parent function $f(x) = |x|$.

Obtaining the graph of $g(x) = a|x - h| + k$ from the graph of $f(x) = |x|$
Vertically stretch or shrink the graph by a factor of $|a|$. Also reflect the graph across the x-axis if the value of a is negative.
• If $|a| > 1$, __stretch__ the graph of $f(x) = |x|$ vertically by a factor of $|a|$.
• If $|a| < 1$, __shrink__ the graph of $f(x) = |x|$ vertically by a factor of $|a|$.
• If $a <$ ___0___, reflect the graph across the x-axis.
Translate the graph h units horizontally.
• If $h > 0$, translate __right__.
• If $h < 0$, translate __left__.
Translate the graph k units vertically.
• If k is positive, translate __up__.
• If k is negative, translate __down__.

© Houghton Mifflin Harcourt Publishing Company

Unit 6   246   Lesson 4

Teaching Strategy

Stress the importance of including the vertex of the graph of the transformed function in the table of values. Have students show the calculations for the y-coordinates given the x-coordinates for the transformed function. For example, if $x = 5$ in part A, have them write

$g(5) = \frac{1}{2}|5 - 3| = \frac{1}{2}|2| = \frac{1}{2} \cdot 2 = 1.$

EXTRA EXAMPLE

Graph each absolute value function. (The parent function $f(x) = |x|$ is shown in gray.)

A. $g(x) = 2|x + 1|$

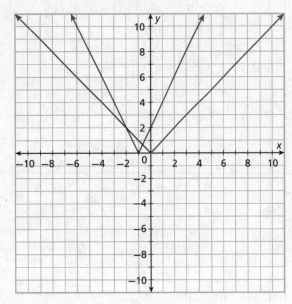

B. $g(x) = \frac{1}{2}|x| + 2$

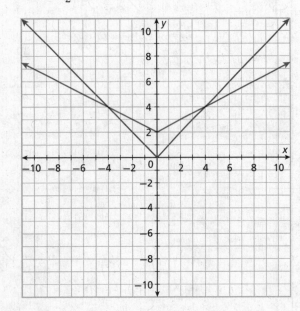

2 EXAMPLE

Questioning Strategies

• What is the vertex of the graph of $g(x)$? **(−1, 3)**

• What will be the effect on the graph of $g(x) = -2|x - (-1)| + 3$ if you replace -1 with 1? **The graph will be translated 1 unit right rather than 1 unit left.**

• What is the effect on the graph of $g(x) = -2|x - (-1)| + 3$ if you replace -2 with 2? **The graph will be reflected in the x-axis.**

Avoid Common Errors

When answering Reflect Question 2c, students may not recognize whether the graph is translated right or left, which depends on the sign of h in $g(x) = a|x - h| + k$. If the expression inside the absolute value bars involves addition, suggest that students rewrite it so that it involves subtraction. So for **2** EXAMPLE , $g(x) = -2|x + 1| + 3 = -2|x - (-1)| + 3$. The value of h is -1, which means that the graph is translated left 1 unit.

EXTRA EXAMPLE

Graph $g(x) = 2|x - 1| - 3$. (The parent function, $f(x) = |x|$, is shown in gray.)

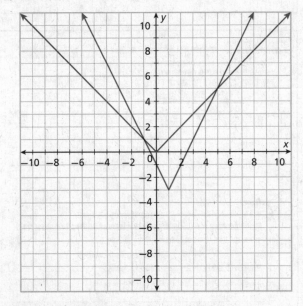

3 EXAMPLE

Questioning Strategies

• What is the slope of each ray from the given graph? How is it related to the value of a? $\frac{1}{3}, -\frac{1}{3}; |a| = \frac{1}{3}$

• How does knowing the vertex and a point of the graph other than the vertex help you find the value of a? **If you have the vertex and a point, you can substitute the coordinates into $g(x) = a|x - h| + k$ to find $g(x)$.**

3 EXAMPLE Writing the Equation for an Absolute Value Function

Write the equation for the absolute value function whose graph is shown.

To write the equation in the form $g(x) = a|x - h| + k$, you need to find the values of a, h, and k.

A Use the coordinates of the vertex to determine the values of h and k.

The vertex is at $(-3, -1)$, so $h = \underline{-3}$ and

$k = \underline{-1}$. Substituting these values into the

general equation for $g(x)$ gives $g(x) = a|x - -3| + -1$.

B Use the coordinates of another point on the graph to determine the value of a.

From the graph you can see that $g(0) = \underline{-2}$. Substituting 0 for x and

$\underline{-2}$ for $g(x)$ into the equation from part A and solving for a gives:

$$-2 = a\,|\,0 - -3\,| + -1$$
$$-\tfrac{1}{3} = a$$

C Write the simplified equation for the function: $g(x) = -\frac{1}{3}|x + 3| - 1$

REFLECT

3a. The graph of $g(x)$ opens down. In what way does this fact help you check that your equation is reasonable?

For the graph to open down, the value of a must be negative, which $-\frac{1}{3}$ is.

3b. The graph of $g(x)$ passes through the point $(-9, -3)$. Show how you can use this fact to check the accuracy of your equation.

Evaluate $g(x)$ when $x = -9$: $g(-9) = -\frac{1}{3}|-9 + 3| - 1 = -3$; this result

agrees with the graph.

3c. If you know the coordinates of the vertex of the graph of an absolute value function, then you know how the graph of the parent function has been translated. Explain why this is so.

The vertex of the graph of the parent function is at (0, 0). If you translate this

point h units horizontally and k units vertically, then the vertex of the translated

graph is at $(0 + h, 0 + k)$, or (h, k).

PRACTICE

Graph each absolute value function.

1. $g(x) = \frac{3}{4}|x + 2|$

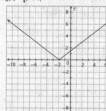

2. $g(x) = 2|x| - 4$

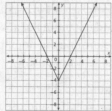

3. $g(x) = -\frac{1}{2}|x + 1|$

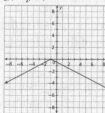

4. $g(x) = -3|x - 3| + 5$

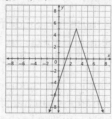

5. $g(x) = 1.5|x - 2| - 3$

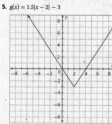

6. $g(x) = \frac{5}{3}|x + 3| - 5$

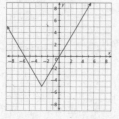

EXTRA EXAMPLE

Write the equation for the absolute value function whose graph is shown.

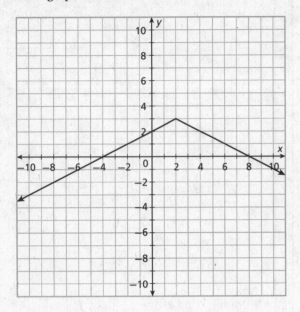

$$g(x) = -\frac{1}{2}|x - 2| + 3$$

MATHEMATICAL PRACTICE — Highlighting the Standards

1 EXAMPLE , **2 EXAMPLE** , and **3 EXAMPLE** provide opportunities to address Mathematical Practice Standard 7 (Look for and make use of structure). Draw students attention to looking for and identifying various combinations of the effects of the constants a, h, and k on the graph of $g(x) = a|x - h| + k$. Point out that relating transformations to a parent graph is also done with other types of functions.

CLOSE

Essential Question

What are the effects of the constants a, h, and k on the graph of g(x) = a|x − h| + k?

If $|a| > 1$, the graph is stretched vertically. If $0 < |a| < 1$, the graph is shrunk vertically. If $a < 0$, the graph is also reflected across the x-axis. The graph is translated h units horizontally and k units vertically.

Summarize

Have students copy the graphic organizer from Reflect Question 2c that summarizes the effects of the constants a, h, and k on $f(x) = a|x|$ into their journals as a reference.

Teaching Strategy

You may want to review the concepts of domain and range with students before assigning Practice Exercise 11.

PRACTICE

Where skills are taught	Where skills are practiced
1 EXAMPLE	EXS. 1–3
2 EXAMPLE	EXS. 4–6
3 EXAMPLE	EXS. 7–10

Exercises 11–12: Students extend their understanding of absolute value graphs to determine the domain and range of absolute value functions.

Exercises 13–15: Students learn the rule $|ab| = |a||b|$ and use it to rewrite absolute value equations so they can be graphed easily.

Exercise 16: Students determine whether the value of a affects the location of the vertex of an absolute value function.

Exercise 17: Students determine that using inverse operations can transform the graph of an absolute value function back to the parent graph.

Write the equation for each absolute value function whose graph is shown.

7.

$g(x) = 2|x - 1| - 5$

8.

$g(x) = -3|x + 2| + 6$

9.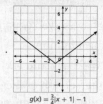

$g(x) = \frac{3}{4}|x + 1| - 1$

10.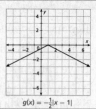

$g(x) = -\frac{1}{2}|x - 1|$

11. The functions that you graphed in Exercises 1–6 are listed in the table below. State the domain and range of each function.

Function	Domain	Range
$g(x) = \frac{3}{4}|x + 2|$	{real numbers}	{real numbers greater than or equal to 0}
$g(x) = 2|x| - 4$	{real numbers}	{real numbers greater than or equal to −4}
$g(x) = -\frac{1}{2}|x + 1|$	{real numbers}	{real numbers less than or equal to 0}
$g(x) = -3|x - 3| + 5$	{real numbers}	{real numbers less than or equal to 5}
$g(x) = 1.5|x - 2| - 3$	{real numbers}	{real numbers greater than or equal to −3}
$g(x) = \frac{5}{3}|x + 3| - 5$	{real numbers}	{real numbers greater than or equal to −5}

12. Describe the domain and range of any function of the form $g(x) = a|x - h| + k$.

Domain = {real numbers}; if $a > 0$, range = {real numbers greater than or equal to k}; if $a < 0$, range = {real numbers less than or equal to k}

13. The definition of absolute value says that if a number x is positive, then $|x| = x$, and if it is negative, then $|x| = -x$. So, if two numbers a and b are both positive, then by the definition of absolute value, $|ab| = ab = |a||b|$. If a is negative and b is positive, then $|ab| = (-a)b = |a||b|$. What happens if a is positive and b is negative, or if a and b are both negative? What rule applies to $|ab|$ in all cases?

If $a > 0$ and $b < 0$, then $|ab| = a(-b) = |a||b|$; if $a < 0$ and $b < 0$, then $|ab| = (-a)(-b) = |a||b|$; in all cases, $|ab| = |a||b|$.

Before graphing, use the rule from Exercise 13 to write each function's equation in the form $g(x) = a|x - h| + k$. Then graph the function.

14. $g(x) = |2x + 8| - 1$

$g(x) = 2|x + 4| - 1$

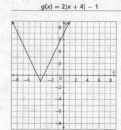

15. $g(x) = \left|\frac{1}{2}x - 2\right| + 3$

$g(x) = \frac{1}{2}|x - 4| + 3$

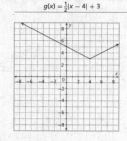

16. Does the value of a affect the location of the vertex for the graph of $g(x) = a|x - h| + k$? Why or why not?

No; although the factor a produces a vertical stretch or shrink and a possible reflection in the x-axis, the vertex is still (0, 0) before the translation of h units horizontally and k units vertically.

17. Suppose you vertically shrink the graph of $g(x) = 2|x + 3|$ by a factor of 0.5 and then translate the result 3 units right. What function has the resulting graph?

You have obtained the graph of the parent function, $f(x) = |x|$.

© Houghton Mifflin Harcourt Publishing Company

6-5 Solving Absolute Value Equations

Essential question: *How can you use graphing to solve equations involving absolute value?*

COMMON CORE Standards for Mathematical Content

CC.9-12.A.CED.1 Create equations ... in one variable and use them to solve problems.*

CC.9-12.A.CED.2 Create equations in two ... variables to represent relationships between quantities; graph equations on coordinate axes with labels and scales.*

CC.9-12.A.REI.11 Explain why the x-coordinates of the points where the graphs of the equations $y = f(x)$ and $y = g(x)$ intersect are the solutions of the equation $f(x) = g(x)$; ... Include cases where $f(x)$ and/or $g(x)$ are linear, ... absolute value ... functions.*

Also: CC.9-12.N.Q.1*, CC.9-12.N.Q.2*, CC.9-12.F.IF.2*, CC.9-12.F.IF.4*, CC.9-12.F.IF.7*, CC.9-12.F.IF.7b*

Prerequisites
Solving linear equations, Lesson 2-1
Graphing absolute value functions, Lesson 6-4

Math Background
Solving equations by graphing is not new for students. Remind them that they solved exponential equations of the form $ab^x = c$ by graphing in Lesson 5-5. To solve an absolute value equation, $a|x - h| + k = c$, first graph the function $f(x) = a|x - h| + k$. Then, graph the horizontal line $g(x) = c$. Estimate the x-coordinates of the points of intersection. There may be 0, 1, or 2 solutions. The exact solutions are found algebraically by isolating the absolute value expression on the left and then setting the expression inside the absolute value bars equal to the number on the right and its opposite. So for $|x + 2| = 8$, the solutions are found by solving $x + 2 = 8$ and $x + 2 = -8$.

INTRODUCE

Remind students that they have solved equations by graphing. Give students the equation $\frac{3}{2}x + 1 = 4$. Have students graph $f(x) = \frac{3}{2}x + 1$ and $g(x) = 4$. Ask students to find the intersection of the graphs, which is at $(2, 4)$. Have students solve the equation algebraically as well. Remind students that the solution, 2, is the x-coordinate of the intersection point.

TEACH

1 EXAMPLE

Questioning Strategies
- In part C, why do you identify the x-coordinate of the intersection point as the solution instead of the y-coordinate? It is the x-coordinate that satisfies the original equation.
- Why is $2|x - 3| + 1 = 5$ separated into two functions in parts A and part B? To solve an equation graphically, you graph each side as a separate function and then find the x-coordinates of any intersection points.

EXTRA EXAMPLE
Solve the equation $3|x - 2| + 1 = 7$ by graphing. **0, 4**

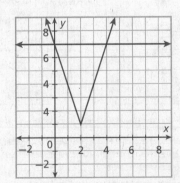

Name _____ Class _____ Date _____

Solving Absolute Value Equations

COMMON CORE

CC.9-12.A.CED.1*,
CC.9-12.A.CED.2*,
CC.9-12.A.REI.11*

Essential question: *How can you use graphing to solve equations involving absolute value?*

The equation $2|x - 3| + 1 = 5$ is an example of an *absolute value equation*.

1 EXAMPLE Solving an Absolute Value Equation by Graphing

Solve the equation $2|x - 3| + 1 = 5$ by graphing.

A Treat the left side of the equation as the absolute value function $f(x) = 2|x - 3| + 1$. Graph the function by following these steps.

- Identify and plot the vertex: __(3, 1)__

- If you move 1 unit to the left or right of the vertex, describe how must you move vertically to get to a point on the graph. Give the coordinates of these points and then plot them.

  __2 units up; (2, 3) and (4, 3)__

- Use the three plotted points to draw the complete graph.

B Treat the right side of the equation as the constant function $g(x) = 5$. Draw the graph of $g(x)$ on the same coordinate plane as the graph of $f(x)$.

C Identify the x-coordinate of each point where the graphs of $f(x)$ and $g(x)$ intersect. Show that each x-coordinate is a solution of $2|x - 3| + 1 = 5$.

__1 and 5; $2|1 - 3| + 1 = 2|-2| + 1 = 4 + 1 = 5$; $2|5 - 3| + 1 = 2|2| + 1 = 4 + 1 = 5$__

REFLECT

1a. Use transformations to justify the steps taken when graphing $f(x)$.

__The graph of the parent function has its vertex at (0, 0), but a translation of 3 units horizontally and 1 unit vertically puts the vertex of the graph of $f(x)$ at (3, 1). Also, the graph of the parent function rises 1 unit vertically when you move 1 unit to the left or right of the vertex, but a vertical stretch by a factor of 2 means that the graph of $f(x)$ will rise 2 units vertically when you move 1 unit to the left or right of the vertex.__

2 EXAMPLE Solving an Absolute Value Equation Using Algebra

Solve the equation $2|x - 3| + 1 = 5$ using algebra.

A Isolate the expression $|x - 3|$.

$2|x - 3| + 1 = 5$		Write the equation.
$\underline{-1 \quad -1}$		Subtract 1 from both sides.
$2|x - 3| = $ __4__		Simplify.
$\dfrac{2|x-3|}{2} = \dfrac{4}{2}$		Divide both sides by 2.
$|x - 3| = $ __2__		Simplify.

B Interpret the equation $|x - 3| = 2$: What numbers have an absolute value equal to 2?

__2 and −2__

C Set the expression inside the absolute value bars equal to each of the numbers from Part B and solve for x.

$x - 3 = $ __2__ or	$x - 3 = $ __−2__	Write an equation for each value of $x - 3$.
$\underline{+3 \quad +3}$	$\underline{+3 \quad +3}$	Add 3 to both sides of each equation.
$x = $ __5__ or	$x = $ __1__	Simplify.

REFLECT

2a. The left side of the equation is the function $f(x) = 2|x - 3| + 1$. Evaluate this function for each solution of the equation. How does this help you check the solutions?

__$f(5) = 2|5 - 3| + 1 = 2|2| + 1 = 4 + 1 = 5$;__

__$f(1) = 2|1 - 3| + 1 = 2|-2| + 1 = 4 + 1 = 5$;__

__the value of the function is 5 in each case, and this is the number__

__on the right side of the equation, so the solutions check.__

2b. Suppose the number on the right side of the equation was −5 instead of 5. What solutions would the equation have? Why? When answering these questions, you may want to refer to the graph of $f(x) = 2|x - 3| + 1$.

__There would be no solutions because the graph of $g(x) = -5$ does not intersect__

__the graph of $f(x) = 2|x - 3| + 1$.__

Questioning Strategies

- Can you predict the number of solutions to the equation $a|x - h| + k = c$ before solving? If $c = k$, the equation becomes $a|x - h| = 0$, and you can predict there will be 1 solution, h. If $c \neq k$, you can predict there will be either 0 or 2 solutions.

EXTRA EXAMPLE

Solve the equation $3|x - 2| + 1 = 7$ using algebra. 0, 4

Questioning Strategies

Why is (20, 2) a point of the graph showing Sal's distance from home? **After 20 minutes, Sal is 20 min × 0.1 mi/min = 2 miles from home. Since the horizontal axis represents time and the vertical axis represents distance, (20, 2) is on the graph.**

Why is the vertex of the graph important? **It is the point at which Sal turns around and starts the return home.**

Avoid Common Errors

Make sure students understand that the y-coordinate shows the distance from home, not the distance traveled.

> MATHEMATICAL PRACTICE
> **Highlighting the Standards**
>
> **3 EXAMPLE** addresses Mathematical Practice Standard 4 (Model with mathematics). Both the graph and the function $d(t) = -0.1|t - 30| + 3$ represent Sal's distance from home at a given time. To find when Sal is a particular distance from home (1 mile in the case of the Example) you can solve the equation either graphically, as in Part C, or algebraically, as in Reflect Question 3a.

EXTRA EXAMPLE

During driving class, Harry drives directly to a point 4 miles away and then reverses his direction to drive back to school. He drives at a constant speed of 0.5 mile per minute. Write and graph a model that gives his distance d (in miles) from school as a function of the elapsed time t (minutes). Use the graph to find the time(s) when Harry is 2 miles from school.
$d(t) = -0.5|x - 8| + 4;$ $t = 4$ min; $t = 12$ min

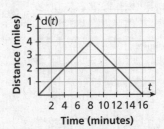

CLOSE

Essential Question

How can you use graphing to solve equations involving absolute value?
Graph two functions, each representing the expression on one side of the equal sign. Find the points where the graphs intersect. The x-coordinates of at those points are the solutions of the equation.

Summarize

Have students write a journal entry in which they describe how to solve $c = a|x - h| + k$ by graphing.

PRACTICE

Where skills are taught	Where skills are practiced
1 EXAMPLE	EXS. 1–3
2 EXAMPLE	EXS. 4–6
3 EXAMPLE	EXS. 7–8

3 EXAMPLE   Solving a Real-World Problem

Sal exercises by running east 3 miles along a road in front of his home and then reversing his direction to return home. He runs at a constant speed of 0.1 mile per minute. Write and graph a model that gives his distance d (in miles) from home as a function of the elapsed time t (in minutes). Use the graph to find the time(s) at which Sal is 1 mile from home.

A Determine the three key values of the distance function:

- When Sal begins his run ($t = 0$ minutes), he is ___0___ miles from home,

  so $d(0) =$ ___0___.

- When Sal is reverses direction, he is ___3___ miles from home.

  He reaches this point in $t = \dfrac{3 \text{ miles}}{0.1 \text{ mile per minute}} = $ ___30___ minutes, so

  $d($ ___30___ $) = $ ___3___.

- When Sal returns home, he is ___0___ miles from home. Because he has

  run a total of 6 miles, he reaches this point in $t = \dfrac{6 \text{ miles}}{0.1 \text{ mile per minute}} = $

  ___60___ minutes, so $d($ ___60___ $) = $ ___0___.

B Add axis labels and scales to the coordinate plane shown, then plot the points $(t, d(t))$ using the time and distance values from part A. The function $d(t)$ is an absolute value function, and the vertex of the function's graph is the point that represents when Sal reverses direction. Draw the complete graph of $d(t)$ and then write the equation for the function.

$d(t) = -0.1|t - 30| + 3$

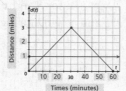

C To find the time(s) when Sal is 1 mile from home, draw the graph of $d(t) = 1$. Find the t-coordinate of each point where the two graphs intersect.

$t = 10$ minutes and $t = 50$ minutes

REFLECT

3a. Show how to use algebra to find the time(s) when Sal is 1 mile from home.

$-0.1|t - 30| + 3 = 1;\ -0.1|t - 30| = -2;\ |t - 30| = 20;\ t - 30 = 20$ or $t - 30 = -20;$

$t = 50$ or $t = 10$

PRACTICE

Solve each absolute value equation by graphing.

1. $-2|x + 1| + 4 = -4$

$x = -5$ or $x = 3$

2. $0.5|x - 3| + 2 = 4$

$x = -1$ or $x = 7$

3. $|x + 2| - 2 = -2$

$x = -2$

Solve each absolute value equation using algebra.

4. $4|x + 3| - 7 = 5$

$x = 0$ or $x = -6$

5. $0.8|x + 4| - 3 = 1$

$x = -9$ or $x = 1$

6. $-3|x - 1| + 5 = 8$

No solution

7. The number of shoppers in a store is modeled by $s(t) = -0.5|t - 288| + 144$ where t is the time (in minutes) since the store opened at 10:00 A.M.

a. For what values of t are there 100 shoppers in the store? ___200 and 376___

b. At what times are there 100 shoppers in the store? ___1:20 P.M. and 4:16 P.M.___

c. What is the greatest number of shoppers in the store? ___144___

d. At what time does the greatest number of shoppers occur? ___2:48 P.M.___

8. On January 1, 2010, Joline deposits $1000 in a bank account that does not earn interest. For the next 12 months she deposits $25 each month. Then she withdraws $25 each month for the next 12 months. On January 1, 2010, Sofia deposits $1100 in an account that earns 0.25% interest each month.

a. Write two models: one for the amount in Joline's account and one for the amount in Sophia's account. State what the variables in your models represent.

Joline: $A(t) = -25|t - 12| + 1300;$ Sophia: $A(t) = 1100(1.0025)^t;$

t is time (in months since January 2010); $A(t)$ is amount (in dollars)

b. In what months and years do the accounts have approximately the same amount, and what are the amounts?

On May 1, 2010, Joline's account has $1100, and Sofia's account has $1111.04;

on July 1, 2011, Joline's account has $1150, and Sofia's account has $1150.66.

FOCUS ON MODELING
Modeling with Absolute Value Functions

Essential question: How can you use an absolute value function to plan a bank shot when playing pool?

⊙ COMMON   Standards for
    CORE   Mathematical Content

The following standards are addressed in this lesson. (An asterisk indicates that a standard is also a Modeling standard.) For more detailed information, see each section of the lesson.

Grade 8: CC.8.G.2, CC.8.G.4

Number and Quantity: CC.9-12.N.Q.1*, CC.9-12.N.Q.2*

Algebra: CC.9-12.A.CED.2*

Functions: CC.9-12.F.IF.2, CC.9-12.F.IF.4*, CC.9-12.F.IF.5*, CC.9-12.F.IF.7*, CC.9-12.F.IF.7b*, CC.9-12.F.BF.1*, CC.9-12.F.BF.1a*

Prerequisites

- Understanding a piecewise function, Lesson 6-1
- Graphing absolute value functions, Lesson 6-4
- Writing the equation of an absolute value function, Lesson 6-4

Math Background

The primary goal of this lesson is to locate the point along a rail of a pool table where a ball must be hit to bank it into a pocket. Because the y-coordinate of the point is already known, the focus is on finding the x-coordinate. In the special case considered in Step 2 of this lesson (where the ball's initial position, B, and final position, B', have the same y-coordinate), it is easy to see that the x-coordinate of the vertex A of the ball's path is simply the average of the x-coordinates of B and B'. That is, $x = \dfrac{x_1 + x_2}{2}$.

A similar formula can be derived for the general case considered in Step 3. Using the equation given as the answer to Reflect Question 3b ($S = (1 + f) \cdot BC$), you can write expressions for S and BC in terms of x, x_1, and x_2 given that $x_1 < x < x_2$ (as in the diagram for Step 3): Since S is the horizontal displacement of the ball from its initial position to its final position, $S = x_2 - x_1$. Since segment BC is horizontal, its

length is just the difference between the x-coordinate of C (which has the same x-coordinate as A) and the x-coordinate of B, or $BC = x - x_1$. Substituting $x_2 - x_1$ for S and $x - x_1$ for BC in $S = (1 + f) \cdot BC$ and solving for x gives the following:

$$x_2 - x_1 = (1 + f)(x - x_1)$$
$$x_2 - x_1 = (1 + f)x - (1 + f)x_1$$
$$x_2 - x_1 + (1 + f)x_1 = (1 + f)x$$
$$x_2 + fx_1 = (1 + f)x$$
$$\frac{fx_1 + x_2}{1 + f} = x$$

This general formula generates the specific formula given in the preceding paragraph when you let $f = 1$.

INTRODUCE

The game of pool involves striking numbered balls with a cue ball, to cause them to roll into one of six pockets at the edges of the table. Frequently the numbered ball is struck in such a way that it bounces off the edge, or rail, of the table. The angle that the ball bounces off the rail will be the same as the angle at which it struck the rail, and the path of the ball looks like the graph of an absolute value function, which is why such a function is a good model for the situation.

TEACH

1 **Place a coordinate system on the playing surface.**

Standards

CC.9-12.N.Q.1 … choose and interpret the scale and the origin in graphs …*

CC.9-12.F.IF.4 For a function that models a relationship between two quantities, … sketch graphs showing key features given a verbal description of the relationship.*

continued

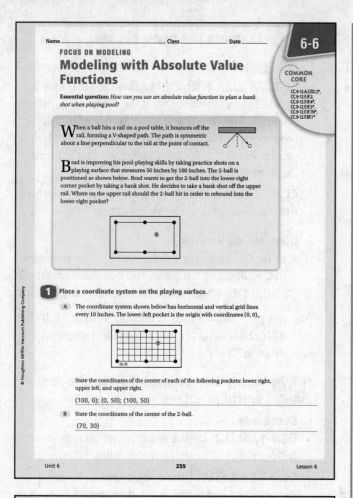

6-6

COMMON
CORE

CC 9-12.A.CED.2*,
CC 9-12.F.IF.2,
CC 9-12.F.IF.4*,
CC 9-12.F.IF.5*,
CC 9-12.F.IF.7b*,
CC 9-12.F.BF.1*

Name_____ Class_____ Date_____

FOCUS ON MODELING

Modeling with Absolute Value Functions

Essential question: *How can you use an absolute value function to plan a bank shot when playing pool?*

When a ball hits a rail on a pool table, it bounces off the rail, forming a V-shaped path. The path is symmetric about a line perpendicular to the rail at the point of contact.

Brad is improving his pool-playing skills by taking practice shots on a playing surface that measures 50 inches by 100 inches. The 2-ball is positioned as shown below. Brad wants to get the 2-ball into the lower-right corner pocket by taking a bank shot. He decides to take a bank shot off the upper rail. Where on the upper rail should the 2-ball hit in order to rebound into the lower-right pocket?

1 Place a coordinate system on the playing surface.

A The coordinate system shown below has horizontal and vertical grid lines every 10 inches. The lower-left pocket is the origin with coordinates (0, 0).

State the coordinates of the center of each of the following pockets: lower right, upper left, and upper right.

(100, 0); (0, 50); (100, 50)

B State the coordinates of the center of the 2-ball.

(70, 30)

REFLECT

1a. Suppose you place the origin of the coordinate system at the center of the side (middle) pocket on the lower rail instead. How does this change the coordinates of the centers of the corner pockets? The coordinates of the center of the 2-ball?

Lower-left pocket: (−50, 0); lower-right pocket: (50, 0); upper-left pocket:

(−50, 50); upper-right pocket: (50, 50); 2-ball: (20, 30)

1b. Using the original coordinate system shown, sketch the path of the 2-ball as it hits the upper rail and rebounds into the lower-right pocket. Explain why the graph of an absolute value function is a good model for the path.

Like the graph of an absolute value function, the path

has a vertex and is symmetric in a vertical line through

its vertex.

1c. Using the original coordinate system, estimate the coordinates of the point where the 2-ball must hit in order to rebound into the lower-right corner pocket.

Answers will vary. Sample answer: (80, 50)

2 Examine a special case.

A In the diagram below, a ball is represented by a point, labeled B, with coordinates (x_1, y_1). The ball strikes a rail at point A and rebounds to a point B' whose y-coordinate is the same as the y-coordinate of the ball's original location. Write the y-coordinate of B' on the diagram.

A(x, y)

B(x₁, y₁)   B′(x₂, y₁)

B State the x-coordinate of point A in terms of x_1 and x_2. Explain your reasoning.
$\frac{x_1 + x_2}{2}$; symmetry tells you that the x-coordinate of A is halfway between the

x-coordinates of B and B′.

1 continued

Questioning Strategies

- Why is it convenient to use $(0, 0)$ as the coordinates of the lower left pocket? **It will make all coordinates of the pool table positive.**

- Suppose you place the origin of the coordinate system at the lower right pocket. How does this change the coordinates of the 2-ball? **The new coordinates are $(-30, 30)$.**

2 Examine a special case.

Standards

CC.8.G.2 Understand that a two-dimensional figure is congruent to another if the second can be obtained from the first by a sequence of rotations, reflections, and translations; given two congruent figures, describe a sequence that exhibits the congruence between them.

CC.9-12.N.Q.2 Define appropriate quantities for the purposes of descriptive modeling.*

Questioning Strategies

- What is the midpoint of $\overline{BB'}$? How is it related to the coordinates of point A? $\left(\dfrac{x_1 + x_2}{2}, y_1\right)$; **point A has the same x-coordinate as the x-coordinate of the midpoint of $\overline{BB'}$, $\dfrac{x_1 + x_2}{2}$.**

- Similar figures have the same shape. Under what circumstances are similar figures congruent? **When they have the same size**

3 Examine the general case.

Standards

CC.8.G.4 Understand that a two-dimensional figure is similar to another if the second can be obtained from the first by a sequence of rotations, reflections, translations, and dilations; given two similar figures, describe a sequence that exhibits the similarity between them.

CC.9-12.N.Q.2 Define appropriate quantities for the purposes of descriptive modeling.*

Questioning Strategies

- In part B, given the relative sizes of the triangles in the diagram, what can you conclude about the value of the scale factor? **It must be greater than 1.**

- Suppose $BC = 9$ inches and the sum $BC + B'C' = 27$ inches. What is f, the scale factor of the dilation? **2**

4 Apply the general case to the real-world problem.

Standards

CC.9-12.N.Q.2 Define appropriate quantities for the purposes of descriptive modeling.*

CC.9-12.A.CED.1 Create equations ... in one variable and use them to solve problems.*

CC.9-12.A.REI.3 Solve linear equations ... in one variable ...

Questioning Strategies

- In part B, why don't you compare the lengths CC' and AC to get a scale factor of $\dfrac{30}{20} = 1.5$? **You must compare the lengths of complete sides triangles, and CC' is not the length of a complete side.**

- What is the ratio of the path lengths BA to AB'? **2.5**

REFLECT

2a. The figure at the right is another representation of the situation. Knowing that m∠BAC = m∠B'AC, what can you say about △BAC and △B'AC? Explain.

The triangles are congruent because △B'AC is a reflection

of △BAC across the line through points A and C.

2b. In the figure, is it correct to say that △B'AC is a dilation of △BAC after △ACB is reflected across the line through points A and C? If so, what is the scale factor of the dilation?

Yes; the scale factor is 1.

3 Examine the general case.

A In the diagram below, the ball at point B strikes a rail at point A and rebounds to a point B' whose y-coordinate is not the same as the y-coordinate of the ball's original location. Write the y-coordinate of B' on the diagram.

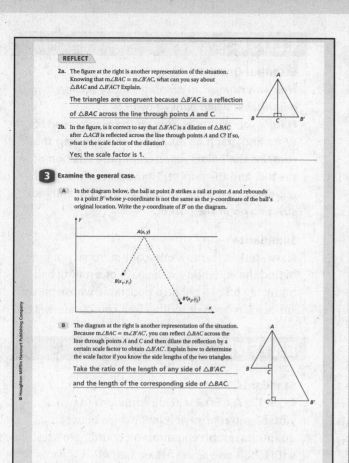

B The diagram at the right is another representation of the situation. Because m∠BAC = m∠B'AC, you can reflect △BAC across the line through points A and C and then dilate the reflection by a certain scale factor to obtain △B'AC'. Explain how to determine the scale factor if you know the side lengths of the two triangles.

Take the ratio of the length of any side of △B'AC'

and the length of the corresponding side of △BAC.

REFLECT

3a. If you know the lengths AC and AC' in the diagram from Step 3B, then you know that the scale factor f for the dilation is $f = \frac{AC'}{AC}$. If you also know the length BC but don't know the length B'C', how can you use BC and f to find B'C'?

Multiply BC by f to obtain B'C'.

3b. In Question 3a, suppose you don't know either the length BC or the length B'C', but you do know the sum S of those lengths. How can you express S only in terms of BC and the scale factor f?

$S = BC + B'C' = BC + f \cdot BC$, or $(1 + f) \cdot BC$

4 Apply the general case to the real-world problem.

A The coordinate system for the pool table is shown below. Write the y-coordinate of A on the diagram.

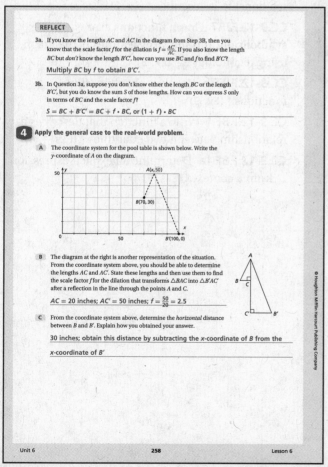

B The diagram at the right is another representation of the situation. From the coordinate system above, you should be able to determine the lengths AC and AC'. State these lengths and then use them to find the scale factor f for the dilation that transforms △BAC into △B'AC' after a reflection in the line through the points A and C.

AC = 20 inches; AC' = 50 inches; $f = \frac{50}{20} = 2.5$

C From the coordinate system above, determine the *horizontal* distance between B and B'. Explain how you obtained your answer.

30 inches; obtain this distance by subtracting the x-coordinate of B from the

x-coordinate of B'

Notes

5 Write the equation for the path of the ball.

Standards

CC.9-12.A.CED.2 Create equations in two or more variables to represent relationships between quantities ...*

CC.9-12.F.IF.2 Use function notation, evaluate functions for inputs in their domains, and interpret statements that use function notation in terms of a context.

CC.9-12.F.BF.1 Write a function that describes a relationship between two quantities.*

CC.9-12.F.BF.1a Determine an explicit expression ... from a context.*

Questioning Strategies

- What points are used to find the absolute value function that models the path? **the vertex $A(78.6, 50)$ and the starting point of the 2-ball, $B(70, 30)$**

- Can the function found in part C be used to model the path of another ball located at $(30, 30)$ that is aimed to bounce off point A into a pocket? Explain. **No; a different function would apply to that path.**

MATHEMATICAL PRACTICE Highlighting the Standards

Writing an absolute value function to model the path of a pool ball addresses Mathematical Practice Standard 4 (Model with mathematics). Draw students' attention to writing and graphing absolute value functions to model the bank shots and using the functions to determine whether shots will be successful. Stress the importance of checking the graphs of their functions to see they correctly model the path of the 2-ball.

Teaching Strategy

Students may have difficulty understanding how the absolute value function can be used to show that the ball goes into the lower-right corner pocket. Focus their attention on the shape of the function's graph, which matches the path of the ball. Therefore the starting and ending points of the ball must lie on that graph.

CLOSE

Essential Question

How can you use an absolute value function to plan a bank shot when playing pool?

Place a coordinate system on the playing surface. Write and graph an absolute value function that contains the points representing the position of the ball and the pocket. The vertex of the graph represents the point on the rail that the ball must strike to go in the pocket.

Summarize

Have students write a one-page summary of how to find the equation for the path of a rolling ball bouncing off of a rail on a pool table whose playing surface has been described by a coordinate system.

EXTEND

Standards

CC.9-12. A.CED.2 Create equations in two ... variables to represent relationships between quantities; graph equations on coordinate axes with labels and scales.* **(Exs. 1, 3, 4)**

CC.9-12.F.IF.5 Relate the domain of a function to its graph and, where applicable, to the quantitative relationship it describes.* **(Ex. 2)**

CC.9-12.F.IF.7 Graph functions expressed symbolically and show key features of the graph, ... using technology ...* **(Ex. 3)**

CC.9-12.F.IF.7b Graph ... absolute value functions.* **(Ex. 3)**

CC.9-12.F.BF.1 Write a function that describes a relationship between two quantities.* **(Exs. 1, 4)**

CC.9-12.F.BF.1a Determine an explicit expression ... from a context.* **(Exs. 1, 4)**

D Find the length BC by recognizing that the sum of BC and $B'C'$ equals the horizontal distance that you found in the previous step.

$BC + B'C' =$	30		Equation for horizontal distance
$BC + $ 2.5 $BC =$	30		Use the scale factor to replace $B'C'$.
3.5 $BC =$	30		Combine like terms.
$BC \approx$	8.6		Solve for BC.

E Find the x-coordinate of point A. Explain your reasoning.

Approximately 78.6; add the length BC to the x-coordinate of B to obtain the

x-coordinate of C, which is the same as the x-coordinate of A

REFLECT

4a. Compare your answer for Step 4E with your estimate from Reflect Question 1b. Are your calculated value and your estimate reasonably close?

78.6 (calculated value) and 80 (estimated value) are reasonably close.

---

5 Write the equation for the path of the ball.

A In Lesson 6-3 you learned that the path of a rolling ball that strikes and bounces off a flat surface can be modeled by the graph of the function $f(x) = a|x - h| + k$. You now know the values of h and k. Write the function using those values.

$f(x) = a|x - 78.6| + 50$

B Find the value of a by using point $B(70, 30)$.

$f(x) = a|x - $ 78.6 $| + $ 50	Write the function.
30 $= a\|$ 70 $- $ 78.6 $| + $ 50	Substitute for x and $f(x)$ using the coordinates of B.
30 $= a\|$ -8.6 $| + $ 50	Simplify inside the absolute value.
30 $= $ 8.6 $a + $ 50	Find the absolute value.
$-20 = $ 8.6 a	Subtract 50 from both sides.
$-2.3 \approx a$	Divide both sides by 8.6.

C Write the function whose graph models the path of the 2-ball. Use the function and the point $B'(100, 0)$ to show that the ball does go into the lower-right corner pocket.

$f(x) = -2.3|x - 78.6| + 50$; since $f(100) = -2.3|100 - 78.6| + 50 = -2.3|21.4| + $

$50 = -49.22 + 50 = 0.78 \approx 0$, so the ball does go into the pocket

---

REFLECT

5a. In Step 5B, the value of a is negative. Explain why this is expected.

The path of the ball is an inverted V, and the graph of an absolute value

function looks the same when $a < 0$.

5b. In Step 5C, the value of the function was not exactly 0. Explain why not.

Both the value of h, 78.6, and the value of a, -2.3, were both rounded, which

caused the value of $f(100)$ to be inexact.

EXTEND

1. Write the absolute value function whose graph models the path of the 2-ball as a piecewise function.

$f(x) = \begin{cases} 2.3(x - 78.6) + 50 & \text{if } 70 \leq x \leq 78.6 \\ -2.3(x - 78.6) + 50 & \text{if } 78.6 < x \leq 100 \end{cases}$

2. For the absolute value function whose graph models the path of the 2-ball, state the domain and range of the function based on the initial and final positions of the ball.

Domain $= \{x \mid 70 \leq x \leq 100\}$; range $= \{y \mid 0 \leq y \leq 50\}$

3. Graph the absolute value function whose graph models the path of the 2-ball on a graphing calculator. Use a viewing window that shows $0 \leq x \leq 100$ and $0 \leq y \leq 50$. How is the function's graph different from the actual path of the ball? Why?

On the graphing calculator, the function's domain is unrestricted, so the graph

includes a segment from about (57, 0) to (70, 30), and this segment is not part

of the ball's actual path.

4. Suppose Brad wants to get the 2-ball into the upper-left corner pocket with a bank shot off the lower rail. Find the coordinates of the point on the lower rail that the ball must hit, and give the equation of the absolute value function whose graph models the path of the ball.

(43.75, 0); $f(x) = 1.14|x - 43.75|$

CORRELATION

Standard	Items
CC.9-12.A.CED.1*	10
CC.9-12.A.CED.2*	7, 9
CC.9-12.A.REI.11*	6
CC.9-12.F.IF.2	1, 10
CC.9-12.F.IF.4*	3
CC.9-12.F.IF.5*	5, 7
CC.9-12.F.IF.7b*	8, 9
CC.9-12.F.BF.1*	4, 7, 9
CC.9-12.F.BF.3	2, 8

TEST PREP DOCTOR ⊕

Multiple Choice: Item 1
- Students who chose **A** did not use the correct part of the domain to find $C(10)$.
- Students who chose **C** or **D** did not multiply the cost of a ticket by the number of tickets.

Multiple Choice: Item 2
- Students who chose **G** did not understand how to correctly apply the value of a to stretch the graph of the absolute value function.
- Students who answered **H** or **J** translated the graph stretched rather than it vertically.

Multiple Choice: Item 3
- Students who chose **B** gave $-h$ as the x-coordinate of the vertex.
- Students who chose **A** or **C** gave $-k$ as the y-coordinate of the vertex.

Multiple Choice: Item 4
- Students who answered **F** switched the values for h and k in the vertex.
- Students who chose **G** had the wrong sign for the y-coordinate of the vertex.
- Students who chose **H** had the wrong sign for the x-coordinate of the vertex.

Multiple Choice: Item 6
- Students can eliminate choices **F** and **J** quickly if they graph $g(x)$ and see that the graph intersects the absolute value graph twice.
- Students who chose **G** found the x-intercepts of the absolute value graph.

Free Response: Item 7
- Students who wrote $d(t) = 30|t - 4- + 120$ forgot to make the value of a in $d(t) = a|t-h| + k$ negative to take into account that the graph opens down.
- Students who wrote $d(t) = -30|t - 120| + 4$ switched the coordinates of the vertex of the graph. They used $(120, 4)$ instead of $(4, 120)$.

Free Response: Item 8
- Students who described the graph as a vertical stretch did not understand that if $0 < a < 1$ in the graph of $g(x) = a|x - h| + k$, then the graph is a vertical shrink with a factor of a.
- Students who wrote that the graph is translated 1 unit right and 4 units down did not know that h is negative in this function, so the graph is translated 1 unit to the left.

Name _____ Class _____ Date _____

MULTIPLE CHOICE

1. The function $C(t)$ gives the cost C of buying t tickets to a museum exhibit when a group discount is offered.

$$C(t) = \begin{cases} 20t \text{ if } 0 \le t < 10 \\ 18t \text{ if } t \ge 10 \end{cases}$$

Which statement describes what $C(10)$ represents?

A. 10 tickets cost $200.

Ⓑ **10 tickets cost $180.**

C. 10 tickets cost $20.

D. 10 tickets cost $18.

2. Which of the following describes a way to graph the function $g(x) = -2|x|$?

Ⓕ **Stretch the graph of $f(x) = |x|$ vertically by a factor of 2. Then reflect the result across the x-axis.**

G. Shrink the graph of $f(x) = |x|$ vertically by a factor of $\frac{1}{2}$. Then reflect the result across the x-axis.

H. Translate the graph of $f(x) = |x|$ down 2 units.

J. Translate the graph of $f(x) = |x|$ right 2 units.

3. What are the coordinates of the vertex of the graph of $f(x) = 3|x + 1| - 4$?

A. $(1, 4)$

B. $(1, -4)$

C. $(-1, 4)$

Ⓓ **$(-1, -4)$**

For Items 4–6, refer to the graph of an absolute value function $f(x)$ shown below.

4. What is the equation for $f(x)$?

F. $f(x) = |x - 1| - 2$

G. $f(x) = |x - 2| + 1$

H. $f(x) = |x + 2| - 1$

Ⓙ **$f(x) = |x - 2| - 1$**

5. What are the domain and range of $f(x)$?

A. Domain: $\{x \mid x \ge -1\}$
Range: {real numbers}

B. Domain: $\{x \mid x \le -1\}$
Range: {real numbers}

Ⓒ **Domain: {real numbers}
Range: $\{y \mid y \ge -1\}$**

D. Domain: {real numbers}
Range: $\{y \mid y \le -1\}$

6. What are the solutions of $f(x) = g(x)$ where $g(x) = 1$?

F. $x = 2$

G. $x = 1$ and $x = 3$

Ⓗ **$x = 0$ and $x = 4$**

J. No solutions

FREE RESPONSE

7. The graph shows Jim's distance from shore as he rows a boat to an island and back to shore.

a. Write the equation for the distance function $d(t)$ where t is the elapsed time of Jim's trip.

$d(t) = -30|t - 4| + 120$ or

$d(t) = \begin{cases} 30t & \text{if } 0 \le t \le 4 \\ 240 - 30t & \text{if } 4 < t \le 8 \end{cases}$

b. What is the domain for this function? What does the maximum domain value represent?

$0 \le t \le 8$; the round-trip time of

8 minutes

8. a. Graph the function $g(x) = \frac{1}{2}|x + 1| - 4$.

b. Describe how to transform the graph of $f(x) = |x|$ to obtain the graph of $g(x) = \frac{1}{2}|x + 1| - 4$.

Shrink the graph of $f(x) = |x|$

vertically by a factor of $\frac{1}{2}$. Then

translate 1 unit left and 4 units

down.

9. A taxicab driver charges $6.00 for any distance less than 1 mile. For distances of 1 mile or more, he charges $6.00 plus $3.00 for each complete mile.

a. Write the equation for the function $C(d)$, which gives the cost C (in dollars) of riding in the taxicab for a distance d (in miles).

$C(d) = 6 + 3[\![d]\!]$

b. Graph the function to show the costs for all distances less than 5 miles. Include labels and scales on your graph.

10. Student enrollment in a county's schools during a 16-year period is modeled by the function $s(t) = -0.3|t - 8| + 11$ where $s(t)$ is the number of students (in thousands) at time t (in number of years since 1990).

a. What was the enrollment in 1990? Show how you found your answer.

8,600; $f(0) = -0.3|0 - 8| + 11 = 8.6$

(thousand)

b. In what year(s) was the enrollment closest to 10,000? Explain how to find the answer.

1995 and 2001; solving

$-0.3|t - 8| + 11 = 10$ gives $t = 4.\overline{6}$

and $t = 11.\overline{3}$, or about 5 and

11 years after 1990.

Quadratic Functions of the Form $f(x) = a(x - h)^2 + k$

Unit Vocabulary

parabola   (7-1)

quadratic
  function   (7-1)

square root   (7-5)

vertex   (7-1)

Quadratic Functions of the Form $f(x) = a(x - h)^2 + k$

Unit Focus

This unit introduces you to quadratic functions and their graphs, called parabolas. You will learn how transformations affect the characteristics of those graphs, such as the location of the vertex and whether the parabola opens up or down. You will also learn how to solve quadratic equations, obtained by setting a quadratic function equal to a constant, both by using graphs and by using square roots. Finally, you will apply all that you have learned about quadratic functions by using them as models for real-world situations.

COMMON
CORE

Unit at a Glance

Lesson		Standards for Mathematical Content
7-1	Translating the Graph of $f(x) = x^2$	CC.9-12.F.IF.2, CC.9-12.F.IF.4*, CC.9-12.F.IF.5*, CC.12.F.IF.7a*, CC.9-12.F.BF.1*, CC.9-12.F.BF.3
7-2	Stretching, Shrinking, and Reflecting the Graph of $f(x) = x^2$	CC.9-12.A.CED.2*, CC.9-12.F.IF.2, CC.9-12.F.IF.4*, CC.9-12.F.IF.7a*, CC.9-12.F.BF.1*, CC.9-12.F.BF.3
7-3	Combining Transformations of the Graph of $f(x) = x^2$	CC.9-12.A.CED.2*, CC.9-12.F.IF.2, CC.9-12.F.IF.4*, CC.9-12.F.IF.7a*, CC.9-12.F.BF.1*, CC.9-12.F.BF.3
7-4	Solving Quadratic Equations Graphically	CC.9-12.A.CED.1*, CC.9-12.A.CED.2*, CC.9-12.A.REI.11*
7-5	Solving Quadratic Equations Using Square Roots	CC.9-12.A.CED.1*, CC.9-12.A.REI.4b
7-6	Modeling with Quadratic Functions	CC.9-12.N.Q.1*, CC.9-12.N.Q.2*, CC.9-12.A.CED.2*, CC.9-12.F.IF.2, CC.9-12.F.IF.4*, CC.9-12.F.BF.1*
	Test Prep	

Unpacking the Common Core State Standards

Use the table to help you understand the Standards for Mathematical Content that are taught in this unit. Refer to the lessons listed after each standard for exploration and practice.

COMMON CORE Standards for Mathematical Content	What It Means For You
CC.9-12.N.Q.1 Use units as a way to understand problems and to guide the solution of multi-step problems; choose and interpret units consistently in formulas; **choose and interpret the scale and the origin in graphs and data displays.*** Lesson 7-6 (Also 7-3)	When making a scatter plot of paired data, you need to consider the least and greatest values of each variable in order to establish an appropriate scale on each axis.
CC.9-12.N.Q.2 Define appropriate quantities for the purpose of descriptive modeling.* Lesson 7-6 (Also 7-3)	When using a function to model real-world data, you need to identify the independent and dependent variables before you can write a rule relating them.
CC.9-12.A.CED.1 Create equations and inequalities in one variable and use them to solve problems.* Lessons 7-4, 7-5 (Also 7-6)	You will use quadratic functions to write quadratic equations in one variable, and you will solve the equations using graphs or square roots.
CC.9-12.A.CED.2 Create equations in two or more variables to represent relationships between quantities; graph equations on coordinate axes with labels and scales.* Lessons 7-1, 7-2, 7-3, 7-4, 7-6	You will learn to graph functions of the form $f(x) = a(x - h)^2 + k$ and to write equations in this form given the graphs of quadratic functions.
CC.9-12.A.REI.4 Solve quadratic equations in one variable. **CC.9-12.A.REI.4b** Solve quadratic equations by inspection (e.g., for $x^2 = 49$), taking square roots, completing the square, the quadratic formula and factoring, as appropriate to the initial form of the equation. Recognize when the quadratic formula gives complex solutions and write them as $a \pm bi$ for real numbers a and b. Lesson 7-5 (Also 7-6)	You will learn that every positive number has two square roots, and you will solve quadratic equations of the form $a(x - h)^2 + k = c$ by isolating the expression $(x - h)^2$ and using the definition of a square root.
CC.9-12.A.REI.11 Explain why the x-coordinates of the points where the graphs of the equations $y = f(x)$ and $y = g(x)$ intersect are the solutions of the equation $f(x) = g(x)$; find the solutions approximately, e.g., using technology to graph the functions, make tables of values, or find successive approximations. Include cases where $f(x)$ and/or $g(x)$ are linear, polynomial, rational, absolute value, exponential, and logarithmic functions.* Lesson 7-4	You will solve quadratic equations graphically by finding the points where the graphs of a quadratic function and a constant function intersect. You will do this by hand as well as by using a graphing calculator.

© Houghton Mifflin Harcourt Publishing Company

Notes

This page lists and explains the Standards for Mathematical Content that are addressed in this unit. For information about the Standards for Mathematical Practice, which are integrated throughout the text, see Teacher Edition pages viii–xi.

Additional Standards in this Unit

CC.9-12.A.SSE.1a Interpret parts of an expression, such as terms, factors, and coefficients.* Lessons 7-4, 7-5

CC.9-12.F.IF.6 Calculate and interpret the average rate of change of a function (presented symbolically or as a table) over a specified interval. Estimate the rate of change from a graph.* Lesson 7-4

CC.9-12.F.IF.9 Compare properties of two functions each represented in a different way (algebraically, graphically, numerically in tables, or by verbal descriptions). Lesson 7-6

CC.9-12.S.ID.6 Represent data on two quantitative variables on a scatter plot, and describe how the variables are related.* Lesson 7-6

CC.9-12.S.ID.6a Fit a function to the data; use functions fitted to data to solve problems in the context of the data.* Lesson 7-6

COMMON CORE Standards for Mathematical Content	What It Means For You
CC.9-12.F.IF.2 Use function notation, evaluate functions for inputs in their domains, and interpret statements that use function notation in terms of a context. Lessons 7-1, 7-2, 7-3, 7-6	You will write quadratic functions using function notation, and you will evaluate them when graphing and modeling.
CC.9-12.F.IF.4 For a function that models a relationship between two quantities, interpret key features of graphs and tables in terms of the quantities, and sketch graphs showing key features given a verbal description of the relationship.* Lessons 7-1, 7-2, 7-3, 7-6 (Also 7-4)	You will learn that the graph of any quadratic function either decreases and then increases or increases and then decreases. The turning point is called the vertex, and the y-coordinate of the vertex is either the function's minimum value or its maximum value. You will also see that the graph of a quadratic function can intersect the x-axis in 0, 1, or 2 points.
CC.9-12.F.IF.5 Relate the domain of a function to its graph and, where applicable, to the quantitative relationship it describes.* Lesson 7-1 (Also 7-3, 7-4)	Quadratic functions are defined for all real numbers. The domain may be restricted, however, in real-world situations modeled by quadratic functions.
CC.9-12.F.IF.7 Graph functions expressed symbolically and show key features of the graph, by hand in simple cases and using technology for more complicated cases.* **CC.9-12.F.IF.7a** Graph linear and quadratic functions and show intercepts, maxima, and minima.* Lessons 7-1, 7-2, 7-3 (Also 7-4)	You will find the maximum and minimum values of quadratic functions as well as the intercepts of those functions. You will discover when quadratic functions increase and when they decrease and use the symmetry of their graphs to help you solve problems.
CC.9-12.F.BF.1 Write a function that describes a relationship between two quantities.* **CC.9-12.F.BF.1a** Determine an explicit expression, a recursive process, or steps for calculation from a context.* Lessons 7-1, 7-2, 7-3, 7-6	You will write equations for quadratic functions that model real-world situations.
CC.9-12.F.BF.3 Identify the effect on the graph of replacing $f(x)$ by $f(x) + k$, $kf(x)$, $f(kx)$, and $f(x + k)$ for specific values of k (both positive and negative); find the value of k given the graphs. Experiment with cases and illustrate an explanation of the effects on the graph using technology. Lessons 7-1, 7-2, 7-3 (Also 7-6)	You will investigate how the values of a, h, and k affect the graph of $f(x) = a(x - h)^2 + k$, and you will learn which quadratic functions are even functions.

© Houghton Mifflin Harcourt Publishing Company

Notes

_____

_____

_____

_____

_____

_____

_____

_____

Notes

_____

_____

_____

_____

_____

_____

_____

_____

_____

_____

_____

_____

_____

_____

_____

_____

_____

_____

_____

_____

_____

_____

_____

_____

_____

_____

_____

_____

_____

_____

_____

_____

Translating the Graph of $f(x) = x^2$

Essential question: *What are the effects of the constants h and k on the graph of $g(x) = (x - h)^2 + k$?*

COMMON **Standards for**
CORE **Mathematical Content**

CC.9-12.A.CED.2 ... graph equations on coordinate axes with labels and scales.*

CC.9-12.F.IF.2 Use function notation, evaluate functions for inputs in their domains ...

CC.9-12.F.IF.4 For a function ... interpret key features of graphs and tables in terms of the quantities ...*

CC.9-12.F.IF.5 Relate the domain of a function to its graph and, where applicable, to the quantitative relationship it describes.*

CC.9-12.F.IF.7a Graph ... quadratic functions and show intercepts, maxima, and minima.*

CC.9-12.F.BF.1 Write a function that describes a relationship between two quantities.*

CC.9-12.F.BF.3 Identify the effect on the graph of replacing $f(x)$ by $f(x) + k$ ... and $f(x + k)$ for specific values of k (both positive and negative); find the value of k given the graphs.

Vocabulary

quadratic function

parabola

vertex

Prerequisites

Functions, Lesson 1-5

Math Background

An even function $f(x)$ has the property that $f(-x) = f(x)$ for all values x in the domain of f, and the graph of an even function has symmetry in the y-axis. The quadratic function $f(x) = x^2$ is the parent function of the general quadratic function $f(x) = ax^2 + bx + c$, where $a \neq 0$. $f(x) = x^2$ is an even function and therefore has symmetry in the y-axis. Its graph is a U-shaped curve called a parabola and the turning point of the parabola is called the vertex. The vertex of $f(x) = x^2$ is the point $(0, 0)$. In this lesson, students will graph quadratic functions of the form $f(x) = x^2 + k$. This graph also will be symmetric in the y-axis, but its vertex will be $(0, k)$. Students also will graph quadratic functions of the form $f(x) = (x - h)^2$. This graph will be translated h units horizontally with vertex $(h, 0)$. It will not be symmetric in the y-axis.

INTRODUCE

Students are familiar with linear functions, absolute value functions, and exponential functions. Ask students to name the characteristics of the graphs of each. Tell students they will be studying another type of function in this lesson, quadratic functions.

Type of Function	Function	Restrictions
Linear	$f(x) = mx + b$	none
Absolute value	$f(x) = |x|$	none
Exponential	$f(x) = ab^x$	$a \neq 0, b > 0, b \neq 1$

Name_____ Class_____ Date_____

Translating the Graph of $f(x) = x^2$

COMMON CORE

CC.9-12.F.IF.2,
CC.9-12.F.IF.4*,
CC.9-12.F.IF.5*,
CC.9-12.F.IF.7a*,
CC.9-12.F.BF.1*,
CC.9-12.F.BF.3

Essential question: *What are the effects of the constants h and k on the graph of g(x) = (x − h)² + k?*

1 ENGAGE   Understanding the Parent Quadratic Function

Any function that can be written as $f(x) = ax^2 + bx + c$ where a, b, and c are constants and $a \neq 0$ is a **quadratic function**. Notice that the highest exponent of the variable x is 2.

The most basic quadratic function is $f(x) = x^2$. It is called the *parent* quadratic function. To graph the parent function, make a table of values like the one below. Then plot the ordered pairs and draw the graph. The U-shaped curve is called a **parabola**. The turning point on the parabola is called its **vertex**.

x	$f(x) = x^2$
−3	9
−2	4
−1	1
0	0
1	1
2	4
3	9

REFLECT

1a. What is the domain of $f(x) = x^2$? What is the range?

Domain = {real numbers}; range = {$y \mid y \geq 0$}

1b. What symmetry does the graph of $f(x) = x^2$ have? Why does it have this symmetry?

Symmetric in the y-axis; the square of any number and the square of its opposite are equal, so the points $(x, f(x))$ and $(-x, f(-x))$ are reflections in the y-axis.

1c. For what values of x is $f(x) = x^2$ increasing? For what values is it decreasing?

Increasing for $x \geq 0$ and decreasing for $x \leq 0$.

2 EXAMPLE   Graphing Functions of the Form g(x) = x² + k

Graph each quadratic function. (The graph of the parent function $f(x) = x^2$ is shown in gray.)

A $g(x) = x^2 + 2$

x	$g(x) = x^2 + 2$
−3	11
−2	6
−1	3
0	2
1	3
2	6
3	11

B $g(x) = x^2 - 2$

x	$g(x) = x^2 - 2$
−3	7
−2	2
−1	−1
0	−2
1	−1
2	2
3	7

REFLECT

2a. How is the graph of $g(x) = x^2 + 2$ related to the graph of $f(x) = x^2$?

Vertical translation of 2 units up

2b. How is the graph of $g(x) = x^2 - 2$ related to the graph of $f(x) = x^2$?

Vertical translation of 2 units down

2c. In general, how is the graph of $g(x) = x^2 + k$ related to the graph of $f(x) = x^2$?

Vertical translation of k units (up if $k > 0$, down if $k < 0$)

1 ENGAGE

Questioning Strategies

- Why is the coefficient a of the quadratic function $f(x) = ax^2 + bx + c$ restricted to non-zero values? **If $a = 0$, then the first term is 0, and $f(x)$ is a linear function.**

- How is the vertex of the graph of the parent quadratic function related to the axis of symmetry? **The vertex is on the y-axis, which is the axis of symmetry for the graph.**

- What other point is on the graph of $f(x) = x^2$ for each point (x, y) that is on the graph? Explain. **The point $(-x, y)$ is also on the graph of $f(x) = x^2$ due to the symmetry of the graph over the y-axis.**

2 EXAMPLE

Questioning Strategies

- How is the graph of $g(x) = x^2 + 2$ related to the graph of $g(x) = x^2 - 2$? **They are both translated graphs of the same parent graph $f(x) = x^2$, but $g(x) = x^2 + 2$ is translated 2 units up and $g(x) = x^2 - 2$ is translated 2 units down.**

- Is the vertex of the graph of $g(x) = x^2 + 2$ the same as the vertex of the graph of $g(x) = x^2 - 2$? **No; $g(x) = x^2 + 2$ has vertex $(0, 2)$, and $g(x) = x^2 - 2$ has vertex $(0, -2)$.**

EXTRA EXAMPLE

Graph each quadratic function. How is each related to the graph of $f(x) = x^2$?

A. $g(x) = x^2 + 3$

The graph is translated 3 units up from the graph of the parent function $f(x) = x^2$. The graph opens upward with the vertex at $(0, 3)$.

B. $g(x) = x^2 - 3$

The graph is translated 3 units down from the graph of the parent function $f(x) = x^2$. The graph opens upward with the vertex at $(0, -3)$.

Questioning Strategies

- How is the graph of $g(x) = (x - 1)^2$ related to the graph of $g(x) = (x + 1)^2$? **They are both translated graphs of the same parent graph $f(x) = x^2$, but the graph of $g(x) = (x - 1)^2$ is translated 1 unit to the right and has vertex $(1, 0)$, while the graph of $g(x) = (x + 1)^2$ is translated 1 unit to the left and has vertex $(-1, 0)$.**

- What is the vertex of $g(x) = (x - h)^2$? **$(h, 0)$**

EXTRA EXAMPLE

Graph each quadratic function. How is each related to the graph of $f(x) = x^2$?

A. $g(x) = (x - 4)^2$

The graph is translated 4 units right from the graph of the parent function $f(x) = x^2$. The graph opens upward with the vertex at $(4, 0)$.

B. $g(x) = (x + 4)^2$

The graph is translated 4 units left from the graph of the parent function $f(x) = x^2$. The graph opens upward with the vertex at $(-4, 0)$.

MATHEMATICAL PRACTICE **Highlighting the Standards**

Examples 2 and 3 include opportunities to address Mathematical Practice Standard 7 (Look for and make use of structure). Students should realize that adding k to x^2 moves the graph up for $k > 0$ or down for $k < 0$ and that subtracting h from x moves the graph left for $h < 0$ or right for $h > 0$. This is true for all nonzero values of k and h. Recognizing this structure allows students to write equations from graphs in Example 4.

3 **E X A M P L E** Graphing Functions of the Form $g(x) = (x - h)^2$

Graph each quadratic function. (The graph of the parent function $f(x) = x^2$ is shown in gray.)

A $g(x) = (x - 1)^2$

x	$g(x) = (x - 1)^2$
−2	9
−1	4
0	1
1	0
2	1
3	4
4	9

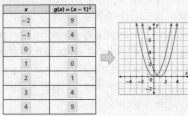

B $g(x) = (x + 1)^2$

x	$g(x) = (x + 1)^2$
−4	9
−3	4
−2	1
−1	0
0	1
1	4
2	9

REFLECT

3a. How is the graph of $g(x) = (x - 1)^2$ related to the graph of $f(x) = x^2$?

Horizontal translation of 1 unit to the right

3b. How is the graph of $g(x) = (x + 1)^2$ related to the graph of $f(x) = x^2$?

Horizontal translation of 1 unit to the left

3c. In general, how is the graph of $g(x) = (x - h)^2$ related to the graph of $f(x) = x^2$?

Horizontal translation of h units (to the right if $h > 0$, to the left if $h < 0$)

---

4 **E X A M P L E** Writing Equations for Quadratic Functions

Write the equation for the quadratic function whose graph is shown.

A Compare the given graph to the graph of the parent function $f(x) = x^2$.

Complete the table below to describe how the parent function must be translated to get the graph shown here.

Type of Translation	Number of Units	Direction
Horizontal Translation	3	To the right
Vertical Translation	2	Up

B Determine the values of h and k for the function $g(x) = (x - h)^2 + k$.

• h is the number of units that the parent function is translated horizontally. For a translation to the right, h is positive; for a translation to the left, h is negative.

• k is the number of units that the parent function is translated vertically. For a translation up, k is positive; for a translation down, k is negative.

So, $h =$ 3 and $k =$ 2 . The equation is $g(x) = (x - 3)^2 + 2$.

REFLECT

4a. What can you do to check that your equation is correct?

Graph the equation to see if the graph is identical to the given one.

4b. If the graph of a quadratic function is a translation of the graph of the parent function, explain how you can use the vertex of the translated graph to help you determine the equation for the function.

If the vertex has coordinates (h, k), then the equation for the function

is $g(x) = (x - h)^2 + k$.

4c. Error Analysis A student says that the graph of $g(x) = (x + 2)^2 + 1$ is the graph of the parent function translated 2 units to the right and 1 unit up. Explain what is incorrect about this statement.

When written in the form $g(x) = (x - h)^2 + k$, the function is $g(x) = (x - (-2))^2 + 1$,

so the parent graph is translated 2 units to the left and 1 unit up.

Notes

Questioning Strategies

- How is the vertex of the graph of $g(x) = (x - h)^2 + k$ related to the vertex of the graph of $f(x) = x^2$? The graph of $f(x) = x^2$ has vertex $(0, 0)$, while the graph of $g(x) = (x - h)^2 + k$ has vertex (h, k).

- How is the graph of $g(x) = (x - h)^2 + k$ related to the graph of $f(x) = x^2$? The graph of $g(x) = (x - h)^2 + k$ is the same shape as the graph of $f(x) = x^2$, but it is translated k units vertically and h units horizontally.

EXTRA EXAMPLE

Write the equation for the quadratic function whose graph is shown.

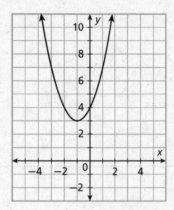

A. Compare the graph to the graph of $f(x) = x^2$. The graph is translated 3 units up and 1 unit left; the vertex is at $(-1, 3)$ instead of $(0, 0)$.

B. Determine the values of h and k for the function $g(x) = (x - h)^2 + k$ and write the function for the graph. $h = -1$; $k = 3$; $g(x) = (x + 1)^2 + 3$

Essential Question

What are the effects of the constants h and k on the graph of g(x) = (x − h)² + k?

The constant h moves the graph of the parent function $f(x) = x^2$ right h units if $h > 0$ or h units left if $h < 0$. The constant k moves the graph up k units if $k > 0$ or down k units if $k < 0$. The vertex of the graph is (h, k).

Summarize

Have students write a journal entry in which they describe the effects of the constants h and k on the graph of $g(x) = (x - h)^2 + k$ by comparing its graph to the graph of the parent function $f(x) = x^2$.

Where skills are taught	Where skills are practiced
2 EXAMPLE	EXS. 1, 2
3 EXAMPLE	EXS. 3, 4
4 EXAMPLE	EXS. 9–12

Exercises 5–8: Students extend what they learned in **4** EXAMPLE to graph quadratic functions of the form $g(x) = (x - h)^2 + k$.

Exercises 13–18: Students use their knowledge of where the vertex is located to find the domain and range of quadratic functions of the form $g(x) = (x - h)^2 + k$. Students should see that the domains do not change, but the ranges do.

Exercise 19: Students should see that a quadratic function of the form $f(x) = x^2 - 1$ is an even function, while $f(x) = (x - 1)^2$ is not. Students should realize that a vertical translation of $f(x) = x^2$ results in an even function, but that a horizontal translation does not.

PRACTICE

Graph each quadratic function.

1. $f(x) = x^2 + 4$

2. $f(x) = x^2 - 5$

3. $f(x) = (x - 2)^2$

4. $f(x) = (x + 3)^2$

5. $f(x) = (x - 5)^2 - 2$

6. $f(x) = (x - 1)^2 + 1$

7. $f(x) = (x + 4)^2 + 3$

8. $f(x) = (x + 2)^2 - 4$

Write a rule for the quadratic function whose graph is shown.

9.

$f(x) = (x - 2)^2 - 3$

10.

$f(x) = (x - 1)^2 + 4$

11.

$f(x) = (x + 3)^2 - 1$

12.

$f(x) = (x + 5)^2 + 4$

Determine the domain and range of the function.

13. $f(x) = (x - 3)^2$

D = {real nos.};

R = $\{y \mid y \geq 0\}$

14. $f(x) = x^2 + 4$

D = {real nos.};

R = $\{y \mid y \geq 4\}$

15. $f(x) = (x + 5)^2$

D = {real nos.};

R = $\{y \mid y \geq 0\}$

16. $f(x) = x^2 - 7$

D = {real nos.};

R = $\{y \mid y \geq -7\}$

17. $f(x) = (x + 1)^2 - 6$

D = {real nos.};

R = $\{y \mid y \geq -6\}$

18. $f(x) = (x - 2)^2 + 8$

D = {real nos.};

R = $\{y \mid y \geq 8\}$

19. A function is called *even* if $f(-x) = f(x)$ for all x in the domain of the function. For instance, if $f(x) = x^2$, then $f(-x) = (-x)^2 = x^2 = f(x)$. In other words, you get the same value when you square $-x$ as you do when you square x. So, $f(x) = x^2$ is an even function.

a. Is $f(x) = x^2 - 1$ an even function? Explain.

Yes; $f(-x) = (-x)^2 - 1 = x^2 - 1 = f(x)$

b. Is $f(x) = (x - 1)^2$ an even function? Explain.

No; $f(-x) = (-x - 1)^2 = (-(x + 1))^2 = (x + 1)^2 \neq f(x)$

Stretching, Shrinking, and Reflecting the Graph of $f(x) = x^2$

Essential question: What is the effect of the constant a on the graph of $g(x) = ax^2$?

Standards for Mathematical Content

CC.9-12.A.CED.2 Create equations in two or more variables to represent relationships between quantities; graph equations on coordinate axes with labels and scales.*

CC.9-12.F.IF.2 Use function notation, evaluate functions for inputs in their domains ...

CC.9-12.F.IF.4 For a function that models a relationship between two quantities, interpret key features of graphs and tables in terms of the quantities ... *

CC.9-12.F.IF.7 Graph functions expressed symbolically and show key features of the graph, by hand in simple cases ... *

CC.9-12.F.IF.7a Graph ... quadratic functions and show intercepts, maxima, and minima.*

CC.9-12.F.BF.1 Write a function that describes a relationship between two quantities.*

CC.9-12.F.BF.3 Identify the effect on the graph of replacing $f(x)$ by ... $kf(x)$ ... for specific values of k (both positive and negative); find the value of k given the graphs ...

Prerequisites
Quadratic Functions, Lesson 7-1

Math Background
A quadratic function of the form $f(x) = ax^2$ is an even function with the parent function $f(x) = x^2$. If $a > 1$, the parabola is stretched vertically. If $0 < a < 1$, then the parabola is shrunk vertically. The new graphs are still symmetric in the y-axis and each has vertex $(0, 0)$. If the value of a is negative, then the parabola is reflected over the x-axis and opens downward.

INTRODUCE

Students will be building their knowledge about quadratic functions and their graphs as they do the lessons in this unit. Review Lesson 7-1 with students as an introduction to Lesson 7-2.

Type of Quadratic	Function	Vertex
Parent	$f(x) = x^2$	$(0, 0)$
Translated Vertically	$f(x) = x^2 + k$	$(0, k)$
Translated Horizontally	$f(x) = (x - h)^2$	$(h, 0)$

TEACH

1 EXAMPLE

Questioning Strategies
- How are the graphs of $g(x) = 2x^2$ and $g(x) = \frac{1}{2}x^2$ similar? How are they different? **The graphs are similar because they both have the same parent graph, $f(x) = x^2$, are both symmetric in the y-axis, and both have the same vertex $(0, 0)$. They are different because the graph of $f(x) = 2x^2$ is a vertical stretch of the graph of $f(x) = x^2$, while the graph of $f(x) = \frac{1}{2}x^2$ is a vertical shrink of the graph of $f(x) = x^2$.**

continued

Stretching, Shrinking, and Reflecting the Graph of $f(x) = x^2$

COMMON CORE

CC.9-12.A.CED.2*,
CC.9-12.F.IF.2,
CC.9-12.F.IF.4*,
CC.9-12.F.IF.7a*,
CC.9-12.F.BF.1*,
CC.9-12.F.BF.3

Essential question: *What is the effect of the constant a on the graph of $g(x) = ax^2$?*

To understand the effect of the constant a on the graph of $g(x) = ax^2$, you will graph the function using various values of a.

1 EXAMPLE Graphing $g(x) = ax^2$ when $a > 0$

Graph each quadratic function. (The graph of the parent function $f(x) = x^2$ is shown in gray.)

A $g(x) = 2x^2$

x	$g(x) = 2x^2$
−3	18
−2	8
−1	2
0	0
1	2
2	8
3	18

B $g(x) = \frac{1}{2}x^2$

x	$g(x) = \frac{1}{2}x^2$
−3	4.5
−2	2
−1	0.5
0	0
1	0.5
2	2
3	4.5

REFLECT

1a. The graph of the parent function $f(x) = x^2$ includes the point $(−1, 1)$ because $f(−1) = (−1)^2 = 1$. The corresponding point on the graph of $g(x) = 2x^2$ is $(−1, 2)$ because $g(−1) = 2(−1)^2 = 2$. In general, how does the y-coordinate of a point on the graph of $g(x) = 2x^2$ compare with the y-coordinate of a point on the graph of $f(x) = x^2$ when the points have the same x-coordinate?

The y-coordinate of a point on the graph of $g(x)$ is 2 times the y-coordinate of a point on the graph of $f(x)$.

1b. Describe how the graph of $g(x) = 2x^2$ compares with the graph of $f(x) = x^2$. Use either the word *stretch* or *shrink*, and include the direction of the movement.

The graph of $g(x)$ is a vertical stretch of the graph of $f(x)$.

1c. How does the y-coordinate of a point on the graph of $g(x) = \frac{1}{2}x^2$ compare with the y-coordinate of a point on the graph of $f(x) = x^2$ when the points have the same x-coordinate?

The y-coordinate of a point on the graph of $g(x)$ is $\frac{1}{2}$ times the y-coordinate of a point on the graph of $f(x)$.

1d. Describe how the graph of $g(x) = \frac{1}{2}x^2$ compares with the graph of $f(x) = x^2$. Use either the word *stretch* or *shrink*, and include the direction of the movement.

The graph of $g(x)$ is a vertical shrink of the graph of $f(x)$.

2 EXAMPLE Graphing $g(x) = ax^2$ when $a < 0$

Graph each quadratic function. (The graph of the parent function $f(x) = x^2$ is shown in gray.)

A $g(x) = −2x^2$

x	$g(x) = −2x^2$
−3	−18
−2	−8
−1	−2
0	0
1	−2
2	−8
3	−18

Questioning Strategies

- Do the graphs in part A and part B have symmetry? If so, what is it? **Yes; they are symmetrical in the y-axis.**

- If (5, 50) is a point of the graph in part A, what is another point? **(−5, 50)**

EXTRA EXAMPLE

Graph each quadratic function. How is each related to the graph of $f(x) = x^2$?

A. $g(x) = 3x^2$

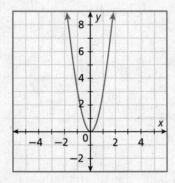

The graph is a vertical stretch of the graph of the parent function $f(x) = x^2$.

B. $g(x) = \frac{1}{3}x^2$

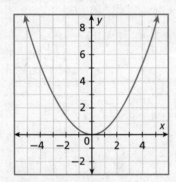

The graph is a vertical shrink of the graph of the parent function $f(x) = x^2$.

Teaching Strategy

Students may perceive the horizontal changes in a graph more readily than the vertical changes, so they may describe a vertical stretch as a horizontal shrink. Explain to students that changes are described in the vertical because they describe changes in the y-value for a given x-value.

Questioning Strategies

- Why do the graphs in part A and part B open downwards? **The y-values are all negative for each point that is not the vertex.**

- How could you use the graphs from the first Example to draw the graphs in this Example? **You could reflect the graphs from the first Example over the x-axis to get the graphs in this Example.**

EXTRA EXAMPLE

Graph each quadratic function. How is each related to the graph of $f(x) = x^2$?

A. $g(x) = -3x^2$

The graph is a vertical stretch of the graph of $f(x) = x^2$ along with a reflection across the x-axis.

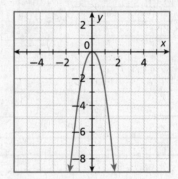

B. $g(x) = -\frac{1}{3}x^2$

The graph is a vertical shrink of the graph of $f(x) = x^2$ along with a reflection across the x-axis.

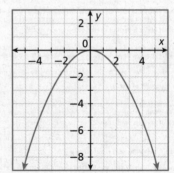

B $g(x) = -\frac{1}{2}x^2$

x	$g(x) = -\frac{1}{2}x^2$
-3	-4.5
-2	-2
-1	-0.5
0	0
1	-0.5
2	-2
3	-4.5

REFLECT

2a. In part A of the previous example, you drew the graph of $g(x) = ax^2$ where $a = 2$. In part A of this example, you drew the graph of $g(x) = ax^2$ where $a = -2$. How do the two graphs compare? How does the graph of $g(x) = -2x^2$ compare with the graph of $f(x) = x^2$?

The graphs are reflections across the x-axis; the graph of $g(x) = -2x^2$ is a vertical

stretch of the graph of $f(x) = x^2$ along with a reflection across the x-axis.

2b. In part B of the previous example, you drew the graph of $g(x) = ax^2$ where $a = \frac{1}{2}$. In part B of this example, you drew the graph of $g(x) = ax^2$ where $a = -\frac{1}{2}$. How do the two graphs compare? How does the graph of $g(x) = -\frac{1}{2}x^2$ compare with the graph of $f(x) = x^2$?

The graphs are reflections across the x-axis; the graph of $g(x) = -\frac{1}{2}x^2$ is a vertical

shrink of the graph of $f(x) = x^2$ along with a reflection across the x-axis.

2c. Summarize your observations about the graph of $g(x) = ax^2$.

Value of a	Vertical stretch or shrink?	Reflection across x-axis?
$a > 1$	Vertical stretch	No
$0 < a < 1$	Vertical shrink	No
$-1 < a < 0$	Vertical shrink	Yes
$a = -1$	No stretch or shrink	Yes
$a < -1$	Vertical stretch	Yes

© Houghton Mifflin Harcourt Publishing Company

Unit 7   275   Lesson 2

Writing Equations from Graphs A function whose graph is a parabola with vertex $(0, 0)$ always has the form $f(x) = ax^2$. To write the rule for the function, you can substitute the x- and y-coordinates of a point on the graph into the equation $y = ax^2$ and solve for a.

3 EXAMPLE   Writing the Equation for a Quadratic Function

Write the equation for the quadratic function whose graph is shown.

Use the point $(2, -1)$ to find a.

$$y = ax^2$$
$$-1 = a\left(\,2\,\right)^2$$
$$-1 = a\left(\,4\,\right)$$
$$-\frac{1}{4} = a$$

The equation for the function is $f(x) = -\frac{1}{4}x^2$.

REFLECT

3a. Without actually graphing the function whose equation you found, how can check that your equation is reasonable?

Because the value of a is between 0 and -1, the graph of the function is a

vertical shrink along with a reflection across the x-axis of the graph of the parent

quadratic function; the given graph has these characteristics.

3b. Error Analysis Knowing that the graph of $f(x) = ax^2$ is a parabola that has its vertex at $(0, 0)$ and passes through the point $(-2, 2)$, a student says that the value of a must be $-\frac{1}{2}$. Explain why this value of a is not reasonable.

If $a = -\frac{1}{2}$, then the graph of the function would be a parabola that lies

(except for its vertex) entirely in Quadrants III and IV, but the given

point lies in Quadrant II.

© Houghton Mifflin Harcourt Publishing Company

Unit 7   276   Lesson 2

Questioning Strategies

- How can you tell immediately that the value of a must be negative? **The graph opens downward, so a must be negative.**

- How does having a point of the parabola other than the vertex help you find the value of a? **If you have a point other than (0, 0), you can substitute the x- and y-values into $f(x) = ax^2$ and solve for a.**

EXTRA EXAMPLE

Write the equation for the function whose graph is shown.

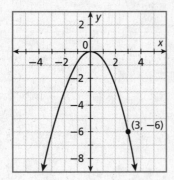

$f(x) = -\frac{2}{3}x^2$

MATHEMATICAL PRACTICE · Highlighting the Standards

Lessons 7-1 and 7-2 include opportunities to address Mathematical Practice Standard 7 (Look for and make use of structure). Draw students attention to how graphs of the form $f(x) = x^2 + k$, $f(x) = (x - h)^2$, and $f(x) = ax^2$ have the same structure as the graph of $f(x) = x^2$ but are translated vertically or horizontally, or are stretched or shrunk vertically. Point out that relating transformations to a parent graph is also done with other types of functions.

Essential Question

What is the effect of the constant a on the graph of $g(x) = ax^2$?

Having a coefficient other than 1 for the x^2-term either stretches or shrinks the graph of the parent quadratic function vertically. If the coefficient is negative, it reflects the graph over the x-axis so that it opens downward (like an arch on a bridge) instead of upward (like a cup). The coefficient does not change the vertex, however, so it is still at the origin.

Summarize

Have students create a table for their notebooks that summarizes how a affects the graph of $f(x) = ax^2$ in relation to the graph of the parent quadratic function.

For these values of a:	The function $f(x) = ax^2$ is a vertical:	And the graph opens:
$0 < a < 1$	shrink	up
$a > 1$	stretch	up
$-1 < a < 0$	shrink	down
$a = -1$	no shrink/ stretch	down
$a < -1$	stretch	down

PRACTICE

Where skills are taught	Where skills are practiced
1 EXAMPLE	EXS. 1, 3, 5, 7
2 EXAMPLE	EXS. 2, 4, 6, 8
3 EXAMPLE	EXS. 9–12

Exercise 13: Students extend what they learned in the Examples to identify when the function $f(x) = ax^2$ has a minimum value or a maximum value and how to find that value.

Exercise 14: Students extend their knowledge of even functions to understand that if $f(x) = x^2$ is even, then $f(x) = ax^2$ is also even.

PRACTICE

Graph each quadratic function.

1. $f(x) = 3x^2$

2. $f(x) = -\frac{3}{4}x^2$

3. $f(x) = 0.6x^2$

4. $f(x) = -1.5x^2$

5. $f(x) = \frac{1}{5}x^2$

6. $f(x) = -2.5x^2$

7. $f(x) = 4x^2$

8. $f(x) = -0.2x^2$

Write the equation for each quadratic function whose graph is shown.

9.

$f(x) = 5x^2$

10.

$f(x) = \frac{2}{3}x^2$

11.

$f(x) = \frac{1}{10}x^2$

12.

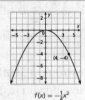

$f(x) = -\frac{1}{4}x^2$

13. A quadratic function has a *minimum value* when the function's graph opens up, and it has a *maximum value* when the function's graph opens down. In each case, the minimum or maximum value is the y-coordinate of the vertex of the function's graph. Under what circumstances does the function $f(x) = ax^2$ have a minimum value? A maximum value? What is the minimum or maximum value in each case?

Minimum value when $a > 0$; maximum value when $a < 0$; minimum or maximum value is 0.

14. A function is called *even* if $f(-x) = f(x)$ for all x in the domain of the function. Show that the function $f(x) = ax^2$ is even for any value of a.

$f(-x) = a(-x)^2 = ax^2 = f(x)$

Combining Transformations of the Graph of $f(x) = x^2$

Essential question: *How can you obtain the graph of $g(x) = a(x - h)^2 + k$ from the graph of $f(x) = x^2$?*

COMMON **Standards for**
CORE **Mathematical Content**

CC.9-12.A.CED.2 Create equations in two or more variables to represent relationships between quantities; graph equations on coordinate axes with labels and scales.*

CC.9-12.F.IF.2 Use function notation, evaluate functions for inputs in their domains ...

CC.9-12.F.IF.4 For a function that models a relationship between two quantities, interpret key features of graphs and tables in terms of the quantities ...*

CC.9-12.F.IF.7 Graph functions expressed symbolically and show key features of the graph, by hand in simple cases ...*

CC.9-12.F.IF.7a Graph ... quadratic functions and show intercepts, maxima, and minima.*

CC.9-12.F.BF.1 Write a function that describes a relationship between two quantities.*

CC.9-12.F.BF.3 Identify the effect on the graph of replacing $f(x)$ by $f(x) + k$, $kf(x)$, ... and $f(x + k)$ for specific values of k (both positive and negative); find the value of k given the graphs. ...

Also: CC.9-12.N.Q.1*, CC.9-12.N.Q.2*, CC.9-12.F.IF.5*

Prerequisites

Graphing quadratics functions, Lessons 7-1 and 7-2

Math Background

The graph of a quadratic function of the form $g(x) = a(x - h)^2 + k$ is a translation of the graph of the function $f(x) = ax^2$ so that the vertex is (h, k). To graph the quadratic function $g(x) = a(x - h)^2 + k$ start with the graph of the parent function $f(x) = x^2$. Then stretch or shrink the graph vertically by a factor of a, and then reflect in the x-axis if $a < 0$. Lastly, translate the graph horizontally h units and vertically k units. The graph is symmetric with respect to a vertical line with equation $x = h$. This line is known as the "axis of symmetry."

INTRODUCE

Remind students that a quadratic function may be of the form $f(x) = ax^2$, where $a \neq 0$. Ask them to graph $f(x) = 3x^2$ and $f(x) = -3x^2$ on the same screen using a graphing calculator and describe what they see. They should see functions that are reflections of each other in the x-axis. Ask them to recall how they represented quadratic functions that are translations to the right or to the left along the x-axis.

TEACH

1 ENGAGE

Questioning Strategies

- How do you justify saying that $f(x) = x^2$ is the parent graph of $g(x) = a(x - h)^2 + k$? The graph of $g(x) = a(x - h)^2 + k$ is a transformation of the graph of $f(x) = x^2$ because the graph of $f(x) = x^2$ is stretched or shrunk by a factor of a, and it is translated h units horizontally and k units vertically.

- How can you tell if the graph of $g(x) = a(x - h)^2 + k$ opens up or down without graphing? Look at the value of a. If $a > 0$, it opens up; if $a < 0$, it opens down.

Name_____ Class_____ Date_____

7-3

Combining Transformations
of the Graph of $f(x) = x^2$

COMMON CORE

CC9-12.A.CED.2*,
CC9-12.F.IF.2,
CC9-12.F.IF.4*,
CC9-12.F.IF.7a*,
CC9-12.F.BF.1*,
CC9-12.F.BF.3

Essential question: *How can you obtain the graph of $g(x) = a(x - h)^2 + k$ from the graph of $f(x) = x^2$?*

1 ENGAGE Understanding How to Graph $g(x) = a(x - h)^2 + k$

The sequence of graphs below shows how you can obtain the graph of $g(x) = 2(x - 3)^2 + 1$ from the graph of the parent quadratic function $f(x) = x^2$ using transformations.

1. Start with the graph of $y = x^2$.

2. Stretch the graph vertically by a factor of 2 to obtain the graph of $y = 2x^2$.

3. Translate the graph of $y = 2x^2$ right 3 units and up 1 unit to obtain the graph of $y = 2(x - 3)^2 + 1$.

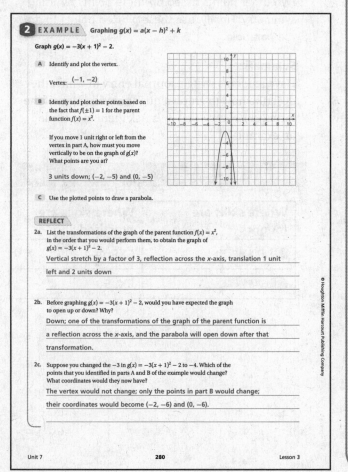

REFLECT

1a. The vertex of the graph of $f(x) = x^2$ is ___(0, 0)___, while the vertex of the

graph of $g(x) = 2(x - 3)^2 + 1$ is ___(3, 1)___.

1b. If you start at the vertex of the graph of $f(x) = x^2$ and move 1 unit to the right or left,

how must you move vertically to get back to the graph? ___1 unit up___

1c. If you start at the vertex of the graph of $g(x) = 2(x - 3)^2 + 1$ and move 1 unit to the

right or left, how must you move vertically to get back to the graph? ___2 units up___

1d. Based on your answers to Questions 1a–c, describe how you could graph
$g(x) = a(x - h)^2 + k$ directly, without using transformed graphs.

Use the points (h, k), $(h - 1, k + a)$, and $(h + 1, k + a)$ to draw the parabola.

Unit 7   **279**   Lesson 3

---

2 EXAMPLE Graphing $g(x) = a(x - h)^2 + k$

Graph $g(x) = -3(x + 1)^2 - 2$.

A Identify and plot the vertex.

Vertex: ___(−1, −2)___

B Identify and plot other points based on the fact that $f(\pm 1) = 1$ for the parent function $f(x) = x^2$.

If you move 1 unit right or left from the vertex in part A, how must you move vertically to be on the graph of $g(x)$? What points are you at?

3 units down; $(-2, -5)$ and $(0, -5)$

C Use the plotted points to draw a parabola.

REFLECT

2a. List the transformations of the graph of the parent function $f(x) = x^2$, in the order that you would perform them, to obtain the graph of $g(x) = -3(x + 1)^2 - 2$.

Vertical stretch by a factor of 3, reflection across the x-axis, translation 1 unit

left and 2 units down

2b. Before graphing $g(x) = -3(x + 1)^2 - 2$, would you have expected the graph to open up or down? Why?

Down; one of the transformations of the graph of the parent function is

a reflection across the x-axis, and the parabola will open down after that

transformation.

2c. Suppose you changed the −3 in $g(x) = -3(x + 1)^2 - 2$ to −4. Which of the points that you identified in parts A and B of the example would change? What coordinates would they now have?

The vertex would not change; only the points in part B would change;

their coordinates would become $(-2, -6)$ and $(0, -6)$.

Unit 7   **280**   Lesson 3

EXAMPLE

Questioning Strategies

- What can you tell about the graph of $g(x)$ from its equation? **The vertex is at $(-1, -2)$ and the graph opens down.**

- Use the graph in part C to find the domain and range of $g(x)$. **domain: all real numbers; range: $y \leq -2$**

EXTRA EXAMPLE
Graph $g(x) = -2(x - 1)^2 + 3$.

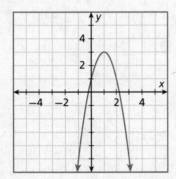

Technology
Encourage students to use graphing calculators to graph functions simultaneously with the parent function to see the effect of changing the parameters a, h, and k.

3 **EXAMPLE**

Questioning Strategies

- What does the y-value of the vertex of this parabola represent? **the height of the paintbrush at 0 seconds**

- Why doesn't $f(2)$ make sense in this situation? **The height of the paintbrush at 2 seconds would be $f(2) = -16(2)^2 + 30 = -34$ feet, which is not possible.**

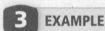

┊**MATHEMATICAL** **Highlighting the**
┊   **PRACTICE**   **Standards**

Example 3 provides an opportunity to address Mathematical Practices Standard 4 (Model with mathematics) because a quadratic function models dropping an object from a given height. Draw students' attention to the vertex (h, k) being the maximum point of the graph and being the values to substitute into the general equation $g(x) = a(x - h)^2 + k$.

EXTRA EXAMPLE
A diver jumps off a cliff into the sea below to search for shells. The diver's height above the sea (in feet) is given by a function of the form $f(t) = a(t - h)^2 + k$, where t is the time (in seconds) since the diver jumped. Use the graph to find an equation for $f(t)$.

A. Identify the vertex. **(0, 40)**

B. Use the graph to find an equation for $f(t)$.
$f(t) = -16t^2 + 40$

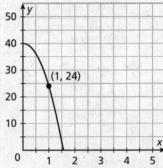

CLOSE

Essential Question
How can you obtain the graph of $g(x) = a(x - h)^2 + k$ from the graph of $f(x) = x^2$?
First, identify the vertex (h, k). Next, identify whether the graph will open up or down by examining a. Then, choose two x-values on one side of the vertex and calculate their y-values. Find two other points based on these points by using symmetry. Finally, use these plotted points to draw the parabola.

Summarize
Have students write a journal entry in which they describe how to graph a quadratic function of the form $g(x) = a(x - h)^2 + k$. Ask them to include an example.

PRACTICE

Where skills are taught	Where skills are practiced
2 EXAMPLE	EXS. 1–4
3 EXAMPLE	EX. 5

3 **EXAMPLE** Writing a Quadratic Function from a Graph

A house painter standing on a ladder drops a paintbrush, which falls to the ground. The paintbrush's height above the ground (in feet) is given by a function of the form $f(t) = a(t - h)^2 + k$ where t is the time (in seconds) since the paintbrush was dropped.

Because $f(t)$ is a quadratic function, its graph is a parabola. Only the portion of the parabola that lies in Quadrant I and on the axes is shown because only nonnegative values of t and $f(t)$ make sense in this situation. The vertex of the parabola lies on the vertical axis.

Use the graph to find an equation for $f(t)$.

A The vertex of the parabola is $(h, k) = \left(\ \underline{0}\ ,\ \underline{30}\ \right)$.

Substitute the values of h and k into the general equation

for $f(t)$ to get $f(t) = a\left(t - \underline{0}\ \right)^2 + \underline{30}$.

B From the graph you can see that $f(1) = \underline{14}$. Substitute 1 for t

and $\underline{14}$ for $f(t)$ to determine the value of a for this function:

$$14 = a\left(1 - 0\right)^2 + 30$$

$$\underline{-16} = a$$

C Write the equation for the function: $f(t) = \underline{-16t^2 + 30}$

REFLECT

3a. Using the graph, estimate how much time elapses until the paintbrush hits

the ground: $t \approx \underline{1.4\ \text{seconds}}$

3b. Using the value of t from Question 3a and the equation for the height function from part C of the example, find the value of $f(t)$. How does this help you check the reasonableness of the equation?

$\underline{f(1.4) = -16(1.5)^2 + 30 = -1.36;\ \text{since } f(1.4)\ \text{is close to 0 as expected from}}$

$\underline{\text{the graph, the equation for the function is reasonable.}}$

© Houghton Mifflin Harcourt Publishing Company

Height (feet) / Time (seconds) graph with point (1, 14)

PRACTICE

Graph each quadratic function.

1. $f(x) = 2(x - 2)^2 + 3$

2. $f(x) = -(x - 1)^2 + 2$

3. $f(x) = \frac{1}{2}(x - 2)^2$

4. $f(x) = -\frac{1}{3}x^2 - 3$

5. A roofer working on a roof accidentally drops a hammer, which falls to the ground. The hammer's height above the ground (in feet) is given by a function of the form $f(t) = a(t - h)^2 + k$ where t is the time (in seconds) since the hammer was dropped.

Because $f(t)$ is a quadratic function, its graph is a parabola. Only the portion of the parabola that lies in Quadrant I and on the axes is shown because only nonnegative values of t and $f(t)$ make sense in this situation. The vertex of the parabola lies on the vertical axis.

Height (feet) / Time (seconds) graph with point (1, 29)

a. Use the graph to find an equation for $f(t)$.

$\underline{f(t) = -16t^2 + 45}$

b. Explain how you can use the graph's t-intercept to check the reasonableness of your equation.

$\underline{\text{The } t\text{-intercept is approximately 1.7 seconds; } f(1.7) = -1.24,\ \text{which is close to 0,}}$

$\underline{\text{so the equation agrees with the graph.}}$

© Houghton Mifflin Harcourt Publishing Company

Notes

Solving Quadratic Equations Graphically

Essential question: *How can you solve a quadratic equation by graphing?*

COMMON **Standards for**
CORE **Mathematical Content**

CC.9-12.A.CED.1 Create equations ... in one variable and use them to solve problems.*

CC.9-12.A.CED.2 Create equations in two or more variables to represent relationships between quantities; graph equations on coordinate axes with labels and scales.*

CC.9-12.A.REI.11 Explain why the x-coordinates of the points where the graphs of the equations $y = f(x)$ and $y = g(x)$ intersect are the solutions of the equation $f(x) = g(x)$; find the solutions approximately, e.g., using technology to graph the functions...*

Also: CC.9-12.A.SSE.1a*, CC.9-12.F.IF.4*, CC.9-12.F.IF.5*, CC.9-12.F.IF.6*, CC.9-12.F.IF.7*, CC.9-12.F.IF.7a*

Prerequisites

Graphing quadratic functions, Lesson 7-3

Math Background

Solving equations by graphing is not new for students. Remind them that they solved equations of the form $c = ab^x$ by graphing in Lesson 5-5. To solve a quadratic equation $c = a(x - h)^2 + k$, first graph the function $f(x) = a(x - h)^2 + k$. Then graph function the $g(x) = c$. Estimate the x-coordinates of the points of intersection. There may be 0, 1, or 2 solutions. Exact solutions will be found algebraically in Lesson 7-5.

INTRODUCE

The graph at the right shows the graphs of $f(x) = 2^x$ and $g(x) = 4$. What are the coordinates of the intersection point? **(2, 4)**

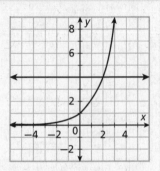

What is the solution to the associated equation $2^x = 4$? **2**

TEACH

1 EXPLORE

Questioning Strategies

- How many points of intersection can a parabola and a line have? **None, one, or two**

- In part C, why do you use the x-coordinate of the intersection point as the solution instead of the y-coordinate? **It is the x-coordinate that satisfies the original associated equation.**

- Can the method described in part C be used to find the intersection of any line and a parabola? **yes**

2 EXAMPLE

Questioning Strategies

- Why is $2(x - 4)^2 + 1 = 7$ separated into two equations in part A and part B? **By separating the equations, you will be graphing a quadratic function and a linear function and then finding their intersection point(s).**

- How can you predict the number of solutions to the equation $3(x + 4)^2 - 2 = c$ before graphing? **Find the y-coordinate of the vertex, −2. Because the graph opens up, if $c < -2$, then there will be no solution. If $c = -2$, there will be one solution. If $c > -2$, there will be two solutions.**

continued

Solving Quadratic Equations Graphically

COMMON CORE

CC.9-12.A.CED.1*,
CC.9-12.A.CED.2*,
CC.9-12.A.REI.11*

Essential question: *How can you solve a quadratic equation by graphing?*

1 EXPLORE Finding Intersections of Lines and Parabolas

The graphs of three quadratic functions are shown.

Parabola A is the graph of $f(x) = x^2$.

Parabola B is the graph of $f(x) = x^2 + 4$.

Parabola C is the graph of $f(x) = x^2 + 8$.

A On the same coordinate grid, graph the function $g(x) = 4$. What type of function is this? Describe its graph.

constant function; horizontal line

B At how many points does the graph of $g(x)$ intersect each parabola?

Intersections with parabola A: 2

Intersections with parabola B: 1

Intersections with parabola C: 0

C Use the graph to find the x-coordinate of each point of intersection of the graph of $g(x)$ and parabola A. Show that each x-coordinate satisfies the equation $x^2 = 4$.

$$x = \pm 2; \ (\pm 2)^2 = 4$$

D Use the graph to find the x-coordinate of each point of intersection of the graph of $g(x)$ and parabola B. Show that each x-coordinate satisfies the equation $x^2 + 4 = 4$.

$$x = 0; \ 0^2 + 4 = 4$$

REFLECT

1a. Describe how you could solve an equation like $x^2 + 5 = 7$ graphically.

Treat each side of the equation as a function and graph it. Find the x-coordinates

of any points of intersection.

You can solve an equation of the form $a(x - h)^2 + k = c$, which is called a *quadratic equation*, by graphing the functions $f(x) = a(x - h)^2 + k$ and $g(x) = c$ and finding the x-coordinate of each point of intersection.

2 EXAMPLE Solving Quadratic Equations Graphically

Solve $2(x - 4)^2 + 1 = 7$.

A Graph $f(x) = 2(x - 4)^2 + 1$.

What is the vertex? (4, 1)

If you move 1 unit right or left from the vertex, how must you move vertically to be on the graph of $f(x)$? What points are you at?

2 units up; (3, 3), (5, 3)

B Graph $g(x) = 7$.

C At how many points do the graphs of $f(x)$ and $g(x)$ intersect? If possible, find the x-coordinate of each point of intersection exactly. Otherwise, give an approximation of the x-coordinate of each point of intersection.

Two points; $x \approx 2.3$ and $x \approx 5.7$

D For each x-value from part C, find the value of $f(x)$. How does this show that you have found actual or approximate solutions of $2(x - 4)^2 + 1 = 7$?

$f(2.3) \approx 2(2.3 - 4)^2 + 1 = 2(-1.7)^2 + 1 = 2(2.89) + 1 = 6.78$; $f(5.7) \approx 2(5.7 - 4)^2 +$

$1 = 2(1.7)^2 + 1 = 2(2.89) + 1 = 6.78$; because the function values are not exactly

equal to 7, the solutions are approximations.

REFLECT

2a. If you solved the equation $4(x - 3)^2 + 1 = 3$ graphically, would you be able to obtain exact or approximate solutions? Explain.

Exact, because the parabola and line intersect at points where the horizontal

and vertical grid lines cross.

2b. For what value of c would the equation $4(x - 3)^2 + 1 = c$ have exactly one solution? How is that solution related to the graph of $f(x)$?

$c = 1$; it is the x-coordinate of the parabola's vertex.

2 EXAMPLE continued

EXTRA EXAMPLE
Solve $3(x-2)^2 + 1 = 8$.
The values of x are approximately 0.5 and 3.5.

Avoid Common Errors
Some students may incorrectly give the y-value of the points of intersection as the solution. Remind students that they are solving the equation for the values of x, not the values of y.

Technology
Students can check their graphs and the points of intersection by using the intersect feature under the CALC menu of a graphing calculator.

3 EXAMPLE

Questioning Strategies
- What do the x- and y-values of the point $(0, 20)$ represent in this problem? The x-value 0 represents the time at which the performer begins to fall. The y-value 20 represents the performer's initial height in feet.

- What do the values on the horizontal axis represent? What do the values on the vertical axis represent? The horizontal axis is the time in seconds; the vertical axis is the height in feet.

- What is $h(2)$? Does it make sense in this situation? $h(2) = -44$; it does not make sense in the problem because height will not be negative.

> MATHEMATICAL PRACTICE **Highlighting the Standards**
>
> **3 EXAMPLE** addresses Mathematical Practice Standard 4 (Model with mathematics). Draw students' attention to the distance model $d(t)$ that represents the distance a falling object falls as a function of time t (in seconds) as $d(t) = 16t^2$. Discuss with students how to distinguish distance fallen from height above the ground. (See Question 3b.)

EXTRA EXAMPLE
While filming an action movie, a car drives off a cliff into a lake. The function $h(t) = -16t^2 + 40$, where t measures the time in seconds, gives the car's height above the water (in feet) as the car falls. The car also hits a tree that is 15 feet above the water. Write and solve an equation to find the elapsed time until the car hits the tree.
Equation: $-16t^2 + 40 = 15$; 1.25 seconds

Differentiated Instruction
Students may benefit from a more visual approach to this example. Have them share their graphs with a partner and describe each step for finding the intersection point of the graphs using the trace and intersect features of the calculator. Ask one student to display the graph on the overhead.

CLOSE

Essential Question
How can you solve a quadratic equation by graphing?
To solve a quadratic equation by graphing, write the equation as two functions: a quadratic function and a linear function. Then graph both the parabola and the line. The x-values of the intersection point(s) of the line and parabola are the solutions to the equation. There can be no solution, one solution, or two solutions.

Summarize
Have students write a journal entry in which they describe how to solve $c = a(x - h)^2 + k$ by graphing.

PRACTICE

Where skills are taught	Where skills are practiced
2 EXAMPLE	EXS. 1–4
3 EXAMPLE	EX. 5

3 **EXAMPLE** Solving a Real-World Problem

While practicing a tightrope walk at a height of 20 feet, a circus performer slips and falls into a safety net 15 feet below. The function $h(t) = -16t^2 + 20$, where t represents time measured in seconds, gives the performer's height above the ground (in feet) as he falls. Write and solve an equation to find the elapsed time until the performer lands in the net.

A Write the equation that you need to solve. $-16t^2 + 20 = 5$

B You will solve the equation using a graphing calculator. Because the calculator requires that you enter functions in terms of x and y, use x and y to write the equations for the two functions that you will graph. $y = -16x^2 + 20; y = 5$

C When setting a viewing window, you need to decide what portion of each axis to use for graphing. What interval on the x-axis and what interval on the y-axis are reasonable for this problem? Explain.

Sample answer: $0 \le x \le 2$ and $0 \le y \le 20$ because only nonnegative values

of x and y are meaningful, the fall will not last more than a couple of seconds,

and the performer's height before the fall is 20 feet.

D Graph the two functions, and use the calculator's trace or intersect feature to find the elapsed time until the performer lands in the net. Is your answer exact or an approximation?

The performer lands in the net in about 1 second; this is an approximate solution.

REFLECT

3a. Although the graphs also intersect to the left of the y-axis, why is that point irrelevant to the problem?

Negative time has no meaning in this problem.

3b. The distance d (in feet) that a falling object travels as a function of time t (in seconds) is given by $d(t) = 16t^2$. Use this fact to explain the model given in the problem, $h(t) = -16t^2 + 20$. In particular, explain why the model includes the constant 20 and why $-16t^2$ includes a negative sign.

The model can be written as $h(t) = 20 - 16t^2$. When you take the performer's

initial height above the ground (20 feet) and subtract the distance he has fallen

for some time t, $16t^2$, you have his current height above the ground, $h(t)$.

3c. At what height would the circus performer have to be for his fall to last exactly 1 second? Explain.

21 feet; the distance-fallen function $d(t) = 16t^2$ has a value of 16 when $t = 1$,

so with the net 5 feet above the ground, the performer would have to be

$5 + 16 = 21$ feet above the ground initially for his fall to last exactly 1 second.

PRACTICE

Solve each quadratic equation by graphing. Indicate whether the solutions are exact or approximate.

1. $(x + 2)^2 - 1 = 3$

$x = -4$ and $x = 0$; exact

2. $2(x - 3)^2 + 1 = 5$

$x \approx 1.6$ and $x \approx 4.4$; approximate

3. $-\frac{1}{2}x^2 + 2 = -4$

$x \approx -3.5$ and $x \approx 3.5$; approximate

4. $-(x - 3)^2 - 2 = -6$

$x = 1$ and $x = 5$; exact

5. As part of an engineering contest, a student who has designed a protective crate for an egg drops the crate from a window 18 feet above the ground. The height (in feet) of the crate as it falls is given by $h(t) = -16t^2 + 18$ where t is the time (in seconds) since the crate was dropped.

a. Write and solve an equation to find the elapsed time until the crate passes a window 10 feet directly below the window from which it was dropped.

$-16t^2 + 18 = 8; t \approx 0.8$ second

b. Write and solve an equation to find the elapsed time until the crate hits the ground.

$-16t^2 + 18 = 0; t \approx 1.1$ seconds

c. Is the crate's rate of fall constant? Explain.

For the first 10 feet, the average rate of fall was $\frac{10 \text{ feet}}{0.8 \text{ second}} = 12.5$ feet per second.

For the remainder of the fall, the average rate of fall was $\frac{18 \text{ feet} - 10 \text{ feet}}{1.1 \text{ seconds} - 0.8 \text{ second}} =$

$\frac{8 \text{ feet}}{0.3 \text{ second}} = 26.7$ feet per second. So, the rate of fall was not constant; in fact,

it was increasing.

© Houghton Mifflin Harcourt Publishing Company

Notes

Solving Quadratic Equations Using Square Roots

Essential question: *How can you solve a quadratic equation using square roots?*

COMMON CORE Standards for Mathematical Content

CC.9-12.A.CED.1 Create equations … in one variable and use them to solve problems.*

CC.9-12.A.REI.4 Solve quadratic equations in one variable.

CC.9-12.A.REI.4b Solve quadratic equations by inspection (e.g., for $x^2 = 49$), taking square roots, …

Also: CC.9-12.A.SSE.1a*

Vocabulary
square root

Prerequisites
Square roots, 8th grade

Math Background
For a positive number a, you write the positive square root of a as $\sqrt{a}$. Likewise, for a positive number b, you write the positive square root of b as $\sqrt{b}$. By the definition of square root, $(\sqrt{a})^2 = a$ and $(\sqrt{b})^2 = b$. Therefore, $ab = (\sqrt{a})^2 (\sqrt{b})^2 = (\sqrt{a} \cdot \sqrt{b})^2$ by the product of powers property. This means, again by the definition of square root, that $\sqrt{a} \cdot \sqrt{b} = \sqrt{ab}$. A similar argument can be made for the quotient property of radicals.

INTRODUCE

A square chessboard has an area of 64 square units. How would you find how many squares are along each side? (You would find the square root of 64, or 8.) Tell students that they will use square roots to help them solve quadratic equations in this lesson.

TEACH

1 ENGAGE

Questioning Strategies

• Why does a positive number have two square roots? If you square of a number and its opposite, you get the same positive number. Thus, every positive number has two square roots, one positive and one negative.

• How is finding square roots related to solving a quadratic equation by graphing? If you find the square roots of a nonnegative number a, this is similar to finding the intersection points of $f(x) = x^2$ and $g(x) = a$ by graphing. Both methods have the solutions $\sqrt{a}$ and $-\sqrt{a}$.

2 EXAMPLE

Questioning Strategies

• Why are there two solutions in parts A and B? When you apply the definition of a square root in the solution, you get two square roots, the positive square root and the negative square root, thus leading to two solutions.

• Why aren't the solutions to part B opposites? After applying the definition of a square root, you need to add 6 to each square root to get the solutions. This creates solutions that are not opposites.

Avoid Common Errors

There are many opportunities for error when solving quadratic equations. As evidenced by parts A and B, students must add, subtract, divide, and take square roots, any of which can lead to an error. Encourage students to work carefully and to check their solutions by substituting them back into the original equation.

Teaching Strategy

You may want to emphasize the importance and order of the steps in part A by asking students to start with a solution like $x = \pm 3\sqrt{3}$ and then work backwards to create their own quadratic equation.

continued

Name_____ Class_____ Date_____

7-5

COMMON
CORE

Solving Quadratic Equations Using Square Roots

CC.9-12.A.CED.1*,
CC.9-12.A.REI.4b

Essential question: How can you solve a quadratic equation using square roots?

1 ENGAGE Understanding Square Roots

You know that $2^2 = 4$ and $(-2)^2 = 4$. The numbers 2 and -2 are called the *square roots* of 4.

If $x^2 = a$, then x is a **square root** of a. Every positive number a has two square roots. This is illustrated in the diagram using the graph of $y = x^2$ and letting $y = a$. Notice that one square root of a is positive and is written $\sqrt{a}$, while the other is negative and is written $-\sqrt{a}$. The symbol $\sqrt{}$ is called a *radical sign*, and the number underneath the radical sign is called the *radicand*.

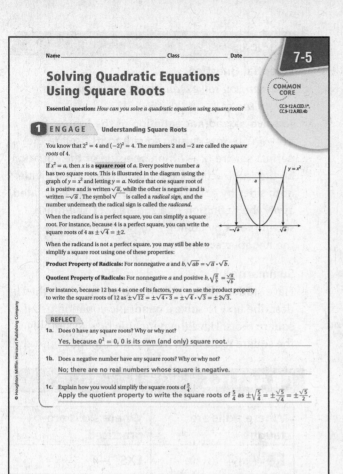

When the radicand is a perfect square, you can simplify a square root. For instance, because 4 is a perfect square, you can write the square roots of 4 as $\pm\sqrt{4} = \pm 2$.

When the radicand is not a perfect square, you may still be able to simplify a square root using one of these properties:

Product Property of Radicals: For nonnegative a and b, $\sqrt{ab} = \sqrt{a} \cdot \sqrt{b}$.

Quotient Property of Radicals: For nonnegative a and positive b, $\sqrt{\frac{a}{b}} = \frac{\sqrt{a}}{\sqrt{b}}$.

For instance, because 12 has 4 as one of its factors, you can use the product property to write the square roots of 12 as $\pm\sqrt{12} = \pm\sqrt{4 \cdot 3} = \pm\sqrt{4} \cdot \sqrt{3} = \pm 2\sqrt{3}$.

REFLECT

1a. Does 0 have any square roots? Why or why not?

Yes, because $0^2 = 0$, 0 is its own (and only) square root.

1b. Does a negative number have any square roots? Why or why not?

No; there are no real numbers whose square is negative.

1c. Explain how you would simplify the square roots of $\frac{5}{4}$.

Apply the quotient property to write the square roots of $\frac{5}{4}$ as $\pm\sqrt{\frac{5}{4}} = \pm\frac{\sqrt{5}}{\sqrt{4}} = \pm\frac{\sqrt{5}}{2}$.

© Houghton Mifflin Harcourt Publishing Company

Unit 7   287   Lesson 5

Solving a quadratic equation algebraically involves isolating the squared expression in the equation. Once you have the equation in the form $(x - h)^2 = c$, you can use the definition of a square root to write $x - h = \pm\sqrt{c}$ and finish solving for x.

2 EXAMPLE Solving Quadratic Equations Algebraically

Solve each quadratic equation.

A $2x^2 - 7 = 9$ Equation to be solved

$\underline{+7 \quad +7}$ Add 7 to both sides.

$2x^2 = 16$ Simplify.

$\dfrac{2x^2}{2} = \dfrac{16}{2}$ Divide both sides by 2.

$x^2 = 8$ Simplify.

$x = \pm\sqrt{8}$ Definition of a square root

$x = \pm 2\sqrt{2}$ Simplify the square roots.

B $-3(x - 6)^2 + 19 = 7$ Equation to be solved

$\underline{-19 \quad -19}$ Subtract 19 from both sides.

$-3(x - 6)^2 = -12$ Simplify.

$\dfrac{-3(x - 6)^2}{-3} = \dfrac{-12}{-3}$ Divide both sides by -3.

$(x - 6)^2 = 4$ Simplify.

$x - 6 = \pm\sqrt{4}$ Definition of a square root

$x - 6 = 2$ $x - 6 = -2$ Simplify the square roots.
      or
$x = 8$ $x = 4$ Add 6 to both sides.

REFLECT

2a. How can you check the solutions of a quadratic equation?

Substitute each solution into the original equation and simplify both sides to see if they are equal.

© Houghton Mifflin Harcourt Publishing Company

Unit 7   288   Lesson 5

EXTRA EXAMPLE

Solve each quadratic equation.

A. $3x^2 + 8 = 83$

$x = 5; x = -5$

B. $-2(x + 8)^2 + 38 = 6$

$x = -4; x = -12$

3 EXAMPLE

Questioning Strategies

- Why is there only one solution to the real-world situation given in the problem? **When you solve the equation that represents the situation, you get a positive and a negative solution. Since t represents time and time cannot be negative, you can reject the negative solution.**

- What equation would you solve if the person in the building dropped the keys from a height of 20 feet? How long would it take for the keys to drop to 4 feet? $-16t^2 + 20 = 4$; 1 sec

EXTRA EXAMPLE

A stunt person for a movie jumps off a window ledge to a buffer area below. The window ledge is 24 feet off the ground. The height (in feet) of the stunt person as he falls is given by the function $h(t) = -16t^2 + 24$, where t is the time in seconds since the person jumped. An awning below the window breaks the fall at a height of 10 feet. Write and solve an equation to find the elapsed time before the stunt person hits the awning.

$-16t^2 + 24 = 10$; 0.9 sec

```
MATHEMATICAL   Highlighting the
   PRACTICE      Standards
```

Example 3 is an opportunity to work in the abstract to solve a quadratic equation and then analyze the result in context. This addresses Mathematical Practices Standard 2 (Reason abstractly and quantitatively). Draw students' attention to the fact that although there are two solutions to the equation, only one makes sense in terms of the problem.

CLOSE

Essential Question

How can you solve a quadratic equation using square roots?

To solve a quadratic equation of the form $a(x - h)^2 + k = c$ using square roots, isolate the perfect square $(x - h)^2$ on one side of the equation by first subtracting k from both sides. Then divide both sides by a. Once the perfect square is isolated, apply the definition of a square root and finish solving for x by adding h to both the positive and the negative square root.

Summarize

Have students write a journal entry in which they describe how to solve a quadratic equation using square roots. Have them include how to simplify the square roots of an irrational number.

PRACTICE

Where skills are taught	Where skills are practiced
1 ENGAGE	EXS. 1–4
2 EXAMPLE	EXS. 5–14
3 EXAMPLE	EX. 15

3 EXAMPLE Solving a Real-World Problem

A person standing on a second-floor balcony drops keys to a friend standing below the balcony. The keys are dropped from a height of 10 feet. The height (in feet) of the keys as they fall is given by the function $h(t) = -16t^2 + 10$ where t is the time (in seconds) since the keys were dropped. The friend catches the keys at a height of 4 feet. Write and solve an equation to find the elapsed time before the keys are caught.

$-16t^2 + 10 = \boxed{4}$	Write the equation to be solved.
$\underline{-10 \quad -10}$	Subtract 10 from both sides.
$-16t^2 = \boxed{-6}$	Simplify.
$\dfrac{-16t^2}{-16} = \dfrac{-6}{-16}$	Divide both sides by -16.
$t^2 = \boxed{0.375}$	Simplify. Express the right side as a decimal.
$t = \pm\sqrt{0.375}$	Definition of a square root.
$t \approx \boxed{\pm 0.6}$	Use a calculator to approximate the square roots.

The elapsed time before the keys are caught is about ___0.6 second___.

REFLECT

3a. Although the equation that you solved has two solutions, one of them is rejected. Why?

A negative time value is meaningless in the context of this problem.

3b. The exact positive solution of the equation is $t = \frac{\sqrt{6}}{4}$. Explain how to obtain this result, and show that it gives the same approximate solution.

Instead of writing $t^2 = 0.375$, write $t^2 = \frac{6}{16}$ so that $t = \pm\sqrt{\frac{6}{16}} = \pm\frac{\sqrt{6}}{\sqrt{16}} = \pm\frac{\sqrt{6}}{4}$;

reject the negative solution. From a calculator, you get $t \approx \frac{2.4}{4} = 0.6$ second.

3c. Suppose the friend decides not to catch the keys and lets them fall to the ground instead. What equation must you solve to find the elapsed time until the keys hit the ground? What is that elapsed time?

$-16t^2 + 10 = 0$; $t \approx 0.8$ second

PRACTICE

1. Write the square roots of 64 in simplified form. ___± 8___

2. Write the square roots of 32 in simplified form. ___$\pm 4\sqrt{2}$___

3. Write the square roots of $\frac{8}{9}$ in simplified form. ___$\pm\frac{2\sqrt{2}}{3}$___

4. Explain why the square roots of 37 cannot be simplified.

37 has no factors that are perfect squares.

Solve each quadratic equation. Simplify solutions when possible.

5. $x^2 = 18$

$x = \pm 3\sqrt{2}$

6. $-4x^2 = -20$

$x = \pm\sqrt{5}$

7. $x^2 + 4 = 10$

$x = \pm\sqrt{6}$

8. $2x^2 = 200$

$x = \pm 10$

9. $(x - 5)^2 = 25$

$x = 0$ or $x = 10$

10. $(x + 1)^2 = 16$

$x = -5$ or $x = 3$

11. $2(x - 7)^2 = 98$

$x = 0$ or $x = 14$

12. $-5(x + 3)^2 = -80$

$x = -7$ or $x = 1$

13. $0.5(x + 2)^2 - 4 = 14$

$x = -8$ or $x = 4$

14. $3(x - 1)^2 + 1 = 19$

$x = 1 \pm\sqrt{6}$

15. To study how high a ball bounces, students drop the ball from various heights. The function $h(t) = -16t^2 + h_0$ gives the height (in feet) of the ball at time t measured in seconds since the ball was dropped from a height h_0.

a. The ball is dropped from a height $h_0 = 8$ feet. Write and solve an equation to find the elapsed time until the ball hits the floor.

$-16t^2 + 8 = 0$; $t \approx 0.7$ second

b. Does doubling the drop height also double the elapsed time until the ball hits the floor? Explain why or why not.

No; if you double the height to 16 and solve $-16t^2 + 16 = 0$, you get

$t = 1$ second, which is not double the elapsed time found in part a.

c. When dropped from a height $h_0 = 16$ feet, the ball rebounds to a height of 8 feet and then falls back to the floor. Find the total time for this to happen. (Assume the ball takes the same time to rebound 8 feet as it does to fall 8 feet.)

About $1 + 0.7 + 0.7 = 2.4$ seconds

FOCUS ON MODELING
Modeling with Quadratic Functions

Essential question: How can you model a car's gas mileage using a quadratic function?

The following standards are addressed in this lesson. (An asterisk indicates that a standard is also a Modeling standard.) For more detailed information, see each section of the lesson.

Number and Quantity: CC.9-12.N.Q.1*, CC.9-12.N.Q.2*

Algebra: CC.9-12.A.CED.1*, CC.9-12.A.CED.2*, CC.9-12.A.REI.4b

Functions: CC.9-12.F.IF.2, CC.9-12.F.IF.4*, CC.9-12.F.IF.9, CC.9-12.F.BF.1*, CC.9-12.F.BF.1a*, CC.9-12.F.BF.3

Statistics and Probability: CC.9-12.S.ID.6*, CC.9-12.S.ID.6a*

Prerequisites

• Write an equation of a quadratic function in vertex form, Lesson 7-3

Math Background

In this lesson, students analyze gas mileage data (in miles per gallon) for a particular year, make, and model car. Students plot the data and sketch a parabola to model it. Then they derive the equation of the parabola in vertex form. To do this, they estimate certain aspects of the graph, including the vertex and another point on the graph. Students should notice that it is not a coincidence that the vertex of their graph is the point (55, 29) and that 55 mph is a common speed limit around the country. This speed limit gives the best gas mileage for this car.

INTRODUCE

Gas mileage has improved over time, reducing both energy consumption and air pollution per mile. You may wish to share with students data showing the increase in gas mileage over the last 30 or 40 years.

TEACH

 Identify the variables and graph the data.

Standards
CC.9-12.N.Q.1 ... choose and interpret the scale and the origin in graphs and data displays.*

CC.9-12.N.Q.2 Define appropriate quantities for the purpose of descriptive modeling.*

CC.9-12.A.CED.2 ...; graph equations on coordinate axes with labels and scales.*

CC.9-12.F.IF.4 For a function that models a relationship between two quantities, interpret key features of graphs and tables ...*

Questioning Strategies

• Why is it important to draw a parabola so that some data points fall below it and some above it? If some of the data points are above and some below the curve, the model is less likely to overestimate or underestimate the mileage.

• Why can't the model for the curve be exponential? An exponential model is always increasing or always decreasing. These data values increase and then decrease.

Name _____ Class _____ Date _____

7-6

COMMON
CORE

FOCUS ON MODELING
Modeling with Quadratic Functions

Essential question: *How can you model a car's gas mileage using a quadratic function?*

CC-9-12.N.Q.1*,
CC-9-12.N.Q.2*,
CC-9-12.A.CED.2*,
CC-9-12.F.IF.2,
CC-9-12.F.IF.4*,
CC-9-12.F.BF.1*

The Center for Transportation Analysis in the Oak Ridge National Laboratory publishes *Transportation Energy Data Book*, which gives data about the transportation industry. One of the book's many data sets is the gas mileage of cars driven at steady speeds. The gas mileage (in miles per gallon) for a particular year, make, and model of car is shown in the table.

As you can see, the gas mileage varies with the speed of the car. How can you predict the car's gas mileage when the car is driven at a speed of 35 miles per hour?

Speed (mph)	Gas mileage (mpg)
40	23.0
50	27.3
55	29.1
60	28.2
70	22.9

1 Identify the variables and graph the data.

A Identify the independent and dependent variables in this situation. State the units associated with each variable.

Independent variable: speed (in miles per hour); dependent variable: gas

mileage (in miles per gallon)

B Explain why it makes sense to use *s* for the independent variable and $m(s)$ for the dependent variable.

The letter *s* is the first letter of *speed*; the letter *m* is the first letter of *mileage*;

$m(s)$ indicates that mileage is a function of speed.

C On the scatter plot given on the next page, label the axes with the quantities they represent and indicate the axis scales by showing numbers for select grid lines. Then plot the ordered pairs of data from the table.

D Sketch a parabola that you think best fits the plotted points. (You will not be able to make the parabola pass through all the points. Instead, you should try to draw the parabola so that some points fall above it and some below it.) Explain why a parabola is a reasonable curve to fit to the data.

As speed increases, the gas mileage increases and then decreases,

so a parabola that opens down is a reasonable fit.

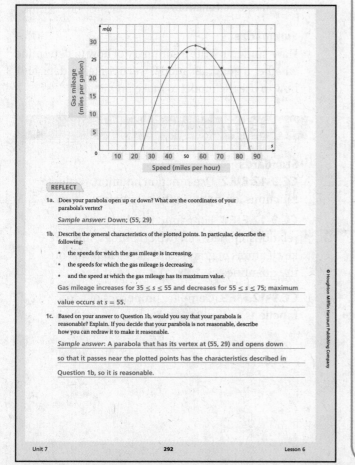

REFLECT

1a. Does your parabola open up or down? What are the coordinates of your parabola's vertex?

Sample answer: Down; (55, 29)

1b. Describe the general characteristics of the plotted points. In particular, describe the following:

• the speeds for which the gas mileage is increasing,

• the speeds for which the gas mileage is decreasing,

• and the speed at which the gas mileage has its maximum value.

Gas mileage increases for $35 \leq s \leq 55$ and decreases for $55 \leq s \leq 75$; maximum

value occurs at $s = 55$.

1c. Based on your answer to Question 1b, would you say that your parabola is reasonable? Explain. If you decide that your parabola is not reasonable, describe how you can redraw it to make it reasonable.

Sample answer: A parabola that has its vertex at (55, 29) and opens down

so that it passes near the plotted points has the characteristics described in

Question 1b, so it is reasonable.

Write the equation for the model.

Standards

CC.9-12. A.CED.2 Create equations in two ...
variables to represent relationships between
quantities; ...*

CC.9-12.F.IF.2 Use function notation, evaluate
functions for inputs in their domains ...

CC.9-12.F.IF.4 For a function that models a
relationship between two quantities, interpret
key features of graphs and tables in terms of the
quantities, ...*

CC.9-12.F.BF.1 Write a function that describes a
relationship between two quantities.*

CC.9-12.F.BF.1a Determine an explicit
expression ... from a context.*

Questioning Strategies

• Will you get the same equation if you use one
of the data points to calculate the value of *a*?
Explain. **It depends. You will if you use a data
point on the parabola, but not if you use a data
point not on the parabola.**

3 **Make a prediction.**

Standards

CC.9-12.F.IF.2 Use function notation, evaluate
functions for inputs in their domains ...

Questioning Strategies

• Why might it be easier to use the original data
to make a prediction about mileage for a speed
of 65 miles per hour than for 35 miles per hour?
Sample answer: **65 miles per hour falls between
data points so you can predict by averaging
mileage. It is more difficult to predict behavior
beyond the data set.**

• How can the model be used to predict the gas
mileage for a given speed? **You can evaluate
the function for that speed to determine the
expected gas mileage at that speed.**

⋮ **MATHEMATICAL** **Highlighting the**
⋮ **PRACTICE** **Standards**

Approximating data points with a smooth
curve addresses Mathematical Practice
Standard 4 (Model with mathematics).
Draw students' attention to the method to
find the quadratic model in Step 2 and how
they interpret the model to discuss driving
at certain speeds in the Extend. Stress the
importance of checking the model with actual
values and not assuming that the model is a
good fit to the data.

CLOSE

Essential Question

*How can you model a car's gas mileage using a
quadratic function?*
To model gas mileage as a function of speed,
graph the given data, draw a parabola that closely
resembles the data, and identify the vertex of the
parabola. Using the vertex and another point of
the parabola, find the value of *a*, and then write
the quadratic function.

Summarize

Have students write a summary of how to determine
whether a quadratic model will fit mileage data, and
how to use the model to make predictions.

EXTEND

Standards

CC.9-12.F.IF.2 Use function notation, evaluate
functions for inputs in their domains ... **(Exs. 1, 2, 3)**

CC.9-12.F.IF.4 For a function that models a
relationship between two quantities, interpret
key features of graphs and tables in terms of
the quantities. ... * **(Ex. 1)**

CC.9-12.F.IF.9 Compare properties of two
functions ... **(Ex. 3)**

2 Write the equation for the model.

A Using the coordinates of the vertex of your parabola, write the equation for a function of the form $m(s) = a(s - h)^2 + k$.

$$m(s) = a\left(s - \boxed{55}\right)^2 + \boxed{29}$$ A sample answer is given.

B The next step is to find the value of a. Does your parabola open up or down? What does this fact tell you about the value of a?

Down; the value of a is negative.

C Choose a point on your parabola other than the vertex. For your chosen point, what is the value of s? What is the value of $m(s)$?

Sample answer: My parabola passes through the point

(45, 26) so $s = 45$ and $m(s) = 26$.

D Substituting the values of s and $m(s)$ from Step C into the equation from Step A results in an equation containing only the unknown a. Solve the equation to find a.

$a = \underline{\text{Sample answer: } -0.03}$

E Write the equation of the function that models the data.

$$m(s) = -0.03\left(s - \boxed{55}\right)^2 + \boxed{29}$$ Answers will vary. A sample answer is given.

REFLECT

2a. Use your model to complete the third column of the table. Compare the predicted gas mileages to the actual ones.

A sample answer based on the model

$m(s) = -0.03(s - 55)^2 + 29$ is given.

Speed	Actual gas mileage	Predicted gas mileage
40	23.0	22.3
50	27.3	28.3
55	29.1	29.0
60	28.2	28.3
70	22.9	22.3

2b. In Step 2C, suppose you chose a different point on your parabola. How would that have affected the equation for your model?

Choosing a different point has no effect on the equation for the model since all points on the parabola satisfy the same equation.

---

3 Make a prediction.

A Using only the given data and not your model, predict what the gas mileage for the car is when it travels at a speed of 35 miles per hour. Explain your reasoning.

Sample answer: 20.5 miles per gallon; the change per unit interval from 40 to 50 mph is about 0.43 mpg/mph and from 50 to 55 mph is about 0.36 mpg/mph. An estimate of the change from 35 to 40 mph is about 0.5 mpg/mph: $23.0 - 5(0.5) = 20.5$ mpg.

B Using the equation of your model from Step 2E, predict what the gas mileage for the car is when it travels at a speed of 35 miles per hour.

Sample answer: $m(35) = -0.03(35 - 55)^2 + 29 = 17$ miles per gallon

REFLECT

3a. At a speed of 35 miles per hour, the car's actual gas mileage is 21.2 miles per gallon. Compare this value with your two predictions.

Sample answer: The actual gas mileage is greater than the predictions.

EXTEND

1. Identify the s-intercepts of your model. Interpret them in the context of the problem. Would you expect the actual data to support this interpretation? Explain.

Sample answer based on the model $m(s) = -0.03(s - 55)^2 + 29$: About 24 and 86; the car's gas mileage at speeds of 24 mph and 86 mph is 0 miles per gallon; no, the car's actual gas mileage will always be greater than 0 no matter at what speed the car is driven.

2. Suppose that when the car was driven at a steady speed, its gas mileage was 25 miles per gallon. Describe how you can use your model to find the car's speed. Is only one speed or more than one speed possible? Explain, and then find the speed(s).

Sample answer based on the model $m(s) = -0.03(s - 55)^2 + 29$: Let $m(s) = 25$ and solve for s; two speeds, because 25 mpg is less than the maximum value of 29.1 mpg; $s \approx 43.5$ mph or $s \approx 66.5$ mph

3. A student found that the gas mileage data for a different car from the same year can be modeled by the function $m(s) = -0.007(s - 40)^2 + 25.5$ where s is the car's speed. Compare this model with the one that you found in Step 2E.

Sample answer: The other car has a lower maximum gas mileage (25.5 mpg), and it achieves this gas mileage at a lower speed (40 mph).

COMMON CORE CORRELATION

Standard	Items
CC.9-12.A.CED.2	13
CC.9-12.A.REI.4b	6, 7, 12, 13
CC.9-12.A.REI.11	12, 13
CC.9-12.F.IF.2	13
CC.9-12.F.IF.4	4, 5, 8, 9, 13
CC.9-12.F.IF.7a	11, 12, 13
CC.9-12.F.BF.3	1, 2, 3, 10, 11

TEST PREP DOCTOR ✛

Multiple Choice: Item 1
- Students who chose **B, C,** or **D** did not understand the concept of parent function.

Multiple Choice: Item 2
- Students who chose **F** did not understand that the value of a must be negative to reflect the parent quadratic function in the x-axis.
- Students who answered **H** or **J** chose a parabola that is shrunk vertically, not stretched vertically. To be stretched vertically, $|a|$ must be greater than 1.

Multiple Choice: Item 3
- Students who chose **A** used $f(x) = a(x + h)^2 + k$ as the general vertex form.
- Students who chose **B** did not understand which variable translates vertically and which translates horizontally.
- Students who chose **D** used $f(x) = a(x - h)^2 - k$ as the general vertex form.

Multiple Choice: Item 4
- Students who answered **G, H,** or **J** chose functions whose vertex is a minimum. They did not understand that for the vertex to be a maximum, the value of a must be negative.

Multiple Choice: Item 6
- Students who chose **G** and **H** did not understand that $2(x - 1)^2 = -2$ cannot have a solution. Students who chose **J** did not understand that a quadratic equation has at most two solutions.

Free Response: Item 11
- Students whose graph has vertex $(0, -3)$ in Item **11a** translated the vertex down instead of up.
- Students whose graph opens upward in Item **11a** did not reflect the graph in the x-axis.
- Students who answered $h(x) = -2(x + 1)^2 + 3$ in Item **11c** translated 1 unit to the left instead of 1 unit to the right.

Free Response: Item 12
- Students who answered "no solution" in Item **12a** may have graphed either $f(x)$ or $g(x)$ incorrectly. There are two solutions.
- Students who answered $\sqrt{5}$ or $-\sqrt{5}$ in Item **12b** did not solve the equations $x + 1 = \sqrt{5}$ and $x + 1 = -\sqrt{5}$.

Name _____ Class _____ Date _____

MULTIPLE CHOICE

1. Which is the parent quadratic function?

(A.) $f(x) = x^2$ C. $f(x) = (x - h)^2 + k$

B. $f(x) = ax^2$ D. $f(x) = a(x - h)^2 + k$

2. The graph of which function is stretched vertically and reflected in the x-axis as compared to the parent quadratic function?

F. $g(x) = 2x^2$ H. $g(x) = 0.4x^2$

(G.) $g(x) = -2x^2$ J. $g(x) = -0.4x^2$

3. The graph of $g(x) = (x - 2)^2 + 3$ can be obtained from the graph of $f(x) = x^2$ using which transformation?

A. Translate −2 units horizontally and 3 units vertically.

B. Translate 3 units horizontally and −2 units vertically.

(C.) Translate 2 units horizontally and 3 units vertically.

D. Translate 2 units horizontally and −3 units vertically.

4. Which function has a maximum value?

(F.) $f(x) = -x^2$ H. $f(x) = x^2 - 5$

G. $f(x) = (x - 10)^2$ J. $f(x) = (x + 100)^2$

5. A parabola has its vertex at (10, 5). One point on the parabola is (12, 8). Which is another point on the parabola?

A. (8, 12)   C. (12, −8)

B. (−12, 8)   (D.) (8, 8)

6. How many real solutions does the equation $2(x - 1)^2 + 5 = 3$ have?

(F.) No solution   H. Two solutions

G. One solution   J. Three solutions

7. What are the solutions of $(x + 9)^2 = 16$?

A. −4 and 4   C. −3 and 3

B. 5 and 13   (D.) −13 and −5

8. Nick made the table below while preparing to graph a quadratic function. What is the vertex of the function's graph?

x	f(x)
1	9
2	6
3	5
4	6
5	9

F. (0, 0)   (H.) (3, 5)

G. (1, 9)   J. (5, 9)

9. The graph of $f(x) = 9x^2 + 3$ has what vertex?

A. (9, 3)   (C.) (0, 3)

B. (3, 0)   D. (9, −3)

10. The graph of which function is shown?

F. $f(x) = \frac{1}{2}(x - 1)^2 - 2$

(G.) $f(x) = \frac{1}{2}(x + 1)^2 - 2$

H. $f(x) = 2(x - 1)^2 + 2$

J. $f(x) = 2(x + 1)^2 - 2$

© Houghton Mifflin Harcourt Publishing Company

FREE RESPONSE

11. a. Graph $g(x) = -2x^2 + 3$.

b. Describe the transformations that you would have to perform on the graph of $f(x) = x^2$ to obtain the graph of $g(x)$.

Vertical stretch by a factor of 2; reflection in the x-axis; translation 3 units up

c. If the graph of $g(x)$ is translated 1 unit to the right to obtain the graph of $h(x)$, what is the equation for $h(x)$?

$h(x) = -2(x - 1)^2 + 3$

12. a. Find the approximate solutions of $(x + 1)^2 + 2 = 7$ by graphing $f(x) = (x + 1)^2 + 2$ and $g(x) = 7$.

$x \approx 1.2$ or $x \approx -3.2$

b. Find the exact solutions of $(x + 1)^2 + 2 = 7$ by using square roots.

$x = -1 + \sqrt{5}$ or $x = -1 - \sqrt{5}$

13. Nicole is bouncing on a trampoline. Her height h (in feet), measured from the surface of the trampoline to the soles of her feet, is given by $h(t) = -16(t - 0.5)^2 + 4$ where t is the time (in seconds) since a bounce began.

a. On the coordinate grid below, add the axis labels and draw the graph of $h(t)$.

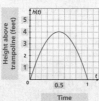

b. Explain the relevance of the statement $h(1) = 0$ in the context of the situation.

The bounce lasts 1 second.

c. What is the maximum height of the bounce? At what time does it occur?

4 feet; 0.5 second

d. Suppose you want to know the time(s) at which Nicole was 3 feet above the trampoline during the bounce. Describe how you can obtain this information from the graph and by using algebra. Then find the time(s).

Graph $g(t) = 3$ and find the t-coordinates of the points of intersection with the graph of $h(t)$; solve the equation $-16(t - 0.5)^2 + 4 = 3$ using square roots; $t = 0.25$ second and $t = 0.75$ second

© Houghton Mifflin Harcourt Publishing Company

UNIT 8

Quadratic Functions of the Form $f(x) = ax^2 + bx + c$

Unit Vocabulary

UNIT 8

Quadratic Functions of the Form $f(x) = ax^2 + bx + c$

Unit Focus

Quadratic functions are examined further in this unit. You will explore several ways to solve quadratic equations of the form $ax^2 + bx + c = 0$. You will graph quadratic functions of the form $f(x) = ax^2 + bx + c$ and use them to model real-world situations.

Unit at a Glance

COMMON CORE

Test Prep

© Houghton Mifflin Harcourt Publishing Company

Unpacking the Common Core State Standards

Use the table to help you understand the Standards for Mathematical Content that are taught in this unit. Refer to the lessons listed after each standard for exploration and practice.

COMMON CORE Standards for Mathematical Content	What It Means For You
CC.9-12.A.SSE.2 Use the structure of an expression to identify ways to rewrite it. Lesson 8-1	When working with quadratic expressions in different forms, you will need to recognize how the forms are related in order to transform expressions from one form to another.
CC.9-12.A.SSE.3 Choose and produce an equivalent form of an expression to reveal and explain properties of the quantity represented by the expression. **CC.9-12.A.SSE.3a** Factor a quadratic expression to reveal the zeros of the function it defines. Lessons 8-2, 8-3, 8-10	You will learn to find the zeros of the quadratic function $f(x) = ax^2 + bx + c$ by factoring the quadratic expression and setting each factor equal to 0.
CC.9-12.A.APR.1 Understand that polynomials form a system analogous to the integers, namely, they are closed under the operations of addition, subtraction, and multiplication; add, subtract, and **multiply polynomials.** Lesson 8-1	You will learn to multiply binomials using the distributive property and FOIL. You will use this knowledge to help you factor polynomials.
CC.9-12.A.CED.1 Create equations and inequalities in one variable and use them to solve problems.* Lessons 8-3, 8-7	You will learn how to create quadratic functions for projectile motion problems. You will then set a function equal to 0 and solve the resulting quadratic equation to determine when a projectile hits ground or water.
CC.9-12.A.CED.2 Create equations in two or more variables to represent relationships between quantities; graph equations on coordinate axes with labels and scales.* Lessons 8-9, 8-10	You will graph quadratic functions of the form $f(x) = ax^2 + bx + c$ by rewriting them in vertex form $f(x) = a(x - h)^2 + k$ and graphing them using the vertex and symmetry.

Unpacking the Common Core State Standards

This page lists and explains the Standards for Mathematical Content that are addressed in this unit. For information about the Standards for Mathematical Practice, which are integrated throughout the text, see Teacher Edition pages viii–xi.

Notes

_____

_____

_____

_____

_____

_____

_____

_____

_____

_____

COMMON CORE Standards for Mathematical Content	What It Means For You
CC.9-12.A.REI.4 Solve quadratic equations in one variable. **CC.9-12.A.REI.4a** Use the method of completing the square to transform any quadratic equation in x into an equation of the form $(x - p)^2 = q$ that has the same solutions. Derive the quadratic formula from this form. **CC.9-12.A.REI.4b** Solve quadratic equations by inspection (e.g., for $x^2 = 49$), taking square roots, completing the square, the quadratic formula and factoring, as appropriate to the initial form of the equation. Recognize when the quadratic formula gives complex solutions and write them as $a \pm bi$ for real numbers a and b. Lessons 8-2, 8-3, 8-4, 8-5, 8-6, 8-7, 8-9, 8-10	You will solve quadratic equations of the form $ax^2 + bx + c = 0$ several different ways including factoring, completing the square, and using the quadratic formula. Although some methods of solving quadratic equations have limitations, you can use the quadratic formula to solve any quadratic equation. As you will see, the derivation of the quadratic formula depends on the method of completing the square.
CC.9-12.A.REI.7 Solve a simple system consisting of a linear equation and a quadratic equation in two variables algebraically and graphically. Lesson 8-9	You will solve systems of linear and quadratic equations algebraically by setting a linear expression equal to a quadratic expression and solving for x. You will also solve the systems graphically, both by hand and by using technology.
CC.9-12.F.IF.2 Use function notation, evaluate functions for inputs in their domains, and interpret statements that use function notation in terms of a context. Lesson 8-10	You will evaluate and interpret functions that model projectile motion.
CC.9-12.F.IF.4 For a function that models a relationship between two quantities, interpret key features of graphs and tables in terms of the quantities, and sketch graphs showing key features given a verbal description of the relationship.* Lessons 8-8, 8-9, 8-10	For a quadratic function that models projectile motion, you will determine the vertex of the function's graph, which gives the projectile's maximum height, as well as the graph's intercepts, which give the projectile's initial height and time in the air.
CC.9-12.F.IF.5 Relate the domain of a function to its graph and, where applicable, to the quantitative relationship it describes.* Lessons 8-8 (Also 8-10)	You will analyze quadratic functions that model real-world situations and interpret their graphs including understanding which portion of the graph makes sense in the given situation.
CC.9-12.F.IF.6 Calculate and interpret the average rate of change of a function (presented symbolically or as a table) over a specified interval. Estimate the rate of change from a graph.* Lesson 8-10	You will calculate the average velocity for a projectile and analyze how the projectile's average velocity changes.

© Houghton Mifflin Harcourt Publishing Company

Notes

_____

_____

_____

_____

_____

_____

_____

_____

_____

_____

COMMON CORE Standards for Mathematical Content	What It Means For You
CC.9-12.F.IF.7 Graph functions expressed symbolically and show key features of the graph, by hand in simple cases and using technology for more complicated cases.* **CC.9-12.F.IF.7a** Graph linear and quadratic functions and show intercepts, maxima, and minima.* Lesson 8-8 (Also 8-10)	You will graph quadratic functions of the form $f(x) = ax^2 + bx + c$ and relate that form to the intercept form and the vertex form of a quadratic function.
CC.9-12.F.IF.8 Write a function defined by an expression in different but equivalent forms to reveal and explain different properties of the function. **CC.9-12.F.IF.8a** Use the process of factoring and completing the square in a quadratic function to show zeros, extreme values, and symmetry of the graph, and interpret these in terms of a context. Lessons 8-2, 8-3, 8-8, 8-10	You will graph quadratic functions of the form $f(x) = ax^2 + bx + c = 0$ by factoring them to find intercepts and by completing the square to find the vertex.
CC.9-12.F.IF.9 Compare properties of two functions each represented in a different way (algebraically, graphically, numerically in tables, or by verbal descriptions). Lesson 8-10	You will compare two quadratic functions modeling projectile motion to see which projectile goes higher and stays in the air longer.
CC.9-12.F.BF.1 Write a function that describes a relationship between two quantities.* **CC.9-12.F.BF.1a** Determine an explicit expression, a recursive process, or steps for calculation from a context.* Lessons 8-3, 8-8, 8-10	You will write a model for the height of a projectile using the quadratic function $h(t) = -16t^2 + vt + h_0$ for situations where you know the projectile's initial vertical velocity v and initial height h_0.

UNIT 8

© Houghton Mifflin Harcourt Publishing Company

Notes

UNIT 8

Multiplying Binomials

Essential question: *How can you use the distributive property to multiply binomials?*

○○○ **COMMON** Standards for
CORE **Mathematical Content**

CC.9-12.A.SSE.2 Use the structure of an expression to identify ways to rewrite it.
CC.9-12.A.APR.1 ... multiply polynomials.

Vocabulary
monomial
polynomial
term
binomial
trinomial

Prerequisites
Exponents, Grade 8
Distributive property, Grade 6

Math Background
Students have already learned about and understood the distributive property. In this lesson, they will extend that knowledge to use the distributive property when multiplying two binomials.

Multiplying two binomials gives students the background needed to factor trinomials, which is a key step in learning to solve quadratic equations.

Trinomials can result from real-world problems. The most well known is projectile motion—objects propelled into the air with only the force of gravity acting on them. Students will model projectile motion later in this unit.

INTRODUCE

Have students recall the distributive property. Remind them that they can use it to solve mental math problems. For example, knowing that $11 = 10 + 1$, students can think of $17 \cdot 11$ as $17 \cdot (10 + 1)$, which is $170 + 17 = 187$. Have students solve several mental math problems like this. They can check their answers by using longhand multiplication or calculators. Be sure to give students several problems that include subtraction, for example: $3 \cdot 29 = 3 \cdot (30 - 1)$.

TEACH

1 EXPLORE

Materials
Algebra tiles

Questioning Strategies
- Which tiles represent the product of $2x$ and $(x + 3)$? both x^2-tiles and the six x-tiles to the right of the x^2-tiles
- Which tiles represent the product of 1 with $(x + 3)$? the x-tile below the x^2-tiles and the three 1-tiles

Differentiated Instruction
A visual of a flatbed copier can help visual learners understand multiplication by using algebra tiles. The vertical tiles on the left edge "sweep" across the horizontal tiles that lie across the top, just as the light bar on a flatbed copier sweeps across the document. As they sweep, they draw out the product tiles. So, as the x-tile on the left sweeps its way across the x-tile above it, it draws out a box as long as itself and as wide as the x-tile above it, resulting in an x^2-tile. As the x-tile on the left continues its sweep, it moves past each 1-tile, resulting in tiles that are as wide as a 1-tile and as long as an x-tile.

8-1

Multiplying Binomials

COMMON CORE

CC.9-12.A.SSE.2,
CC.9-12.A.APR.1

Essential question: *How can you use the distributive property to multiply binomials?*

A **monomial** is a number, a variable, or the product of a number and one or more variables raised to whole number powers, such as 5, x, $-8y$, and $3x^2y^4$. A **polynomial** is a monomial or a sum of monomials. Each monomial in the expression is called a **term**. A polynomial with two terms is a **binomial**. You can multiply two binomials by using algebra tiles.

1 EXPLORE Multiplying Two Binomials Using Algebra Tiles

To use algebra tiles to multiply $(2x + 1)(x + 3)$, first represent $2x + 1$ vertically along the left side of an algebra tile diagram and $x + 3$ horizontally along the top. Then use x^2-tiles, x-tiles, and 1-tiles to complete the diagram, as shown below.

$$2x(x + 3) = \boxed{2}\ x^2 + \boxed{6}\ x$$

$$1(x + 3) = \underline{\qquad \boxed{1}\ x + \boxed{3}\ }$$

$$\boxed{2}\ x^2 + \boxed{7}\ x + \boxed{3}$$

$$(2x + 1)(x + 3) = \boxed{2}\ x^2 + \boxed{7}\ x + \boxed{3}$$

The product is a **trinomial**, a polynomial with three terms.

REFLECT

1a. Look at the algebra tile diagram. What two terms in the original binomials combine to form the x^2-term in the trinomial? How do they combine (by multiplying, by adding, or by subtracting)?

2x and x, by multiplying

1b. Look at the algebra tile diagram. What two terms in the original binomials combine to form the constant term in the trinomial? How do they combine (by multiplying, by adding, or by subtracting)?

1 and 3, by multiplying

© Houghton Mifflin Harcourt Publishing Company

1c. Look at the algebra tile diagram. Show how the terms of the original binomials combine to form the x-term in the trinomial.

$2x \cdot 3 + 1 \cdot x = 7x$

1d. You can verify that the expressions are equivalent by substituting a value for x into both expressions and simplifying to show that they are equal. Verify that the expressions are equivalent. Use $x = 4$.

$$(2 \cdot 4 + 1)(4 + 3) \stackrel{?}{=} 2 \cdot 4^2 + 7 \cdot 4 + 3$$
$$9 \cdot 7 \stackrel{?}{=} 2 \cdot 16 + 28 + 3$$
$$63 \stackrel{?}{=} 32 + 28 + 3$$
$$63 = 63$$

1e. Suppose you want to use algebra tiles to find the product $(2x + 1)(x + 2)$. Describe how you can modify the algebra tile diagram to find the product.

Remove the last column of tiles from the diagram. The product

becomes $2x^2 + 5x + 2$.

1f. Suppose you want to use algebra tiles to find the product $(2x + 2)(x + 3)$. Describe how you can modify the algebra tile diagram to find the answer.

Add a row of tiles to the bottom of the diagram that is identical to the bottom

row of the existing diagram. This adds one x-tile and three 1-tiles to the product,

so the product becomes $2x^2 + 8x + 6$.

2 ENGAGE Multiplying Binomials Using the Distributive Property

Using algebra tiles to multiply two binomials is a useful tool for understanding how the two binomials are being multiplied. However, it is not a very practical method for everyday use. Using the distributive property is.

To multiply $(2x + 1)(x + 3)$ using the distributive property, you distribute the binomial $x + 3$ to each term of $2x + 1$. Then you distribute the monomial $2x$ to each term of $x + 3$ as well as the monomial 1 to each term of $x + 3$.

$$(2x + 1)(x + 3) = 2x(x + 3) + 1(x + 3)$$
$$= 2x^2 + 6x + x + 3$$
$$= 2x^2 + 7x + 3$$

Notice that the product found using algebra tiles in the Explore is the same as the product found here using the distributive property. Thus, the two methods are equivalent.

To multiply $(4x - 7)(3x + 6)$ using the distributive property, you should think of $4x - 7$ as $4x + (-7)$ and therefore keep the negative sign with the 7.

$$(4x - 7)(3x + 6) = 4x(3x + 6) - 7(3x + 6)$$
$$= 12x^2 + 24x - 21x - 42$$
$$= 12x^2 + 3x - 42$$

© Houghton Mifflin Harcourt Publishing Company

Questioning Strategies

- In the Explore, how many terms resulted from multiplying $2x$ and $(x + 3)$? two terms How many terms resulted from multiplying 1 and $(x + 3)$? two terms So, before combining like terms, how many terms resulted from multiplying $(2x + 1)$ and $(x + 3)$? four terms

- What does the word FOIL represent? First, Outer, Inner, and Last

- What do the words represented by FOIL correspond to? the four terms in the two binomials that are being multiplied

---

```
     ⋮  MATHEMATICAL    Highlighting
     ⋮      PRACTICE     the Standards
```

2 ENGAGE and its Reflect questions offer an opportunity to address Mathematical Practice Standard 2 (Reasoning abstractly and quantitatively). Students use the mnemonic FOIL to contextualize the repeated application of the distributive property to the multiplication of two binomials.

Students who recognize that the words associated with FOIL represent the four terms resulting from multiplying two binomials will be able to quickly perform the multiplication. Relating the words to the terms of the resulting trinomial allows students to relate the coefficients of the trinomial to the original binomials. This gives students the background needed to recognize patterns that will be used in factoring trinomials.

---

3 EXAMPLE

Questioning Strategies

- Why is the sign in front of the product of the inner term negative? The product of the inner term is the product of a negative number, -5, and a term with a positive coefficient, 3.

- Why is the sign in front of the product of the last terms negative? The product of the last terms is the product of a negative number, -5, and a positive number, 6.

EXTRA EXAMPLE

Multiply $(8x - 3)(3x + 5)$ using the FOIL method. $24x^2 + 31x - 15$

Avoid Common Errors

Students sometimes overlook the subtraction sign in binomials of the form $ax - b$. Have students rewrite the binomial as $ax + (-b)$ so that it is clear to them that the constant in the binomial is negative. Highlighting or circling negative constants and coefficients is also a good idea so that students pay attention to them as they multiply binomials.

4 EXAMPLE

Questioning Strategies

- When squaring binomials, how many terms do you expect in the answer? three terms

- What do you notice about the product of the inside terms and the product of the outside terms when squaring binomials? They are the same. Why? They result from multiplying the x-term in one binomial by the constant in the other. Since the x-terms and the constants are the same, the products are the same.

- What do you notice about the product of the inner terms and the product of the outer terms with a sum and difference product? The product of the inner terms and the product of the outer terms are opposites, and their sum is zero.

- In a sum and difference product, what can you say about the sign of the last term? The sum of the last term is always negative since you are multiplying a positive constant and a negative constant.

EXTRA EXAMPLE

Multiply using FOIL.

A. $(4y + 5)^2$ $16y^2 + 40y + 25$

B. $(4y - 5)^2$ $16y^2 - 40y + 25$

C. $(4y + 5)(4y - 5)$ $16y^2 - 25$

This method of using the distributive property to multiply two binomials is referred to as the FOIL method. The letters of the word FOIL stand for First, Outer, Inner, and Last and will help you remember how to use the distributive property to multiply binomials.

You apply the FOIL method by multiplying each of the four pairs of terms described below and then simplifying the resulting polynomial.

- **F**irst refers to the first terms of each binomial.
- **O**uter refers to the two terms on the outside of the expression.
- **I**nner refers to the two terms on the inside of the expression.
- **L**ast refers to the last terms of each binomial.

Now multiply $(7x - 1)(3x - 5)$ using FOIL. Again, think of $7x - 1$ as $7x + (-1)$ and $3x - 5$ as $3x + (-5)$. This results in a positive constant term of 5 because $(-1)(-5) = 5$.

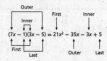

$$(7x - 1)(3x - 5) = 21x^2 - 35x - 3x + 5$$

$$(7x - 1)(3x - 5) = 21x^2 - 38x + 5$$

Notice that the trinomials are written with variable terms in descending order of exponents and with the constant term last. This is a standard form for writing polynomials: Starting with the variable term with the greatest exponent, write the other variable terms in descending order of their exponents, and put the constant term last.

REFLECT

2a. Refer back to the Explore. Using the tiles, you multiplied $2x$ by $\left(x + \boxed{3}\right)$ and then multiplied 1 by $\left(x + \boxed{3}\right)$. You are using the __distributive__ property.

2b. In FOIL, which of the products combine to form the x-term?

Outer and Inner

2c. In FOIL, which of the products combine to form the constant term?

Last

2d. In FOIL, which of the products combine to form the x^2-term?

First

2e. Two binomials are multiplied to form a trinomial. When is the constant term of the trinomial positive? When is it negative?

when the original constants are both positive or both negative; when one original

constant is positive and the other is negative

---

3 EXAMPLE   Multiplying Two Binomials Using FOIL

Multiply $(12x - 5)(3x + 6)$ using the FOIL method.

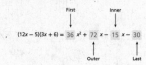

$$(12x - 5)(3x + 6) = 36 \, x^2 + 72 \, x - 15 \, x - 30$$

$$(12x - 5)(3x + 6) = \underline{36x^2 + 57x - 30}$$

REFLECT

3a. How does the final x-term in the answer to the Example relate to your answer to Question 2b? Explain.

The final x-term, $57x$, is the sum of the outer product, $72x$, and the inner

product, $-15x$.

3b. How does the final constant in the answer to the Example relate to your answer to Question 2c? Explain.

The final constant term, -30, is the product of the two last terms, -5 and 6.

3c. How does the final x^2-term in the answer to the Example relate to your answer to Question 2d? Explain.

The final x^2-term, $36x^2$, is the product of the two first terms, $12x$ and $3x$.

3d. Suppose the problem in the example were $(12x - 5)(3x + 2)$. Would the x^2-term in the product change? Would the x-term change? Would the constant term change? Explain your reasoning.

No; yes; yes; the first terms are the same, and the x^2-term only depends on the

first terms, so the x^2-term doesn't change. One of the outer terms is different,

and the product of the outer terms affects the x-term, so the x-term will change.

One of the last terms is different, and the product of the last terms produces the

constant term, so the constant term will change.

3e. Multiply $(12x - 5)(3x + 2)$.

$36x^2 + 9x - 10$

Avoid Common Errors

When students see a square of a binomial such as $(2x + 1)^2$, they are likely to square only the two terms, losing the x-term of the trinomial. To avoid this error, have students rewrite the expression to show the multiplication:
$(2x + 1)^2 = (2x + 1)(2x + 1)$.

CLOSE

Essential Question

How can you use the distributive property to multiply binomials?

Multiplying binomials involves first distributing binomial A to each term of the binomial B and then distributing each term of binomial B to the terms of binomial A. In effect, each term of one binomial is multiplied by each term of the other binomial through the distributive process.

Summarize

Have students write a journal entry in which they describe how to multiply two binomials using the distributive property and FOIL.

PRACTICE

Where skills are taught	Where skills are practiced
3 EXAMPLE	EXS. 7, 8, 11, 12
4 EXAMPLE	EXS. 9, 10, 13, 14

Exercises 1–6: Students review vocabulary terms by identifying an expression as a monomial, binomial, trinomial, or polynomial.

Exercise 15: Students extend what they learned in 4 EXAMPLE (squaring a binomial) and relate it to their prior knowledge of the vertex form of a quadratic function. They now see that it's possible to rewrite any quadratic function in vertex form so that it is in standard form.

The special products $(ax + b)^2$, $(ax - b)^2$, and $(ax + b)(ax - b)$ can all be found using the FOIL method. The products $(ax + b)^2$ and $(ax - b)^2$ are called *squares of binomials* and the product $(ax + b)(ax - b)$ is called the *sum and difference product*.

4 EXAMPLE Multiplying Special Cases

A Multiply $(2x + 5)^2$ using FOIL.

$(2x + 5)^2 = (2x + 5)(2x + 5) = \underline{4x^2 + 10x + 10x + 25}$

$\qquad\qquad\qquad = \underline{4x^2 + 20x + 25}$

B Multiply $(2x - 5)^2$ using FOIL.

$(2x - 5)^2 = (2x - 5)(2x - 5) = \underline{4x^2 - 10x - 10x + 25}$

$\qquad\qquad\qquad = \underline{4x^2 - 20x + 25}$

C Multiply $(2x - 5)(2x + 5)$ using FOIL.

$(2x - 5)(2x + 5) = \underline{4x^2 + 10x - 10x - 25}$

$\qquad\qquad\qquad = \underline{4x^2 - 25}$

REFLECT

4a. In the final answer of Part A, which two terms of the trinomial are perfect squares? How can you use the coefficients 2 and 5 to produce the coefficient of x in the product? Generalize these results to write a rule for the product $(ax + b)^2$ in terms of a, b, and x.

$4x^2$ and 25; $20x = 2(2)(5)x$; $(ax)^2 + 2abx + b^2$

4b. In the final answer of Part B, which two terms of the trinomial are perfect squares? How can you use the coefficients 2 and 5 to produce the coefficient of x in the product? Generalize these results to write a rule for the product $(ax - b)^2$ in terms of a, b, and x.

$4x^2$ and 25; $-20x = -2(2)(5)x$; $(ax)^2 - 2abx + b^2$

4c. In the final answer of Part C, which two terms of the trinomial are perfect squares? What is the coefficient of the x-term and how was it created? Generalize these results to write a rule for the product $(ax - b)(ax + b)$ in terms of a, b, and x.

$4x^2$ and 25; There is no x-term; the coefficient is 0 because

$10x + (-10x) = 0$; $(ax)^2 - b^2$

4d. In Part C, suppose the product had been $(2x + 5)(2x - 5)$. Would the answer have been different? Explain.

No; multiplication is commutative, so $(2x - 5)(2x + 5) = (2x + 5)(2x - 5) = 4x^2 - 25$.

© Houghton Mifflin Harcourt Publishing Company

PRACTICE

Classify the expression as a monomial, binomial, trinomial, or polynomial. Use the most descriptive term.

1. $3x^2$ _monomial_

2. $3x^2 - 4$ _binomial_

3. $18x^3 + 5x^2 - 2x + 29$ _polynomial_

4. $x - 12$ _binomial_

5. $4x + x^2 + 1$ _trinomial_

6. $y^2 + 17$ _binomial_

Find each product.

7. $(x + 2)(x + 3)$

$x^2 + 5x + 6$

8. $(x + 7)(x + 11)$

$x^2 + 18x + 77$

9. $(x + 4)^2$

$x^2 + 8x + 16$

10. $(x - 1)(x + 1)$

$x^2 - 1$

11. $(2x + 13)(x - 6)$

$2x^2 + x - 78$

12. $(2x - 5)(3x + 1)$

$6x^2 - 13x - 5$

13. $(3x - 8)^2$

$9x^2 - 48x + 64$

14. $(9x - 7)(9x + 7)$

$81x^2 - 49$

15. The *vertex form* of a quadratic function is $f(x) = a(x - h)^2 + k$. Use your knowledge about multiplying binomials to complete the following.

$f(x) = a(x - h)\left(\boxed{x} - \boxed{h}\right) + k$ Write as a product of two binomials.

$= a\left(x^2 - 2hx + \boxed{h}^2\right) + k$ Multiply the binomials.

$= ax^2 - 2ah\,x + ah^2 + k$ Distribute the constant a.

Compare this rewritten form to the standard form of a quadratic function, $f(x) = ax^2 + bx + c$. Discuss how b and c relate to the rewritten function. How can you rewrite a quadratic function in vertex form so that it is in standard form?

$b = -2ah$; $c = ah^2 + k$; a becomes the coefficient of x^2, $-2ah$ becomes the

coefficient of x, and $ah^2 + k$ becomes the constant term.

© Houghton Mifflin Harcourt Publishing Company

Solving $x^2 + bx + c = 0$ by Factoring

Essential question: *How can you use factoring to solve quadratic equations in standard form when a = 1?*

COMMON CORE Standards for Mathematical Content

CC.9-12.A.SSE.3 Choose and produce an equivalent form of an expression to reveal and explain properties of the quantity represented by the expression.*

CC.9-12.A.SSE.3a Factor a quadratic expression to reveal the zeros of the function it defines.*

CC.9-12.A.REI.4 Solve quadratic equations in one variable.

CC.9-12.A.REI.4b Solve quadratic equations by ... factoring ...

CC.9-12.F.IF.8 Write a function defined by an expression in different but equivalent forms to reveal and explain different properties of the function.

CC.9-12.F.IF.8a Use the process of factoring ... in a quadratic function to show zeros ...

Vocabulary

zeros

zero-product property

Prerequisites

Multiplying binomials, Lesson 8-1

Math Background

In this unit, students will learn several ways to solve quadratic equations. In this lesson, they will learn how to use factoring. In later lessons, they will learn how to solve by completing the square and by using the quadratic formula.

While many students gravitate toward using the quadratic formula (once they know it), that is not always the fastest or most useful method. Some quadratic equations, such as $x^2 + 4x + 3 = 0$, are solved easily by factoring. The factors are obvious: $(x + 1)$ and $(x + 3)$. The zero-product property then says the solutions are -1 and -3.

In this lesson, a connection is made between factoring and the zeros of a quadratic function: If the rule for the function can be factored, then the zero-product property can be used to find the values of x for which $f(x) = 0$. Students will later learn that the zeros of a function are the x-intercepts of its graph.

INTRODUCE

Completing several warm-up exercises will help students see how to factor quadratic equations.

Ask students to use FOIL to multiply:

A. $(x + 4)(x + 3)$ $x^2 + 7x + 12$

B. $(x - 5)(x + 2)$ $x^2 - 3x - 10$

C. $(x + 3)^2$ $x^2 + 6x + 9$

Next, have students factor the following numbers into all possible different *pairs* of integer factors.

A. 12 1 and 12, 2 and 6, 3 and 4, −1 and −12, −2 and −6, −3 and −4

B. −10 −1 and 10, −2 and 5, 2 and −5, 1 and −10

C. 9 1 and 9, 3 and 3, −1 and −9, −3 and −3

Then ask students how one of each of these pairs of factors is related to each multiplication.

TEACH

1 ENGAGE

Questioning Strategies

• When you factor a trinomial, what type of expression do you expect? **the product of two binomials**

• Using FOIL, which two terms produce the x^2-term in the trinomial? **the first** Using FOIL, which two terms produce the constant term in the trinomial? **the last** Using FOIL, which terms produce the x-term in the trinomial? **the sum of the product of the inner terms and the product of the outer terms**

• When factoring a trinomial, why do you factor the constant into pairs of factors rather than find prime factors? **The constant term comes from multiplying the constant terms of two binomials. So, you need two factors that may not be prime.**

Name _____ Class _____ Date _____

Solving $x^2 + bx + c = 0$ by Factoring

Essential question: *How can you use factoring to solve quadratic equations in standard form when a = 1?*

COMMON
CORE

CC-9-12.A.SSE.3,
CC-9-12.A.SSE.3a,
CC-9-12.A.REI.4,
CC-9-12.A.REI.4b,
CC-9-12.F.IF.8,
CC-9-12.F.IF.8a

1 ENGAGE Factoring Trinomials

You know how to multiply binomials: for example, $(x + 7)^2 = x^2 + 14x + 49$. In this lesson, you will learn how to reverse this process and factor trinomials.

There are several important things you should remember from multiplying binomials.

- Using FOIL, the constant term in the trinomial is a result of multiplying the *last* terms in the two binomials.
- Using FOIL, the *x*-term results from adding the products of the *outside* terms and *inside* terms.

You can factor $x^2 + 10x + 25$ by working FOIL backward. Both signs in the trinomial are plus signs, so you know both binomials are of the form *x plus something*. Therefore, you can set up the factoring as shown below.

$$x^2 + 10x + 25 = (x + \boxed{?})(x + \boxed{?})$$

To find the constant terms in the binomials, use the information above and follow the steps below.

1) The constant term in the trinomial, 25, is the product of the last terms in the two binomials. Factor 25 into pairs. The factor pairs are shown in the table at the right.

2) The correct factor pair is the one whose sum is the coefficient of *x* in the trinomial.

3) Complete the binomial expression with the appropriate numbers.

$$x^2 + 10x + 25 = \left(x + \boxed{5}\right)\left(x + \boxed{5}\right)$$

Factors of 25	Sum of Factors
1 and 25	26
5 and 5	10 ✓

You should recognize this as one of the special cases presented in Lesson 8-1. It is $(x + 5)^2$. When factoring trinomials, it is convenient to keep the special cases in mind. They are listed below for reference.

$a^2 + 2ab + b^2 = (a + b)^2$ Perfect square trinomial pattern

$a^2 - 2ab + b^2 = (a - b)^2$ Perfect square trinomial pattern

$a^2 - b^2 = (a + b)(a - b)$ Difference of squares pattern

Not all trinomials that you need to factor will be one of the special cases. The three-step procedure outlined above works for all factoring problems, not just the special cases.

REFLECT

1a. You want to factor $x^2 - 6x + 8$. What factoring pattern would you set up to begin the process? Explain.

The first sign is − and the second is +. To get a negative *x*-term and a positive constant, both binomials must be $(x - \boxed{?})$. The pattern is $(x - \boxed{?})(x - \boxed{?})$.

1b. You want to factor $x^2 - 2x - 15$. What factoring pattern would you set up to begin the process? Explain. Would this pattern also work for $x^2 + 2x - 15$? Explain.

Both signs are −. To get a negative *x*-term and a negative constant, one binomial must be $(x + \boxed{?})$ and the other must be $(x - \boxed{?})$. The pattern is $(x + \boxed{?})(x - \boxed{?})$.

Yes; the positive *x*-term and the negative constant also require the pattern to be $(x + \boxed{?})(x - \boxed{?})$.

2 EXAMPLE Factoring Trinomials

A Factor $x^2 + 3x - 10$.

The constant is negative, so you know one binomial will have a subtraction sign.

$$x^2 + 3x - 10 = (x + \boxed{?})(x - \boxed{?})$$

Complete the table at the right. Note that you are finding the factors of −10, not 10. Since the coefficient of *x* is positive, the factor with the greater absolute value will be positive (and the other factor will be negative).

Factors of −10	Sum of Factors
−1 and 10	9
−2 and 5	3

$$x^2 + 3x - 10 = \left(x + \boxed{5}\right)\left(x - \boxed{2}\right)$$

B Factor $x^2 - 8x - 48$.

The constant is negative, so you know one binomial will have a subtraction sign.

$$x^2 - 8x - 48 = (x + \boxed{?})(x - \boxed{?})$$

Complete the table at the right. Since the coefficient of *x* is negative, the factor with the greater absolute value will be negative (and the other factor will be positive).

$$x^2 - 8x - 48 = \left(x + \boxed{4}\right)\left(x - \boxed{12}\right)$$

Factors of −48	Sum of Factors
1 and −48	−47
2 and −24	−22
3 and −16	−13
4 and −12	−8
6 and −8	−2

Differentiated Instruction

If students are having difficulty in factoring trinomials, algebra tiles can help them visualize the process. Give students algebra tiles to represent the trinomial $x^2 + 6x + 5$ (one x^2-tile, six x-tiles, and five 1-tiles). You can either arrange the tiles for students or have the students arrange the tiles to make a rectangle as shown below. Students should write the trinomial $x^2 + 6x + 5$ that is depicted by the tiles.

Next, have students place x-tiles and 1-tiles to the left of and above the rectangle. These tiles represent the binomials that are multiplied to obtain the trinomial. In this case, the binomials are $x + 5$ across the top and $x + 1$ arranged vertically on the left side. Students can then determine that $x^2 + 6x + 5 = (x + 5)(x + 1)$.

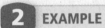 **EXAMPLE**

Questioning Strategies

- In part A, explain what would happen to the coefficient of x if the greater of the factor pair were negative. **The coefficient of x would be negative.**

- If the problem in part A were to factor $x^2 - 3x - 10$, what would be the factored form? **$(x - 5)(x + 2)$**

- How are the factored forms of $x^2 - 3x - 10$ and $x^2 + 3x - 10$ alike? How are they different? **The factored forms have the same coefficients for x and the same numbers as constants. The difference is in which binomial involves subtraction.**

- After completing part B, determine the factors of $x^2 + 8x - 48$. **$(x - 4)(x + 12)$**

Factor.

A. $y^2 + 5y + 6$ $(y + 3)(y + 2)$

B. $z^2 - 9z - 22$ $(z - 11)(z + 2)$

3 **ENGAGE**

Questioning Strategies

- What is true if you multiply any real number by zero? **The product is zero.**

- How many solutions do you expect if you solve the equation $x(x - 4) = 0$? **two**

- How would you solve the equation $x(x - 4) = 0$? **Set $x = 0$ and $x - 4 = 0$. These will give the two solutions.**

- How can you check to see whether your solutions are correct? **Substitute them into the original equation.**

| MATHEMATICAL PRACTICE | Highlighting the Standards |

3 ENGAGE and its Reflect questions offer an opportunity to address Mathematical Practice Standard 1 (Make sense of problems and persevere in solving them). Students will need to continually ask themselves whether the factor pairs they find make sense for the problem. They will need to analyze the equation and make conjectures about the form of the binomial factors. Also, recognizing special cases will help them solve problems quickly and efficiently.

REFLECT

2a. Complete the table below. Assume that b, c, p, and q are positive numbers.

Trinomial	Form of Binomial Factors
$x^2 + bx + c$	$(x + p)(x + q)$
$x^2 - bx + c$	$(x - p)(x - q)$
$x^2 - bx - c$ or $x^2 + bx - c$	$(x + p)(x - q)$

For the last row in the table, explain how to determine which factor contains a $+$ sign and which factor contains a $-$ sign.

If the sign before bx is $-$, then the factor involving the larger of p or q will have a $-$ sign. If the sign before bx is $+$, then the factor involving the larger of p or q will have a $+$ sign.

3 ENGAGE Understanding the Zero-Product Property and Recognizing Zeros of Quadratic Functions

You already know how to solve simple quadratic equations. For example, you can solve the equation $x^2 = 36$ by using the definition of __square root__. The solutions of the equation are $x = \underline{6}$ and $x = \underline{-6}$.

Another method for solving $x^2 = 36$ involves factoring. Start by subtracting 36 from both sides, resulting in $x^2 - 36 = 0$. This makes the left side of the equation a difference of two squares that can be factored as $(x + 6)(x - 6)$.

The **zero-product property** states that the product of any group of numbers is 0 if at least one of the numbers is 0 because 0 times any number is 0. Applying the zero-product property to $(x + 6)(x - 6) = 0$ gives the following:

$$x + \underline{6} = 0 \quad \text{or} \quad x - \underline{6} = 0$$
$$x = \underline{-6} \quad \text{or} \quad x = \underline{6}$$

The solutions of the equation $x^2 - 36 = 0$ are called the **zeros** of the related function $f(x) = x^2 - 36$ because they satisfy the equation $f(x) = 0$. To see this, you can substitute 6 and -6 for x in $f(x) = x^2 - 36$. The result is $f(6) = 0$ and $f(-6) = 0$.

REFLECT

3a. Describe how to use the zero-product property to solve the equation $(x + 4)(x - 12) = 0$. Then identify the solutions.

Set each factor equal to zero and solve: $x + 4 = 0$ or $x - 12 = 0$; -4, 12

3b. How can you use your answer to Question 3a to identify the zeros of the function $f(x) = x^2 - 8x - 48$?

By factoring, the function can be written $f(x) = (x + 4)(x - 12)$. The zeros of $f(x)$ are the values of x where $f(x) = 0$, which are -4 and 12.

Unit 8   309   Lesson 2

You can use the zero-product property to solve any quadratic equation written in standard form, $ax^2 + bx + c = 0$, provided the quadratic expression is factorable. You can also use the zero-product property to find the zeros of any quadratic function $f(x) = ax^2 + bx + c$ whose rule is factorable once you set $f(x)$ equal to 0.

4 EXAMPLE Solving a Quadratic Equation

Find the solutions of $x^2 + 13x = -36$.

A Write the equation in standard form. $x^2 + 13x + 36 = 0$

B Factor the trinomial. The constant term is positive so its factors are either both positive or both negative. The coefficient of x is positive, so both factors of the constant term must be __positive__. The binomial factors will be of the form $(x + p)(x + q)$.

Factors of 36	Sum of Factors
1 and 36	37
2 and 18	20
3 and 12	15
4 and 9	13
6 and 6	12

The factored trinomial is $(x + 4)(x + 9)$, so the equation becomes $(x + 4)(x + 9) = 0$.

C Use the zero-product property.

$$x + 4 = 0 \quad \text{or} \quad x + 9 = 0$$
$$x = \underline{-4} \quad \text{or} \quad x = \underline{-9}$$

REFLECT

4a. Suppose the equation was $x^2 - 13x = -36$. Describe how solving the equation would be different than what is shown in the Example. Find the solutions of the equation.

In standard form, the equation would be $x^2 - 13x + 36 = 0$. Because the sign of the x-term is $-$, use the factoring pattern $(x - p)(x - q)$ instead of $(x + p)(x + q)$. The equation becomes $(x - 4)(x - 9) = 0$ with solutions 4 and 9.

4b. Can the zero-product property be used to solve any quadratic equation? If so, explain why. If not, give an example of an equation that cannot be solved.

No; the equation $x^2 + 2x + 2 = 0$, for instance, cannot be solved because $x^2 + 2x + 2$ is not factorable.

Unit 8   310   Lesson 2

Questioning Strategies

- Why must you put the equation in standard form before solving? **To solve the equation by factoring and applying the zero-product property, you need to have 0 on one side of the equals sign.**

- How do you decide which factor pair to use? **Use the pair whose sum is 13.**

Avoid Common Errors

Students may try to solve quadratic equations by factoring without first putting the equation in standard form. One way to help students understand the importance of writing the equation in standard form is to ask them to explain the zero-product property and how it is used. Then ask them about the underlying assumption of the zero-product property. (The product of the factors must equal zero.) When students realize that the zero-product property can be applied only to an expression that equals zero, they will understand the importance of first writing the equation in standard form. Getting used to putting a quadratic equation in standard form as a first step will also help students later when they are using the quadratic formula.

EXTRA EXAMPLE
Find the solutions of $x^2 - 2x = 35$. **−5, 7**

Questioning Strategies

- When writing $x^2 - 4x - 12 = 0$ in the form $(x + p)(x - q) = 0$ where p and q are positive, which number, p or q, is greater? Why? **q is greater because the coefficient of the x-term is negative and equal to $p - q$, which is negative when $p > q$.**

- After writing $x^2 - 4x - 12 = 0$ in the form $(x + p)(x - q) = 0$, can you conclude that p and q are the zeros of the function? Explain. **No; you still have to apply the zero-product property and solve $x + p = 0$ and $x - q = 0$, which results in the zeros $-p$ and q.**

EXTRA EXAMPLE
Find the zeros of the function $f(x) = x^2 - 10x + 16$.
2, 8

CLOSE

Essential Question

How can you use factoring to solve quadratic equations in standard form when a = 1?
Trinomials can be factored into two binomials by finding factor pairs for the constant term and determining which factor pair sums to the coefficient of the x-term. Using the zero-product property, you can set each binomial equal to 0 and solve to get the solutions of the equation.

Summarize

Have students create a flowchart like the one below for factoring trinomials of the form $x^2 + bx + c$.

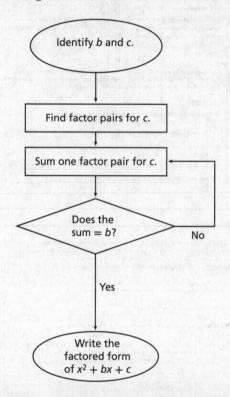

PRACTICE

Where skills are taught	Where skills are practiced
2 EXAMPLE	EXS. 1–10
4 EXAMPLE	EXS. 11–20
5 EXAMPLE	EXS. 21–24

5 EXAMPLE Finding the Zeros of a Quadratic Function

Find the zeros of $f(x) = x^2 - 4x - 12$.

A Set the function equal to 0 and recognize the factoring pattern.

$$x^2 - 4x - 12 = \boxed{0}$$

$$\left(x + p\right)\left(x - q\right) = \boxed{0}$$

Explain your choice of factoring pattern.

The constant term is negative, so one of its factors must be positive and the

other negative.

B Find the factors of -12 that have a sum of -4. Then write the equation in factored form.

Factors of -12	Sum of Factors
1 and -12	-11
2 and -6	-4
3 and -4	-1

So, the factored form of the equation is $\left(x + \boxed{2}\right)\left(x - \boxed{6}\right) = 0$.

C Use the zero-product property to solve the equation and identify the zeros.

$$x + \boxed{2} = 0 \qquad \text{or} \qquad x - \boxed{6} = 0$$

$$x = \boxed{-2} \qquad \text{or} \qquad x = \boxed{6}$$

So, the zeros of $f(x) = x^2 - 4x - 12$ are $\boxed{-2}$ and $\boxed{6}$.

REFLECT

5a. Show that each zero satisfies $f(x) = 0$.

$f(-2) = (-2)^2 - 4(-2) - 12 = 4 + 8 - 12 = 0$; $f(6) = 6^2 - 4(6) - 12 = 36 - 24 - 12 = 0$

5b. If you were to graph the function $f(x) = x^2 - 4x - 12$, what points would be associated with the zeros of the function? What is special about these points and their x-coordinates?

$(-2, 0)$ and $(6, 0)$; these points lie on the x-axis, so they are the points where the

graph intersects the x-axis, and their x-coordinates are the graph's x-intercepts.

PRACTICE

Complete the factorization of the polynomial.

1. $t^2 + 6t + 5 = (t + 5)(t + \boxed{1})$

2. $z^2 - 121 = (z + 11)(z - \boxed{11})$

3. $d^2 + 5d - 24 = (d + \boxed{8})(d - 3)$

4. $x^4 - 4 = (x^2 + \boxed{2})(x^2 - 2)$

Factor the polynomial.

5. $y^2 + 3y - 4$

$(y + 4)(y - 1)$

6. $x^2 - 2x + 1$

$(x - 1)^2$

7. $p^2 - 2p - 24$

$(p - 6)(p + 4)$

8. $g^2 - 100$

$(g - 10)(g + 10)$

9. $z^2 - 7z + 12$

$(z - 3)(z - 4)$

10. $q^2 + 25q + 100$

$(q + 20)(q + 5)$

Solve.

11. $m^2 + 8m + 16 = 0$

-4

12. $n^2 - 10n = 24$

$12, -2$

13. $x^2 + 25x = 0$

$0, -25$

14. $y^2 - 30 = 13y$

$15, -2$

15. $z^2 - 9 = 0$

$3, -3$

16. $p^2 = 54 - 3p$

$6, -9$

17. $x^2 + 11x - 42 = 0$

$3, -14$

18. $g^2 - 14g = 51$

$-3, 17$

19. $n^2 - 81 = 0$

$9, -9$

20. $y^2 = 25y$

$0, 25$

Find the zeros of the function.

21. $f(x) = x^2 + 11x + 30$

$-6, -5$

22. $f(x) = x^2 - x - 20$

$-4, 5$

23. $f(x) = x^2 + 6x - 7$

$-7, 1$

24. $f(x) = x^2 + 2x + 1$

-1

Solving $ax^2 + bx + c = 0$ by Factoring

Essential question: *How can you use factoring to solve $ax^2 + bx + c = 0$ when $a \neq 1$?*

∴COMMON∴ **Standards for**
∴CORE∴ **Mathematical Content**

CC.9-12.A.SSE.3 Choose and produce an equivalent form of an expression to reveal and explain properties of the quantity represented by the expression.*

CC.9-12.A.SSE.3a Factor a quadratic expression to reveal the zeros of the function it defines.*

CC.9-12.A.REI.4 Solve quadratic equations in one variable.

CC.9-12.A.REI.4b Solve quadratic equations by ... factoring ...

CC.9-12.F.IF.8 Write a function defined by an expression in different but equivalent forms to reveal and explain different properties of the function.

CC.9-12.F.IF.8a Use the process of factoring ... in a quadratic function to show zeros.

CC.9-12.F.BF.1 Write a function that describes a relationship between two quantities.*

CC.9-12.F.BF.1a Determine an explicit expression ... from a context.*

Prerequisites

Factoring $x^2 + bx + c = 0$, Lesson 8-2

Math Background

In the last lesson, students learned how to factor and solve equations of the form $x^2 + bx + c = 0$. In this lesson, students will factor and solve equations where the x^2-term has a coefficient other than 1.

Quadratic equations were first examined probably starting in Babylonia 4000 years ago. Around 800 BCE in India, geometric methods were used to solve quadratic equations. These methods were similar to the method of completing the square, which was developed between 300 and 200 BCE. (Students will study how to complete the square in Lessons 8-4 and 8-5.)

Both Euclid and Pythagoras grappled with finding a formula or procedure for solving quadratic equations. It was not until around 600 CE that the first explicit solution to the standard form of the equation was given, although it was not completely general. The practical notation using the symbols and methods currently in use was developed during the 15th century.

INTRODUCE

Conduct a warm-up exercise with students working individually or in pairs. To start, give them two numbers, for example, 6 and 4, and have them find the factor pairs for each number. Next, have them multiply one member of the factor pair for the first number by one member of the factor pair for the second number. Then, have them multiply the remaining two members of the factor pairs. Finally, have them sum the products. For instance, a factor pair of 6 is 2 and 3, a factor pair of 4 is 1 and 4, and $2 \cdot 4 + 3 \cdot 1 = 11$.

Now, give students a pair of numbers and have them find the sum of factor pair products as before, but this time with the goal of generating a specific number. Here are three examples of using factor pairs of the first two numbers to generate the third number.

A. 4 and 10 → 14 $2 \cdot 5 + 2 \cdot 2 = 14$

B. 3 and 21 → 16 $3 \cdot 3 + 1 \cdot 7 = 16$

C. 4 and 15 → −16 $2(-5) + 2(-3) = -16$

Note that in part C, students must recognize they can use two negative factors (−5 and −3) to obtain −16.

Name_____ Class_____ Date_____

Solving $ax^2 + bx + c = 0$ by Factoring

COMMON CORE
CC.9-12.A.SSE.3a,
CC.9-12.A.CED.1*,
CC.9-12.A.REL4,
CC.9-12.A.REL4b,
CC.9-12.F.IF.8a,
CC.9-12.F.BF.1*

Essential question: *How can you use factoring to solve $ax^2 + bx + c = 0$ when $a \neq 1$?*

You have learned how to factor $ax^2 + bx + c$ when $a = 1$ by identifying the correct pair of factors of c whose sum is b. But what if the coefficient of x^2 is not 1?

First, review binomial multiplication. The product $(2x + 5)(3x + 2)$ is found by using FOIL.

$$(2x + 5)(3x + 2) = 6x^2 + 4x + 15x + 10 = 6x^2 + 19x + 10$$
$$\text{F} \qquad \text{O} \quad \text{I} \qquad \text{L}$$

F The product of the coefficients of the **first** terms is a.

O
I } The sum of the coefficients of the **outer** and **inner** products is b.

L The product of the **last** terms is c.

To factor $ax^2 + bx + c$, you need to reverse this process. Start by listing the possible factor pairs of a and c. Then use trial and error to find a sum of b for the outer and inner products.

1 EXAMPLE Factoring $ax^2 + bx + c$

Factor $5n^2 + 11n + 2$.

A First list the possible factor pairs for both a and c. All of the signs of the terms are positive, so the factors of a and c must all be positive.

The only factor pair for a is __1__, __5__. The only factor pair for c is __1__, __2__.

B Choose the arrangement of the factor pairs that makes $b = 11$. Check your result by multiplying.

$$5n^2 + 11n + 2 = \left(\; 1 \; n + \; 2 \;\right)\left(\; 5 \; n + \; 1 \;\right)$$

REFLECT

1a. What other arrangement of factor pairs is possible for a and c? What is the resulting product, and how is it different from $5n^2 + 11n + 2$?

$(n + 1)(5n + 2)$; the product is $5n^2 + 7n + 2$; the middle term is different.

1b. If a is positive, b is negative, and c is positive, what are the signs of the factors of a and c that you are looking for?

The factors of a are both positive, and the factors of c are both negative.

Unit 8   313   Lesson 3

1c. If a is positive, b is negative, and c is negative, what are the signs of the factors of a and c that you are looking for?

Both factors of a are positive. One factor of c is positive. The other is negative.

If a and c have a lot of factors, there are many possible arrangements. One way to quickly check each arrangement is shown below, using the trinomial $5n^2 + 11n + 2$. List the factor pairs of a and c vertically, then multiply diagonally, and add.

Factors of a	Factors of c	Inner and Outer products
1	2	10
5	1	1
		$\overline{11}$ ← Sum

If the sum is correct, the factors are read across: $(1n + 2)$ and $(5n + 1)$.

2 EXAMPLE Factoring $ax^2 + bx + c$

Factor $6x^2 - 13x - 8$.

A First list the possible factor pairs for both a and c. Because c is negative, one of the factors of c must be positive, and the other must be negative.

The factor pairs for a are: __1__, __6__ and __2__, __3__.

The factor pairs for c are: __1__, __-8__; __-1__, __8__; __2__, __-4__; __-4__, __4__.

B Choose the arrangement of factor pairs that makes $b = -13$. Each factor pair of a can be arranged in two ways with each factor pair of c, so there are 16 possible arrangements. Three are shown below.

$$6x^2 - 13x - 8 = \left(\; 2 \; x + \; 1 \;\right)\left(\; 3 \; x - \; 8 \;\right)$$

REFLECT

2a. If you know the factors of $6x^2 - 13x - 8$, how could you easily factor $6x^2 + 13x - 8$?

Keep the terms of the factors the same, but switch the $+$ and $-$ signs.

2b. What fact about the sign of the sum can you use so that you need to test at most half of the possible arrangements?

If the sum is the correct number with the wrong sign, then the factors are

correct except that the negative sign is with the wrong factor of c.

Unit 8   314   Lesson 3

1 EXAMPLE

Questioning Strategies

- Why is there only one factor pair for a and for c? In both cases, the numbers are prime (5 for a and 2 for c), and the only factors of a prime number are itself and 1.

- Why are you looking for an arrangement of the factor pairs that makes $b = 11$? The coefficient of the middle term in the equation is 11, so b must equal 11 if the factoring is to be correct.

- If there are three factor pairs for a and one factor pair for c, how many possible arrangements of factor pairs are there? 6

EXTRA EXAMPLE

Factor $3x^2 + 10x + 7$. $(3x + 7)(x + 1)$

Teaching Strategy

In this example, since there is only factor pair for each number, determining how to arrange the numbers in the binomial is relatively easy. However, it can be difficult for students to keep track of all possible combinations and which ones they have already tried. An alternative to the method shown in 1 EXAMPLE is for students to make a table like the one below.

a	Possibilities for b	c
1, 5	$1 \cdot 1 + 5 \cdot 2 = 11$ ✓	1, 2
1, 5	$1 \cdot 2 + 5 \cdot 1 = 7$	2, 1

This will help students see that factor pairs can be combined in more than one way. Allotting two rows to each factor pair of a allows students to write both permutations of the factor pairs for c.

2 EXAMPLE

Questioning Strategies

- What is the difference between this example and the previous example? This example has negative values for b and c and more than one set of factor pairs for a and c.

- Why is one of the factors in each factor pair for c negative? Because c is negative, it must have one positive and one negative factor.

EXTRA EXAMPLE

Factor $4x^2 - 16x + 15$. $(2x - 5)(2x - 3)$

> ⋮ MATHEMATICAL **Highlighting**
> PRACTICE **the Standards**
>
> 2 EXAMPLE and its Reflect questions offer an opportunity to address Mathematical Practice Standard 7 (Look for and make use of structure). Students will need to recognize the factor pairs of a and c that give the correct value of b. They will need to take a structured approach to determining the factor pairs that result in the correct trinomial.
>
> In this lesson, students must also recognize that the zero-product property can be applied only to quadratic equations in standard form because the property cannot be applied to equations equal to a number other than zero.
>
> Recognizing special cases will help students solve problems quickly and efficiently.

3 EXAMPLE

Questioning Strategies

- Is $7x^2 + 20x = x + 6$ a quadratic equation? How can you tell? Yes; each side is a polynomial and the highest degree is 2.

- In step B of the example, one binomial has a plus sign, while the other has a minus sign. Why? The constant is negative, so its factors must have opposite signs, which leads to the factoring pattern $(mx + p)(nx - q)$ where p and q are positive.

EXTRA EXAMPLE

Solve $5x^2 = -3x^2 + 3x + 5$ by factoring.
$x = -\frac{5}{8}$; $x = 1$

To solve a quadratic equation by factoring, first rewrite the equation so one side equals 0, then factor. By the zero-product property, at least one of the factors must equal 0. Set each factor equal to 0 and solve each linear equation separately to find the solutions.

3 EXAMPLE Solving $ax^2 + bx + c = 0$ by Factoring

Solve $7x^2 + 20x = x + 6$ by factoring.

A Use the addition and subtraction properties of equality as needed to rewrite the equation so that one side equals 0.

$$\underline{7x^2 + 19x - 6} = 0$$

B Factor the left side of the equation.

$$\left(\boxed{1}\,x + \boxed{3}\right)\left(\boxed{7}\,x - \boxed{2}\right) = 0$$

C Set each factor equal to 0, and solve.

$$\boxed{1}\,x + \boxed{3} = 0 \qquad \text{or} \qquad \boxed{7}\,x - \boxed{2} = 0$$

$$x = -3 \qquad \text{or} \qquad x = \frac{2}{7}$$

REFLECT

3a. Why is it necessary to rewrite the equation so that one side equals 0 before factoring?

To use the zero-product property, the product of the factors must equal 0.

3b. How is solving the equation $7x^2 + 12x = x + 6$ like solving the equation in the Example and how is it different?

Sample answer: In both cases you first rewrite the equation so that one side equals 0 and then factor. Because the x-term is $11x$ rather than $19x$, you factor as $(7x - 3)(x + 2)$, and the solutions are -2 and $\frac{3}{7}$.

3c. How could you write a quadratic equation in standard form with solutions $x = \frac{1}{4}$ and $x = -\frac{3}{2}$?

Sample answer: Rewrite each solution as an equation with one side equal to 0: $4x - 1 = 0$ and $2x + 3 = 0$. The left side of each equation is a factor of the quadratic equation: $(4x - 1)(2x + 3) = 0$. Multiply using FOIL: $8x^2 + 10x - 3 = 0$.

© Houghton Mifflin Harcourt Publishing Company

Special Cases The following example includes some special cases to consider.

1. Always look for a common factor before you begin. If $c = 0$, then x is a common factor of $ax^2 + bx$.
2. Consider the perfect square trinomial and difference of squares patterns:
$$(a + b)^2 = a^2 + 2ab + b^2$$
$$(a - b)^2 = a^2 - 2ab + b^2$$
$$(a + b)(a - b) = a^2 - b^2$$

4 EXAMPLE Solving $ax^2 + bx + c = 0$ by Factoring

Solve the equation by factoring.

A $12x^2 + 6x - 6 = 0$

Both a and c have many factor pairs, so there are a lot of possible factors. However, notice that 6 is a common factor for each term.

$6\left(2x^2 + x - 1\right) = 0$	First, factor out the 6.
$6\left(x + 1\right)\left(2x - 1\right) = 0$	Factor the remaining trinomial.
$x + 1 = 0$ or $2x - 1 = 0$	Set each factor equal to 0.
$x = -1$ or $x = \frac{1}{2}$	Solve.

B $4x^2 - 25 = 0$

The left side of the equation has the form $a^2 - b^2$, a difference of squares.

$a^2 = 4x^2$, so $a = \underline{2x}$, and $b^2 = 25$, so $b = \underline{5}$.

$\left(2x + 5\right)\left(2x - 5\right) = 0$	Factor the difference of squares.
$2x + 5 = 0$ or $2x - 5 = 0$	Set each factor equal to 0.
$x = -\frac{5}{2}$ or $x = \frac{5}{2}$	Solve.

C $3x^2 + 9x = 0$

Because $c = 0$, x is a common factor. There is also a common factor of 3.

$3x\left(x + 3\right) = 0$	Factor out the common factor.
$3x = 0$ or $x + 3 = 0$	Set each factor equal to 0.
$x = 0$ or $x = -3$	Solve.

© Houghton Mifflin Harcourt Publishing Company

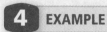

4 EXAMPLE

Questioning Strategies

• In part A, the first step is to factor out 6. What does that do to the number of factor pairs for a? It reduces the number from three factor pairs to one factor pair.

• What does factoring out 6 do to the number of factor pairs for c? It reduces the number from two factor pairs to one factor pair.

• How does factoring out 6 make the trinomial easier to factor? There are not as many factor pairs to check.

• How else could you solve the equation in part B? By using square roots; add 25 to both sides and then divide both sides by 4. Finally, apply the definition of square root.

EXTRA EXAMPLE

Solve by factoring.

A. $4x^2 + 10 = -14x$ $x = -2.5, x = -1$

B. $9x^2 = 121$ $x = -\frac{11}{3}; x = \frac{11}{3}$

C. $9y^2 = 81y$ $y = 0, y = 9$

5 EXAMPLE

Questioning Strategies

• What starting conditions are you given in the problem? $h = 3$ meters, and $v = 14$ meters per second

• What quantity are you looking for? time

EXTRA EXAMPLE

A child is tossing a ball up in the air and catching it. The equation that models the ball's height $h(t)$ above the child's hand as a function of time t is $h(t) = -5t^2 + vt$ where v is the initial upward velocity. If the initial upward velocity of the ball is 5 meters per second, for how long is the ball in the air before the child catches it again? **1 sec**

CLOSE

Essential Question

How can you use factoring to solve $ax^2 + bx + c = 0$ when $a \neq 1$?

Find factor pairs for a and c and determine which arrangement of factor pairs will produce b. Factor the equation and use the zero-product property to set each binomial factor equal to 0 and solve for x.

Summarize

Have students create a flowchart like the one below for factoring trinomials of the form $ax^2 + bx + c$.

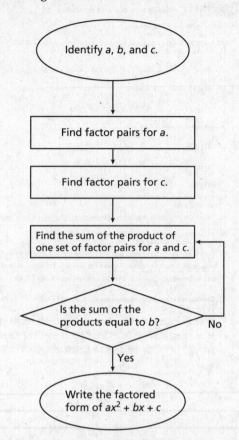

PRACTICE

Where skills are taught	Where skills are practiced
1 EXAMPLE	EXS. 1, 2
2 EXAMPLE	EXS. 3, 4
3 EXAMPLE	EXS. 5–9
4 EXAMPLE	EXS. 10–14
5 EXAMPLE	EX. 15

REFLECT

4a. Why can you ignore the common factor of 6 in Part A once it is factored out?

Because 6 cannot equal 0 it does not have to be considered as a solution.

4b. Why can't you ignore the common factor of $3x$ in part C?

Because $3x$ can equal 0 it has to be considered. $3x = 0$ implies $x = 0$.

5 EXAMPLE Modeling the Height of a Diver

Physics students are measuring the heights and times of divers jumping off diving boards. The function that models a diver's height (in meters) above the water is

$$h(t) = -5t^2 + vt + h_0$$

where v is the diver's initial upward velocity in meters per second, h_0 is the diver's height above the water in meters, and t is the time in seconds. A diver who is 3 meters above the water jumps off a diving board with an initial upward velocity of 14 m/s. How many seconds will it take for the diver to hit the water? That is, when does $h(t) = 0$?

A Write the equation $h(t) = 0$, substituting in known values. $\quad -5t^2 + \boxed{14}\ t + \boxed{3} = 0$

B Factor the left side of the equation. $\qquad \left(-t + 3\right)\left(5t + 1\right) = 0$

C Set each factor equal to zero and solve. $\qquad t = \dfrac{3}{}$ or $t = \dfrac{-0.2}{}$

D Which value of t makes sense in the context of the problem? Why?

$t = 3$, because the negative value represents a time before the diver jumped.

REFLECT

5a. Suppose a diver who is 10 meters above the water jumps off a diving board with an initial upward velocity of 5 m/s. How many seconds will it take for the diver to hit the water? Explain your reasoning.

2 seconds; you solve the equation $-5t^2 + 5t + 10 = 0$ by factoring to get

$-5(t - 2)(t + 1) = 0$ and setting the factors equal to 0. Only the positive

solution makes sense, which is $t = 2$ seconds.

5b. If an object is dropped, its initial velocity is 0. How would this affect the function that models the object's height?

The middle term would be 0, so the function would be $h(t) = -5t^2 + h_0$.

PRACTICE

Factor.

1. $2x^2 + 15x + 7$

$(2x + 1)(x + 7)$

2. $7z^2 - 30z + 27$

$(z - 3)(7z - 9)$

3. $8x^2 - 10x - 3$

$(4x + 1)(2x - 3)$

4. $30d^2 + 7d - 15$

$(6d + 5)(5d - 3)$

Solve by factoring.

5. $10g^2 + 23g + 12 = 0$

$-\dfrac{3}{2}, -\dfrac{4}{5}$

6. $5y^2 - 2y - 7 = 0$

$\dfrac{7}{5}, -1$

7. $2n^2 + 15 = 11n$

$\dfrac{5}{2}, 3$

8. $6a^2 + 10a = 3a + 10$

$\dfrac{5}{6}, -2$

9. $12x^2 - x = 20$

$\dfrac{4}{3}, -\dfrac{5}{4}$

10. $9z^2 - 25 = 0$

$\dfrac{5}{3}, -\dfrac{5}{3}$

11. $36h^2 - 12h + 1 = 0$

$\dfrac{1}{6}$

12. $12n^2 + 48 = 80n$

$6, \dfrac{2}{3}$

13. $18x^2 + 24x = -8$

$-\dfrac{2}{3}$

14. $12y^2 + 3y = 54$

$-\dfrac{9}{4}, 2$

15. A dolphin bounces a ball off its nose at an initial upward velocity of 6 m/s to a trainer lying on a 1-meter high platform. The function $h(t) = -5t^2 + vt$ models the ball's height (in meters) above the water, where v is the initial upward velocity of the ball in meters per second.

a. Write an equation to find the time when $h(t) = 1$.

$-5t^2 + \boxed{6}\ t = \boxed{1}$

b. Solve the equation to find the two values for t.

$t = \dfrac{0.2}{}$ or $t = \dfrac{1}{}$

c. Explain the two values for t in the context of the situation.

The ball will reach the trainer in 0.2 second. If the trainer misses, the ball

goes up, and comes back down, reaching the trainer again 1 second after

the dolphin bounces it.

Solving $x^2 + bx + c = 0$ by Completing the Square

Essential question: *How can you solve $x^2 + bx + c = 0$ without factoring?*

COMMON CORE

Standards for Mathematical Content

CC.9-12.A.REI.4 Solve quadratic equations in one variable.

CC.9-12.A.REI.4a Use the method of completing the square to transform any quadratic equation in x into an equation of the form $(x - p)^2 = q$ that has the same solutions ...

CC.9-12.A.REI.4b Solve quadratic equations by ... completing the square ...

Vocabulary
completing the square

Prerequisites
Solving $x^2 + bx + c = 0$ by factoring, Lesson 8-2

Math Background
Students have learned to solve quadratic equations by factoring. In this lesson and the next, students will learn to solve quadratic equations by completing the square. Note that these two lessons follow the same progression as that of the previous two: 1) completing the square when $a = 1$, and then 2) completing the square when $a \neq 1$.

It is important that students not only learn each method for solving quadratic equations but also learn to identify when a certain method is the best approach. Solving by factoring works well when there are not a lot of factor pairs to try or when the factors are obvious. Completing the square is a good method when the equation is difficult to factor or cannot be factored.

INTRODUCE

Conduct a warm-up exercise. Have students square the binomials below.

$(x + 1)^2$ $x^2 + 2x + 1$

$(x + 2)^2$ $x^2 + 4x + 4$

$(x + 3)^2$ $x^2 + 6x + 9$

$(x + 4)^2$ $x^2 + 8x + 16$

Ask leading questions until students have clearly indicated they recognize the pattern $(x + a)^2 = x^2 + 2ax + a^2$.

Then have students quickly square the binomials below. They should be able to use the pattern from above, just slightly adjusted.

$(x - 1)^2$ $x^2 - 2x + 1$

$(x - 2)^2$ $x^2 - 4x + 4$

$(x - 3)^2$ $x^2 - 6x + 9$

$(x - 4)^2$ $x^2 - 8x + 16$

Recognizing and internalizing these patterns will aid students as they learn to complete the square to solve quadratic equations.

1 EXPLORE

Materials
Algebra tiles

Questioning Strategies
- What shape do the algebra tiles make in the Explore activity? **a square**

- Why do you think adding the nine 1-tiles is called "completing the square"? **Without the 1-tiles, the diagram is not a complete square. Adding the tiles completes the square.**

- Can you complete a square using 1-tiles if you start with an x^2-tile and four x-tiles? If so, how? **Yes; add four 1-tiles.**

8-4

Name_____ Class_____ Date_____

Solving $x^2 + bx + c = 0$ by Completing the Square

COMMON CORE

CC.9-12.A.REI.4,
CC.9-12.A.REI.4a,
CC.9-12.A.REI.4b

Essential question: *How can you solve $x^2 + bx + c = 0$ without factoring?*

1 EXPLORE Completing the Square

The diagram below represents the expression $x^2 + 6x + c$ with the constant term missing.

A Complete the diagram by filling the bottom right corner with 1-tiles to form a square.

B How many 1-tiles did you add to the expression? __9__

C Write the trinomial represented by the algebra tiles for the complete square.

   $1\ x^2 + 6\ x + 9$

D You should recognize this trinomial as an example of the special case $(a + b)^2 = a^2 + 2ab + b^2$. Recall that trinomials of this form are called perfect square trinomials. Since the trinomial is a perfect square, you can factor it into two binomials that are the same.

   $1\ x^2 + 6\ x + 9 = \left(\ 1\ x + \ 3\ \right)^2$

REFLECT

1a. Look at the algebra tiles above. The x-tiles are divided equally, with 3 on the right and bottom sides of the x^2-tile. How does the number 3 relate to the total number of x-tiles? How does the number 3 relate to the number of 1-tiles you added?

   3 is half of 6. The number added, 9, is 3^2.

1b. How would algebra tiles be arranged to form a perfect square trinomial $x^2 + 8x + c$? How many 1-tiles must be added? How is this number related to the number of x-tiles?

   Arrange 4 x-tiles on the right and bottom sides of the x^2-tile. Add 16 1-tiles to complete the square. 16 is 4^2 and 4 is one-half the number of x-tiles.

© Houghton Mifflin Harcourt Publishing Company

Unit 8   319   Lesson 4

Completing the Square   Finding the value of c needed to make an expression such as $x^2 + 6x + c$ into a perfect square trinomial is called **completing the square**.

Using algebra tiles, half of the x-tiles are placed along the right and bottom sides of the x^2-tile. The number of 1-tiles added is the square of the number of x-tiles on either side of the x^2-tile.

To complete the square for the expression $x^2 + bx + c$, replace c with $\left(\frac{b}{2}\right)^2$. The perfect square trinomial is $x^2 + bx + \left(\frac{b}{2}\right)^2$ and factors as $\left(x + \frac{b}{2}\right)^2$.

2 EXAMPLE Completing the Square

Complete the square to form a perfect square trinomial. Then factor the trinomial.

A $x^2 + 12x + c$

   Identify b. $b = \underline{\ 12\ }$

   Find c. $c = \left(\frac{b}{2}\right)^2 = \left(\frac{12}{2}\right)^2 = \underline{\ 6\ }$

   Write the trinomial. $x^2 + 12x + 36$

   Factor the trinomial. $x^2 + 12x + 36 = \left(\ x + 6\ \right)^2$

B $z^2 - 26z + c$

   Identify b. $b = \underline{\ -26\ }$

   Find c. $c = \left(\frac{b}{2}\right)^2 = \left(\frac{-26}{2}\right)^2 = \underline{\ 169\ }$

   Write the trinomial. $z^2 + \underline{-26}\ z + \underline{169}$

   Factor the trinomial. $z^2 + \underline{-26}\ z + \underline{169} = \left(\ z - 13\ \right)^2$

REFLECT

2a. In Part A, b is positive and in Part B, b is negative. Does this affect the sign of c? Why or why not?

   The sign of b has no effect on the sign of c because $c = \left(\frac{b}{2}\right)^2$ and a nonzero number

   squared is always positive. Thus, c is always positive.

2b. How can you confirm that you have factored each trinomial correctly?

   Use FOIL to square the binomial to make sure that the result is equal to the

   trinomial being factored.

© Houghton Mifflin Harcourt Publishing Company

Unit 8   320   Lesson 4

Teaching Strategy

At the end of the Explore, ask students how the constant is related to the coefficient of x in the trinomial $x^2 + 2ax + a^2$. They should recognize that the constant is the square of half of the coefficient of x. This is the pattern students should have internalized in the warm-up activity.

TEACH

2 EXAMPLE

Questioning Strategies

- For the standard form of a quadratic expression, describe b in words. It is the coefficient of x. For the standard form of a quadratic expression, describe c in words. It is the constant term.

- For a perfect square trinomial, what is the mathematical relationship between b and c? $c = \left(\frac{b}{2}\right)^2$

EXTRA EXAMPLE

Complete the square to form a perfect square trinomial. Then factor the expression.

A. $x^2 + 36x + c$ $x^2 + 36x + 324 = (x + 18)^2$

B. $z^2 - 8z + c$ $z^2 - 8z + 16 = (z - 4)^2$

3 ENGAGE

Questioning Strategies

- Do you use the zero-product property to solve when completing the square? Explain. No. This equation is not equal to zero on one side. Instead of using the zero-product property, you apply the definition of square root.

- Why is applying the definition of square root a good way to solve these equations? Because you first make one side a perfect square trinomial, you end up with an equation of the form (expression)^2 = number, and the definition of square root tells you that what is being squared must be a square root of the number as long as the number is nonnegative.

Differentiated Instruction

When solving an equation like $x^2 + 4x = 5$, students can use algebra tiles to complete the square on $x^2 + 4x$. If they need further visualization, they can use a large "=" and construct the entire equation using algebra tiles. When they add 4 to one side of the equation to complete the square, they need to add 4 to the other side to maintain the equality. They should form a square with nine 1-tiles so that they can compare the side lengths of the two squares. On the left, the side length is $x + 2$, while on the right, the side length is 3, so $x + 2 = 3$. Point out that thinking in terms of lengths means that the other possibility, $x + 2 = -3$, is overlooked.

> ⋮ **MATHEMATICAL PRACTICE**   **Highlighting the Standards**
>
> **3 ENGAGE** and its Reflect questions offer an opportunity to address Mathematical Practice Standard 6 (Attend to precision). Students will need to be precise with their terminology regarding the coefficients and constants in the quadratic equation and with the numbers they are adding to both sides.
>
> Students will need to recognize and internalize the fact that the symbols a, b, and c represent specific things, such as b being the coefficient of x. At times, different students may use different symbols. As long as they stay consistent, they should be able to explain their work to others using what the symbols represent.

4 EXAMPLE

Questioning Strategies

- How is the first step in solving a quadratic equation by completing the square different from solving one by factoring? The first step when completing the square is to put the variable terms on one side of the equation and the constant on the other. When factoring, the first step is to put the equation in standard form.

- Will the number added to both sides of $x^2 + bx = c$ always be positive? Explain. Yes; even if the coefficient of x is negative, since you ultimately square half of a number you will always add a positive number to both sides.

3 ENGAGE — Solving Quadratic Equations by Completing the Square

You have solved quadratic equations by factoring and using the zero-product property. You can also solve quadratic equations by completing the square. This method is especially useful if the quadratic equation is difficult or impossible to factor. To solve a quadratic equation by completing the square, follow these steps:

1. Write the equation in the form $x^2 + bx = c$.

2. Complete the square by adding $\left(\frac{b}{2}\right)^2$ to both sides of the equation.

3. Factor the perfect square trinomial.

4. Apply the definition of a square root.

5. Write two equations, one using the positive square root and one using the negative square root.

6. Solve both equations.

REFLECT

3a. Which property explains why you need to add $\left(\frac{b}{2}\right)^2$ to both sides of the equation?

Addition Property of Equality

3b. What would be the first two steps in solving $x^2 + 10x - 11 = 0$ by completing the square?

First, add 11 to both sides to get $x^2 + 10x = 11$. Then add $\left(\frac{10}{2}\right)^2 = 25$ to both sides to get $x^2 + 10x + 25 = 36$.

3c. Could you use another method besides completing the square to solve the equation $x^2 + 10x - 11 = 0$? If so, describe how you would apply the alternate method.

Yes; you could factor the trinomial and use the zero-product property.

You would get $(x + 11)(x - 1) = 0$, and the solutions are -11 and 1.

3d. How would you apply the definition of a square root to eliminate the exponent in the equation $(x + 5)^2 = 36$?

If $a^2 = b$, then a is a square root of b. So, because $(x + 5)^2 = 36$,

$x + 5 = \pm\sqrt{36}$, which can be written $x + 5 = \pm 6$.

3e. Look at step 4 above. Explain why there can be two, one, or zero real solutions of a quadratic equation.

If the right side of the equation is positive, it has a positive square root and

a negative square root. If it is zero, there is only one square root, and if it is

negative, there is no real square root.

---

4 EXAMPLE — Solving Quadratic Equations by Completing the Square

Solve the equation by completing the square.

A $x^2 - 2x - 1 = 0$

Write the equation in the form $x^2 + bx = c$.	$x^2 - 2x = 1$
Add $\left(\frac{b}{2}\right)^2$ to both sides of the equation.	$x^2 - 2x + 1 = 1 + 1$
Factor the perfect square trinomial.	$(x - 1)^2 = 2$
Apply the definition of a square root.	$x - 1 = \pm\sqrt{2}$
Write two equations.	$x - 1 = \sqrt{2}$ or $x - 1 = -\sqrt{2}$
Solve the equations.	$1 + \sqrt{2},\ 1 - \sqrt{2}$

B $x^2 - 8x + 16 = 0$

Write the equation in the form $x^2 + bx = c$.	$x^2 - 8x = -16$
Add $\left(\frac{b}{2}\right)^2$ to both sides of the equation.	$x^2 - 8x + 16 = -16 + 16$
Factor the perfect square trinomial.	$(x - 4)^2 = 0$
Apply the definition of a square root.	$x - 4 = \pm\sqrt{0}$
Write two equations.	$x - 4 = 0$ or $x - 4 = 0$
Solve the equations.	4

REFLECT

4a. Can you solve either equation by factoring? If so, which method is easier?

The equation $x^2 - 2x - 1 = 0$ cannot be solved by factoring. The equation

$x^2 - 8x + 16 = 0$ can more easily be solved by factoring the left side as $(x - 4)^2$.

Set $x - 4$ equal to 0 and solve to get $x = 4$.

4b. Use completing the square to explain why $x^2 - 2x + 3 = 0$ has no solution.

First, rewrite the equation as $x^2 - 2x = -3$. Adding 1 to both sides to complete the

square gives $x^2 - 2x + 1 = -3 + 1$. Factoring the left side results in $(x - 1)^2 = -2$.

The right side is negative, so it has no real square roots. There are no real solutions.

4c. What method would you use to solve the equation $x^2 + 3x - 4 = 0$? Explain why you would choose this method.

Sample answer: Factor and apply the zero-product property. This method is easier

because the trinomial can be factored and completing the square when b is odd

involves fractions.

Notes

Solve the equation by completing the square.

A. $x^2 + 4x - 6 = 0$ $x = -2 \pm \sqrt{10}$

B. $x^2 - 10x + 5 = 0$ $x = 5 \pm 2\sqrt{5}$

Avoid Common Errors

Students often forget to add $\left(\frac{b}{2}\right)^2$ to *both* sides of the equation. To help students remember to do this, when they write the equation with the variable terms on one side and the constant on the other side, have them leave room for $\left(\frac{b}{2}\right)^2$ on both sides and put in + signs immediately as a reminder. Example:

$x^2 - 2x - 1 = 0$

$x^2 - 2x + \underline{\hspace{1cm}} = 1 + \underline{\hspace{1cm}}$

The blank line on each side of the equation is a visual reminder to add $\left(\frac{b}{2}\right)^2$ to *both* sides of the equation.

CLOSE

Essential Question

How can you solve $x^2 + bx + c = 0$ without factoring?

You can solve $x^2 + bx + c = 0$ by completing the square. Move the constant to one side of the equation. Then add a constant to both sides. The constant is chosen to make a perfect square trinomial. In the case when $a = 1$, that constant is $\left(\frac{b}{2}\right)^2$. Once the trinomial is written as the square of a binomial, the definition of square root can be invoked (provided the constant on the other side is nonnegative), resulting in the binomial being equal to plus or minus the square root of the constant. By considering each case (positive square root, negative square root) separately, you can finish solving for *x*.

Summarize

Have students write a journal entry about completing the square. They should describe patterns they expect to see as they go through the process.

PRACTICE

Where skills are taught	Where skills are practiced
1 EXPLORE	EX. 1
2 EXAMPLE	EXS. 2–5
4 EXAMPLE	EXS. 6–15

PRACTICE

1. The diagram represents the expression $x^2 + 4x + c$ with the constant term missing. Complete the square by filling in the bottom right corner with 1-tiles, and write the expression as a trinomial and in factored form.

$x^2 + 4x + 4; (x + 2)^2$

Complete the square to form a perfect square trinomial. Then factor the trinomial.

2. $m^2 + 10m +$ ⬚25⬚

$(m + 5)^2$

3. $g^2 - 20g +$ ⬚100⬚

$(g - 10)^2$

4. $y^2 + 2y +$ ⬚1⬚

$(y + 1)^2$

5. $w^2 - 11w + \dfrac{121}{4}$

$\left(w - \dfrac{11}{2}\right)^2$

Solve the equation by completing the square.

6. $s^2 + 15s = -56$

$-7, -8$

7. $r^2 - 4r = 165$

$15, -11$

8. $y^2 + 19y + 78 = 0$

$-6, -13$

9. $x^2 - 19x + 84 = 0$

$7, 12$

10. $t^2 + 2t - 224 = 0$

$14, -16$

11. $x^2 + 18x - 175 = 0$

$-25, 7$

12. $g^2 + 3g = -6$

no real solutions

13. $p^2 - 3p = 18$

$6, -3$

14. $z^2 = 6z - 2$

$3 + \sqrt{7}, 3 - \sqrt{7}$

15. $x^2 + 25 = 10x$

5

© Houghton Mifflin Harcourt Publishing Company

Solving $ax^2 + bx + c = 0$ by Completing the Square

Essential question: *How can you solve $ax^2 + bx + c = 0$ by completing the square when $a \neq 1$?*

COMMON **Standards for**
CORE **Mathematical Content**

CC.9-12.A.REI.4 Solve quadratic equations in one variable.

CC.9-12.A.REI.4a Use the method of completing the square to transform any quadratic equation in x into an equation of the form $(x - p)^2 = q$ that has the same solutions. ...

CC.9-12.A.REI.4b Solve quadratic equations by ... completing the square ...

Prerequisites

Solving $x^2 + bx + c = 0$ by completing the square, Lesson 8-4

Math Background

This lesson builds on the previous lesson. The difference is that a is no longer required to be 1. Drawing on the similarities of the previous lesson will be very helpful for students. The method of completing the square taught in this lesson prepares students to derive the quadratic formula in Lesson 8-6.

INTRODUCE

Conduct a warm-up exercise to review completing the square when $a = 1$ and to generate perfect square trinomials.

Have students complete the square for the expressions below.

$x^2 - 2x + c$ **1**

$x^2 + 8x + c$ **16**

$x^2 + 20x + c$ **100**

$x^2 - 100x + c$ **2500**

Next, have students square the binomials below.

$(2x + 1)^2$ **$4x^2 + 4x + 1$**

$(3x + 2)^2$ **$9x^2 + 12x + 4$**

$(5x + 3)^2$ **$25x^2 + 30x + 9$**

$(3x + 4)^2$ **$9x^2 + 24x + 16$**

TEACH

1 EXPLORE

Materials
Algebra tiles

Questioning Strategies

- What final shape do the algebra tiles make in the Explore? **a square**

- What shape do the x^2-tiles make? **a square** What does this tell you about the number of x^2-tiles that must be present to complete the square? **The number of x^2-tiles must be a perfect square.**

2 EXAMPLE

Questioning Strategies

- What is the purpose of adding a number to both sides in step A? **To make the left side a perfect square trinomial**

- Compare the numbers you add to make the trinomial a perfect square when $a = 1$ and when $a \neq 1$. How are the numbers related? **The number you add when $a \neq 1$ is $\left(\frac{b^2}{4a}\right)$. When $a = 1$, the number becomes $\left(\frac{b^2}{4 \cdot 1}\right)$ or $\left(\frac{b}{2}\right)^2$. So, the number added when $a = 1$ is the simplified version of what is added when $a \neq 1$.**

EXTRA EXAMPLE
Solve $9x^2 - 6x = 8$ by completing the square.
$x = -\frac{2}{3}, x = \frac{4}{3}$

8-5

Name_____ Class_____ Date_____

Solving $ax^2 + bx + c = 0$ by Completing the Square

COMMON CORE

CC.9-12.A.REI.4
CC.9-12.A.REI.4a
CC.9-12.A.REI.4b

Essential question: *How can you solve $ax^2 + bx + c = 0$ by completing the square when $a \neq 1$?*

You already know how to complete the square to solve equations of the form $x^2 + bx = c$. To solve equations of the form $ax^2 + bx = c$ where $a \neq 1$ by completing the square, you could divide each term by a to eliminate the coefficient of x^2. However, in this lesson you will explore a direct method for solving $ax^2 + bx = c$ where $a \neq 1$ by completing the square.

1 EXPLORE Completing the Square for $ax^2 + bx$ when $a \neq 1$

A Refer to the algebra tile diagram shown below. Which expression is represented by the tiles?

$4x^2 + 8x$

Complete the square by filling the bottom right corner with 1-tiles. How many 1-tiles did you add to the diagram? ___4___

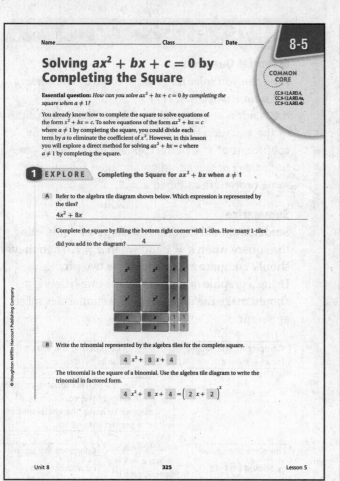

B Write the trinomial represented by the algebra tiles for the complete square.

$4\,x^2 + 8\,x + 4$

The trinomial is the square of a binomial. Use the algebra tile diagram to write the trinomial in factored form.

$4\,x^2 + 8\,x + 4 = \left(2\,x + 2\right)^2$

© Houghton Mifflin Harcourt Publishing Company

REFLECT

1a. The coefficient of x^2 in the trinomial is 4. What is it about the number 4 that makes it possible to arrange the x^2-tiles as shown to complete the square?

4 is a perfect square, allowing the x^2-tiles to be arranged in a square.

1b. When you complete the square for $ax^2 + bx$ with $a \neq 1$, is the number you add $\left(\frac{b}{2}\right)^2$? Why or why not?

No; if $a \neq 1$, $ax^2 + bx + \frac{b^2}{4}$ is not a perfect square trinomial.

Completing the Square when a is a Perfect Square To find the value of c for which $ax^2 + bx + c$ is a perfect square when a is a perfect square, write $ax^2 + bx + c = (mx + n)^2$. Use FOIL to multiply $(mx + n)^2$, and compare the coefficients.

$$ax^2 + bx + c = (mx + n)^2$$
$$= m^2x^2 + 2mnx + n^2$$

Corresponding coefficients must be equal, so $a = m^2$, $b = 2mn$, and $c = n^2$. Thus, $m = \sqrt{a}$ and $n = \frac{b}{2m} = \frac{b}{2\sqrt{a}}$. The constant term, c, is $n^2 = \left(\frac{b}{2\sqrt{a}}\right)^2 = \frac{b^2}{4a}$. (Alternately, $m = -\sqrt{a}$ and $n = -\frac{b}{2\sqrt{a}}$. However, this does not change the overall result, so you need only consider the case of $m = \sqrt{a}$.)

2 EXAMPLE Solving $ax^2 + bx = c$ when a is a Perfect Square

Solve $4x^2 + 8x = 21$ by completing the square.

A Add $\frac{b^2}{4a}$ to both sides of the equation. Since $a = \underline{4}$ and $b = \underline{8}$, $\frac{b^2}{4a} = \frac{\underline{8}^2}{4\left(\underline{4}\right)} = \underline{4}$.

$4x^2 + 8x + \underline{4} = 21 + \underline{4}$

B Factor the left side of the equation as a perfect square trinomial.

$\left(\underline{2}\,x + \underline{2}\right)^2 = \underline{25}$

C Apply the definition of a square root. Write two equations, and solve each equation to find the two solutions.

$\left(\underline{2}\,x + \underline{2}\right) = \pm\,\underline{5}$

$\underline{2}\,x + \underline{2} = \underline{5}$ or $\underline{2}\,x + \underline{2} = -\,\underline{5}$

$x = \underline{1.5}$ or $x = \underline{-3.5}$

© Houghton Mifflin Harcourt Publishing Company

2 EXAMPLE and its Reflect questions offer an opportunity to address Mathematical Practice Standard 6 (Attend to precision). As with the last lesson, students will need to be precise with their terminology regarding the coefficients and constants in the quadratic equation and with the numbers they are multiplying by or adding to both sides.

Students will need to recognize and internalize the fact that the symbols a, b, and c represent specific things, such as b being the coefficient of x. At times, different students may use different symbols. As long as they stay consistent, they should be able to explain their work to others using what the symbols represent.

3 EXAMPLE

Questioning Strategies

- What are the first ten perfect squares, starting with 1? **1, 4, 9, 16, 25, 36, 49, 64, 81, 100**

- When solving $ax^2 + bx = c$ by completing the square, does c need to be a perfect square? **no**

EXTRA EXAMPLE

Solve $12x^2 + 4x = 7$. Leave your answer in exact form.

$$x = \frac{-1 \pm \sqrt{22}}{6}$$

CLOSE

Essential Question

How can you solve $ax^2 + bx + c = 0$ by completing the square when $a \neq 1$?

If a is not a perfect square, first multiply both sides of the equation by a number that will make the coefficient of x^2 a perfect square. Next, add $\frac{b^2}{4a}$ to both sides of the equation and then follow the same procedure as when $a = 1$.

Summarize

Students should describe the steps for completing the square when $a = 1$ and when $a \neq 1$. Then they should compare and contrast the two processes. Using a graphic organizer like the one below should make the differences and similarities more apparent.

Completing the square for $x^2 + bx = c$		Completing the square for $ax^2 + bx = c$
No matching step		If a is not a perfect square, multiply both sides of the equation by a number to make the coefficient of x^2 a perfect square.
Complete the square by adding $\left(\frac{b}{2}\right)^2$ to both sides.	Number added when $a = 1$ is a special case of number added when $a \neq 1$.	Complete the square by adding $\frac{b^2}{4a}$ to both sides.
Factor the perfect square trinomial.	Same	Factor the perfect square trinomial.
Apply the definition of square root.	Same	Apply the definition of square root.
Write two equations.	Same	Write two equations.
Solve both equations.	Same	Solve both equations.

PRACTICE

Where skills are taught	Where skills are practiced
2 EXAMPLE	EXS. 1–4
3 EXAMPLE	EXS. 5–6

Exercise 7: Students write a quadratic equation to model a real-world situation and solve it by completing the square.

REFLECT

2a. Compare the steps for solving an equation of the form $ax^2 + bx = c$ when $a \neq 1$ and a is a perfect square with solving $x^2 + bx = c$.

When solving $ax^2 + bx = c$, you add $\frac{b^2}{4a}$ to both sides of the equation. When solving $x^2 + bx = c$, you add $\left(\frac{b}{2}\right)^2 = \frac{b^2}{4}$ to both sides of the equation. If $a = 1$, the added terms are the same. The remaining steps are the same for both equations.

2b. Why does a have to be a perfect square for this procedure to work?

If a is not a perfect square, then $ax^2 + bx$ plus the added constant term cannot be factored as the square of a binomial.

Completing the Square when a is Not a Perfect Square To find the value of c for which $ax^2 + bx + c$ is a perfect square when a is not a perfect square, you can multiply each term by a number that makes the coefficient of x^2 be a perfect square. One possible value is a. Remember that when you are solving an equation by completing the square, you need to multiply both sides by a. Then solve in the same manner as before.

3 E X A M P L E   Solving $ax^2 + bx = c$ when a is Not a Perfect Square

Solve $2x^2 + 6x = 5$. Leave your answer in exact form.

A The coefficient of x^2 is not a perfect square. Multiply both sides by 2.

$$2(2x^2 + 6x) = 2(5)$$

$$\boxed{4}\ x^2 + \boxed{12}\ x = 10$$

B Add $\frac{b^2}{4a}$ to both sides of the equation. In this case, $\frac{b^2}{4a} = \frac{12^2}{4(\boxed{4})} = \boxed{9}$.

$$\boxed{4}\ x^2 + \boxed{12}\ x + \boxed{9} = 10 + \boxed{9}$$

C Factor the left side of the equation as a perfect square trinomial.

$$\left(\boxed{2}\ x + \boxed{3}\right)^2 = 19$$

D Apply the definition of a square root. Write two equations, and solve each equation to find the two solutions.

$$\left(\boxed{2}\ x + \boxed{3}\right) = \pm\sqrt{19}$$

$$\boxed{2}\ x + \boxed{3} = \sqrt{19} \quad \text{or} \quad \boxed{2}\ x + \boxed{3} = -\sqrt{19}$$

$$x = \frac{\sqrt{19} - 3}{2} \quad \text{or} \quad x = \frac{-\sqrt{19} - 3}{2}$$

REFLECT

3a. Why is 2 the best value to multiply both sides of the equation by before completing the square? Are other values possible? Explain.

The value 2 creates the smallest perfect square coefficient of x^2 and is easiest to compute with. Other values of the form $2n^2$, where n is a whole number greater than 1, are possible.

3b. You want to solve $12x^2 - 3x = 51$ by completing the square. What is the smallest whole number you could multiply 12 by? Explain.

3; multiplying 12 by 3 results in 36, a perfect square.

PRACTICE

Solve the equation by completing the square.

1. $9z^2 + 48z = 36$

$$\frac{2}{3}, -6$$

2. $49x^2 + 28x = 60$

$$\frac{6}{7}, -\frac{10}{7}$$

3. $121r^2 - 44r = 5$

$$-\frac{1}{11}, \frac{5}{11}$$

4. $4x^2 + 20x - 11 = 0$

$$\frac{1}{2}, -\frac{11}{2}$$

5. $2x^2 + 9 = 9x$

$$3, \frac{3}{2}$$

6. $3x^2 + 4x = 20$

$$\frac{4}{3}, -5$$

7. A carpenter is making the tabletop shown below. The surface area will be 24 square feet.

a. Write an equation to represent this situation.

$$(3x + 2)(x + 1) = 24$$

b. Solve the equation. Which solution(s) make sense in this situation? Explain.

$2, -\frac{11}{3}$; 2; only the positive solution produces positive side lengths.

c. What are the dimensions of the tabletop?

8 ft by 3 ft

Deriving the Quadratic Formula

Essential question: *What is the quadratic formula and how can you derive it from $ax^2 + bx + c = 0$?*

Standards for Mathematical Content

CC.9-12.A.REI.4 Solve quadratic equations in one variable.

CC.9-12.A.REI.4a Use the method of completing the square to transform any quadratic equation in x into an equation of the form $(x - p)^2 = q$ that has the same solutions. Derive the quadratic formula from this form.

CC.9-12.A.REI.4b Solve quadratic equations by ... completing the square ...

Vocabulary
quadratic formula

Prerequisites
Solving $ax^2 + bx + c = 0$ when $a \neq 1$, Lesson 8-5

Math Background
The quadratic formula can be used to solve any quadratic equation, including those that arise from finding the zeros of a quadratic function or the x-intercepts of a quadratic function's graph. The derivation of the quadratic formula is a direct application of completing the square.

INTRODUCE

Remind students of the steps for completing the square for $ax^2 + bx = c$ when a is not a perfect square. Explain to them that they will be completing the square on the general equation, an equation with letters instead of numbers.

TEACH

 **EXPLORE**

Questioning Strategies
- In step C, what is the coefficient of x^2? $4a^2$
- What is the coefficient of x? $4ab$
- If you square the coefficient of x and divide it by 4 times the coefficient of x^2, what do you get? b^2

Teaching Strategy
To help students follow the derivation of the quadratic formula, you may want to have students assign specific values to a, b, and c and show what each step of the derivation looks like in terms of those values to check the reasonableness of those steps.

MATHEMATICAL PRACTICE | **Highlighting the Standards**

1 EXPLORE and its Reflect questions offer an opportunity to address Mathematical Practice Standard 2 (Reason abstractly and quantitatively). Students will perform a derivation of the quadratic formula. They will be working with the general form of the quadratic equation—all letters and no numbers. The Reflect questions will specifically ask students to explain the steps in the derivation and even derive the formula in another way.

CLOSE

Essential Question
What is the quadratic formula and how can you derive it from $ax^2 + bx + c = 0$?
$x = \dfrac{-b \pm \sqrt{b^2 - 4ac}}{2a}$; it is derived by completing the square on the standard form of a quadratic equation, $ax^2 + bx + c = 0$.

Summarize
Have students write the steps of the derivation and then write the description of each step (such as "apply the definition of square root") next to the step.

Name_____ Class_____ Date_____

8-6

Deriving the Quadratic Formula

COMMON CORE

CC.9-12.A.REI.4
CC.9-12.A.REI.4a
CC.9-12.A.REI.4b

Essential question: *What is the quadratic formula and how can you derive it from $ax^2 + bx + c = 0$?*

You have learned how to solve quadratic equations by completing the square. In this lesson, you will complete the square on the general form of a quadratic equation to derive a formula that can be used to solve any quadratic equation.

1 EXPLORE   Deriving the Quadratic Formula

Solve the general form of the quadratic equation, $ax^2 + bx + c = 0$, by completing the square to find the values of x in terms of a, b, and c.

A   Subtract c from both sides of the equation.

$$ax^2 + bx = -c$$

B   Multiply both sides of the equation by $4a$ to make the coefficient of x^2 a perfect square.

$$4a^2x^2 + 4ab\,x = -4ac$$

C   Add b^2 to both sides of the equation to complete the square. Then write the trinomial as the square of a binomial.

$$4a^2x^2 + 4abx + b^2 = -4ac + b^2$$

$$\left(\,2ax + b\,\right)^2 = b^2 - 4ac$$

D   Apply the definition of a square root and solve for x.

$$2ax + b = \pm\sqrt{\,b^2 - 4ac\,}$$

$$2ax = -\,b\,\pm\sqrt{\,b^2 - 4ac\,}$$

$$x = \frac{-b \pm \sqrt{b^2 - 4ac}}{2a}$$

The formula $x = \frac{-b \pm \sqrt{b^2 - 4ac}}{2a}$ is called the **quadratic formula**.
For any quadratic equation written in standard form, $ax^2 + bx + c = 0$,
the quadratic formula gives the solutions of the equation.

REFLECT

1a. In Part B, why did you multiply both sides of the equation by $4a$?

To make the coefficient of x^2 a perfect square. It would also be possible

to multiply by a.

1b. In Part C, explain why you added b^2 to each side to complete the square.

To make a perfect square trinomial, you add the square of the coefficient of x

divided by the product of 4 and the coefficient of x^2, which is $\frac{(4ab)^2}{4(4a^2)} = \frac{16a^2b^2}{16a^2} = b^2$.

1c. Provided the expression under the radical sign, $b^2 - 4ac$, is positive, how many solutions will the quadratic formula give for a quadratic equation? Explain.

Two; when you apply the definition of a square root, you get both a positive

and a negative square root. This results in two solutions.

1d. If the expression under the radical sign, $b^2 - 4ac$, is 0, how many solutions will the quadratic formula give for a quadratic equation? What if the expression is negative?

One solution; no real solutions

1e. Another method of deriving the quadratic formula is to first divide each term by a, and then complete the square. Complete the derivation below. (In this derivation, you will use the quotient property of square roots, which says that $\sqrt{\frac{a}{b}} = \frac{\sqrt{a}}{\sqrt{b}}$. For a square root of a fraction, this property allows you to simplify the numerator and denominator separately. For instance, $\sqrt{\frac{5}{9}} = \frac{\sqrt{5}}{\sqrt{9}} = \frac{\sqrt{5}}{3}$.)

$ax^2 + bx + c = 0$	
$ax^2 + bx = -c$	Subtract c from both sides.
$x^2 + \dfrac{b}{a}x = -\dfrac{c}{a}$	Divide each term by a.
$x^2 + \dfrac{b}{a}x + \left(\dfrac{b}{2a}\right)^2 = \left(\dfrac{b}{2a}\right)^2 - \dfrac{c}{a}$	Add $\left(\dfrac{b}{2a}\right)^2$ to both sides to complete the square.
$\left(x + \dfrac{b}{2a}\right)^2 = \dfrac{b^2 - 4ac}{4a^2}$	Factor the left side, and write the right side as a single fraction.
$x + \dfrac{b}{2a} = \pm\sqrt{\dfrac{b^2 - 4ac}{4a^2}}$	Apply the definition of a square root.
$x + \dfrac{b}{2a} = \pm\dfrac{\sqrt{b^2 - 4ac}}{\sqrt{4a^2}}$	Apply the quotient property of radicals.
$x + \dfrac{b}{2a} = \pm\dfrac{\sqrt{b^2 - 4ac}}{2a}$	Simplify the radical in the denominator.
$x = \dfrac{-b \pm \sqrt{b^2 - 4ac}}{2a}$	Solve for x.

Using the Quadratic Formula

Essential question: *How do you solve quadratic equations using the quadratic formula?*

COMMON CORE Standards for Mathematical Content

CC.9-12.A.CED.1* Create equations ... in one variable and use them to solve problems.

CC.9-12.A.REI.4 Solve quadratic equations in one variable.

CC.9-12.A.REI.4b Solve quadratic equations by ... the quadratic formula ...

Vocabulary
discriminant

Prerequisites
Quadratic formula, Lesson 8-6

Math Background
The quadratic formula can be used to solve any quadratic equation, but it is not always the quickest or easiest method. Students should learn when to apply it and when to use other methods. In Algebra 2, the formula will provide the basis for solving quadratic equations with imaginary solutions.

INTRODUCE

Remind students of the formula for finding the slope of a line and the importance of substituting the x- and y-values appropriately. Inform students that using the quadratic formula will require the same attention to detail in identifying quantities and keeping track of signs.

TEACH

1 ENGAGE

Questioning Strategies

- Look at the quadratic formula. Why does it generate two solutions? **The plus or minus sign in front of the square root indicates that you must both add and subtract the square root. This gives two solutions.**

- What are the steps for solving a quadratic equation by using the quadratic formula? **First, write the equation in standard form. Next, identify the values of a, b, and c. Then, substitute into the quadratic formula. Finally, simplify.**

2 EXAMPLE

Questioning Strategies

- Look at the equation in part A. What is another method that you could use to solve it? Explain. **Factoring; the equation is factorable and factors as $(3x + 4)(2x - 1)$.**

- Is the discriminant for part A positive, negative, or zero? **positive** How many real solutions do you expect? **two**

- Look at the equation in part B. What is another method that you could use to solve it? Explain. **This equation cannot be factored, so you can complete the square to solve it.**

Teaching Strategy
Students should be encouraged to always check that the equation is in standard form; if it is not, they should rewrite it in standard form. Below that, students should explicitly note the values of a, b, and c. After that, they should write the general quadratic formula. Then, they can substitute values and solve.

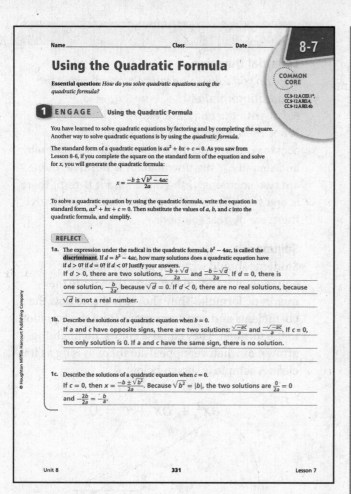

Name _____ **Class** _____ **Date** _____

8-7

Using the Quadratic Formula

Essential question: *How do you solve quadratic equations using the quadratic formula?*

COMMON
CORE

CC.9-12.A.CED.1*,
CC.9-12.A.REI.4,
CC.9-12.A.REI.4b

1 ENGAGE   Using the Quadratic Formula

You have learned to solve quadratic equations by factoring and by completing the square. Another way to solve quadratic equations is by using the *quadratic formula*.

The standard form of a quadratic equation is $ax^2 + bx + c = 0$. As you saw from Lesson 8-6, if you complete the square on the standard form of the equation and solve for *x*, you will generate the quadratic formula:

$$x = \frac{-b \pm \sqrt{b^2 - 4ac}}{2a}$$

To solve a quadratic equation by using the quadratic formula, write the equation in standard form, $ax^2 + bx + c = 0$. Then substitute the values of *a*, *b*, and *c* into the quadratic formula, and simplify.

REFLECT

1a. The expression under the radical in the quadratic formula, $b^2 - 4ac$, is called the **discriminant**. If $d = b^2 - 4ac$, how many solutions does a quadratic equation have if $d > 0$? if $d = 0$? if $d < 0$? Justify your answers.

If $d > 0$, there are two solutions, $\frac{-b + \sqrt{d}}{2a}$ and $\frac{-b - \sqrt{d}}{2a}$. If $d = 0$, there is

one solution, $-\frac{b}{2a}$, because $\sqrt{d} = 0$. If $d < 0$, there are no real solutions, because

$\sqrt{d}$ is not a real number.

1b. Describe the solutions of a quadratic equation when $b = 0$.

If *a* and *c* have opposite signs, there are two solutions: $\frac{\sqrt{-ac}}{a}$ and $\frac{-\sqrt{-ac}}{a}$. If $c = 0$,

the only solution is 0. If *a* and *c* have the same sign, there is no solution.

1c. Describe the solutions of a quadratic equation when $c = 0$.

If $c = 0$, then $x = \frac{-b \pm \sqrt{b^2}}{2a}$. Because $\sqrt{b^2} = |b|$, the two solutions are $\frac{0}{2a} = 0$

and $\frac{-2b}{2a} = -\frac{b}{a}$.

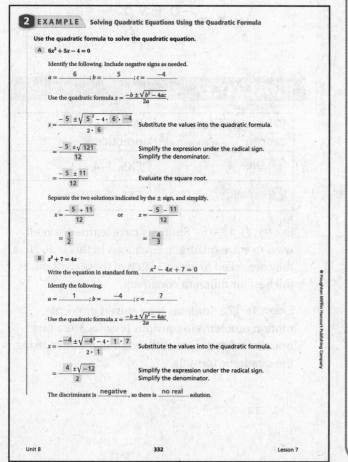

2 EXAMPLE   Solving Quadratic Equations Using the Quadratic Formula

Use the quadratic formula to solve the quadratic equation.

A $6x^2 + 5x - 4 = 0$

Identify the following. Include negative signs as needed.

$a = \underline{6}$; $b = \underline{5}$; $c = \underline{-4}$

Use the quadratic formula $x = \frac{-b \pm \sqrt{b^2 - 4ac}}{2a}$.

$x = \frac{-5 \pm \sqrt{5^2 - 4 \cdot 6 \cdot -4}}{2 \cdot 6}$ Substitute the values into the quadratic formula.

$= \frac{-5 \pm \sqrt{121}}{12}$ Simplify the expression under the radical sign.
Simplify the denominator.

$= \frac{-5 \pm 11}{12}$ Evaluate the square root.

Separate the two solutions indicated by the $\pm$ sign, and simplify.

$x = \frac{-5 + 11}{12}$ or $x = \frac{-5 - 11}{12}$

$= \frac{1}{2}$ $= -\frac{4}{3}$

B $x^2 + 7 = 4x$

Write the equation in standard form. $x^2 - 4x + 7 = 0$

Identify the following.

$a = \underline{1}$; $b = \underline{-4}$; $c = \underline{7}$

Use the quadratic formula $x = \frac{-b \pm \sqrt{b^2 - 4ac}}{2a}$.

$x = \frac{-4 \pm \sqrt{-4^2 - 4 \cdot 1 \cdot 7}}{2 \cdot 1}$ Substitute the values into the quadratic formula.

$= \frac{4 \pm \sqrt{-12}}{2}$ Simplify the expression under the radical sign.
Simplify the denominator.

The discriminant is _negative_, so there is _no real_ solution.

Differentiated Instruction

A good activity for visual learners is to use sticky notes that show the coefficients and constant of a quadratic equation. Extra coefficients and constants for each equation should be placed next to the equation. Write the quadratic formula below the equation. Have students move the sticky notes to the appropriate place in the formula and then evaluate the formula to solve the equation.

EXTRA EXAMPLE

Use the quadratic formula to solve the equation.

A. $21x^2 - 5 - 8x = 0$ $x = -\frac{1}{3}, x = \frac{5}{7}$

B. $3x^2 + 24x = -47$ no real solution

C. $4x^2 + 9 = 12x$ $x = \frac{3}{2}$

MATHEMATICAL PRACTICE · Highlighting the Standards

2 EXAMPLE and its Reflect questions offer an opportunity to address Mathematical Practice Standard 6 (Attend to precision). Given quadratic equations, students must correctly identify the values of a, b, and c and then correctly substitute them into the quadratic formula. As students do their calculations, they need to attend to whether numbers are positive or negative. They also need to check the discriminant to determine whether the equation has real solutions.

Essential Question

How do you solve quadratic equations using the quadratic formula?

First, write the quadratic equation in standard form. Then, identify the coefficients and the constant, substitute their values into the formula, and simplify. If the discriminant is positive, there are two solutions; if the discriminant is zero, there is one solution; and if the discriminant is negative, there are no real solutions.

Summarize

Students should write the general quadratic equation in standard form and then write the quadratic formula. They should indicate how the coefficients and constants move from the equation to the formula. They can use colors, highlighting, arrows, or whatever appeals to them as long as it is clear. A sample is shown below.

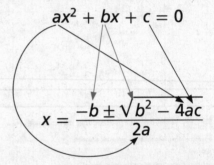

$$ax^2 + bx + c = 0$$

$$x = \frac{-b \pm \sqrt{b^2 - 4ac}}{2a}$$

PRACTICE

Where skills are taught	Where skills are practiced
1 ENGAGE	EXS. 1–4
2 EXAMPLE	EXS. 5–12

Exercises 13–16: Students have learned several ways to solve quadratic equations in this unit. Here they are asked to justify which of these methods is the best for different equations.

Exercise 17: Students have solved projectile motion problems in previous lessons. Here they practice solving a projectile motion problem using the quadratic formula.

C $5x^2 + 9.8 = -14x$

Write the equation in standard form. $\underline{5x^2 + 14x + 9.8 = 0}$

Identify the following.

$a = \underline{5}$; $b = \underline{14}$; $c = \underline{9.8}$

Use the quadratic formula $x = \dfrac{-b \pm \sqrt{b^2 - 4ac}}{2a}$.

$x = \dfrac{-14 \pm \sqrt{14^2 - 4 \cdot 5 \cdot 9.8}}{2 \cdot 5}$ Substitute the values into the quadratic formula.

$= \dfrac{-14 \pm \sqrt{0}}{10}$ Simplify the expression under the radical sign.
Simplify the denominator.

$= \dfrac{-14 \pm 0}{10}$ Take the square root.

The discriminant is $\underline{0}$, so there is $\underline{\text{one}}$ solution.

$x = -\dfrac{7}{5}$

REFLECT

2a. Is it possible to solve the equation from Part A by factoring? Explain.

Yes; the equation from Part A can be solved by factoring the expression

$6x^2 + 5x - 4$ as $(2x - 1)(3x + 4)$.

2b. Is it possible to solve the equation from Part B by factoring? Explain.

No; the expression $x^2 - 4x + 7$ cannot be factored because the

factors of 7, 1 and 7 or −1 and −7, do not have a sum of −4.

2c. Is it possible to solve the equation from Part C by factoring? Explain.

Yes; the equation can be solved by multiplying both sides by 5 to get the perfect

square trinomial $25x^2 + 70x + 49$ on the left side, and the factored form of the

trinomial is $(7x + 5)^2$.

PRACTICE

State how many real solutions the equation has. Do not solve the equation.

1. $3x^2 + 8x + 6 = 0$ $\underline{0}$
2. $z^2 = 9$ $\underline{2}$
3. $9d^2 + 16 = 24d$ $\underline{1}$
4. $-2x^2 = 25 - 10x$ $\underline{0}$

Solve the equation using the quadratic formula. Round to the nearest hundredth, if necessary.

5. $16 + r^2 - 8r = 0$
4

6. $3x^2 = 10 - 4x$
1.28, −2.61

7. $2s^2 = 98$
7, −7

8. $z^2 = 2.5z$
0, 2.5

9. $3x^2 + 16x - 84 = 0$
3.26, −8.59

10. $34z^2 + 19z = 15$
0.44, −1

11. $6q^2 + 25q + 24 = 0$
−1.5, −2.67

12. $7x^2 + 100x = 4$
0.04, −14.33

State what method you would use to solve the equation. Justify your answer.
You do not need to solve the equation.

13. $4x^2 + 25 = 20x$

Factor. $4x^2 - 20x + 25$ is a perfect square trinomial.

14. $2z^2 = 20$

Apply the definition of a square root after dividing by 2. There is no x-term.

15. $4x^2 + 25 = 18x$

Quadratic formula. $4x^2 - 18x + 25$ cannot be factored.

16. $g^2 - 3g - 4 = 0$

Factor. $g^2 - 3g - 4$ is easily factored.

17. A football player kicks a ball with an initial upward velocity of 47 feet per second. The initial height of the ball is 3 feet. The function $h(t) = -16t^2 + vt + h_0$ models the height (in feet) of the ball, where v is the initial upward velocity and h_0 is the initial height. If no one catches the ball, how long will it be in the air?

3 seconds

Graphing Functions of the Form $f(x) = ax^2 + bx + c$

Essential question: How can you describe key attributes of the graph of $f(x) = ax^2 + bx + c$ by analyzing its equation?

COMMON CORE Standards for Mathematical Content

CC.9-12.F.IF.4 For a function that models a relationship between two quantities, interpret key features of graphs and tables in terms of the quantities, and sketch graphs showing key features given a verbal description of the relationship.*

CC.9-12.F.IF.5 Relate the domain of a function to its graph and, where applicable, to the quantitative relationship it describes.*

CC.9-12.F.IF.7 Graph functions expressed symbolically and show key features of the graph ...*

CC.9-12.F.IF.7a Graph ... quadratic functions and show intercepts, maxima, and minima.*

CC.9-12.F.IF.8 Write a function defined by an expression in different but equivalent forms to reveal and explain different properties of the function.

CC.9-12.F.IF.8a Use the process of factoring ... in a quadratic function to show zeros ...

CC.9-12.F.BF.1 Write a function that describes a relationship between two quantities.*

Prerequisites

Transformations of the graph of $f(x) = x^2$, Lesson 7-3

Factoring and completing the square to solve equations of the form $ax^2 + bx + c = 0$, Lessons 8-3 and 8-5

Math Background

In Unit 7, students graphed quadratic functions in vertex form. Now, they will graph quadratic functions in standard form. They will describe key attributes of the graph (vertex, maximum or minimum, and intercepts) by analyzing the equation.

INTRODUCE

Remind students that they have graphed quadratic functions of the form $f(x) = a(x - h)^2 + k$. This is called the vertex form of the function because the graph's vertex is (h, k). If $a < 0$, the graph opens downward and the y-coordinate of the vertex is the function's maximum value. If $a > 0$, the graph opens upward and the y-coordinate of the vertex is the function's minimum value. Ask students to relate the symmetry of a parabola to its vertex.

TEACH

 EXAMPLE

Questioning Strategies

- How does factoring generate the x-intercepts of the function's graph? **The points where the graph of $f(x)$ crosses the x-axis have y-values that are 0, so the x-intercepts are found by solving the equation $f(x) = 0$, which can be done by factoring $f(x)$ and applying the zero-product property.**

- If you fold the parabola along its axis of symmetry, where would the two sides of the parabola be in relation to each other? **One side of the parabola would coincide with the other side.**

- If you folded the parabola along its axis of symmetry, where would the points where the x-intercepts occur be in relation to each other? **They would coincide.**

- If you know the coordinates of a point on a parabola, how can you find the coordinates of its reflection across the axis of symmetry? **The reflection will have the same y-value as the given point and be the same distance but opposite direction from the axis of symmetry.**

Technology

Students can use a graphing calculator to graph the function in the Example as a check on their work. When doing this as a check, students should always graph the original function, not the rewritten one. That way, any errors they may have made are not included in the check.

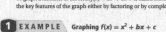

Name_____ Class_____ Date_____

8-8

COMMON
CORE

CC.9-12.F.IF.4*
CC.9-12.F.IF.5*
CC.9-12.F.IF.7a*
CC.9-12.F.IF.8a
CC.9-12.F.BF.1*

Graphing Functions of the Form
$f(x) = ax^2 + bx + c$

Essential question: *How can you describe key attributes of the graph of*
$f(x) = ax^2 + bx + c$ by analyzing its equation?

To graph a function of the form $f(x) = ax^2 + bx + c$, called *standard form*, you can analyze
the key features of the graph either by factoring or by completing the square.

1 EXAMPLE Graphing $f(x) = x^2 + bx + c$

Graph the function $f(x) = x^2 + 2x - 3$ by factoring.

A You can determine the *x*-intercepts of the graph by factoring to solve $f(x) = 0$:

$f(x) = x^2 + 2x - 3 = (x - \boxed{1})(x + \boxed{3})$, so $f(x) = 0$ when $x = \underline{\ \ 1\ \ }$ or

$x = \underline{\ \ -3\ \ }$

The graph of $f(x) = x^2 + 2x - 3$ intersects the *x*-axis at $\left(\boxed{1},\ \boxed{0}\right)$ and $\left(\boxed{-3},\ \boxed{0}\right)$.

B The axis of symmetry of the graph is a vertical line that is halfway between the two
x-intercepts and passes through the vertex. The axis of symmetry is $x = -1$. So, the
vertex is $\left(\boxed{-1},\ \boxed{-4}\right)$.

C Find another point on the graph and reflect it across the axis of symmetry. Use the
point (2, 5). The *x*-value is 3 units from the axis of symmetry, so its reflection is
$\left(\boxed{-4},\ \boxed{5}\right)$.

D Use the five points to graph the function.

REFLECT

1a. A useful point to plot is where the *y*-intercept occurs. How can you find
the *y*-intercept? What point is the reflection across the axis of symmetry of
the point where the *y*-intercept occurs?

The *y*-intercept is $f(0) = c$. In this case, $f(0) = -3$.

The reflection of $(0, -3)$ across the axis of symmetry is $(-2, -3)$.

© Houghton Mifflin Harcourt Publishing Company

If the function cannot be factored, complete the square to rewrite the function in *vertex
form*: $f(x) = a(x - h)^2 + k$. Completing the square in this situation is similar to solving
equations by completing the square, but instead of adding a term to both sides of the
equation, you will both add and subtract it from the function's rule.

2 EXAMPLE Graphing $f(x) = ax^2 + bx + c$

Graph the function $f(x) = -3x^2 + 6x + 1$ by completing the square.

A Complete the square to write the function in the form $f(x) = a(x - h)^2 + k$. Start
by disregarding the constant term. Factor -3 from the first two terms, paying close
attention to the signs of the terms.

$f(x) = -3\left(\boxed{x^2 - 2x}\right) + 1$ Factor.

$= -3\left(x^2 - 2x + \boxed{1} - \boxed{1}\right) + 1$ Complete the square within the parentheses.

$= -3\left(\left(\boxed{x - 1}\right)^2 - \boxed{1}\right) + 1$ Factor the first three terms in parentheses using the perfect square trinomial pattern.

$= -3\left(\boxed{x - 1}\right)^2 + \boxed{3} + 1$ Distribute the -3.

$= -3\left(\boxed{x - 1}\right)^2 + \boxed{4}$ Combine the last two terms.

Write the coordinates of the vertex (h, k). $\left(\boxed{1},\ \boxed{4}\right)$

B Graph the function by plotting another point besides the vertex and reflecting the

point across the axis of symmetry. The axis of symmetry is $x = \underline{\ \ 1\ \ }$. Since

$f(2) = \underline{\ \ 1\ \ }$, the point $\left(2,\ \boxed{1}\right)$ is on the graph. Reflecting this point across the

axis of symmetry gives the point $\left(\boxed{0},\ \boxed{1}\right)$.

C Based on the fact that $a = -3$, confirm that the graph has the characteristics you

would expect by comparing it with the graph of the parent function, $f(x) = x^2$. The

graph should be a vertical $\underline{\ \ \text{stretch}\ \ }$ of the graph of the parent function as well

as a reflection across the $\underline{\ \ \text{x-axis}\ \ }$, which means that the graph should open

$\underline{\ \ \text{down}\ \ }$. Does the graph that you drew have these characteristics? $\underline{\ \ \text{Yes}\ \ }$

© Houghton Mifflin Harcourt Publishing Company

Graph the function $f(x) = x^2 - 4x - 5$ by factoring.
$f(x) = (x + 1)(x - 5)$

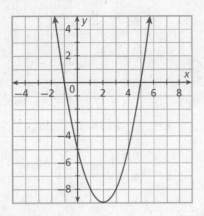

Graph the function $f(x) = -2x^2 - 12x - 17$ by completing the square.
$f(x) = -2(x + 3)^2 + 1$

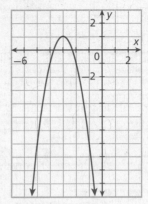

2 **EXAMPLE**

Questioning Strategies

- To convert from the standard form of a quadratic equation to the vertex form, what do you do? **Factor the coefficient *a* from the first two terms and then complete the square on the expression in parentheses.**

- Since you add a number to only one side of the equation rather than to both, what must you do to preserve equality? **After you add the number, you subtract it from the same side.**

3 **EXAMPLE**

Questioning Strategies

- Describe in words what the ball does. **The ball moves upward until it reaches its maximum height; then, it falls to the ground at the base of the cliff.**

- Describe in words how the vertex of the graph relating time and height relates to the motion of the ball. **The value of *h*(*t*) at the vertex is the ball's greatest height. The value of *t* at the vertex is the amount of time it takes the ball to reach its greatest height.**

- You know that the graph of a quadratic function is a parabola. Why isn't the complete parabola drawn when graphing *h*(*t*)? **Time and distance are both nonnegative, and this restricts the graph to first-quadrant values.**

```
············
·  MATHEMATICAL    Highlighting
·  PRACTICE        the Standards
············
```

1 EXAMPLE , **2** EXAMPLE , and their Reflect questions offer an opportunity to address Mathematical Practice Standard 1 (Make sense of problems and persevere in solving them). Students must decide whether to graph by factoring or by completing the square. The first step on this solution pathway is to determine whether the equation can be factored. Students need to persevere in checking factors to determine factorability. Should the equation be non-factorable, students must use completing the square to graph. Students can check the accuracy of their hand-drawn graphs by using a graphing calculator.

REFLECT

2a. Why did you add and subtract within the parentheses when completing the square?

You need to add 1 to $x^2 - 2x$ inside the parentheses to complete the square.

In order to keep the function's rule unchanged, you need to subtract 1 inside the

parentheses to balance adding 1.

2b. Why did you multiply both $(x - 1)^2$ and -1 by -3 in the fourth step? Why did you not multiply 1 by -3 in the same step?

Both $(x - 1)^2$ and -1 are inside the parentheses that have -3 in front of them.

Therefore, -3 is distributed to both terms. The 1, however, is outside these

parentheses and not subject to the distributive property.

2c. State the domain and range of the function.

Domain: all real numbers; Range: $f(x) \leq 4$

2d. Suppose the function were $g(x) = -3x^2 + 6x - 2$ instead of $f(x) = -3x^2 + 6x + 1$. Would you complete the square any differently? Why or why not? What is the vertex form of the function $g(x)$? How does the graph of $g(x)$ compare with the graph of $f(x)$? What are the domain and range of $g(x)$?

No; only the constant term of the functions is different. When you complete the

square, you disregard the constant term; $g(x) = -3(x - 1)^2 + 1$; the graph of $g(x)$

is a translation down by 3 units of the graph of $f(x)$; Domain: all real numbers;

Range: $g(x) \leq 1$

2e. It is useful to have a general expression for the vertex form and of the vertex in terms of a, b, and c. Complete the steps below on $f(x) = ax^2 + bx + c$ to write a general expression for the vertex form of a function and of the vertex (h, k) of the function.

$$f(x) = a\left(x^2 + \frac{b}{a}x\right) + c \qquad \text{Factor out the } a \text{ from the first two terms.}$$

$$= a\left(x^2 + \frac{b}{a}x + \left(\frac{b}{2a}\right)^2 - \left(\frac{b}{2a}\right)^2\right) + c \qquad \text{Complete the square within the parentheses.}$$

$$= a\left(\left(x + \frac{b}{2a}\right)^2 - \frac{b^2}{4a^2}\right) + c \qquad \text{Factor the perfect square trinomial.}$$

$$= a\left(x + \frac{b}{2a}\right)^2 - \frac{b^2}{4a} + c \qquad \text{Distribute the } a.$$

Write the coordinates of the vertex (h, k). $\left(-\dfrac{b}{2a}, \ -\dfrac{b^2}{4a} + c\right)$

Projectile Motion The height of an object moving under the force of gravity, with no other forces acting on it, can be modeled by the following quadratic function.

$$h(t) = -16t^2 + vt + h_0$$

The variables in the function represent the following quantities:

t is the time in seconds,

$h(t)$ is the height of the object above the ground in feet,

v is the initial vertical velocity of the object in feet per second, and

h_0 is the initial height of the object in feet.

3 **EXAMPLE**   Graphing a Projectile Motion Model

A person standing at the edge of a 48-foot cliff tosses a ball up and just off the edge of the cliff with an initial upward velocity of 8 feet per second. Graph the function that models the motion of the ball.

A   Identify the values of v and h_0 for the projectile motion function.

Initial vertical velocity, $v = $ _____8 feet per second_____

Initial height, $h_0 = $ _____48 feet_____

B   Write the equation for the projectile motion function.

$h(t) = -16t^2 + 8t + 48$

C   Complete the square to find the vertex of the function's graph.

$$h(t) = -16t^2 + 8\ t + 48$$

$$= -16\left(t^2 - \frac{1}{2}t\right) + 48 \qquad \text{Factor out } -16.$$

$$= -16\left(t^2 - \frac{1}{2}t + \frac{1}{16} - \frac{1}{16}\right) + 48 \qquad \text{Complete the square.}$$

$$= -16\left(\left(t - \frac{1}{4}\right)^2 - \frac{1}{16}\right) + 48 \qquad \text{Factor the perfect square trinomial.}$$

$$= -16\left(t - \frac{1}{4}\right)^2 + 1 + 48 \qquad \text{Distribute the } -16.$$

$$= -16\left(t - \frac{1}{4}\right)^2 + 49 \qquad \text{Combine the last two terms.}$$

Write the coordinates of the vertex. $\left(\dfrac{1}{4}, 49\right)$

Notes

The function $h(t) = -16t^2 + vt + h_0$ models projectile motion. A diver who is 3 feet above the water jumps off a diving board with an initial upward velocity of 12 feet per second. Write and graph the function that models the diver's height as a function of time.

$h(t) = -16t^2 + 12t + 3$

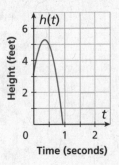

CLOSE

Essential Question

How can you describe key attributes of the graph of $f(x) = ax^2 + bx + c$ *by analyzing its equation?*
Quadratic equations can be written in various forms. The *intercept form* gives you the x-intercepts of the function's graph. The *vertex form* of the equation gives you the vertex of the function's graph. To change from standard form to intercept form, you factor. To change from standard form to vertex form, you complete the square.

Summarize

Students should create a graph labeled to show the relationship between the graph and the three forms (standard, intercept, and vertex) of a quadratic function. Students should choose a function with at least one x-intercept. A sample is shown.

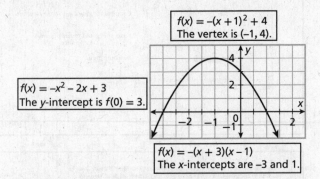

PRACTICE

Where skills are taught	Where skills are practiced
1 EXAMPLE	EX. 1, 2
2 EXAMPLE	EXS. 3, 4
3 EXAMPLE	EX. 5

D Graph the function by plotting a couple of points besides the vertex. Because only nonnegative values of t and $h(t)$ make sense for this situation, one point that you should plot is the point where the $h(t)$-intercept occurs. Since $h(0) = \underline{48}$, the graph starts at the point $\left(0, 48\right)$. Determining when the ball hits the ground gives you another point that you can plot:

$$h(t) = 0$$
$$-16\left(t - \tfrac{1}{4}\right)^2 + 49 = 0$$
$$-16\left(t - \tfrac{1}{4}\right)^2 = -49$$
$$\left(t - \tfrac{1}{4}\right)^2 = \tfrac{49}{16}$$
$$t - \tfrac{1}{4} = \pm\sqrt{\tfrac{49}{16}}$$
$$t - \tfrac{1}{4} = \pm\tfrac{7}{4}$$
$$t = \tfrac{1}{4} \pm \tfrac{7}{4} = \underline{2} \text{ or } -1.5$$

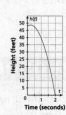

Reject the negative t-value. So, $\left(2, 0\right)$ is another point on the graph.

REFLECT

3a. How long is the ball in the air? When is the ball at its highest? What is its height at that time?

2 seconds; at 0.25 second; 49 feet

3b. State the domain and range of the function in the context of the situation.

Domain: $0 \le t \le 2$; Range: $0 \le h(t) \le 49$

3c. The units of $h(t)$ and h_0 are in feet, the units of t are in seconds, and the units of v are in feet per second. What are the units of the coefficient -16? Explain.

Feet per second squared, or $\frac{ft}{s^2}$; in order for the units of $h(t)$ to be in feet, the units of each term must be in feet. -16 is multiplied by a time in seconds squared, so the units of -16 must be feet per second squared.

PRACTICE

Write the rule for the quadratic function in the form you would use to graph it. Then graph the function.

1. $f(x) = x^2 + 4x + 3$

$f(x) = (x + 3)(x + 1)$

2. $f(x) = x^2 - 6x + 11$

$f(x) = (x - 3)^2 + 2$

3. $f(x) = -x^2 + 2x - 2$

$f(x) = -(x - 1)^2 - 1$

4. $f(x) = \tfrac{1}{2}x^2 - 4x + 5$

$f(x) = \tfrac{1}{2}(x - 4)^2 - 3$

5. A model rocket is launched from a 12-foot platform with an initial upward velocity of 64 feet per second.

a. Write a quadratic function in standard form that models the height of the rocket.

$h(t) = -16t^2 + 64t + 12$

b. Write the quadratic function in vertex form that models the height of the rocket.

$h(t) = -16(t - 2)^2 + 76$

c. Graph the function.

d. State the domain and range of the function in the context of the situation.

Domain: $0 \le t \le 4.18$ (approximately); Range: $0 \le h(t) \le 76$

Solving Systems of Linear and Quadratic Equations

Essential question: *How can you solve a system of equations when one equation is linear and the other is quadratic?*

COMMON **Standards for**
CORE **Mathematical Content**

CC.9-12.A.CED.2* Create equations in two or more variables to represent relationships between quantities; graph equations on coordinate axes with labels and scales.

CC.9-12.A.REI.4 Solve quadratic equations in one variable.

CC.9-12.A.REI.4b Solve quadratic equations by ... the quadratic formula and factoring ...

CC.9-12.A.REI.7 Solve a simple system consisting of a linear equation and a quadratic equation in two variables algebraically and graphically.

CC.9-12.F.IF.4 For a function that models a relationship between two quantities, interpret key features of graphs and tables in terms of the quantities, and sketch graphs showing key features given a verbal description of the relationship.*

Prerequisites

Graphing $f(x) = ax^2 + bx + c$, Lesson 8-8

Solving linear systems, Lessons 3-1 through 3-4

Math Background

Students solved systems of linear equations both graphically and algebraically in Unit 3. Have students recall that a system of linear equations can have at most one solution, and may have no solutions at all. Ask students to think about how many possible solutions can exist for a system that involves a linear equation and a quadratic equation. Ask them to give examples of these situations by sketching graphs to represent each case.

INTRODUCE

Students have solved systems of equations before. Ask them to name different methods for solving systems of linear equations. (They might come up with graphing, substitution, or elimination.) Focus on the graphing and substitution methods and ask questions to elicit details from the students of how to implement those methods.

TEACH

1 EXAMPLE

Questioning Strategies

• When solving systems of equations by graphing, how do you find the solution(s)? **Find the points where the graphs intersect.**

• In what form is the quadratic function $g(x)$? **vertex form**

• How does symmetry help you graph a quadratic function in vertex form? **You already know the axis of symmetry. It is relatively easy to choose two points on one side of the axis and then reflect them across the axis.**

• Which way does the parabola open and why? **down; because $a < 0$**

• In what form is the linear function $f(x)$? **slope-intercept form**

• How do the slope and y-intercept help you graph the line? **Start at the y-intercept of 48. Move down 8 units and right 1 unit to (1, 40). Draw the line through (0, 48) and (1, 40).**

EXTRA EXAMPLE

Solve the system of equations $g(x) = 2x - 2$ and $h(x) = 4(x + 2)^2 - 6$.
(−1.5, −5) and (−2, −6)

8-9

Solving Systems of Linear and Quadratic Equations

COMMON
CORE

CC.9-12.A.CED.2*,
CC.9-12.A.REI.4,
CC.9-12.A.REI.4b,
CC.9-12.A.REI.7,
CC.9-12.F.IF.4*

Essential question: *How can you solve a system of equations when one equation is linear and the other is quadratic?*

To estimate the solution to a system of equations, you can graph both equations on the same coordinate plane and find the intersection points. Or you can solve the equations algebraically using substitution or elimination.

1 EXAMPLE   Solving by Graphing and Algebraically

Solve the system of equations.

$$f(x) = -8x + 48$$
$$g(x) = -2(x - 2)^2 + 32$$

A   Solve the system of equations by graphing.

Start by graphing the quadratic function. The vertex is (2 , 32). Describe the transformation of the parent quadratic function that produces the graph of $g(x)$.

The parent graph is vertically stretched by a factor of 2 and reflected across the

x-axis, then translated 2 units right and 32 units up.

To make the graph more accurate, plot the points where the x-intercepts occur. The x-intercepts are the solutions of the equation $g(x) = 0$:

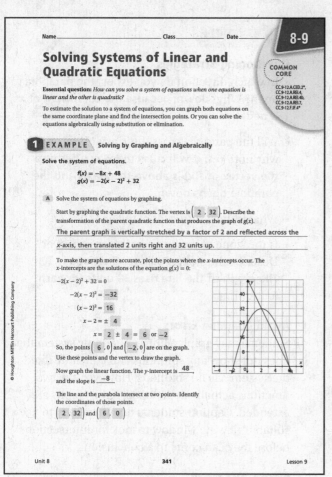

$$-2(x - 2)^2 + 32 = 0$$
$$-2(x - 2)^2 = -32$$
$$(x - 2)^2 = 16$$
$$x - 2 = \pm\ 4$$
$$x = 2 \pm 4 = 6 \text{ or } -2$$

So, the points (6 , 0) and (-2 , 0) are on the graph. Use these points and the vertex to draw the graph.

Now graph the linear function. The y-intercept is 48, and the slope is -8.

The line and the parabola intersect at two points. Identify the coordinates of those points.

(2 , 32) and (6 , 0)

© Houghton Mifflin Harcourt Publishing Company

B   Solve the system of equations algebraically.

Write the functions in terms of y.

$$y = -8x + 48$$
$$y = -2(x - 2)^2 + 32$$

Both equations are solved for y, so set the right sides equal to each other and solve for x.

$$-8x + 48 = -2(x - 2)^2 + 32$$

$-8x + 48 = -2x^2 + 8x + 24$ Simplify the right side.

$\underline{8x - 48 = \qquad\quad 8x - 48}$ Add 8x − 48 to both sides.

$0 = -2x^2 + 16x - 24$ Simplify both sides.

$0 = -2(x - 2)(x - 6)$ Factor the right side.

$x = 2$ or $x = 6$ Use the zero-product property to solve for x.

Substitute these values of x into the equation of the line to find the corresponding y-values.

$$y = -8(2) + 48 = \underline{32}$$
$$y = -8(6) + 48 = \underline{0}$$

The solutions are (2 , 32) and (6 , 0).

REFLECT

1a. If the linear function was $f(x) = 8x + 48$, how many solutions would there be? Justify your answer.

None; the line would be entirely above the parabola, so they would not intersect.

There would be no solutions.

1b. When solving algebraically, why do you substitute the x-values into the equation of the line instead of the equation of the parabola?

The computations are simpler for the linear equation.

1c. Explain the relationship between the intersection points of the graphs and the solutions of the system of equations.

The coordinates of the intersection points are the values of x and y that make both

equations true.

1d. Describe how to check that the solutions are correct.

Sample answer: Confirm that $f(2) = g(2)$ and $f(6) = g(6)$.

© Houghton Mifflin Harcourt Publishing Company

Notes

Differentiated Instruction

Visual learners can be introduced to solving systems of equations by using technology to graph the system given in the Example and find the intersection points. They can substitute the x-value of each point of intersection into each equation to prove to themselves that both equations have the same y-value. They can then choose different x-values and substitute them into each equation. They should see that the equations have different values for y. Have them locate these points on the graphs. This will show them that the line and the parabola do not intersect at these points.

2 EXPLORE

Questioning Strategies

• Is there a case where a line and a parabola would *not* intersect? If so, give an example. **Yes; example: if the parabola opened down with a vertex of (0, 0) and the line was $y = 3$**

• Two lines that are parallel don't intersect. If a line and a parabola don't intersect, are they parallel? Explain. **No; parallel lines are the same distance apart everywhere. Since the slope of a parabola changes and the slope of a line is constant, the line and parabola cannot be parallel.**

Teaching Strategy

Draw a parabola on the board and have students copy it. Ask them to (a) draw a line that intersects the parabola at two points, (b) draw a line that intersects the parabola at just one point, and (c) draw a line that does not intersect the parabola. Explain how many solutions a linear-quadratic system can have.

3 EXAMPLE

Questioning Strategies

• In which direction do you expect the parabola to open? Why? **down; because the coefficient of x^2 is negative**

• Will the parabola cross the x-axis? Why or why not? **Yes; it will cross the x-axis because the vertex of $f(x)$ is above the x-axis and the parabola opens down.**

• What is the y-intercept of the line? **0**

• Is the slope of the line positive or negative? Describe the slope. **Positive; the slope is 30. The graph of the line rises 30 units for each unit of run.**

Avoid Common Errors

Students may graph a linear-quadratic system that does not show any solutions and conclude that the system has no solutions. However, the two functions actually do intersect if the graphs are extended. Caution students that they need to use a suitable viewing window to look for intersections before they can come to a conclusion.

EXTRA EXAMPLE

Use a graphing calculator to solve the system of equations $f(x) = -5x^2 + 150x$ and $g(x) = 25x$. **(0, 0) and (25, 625)**

MATHEMATICAL PRACTICE **Highlighting the Standards**

1 EXAMPLE and **3 EXAMPLE** along with their Reflect questions offer an opportunity to address Mathematical Practice Standard 5 (Use tools appropriately). Students can use technology to graph the systems of equations and the *Intersect* feature to find the solutions. They should recognize when this results in approximate solutions.

Students should always check their answers. They can use calculators to find $f(x)$ and $g(x)$ for the values of x they have found.

2 EXPLORE Determining the Possible Number of Solutions

In the previous example, the system of equations had two solutions. You can use a graph to understand other possible numbers of solutions of a system of equations involving a linear equation and a quadratic equation.

The graph of the quadratic function $f(x) = -x^2 + 10x - 27$ is shown below.

Graph each linear function below on the same coordinate plane as the parabola.

Line 1: $g(x) = 2x - 11$

Line 2: $h(x) = -2x + 14$

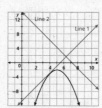

REFLECT

2a. At how many points do the parabola and Line 1 intersect? ___1___

How many solutions are there for the system consisting of the quadratic function and the first linear function? ___1___

2b. At how many points do the parabola and Line 2 intersect? ___0___

How many solutions are there for the system consisting of the quadratic function and the second linear function? ___0___

2c. A system of equations consisting of one quadratic equation and one linear equation can have ___0___, ___1___, or 2 real solutions.

2d. How many solutions does the following system of equations have? Explain your reasoning.

$$f(x) = -x^2 + 10x - 27$$
$$k(x) = -x + 1$$

2 solutions; if you graph $k(x)$ on the coordinate plane above, you will see that the line and parabola intersect at points $(4, -3)$ and $(7, -6)$.

2e. How many solutions does the following system of equations have? Explain your reasoning.

$$f(x) = -x^2 + 10x - 27$$
$$p(x) = -2$$

1 solution; the graph of $p(x)$ is a horizontal line through -2 on the y-axis, and it intersects the graph of $f(x)$ at its vertex, $(5, -2)$.

You can use the Intersect feature on a graphing calculator to solve systems of equations.

3 EXAMPLE Solving Systems Using Technology

Use a graphing calculator to solve the system of equations.

$$f(x) = -4.9x^2 + 50x + 25$$
$$g(x) = 30x$$

A Enter the functions as Y_1 and Y_2 on a graphing calculator. Then graph both functions. Sketch the graphs on the coordinate plane at the right.

Estimate the solutions of the system from the graph.

$(-1, -30)$ and $(5, 150)$

B Solve the system directly by using the Intersect feature of the graphing calculator.

Press 2nd and CALC, then select Intersect. Press Enter for the first curve and again for the second curve. For Guess?, press the left or right arrows to move the cursor close to one of the intersections, then press Enter again. Repeat, moving the cursor close to the other intersection to find the second solution. Round your solutions to the nearest tenth.

$(-1.0, -30.1)$ and $(5.1, 152.5)$

REFLECT

3a. Are the solutions you get using the Intersect feature of a graphing calculator always exact? Explain.

No; the values may be rounded in the calculator.

3b. How can you check the accuracy of your estimated solutions?

Substitute the values into the original equations, and simplify.

3c. Use a graphing calculator to solve the system of equations $f(x)$ and $h(x)$ where $h(x) = 30x + 50$. What is the result? Explain.

The calculator produces an error message, because the graphs don't intersect, so there is no solution to the system.

Essential Question

How can you solve a system of equations when one equation is linear and the other is quadratic?
Systems of equations can be solved by graphing both equations and looking for the intersection points of the graphs. They can be solved algebraically by writing both equations in the form "y = expression in x" and setting the expressions equal to each other in order to solve for x.

Summarize

Students should create a graphic organizer depicting linear-quadratic systems with no solutions, with one solution, and with two solutions. They should include notes about solving them by using technology, by graphing, and algebraically. A sample is shown below.

> To find the intersections of Line 1 and the parabola, use the Intersect feature on your graphing calculator.

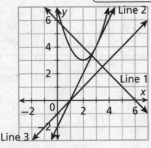

> To see that Line 3 and the parabola do not intersect, graph by hand.

> To find the intersection of Line 2 and the parabola, solve each equation for y, set them equal to each other, and find x. Then, substitute back in to find y.

Where skills are taught	Where skills are practiced
1 EXAMPLE	EXS. 1–6, 9–12
2 EXAMPLE	EXS. 7, 8
3 EXAMPLE	EXS. 13, 14

PRACTICE

Solve the system of equations algebraically. Round to the nearest tenth, if necessary.

1. $f(x) = x^2 - 2$
$g(x) = -2$

    $(0, -2)$

2. $y = (x - 3)^2$
$y = x$

    $(1.7, 1.7)$ and $(5.3, 5.3)$

3. $y = -2x^2 - 4x + 1$
$y = -\frac{1}{2}x + 3$

    No solution

4. $f(x) = x^2$
$g(x) = 1$

    $(1, 1)$ and $(-1, 1)$

5. $y = x^2 + 4x - 5$
$y = 3x - 2$

    $(1.3, 1.9)$ and $(-2.3, -8.9)$

6. $f(x) = -16x^2 + 15x + 10$
$g(x) = 14 - x$

    $(0.5, 13.5)$

The graph of a system of equations is shown. State how many solutions the system has. Then estimate the solution(s).

7.   2

    $(-6.25, 16)$, $(0.5, -11)$

8.   1

    $(1, 4)$

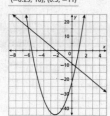

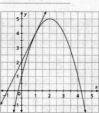

© Houghton Mifflin Harcourt Publishing Company

Estimate the solutions to the system of equations graphically. Confirm the solutions by substituting the values into the equations.

9. $f(x) = x^2$
$g(x) = 1$

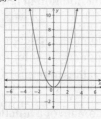

    $(1, 1)$ and $(-1, 1)$

10. $y = x^2 - 1$
$y = 0.5x - 3$

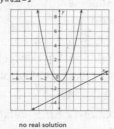

    no real solution

11. $f(x) = -16x^2 + 15x + 10$
$g(x) = 14 - x$

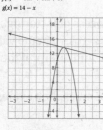

    $(0.5, 13.5)$

12. $f(x) = 3(x - 1)^2 + 4$
$g(x) = -4x + 9$

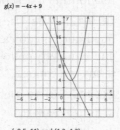

    $(-0.5, 11)$ and $(1.2, 4.3)$

Solve the system of equations using the Intersect feature of a graphing calculator. Round your answers to the nearest tenth.

13. $y = -x^2 + 6x + 7$
$y = 2x + 6$

    $(-0.2, 5.5)$ and $(4.2, 14.5)$

14. $f(x) = -x^2 + x - 2$
$g(x) = 2x - 3$

    $(-1.6, -6.2)$ and $(0.6, -1.8)$

© Houghton Mifflin Harcourt Publishing Company

FOCUS ON MODELING
Modeling with Quadratic Functions

Essential question: *How can you use quadratic functions to compare the motions of two baseballs that are thrown into the air?*

Standards for Mathematical Content

The following standards are addressed in this lesson. (An asterisk indicates that a standard is also a Modeling standard.) For more detailed information, see each section of the lesson.

Number and Quantity: CC.9-12.N.Q.2*

Algebra: CC.9-12.A.SSE.3a, CC.9-12.A.CED.2*, CC.9-12.A.REI.4a, CC.9-12.A.REI.4b

Functions: CC.9-12.F.IF.2, CC.9-12.F.IF.4*, CC.9-12.F.IF.5*, CC.9-12.F.IF.6*, CC.9-12.F.IF.8a, CC.9-12.F.IF.9, CC.9-12.F.BF.1a

Prerequisites

Solving quadratic functions by factoring, Lessons 8-2 and 8-3

Solving quadratic functions by completing the square, Lessons 8-4 and 8-5

The quadratic formula, Lesson 8-7

Math Background

Projectile motion refers to an object that is launched with an initial velocity and is subsequently acted upon only by the downward effect of gravitational acceleration. In most algebra applications, the effects of air resistance are ignored. Note that when a ball or another object is thrown into the air, the upward direction is taken as the positive direction. For this reason, gravitational acceleration, which pulls objects downward, is negative. On Earth, this constant force is -16 ft/s^2 (feet per second per second) or -9.8 m/s^2 (meters per second per second).

INTRODUCE

Discuss the problem that is posed at the beginning of the lesson. You may wish to draw a sketch on the board to show the cliff, the beach, and the positions of the two people who throw baseballs into the air. Be sure students understand that at the level of the beach the height is 0 feet. Point out that Franco throws his baseball with less initial velocity

but a greater initial height because he is standing on a cliff above the beach. You might want to have students guess which baseball reaches a greater maximum height. Then have students revisit their guesses at the end of the lesson.

TEACH

1 Find the maximum height of Franco's baseball.

Standards

CC.9-12.N.Q.2 Define appropriate quantities for the purpose of descriptive modeling.*

CC.9-12.A.SSE.3a Factor a quadratic expression to reveal the zeros of the function it defines.

CC.9-12.A.CED.2 Create equations in two or more variables to represent relationships between quantities ...*

CC.9-12.F.IF.2 Use function notation, evaluate functions for inputs in their domains, and interpret statements that use function notation in terms of a context.

CC.9-12.F.IF.4 For a function that models a relationship between two quantities, interpret key features of graphs and tables in terms of the quantities ...*

CC.9-12.F.IF.5 Relate the domain of a function to its graph and, where applicable, to the quantitative relationship it describes.*

CC.9-12.F.IF.8a Use the process of factoring ... in a quadratic function to show zeros, extreme values, and symmetry of the graph, and interpret these in terms of a context.

CC.9-12.F.BF.1a Determine an explicit expression ... from a context.*

Questioning Strategies

• How do you know the maximum height of Franco's baseball will be greater than 48 feet? **The ball starts at an initial height of 48 feet, and Franco throws the ball upward.**

continued

Name _____ Class _____ Date _____

FOCUS ON MODELING

Modeling with Quadratic Functions

8-10

COMMON CORE
CC.9-12.A.SSE.3a,
CC.9-12.A.REI.4a,
CC.9-12.A.REI.4b,
CC.9-12.F.IF.4*,
CC.9-12.F.IF.4*,
CC.9-12.F.IF.8a

Essential question: *How can you use quadratic functions to compare the motions of two baseballs that are thrown into the air?*

Franco and Grace each throw a baseball vertically into the air at the same time. Franco throws his baseball while standing on a cliff so that the baseball lands on a beach below. Grace throws her baseball into the air while standing on the beach. The table gives the initial vertical velocity v and the initial height h_0 at which each baseball is thrown. How do the motions of the two baseballs compare?

	Initial Velocity (ft/s)	Initial Height (ft)
Franco's baseball	32	48
Grace's baseball	64	3

1 Find the maximum height of Franco's baseball.

A The height in feet of an object thrown into the air with an initial vertical velocity of v feet per second and an initial height of h_0 feet is

$$f(t) = -16t^2 + vt + h_0,$$

where t is the time in seconds. Write a function $f(t)$ that models the height of Franco's baseball.

$f(t) = -16t^2 + 32t + 48$

B To find the maximum height of Franco's baseball, first factor the quadratic expression you wrote in order to find the t-intercepts of the function's graph.

$-16t^2 + 32\ t + 48 = -16\left(t^2 -\ 2\ t -\ 3\ \right)$

$= -16\left(t +\ 1\ \right)\left(t -\ 3\ \right)$

So, the graph of $f(t)$ intersects the t-axis at $t =\ \underline{-1}\ $ and at $t =\ \underline{3}\ $.
The axis of symmetry of the graph of $f(t)$ is a vertical line that is halfway between the two t-intercepts and passes through the vertex.
The axis of symmetry is the line $t =\ \underline{1}\ $ and the vertex is $\underline{(1, 64)}$.
So, the maximum height of Franco's baseball is $\underline{64}$ feet.

REFLECT

1a. Evaluate $f(t)$ at $t = 0$. What does this value tell you?

$f(0) = 48$; before Franco throws the baseball, it is 48 feet above the beach.

1b. Explain how you used the vertex of the graph of $f(t)$ to find the maximum height of Franco's baseball.

Because the coefficient of the t^2-term is negative, the graph of $f(t)$ is a parabola

that opens downward, so the $h(t)$-value of the vertex is the maximum height.

1c. How long after Franco's baseball is thrown into the air does it reach its maximum height? How do you know?

1 second; the vertex (1, 64) tells you that the maximum height of 64 feet is

attained when $t = 1$.

1d. What is the domain of $f(t)$? How do the t-intercepts help you determine the domain?

$0 \le t \le 3$; $f(t)$ represents a height, so it must be nonnegative; this occurs

between the t-intercepts, -1 and 3. However, t represents time, so it must

also be nonnegative, i.e., $t \ge 0$.

2 Find the maximum height of Grace's baseball.

A Write a function $g(t)$ that models the height of Grace's baseball.

$g(t) = -16t^2 + 64t + 3$

B To find the maximum height of Grace's baseball, first complete the square to write the function in vertex form, $g(t) = a(t - h)^2 + k$.

$g(t) = -16t^2 +\ 64\ t + 3$	Write the function in standard form.
$= -16\left(t^2 -\ 4\ t\right) + 3$	Factor -16 from the first two terms.
$= -16\left(t^2 -\ 4\ t +\ 4\ -\ 4\ \right) + 3$	Complete the square within the parentheses.
$= -16\left(\left(t -\ 2\ \right)^2 -\ 4\ \right) + 3$	Factor the first three terms in the parentheses using the perfect square trinomial pattern.
$= -16\left(t -\ 2\ \right)^2 + 64 + 3$	Distribute the -16.
$= -16\left(t -\ 2\ \right)^2 + 67$	Combine the last two terms.

The vertex of the graph of $g(t)$ is $\underline{(2, 67)}$.
So, the maximum height of Grace's baseball is $\underline{67}$ feet.

REFLECT

2a. Evaluate $g(t)$ at $t = 0$. What does this value tell you?

$g(0) = 3$; before Grace throws the baseball, it is 3 feet above the beach.

2b. How long after Grace's baseball is thrown into the air does it reach its maximum height? How do you know?

2 seconds; the vertex (2, 67) tells you that the maximum of 67 feet is attained

when $t = 2$.

© Houghton Mifflin Harcourt Publishing Company

1 continued

- If you know the two x-intercepts of a parabola, how do you find the vertex? **Find the average of the two x-intercepts. This gives the x-coordinate of the vertex. Substitute the x-coordinate into the equation of the parabola to find the y-coordinate of the vertex.**

- Suppose Franco threw the baseball downward with an initial vertical velocity of 32 ft/s. How would the function $f(t)$ be different in this case? **In this case v would be -32 ft/s, and the function would be $f(t) = -16t^2 - 32t + 48$.**

2 **Find the maximum height of Grace's baseball.**

Standards

CC.9-12.N.Q.2 Define appropriate quantities for the purpose of descriptive modeling.*

CC.9-12.A.CED.2 Create equations in two ... variables to represent relationships between quantities ...*

CC.9-12.A.REI.4a Use the method of completing the square to transform any quadratic equation in x into an equation of the form $(x - p)^2 = q$ that has the same solutions.

CC.9-12.F.IF.2 Use function notation, evaluate functions for inputs in their domains, and interpret statements that use function notation in terms of a context.

CC.9-12.F.IF.4 For a function that models a relationship between two quantities, interpret key features of graphs and tables in terms of the quantities ...*

CC.9-12.F.IF.8a Use the process of ... completing the square in a quadratic function to show zeros, extreme values, and symmetry of the graph, and interpret these in terms of a context.

CC.9-12.F.BF.1a Determine an explicit expression ... from a context.*

Questioning Strategies

- Why do you use a different method to find the maximum height of Grace's baseball? **The function that models the height of Grace's baseball cannot be factored easily.**

- What vertical distance does Grace's baseball travel as it moves from its starting position to its maximum height? **64 ft**

Avoid Common Errors

Remind students that when they add a constant to make the expression in parentheses a perfect square

trinomial, they must also subtract the constant within the parentheses to maintain balance.

3 **Determine when Franco's baseball hits the ground.**

Standards

CC.9-12.A.SSE.3a Factor a quadratic expression to reveal the zeros of the function it defines.

CC.9-12.A.REI.4b Solve quadratic equations by ... factoring, as appropriate to the initial form of the equation.

CC.9-12.F.IF.4 For a function that models a relationship between two quantities, interpret key features of graphs and tables in terms of the quantities ...*

CC.9-12.F.IF.8a Use the process of factoring ... in a quadratic function to show zeros, extreme values, and symmetry of the graph, and interpret these in terms of a context.

Also: CC.9-12.F.IF.7a*

Questioning Strategies

- What is the first step in solving $-16t^2 + 32t + 48 = 0$ by factoring? Why? **Divide both sides of the equation by -16. This makes the coefficient of the t^2-term equal to 1, so the equation is easier to factor.**

- Does it make sense to draw arrows on the ends of the graph? Why or why not? **No; the domain is $0 \leq t \leq 3$, so the graph does not continue outside the first quadrant.**

MATHEMATICAL PRACTICE   **Highlighting the Standards**

Mathematical Practice Standard 4 (Model with mathematics) emphasizes that mathematically proficient students "routinely interpret their mathematical results in the context of the situation and reflect on whether the results make sense." To address this standard, have students check that their graph matches what they know about the motion of Franco's baseball. For example, students should recognize that the parabola lies on or above the t-axis for $0 \leq t \leq 3$ and that this corresponds to the fact that the baseball is in the air from 0 to 3 seconds. Encourage students to describe other connections between the graph and the real-world situation.

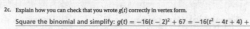

2c. Explain how you can check that you wrote $g(t)$ correctly in vertex form.

Square the binomial and simplify: $g(t) = -16(t - 2)^2 + 67 = -16(t^2 - 4t + 4) +$

$67 = -16t^2 + 64t - 64 + 67 = -16t^2 + 64t + 3$, which is the original function

in standard form.

3 Determine when Franco's baseball hits the ground.

A At the moment when Franco's baseball hits the ground and lands on the beach, what must be true about $f(t)$? Why?

$f(t) = 0$; the height of the baseball is 0 when it lands on the beach.

B Write an equation you can solve to determine when Franco's baseball hits the ground.

$-16t^2 + 32t + 48 = 0$

C Show how to solve the equation by factoring.

$-16t^2 + 32t + 48 = 0$, which means $-16(t^2 - 2t - 3) = 0$.

This implies $-16(t - 3)(t + 1) = 0$. So $t = 3$ or $t = -1$.

D Interpret your solutions. When does Franco's baseball hit the ground?

It hits the ground in 3 seconds. The other solution, −1, does not make sense in

the context of the problem since time cannot be negative.

E Use everything you know about $f(t)$ to draw the graph of the function on the coordinate plane at right. Be sure to label the points representing the vertex, where the $f(t)$-intercept occurs, and where the t-intercept occurs.

Explain how the time when Franco's baseball hits the ground is represented in your graph.

The time is the t-intercept, which is the

t-coordinate of the point (3, 0).

Franco's Baseball

[graph: Height (feet) vs Time (sec), points (1, 64), (0, 48), (3, 0)]

REFLECT

3a. Does Franco's baseball take as much time going up as it does coming down? Why or why not?

No; the baseball goes up for 1 second until it reaches its maximum. Then it

comes down for 2 seconds, until it hits the ground.

© Houghton Mifflin Harcourt Publishing Company

---

4 Determine when Grace's baseball hits the ground.

A At the moment when Grace's baseball hits the ground and lands on the beach, what must be true about $g(t)$? Why?

$g(t) = 0$; the height of baseball is 0 when it lands on the beach.

B Write an equation you can solve to find out when Grace's baseball hits the ground.

$-16t^2 + 64t + 3 = 0$

C Use the quadratic formula to solve the equation.

$a = -16$; $b = 64$; $c = 3$

$t = \dfrac{-b \pm \sqrt{b^2 - 4ac}}{2a}$ Use the quadratic formula.

$t = \dfrac{-64 \pm \sqrt{64^2 - 4 \cdot (-16) \cdot 3}}{2 \cdot (-16)}$ Substitute the values of a, b, and c.

$t = \dfrac{-64 \pm \sqrt{4288}}{-32}$ Simplify the expression under the radical. Simplify the denominator.

$t \approx -0.05$ or $t \approx 4.05$ Use a calculator. Round to the nearest hundredth.

D Interpret your solutions. When does Grace's baseball hit the ground?

It hits the ground in 4.05 seconds. The other solution, −0.05, does not make

sense in the context of the problem since time cannot be negative.

E Use everything you know about $g(t)$ to draw the graph of the function on the coordinate plane at right. Be sure to label the points representing the vertex, where the $g(t)$-intercept occurs, and where the t-intercept occurs.

Explain how the time when Grace's baseball hits the ground is represented in your graph.

The time is the t-intercept, which is the

t-coordinate of the point (4.05, 0).

Grace's Baseball

[graph: Height (feet) vs Time (sec), points (2, 67), (0, 3), (4.05, 0)]

REFLECT

4a. A student claims that Grace's baseball takes about the same amount of time going up as it does coming down. Do you agree? Why or why not?

Agree; the baseball goes up for 2 seconds until it reaches its maximum.

Then it comes down for 2.05 seconds, until it hits the ground.

© Houghton Mifflin Harcourt Publishing Company

4 Determine when Grace's baseball hits the ground.

Standards

CC.9-12.A.REI.4b Solve quadratic equations by ... the quadratic formula ... as appropriate to the initial form of the equation. ...

CC.9-12.F.IF.4 For a function that models a relationship between two quantities, interpret key features of graphs and tables in terms of the quantities ...*

CC.9-12.F.IF.5 Relate the domain of a function to its graph and, where applicable, to the quantitative relationship it describes.*

Also: CC.9-12.F.IF.7a*

Questioning Strategies

- Why does it make sense to use the quadratic formula to solve the equation $-16t^2 + 64t + 3 = 0$? **The equation cannot be factored easily.**

- How does the graph of $g(t)$ compare with the graph of $f(t)$? **Both are downward-opening parabolas, but the starting point of the graph of $g(t)$ is lower than the starting point of the graph of $f(t)$.**

5 Compare the motions of the two baseballs.

Standards

CC.9-12.F.IF.4 For a function that models a relationship between two quantities, interpret key features of graphs and tables in terms of the quantities ...*

CC.9-12.F.IF.9 Compare properties of two functions each represented in a different way (algebraically, graphically, numerically in tables, or by verbal descriptions).

Questioning Strategies

- How do you find the total vertical distance traveled by Franco's baseball? **The upward distance (16 ft) + the downward distance (64 ft) = the total distance (80 ft).**

- Overall, how much farther does Grace's baseball travel vertically than Franco's baseball? **51 ft**

CLOSE

Essential Question

How can you use quadratic functions to compare the motions of two baseballs that are thrown into the air?

Use factoring or completing the square to determine the vertex of the graph of each quadratic function. This makes it possible to determine the maximum heights of the baseballs. Use factoring or the quadratic formula to find the positive t-intercept of the graph of each function. This tells you how long it takes each baseball to hit the ground after being thrown.

Summarize

Have students draw a series of time-lapse graphs that show the vertical positions of the two baseballs at various times. Students should label the graphs with heights, distances, and/or times, as appropriate.

EXTEND

Standards

CC.9-12.F.IF.2 Use function notation, evaluate functions for inputs in their domains, and interpret statements that use function notation in terms of a context. (Ex. 2)

CC.9-12.F.IF.4 For a function that models a relationship between two quantities, interpret key features of ... tables in terms of the quantities ...* (Exs. 1–5)

CC.9-12.F.IF.6 Calculate and interpret the average rate of change of a function (presented symbolically or as a table) over a specified interval. ...* (Exs. 2–5)

4b. What is the domain of $g(t)$?

$0 \leq t \leq 4.05$

4c. Explain how you can use your graph to estimate when Grace's baseball is at a height of 50 feet.

Draw the horizontal line $g(t) = 50$ and find the points where the line and the

parabola intersect. These are approximately at $t = 1$ and $t = 3$.

4d. Explain how you can use your calculator to find more precise estimates of the times when Grace's baseball is at a height of 50 feet.

Graph $g(t)$ and the line $g(t) = 50$. Use the Intersect feature to find the points of

intersection. These are at $t \approx 0.97$ and $t \approx 3.03$.

4e. Why does it make sense that there are two times when Grace's baseball is at a height of 50 feet?

The baseball is at this height once on the way up and once on the way down.

5 Compare the motions of the two baseballs.

A Complete the table to compare the motions of the two baseballs. You have already determined some of the required values. You will need to use your equations and/or graphs to determine others.

	Maximum Height (ft)	Time Spent in the Air (sec)	Total Vertical Distance Traveled (ft)
Franco's baseball	64	3	80
Grace's baseball	67	4.05	131

B Which baseball has greater values in every column of the table? Why do you think this is the case?

Grace's baseball; she threw the ball with a greater initial vertical velocity,

which made it travel farther vertically and stay in the air longer.

REFLECT

5a. How did you find the total vertical distance traveled by each baseball?

Use the graph to find the distance the baseball travels from its starting height

to the maximum height and then add the distance the baseball travels from the

maximum height back to the ground.

EXTEND

1. Complete the table for the motion of Grace's baseball.

Time (sec)	0	1	2	3	4
Height (ft)	3	51	67	51	3

Describe any symmetry in the table. Explain why this makes sense.

The heights are symmetric. This makes sense because the line $t = 2$ is a

line of symmetry for the graph of $g(t)$.

2. The average rate of change of the function $g(t)$ over an interval is

$$\frac{\text{change in } g(t)}{\text{change in } t} = \frac{g(t_2) - g(t_1)}{t_2 - t_1}.$$

For example, from $t = 0$ to $t = 1$, the average rate of change of $g(t)$ is $\frac{51 - 3}{1 - 0} = \frac{48}{1}$ or 48 ft/sec. This is the average velocity of the baseball during the first second of its motion. Find the average rate of change of $g(t)$ for the other intervals in the table.

Interval	From $t = 0$ to $t = 1$	From $t = 1$ to $t = 2$	From $t = 2$ to $t = 3$	From $t = 3$ to $t = 4$
Average Rate of Change (ft/sec)	48	16	−16	−48

3. When is the average rate of change is positive? When is it negative?

The average rate of change is positive when the baseball is moving upward; the

average rate of change is negative when the baseball is moving downward.

4. Is the average rate of change greater during the first second of the baseball's motion or during the next second of its motion? Explain why this is so.

The average rate of change is greater during the first second; during the

next second the baseball is slowing down due to gravity as it approaches its

maximum height.

5. What do you find if you calculate the average rate of change over the interval from $t = 1$ to $t = 3$? Why does this happen?

The average rate of change is 0. The baseball's positive and negative velocities

over this interval are averaging to 0.

COMMON CORE CORRELATION

Standard	Items
CC.9-12.A.APR.1	1, 11
CC.9-12.A.SSE.3a	2, 3
CC.9-12.A.CED.1	12
CC.9-12.A.REI.4a	4
CC.9-12.A.REI.4b	5, 6, 8, 9, 13, 15
CC.9-12.A.REI.7	7, 14
CC.9-12.F.IF.9	10

TEST PREP DOCTOR ⊕

Multiple Choice: Item 1
- Students who chose **B** or **D** did not carry the negative sign with the 9 when multiplying the last terms to find the constant.
- Students who chose **C** forgot to add the product of the inner terms to the product of the outer terms.

Multiple Choice: Item 2
- Students who chose **H** or **J** factored the 8 instead of the 7.
- Students who chose **F** most likely read their solutions directly from the binomials instead of using the zero-product property to solve the equation.

Multiple Choice: Item 4
- Students who chose **H** or **J** were using the constant 12 instead of the coefficient of r, -5, to determine the number to add.
- Students who chose **G** forgot to divide 5 by 2 before squaring.

Multiple Choice: Item 10
- Students who chose **F** or **G** did not include the x-value of the vertex in the parentheses. These two answers are for a vertical translation of the parent graph rather than a horizontal translation.
- Students who chose **H** may not have understood that the vertex form is $y = (x - h)^2 + k$, not $y = (x + h)^2 + k$.

Free Response: Item 13
- Students who gave a solution to this equation miscalculated the discriminant or ignored the fact that it is negative.

Free Response: Item 15
- Students who gave incorrect answers may have completed the square incorrectly. Students who gave their answers as **5.32** and **−5.32** forgot to subtract 2.5 from the square roots of 28.25 and then divide by 2 to find x.

Notes

Name _____ Class _____ Date _____

MULTIPLE CHOICE

1. What is the product $(2x - 9)(3x + 5)$?

(A) $6x^2 - 17x - 45$

B. $6x^2 - 21x + 45$

C. $6x^2 + 10x - 45$

D. $6x^2 + 37x + 45$

2. What are the solutions of $y^2 - 8y + 7 = 0$?

F. $-1, -7$ H. $-1, -8$

(G) $1, 7$ J. $1, 8$

3. What is the factored form of $5z^2 + 9z - 2$?

A. $(5z - 2)(z + 1)$

B. $(5z + 2)(z - 1)$

(C) $(5z - 1)(z + 2)$

D. $(5z + 1)(z - 2)$

4. What number should be added to both sides to complete the square on $r^2 - 5r = 12$?

(F) 6.25 H. 36

G. 25 J. 144

5. What is the *best* first step to solve $2x^2 = x + 1$ by completing the square?

A. Put the equation in standard form.

B. Divide both sides by 2.

(C) Subtract x from both sides.

D. Add 0.25 to both sides.

6. To solve the equation below by completing the square, you could multiply both sides of the equation by which number?

$$3x^2 - 7x = 8$$

(F) 3 H. -7

G. $3x$ J. 8

7. What are the solutions of the following system of equations?

$$f(x) = x^2 - 4x + 13$$
$$g(x) = x + 9$$

A. $(0, 4); (0, 13)$

B. $(0, 10); (4, 13)$

(C) $(1, 10); (4, 13)$

D. $(2, 9); (0, 9)$

8. What values of a, b, and c should be substituted in the quadratic formula to solve $5x^2 - 3x + 2 = 0$?

F. $a = 5; b = -3; c = -2$

G. $a = 5; b = 3; c = -2$

H. $a = 5; b = 3; c = 2$

(J) $a = 5; b = -3; c = 2$

9. What does it mean if the value under the radical sign in the quadratic formula is negative?

A. The quadratic equation has one solution.

B. The quadratic equation has two solutions.

(C) The quadratic equation has no solution.

D. There is an error in the calculations.

10. The graph of which function is shown?

F. $f(x) = x^2 - 2$

G. $f(x) = x^2 + 2$

H. $f(x) = x^2 + 4x + 4$

(J) $f(x) = x^2 - 4x + 4$

FREE RESPONSE

11. Complete the diagram and the equation that represent the binomial multiplication shown by the algebra tiles.

$$(x + 2)\left(\boxed{x} + \boxed{1} \right) = x^2 + 3x + 2$$

12. A diver leaves a 3-foot-high diving board with an initial upward velocity of 11 feet per second. Use the projectile motion model, $h(t) = -16t^2 + vt + h_0$, for the following.

a. Write the function that represents the diver's height as a function of time.

$$h(t) = -16t^2 + 11t + 3$$

b. Graph the function.

Height (feet) vs Time (seconds)

c. What is the diver's maximum height above the water?

$$4.9 \text{ ft}$$

d. How much time elapses before the diver enters the water? Round your answer to the nearest hundredth of a second.

$$0.90 \text{ s}$$

e. What is the domain and range of the function in terms of the situation?

$$D: 0 \le t \le 0.9; \ R: 0 \le h(t) \le 4.9$$

13. Solve the quadratic equation. Tell which method you used and explain why.

$$0 = 3x^2 - 4x + 12$$

No solution; solve by using the quadratic formula because the right side of the equation does not factor.

14. Solve the system of equations algebraically. What do the solutions tell you about the graphs of the two functions?

$$f(x) = -3x^2 + 3x + 4$$
$$g(x) = -6x + 4$$

$(0, 4)$ and $(3, -14)$; The graphs intersect at these two points.

15. Solve the quadratic equation by completing the square. Show all work. Round solutions to the nearest tenth, if necessary.

$$11 = 2x^2 + 5x$$
$$11 = 2x^2 + 5x$$
$$22 = 4x^2 + 10x$$
$$22 + \frac{25}{4} = 4x^2 + 10x + \frac{25}{4}$$
$$28.25 = \left(2x + \frac{5}{2}\right)^2$$
$$\pm\sqrt{28.25} = 2x + \frac{5}{2}$$
$$2x + \frac{5}{2} \approx 5.32 \quad \text{or} \quad 2x + \frac{5}{2} \approx -5.32$$
$$x \approx 1.4 \quad \text{or} \quad x \approx -3.9$$

© Houghton Mifflin Harcourt Publishing Company

Data Analysis

Unit Vocabulary

conditional relative frequency	(9-5)
first quartile	(9-1)
interquartile range	(9-1)
joint relative frequency	(9-5)
marginal relative frequency	(9-5)
mean	(9-1)
median	(9-1)
outlier	(9-2)
range	(9-1)
skewed to the left	(9-2)
skewed to the right	(9-2)
standard deviation	(9-1)
statistics	(9-1)
symmetric	(9-2)
third quartile	(9-1)
two-way frequency table	(9-5)
two-way relative frequency table	(9-5)

UNIT 9

Data Analysis

Unit Focus

In this unit you will learn how to display and analyze data. You will begin by calculating statistics that locate the center and measure the spread of a set of numerical data. Then you will see how displaying numerical data in various ways helps you make sense of data, especially when the amount of data is substantial. By comparing data displays for two sets of numerical data, you will be able to draw conclusions about how one set differs from another. Finally, you will learn how to organize and analyze categorical data by using relative frequencies.

Unit at a Glance

COMMON CORE

Lesson		Standards for Mathematical Content
9-1	Measures of Center and Spread	CC.9-12.S.ID.2*
9-2	Data Distributions and Outliers	CC.9-12.S.ID.1*, CC.9-12.S.ID.2*, CC.9-12.S.ID.3*
9-3	Histograms	CC.9-12.S.ID.1*, CC.9-12.S.ID.2*
9-4	Box Plots	CC.9-12.S.ID.1*, CC.9-12.S.ID.2*
9-5	Two-Way Frequency Tables	CC.9-12.S.ID.5*
	Test Prep	

© Houghton Mifflin Harcourt Publishing Company

Unit 9　　　355　　　Data Analysis

This page lists and explains the Standards for Mathematical Content that are addressed in this unit. For information about the Standards for Mathematical Practice, which are integrated throughout the text, see Teacher Edition pages viii–xi.

Unpacking the Common Core State Standards

Use the table to help you understand the Standards for Mathematical Content that are taught in this unit. Refer to the lessons listed after each standard for exploration and practice.

COMMON CORE Standards for Mathematical Content	What It Means For You
CC.9-12.S.ID.1 Represent data with plots on the real number line (dot plots, histograms, and box plots).* Lessons 9-2, 9-3, 9-4	You will see how different data displays reveal different aspects of a data set. Data displays are useful in making sense of raw data, such as long lists of numbers.
CC.9-12.S.ID.2 Use statistics appropriate to the shape of the data distribution to compare center (median, mean) and spread (interquartile range, standard deviation) of two or more different data sets.* Lessons 9-1, 9-2, 9-3, 9-4	You will see that there are a variety of statistics that can be used to describe a single data set. You will learn that some statistics are more useful than others in describing certain data sets.
CC.9-12.S.ID.3 Interpret differences in shape, center, and spread in the context of the data sets, accounting for possible effects of extreme data points (outliers).* Lesson 9-2	A real-world data set may include extreme data values. Knowing how to recognize extreme data values is important so that the unusual does not cloud your picture of what is typical.
CC.9-12.S.ID.5 Summarize categorical data for two categories in two-way frequency tables. Interpret relative frequencies in the context of the data (including joint, marginal, and conditional relative frequencies). Recognize possible associations and trends in the data.* Lesson 9-5	In most of this unit, you will focus on analyzing numerical data. However, it is also important to learn how to display and make sense of data that involve categories, such as gender and favorite type of pet.

Notes

_____

_____

_____

_____

_____

_____

_____

_____

_____

Measures of Center and Spread

Essential question: *What statistics can you use to characterize and compare the center and spread of data sets?*

COMMON CORE **Standards for Mathematical Content**

CC.9-12.S.ID.2 Use statistics appropriate to the shape of the data distribution to compare center (median, mean) and spread (interquartile range, standard deviation) of two or more different data sets.*

Vocabulary

mean, median, first quartile, third quartile, range, interquartile range, standard deviation, statistics

Math Background

Students are familiar with how to find the mean, median, and interquartile range as a way of summarizing a data set. Students are also familiar with making a box plot using quartiles and the definition of IQR. Measures of center like mean and median are ways of summarizing a data set by using a single value to describe the center of that set of data. Each measure provides a slightly different perspective on the data set. Students should recognize that the mean of a data set may not actually be one of the data values in the data set, and that the same is true for the median.

One measure of spread of a data set is the interquartile range (IQR). Another measure of spread is standard deviation, which is related to the distance of each data value from the mean.

INTRODUCE

Remind students of the definitions of mean, median, and interquartile range. The *mean* is the average of the data values, or the sum of the values in the set divided by the number of values in the set. When the data values are in numerical order, the median is the middle value if there is an odd number of values or the mean of the two middle values if there is an even number of values. The *interquartile range* (IQR) of a data set is the difference between the third and first quartiles. It represents the range of the middle half of the data.

TEACH

 EXAMPLE

Questioning Strategies

- Describe how to find the first quartile of the data set. The first quartile is the median of the lower half of the data set. The lower half of the data set has two values, 77 and 84, so the first quartile is the mean of those two values: $\frac{77 + 84}{2} = 80.5$.

- Describe how to find the third quartile of the data set. The third quartile is the median of the upper half of the data set. The upper half of the data set has two values, 90 and 93, so the third quartile is the mean of those two values: $\frac{90 + 93}{2} = 91.5$.

Teaching Strategy

Ask students to give examples of questions about the data set that can be answered by finding a measure of center ("What was the average April temperature in Boston for the five years?") and questions that can be answered by finding a measure of spread ("What was the difference between the highest and lowest April temperatures in Boston for the five years?")

EXTRA EXAMPLE

The number of wins per nation for the Tour de France bicycling race is 36 (France), 18 (Belgium), 12 (Spain), 10 (United States), and 9 (Italy). Find the mean, median, first quartile, third quartile, and interquartile range for the data set. **17, 12, 9.5, 27, 17.5**

Avoid Common Errors

Students may include the median in the upper and lower halves of the data set when finding Q_1 and Q_3. Remind them that the median is not included.

Name_____ Class_____ Date_____

Measures of Center and Spread

Essential question: *What statistics can you use to characterize and compare the center and spread of data sets?*

Two commonly used measures of the center of a set of numerical data are the *mean* and *median*. Let *n* be the number of data values. The **mean** is the sum of the data values divided by *n*. When the data values are ordered from least to greatest, the **median** is either the middle value if *n* is odd or the average of the two middle values if *n* is even. The median divides the data set into two halves. The **first quartile** (Q_1) of a data set is the median of the lower half of the data. The **third quartile** (Q_3) is the median of the upper half.

Two commonly used measures of the spread of a set of numerical data are the *range* and *interquartile range*. The **range** is the difference between the greatest data value and the least data value. The **interquartile range** (IQR) is the difference between the third quartile and first quartile: IQR = $Q_3 - Q_1$.

1 EXAMPLE Finding Mean, Median, Range, and Interquartile Range

The April high temperatures (in degrees Fahrenheit) for five consecutive years in Boston are listed below. Find the mean, median, range, and interquartile range for this data set.

$$77 \quad 86 \quad 84 \quad 93 \quad 90$$

A Find the mean.

$$\text{Mean} = \frac{77 + 86 + 84 + 93 + 90}{5} = \frac{430}{5} = 86$$

B Find the median.

Write the data values from least to greatest: $\underline{77 \ 84 \ 86 \ 90 \ 93}$

Identify the middle value: $\underline{86}$

C Find the range.

Range = 93 − 77 = 16

D Find the interquartile range.

Find the first and third quartiles. Do not include the median as part of either the lower half or the upper half of the data.

$$Q_1 = \frac{77 + 84}{2} = 80.5 \text{ and } Q_3 = \frac{90 + 93}{2} = 91.5$$

Find the difference between Q_3 and Q_1: IQR = 91.5 − 80.5 = 11

REFLECT

1a. If 90°F is replaced with 92°F, will the median or mean change? Explain.

The median will still be 86, because it will still be the middle number. The mean will increase to 86.4 because the sum of the data values will increase.

1b. Why is the IQR less than the range?

Unlike the range, the IQR does not use extreme values, so the difference in the values is less.

Standard Deviation Another measure of spread is **standard deviation**. It is found by squaring the deviations of the data values from the mean of the data values, then finding the mean of those squared deviations, and finally taking the square root of the mean of the squared deviations. The steps for calculating standard deviation are listed below.

1. Calculate the mean, $\bar{x}$.
2. Calculate each data value's deviation from the mean by finding $x - \bar{x}$ for each data value x.
3. Find $(x - \bar{x})^2$, the square of each deviation.
4. Find the mean of the squared deviations.
5. Take the square root of the mean of the squared deviations.

2 EXAMPLE Calculating the Standard Deviation

Calculate the standard deviation for the data from the previous example.

A Complete the table using the fact that the mean of the data is $\bar{x} = 86$.

Data value, x	Deviation from mean, $x - \bar{x}$	Squared deviation, $(x - \bar{x})^2$
77	77 − 86 = −9	$(-9)^2 = 81$
86	86 − 86 = 0	$0^2 = 0$
84	84 − 86 = −2	$(-2)^2 = 4$
93	93 − 86 = 7	$7^2 = 49$
90	90 − 86 = 4	$4^2 = 16$

B Find the mean of the squared deviations.

$$\text{Mean} = \frac{81 + 0 + 4 + 49 + 16}{5} = \frac{150}{5} = 30$$

C Take the square root of the mean of the squared deviations. Use a calculator, and round to the nearest tenth.

Square root of mean = $\sqrt{30} \approx 5.5$

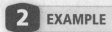

2 EXAMPLE

Questioning Strategies

- What does the standard deviation tell you? **Standard deviation tells you how spread out the data values are.**

- What symbol is used to represent the mean? $\bar{x}$

- In the second column of the table in part A, you subtract the mean from the data value to find the deviation from the mean. Can you subtract the data value from the mean instead? **Yes, the result will be the same when you square the deviation in the third column of the table. For example, $77 - 86 = -9$ and $(-9)^2 = 81$, and $86 - 77 = 9$ and $9^2 = 81$.**

- How is the standard deviation different from the range or the IQR as a measure of spread? **The standard deviation is a measure of spread that is calculated by using the mean. The range is a measure of spread, but it is not based on any measure of center for the data set. The IQR depends on the median.**

Teaching Strategy

Review the concept of the interquartile range and ask students whether they can think of other ways to describe the spread of a data set. Point out that the IQR depends on the median as a measure of center, and ask students whether they can think of a way to measure spread that depends on the mean. Some students may come up with the idea of finding the deviation of each data value from the mean and then finding the average of those deviations. Point out that if deviations for values less than the mean are represented as negative numbers and deviations for values greater than the mean are represented as positive numbers, adding the deviations will result in a total of zero. Use this as an opportunity to discuss why the deviation is squared rather than being left as is.

Differentiated Instruction

Visual and kinesthetic learners may benefit from plotting the values on a number line, marking the mean, and identifying the distance of each data value from the mean.

EXTRA EXAMPLE

Calculate the standard deviation for the data from the Extra Example for **1 EXAMPLE**. 10

3 EXAMPLE

Questioning Strategies

- In part B, a calculator is used to find the measures of center and spread. The resulting screen is shown, but the median is not displayed. How can you find the median? **Use the arrow keys to scroll down and display the median, as well as the values for Q_1 and Q_3.**

- If you don't have a graphing calculator, can you find the standard deviation using pencil and paper? **Yes, you can follow the same steps as in 2 EXAMPLE, although for a data set this large, the process would be time consuming.**

- In part B, are the answers reasonable? Explain. **The measures of center are reasonable since players often enter professional football and baseball after they graduate from college, and they play for several years. Professional baseball players often play in the minor leagues for several years before they reach the major leagues, which is one explanation for why pro football players tend to be younger than big-league baseball players.**

Technology

Explain that measures of center and spread can also be found using a spreadsheet. Point out that this may be preferable in many cases since the results can be more easily saved. Also, if statistics are calculated using a spreadsheet, results can be copied and pasted into word processing documents or used in presentation software. If spreadsheet software is available, demonstrate how to enter the data into cells of the spreadsheet and use the statistical functions available with the software.

REFLECT

2a. What is the mean of the deviations *before* squaring? Use your answer to explain why squaring the deviations is reasonable.

0; squaring the deviations is reasonable because it prevents the positive and negative deviations from averaging to 0.

2b. In terms of the data values used, what makes calculating the standard deviation different from calculating the range?

The standard deviation uses all data values, not just the extreme ones.

2c. What must be true about a data set if the standard deviation is 0? Explain.

The data values must all be equal; if the mean of the squared deviations is 0, then the deviations must all be 0, so each value is equal to the mean.

Numbers that characterize a data set, such as measures of center and spread, are called **statistics**. They are useful when comparing large sets of data.

3 EXAMPLE Comparing Statistics for Related Data Sets

The tables below list the average ages of players on 15 teams randomly selected from the 2010 teams in the National Football League (NFL) and Major League Baseball (MLB). Compare the average ages of NFL players to the average ages of MLB players.

NFL Players' Average Ages	
Team	**Average Age**
Bears	25.8
Bengals	26.0
Broncos	26.3
Chiefs	25.7
Colts	25.1
Eagles	25.2
Jets	26.1
Lions	26.4
Packers	25.9
Patriots	26.6
Saints	26.3
Seahawks	26.2
Steelers	26.8
Texans	25.6
Titans	25.7

MLB Players' Average Ages	
Team	**Average Age**
Astros	28.5
Cardinals	29.0
Cubs	28.0
Diamondbacks	27.8
Dodgers	29.5
Giants	29.1
Marlins	26.9
Mets	28.9
Nationals	28.6
Padres	28.7
Pirates	26.9
Phillies	30.5
Reds	28.7
Rockies	28.9
Yankees	29.3

A On a graphing calculator, enter the two sets of data into two lists, L_1 and L_2. Examine the data as you enter the values, and record your general impressions about how the data sets compare before calculating any statistics.

Answers will vary. Sample answer: Both the center and spread for the NFL players seem to be less than for the MLB players.

B Calculate the statistics for the NFL data in list L_1. Then do the same for the MLB data in L_2. Record the results in the table below. Your calculator may use the following notations and abbreviations for the statistics you're interested in.

Mean: $\bar{x}$

Median: Med

IQR: May not be reported directly, but can be obtained by subtracting Q_1 from Q_3

Standard deviation: σx

	Center		Spread	
	Mean	**Median**	**IQR** $(Q_3 - Q_1)$	**Standard Deviation**
NFL	25.98	26.00	0.60	0.46
MLB	28.62	28.70	1.10	0.91

C Compare the corresponding statistics for the NFL data and the MLB data. Are your comparisons consistent for the two measures of center and the two measures of spread? Do your comparisons agree with your general impressions from Part A?

In each case, the statistic for the NFL is less than the corresponding statistic for the MLB. There are no inconsistencies between the two measures of center or the two measures of spread. Answers about agreement with general impressions from Part A will vary, but the statistics support those students who said that NFL's center and spread are less.

© Houghton Mifflin Harcourt Publishing Company

MATHEMATICAL PRACTICE — Highlighting the Standards

3 EXAMPLE and its Reflect questions offer an opportunity to address Mathematical Practice Standard 1 (Make sense of problems and persevere in solving them). Students solve real-world statistical analysis problems by forming general impressions while entering the data into a calculator, obtaining the statistics and organizing them into a table, and then analyzing the results to make and justify conclusions.

EXTRA EXAMPLE

The lists below show average yearly gold prices for two 10-year periods.

1990–1999: $386.20, $353.15, $333.00, $391.75, $383.25, $387.00, $369.00, $287.05, $288.70, $290.25

2000–2009: $279.11, $271.04, $309.73, $363.38, $409.72, $444.74, $603.46, $695.39, $871.96, $972.35

Calculate the mean, median, standard deviation, and IQR and compare the corresponding statistics.

For 1990–1999, mean is $346.94, median is $361.08, standard deviation is $41.70, and IQR is $95.95. For 2000–2009, mean is $522.09, median is $427.23, standard deviation is $239.32, and IQR is $385.66. Both measures of center and measures of spread for 1990–1999 are significantly less than those for 2000–2009.

Essential Question

What statistics can you use to characterize and compare the center and spread of data sets?
You can use the mean and median to characterize and compare the center of data sets. You can use the interquartile range and the standard deviation to characterize and compare the spread of data sets.

Summarize

Have students collect or research their own data, perform calculations for measures of center and spread, and draw conclusions based on their calculations. Students can collect data related to their lives or they can be directed to online resources like the *Statistical Abstract of the United States,* which can be found at www.census.gov.

PRACTICE

Where skills are taught	Where skills are practiced
1 EXAMPLE	EXS. 1–4
2 EXAMPLE	EX. 5
3 EXAMPLE	EX. 7

Exercise 6: Students extend their understanding of measures of center and spread by analyzing how a change in the data affects these measures.

REFLECT

3a. Based on a comparison of the measures of center, what conclusion can you draw about the typical age of an NFL player and of an MLB player?

A typical NFL player tends to be younger than a typical MLB player.

3b. Based on a comparison of the measures of spread, what conclusion can you draw about variation in the ages of NFL players and of MLB players?

The ages of NFL players vary a little less than the ages of MLB players.

3c. What do you notice about the mean and median for the NFL? For the MLB?

The mean and median are roughly equal for both the NFL and MLB.

3d. What do you notice about the IQR and standard deviation for the NFL? For the MLB?

The IQR is a little greater than the standard deviation for both the NFL and MLB.

PRACTICE

The numbers of students in each of a school's six Algebra 1 classes are listed below. Find each statistic for this data set.

$$28 \quad 30 \quad 29 \quad 26 \quad 31 \quad 30$$

1. Mean = 29

2. Median = 29.5

3. Range = 5

4. IQR = 2

5. Find the standard deviation of the Algebra 1 class data by completing the table and doing the calculations below it.

Data value, x	Deviation from mean, $x - \bar{x}$	Squared deviation, $(x - \bar{x})^2$
28	$28 - 29 = -1$	$(-1)^2 = 1$
30	$30 - 29 = 1$	$1^2 = 1$
29	$29 - 29 = 0$	$0^2 = 0$
26	$26 - 29 = -3$	$(-3)^2 = 9$
31	$31 - 29 = 2$	$2^2 = 4$
30	$30 - 29 = 1$	$1^2 = 1$

Mean of squared deviations = $2.\overline{6}$

Standard deviation ≈ 1.6

6. Error Analysis Suppose a student in the Algebra 1 class with 31 students transfers to the class with 26 students. The student claims that the measures of center and the measures of spread will all change. Correct the student's error.

The mean and the median do not change; of the measures of spread, the

range decreases from 5 to 3 and the standard deviation decreases from 1.6

to 1.2 while the IQR remains unchanged.

7. The table lists the heights (in centimeters) of 8 males and 8 females on the U.S. Olympic swim team, all randomly selected from swimmers on the team who participated in the 2008 Olympic Games held in Beijing, China.

Heights of Olympic male swimmers	196	188	196	185	203	183	183	196
Heights of Olympic female swimmers	173	170	178	175	173	180	180	175

a. Use a graphing calculator to complete the table below.

	Center		Spread	
	Mean	Median	IQR $(Q_3 - Q_1)$	Standard deviation
Olympic male swimmers	191.25	192	12	7.00
Olympic female swimmers	175.5	175	5	3.35

b. Discuss the consistency of the measures of center for male swimmers and the measures of center for female swimmers, and then compare the measures of center for male and female swimmers.

For male swimmers and for female swimmers, the measures of center are

approximately equal, so they are consistent. On average, a male swimmer

is $192 - 175 = 17$ cm taller than a female swimmer.

c. What do the measures of spread tell you about the variation in the heights of the male and female swimmers?

There is about twice as much variation in the heights of the male

swimmers as there is in the heights of the female swimmers.

Data Distributions and Outliers

Essential question: *Which statistics are most affected by outliers, and what shapes can data distributions have?*

COMMON CORE Standards for Mathematical Content

CC.9-12.S.ID.1 Represent data with plots on the real number line (dot plots, histograms, and box plots).*

CC.9-12.S.ID.2 Use statistics appropriate to the shape of the data distribution to compare center (median, mean) and spread (interquartile range, standard deviation) of two or more different data sets.*

CC.9-12.S.ID.3 Interpret differences in shape, center, and spread in the context of the data sets, accounting for possible effects of extreme data points (outliers).*

Vocabulary

outlier, symmetric, skewed to the left, skewed to the right

Prerequisites

Measures of center and spread, Lesson 9-1

Math Background

Students are familiar with how to make line plots and how to find the interquartile range (IQR) of a data set. In this lesson, students will be introduced to outliers in data sets. An outlier is a value that is very different from the other values in a data set and can be defined as any data value whose distance is more than $1.5 \times$ IQR below Q_1 (the first quartile) or more than $1.5 \times$ IQR above Q_3 (the third quartile). The presence or lack of an outlier can be used to determine whether the mean or the median better describes the center of a data set.

Students will analyze how adding an outlier affects measures of center and spread. Students are then introduced to analyzing a data set by its shape and describing a data set as symmetric or skewed. Finally, students learn how the shape of a data set affects the statistics used to characterize the data.

INTRODUCE

Review with students how to draw a line plot for a data set and how to find the mean and median.

TEACH

1 EXAMPLE

Questioning Strategies

- How can you find the median of the data set using the line plot? A line plot uses Xs to display data ordered from least to greatest. There are 12 data values in this data set, so the median is the mean of the 6th and 7th values. On the line plot, the 6th and 7th values are represented by the 6th and 7th Xs from the left, which are both 40.

- How can you find Q_1 and Q_3 of the data set using the line plot? Explain. Q_1 is the median of the lower half of the data set, or the mean of the 3rd and 4th values. On the line plot, the 3rd and 4th values are represented by the 3rd and 4th Xs from the left, which are both 35. Finding Q_3 entails a similar process with the 9th and 10th Xs, which are both 45.

- Describe how to find the interquartile range of the data set. Since the IQR of a data set is the difference between the 3rd and 1st quartiles, the IQR is $45 - 35 = 10$.

- Describe how to find the standard deviation of the data set. Find the deviations from the mean, square the deviations, find the mean of the squared deviations, and then take the square root of the mean of the squared deviations.

Teaching Strategy

Review how to find the mean, the median, Q_1, Q_3, the interquartile range, and the standard deviation. Ask students to describe how the interquartile range and standard deviation can be used to draw conclusions about the spread of a data set.

Data Distributions and Outliers

9-2

COMMON CORE

CC.9-12.S.ID.1*,
CC.9-12.S.ID.2*,
CC.9-12.S.ID.3*

Name_____ Class_____ Date_____

Essential question: Which statistics are most affected by outliers, and what shapes can data distributions have?

1 EXAMPLE   Using Line Plots to Display Data

Twelve employees at a small company make the following annual salaries (in thousands of dollars): 25, 30, 35, 35, 35, 40, 40, 40, 45, 45, 50, 60.

A Create a line plot of the data by putting an X above the number line to represent each data value. Stack the Xs for repeated data values.

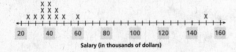

Salary (in thousands of dollars)

B Complete the table. Round to the nearest hundredth, if necessary.

Mean	Median	Range	IQR	Standard deviation
40	40	35	10	8.90

REFLECT

1a. *Quantitative data* are numbers, such as counts or measurements. *Qualitative data* are categories, such as attributes or preferences. For example, employees' salaries are quantitative data while employees' positions within a company are qualitative data. Is it appropriate to use a line plot for displaying quantitative data, qualitative data, or both? Explain.

Quantitative data; a line plot uses a number line, so it is appropriate only for

displaying quantitative data.

1b. The line plot allows you to see how the data are distributed. Describe the overall shape of the distribution of employees' salaries.

The distribution is mounded near the center and trails off at the ends.

1c. When you examine the line plot, do any data values appear to be different than the others? Explain.

The data value 60 appeared separated from the other data values.

Outliers An **outlier** is a value in a data set that is relatively much greater or much less than most of the other values in the data set. Outliers are determined using either the IQR or the standard deviation. Below is one way to determine whether a data value is an outlier.

Determining Whether a Data Value Is an Outlier
A data value x is an outlier if $x < Q_1 - 1.5(IQR)$ or if $x > Q_3 + 1.5(IQR)$.

2 EXPLORE   Investigating the Effect of an Outlier in a Data Set

Suppose the list of salaries in the previous example is expanded to include the owner's salary, which is $150,000. Now the list of salaries is: 25, 30, 35, 35, 35, 40, 40, 40, 45, 45, 50, 60, 150.

A Create a line plot for the revised data set. Choose an appropriate scale for the number line.

Salary (in thousands of dollars)

B Complete the table. Use a calculator and round to the nearest hundredth, if necessary.

Mean	Median	Range	IQR	Standard deviation
48.46	40	125	12.5	30.53

C Complete each sentence by stating whether the statistic increased, decreased, or stayed the same when the data value 150 was added to the original data set. If the statistic increased or decreased, say by what amount.

The mean _____ increased by 8.46 _____.

The median _____ stayed the same _____

The range _____ increased by 90 _____

The IQR _____ increased by 2.5 _____.

The standard deviation _____ increased by 21.63 _____

EXTRA EXAMPLE

Twelve students in a math class have the following quiz scores: 75, 70, 75, 80, 85, 80, 90, 90, 85, 70, 80, 80. Create a line plot for the data by putting an X above the number line to represent each data point. Determine the mean, median, range, IQR, and standard deviation.

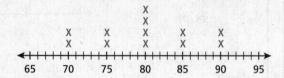

The mean is 80, the median is 80, the range is 20, the IQR is 10, and the standard deviation is 6.45.

Avoid Common Errors

When calculating the first and third quartiles, students often use the mean instead of the median. Review the steps for finding Q_1 and Q_3. Students also often forget to take the square root of the mean of the squared deviations when calculating standard deviation. Review the five steps for calculating the standard deviation. Have students make a chart outlining steps for finding Q_1, Q_3, IQR, and standard deviation to help them remember.

2 EXPLORE

Questioning Strategies

- How can an outlier affect the measure of center of a data set? If a data set includes an outlier, the mean can be increased or decreased significantly. This can result in a measure of center that is misleading. The majority of data values cluster closer to the mean calculated without including the outlier.

- In part C, why did Q_1 stay the same when including the outlier? Since the outlier is much greater than the other data values, it did not change the calculations for Q_1, the median of the lower half of the data.

- Suppose the list of salaries in **1 EXAMPLE** includes a part-time employee's salary, which is $10,000, but does not include the owner's salary. Which statistics change or stay the same when the new value is added to the original data set? The mean is 37.69, a decrease of 2.31; the median stays the same, 40; the range is 50, an increase of 15; the IQR is 12.5, an increase of 2.5; and the standard deviation is 11.7, an increase of 3.05.

Differentiated Learning

English language learners may benefit from acting out a real-world example of how adding an outlier to a data set affects measures of center and spread. For example, have five students in the class each use pieces of paper (or pennies or markers) to represent a number of dollars ranging from 1 to 5. Have students use the pieces of paper to calculate the mean. Then, have a sixth student with $25 (25 pieces of paper) join the group. Again, use the pieces of paper to find the mean. Ask whether the new mean is a reasonable measure of center.

3 EXAMPLE

Questioning Strategies

- If a line plot is skewed to the left, how are the data distributed? Most of the data values are clustered on the right, with a tail to the left of the cluster.

- If a line plot is skewed to the right, how are the data distributed? Most of the data values are clustered on the left, with a tail to the right of the cluster.

- If a line plot is symmetric, how are the data distributed? The distribution is centered on one value, with the data values on the left balanced with the data values on the right.

REFLECT

2a. Show that the data value 150 is an outlier, but the data value 60 is not. Use the inequalities given at the top of the previous page to support your answer.

For either data value to be an outlier, it would have to be greater than

$Q_3 + 1.5(IQR) = 47.5 + 1.5(12.5) = 66.25$. So, 150 is an outlier, but 60 is not.

2b. What effect does the outlier have on the overall shape of the distribution?

It lengthens the tail to the right of the distribution's center.

2c. For the original data set, you can conclude that the salary of a typical employee is $40,000 regardless of whether you used the mean or the median. For the revised data set, you could say that the salary of a typical employee is either $48,500 or $40,000 depending on whether you used the mean or the median. Which average salary is more reasonable for the revised data set? Explain your reasoning.

$40,000; all but one of the employees at the company have salaries that are

close to $40,000.

2d. Based on how the IQR and standard deviation are calculated, explain why the IQR was only slightly affected by the addition of the outlier while the standard deviation was dramatically changed.

The IQR is calculated using only Q_1 and Q_3. The standard deviation is

calculated using all data values, and the addition of the outlier, which

was so much greater than the other data values, greatly increased the

standard deviation.

2e. Because the median and the IQR are based on quartiles while the standard deviation is based on the mean, the center and spread of a data set are usually reported either as the median and IQR or as the mean and standard deviation. Which pair of statistics would you use for a data set that includes one or more outliers? Explain.

Median and IQR; these statistics are affected less (if at all) by outliers than are

the mean and standard deviation.

Shapes of Distributions A data distribution can be described as **symmetric**, **skewed to the left**, or **skewed to the right** depending on the general shape of the distribution in a line plot or other data display.

Skewed to the Left	Symmetric	Skewed to the Right
X X X X X X X X X X X X X	X X X X X X X X X X X X X X X	X X X X X X X X X X X X

3 EXAMPLE Comparing Data Distributions

The tables list Sierra's and Jacey's scores on math tests in each quarter of the school year. Create a line plot for each student's scores and identify the distribution as symmetric, skewed to the left, or skewed to the right.

Sierra's Scores			
I	II	III	IV
88	86	92	88
94	90	87	91
91	95	94	91
92	91	88	93
90	94	96	89

Jacey's Scores			
I	II	III	IV
89	76	87	82
83	86	86	85
86	87	72	86
83	88	73	88
87	90	84	89

A Create and examine a line plot for Sierra's scores.

Sierra's Test Scores

The distribution is centered on one value (91) with the data values to the left of the center balanced with the data values to the right, so the distribution is symmetric.

B Create and examine a line plot for Jacey's scores.

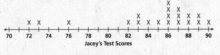

Jacey's Test Scores

The data values cluster on the right with a few data values spread out to the left of the cluster, so the distribution is skewed to the left.

Avoid Common Errors

Students often confuse the terms "skewed to the left" and "skewed to the right." Even though they may be able to identify a distribution as being skewed, they may have trouble remembering how that is related to the direction. Encourage students to come up with a mnemonic that may help them remember. For example, students may easily remember how the "tail" of a data distribution looks on a line plot. Have them think that "tail" and "skew" both have four letters, and that a data distribution is skewed in the direction of its tail.

EXTRA EXAMPLE

The lists below show the results of a survey in which students were asked how many sisters and brothers they have.

Sisters: 2, 4, 1, 0, 2, 0, 1, 3, 1, 2, 3, 2, 3, 4
Brothers: 0, 2, 0, 1, 0, 0, 1, 5, 1, 2, 1, 1, 6, 2, 2, 3

Describe the data distributions for both sets of data and identify each distribution as symmetric, skewed to the left, or skewed to the right. **For the data set for sisters, the distribution is symmetric with data values centered close to 2. For the data set for brothers, the distribution is skewed right.**

MATHEMATICAL PRACTICE Highlighting the Standards

3 EXAMPLE and its Reflect questions offer an opportunity to address Mathematical Practice Standard 2 (Reason abstractly and quantitatively). Students solve real-world statistical analysis problems by creating line plots for data sets, analyzing the shapes of the distributions, recognizing how the shapes affect the measures of center and spread, and making comparisons of the data sets.

Essential Question

Which statistics are most affected by outliers, and what shapes can data distributions have?
Outliers affect the mean more than the median, and they affect the standard deviation more than the IQR. Data distributions can be described generally as symmetric, skewed to the left, or skewed to the right.

Summarize

Have students collect or research their own data, creating a line plot and calculating measures of center and spread. Next, have them check for outliers and recalculate the statistics after excluding the outliers. Then, have them draw conclusions, identifying whether the distribution is symmetric, skewed to the right, or skewed to the left. Students can collect data related to their lives, or they can be directed to online resources like the *Statistical Abstract of the United States,* which can be found at www.census.gov.

PRACTICE

Where skills are taught	Where skills are practiced
1 EXAMPLE	EXS. 1, 3a, 3b
2 EXPLORE	EXS. 2, 3c
3 EXAMPLE	EXS. 3d, 3e

Exercise 4: Students extend their understanding of outliers and data distributions by creating their own symmetric data set with at least one outlier.

Exercise 5: Students extend their understanding of outliers and data distributions by determining that the mean and standard deviation would more accurately represent the data set if an outlier were removed.

REFLECT

3a. Find the mean and median for Sierra's test scores. How do they compare?

Mean = 91; median = 91; they are equal.

3b. Will the mean and median in a symmetric distribution always be equal or approximately equal? Explain.

Yes; the median is the middle data value, and the mean will be equal to

(or close to) the middle value because for every data value that is a certain

distance to the left of the middle value there is another data value that is

the same (or nearly the same) distance to the right of the middle value.

3c. Find the mean and median for Jacey's test scores. How do they compare?

Mean = 84.35; median = 86; the mean is less than the median.

3d. Will the mean and median in a skewed distribution always be different? Explain.

Yes; because a skewed distribution has a tail that is longer on one side of the

middle data value (the median) than on the other, the data values in the longer

tail will pull the mean toward them.

PRACTICE

1. a. Rounded to the nearest $50,000, the values (in thousands of dollars) of homes sold by a realtor are listed below. Use the number line to create a line plot for the data set.

300 250 200 250 350

400 300 250 400 300

```
        X    X
        X    X
  X     X    X       X
X   X   X    X    X   X
200  250  300  350  400
  Values of Homes
(in thousands of dollars)
```

b. Suppose the realtor sells a home with a value of $650,000. Which statistics are affected when 650 is included in the data set?

The mean, range, IQR, and standard deviation

c. Would 650 be considered an outlier? Explain.

Yes; Q_3 = 400 and IQR = 150, so any value greater than 400 + 1.5(150) = 625 is

an outlier.

2. In Exercise 1, find the mean and median for the data set with and without the data value 650. Why might the realtor want to use the mean instead of the median when advertising the typical value of homes sold?

Without: mean = median = 300; with: mean ≈ 332, median = 300; mean suggests

realtor sells homes for higher values

3. The table shows Chloe's scores on math tests in each quarter of the school year.

Chloe's Scores			
I	II	III	IV
74	77	79	74
78	75	76	77
82	80	74	76
76	75	77	78
85	77	87	85

a. Use the number line below to create a line plot for Chloe's scores.

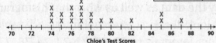

```
                 X
           X     X
     X     X X   X
     X X X X X X X   X     X   X
  70  72  74  76  78  80  82  84  86  88  90
           Chloe's Test Scores
```

b. Complete the table below for the data set.

Mean	Median	Range	IQR	Standard deviation
78.1	77	13	4	3.75

c. Identify any outliers in the data set. Which of the statistics from the table above would change if the outliers were removed?

87; the mean, range, and standard deviation would change.

d. Describe the shape of the distribution.

Skewed to the right

e. Which measure of center and which measure of spread should be used to characterize the data? Explain.

Median and IQR because they are not affected by the outlier

4. Give an example of a data set with a symmetric distribution that also includes one or more outliers.

Sample answer: 10, 23, 23, 25, 25, 25, 26, 26, 40

5. Suppose that a data set has an approximately symmetric distribution, with one outlier. What could you do if you wanted to use the mean and standard deviation to characterize the data?

Remove the outlier from the data set before calculating the statistics.

9-3 Histograms

Essential question: *How can you estimate statistics from data displayed in a histogram?*

COMMON CORE **Standards for Mathematical Content**

CC.9-12.S.ID.1 Represent data with plots on the real number line (dot plots, histograms, and box plots).*

CC.9-12.S.ID.2 Use statistics appropriate to the shape of the data distribution to compare center (median, mean) and spread (interquartile range, standard deviation) of two or more different data sets.*

Prerequisites

Data distributions and outliers, Lesson 9-2

Math Background

Students will create histograms to display a set of data summarized in a frequency table. The *frequency* of a data value is the number of times it occurs. A *frequency table* shows the frequency of each data value. If the data are grouped into intervals, the table shows the frequency for each interval. A *histogram* is a type of bar graph used to display the frequency of data grouped into adjoining intervals of equal width. This means that the bars of the histogram will have equal width and consecutive bars will touch each other.

INTRODUCE

Review the process for creating histograms to display and analyze data sets. Tell students that it is helpful to first order the data from least to greatest, if the data have not already been ordered. Point out that, in general, frequency tables should have between four and seven intervals.

TEACH

 EXAMPLE

Questioning Strategies

- What does the vertical axis in a histogram represent? frequency

- Does a histogram show individual data values? No, a histogram gives a quick visual representation of intervals of data.

Teaching Strategy

Remind students that each bar in a histogram represents an interval and that the bars should have equal width. Discuss reasons why each interval in this frequency table represents a 10-year span instead of a 5-year span or a 20-year span. Point out that even though individual data values are not shown in a histogram, the histogram can be used to estimate measures of center and spread.

EXTRA EXAMPLE

Listed below are the heights in inches of basketball players on a high school basketball team.

68, 69, 71, 72, 72, 72, 73, 73, 74, 75, 76, 76, 77, 79

Describe how you would create a histogram to display the data as well as what that histogram would look like. First, create a frequency table with four intervals of 68–70, 71–73, 74–76, 77–79; then, tally the frequencies. Use the data in the table to create the histogram that has a horizontal axis labeled "Height (in.)" with four intervals labeled the same as those in the frequency table. The vertical axis is labeled "Frequency" with a scale from 0 to 10. Above the intervals are bars of heights 2, 6, 4, and 2, respectively.

Name_____ Class_____ Date_____

9-3

COMMON CORE

CC.9-12.S.ID.1*,
CC.9-12.S.ID.2*

Histograms

Essential question: *How can you estimate statistics from data displayed in a histogram?*

Like a line plot, a histogram uses a number line to display data. Rather than display the data values individually as a line plot does, a histogram groups the data values into adjoining intervals of equal width and uses the heights of bars to indicate the number of data values that occur in each interval.

The number of data values in an interval is called the *frequency* of the interval. A histogram has a vertical frequency axis so that you can read the frequency for each interval. In the histogram at the right, you can see that 3 students had test scores in the interval 60–69, 9 students had test scores in the interval 70–79, and so on.

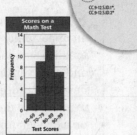

Scores on a Math Test

1 EXAMPLE Creating a Histogram

Listed below are the ages of the 100 U.S. senators at the time that the 112th Congress began on January 3, 2011. Create a histogram for this data set.

39, 39, 42, 44, 46, 47, 47, 47, 48, 49, 49, 49, 50, 50, 51, 51, 52, 52, 53, 53, 54, 54, 55, 55, 55, 55, 55, 55, 55, 56, 56, 57, 57, 57, 58, 58, 58, 58, 58, 59, 59, 59, 59, 60, 60, 60, 60, 60, 60, 60, 61, 61, 62, 62, 62, 63, 63, 63, 63, 64, 64, 64, 64, 66, 66, 66, 67, 67, 67, 67, 67, 67, 67, 68, 68, 68, 68, 69, 69, 69, 70, 70, 70, 71, 71, 73, 73, 74, 74, 74, 75, 76, 76, 76, 76, 77, 77, 78, 86, 86, 86

A Create a frequency table. To do so, you must decide what the interval width will be and where to start the first interval. Since the data are ages that run from 39 to 86, you might decide to use an interval width of 10 and start the first interval at 30. So, the first interval includes any Senator who is in his or her 30s.

Use the data to complete the table at the right. When done, be sure to check that the sum of the frequencies is 100.

Age Interval	Frequency
30–39	2
40–49	10
50–59	30
60–69	37
70–79	18
80–89	3

B Use the frequency table to complete the histogram.

Ages of U.S. Senators at the Start of the 112th Congress

REFLECT

1a. Describe the shape of the distribution. Is it approximately symmetric, skewed to the right, or skewed to the left? Explain.

The distribution is approximately symmetric, because the frequencies are

very roughly equal for the intervals 30–39 and 80–89, for the intervals

40–49 and 70–79, and for the intervals 50–59 and 60–69.

1b. Estimate the center of the distribution. Explain your reasoning.

Answers will vary. Sample answer: 65; the center must be slightly greater

than 60 because there are more data values over 60 than under 60.

1c. Using the histogram alone, and not the data values on the first page of this lesson, estimate the maximum possible range and the minimum possible range. Explain your reasoning.

The maximum possible range is 59 years; the minimum possible range is

41 years; the least possible data value in the first interval is 30, and the

greatest possible data value in the last interval is 89, and 89 − 30 = 59. The

greatest possible data value in the first interval is 39 and the least possible

data value in the last interval is 80, and 80 − 39 = 41.

Questioning Strategies

• Suppose all ages in the 30–39 interval were 39 years, all ages in the 40–49 interval were 49 years, and so on. How would the actual mean be related to the estimated mean? The actual mean would be greater than the estimated mean, because the estimated mean is calculated with all ages at the midpoints of the intervals (35 years, 45 years, and so on).

• Is the median of a data set always represented in one of the middle intervals of a histogram? No, if the data distribution is skewed to the left or right, the median value may be represented in an interval on either end. For example, if more than half the senators were 80–89 years old, the median would be in the rightmost interval.

Differentiated Learning

While visual learners may be comfortable with the general visual representation of a data set, analytical learners may be troubled by the fact that specific data values are not represented. These analytical learners may benefit from sketching the histogram on a piece of paper and writing the actual data values into their corresponding intervals to better understand how the estimates are made. English language learners may also benefit from this additional step, which connects the numeric data set to its visual representation.

EXTRA EXAMPLE

Suppose you have only the histogram from the Extra Example for **1** EXAMPLE as a reference. Estimate the mean and median from the histogram and describe the steps you followed.

Mean ≈ 73; $\dfrac{2 \cdot 69 + 6 \cdot 72 + 4 \cdot 75 + 2 \cdot 78}{14} = \dfrac{1026}{14}$

≈ 73; median ≈ 73; the median is the average of the 5th and 6th values in an interval with 6 values, so it is approximately the sum of the interval's least value and 92% of the interval width, 2. Median $\approx 71 + 0.92(2) \approx 73$

2 EXAMPLE and its Reflect questions offer an opportunity to address Mathematical Practice Standard 1 (Make sense of problems and persevere in solving them). Students develop a process to estimate the mean, the median, and the IQR of a data set based solely on a histogram. Their solutions are expressed in real-world contexts and involve classifying the distribution as symmetric, skewed right, or skewed left.

CLOSE

Essential Question

How can you estimate statistics from data displayed in a histogram?
By looking at a histogram, you can tell which interval contains the median and estimate its value. You can estimate the mean using the frequency and midpoint values of each interval. A histogram provides adequate information with which to make reasonable estimates of the mean, median, IQR, and standard deviation.

Summarize

Have students collect or research their own data and make a histogram to display the data. Also have students share their histograms with a classmate so that the classmate can use it to estimate measures of center and spread.

PRACTICE

Where skills are taught	Where skills are practiced
1 EXAMPLE	EXS. 1a, 1b, 1c
2 EXAMPLE	EX. 1d

Exercise 2: Students build on what they already know about estimating the mean from a histogram to estimate the standard deviation from the histogram.

2 EXAMPLE Estimating Statistics from a Histogram

Although the first page of this lesson listed the ages all 100 senators, suppose you have only the histogram on the second page as a reference. Show how to estimate the mean and the median ages from the histogram.

A Estimate the mean. You know the frequency of each interval, but you don't know the individual data values. Use the midpoint of the interval as a substitute for each of those values. So, for the interval 30–39, you can estimate the sum of the data values by multiplying the midpoint, 35, by the frequency, 2. Complete the calculation below, rounding the final result to the nearest whole number.

$$\text{Mean} \approx \frac{35 \cdot 2 + 45 \cdot 10 + 55 \cdot 30 + 65 \cdot 37 + 75 \cdot 18 + 85 \cdot 3}{100}$$

$$= \frac{6180}{100} \approx 62$$

B Estimate the median. The median is the average of the 50th and 51st data values. In what interval do these values fall? Explain.

The 50th and 51st values fall in the interval 60–69 because there are 2 + 10 +

30 = 42 values to the left of the interval and 30 values in the interval.

The median is the average of the 8th and 9th values in an interval with 37 values, so you can estimate that the median is the sum of the interval's least value and $\frac{8.5}{37} \approx 20\%$ of the interval width, 10. So, what is the estimate?

Median ≈ 60 + 0.2(10) = 62

REFLECT

2a. How do the estimates of the mean and median support the observation that the distribution is approximately symmetric?

In a symmetric distribution, the mean and median are equal, which is true

of these estimates.

2b. Describe how you could estimate the IQR. Then give your estimate.

Follow a procedure like the one for estimating the median in order to estimate

Q_1 and Q_3: $Q_1 \approx 50 + \frac{13.5}{30} \cdot 10 \approx 55$ and $Q_3 \approx 60 + \frac{33.5}{37} \cdot 10 \approx 69$,

so IQR ≈ 69 − 55 = 14.

PRACTICE

1. The ages of the first 44 U.S. presidents on the date of their first inauguration are listed below.

42, 43, 46, 46, 47, 47, 48, 49, 49, 50, 51, 51, 51, 51, 51, 52, 52, 54, 54, 54, 54, 55, 55, 55, 55, 56, 56, 56, 57, 57, 57, 57, 57, 58, 60, 61, 61, 61, 62, 64, 64, 65, 68, 69

a. Complete the frequency table by organizing the data into six equal intervals.

Age Interval	Frequency
41–45	2
46–50	8
51–55	16
56–60	9
61–65	7
66–70	2

b. Use the frequency table to complete the histogram.

Ages of U.S. Presidents on the Date of Their First Inauguration

c. Describe the shape of the distribution. What measures of center and spread would you use to characterize the data? Why?

Skewed to the right; the median and IQR because they are not as affected by

the data values in the right tail as the mean and standard deviation are.

d. Use the histogram to estimate the median and IQR.
Median ≈ $51 + \frac{12.5}{16} \cdot 5 \approx 55$; $Q_1 \approx 51 + \frac{1.5}{16} \cdot 5 \approx 51$ and

$Q_3 \approx 56 + \frac{7.5}{9} \cdot 5 \approx 60$; so IQR ≈ 60 − 51 = 9

2. Describe a way to estimate the standard deviation from a histogram.

Estimate the mean, square the deviation of the midpoint of each interval from

the mean, multiply each squared deviation by its frequency, add the products and

divide by the sum of the frequencies, then take the square root.

Notes

Box Plots

Essential question: How can you compare data sets using box plots?

COMMON
CORE

**Standards for
Mathematical Content**

CC.9-12.S.ID.1 Represent data with plots on the real number line (dot plots, histograms, and box plots).*

CC.9-12.S.ID.2 Use statistics appropriate to the shape of the data distribution to compare center (median, mean) and spread (interquartile range, standard deviation) of two or more different data sets.*

Prerequisites

Measures of center and spread, Lesson 9-1

Data distributions and outliers, Lesson 9-2

Math Background

Students are familiar with how to find the mean, median, and interquartile range of a data set. Students are also familiar with making a box plot using quartiles and the definition of IQR. They are familiar with using measures of center (mean, median) and spread (range, interquartile range, standard deviation) to compare sets of data. Box plots provide a unique way to compare data sets in that they can be positioned together above the same number line so that comparisons can be made simply by looking at the plots.

INTRODUCE

Review the process for creating box plots to display and analyze data sets. Tell students that it is helpful to first order the data from least to greatest, if the data have not already been ordered. Have students recall how to identify the median, first and third quartiles, and minimum and maximum of a data set. Review the steps for constructing a box plot by plotting these five values above a number line and using the points to draw the box plot.

TEACH

1 EXAMPLE

Questioning Strategies

- Based on the appearance of the box plot, describe the shape of the distribution if it were displayed as a line plot. **The data distribution would be skewed right. There would be more Xs clustered on the left side of the graph than on the right.**

- Can you find the exact mean of a data set by looking at its box plot? **No, a box plot shows only the median; you need to know the actual data values to find the exact mean.**

Teaching Strategy

Help students better understand how a box plot shows the distribution of data by making comparisons with line plots. Draw a box plot and a line plot for the same set of data above the same number line. Compare how both data displays show measures of center and spread.

EXTRA EXAMPLE

The scores for a midterm exam are listed below and displayed in the box plot.

57, 59, 60, 62, 65, 71, 74, 78, 80, 81, 83, 84, 88, 95, 99

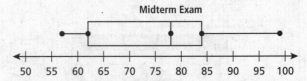

Midterm Exam

Use the box plot to determine the minimum, first quartile, median, third quartile, and maximum of the data set. Describe the distribution of the data.
Minimum: 57; Q_1: 62; median: 78; Q_3: 84; maximum: 99; the data distribution is skewed to the right.

Name_____ Class_____ Date_____

Box Plots

9-4

Essential question: *How can you compare data sets using box plots?*

COMMON
CORE

CC.9-12.S.ID.1*,
CC.9-12.S.ID.2*

1 EXAMPLE Interpreting a Box Plot

The table lists the total number of home runs hit at home games by each team in Major League Baseball (MLB) during the 2010 season. The data are displayed in the box plot below the table. Identify the statistics that are represented in the box plot, and describe the distribution of the data.

Home Runs in 2010 MLB Games Played at Home

Team	Home Runs	Team	Home Runs	Team	Home Runs
Toronto	146	Tampa Bay	78	Cleveland	64
NY Yankees	115	San Francisco	75	Pittsburgh	64
Chicago Sox	111	Atlanta	74	Houston	63
Colorado	108	Chicago Cubs	74	NY Mets	63
Cincinnati	102	Washington	74	LA Dodgers	61
Milwaukee	100	Baltimore	72	Kansas City	60
Boston	98	Detroit	70	San Diego	59
Arizona	98	LA Angels	69	Minnesota	52
Philadelphia	94	Florida	69	Oakland	46
Texas	93	St. Louis	67	Seattle	35

Home Runs in 2010 MLB Games Played at Home

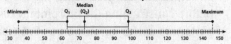

A A box plot displays a five-number summary of a data set. The five numbers are the statistics listed below. Use the box plot to determine each statistic.

Minimum	First Quartile	Median	Third Quartile	Maximum
35	63	73	98	146

B A box plot also shows the distribution of the data. Find the range of the lower half and the upper half of the data.

Range of lower half: __38__   Range of upper half: __73__

The data are more spread out in the upper half than the lower half, so the distribution is skewed to the right.

Unit 9   373   Lesson 4

© Houghton Mifflin Harcourt Publishing Company

REFLECT

1a. The lines that extend from the box in a box plot are sometimes called "whiskers." What *part* (lower, middle, or upper) and about what *percent* of the data does the box represent? What part and about what percent does each whisker represent?

Box: middle 50%; left whisker: lower 25%; right whisker: upper 25%

1b. Which measures of spread can be determined from the box plot, and how are they found? Calculate each measure.

The range is the width of the entire box plot: $146 - 35 = 111$. The IQR

is the width of the box: $98 - 63 = 35$.

1c. In the table, the data value 146 appears to be much greater than the other data values. Determine whether 146 is an outlier.

$Q_3 + 1.5(\text{IQR}) = 98 + 1.5(35) = 150.5$; since $146 < 150.5$, 146 is not an outlier.

1d. The mean of the data is about 78.5. Use the shape of the distribution to explain why the mean is greater than the median.

Because the data in the upper half are more spread out than the data in the lower

half, the mean will be increased by the data values in the upper half but the

median will not be affected by them.

2 EXAMPLE Comparing Data Using Box Plots

The table lists the total number of home runs hit at away games by each team in Major League Baseball (MLB) during the 2010 season. Display the data in a box plot.

Home Runs in 2010 MLB Games Played Away

Team	Home Runs	Team	Home Runs	Team	Home Runs
Boston	113	Milwaukee	82	Atlanta	65
Toronto	111	Arizona	82	NY Mets	65
Minnesota	90	Tampa Bay	82	Colorado	65
San Francisco	87	Chicago Cubs	75	Cleveland	64
LA Angels	86	Washington	75	Oakland	63
NY Yankees	86	San Diego	73	Pittsburgh	62
Cincinnati	86	Philadelphia	72	Baltimore	61
St. Louis	83	Texas	69	Kansas City	61
Florida	83	Chicago Sox	66	LA Dodgers	59
Detroit	82	Seattle	66	Houston	45

Unit 9   374   Lesson 4

© Houghton Mifflin Harcourt Publishing Company

Questioning Strategies

- What are the mean and the median of the away-game data when the outliers are included? when they are excluded? If outliers are included, the mean is 75.3, and the median is 74. If they are excluded, the mean is 72.7, and the median is 72.5.

- What conclusion can you draw about the effect of the outliers on both the center and the shape of the distribution? The outliers increase both the median and, to a greater extent, the mean. That the median and mean are almost equal without the outliers suggests that the distribution is more symmetric when the outliers are excluded.

Avoid Common Errors

Remind students that to compare data sets by comparing box plots that are positioned one above the other, both box plots should be drawn using the same number line. If students want to compare box plots that are created using number lines with different scales, they should make comparisons by identifying and comparing corresponding statistics.

EXTRA EXAMPLE

The scores for a final exam are listed below.

51, 53, 69, 75, 75, 78, 79, 80, 81, 81, 82, 85, 85, 88, 90

The box plot below displays the data from the midterm exam. Draw a second box plot that displays the data from the final exam, showing any outliers as individual dots.

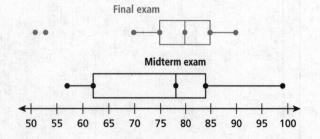

Final exam

Midterm exam

50 55 60 65 70 75 80 85 90 95 100

CLOSE

Essential Question

How can you compare data sets using box plots?
Create the box plot for each data set, using the same number line, positioning one box plot above the other. Identify any outliers. If there are outliers, identify the fences, draw the whiskers to extend only to the least and greatest data values that lie within the fences, and show the outliers as individual dots. Finally, use the box plots to compare the center, spread, and shape of the two distributions.

Summarize

Have students collect or research their own data for two data sets that can be compared, such as sports data for home and away games or weather data for different months. Have students create box plots that display both sets of data one above the other. Then, have them compare the data sets by drawing conclusions about the centers, spreads, and shapes of the two distributions.

PRACTICE

Where skills are taught	Where skills are practiced
1 EXAMPLE	EX. 1a
2 EXAMPLE	EXS. 1b, 1c

A Find the values for the five-number summary.

Minimum	First Quartile	Median	Third Quartile	Maximum
45	65	74	83	113

B Determine whether the data set includes any outliers. Begin by finding the value of each expression below using the fact that the IQR $= Q_3 - Q_1 = 83 - 65 = 18$.

$Q_1 - 1.5(\text{IQR}) =$ ___38___ $Q_3 + 1.5(\text{IQR}) =$ ___110___

These values are sometimes called *fences* because they form the boundaries outside of which a data value is considered to be an outlier. Which data values, if any, are outliers for the away-game data? Why?

111 and 113 are both outliers because each is greater than 110.

C The box plot shown below displays the number of home runs hit at home games during the 2010 MLB season. Draw a second box plot that displays the data for away games. The whiskers should extend only to the least and greatest data values that lie within the fences established in Part B. Show any outliers as individual dots.

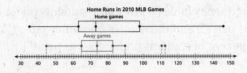

Home Runs in 2010 MLB Games
Home games

Away games

30   40   50   60   70   80   90   100   110   120   130   140   150

REFLECT

2a. Use the box plots to compare the center, spread, and shape of the two data distributions. Ignore any outliers.

The two distributions have approximately the same center, but the spread for home games is much greater than the spread for away games. The distribution for away games is more symmetric than the distribution for home games.

PRACTICE

1. The table shows the 2010 average salary for an MLB player by team for both the American League (AL) and the National League (NL).

a. Find the values for the five-number summary for each league.

	AL	NL
Min.	1.7	1.3
Q_1	2.1	2.2
Median	3.3	3.0
Q_3	4.2	3.7
Max.	8.3	5.4

MLB Players' Average 2010 Salaries (in Millions of Dollars)			
American League		**National League**	
Team	**Salary**	**Team**	**Salary**
New York	8.3	Chicago	5.4
Boston	5.6	Philadelphia	5.1
Detroit	4.6	New York	5.1
Chicago	4.2	St. Louis	3.7
Los Angeles	3.6	Los Angeles	3.7
Seattle	3.5	San Francisco	3.5
Minnesota	3.5	Houston	3.3
Baltimore	3.1	Atlanta	3.1
Tampa Bay	2.7	Colorado	2.9
Kansas City	2.5	Milwaukee	2.8
Cleveland	2.1	Cincinnati	2.8
Toronto	2.1	Arizona	2.3
Texas	1.9	Florida	2.1
Oakland	1.7	Washington	2.0
		San Diego	1.5
		Pittsburgh	1.3

b. Complete the scale on the number line below. Then use the number line to create two box plots, one for each league. Show any outliers as individual dots.

MLB Player's Average 2010 Salaries (in Millions of Dollars)

National League

American League

1.0   2.0   3.0   4.0   5.0   6.0   7.0   8.0   9.0

c. Compare the center, spread, and shape of the two data distributions. Ignore any outliers.

The center for the AL is slightly greater than the center for the NL. The spread of the middle 50% for the AL is also greater than the spread of the middle 50% for the NL. For both distributions, the spread of the upper and lower halves (ignoring the AL outlier) are approximately equal, so the two distributions are approximately symmetric.

Two-Way Frequency Tables

Essential question: How can categorical data be organized and analyzed?

COMMON CORE Standards for Mathematical Content

CC.9-12.S.ID.5 Summarize categorical data for two categories in two-way frequency tables. Interpret relative frequencies in the context of the data (including joint, marginal, and conditional relative frequencies). Recognize possible associations and trends in the data.*

Vocabulary

two-way frequency table, joint relative frequency, marginal relative frequency, two-way relative frequency table, conditional relative frequency

Math Background

Previous lessons in Unit 9 have involved numerical data that could be displayed using a number line. In this lesson, students will work with categorical data, organizing the data in tables.

INTRODUCE

Briefly review the data displays and analysis techniques covered so far in this unit, emphasizing that the data are numeric. Explain that students will be working with a different type of data, involving categories rather than numbers.

TEACH

1 EXAMPLE

Questioning Strategies

• What is an advantage of displaying categorical data in a relative frequency table instead of a frequency table? You can easily see what part of the whole data set is represented by each category of data.

• When the pet data are represented in the relative frequency table shown in part B, is there any way to determine the number of students who were surveyed? No; if you don't already know how many students were surveyed, you cannot determine this information.

Teaching Strategy

Ask students to give examples of questions about the data set that can be answered by looking at the frequency table ("How many students prefer dogs as pets?") and the relative frequency table ("What percent of students prefer dogs as pets?")

EXTRA EXAMPLE

In a survey, 4 students prefer vanilla, 10 prefer chocolate, and 6 prefer other flavors of frozen yogurt. Create a relative frequency table that uses percents.

Preferred Flavor	Vanilla	Chocolate	Other	TOTAL
Relative Frequency	20%	50%	30%	100%

2 EXAMPLE

Questioning Strategies

• What does it mean if you create a two-way frequency table and the sum of the row totals is different from the sum of the column totals? You have made an error in addition.

• Could the table also be organized with rows for Preferred Pet and columns for Gender? yes, as long as the data values are entered in the correct cells of the table

EXTRA EXAMPLE

In the survey from the previous Extra Example, 1 boy and 3 girls prefer vanilla, 6 boys and 4 girls prefer chocolate, and 4 boys and 2 girls prefer other flavors of frozen yogurt. Complete the two-way frequency table below.

Preferred Flavor / Gender	Vanilla	Chocolate	Other	TOTAL
Boy	1	6	4	11
Girl	3	4	2	9
TOTAL	4	10	6	20

Name_____ Class_____ Date_____

9-5

Two-Way Frequency Tables

Essential question: *How can categorical data be organized and analyzed?*

COMMON CORE

CC.9-12.S.ID.5*

In previous lessons, you worked with numerical data involving variables such as age and height. In this lesson, you will analyze *categorical* data that involve variables such as pet preference and gender.

1 EXAMPLE Creating a Relative Frequency Table

The frequency table below shows the results of a survey that Jenna took at her school. She asked 40 randomly selected students whether they preferred dogs, cats, or other pets. Convert this table to a *relative frequency* table that uses decimals as well as one that uses percents.

Preferred Pet	Dog	Cat	Other	Total
Frequency	18	12	10	40

A Divide the numbers in the frequency table by the total to obtain relative frequencies as decimals. Record the results in the table below.

Preferred Pet	Dog	Cat	Other	Total
Relative Frequency	$\frac{18}{40} = 0.45$	$\frac{12}{40} = 0.3$	$\frac{10}{40} = 0.25$	$\frac{40}{40} = 1$

B Write the decimals as percents in the table below.

Preferred Pet	Dog	Cat	Other	Total
Relative Frequency	45%	30%	25%	100%

REFLECT

1a. How can you check that you have correctly converted frequencies to relative frequencies?

The sum of the relative frequencies as decimals should be 1; the sum of the relative frequencies as percents should be 100%.

1b. Explain why the number in the Total column of a relative frequency table is always 1 or 100%.

To obtain a relative frequency from a frequency, you divide the frequency by the total. The total divided by itself will always equal 1 or 100%.

In the previous example, the categorical variable was pet preference, and the variable had three possible data values: dog, cat, and other. The frequency table listed the frequency for each value of that single variable. If you have two categorical variables whose values have been paired, you list the frequencies of the paired values in a **two-way frequency table**.

2 EXAMPLE Creating a Two-Way Frequency Table

For her survey, Jenna also recorded the gender of each student. The results are shown in the two-way frequency table below. Each entry is the frequency of students who prefer a certain pet *and* are a certain gender. For instance, 8 girls prefer dogs as pets. Complete the table.

Gender \ Preferred Pet	Dog	Cat	Other	Total
Girl	8	7	1	16
Boy	10	5	9	24
Total	18	12	10	40

A Find the total for each gender by adding the frequencies in each row. Write the row totals in the Total column.

B Find the total for each preferred pet by adding the frequencies in each column. Write the column totals in the Total row.

C Find the grand total, which is the sum of the row totals as well as the sum of the column totals. Write the grand total in the lower-right corner of the table (the intersection of the Total column and the Total row).

REFLECT

2a. Where have you seen the numbers in the Total row before?

They are from the frequency table in the previous example.

2b. In terms of Jenna's survey, what does the grand total represent?

The number of students surveyed

You can obtain the following *relative* frequencies from a two-way frequency table:

- A **joint relative frequency** is found by dividing a frequency that is not in the Total row or the Total column by the grand total.
- A **marginal relative frequency** is found by dividing a row total or a column total by the grand total.

Questioning Strategies

- In the two-way relative frequency table in part A, what question could have "12.5%" as its answer? **Of the students surveyed, what percent are boys who prefer cats as pets?**

- In the two-way relative frequency table in part A, what question could have "40%" as its answer? **Of the students surveyed, what percent are girls?**

Differentiated Instruction

Visual and English language learners may benefit from shading in one color the part of a two-way frequency table that represents joint relative frequencies (i.e., cells at the intersection of two categories) and shading in another color the part of the table that represents marginal relative frequencies (i.e., row or column totals).

| 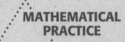 **MATHEMATICAL PRACTICE** | **Highlighting the Standards** |

3 EXAMPLE and its Reflect questions offer an opportunity to address Mathematical Practice Standard 8 (Look for and express regularity in repeated reasoning). As students repeat calculations for each cell in the two-way relative frequency table, they become increasingly proficient in the process of calculating relative frequency. In addition, they generalize the process so they can apply the same calculations and reasoning to any categorical data set organized in a two-way frequency table.

EXTRA EXAMPLE

Create a two-way relative frequency table for the data in the previous Extra Example. Write the relative frequencies as decimals.

Preferred Flavor / Gender	Vanilla	Chocolate	Other	TOTAL
Boy	0.05	0.3	0.2	0.55
Girl	0.15	0.2	0.1	0.45
TOTAL	0.2	0.5	0.3	1

Questioning Strategies

- If you find the conditional relative frequency that a student is a girl, given that the student prefers dogs as pets, and add that to the conditional relative frequency that a student is a boy, given that the student prefers dogs as pets, what is the sum if the relative frequencies are written as decimals? **1**

- What will be the sum if you add the same two conditional relative frequencies as above, changing the condition to students who prefer other pets and writing the conditional relative frequencies as percents instead of decimals? **100%**

Avoid Common Errors

Students may divide the frequency by the grand total instead of the frequency's row total or the frequency's column total when finding conditional relative frequencies. Suggest that they outline or highlight the row or column that is "given." For example, a question that asks for a conditional relative frequency is often of the form "What is the relative frequency that an item of data is in one category, given that the item is in another category?" By outlining or highlighting the "given" category, students should understand that this is the only part of the table that is relevant to the question and should therefore divide by the row or column total for that category.

EXTRA EXAMPLE

Use the two-way frequency table in the Extra Example for **2** EXAMPLE to find the conditional relative frequency that a student prefers vanilla frozen yogurt, given that the student is a boy, and the conditional relative frequency that a student surveyed is a boy, given that the student prefers vanilla frozen yogurt. Express each answer as a decimal and as a percent. $\frac{1}{11} \approx 0.09$, or 9%; $\frac{1}{4} = 0.25$, or 25%.

A **two-way relative frequency table** displays both joint relative frequencies and marginal relative frequencies.

3 EXAMPLE Creating a Two-Way Relative Frequency Table

Create a two-way relative frequency table for Jenna's data.

A Divide each number in the two-way frequency table from the previous example by the grand total. Write the quotients as decimals.

Preferred Pet / Gender	Dog	Cat	Other	Total
Girl	$\frac{8}{40} = 0.2$	$\frac{7}{40} = 0.175$	$\frac{1}{40} = 0.025$	$\frac{16}{40} = 0.4$
Boy	$\frac{10}{40} = 0.25$	$\frac{5}{40} = 0.125$	$\frac{9}{40} = 0.225$	$\frac{24}{40} = 0.6$
Total	$\frac{18}{40} = 0.45$	$\frac{12}{40} = 0.3$	$\frac{10}{40} = 0.25$	$\frac{40}{40} = 1$

B Check by adding the joint relative frequencies in a row or column to see if the sum equals the row or column's marginal relative frequency.

Girl row: $0.2 + 0.175 + 0.025 = 0.4$

Boy row: $0.25 + 0.125 + 0.225 = 0.6$

Dog column: $0.2 + 0.25 = 0.45$

Cat column: $0.175 + 0.125 = 0.3$

Other column: $0.025 + 0.225 = 0.25$

REFLECT

3a. A joint relative frequency in a two-way relative frequency table tells you what portion of the entire data set falls into the intersection of a particular value of one variable and a particular value of the other variable. For instance, the joint relative frequency of students surveyed who are girls *and* prefer dogs as pets is 0.2, or 20%. What is the joint relative frequency of students surveyed who are boys and prefer cats as pets?

0.125, or 12.5%

3b. A marginal relative frequency in a two-way relative frequency table tells you what portion of the entire data set represents a particular value of just one of the variables. For instance, the marginal relative frequency of students surveyed who prefer dogs as pets is 0.45, or 45%. What is the marginal relative frequency of students surveyed who are girls?

0.4, or 40%

One other type of relative frequency that you can obtain from a two-way frequency table is a *conditional relative frequency*. A **conditional relative frequency** is found by dividing a frequency that is not in the Total row or the Total column by the frequency's row total or column total.

4 EXAMPLE Calculating Conditional Relative Frequencies

From Jenna's two-way frequency table you know that 16 students surveyed are girls and 12 students surveyed prefer cats as pets. You also know that 7 students surveyed are girls who prefer cats as pets. Use this information to find each conditional relative frequency.

A Find the conditional relative frequency that a student surveyed prefers cats as pets, given that the student is a girl.

Divide the number of girls who prefer cats as pets by the number of girls. Express your answer as a decimal and as a percent.
$\frac{7}{16} = 0.4375$, or 43.75%

B Find the conditional relative frequency that a student surveyed is a girl, given that the student prefers cats as pets.

Divide the number of girls who prefer cats as pets by the number of students who prefer cats as pets. Express your answer as a decimal and as a percent.
$\frac{7}{12} \approx 0.583$, or about 58.3%

REFLECT

4a. When calculating a conditional relative frequency, why do you divide by a row total or a column total and not by the grand total?

The "given" in a conditional relative frequency restricts the discussion to a single row or column of a two-way frequency table. A conditional relative frequency is the portion of the data in just that row or column (not the portion of all data) that meets a certain criterion.

4b. You can obtain conditional relative frequencies from a two-way *relative* frequency table. For instance, in Jenna's survey, the relative frequency of girls who prefer cats as pets is 0.175, and the relative frequency of girls is 0.4. Find the conditional relative frequency that a student surveyed prefers cats as pets, given that the student is a girl.
$\frac{0.175}{0.4} = 0.4375$, or 43.75%

Questioning Strategies

- If you know that a student prefers cats as pets, what prediction can you make about the student's gender given the conditional relative frequencies? The student is more likely to be a girl.

- If you know that a student prefers other pets, what prediction can you make about the student's gender given the conditional relative frequencies? The student is more likely to be a boy.

EXTRA EXAMPLE

Use the two-way frequency table in the Extra Example for **2** EXAMPLE to investigate the possible influence of gender on frozen yogurt flavor preference.

A. Identify the percent of all students surveyed who are boys. 60%

B. Determine each conditional relative frequency: percent who are boys, given a preference for vanilla frozen yogurt; percent who are boys, given a preference for chocolate frozen yogurt; and percent who are boys, given a preference for other flavors of frozen yogurt. 25%; 60%; 67%

C. Interpret the results by comparing each conditional relative frequency to the percent of all students surveyed who are boys.

The percent of boys who prefer vanilla is much less than 60%, so boys are less likely to prefer vanilla than girls. The percent of boys who prefer chocolate is the same as 60%, so gender does not appear to influence preference for chocolate. The percent of boys who prefer other flavors is greater than 60%, so boys are more likely to prefer other flavors of frozen yogurt than girls.

CLOSE

Essential Question

How can categorical data be organized and analyzed?

You can use frequency tables and two-way frequency tables to show the frequency for each category or category pair. You can use relative frequency tables and two-way relative frequency tables to show what part of the whole data set is represented by each category or category pair, expressing the relative frequencies as decimals or percents. From these tables you can obtain joint relative frequencies and marginal relative frequencies.

You can also calculate conditional relative frequencies, which can help you recognize possible associations in the data.

Summarize

Have students conduct their own surveys using gender and a three-category variable of their choice. Then, have students organize the data in two-way frequency and relative frequency tables using the calculations they learned in the lesson, and have them find conditional relative frequencies based on their calculations. Finally, have students use the conditional relative frequencies to analyze the data to investigate any possible influence of gender on the other variable.

PRACTICE

Where skills are taught	Where skills are practiced
1 EXAMPLE	EX. 1
2 EXAMPLE	EX. 1
3 EXAMPLE	EXS. 2, 3a, 3b
4 EXAMPLE	EX. 3c
5 EXAMPLE	EX. 4

5 EXAMPLE Finding Possible Associations Between Variables

Jenna conducted her survey because she was interested in the question, "Does gender influence what type of pet people prefer?" If there is no influence, then the distribution of gender within each subgroup of pet preference should roughly equal the distribution of gender within the whole group. Use the results of Jenna's survey to investigate possible influences of gender on pet preference.

A Identify the percent of all students surveyed who are girls: __40%__

B Determine each conditional relative frequency.

Of the 18 students who prefer dogs as pets, 8 are girls.
Percent who are girls, given a preference for dogs as pets: __44%__

Of the 12 students who prefer cats as pets, 7 are girls.
Percent who are girls, given a preference for cats as pets: __58%__

Of the 10 students who prefer other pets, 1 is a girl.
Percent who are girls, given a preference for other pets: __10%__

C Interpret the results by comparing each conditional relative frequency to the percent of all students surveyed who are girls.

The percent of girls among students who prefer dogs is fairly close to 40%, so gender does not appear to influence preference for dogs.

The percent of girls among students who prefer cats is much greater than 40%. What conclusion might you draw in this case?

Girls are more likely than boys to prefer cats as pets.

The percent of girls among students who prefer other pets is much less than 25%. What conclusion might you draw in this case?

Girls are less likely than boys to prefer other pets.

REFLECT

5a. Suppose you analyzed the data by focusing on boys rather than girls. How would the percent in Part A change? How would the percents in Part B change? How would the conclusions in Part C change?

Part A: 40% becomes 60%; Part B: 44% becomes 56%, 58% becomes 42%, and

10% becomes 90%; Part C: conclusions would not change.

5b. For pet preference to be completely uninfluenced by gender, about how many girls would have to prefer each type of pet? Explain.

40% of 18, or about 7, would have to prefer dogs; 40% of 12, or 5, would

have to prefer cats; 40% of 10, or 4, would have to prefer other pets.

PRACTICE

Antonio surveyed 60 of his classmates about their participation in school activities as well as whether they have a part-time job. The results are shown in the two-way frequency table below. Use the table to complete the exercises.

Job \ Activity	Clubs Only	Sports Only	Both	Neither	Total
Yes	12	13	16	4	45
No	3	5	5	2	15
Total	15	18	21	6	60

1. Complete the table by finding the row totals, column totals, and grand total.

2. Create a two-way relative frequency table using decimals.

Job \ Activity	Clubs Only	Sports Only	Both	Neither	Total
Yes	$\frac{12}{60} = 0.2$	$\frac{13}{60} \approx 0.217$	$\frac{16}{60} \approx 0.267$	$\frac{4}{60} \approx 0.067$	$\frac{45}{60} = 0.75$
No	$\frac{3}{60} = 0.05$	$\frac{5}{60} \approx 0.083$	$\frac{5}{60} \approx 0.083$	$\frac{2}{60} \approx 0.033$	$\frac{15}{60} = 0.25$
Total	$\frac{15}{60} = 0.25$	$\frac{18}{60} = 0.3$	$\frac{21}{60} = 0.35$	$\frac{6}{60} = 0.1$	$\frac{60}{60} = 1$

3. Give each relative frequency as a percent.

a. The joint relative frequency of students surveyed who participate in school clubs only and have part-time jobs: __20%__

b. The marginal relative frequency of students surveyed who do not have a part-time job: __25%__

c. The conditional relative frequency that a student surveyed participates in both school clubs and sports, given that the student has a part-time job: __About 36%__

4. Discuss possible influences of having a part-time job on participation in school activities. Support your response with an analysis of the data.

There does not appear to be any influence; within each category of school activity,

the percent of students who have a part-time job is fairly close to 75%, the

percent for the whole group.

CORRELATION

Standard	Items
CC.9-12.S.ID.1*	9
CC.9-12.S.ID.2*	3, 6
CC.9-12.S.ID.3*	1, 2, 4, 5, 7, 8, 10
CC.9-12.S.ID.5*	11, 12, 13, 14, 15

TEST PREP DOCTOR ⊕

Multiple Choice: Item 2

- Students who chose **G** or **H** did not understand that since the distribution for the second test is perfectly symmetric, the mean and median are the same.

- Students who chose **J** did not understand that the first test had data values that would result in the median's being greater than the mean.

Multiple Choice: Item 3

- Students who chose **B** may have confused the median with the mean.

- Students who chose **C** did not understand that the two lowest scores of 82 and 86 on the first test unduly influenced the mean, making it a poor measure of center.

- Students who chose **D** did not understand that the median is appropriate for comparing these two sets of test scores.

Multiple Choice: Item 4

- Students who chose **F** may not have understood that when a distribution is skewed in a particular direction, the tail is in that direction.

- Students who chose **H** or **J** may not have understood what it means for a distribution to be skewed.

Free Response: Item 7

- Students who described the distribution as symmetric may not have understood that the line in the center of the box represents the median of the data set, so that the data values are not balanced on either side of the center.

- Students who described the distribution as skewed to the left may not have understood that when a distribution is skewed in a particular direction, the tail is in that direction. Or they may not have known how to interpret from the plot that half of the data values are clustered between 5.5 and 8, while the other half are spread out between 8 and 12.

Free Response: Item 8

- Students who said that the price of the car would not be an outlier may not have known the formula for determining when a data value is an outlier. They may also have determined incorrect values for Q_3 or the IQR.

Free Response: Item 11

- Students who entered incorrect values in the subject and gender rows and columns may have made errors in their arithmetic or may not have divided by the grand total of 40.

- Students who entered incorrect values in the total row or total column may have added incorrectly.

Free Response: Item 14

- Students who answered 0.3, or 30%, may have calculated the conditional relative frequency that a surveyed student is a girl, given that the student prefers another subject. Students who answered 7.5% gave the joint relative frequency of students who are girls and prefer another subject.

Name _____ Class _____ Date _____

MULTIPLE CHOICE

For Items 1–3, use the line plots below.

Class Scores on First Test (top) and Second Test (bottom)

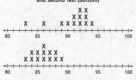

For Items 4–6, use the histograms below.

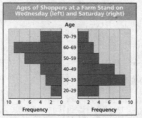

1. How do the medians of the two sets of test scores compare?

   Ⓐ The median for the first test is greater than the median for the second test.

   B. The median for the first test is less than the median for the second test.

   C. The medians for the first and second tests are equal.

   D. The relationship cannot be determined.

2. For which test is the median greater than the mean?

   Ⓕ First test only

   G. Second test only

   H. Both tests

   J. Neither test

3. Which measure of center is appropriate for comparing the two sets of test scores?

   Ⓐ The median only

   B. The mean only

   C. Either the median or the mean

   D. Neither the median nor the mean

4. Which distribution is skewed toward older ages?

   F. Only the Wednesday distribution

   Ⓖ Only the Saturday distribution

   H. Both distributions

   J. Neither distribution

5. How do the spreads of the two distributions compare?

   A. The spread for the Wednesday data is much greater than the spread for the Saturday data.

   B. The spread for the Wednesday data is much less than the spread for the Saturday data.

   Ⓒ The spreads are roughly equal.

   D. The relationship cannot be determined.

6. Which measure of spread is appropriate for comparing the sets of ages?

   Ⓕ The interquartile range only

   G. The standard deviation only

   H. Either the interquartile range or the standard deviation

   J. Neither the interquartile range nor the standard deviation

FREE RESPONSE

For Items 7–10, use the box plot below.

Prices (in Thousands of Dollars) of Vehicles at a Used-Car Dealership

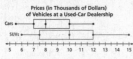

7. Describe the distribution of the prices of the used cars.

   The prices are skewed to the right (toward higher prices).

8. Suppose the dealership acquires a used luxury car that it intends to sell for $15,000. Would the price of the car be an outlier? Explain. (Assume that when the car's price is included in the data set, it has no effect on Q_3.)

   Yes; $Q_3 = 10$ and IQR = 3, so Q_3 + 1.5(IQR) = 14.5 and 15 > 14.5

9. The dealership also sells used SUVs. The prices (in thousands of dollars) of the SUVs are listed below. Add a box plot for the SUVs to the data display above.

   6, 6, 7.5, 7.5, 8, 9, 11, 11, 11, 13, 14, 15

10. Compare the distribution of prices for the used SUVs with the distribution of prices for the used cars.

   The distribution of prices for the used SUVs is more symmetric than the distribution of prices for the used cars. The prices of the used SUVs have a greater median and are more spread out than the prices of the used cars.

Derrick surveyed 40 of his classmates by asking each of them whether his or her favorite subject is math, English, or another subject. He also recorded the gender of each classmate surveyed. He recorded his results in the two-way frequency table below. Use the table to complete Items 11–15.

Gender\Subject	Math	English	Other	Total
Girl	7	10	3	20
Boy	9	4	7	20
Total	16	14	10	40

11. Create a two-way *relative* frequency table for the data using decimals.

Gender\Subject	Math	English	Other	Total
Girl	0.175	0.25	0.075	0.5
Boy	0.225	0.1	0.175	0.5
Total	0.4	0.35	0.25	1

12. Find the joint relative frequency of surveyed students who are girls and prefer English.

   0.25, or 25%

13. Find the marginal relative frequency of surveyed students who prefer math.

   0.4, or 40%

14. Find the conditional relative frequency that a surveyed student prefers another subject, given that the student is a girl.

   0.15, or 15%

15. Discuss possible influences of gender on favorite subject.

   If gender had no influence, then the number of boys and girls who prefer a subject should be roughly equal. That is the case for math, but not for English or other subjects.

Correlation of *On Core Mathematics* to the Common Core State Standards

Standards	Algebra 1	Geometry	Algebra 2
Number and Quantity			
The Real Number System			
CC.9-12.N.RN.1 Explain how the definition of the meaning of rational exponents follows from extending the properties of integer exponents to those values, allowing for a notation for radicals in terms of rational exponents.			Lesson 1-2
CC.9-12.N.RN.2 Rewrite expressions involving radicals and rational exponents using the properties of exponents.			Lesson 1-2
CC.9-12.N.RN.3 Explain why the sum or product of two rational numbers is rational; that the sum of a rational number and an irrational number is irrational; and that the product of a nonzero rational number and an irrational number is irrational.			Lesson 1-1
Quantities			
CC.9-12.N.Q.1 Use units as a way to understand problems and to guide the solution of multi-step problems; choose and interpret units consistently in formulas; choose and interpret the scale and the origin in graphs and data displays.*	Lessons 1-1, 1-2, 1-3, 1-5, 1-6, 2-3, 2-8, 3-6, 4-2, 4-3, 7-6		Lesson 2-6
CC.9-12.N.Q.2 Define appropriate quantities for the purpose of descriptive modeling.*	Lessons 1-3, 1-4, 2-3, 2-8, 3-6, 7-6		
CC.9-12.N.Q.3 Choose a level of accuracy appropriate to limitations on measurement when reporting quantities.*		Lesson 9-1	
The Complex Number System			
CC.9-12.N.CN.1 Know there is a complex number i such that $i^2 = -1$, and every complex number has the form $a + bi$ with a and b real.			Lesson 1-3
CC.9-12.N.CN.2 Use the relation $i^2 = -1$ and the commutative, associative, and distributive properties to add, subtract, and multiply complex numbers.			Lesson 1-3
CC.9-12.N.CN.3(+) Find the conjugate of a complex number; use conjugates to find moduli and quotients of complex numbers.			Lesson 1-4

(+) Advanced   * = Also a Modeling Standard

Standards	Algebra 1	Geometry	Algebra 2
CC.9-12.N.CN.7 Solve quadratic equations with real coefficients that have complex solutions.			Lesson 1-5
CC.9-12.N.CN.9(+) Know the Fundamental Theorem of Algebra; show that it is true for quadratic polynomials.			Lesson 3-10
Algebra			
Seeing Structure in Expressions			
CC.9-12.A.SSE.1 Interpret expressions that represent a quantity in terms of its context.* **a.** Interpret parts of an expression, such as terms, factors, and coefficients. **b.** Interpret complicated expressions by viewing one or more of their parts as a single entity.	Lessons 1-1, 1-2, 1-3, 2-8		Lessons 2-6, 3-5, 3-11, 4-4, 4-5, 9-4, 9-5
CC.9-12.A.SSE.2 Use the structure of an expression to identify ways to rewrite it.	Lessons 1-2, 1-3, 2-1, 2-2, 8-1		Lessons 3-9, 3-10
CC.9-12.A.SSE.3 Choose and produce an equivalent form of an expression to reveal and explain properties of the quantity represented by the expression. **a.** Factor a quadratic expression to reveal the zeros of the function it defines. **b.** Complete the square in a quadratic expression to reveal the maximum or minimum value of the function it defines. **c.** Use the properties of exponents to transform expressions for exponential functions.	Lessons 8-2, 8-3, 8-10		Lessons 2-4, 2-5, 6-4, 6-6
CC.9-12.A.SSE.4 Derive the formula for the sum of a finite geometric series (when the common ratio is not 1), and use the formula to solve problems.			Lessons 9-4, 9-5
Arithmetic with Polynomials and Rational Expressions			
CC.9-12.A.APR.1 Understand that polynomials form a system analogous to the integers, namely, they are closed under the operations of addition, subtraction, and multiplication; add, subtract, and multiply polynomials.	Lessons 4-6, 8-1		Lessons 3-5, 3-6, 3-7, 3-8
CC.9-12.A.APR.2 Know and apply the Remainder Theorem: For a polynomial $p(x)$ and a number a, the remainder on division by $x - a$ is $p(a)$, so $p(a) = 0$ if and only if $(x - a)$ is a factor of $p(x)$.			Lesson 3-8
CC.9-12.A.APR.3 Identify zeros of polynomials when suitable factorizations are available, and use the zeros to construct a rough graph of the function defined by the polynomial.			Lesson 3-9
CC.9-12.A.APR.4 Prove polynomial identities and use them to describe numerical relationships.			Lesson 3-6

(+) Advanced   * = Also a Modeling Standard

Standards	Algebra 1	Geometry	Algebra 2
CC.9-12.A.APR.5(+) Know and apply the Binomial Theorem for the expansion of $(x + y)^n$ in powers of x and y for a positive integer n, where x and y are any numbers, with coefficients determined for example by Pascal's Triangle. (The Binomial Theorem can be proved by mathematical induction or by a combinatorial argument.)			Lesson 3-7
CC.9-12.A.APR.6 Rewrite simple rational expressions in different forms; write $a(x)/b(x)$ in the form $q(x) + r(x)/b(x)$, where $a(x)$, $b(x)$, $q(x)$, and $r(x)$ are polynomials with the degree of $r(x)$ less than the degree of $b(x)$, using inspection, long division, or, for the more complicated examples, a computer algebra system.			Lesson 4-3
CC.9-12.A.APR.7(+) Understand that rational expressions form a system analogous to the rational numbers, closed under addition, subtraction, multiplication, and division by a nonzero rational expression; add, subtract, multiply, and divide rational expressions.			Lessons 4-4, 4-5
Creating Equations			
CC.9-12.A.CED.1 Create equations and inequalities in one variable and use them to solve problems.*	Lessons 1-4, 2-3, 5-5, 6-5, 7-4, 7-5, 8-3, 8-7		Lessons 3-11, 4-6, 6-7, 7-4
CC.9-12.A.CED.2 Create equations in two or more variables to represent relationships between quantities; graph equations on coordinate axes with labels and scales.*	Lessons 2-3, 2-5, 2-8, 3-6, 4-2, 4-3, 4-5, 4-6, 5-1, 5-5, 5-6, 5-8, 6-1, 6-2, 6-3, 6-4, 6-5, 6-6, 7-1, 7-2, 7-3, 7-4, 7-6, 8-9, 8-10		Lessons 2-3, 2-4, 2-5, 2-6, 3-9, 3-11, 4-1, 4-2, 4-3, 4-7, 5-1, 5-2, 5-3, 5-5, 5-6, 6-2, 6-3, 6-4, 6-5, 6-6, 7-5, 8-9
CC.9-12.A.CED.3 Represent constraints by equations or inequalities, and by systems of equations and/or inequalities, and interpret solutions as viable or nonviable options in a modeling context.*	Lessons 1-4, 2-3, 2-8, 3-6		Lessons 2-6, 3-11, 9-5
CC.9-12.A.CED.4 Rearrange formulas to highlight a quantity of interest, using the same reasoning as in solving equations.*	Lesson 2-5		Lesson 7-5
Reasoning with Equations and Inequalities			
CC.9-12.A.REI.1. Explain each step in solving a simple equation as following from the equality of numbers asserted at the previous step, starting from the assumption that the original equation has a solution. Construct a viable argument to justify a solution method.	Lessons 2-1, 2-2, 2-4		
CC.9-12.A.REI.2 Solve simple rational and radical equations in one variable, and give examples showing how extraneous solutions may arise.			Lessons 4-6, 5-7
CC.9-12.A.REI.3 Solve linear equations and inequalities in one variable, including equations with coefficients represented by letters.	Lessons 2-1, 2-2, 2-3, 2-4		

(+) Advanced   * = Also a Modeling Standard

Standards	Algebra 1	Geometry	Algebra 2
CC.9-12.A.REI.4 Solve quadratic equations in one variable. **a.** Use the method of completing the square to transform any quadratic equation in x into an equation of the form $(x - p)^2 = q$ that has the same solutions. Derive the quadratic formula from this form. **b.** Solve quadratic equations by inspection (e.g., for $x^2 = 49$), taking square roots, completing the square, the quadratic formula and factoring, as appropriate to the initial form of the equation. Recognize when the quadratic formula gives complex solutions and write them as $a \pm bi$ for real numbers a and b.	**Lessons 7-5, 8-2, 8-3, 8-4, 8-5, 8-6, 8-7, 8-9, 8-10**		Lesson 1-5
CC.9-12.A.REI.5 Prove that, given a system of two equations in two variables, replacing one equation by the sum of that equation and a multiple of the other produces a system with the same solutions.	**Lesson 3-4**		
CC.9-12.A.REI.6 Solve systems of linear equations exactly and approximately (e.g., with graphs), focusing on pairs of linear equations in two variables.	**Lessons 3-1, 3-2, 3-3, 3-4, 3-6**		
CC.9-12.A.REI.7 Solve a simple system consisting of a linear equation and a quadratic equation in two variables algebraically and graphically.	**Lesson 8-9**	Lesson 8-7	
CC.9-12.A.REI.10 Understand that the graph of an equation in two variables is the set of all its solutions plotted in the coordinate plane, often forming a curve (which could be a line).	**Lessons 2-6, 2-7**		
CC.9-12.A.REI.11 Explain why the x-coordinates of the points where the graphs of the equations $y = f(x)$ and $y = g(x)$ intersect are the solutions of the equation $f(x) = g(x)$; find the solutions approximately, e.g., using technology to graph the functions, make tables of values, or find successive approximations. Include cases where $f(x)$ and/or $g(x)$ are linear, polynomial, rational, absolute value, exponential, and logarithmic functions.*	**Lessons 4-5, 5-5, 5-8, 6-5, 7-4**		Lessons 4-6, 5-7, 6-7, 7-4
CC.9-12.A.REI.12 Graph the solutions to a linear inequality in two variables as a half-plane (excluding the boundary in the case of a strict inequality), and graph the solution set to a system of linear inequalities in two variables as the intersection of the corresponding half-planes.	**Lessons 2-6, 2-7, 3-5, 3-6**		
Functions			
Interpreting Functions			
CC.9-12.F.IF.1 Understand that a function from one set (called the domain) to another set (called the range) assigns to each element of the domain exactly one element of the range. If f is a function and x is an element of its domain, then $f(x)$ denotes the output of f corresponding to the input x. The graph of f is the graph of the equation $y = f(x)$.	**Lessons 1-5, 1-6, 4-2, 4-7, 5-2**		Lesson 8-3

(+) Advanced   * = Also a Modeling Standard

On Core Mathematics Algebra 1

Common Core Correlations

Standards	Algebra 1	Geometry	Algebra 2
CC.9-12.F.IF.2 Use function notation, evaluate functions for inputs in their domains, and interpret statements that use function notation in terms of a context.	**Lessons 1-5, 1-6, 4-1, 4-2, 4-7, 5-1, 6-1, 6-2, 6-3, 6-4, 6-6, 7-1, 7-2, 7-3, 7-6, 8-10**		Lessons 2-1, 2-2, 2-3, 2-4, 2-5, 2-6, 3-4, 4-1, 4-2, 4-3, 4-7, 5-1, 5-2, 5-3, 5-5, 5-6, 6-1, 6-2, 6-3, 6-4, 6-5, 7-1, 7-5, 8-9, 9-1
CC.9-12.F.IF.3 Recognize that sequences are functions, sometimes defined recursively, whose domain is a subset of the integers.	**Lessons 4-1, 5-1**		Lesson 9-1
CC.9-12.F.IF.4 For a function that models a relationship between two quantities, interpret key features of graphs and tables in terms of the quantities, and sketch graphs showing key features given a verbal description of the relationship.*	**Lessons 4-3, 4-4, 4-5, 5-3, 5-4, 6-1, 6-6, 7-1, 7-2, 7-3, 7-6, 8-8, 8-9, 8-10**		Lessons 2-6, 3-11, 4-1, 4-2, 4-3, 4-7, 5-5, 5-6, 6-2, 6-3, 6-6, 7-5, 8-9
CC.9-12.F.IF.5 Relate the domain of a function to its graph and, where applicable, to the quantitative relationship it describes.*	**Lessons 1-5, 1-6, 4-1, 4-2, 5-1, 5-2, 5-8, 6-1, 6-6, 7-1, 8-8**		Lessons 2-6, 3-11
CC.9-12.F.IF.6 Calculate and interpret the average rate of change of a function (presented symbolically or as a table) over a specified interval. Estimate the rate of change from a graph.*	**Lessons 4-3, 4-5, 8-10**		Lessons 2-6
CC.9-12.F.IF.7 Graph functions expressed symbolically and show key features of the graph, by hand in simple cases and using technology for more complicated cases.* **a.** Graph linear and quadratic functions and show intercepts, maxima, and minima. **b.** Graph square root, cube root, and piecewise-defined functions, including step functions and absolute value functions. **c.** Graph polynomial functions, identifying zeros when suitable factorizations are available, and showing end behavior. **d.** (+) Graph rational functions, identifying zeros and asymptotes when suitable factorizations are available, and showing end behavior. **e.** Graph exponential and logarithmic functions, showing intercepts and end behavior, and trigonometric functions, showing period, midline, and amplitude.	**Lessons 4-1, 4-3, 4-5, 5-1, 5-2, 5-3, 5-8, 6-1, 6-2, 6-3, 6-4, 6-6, 7-1, 7-2, 7-3, 8-8**		Lessons 2-1, 2-2, 2-3, 2-4, 2-5, 2-6, 3-1, 3-2, 3-3, 3-4, 3-9, 3-11, 4-1, 4-2, 4-3, 4-7, 5-1, 5-2, 5-3, 5-4, 5-5, 5-6, 6-1, 6-2, 6-3, 6-4, 6-5, 6-6, 6-7, 7-1, 7-2, 8-5, 8-6, 8-7, 8-8, 8-9
CC.9-12.F.IF.8 Write a function defined by an expression in different but equivalent forms to reveal and explain different properties of the function. **a.** Use the process of factoring and completing the square in a quadratic function to show zeros, extreme values, and symmetry of the graph, and interpret these in terms of a context. **b.** Use the properties of exponents to interpret expressions for exponential functions.	**Lessons 8-2, 8-3, 8-8, 8-10**		Lessons 2-4, 2-5, 6-4, 6-6
CC.9-12.F.IF.9 Compare properties of two functions each represented in a different way (algebraically, graphically, numerically in tables, or by verbal descriptions).	**Lessons 4-2, 8-10**		Lesson 4-7

(+) Advanced   * = Also a Modeling Standard

Standards	Algebra 1	Geometry	Algebra 2
Building Functions			
CC.9-12.F.BF.1 Write a function that describes a relationship between two quantities.* a. Determine an explicit expression, a recursive process, or steps for calculation from a context. b. Combine standard function types using arithmetic operations. c. (+) Compose functions.	Lessons 1-6, 2-3, 2-8, 4-5, 4-6, 4-9, 5-5, 5-6, 5-8, 6-1, 6-2, 6-3, 6-4, 6-6, 7-1, 7-2, 7-3, 7-6, 8-3, 8-8, 8-10		Lessons 2-6, 3-5, 3-11, 4-1, 4-2, 4-3, 4-4, 4-5, 4-7, 5-5, 5-6, 6-2, 6-3, 6-4, 6-6, 7-5, 8-9, 9-1, 9-2, 9-3
CC.9-12.F.BF.2 Write arithmetic and geometric sequences both recursively and with an explicit formula, use them to model situations, and translate between the two forms.*	Lesson 4-1		Lessons 9-2, 9-3
CC.9-12.F.BF.3 Identify the effect on the graph of replacing $f(x)$ by $f(x) + k$, $kf(x)$, $f(kx)$, and $f(x + k)$ for specific values of k (both positive and negative); find the value of k given the graphs. Experiment with cases and illustrate an explanation of the effects on the graph using technology.	Lessons 4-4, 5-4, 6-2, 6-3, 6-4, 7-1, 7-2, 7-3		Lessons 2-1, 2-2, 2-3, 3-1, 3-2, 3-3, 4-1, 4-2, 5-4, 6-2, 6-3, 6-4, 6-5, 7-2, 8-7, 8-8, 8-9
CC.9-12.F.BF.4 Find inverse functions. a. Solve an equation of the form $f(x) = c$ for a simple function f that has an inverse and write an expression for the inverse. b. (+) Verify by composition that one function is the inverse of another. c. (+) Read values of an inverse function from a graph or a table, given that the function has an inverse. d. (+) Produce an invertible function from a non-invertible function by restricting the domain.	Lesson 4-7		Lessons 5-1, 5-2, 5-3, 5-5, 5-6
CC.9-12.F.BF.5(+) Understand the inverse relationship between exponents and logarithms and use this relationship to solve problems involving logarithms and exponents.			Lessons 7-1, 7-3
Linear, Quadratic, and Exponential Models			
CC.9-12.F.LE.1 Distinguish between situations that can be modeled with linear functions and with exponential functions.* a. Prove that linear functions grow by equal differences over equal intervals, and that exponential functions grow by equal factors over equal intervals. b. Recognize situations in which one quantity changes at a constant rate per unit interval relative to another. c. Recognize situations in which a quantity grows or decays by a constant percent rate per unit interval relative to another.	Lessons 5-2, 5-3, 5-6, 5-7, 5-8		
CC.9-12.F.LE.2 Construct linear and exponential functions, including arithmetic and geometric sequences, given a graph, a description of a relationship, or two input-output pairs (include reading these from a table).*	Lessons 4-5, 4-6, 5-1, 5-2, 5-3, 5-5, 5-8		Lessons 6-2, 6-3, 6-4, 6-5, 9-2, 9-3

(+) Advanced   * = Also a Modeling Standard

Standards	Algebra 1	Geometry	Algebra 2
CC.9-12.F.LE.3 Observe using graphs and tables that a quantity increasing exponentially eventually exceeds a quantity increasing linearly, quadratically, or (more generally) as a polynomial function.*	Lesson 5-7		Lessons 6-1, 6-6
CC.9-12.F.LE.4 For exponential models, express as a logarithm the solution to $ab^{ct} = d$ where a, c, and d are numbers and the base b is 2, 10, or e; evaluate the logarithm using technology.*			Lesson 7-4
CC.9-12.F.LE.5 Interpret the parameters in a linear or exponential function in terms of a context.*	Lessons 4-4, 4-5, 4-6, 4-9, 4-10, 5-2, 5-3, 5-6, 5-8		Lessons 6-4, 6-5
Trigonometric Functions			
CC.9-12.F.TF.1 Understand radian measure of an angle as the length of the arc on the unit circle subtended by the angle.			Lesson 8-2
CC.9-12.F.TF.2 Explain how the unit circle in the coordinate plane enables the extension of trigonometric functions to all real numbers, interpreted as radian measures of angles traversed counterclockwise around the unit circle.			Lesson 8-3
CC.9-12.F.TF.3(+) Use special triangles to determine geometrically the values of sine, cosine, tangent for $\pi/3$, $\pi/4$ and $\pi/6$, and use the unit circle to express the values of sine, cosines, and tangent for x, $\pi + x$, and $2\pi - x$ in terms of their values for x, where x is any real number.			Lesson 8-3
CC.9-12.F.TF.4(+) Use the unit circle to explain symmetry (odd and even) and periodicity of trigonometric functions.			Lessons 8-5, 8-6
CC.9-12.F.TF.5 Choose trigonometric functions to model periodic phenomena with specified amplitude, frequency, and midline.*			Lesson 8-9
CC.9-12.F.TF.8 Prove the Pythagorean identity $\sin^2(\theta) + \cos^2(\theta) = 1$ and use it to calculate trigonometric ratios.			Lesson 8-4
Geometry			
Congruence			
CC.9-12.G.CO.1 Know precise definitions of angle, circle, perpendicular line, parallel line, and line segment, based on the undefined notions of point, line, distance along a line, and distance around a circular arc.		Lessons 1-1, 1-4, 1-5, 9-4	
CC.9-12.G.CO.2 Represent transformations in the plane using, e.g., transparencies and geometry software; describe transformations as functions that take points in the plane as inputs and give other points as outputs. Compare transformations that preserve distance and angle to those that do not (e.g., translation versus horizontal stretch).		Lessons 2-1, 2-2, 2-3, 2-4, 2-5, 2-6, 5-1, 5-2	

(+) Advanced   * = Also a Modeling Standard

Standards	Algebra 1	Geometry	Algebra 2
CC.9-12.G.CO.3 Given a rectangle, parallelogram, trapezoid, or regular polygon, describe the rotations and reflections that carry it onto itself.		Lesson 4-1	
CC.9-12.G.CO.4 Develop definitions of rotations, reflections, and translations in terms of angles, circles, perpendicular lines, parallel lines, and line segments.		Lessons 2-2, 2-5, 2-6	
CC.9-12.G.CO.5 Given a geometric figure and a rotation, reflection, or translation, draw the transformed figure using, e.g., graph paper, tracing paper, or geometry software. Specify a sequence of transformations that will carry a given figure onto another.		Lessons 2-2, 2-5, 2-6, 3-1	
CC.9-12.G.CO.6 Use geometric descriptions of rigid motions to transform figures and to predict the effect of a given rigid motion on a given figure; given two figures, use the definition of congruence in terms of rigid motions to decide if they are congruent.		Lessons 2-2, 2-5, 2-6, 3-1	
CC.9-12.G.CO.7 Use the definition of congruence in terms of rigid motions to show that two triangles are congruent if and only if corresponding pairs of sides and corresponding pairs of angles are congruent.		Lessons 3-2, 3-3	
CC.9-12.G.CO.8 Explain how the criteria for triangle congruence (ASA, SAS, and SSS) follow from the definition of congruence in terms of rigid motions.		Lesson 3-3	
CC.9-12.G.CO.9 Prove geometric theorems about lines and angles.		Lessons 1-6, 1-7, 2-3, 2-4	
CC.9-12.G.CO.10 Prove theorems about triangles.		Lessons 3-5, 3-6, 3-7, 3-8, 3-9	
CC.9-12.G.CO.11 Prove theorems about parallelograms.		Lessons 4-2, 4-3, 4-4, 4-5	
CC.9-12.G.CO.12 Make formal geometric constructions with a variety of tools and methods (compass and straightedge, string, reflective devices, paper folding, dynamic geometry software, etc.).		Lessons 1-1, 1-4, 1-5	
CC.9-12.G.CO.13 Construct an equilateral triangle, a square, and a regular hexagon inscribed in a circle.		Lesson 7-3	
Similarity, Right Triangles, and Trigonometry			
CC.9-12.G.SRT.1 Verify experimentally the properties of dilations given by a center and a scale factor: **a.** A dilation takes a line not passing through the center of the dilation to a parallel line, and leaves a line passing through the center unchanged. **b.** The dilation of a line segment is longer or shorter in the ratio given by the scale factor.		Lesson 5-1	

(+) Advanced   * = Also a Modeling Standard

Standards	Algebra 1	Geometry	Algebra 2
CC.9-12.G.SRT.2 Given two figures, use the definition of similarity in terms of similarity transformations to decide if they are similar; explain using similarity transformations the meaning of similarity for triangles as the equality of all corresponding angles and the proportionality of all corresponding pairs of sides.		Lessons 5-3, 5-4	
CC.9-12.G.SRT.3 Use the properties of similarity transformations to establish the AA criterion for two triangles to be similar.		Lesson 5-4	
CC.9-12.G.SRT.4 Prove theorems about triangles.		Lessons 5-6, 5-7	
CC.9-12.G.SRT.5 Use congruence and similarity criteria for triangles to solve problems and prove relationships in geometric figures.		Lessons 3-4, 4-2, 4-3, 4-4, 4-5, 5-5, 5-6, 5-7	
CC.9-12.G.SRT.6 Understand that by similarity, side ratios in right triangles are properties of the angles in the triangle, leading to definitions of trigonometric ratios for acute angles.		Lessons 6-1, 6-2, 6-3	
CC.9-12.G.SRT.7 Explain and use the relationship between the sine and cosine of complementary angles.		Lessons 6-2, 6-3	
CC.9-12.G.SRT.8 Use trigonometric ratios and the Pythagorean Theorem to solve right triangles in applied problems.		Lesson 6-4	
CC.9-12.G.SRT.9(+) Derive the formula $A = 1/2\ ab\ \sin(C)$ for the area of a triangle by drawing an auxiliary line from a vertex perpendicular to the opposite side.		Lesson 6-5	
CC.9-12.G.SRT.10(+) Prove the Laws of Sines and Cosines and use them to solve problems.		Lessons 6-6, 6-7	
CC.9-12.G.SRT.11(+) Understand and apply the Law of Sines and the Law of Cosines to find unknown measurements in right and non-right triangles (e.g., surveying problems, resultant forces).		Lessons 6-6, 6-7	
Circles			
CC.9-12.G.C.1 Prove that all circles are similar.		Lesson 5-3	
CC.9-12.G.C.2 Identify and describe relationships among inscribed angles, radii, and chords.		Lessons 7-1, 7-5	
CC.9-12.G.C.3 Construct the inscribed and circumscribed circles of a triangle, and prove properties of angles for a quadrilateral inscribed in a circle.		Lessons 7-2, 7-4, 7-6	
CC.9-12.G.C.4(+) Construct a tangent line from a point outside a given circle to the circle.		Lesson 7-5	

(+) Advanced   * = Also a Modeling Standard

Standards	Algebra 1	Geometry	Algebra 2
CC.9-12.G.C.5 Derive using similarity the fact that the length of the arc intercepted by an angle is proportional to the radius, and define the radian measure of the angle as the constant of proportionality; derive the formula for the area of a sector.		Lessons 9-4, 9-5	Lesson 8-1
Expressing Geometric Properties with Equations			
CC.9-12.G.GPE.1 Derive the equation of a circle of given center and radius using the Pythagorean Theorem; complete the square to find the center and radius of a circle given by an equation.		Lesson 8-1	
CC.9-12.G.GPE.2 Derive the equation of a parabola given a focus and directrix.		Lesson 8-2	
CC.9-12.G.GPE.4 Use coordinates to prove simple geometric theorems algebraically.		Lessons 1-2, 1-3, 3-7, 3-8, 3-9, 8-1, 8-6	
CC.9-12.G.GPE.5 Prove the slope criteria for parallel and perpendicular lines and use them to solve geometric problems (e.g., find the equation of line parallel or perpendicular to a given line that passes through a given point).		Lessons 8-4, 8-5	
CC.9-12.G.GPE.6 Find the point on a directed line segment between two given points that partitions the segment in a given ratio.		Lesson 8-3	
CC.9-12.G.GPE.7 Use coordinates to compute perimeters of polygons and areas of triangles and rectangles, e.g., using the distance formula.*		Lesson 9-2	
Geometric Measurement and Dimension			
CC.9-12.G.GMD.1 Give an informal argument for the formulas for the circumference of a circle, area of a circle, volume of a cylinder, pyramid, and cone.		Lessons 9-3, 9-5, 10-2, 10-3, 10-4	
CC.9-12.G.GMD.2(+) Give an informal argument using Cavalieri's principle for the formulas for the volume of a sphere and other solid figures.		Lessons 10-2, 10-5	
CC.9-12.G.GMD.3 Use volume formulas for cylinders, pyramids, cones, and spheres to solve problems.*		Lessons 10-2, 10-3, 10-4, 10-5, 10-6	
CC.9-12.G.GMD.4 Identify the shapes of two-dimensional cross-sections of three-dimensional objects, and identify three-dimensional objects generated by rotations of two-dimensional objects.		Lesson 10-1	

(+) Advanced   * = Also a Modeling Standard

Standards	Algebra 1	Geometry	Algebra 2
Modeling with Geometry			
CC.9-12.G.MG.1 Use geometric shapes, their measures, and their properties to describe objects (e.g., modeling a tree trunk or a human torso as a cylinder).*		Lessons 9-2, 9-3, 10-2	
CC.9-12.G.MG.2 Apply concepts of density based on area and volume in modeling situations (e.g., persons per square mile, BTUs per cubic foot).*		Lessons 9-2, 10-2, 10-5	
CC.9-12.G.MG.3 Apply geometric methods to solve design problems (e.g., designing an object or structure to satisfy physical constraints or minimize cost; working with typographic grid systems based on ratios).*		Lessons 5-5, 10-6	
Statistics and Probability			
Interpreting Categorical and Quantitative Data			
CC.9-12.S.ID.1 Represent data with plots on the real number line (dot plots, histograms, and box plots).*	Lessons 9-2, 9-3, 9-4		Lessons 10-2, 10-3
CC.9-12.S.ID.2 Use statistics appropriate to the shape of the data distribution to compare center (median, mean) and spread (interquartile range, standard deviation) of two or more different data sets.*	Lessons 9-1, 9-2, 9-3, 9-4		
CC.9-12.S.ID.3 Interpret differences in shape, center, and spread in the context of the data sets, accounting for possible effects of extreme data points (outliers).*	Lesson 9-2		Lesson 10-2
CC.9-12.S.ID.4 Use the mean and standard deviation of a data set to fit it to a normal distribution and to estimate population percentages. Recognize that there are data sets for which such a procedure is not appropriate. Use calculators, spreadsheets, and tables to estimate areas under the normal curve.*			Lesson 10-4
CC.9-12.S.ID.5 Summarize categorical data for two categories in two-way frequency tables. Interpret relative frequencies in the context of the data (including joint, marginal, and conditional relative frequencies). Recognize possible associations and trends in the data.*	Lesson 9-5		
CC.9-12.S.ID.6 Represent data on two quantitative variables on a scatter plot, and describe how the variables are related.* **a.** Fit a function to the data; use functions fitted to data to solve problems in the context of the data. **b.** Informally assess the fit of a function by plotting and analyzing residuals. **c.** Fit a linear function for a scatter plot that suggests a linear association.	Lessons 4-9, 4-10, 5-6, 5-8		Lessons 5-5, 5-6, 6-6

(+) Advanced   * = Also a Modeling Standard

Standards	Algebra 1	Geometry	Algebra 2
CC.9-12.S.ID.7 Interpret the slope (rate of change) and the intercept (constant term) of a linear model in the context of the data.*	Lessons 4-9, 4-10		
CC.9-12.S.ID.8 Compute (using technology) and interpret the correlation coefficient of a linear fit.*	Lessons 4-8, 4-10		
CC.9-12.S.ID.9 Distinguish between correlation and causation.*	Lesson 4-8		
Making Inferences and Justifying Conclusions			
CC.9-12.S.IC.1 Understand statistics as a process for making inferences about population parameters based on a random sample from that population.*			Lesson 10-1
CC.9-12.S.IC.2 Decide if a specified model is consistent with results from a given data-generating process, e.g., using simulation.*			Lesson 10-3
CC.9-12.S.IC.3 Recognize the purposes of and differences among sample surveys, experiments, and observational studies; explain how randomization relates to each.*			Lesson 10-7
CC.9-12.S.IC.4 Use data from a sample survey to estimate a population mean or proportion; develop a margin of error through the use of simulation models for random sampling.*			Lessons 10-5, 10-6
CC.9-12.S.IC.5 Use data from a randomized experiment to compare two treatments; use simulations to decide if differences between parameters are significant.*			Lesson 10-8
CC.9-12.S.IC.6 Evaluate reports based on data.*	Lesson 4-8		Lesson 10-7
Conditional Probability and the Rules of Probability			
CC.9-12.S.CP.1 Describe events as subsets of a sample space (the set of outcomes) using characteristics (or categories) of the outcomes, or as unions, intersections, or complements of other events ("or," "and," "not").*		Lesson 11-1	
CC.9-12.S.CP.2 Understand that two events A and B are independent if the probability of A and B occurring together is the product of their probabilities, and use this characterization to determine if they are independent.*		Lesson 11-7	
CC.9-12.S.CP.3 Understand the conditional probability of A given B as $P(A$ and $B)/P(B)$, and interpret independence of A and B as saying that the conditional probability of A given B is the same as the probability of A, and the conditional probability of B given A is the same as the probability of B.*		Lessons 11-6, 11-7	

(+) Advanced   * = Also a Modeling Standard

Standards	Algebra 1	Geometry	Algebra 2
CC.9-12.S.CP.4 Construct and interpret two-way frequency tables of data when two categories are associated with each object being classified. Use the two-way table as a sample space to decide if events are independent and to approximate conditional probabilities.*		Lessons 11-6, 11-7, 11-10	
CC.9-12.S.CP.5 Recognize and explain the concepts of conditional probability and independence in everyday language and everyday situations.*		Lessons 11-6, 11-7	
CC.9-12.S.CP.6 Find the conditional probability of A given B as the fraction of B's outcomes that also belong to A, and interpret the answer in terms of the model.*		Lesson 11-6	
CC.9-12.S.CP.7 Apply the Addition Rule, $P(A \text{ or } B) = P(A) + P(B) - P(A \text{ and } B)$, and interpret the answer in terms of the model.*		Lesson 11-5	
CC.9-12.S.CP.8(+) Apply the general Multiplication Rule in a uniform probability model, $P(A \text{ and } B) = P(A)P(B|A) = P(B)P(A|B)$, and interpret the answer in terms of the model.*		Lesson 11-8	
CC.9-12.S.CP.9(+) Use permutations and combinations to compute probabilities of compound events and solve problems.*		Lessons 11-3, 11-4	
Using Probability to Make Decisions			
CC.9-12.S.MD.6(+) Use probabilities to make fair decisions (e.g., drawing by lots, using a random number generator).*		Lessons 11-2, 11-9	
CC.9-12.S.MD.7(+) Analyze decisions and strategies using probability concepts (e.g., product testing, medical testing, pulling a hockey goalie at the end of a game).*		Lesson 11-10	

(+) Advanced   * = Also a Modeling Standard